Tokyo

timeout.com/tokyo

Published by Time Out Guides Ltd, a wholly owned subsidiary of Time Out Group Ltd.
Time Out and the Time Out logo are trademarks of Time Out Group Ltd.

© Time Out Group Ltd 2007
Previous editions 1999, 2001, 2003, 2005.

10 9 8 7 6 5 4 3 2 1

This edition first published in Great Britain in 2007 by Ebury Publishing
A Random House Group Company
20 Vauxhall Bridge Road, London SW1V 2SA

Random House Australia Pty Limited 20 Alfred Street, Milsons Point, Sydney, New South Wales 2061, Australia
Random House New Zealand Limited 18 Poland Road, Glenfield, Auckland 10, New Zealand
Random House South Africa (Pty) Limited Isle of Houghton, Corner Boundary
Road & Carse O'Gowrie, Houghton 2198, South Africa

Random House UK Limited Reg. No. 954009

For details of distribution in the Americas, see www.timeout.com

ISBN 10: 1-84670-016-7
ISBN 13: 978184670 0163

A CIP catalogue record for this book is available from the British Library

Printed and bound by Firmengruppe APPL, aprinta druck, Wemding, Germany

The Random House Group Limited makes every effort to ensure that the papers used in our books are made from trees
that have been legally sourced from well-managed and credibly certified forests. Our paper procurement policy can
be found on www.randomhouse.co.uk.

Time Out Guides Limited
Universal House
251 Tottenham Court Road
London W1T 7AB
Tel + 44 (0)20 7813 3000
Fax + 44 (0)20 7813 6001
Email guides@timeout.com
www.timeout.com

Editorial

Editor Nicholas Coldicott
Deputy Editor Emma Howarth
Copy Editors Ismay Atkins, Anna Norman
Editorial Assistance Charlotte Thomas
Researchers Iida Marie, Kodama Chie
Listings Checkers James Catchpole, Ogino Yucary,
  Inada Sumiyo, Sugimoto Ayaka, Tagawa Reiko,
  Takahashi Yusuke, Tsuji Eri
Proofreader Sylvia Tombesi-Walton
Indexer Jackie Brind

Managing Director Peter Fiennes
Financial Director Gareth Garner
Editorial Director Ruth Jarvis
Deputy Series Editor Dominic Earle
Editorial Manager Holly Pick

Design

Art Director Scott Moore
Art Editor Pinelope Kourmouzoglou
Senior Designer Josephine Spencer
Graphic Designer Henry Elphick
Junior Graphic Designer Kei Ishimaru
Digital Imaging Simon Foster
Ad Make-up Jenni Prichard

Picture Desk

Picture Editor Jael Marschner
Deputy Picture Editor Tracey Kerrigan
Picture Researcher Helen McFarland

Advertising

Sales Director Mark Phillips
International Sales Manager Fred Durman
International Sales Consultant Ross Canadé
International Sales Executive Simon Davies
Advertising Assistant Kate Staddon

Marketing

Group Marketing Director John Luck
Marketing Manager Yvonne Poon
Sales and Marketing Director North America Lisa Levinson

Production

Group Production Director Mark Lamond
Production Manager Brendan McKeown
Production Coordinator Caroline Bradford

Time Out Group

Chairman Tony Elliott
Financial Director Richard Waterlow
Time Out Magazine Ltd MD David Pepper
Group General Manager/Director Nichola Coulthard
Time Out Communications Ltd MD David Pepper
Time Out International MD Cathy Runciman
Group Art Director John Oakey
Group IT Director Simon Chappell

Contributors

Introduction Nicholas Coldicott. **History** Steve Walsh (*Suicidal samurai* James Hardy). **Tokyo Today** Lee Brown (*A tale of two princesses* Iida Marie). **Architecture** Steve Walsh. **Otaku** Patrick Macias (*Tokyo tribes* Kodama Chie, Patrick Macias). **Where to Stay** Tama Miyake Lung (*Sisters are doing it by themselves* Kodama Chie). **Introduction** Nicholas Coldicott. **Asakusa** Stephen Forster (*Old soaks* Nicholas Coldicott). **Ebisu & Daikanyama** Martin Webb. **Ginza** Nicholas Coldicott (*Something fishy* Yukari Pratt). **Harajuku & Aoyama** Martin Webb (*Gotta have faith* Stephen Forster). **Ikebukuro** Tom Baker (*How to play pachinko* Clive France). **Marunouchi** Nicholas Coldicott (*Walk on Old Tokyo* James Hardy). **Odaiba** John Paul Catton. **Roppongi** Nicholas Coldicott (*Tokyo Midtown* Martin Webb). **Shibuya** Simeon Paterson (*Animania, Walk on People watching* Nicholas Coldicott). **Shinjuku** Rob Schwartz (*Manga mania* Paul Gravett; *Hey, big spender?* Charles Spreckley). **Ueno** Stephen Forster. **Yanaka** Stephen Forster. **Further Afield: Naka Meguro** Martin Webb; **Shimo-Kitazawa** John Paul Catton; **The Chuo Line** James Barrett. **Restaurants** Robbie Swinnerton (*Shojin ryori* Nicholas Coldicott; *Menu Reader* Hosose Masami). **Bars** Nicholas Coldicott (*Local potions* John Gauntner). **Coffee Shops** Nicholas Coldicott (*Drink your greens* Kobayashi Chikako). **Shops & Services** Martin Webb (*Treats abound underground* Yukari Pratt; *Present perfect, Vending machines* John Paul Catton). **Festivals & Events** Kodama Chie (*Superstitions* Yoko Hoshino-Krause). **Children** Obe Mitsuru, Obe Rie. **Clubs** Simeon Paterson, Jeff Richards. **Film** Rob Schwartz (*Weeper reapers* Mark Schilling). **Galleries** Samantha Sinnayah. **Gay & Lesbian** Ken Panadero. **Music: Classical** Dan Grunebaum; **Jazz** James Catchpole; **Rock & pop** Rob Schwartz (*Big in Japan* David Hickey). **Performing Arts** Dan Grunebaum (*Noh future* Mark Buckton). **Sport & Fitness** Fred Varcoe (*Straight outta Mongolia* Mark Buckton). **Yokohama** Robbie Swinnerton. **Hakone** Nigel Kendall. **Kamakura** Robbie Swinnerton. **Nikko** Robbie Swinnerton. **Other Trips** Clive France (*Climbing Mt Fuji* Nicholas Coldicott). **Getting Around, Resources** Tagawa Reiko. **Getting by in Japanese** Hosose Masami, Adam Barnes.

Maps john@jsgraphics.co.uk.

Photography by Fumie Suzuki, except: pages 12, 275 Karl Blackwell; page 15 Bass Museum of Art/Corbis; page 16 Bettmann/Corbis; pages 19, 24, 264, 271 Getty Images; page 207 Courtesy of WMI Japan; pages 212, 214, 286, 293, 296 JNTO/www.seejapan.co.uk; page 235 Paul Yeung/Reuters; page 263 MOR/Alamy; page 272 FEG Inc.

The following images were provided by the featured establishments/artists: pages 55, 113, 250, 256.

The Editor would like to thank Yamada Takanari and Kylie Clark of the JNTO, Chujo Ayako, Emma Doherty, Hase Eriko, Hayakawa Chie, Hirokawa Masanori, Kei Ishimaru, Kodama Chie, Kojima Kei, Cristoph Mark, Mizoguchi Masako, Sakamoto Shintaro, Justin Simon, Tagawa Reiko, Mark Thompson and all contributors to previous editions of *Time Out Tokyo*, whose work forms the basis for parts of this book.

Contents

Introduction

It's time to call it: Tokyo is now one of the great destinations on the global tourist trail. It's still bewildering, frenetic, overpopulated and arguably short of traditional tourist sights. But, as with all good cites, Tokyo is about submitting to the chaos. The 33 million residents of metropolitan Tokyo form a capital that commands global attention on a political, financial and cultural level. For fashion, design, music or shameless consumerism Tokyo rivals any place on the planet. It's a city that knows its history, but embraces the future with far more fervour.

The frail economy of the 1990s and early noughties is now a vigorous, confident machine again, fostering frantic investment in all the major sub centres. Spectacular architecture, luxury hotels and big brand boutiques are springing up rapidly, but this time around there's a more purse-friendly side to complement it. Tokyo's fearsome reputation as a budget-gobbling black spot is no longer warranted. You'll find affordable highlights listed throughout this guide.

The other great tourist deterrent, language, is nothing like the problem it used to be. English is so prevalent on signs and menus that, other than in traditional Japanese restaurants, if you can't read it you probably don't need to. Spoken English ability is much more varied, but people are usually friendly enough to try.

Visitors to Tokyo will be struck by the contrasts of a conservative city with an obsession for innovation. Where else could you find a grand shrine sitting quietly beside brothels in a notorious red light district? Tokyo excels in unlikely juxtapositions, and that's just part of the fun. You'd need decades to understand this city, but you'll enjoy it the minute you arrive.

ABOUT THE TIME OUT CITY GUIDES

Time Out Tokyo is one of an expanding series of Time Out City Guides produced by the people behind London and New York's successful listings magazines. Our guides are all written and updated by resident experts who have striven to provide you with all the most up-to-date information you'll need to explore the city, whether you're a local or first-time visitor.

THE LOWDOWN ON THE LISTINGS

Above all, we've tried to make this book as useful as possible. Addresses, telephone numbers, websites, transport information, opening times, admission prices and credit card details are all included in our listings. And, as far as possible, we've given details of facilities, services and events, all checked and correct at the time we went to press. However, in Tokyo, businesses open and close with lightning speed. Furthermore, many restaurants and bars can close unexpectedly for the day at the whim of the owner. Before you go out of your way to visit a particular venue, we would advise you, whenever possible, to phone and check opening times. While every effort has been made to ensure the accuracy of the information contained here, the publishers cannot accept responsibility for any errors it may contain.

PRICES AND PAYMENT

Prices throughout this guide are given in Japanese yen (¥). The prices we've supplied should be treated as guidelines, not gospel. If they vary wildly from those we've quoted, please write and let us know. We aim to give the best and most up-to-date advice, so we always want to know if you've been badly treated or overcharged, or if (as we hope) you've been pleasantly surprised.

We have noted whether venues take credit cards, but have only listed the major cards – American Express (**AmEx**), Diners Club (**DC**), **JCB**, MasterCard (**MC**) and Visa (**V**). Note that most small businesses and tourist sights in Japan do not accept credit cards.

THE LIE OF THE LAND

Tokyo is divided into 23 wards (ku), which are given in addresses. These are shown on the map on pp60-1, which also provides an overview of central Tokyo and the specific areas covered by this guide. All listings contain the name of the nearest station(s), the train and subway lines that serve that station, and the most convenient station exit(s). Map references are also provided where possible, referring to the street maps in the Sightseeing section starting on p57, on which local sights and eating, drinking, arts and entertainment recommendations are clearly marked. See also p7 Finding your way around.

TELEPHONE NUMBERS

The area code for central Tokyo is 03. This is always followed by an eight-digit number. Telephone numbers given in this guide omit the 03 prefix as you don't need to dial this when in Tokyo. The outlying areas of Tokyo have different codes. For such places, the full number is provided. Numbers starting with the prefix 0120 are freephone numbers, while most mobile phone numbers in Japan begin with 090. The international dialling code for Japan is 81 (from the UK dial 00 81 (0) 3, followed by the number). For more details, see p311.

ESSENTIAL INFORMATION

For all the practical information you'll need for visiting the city – including visa and customs information, advice on facilities for the disabled, emergency telephone numbers and medical services, plus a list of useful websites and the full lowdown on Tokyo's vast, amazingly efficient rail and subway networks – turn to the Directory chapter. You'll find it at the back of the guide, starting on p299.

A full map of all rail and subway services in Greater Tokyo is on pp332-3, and a map of the subway system only on pp334-5.

Advertisers

We would like to stress that no establishment has been included in this guide because it has advertised in any of our publications and no payment of any kind has influenced any review. The opinions given in this book are those of Time Out writers and entirely independent.

There is an online version of this book, along with guides to over 100 international cities, at **www.timeout.com**.

LET US KNOW WHAT YOU THINK

We hope you enjoy *Time Out Tokyo*, and we'd really like to know what you think of it. We welcome tips and recommendations for places that you believe we should include in future editions and take notice of your criticism of our choices. You can email us at guides@timeout.com or write to us at Time Out Guides, Universal House, 251 Tottenham Court Road, London, W1T 7AB.

Finding your way around

Confusingly for the visitor, few streets in Tokyo have names. And when they do, those names never appear in addresses. Tokyo's street signs are small plaques attached to buildings and lamp posts with a series of digits that act almost like co-ordinates.

Navigating without street names is of course problematic, but take comfort in the fact that it's difficult for locals too. And, because it's the norm, there are various sources of help. Giving directions is part of the job for the staff of the ubiquitous police boxes (*koban*). They will need to know the numerical code for the building, which we give at the start of each address.

Maps showing the buildings and their codes are found at most station exits. A bilingual street atlas, available from major book shops, will make life even easier. And we have marked the exact locations of the majority of the destinations listed in this book on the maps in the Sightseeing chapters. For more information, see p303.

In Context

Roppongi Hills.*See p191.*

History

The tempestuous path from fishing village to metropolis.

Archaeological evidence suggests that the Tokyo metropolitan area was inhabited as long ago as the late Paleolithic period, and various stone tools belonging to the hunter-gatherers of pre-ceramic culture have been discovered at sites including Nogawa, in western Tokyo prefecture.

Pottery featuring rope-cord patterns developed in Japan during the so-called Jomon period (10,000-300 BC). Around 6,000 years ago, Tokyo Bay rose as far as the edge of the high ground that makes up the central *yamanote* area of the modern city; its retreat left behind a marshy shoreline that provided a rich food source. The late Jomon shell mounds at Omori, identified in 1877 by US zoologist ES Morse as he gazed from the window of a Shinbashi-Yokohama train, were the site of Japan's very first modern archaeological dig and forerunner to a long line of similar excavations.

The Yayoi period (300 BC-AD 300) is named after the Yayoi-cho district near Tokyo University in Hongo, where in 1884 the Mukogaoka shell mound yielded the first evidence of a more sophisticated form of pottery. Along with other advances such as wet-rice cultivation and the use of iron, this seems to have been introduced from the Asian mainland. Only after arriving on the southern island of Kyushu did new techniques spread through to the main island of Honshu.

KYOTO: THE FIRST IMPERIAL CAPITAL

Kanto (the region in which Tokyo sits) remained a distant outpost as the early Japanese state started to form around the Yamato court, which emerged in the fourth century as a loose confederation of chieftains in what is now Nara prefecture before extending to other parts of the country. Chinese ideographs and Buddhism arrived via the Korean peninsula.

The Senso-ji temple (*see p68*) in Asakusa supposedly dates from 628, when two fishermen are said to have discovered a gold statue of the *bodhisattva* Kannon in their nets. Under Taika Reform from 645, the land on which Tokyo now stands became part of Musashi province, governed from Kokufu (modern-day Fuchu City). State administration was centralised in emulation of the Tang imperial model and China's advanced civilisation exerted a strong influence.

After the imperial capital was moved to Heian (now Kyoto) in 794, a Japanese court culture flourished. The invention of the *kana* syllabary helped the writing of classics such as Sei Shonagon's *Pillow Book* and Lady Murasaki's *Tale of Genji*. The emperors were largely figureheads, manipulated by powerful regents from the dominant Fujiwara family. But the political power of the Kyoto court nobles went into slow decline as control of the regions fell into the hands of local military aristocracy.

An early revolt against Kyoto rule was staged by Taira no Masakado, a tenth-century rebel. According to one version of the story, in 931 a quarrel over a woman among different members of the 'Eight Bands of Taira from the East' into full-scale military conflict, during which Masakado won control of all eight provinces of Kanto. He then declared himself emperor of a new autonomous state.

After defeat by central government forces in 940, grisly evidence of Masakado's demise was dispatched to Kyoto. Legend has it that his severed head took to the skies and flew back to be reunited with his other remains in the fishing village of Shibasaki. The site is now in the Otemachi financial district but has remained untouched by generations of city builders, perhaps fearful of Masakado's vengeful spirit.

Tokyo's original name, Edo ('Rivergate'), is thought to derive from a settlement near where the Sumida river enters Tokyo Bay. Its first-known use goes back to a minor member of the Taira clan, Edo Shigenaga, who is thought to have adopted it after making his home in the area. In August 1180 Shigenaga attacked the forces of Miura Yoshizumi, an ally of the rival Minamoto clan. He switched sides three months later, though, just as shogun-to-be Minamoto no Yoritomo entered Musashi province.

By the late 12th century the rise of provincial warrior clans had developed into the struggle between the Taira and Minamoto families, later chronicled in *The Tale of Heike*. After Minamoto no Yoritomo wiped out the last of the Tairas in 1185, the emperor dubbed him Seii Tai Shogun ('Barbarian-Subduing Generalissimo'). Yoritomo shunned Kyoto, setting up his government in Kamakura (*see pp288-291*).

THE WAY OF THE WARRIOR

This inaugurated a period of military rule that was to last till the 19th century. *Bushido*, 'the way of the warrior', emphasised martial virtues, while the samurai class emerged as a powerful force in feudal society. Nevertheless, attempted Mongol invasions in 1274 and 1281 were only driven back by stormy seas off Kyushu, something attributed to the *kamikaze*, or 'wind of the gods'. Dissatisfaction grew with the Kamakura government, and in 1333 Ashikaga Takauji established a new shogunate in the Muromachi district of Kyoto.

The first castle at Edo was erected in 1457 by Ota Dokan, a *waka* poet known as Ota Sekenaga before taking a monk's tonsure in 1478, and now celebrated as Tokyo's founder. Above the Hibiya inlet, he constructed fortifications overlooking the entrance to the Kanto plain for northbound travellers along the Pacific sea road. To improve navigation, he also diverted the Hira river east at Kandabashi to form the Nihonbashi river.

In 1486, during a military clash between branches of the locally powerful Uesugi family, Ota was falsely accused of betraying his lord, and met his end at the home of Uesugi Sadamasa in Sagami (modern-day Kanagawa).

'In an age when London still had under one million people, Edo was the world's biggest metropolis.'

Central government authority largely disappeared following the Onin War (1467-77), as regional lords, or *daimyo*, fought for dominance. Only after a century of on-off civil strife did the country begin to regain unity under Oda Nobunaga, although his assassination in 1582 meant that final reunification was left to Toyotomi Hideyoshi. In 1590 Hideyoshi established control of the Kanto region after successfully besieging Odawara Castle, stronghold of the powerful Go-Hojo family.

Hideyoshi ordered his ally Tokugawa Ieyasu to exchange his lands in Shizuoka and Aichi for the former Go-Hojo domains in Kanto. Rather than Odawara (which lies in present-day

Kanagawa prefecture), Ieyasu chose Edo as his headquarters. A new castle was built on the site of Ota Dokan's crumbling fortifications. After Hideyoshi's death, Ieyasu was victorious in the struggle for national power at the Battle of Sekigahara in 1600, and three years later was named shogun. The emperor remained in Kyoto, but Edo became the government capital of Japan.

EDO ERA (1600-1868)

When Ieyasu arrived in 1590, Edo was little more than a few houses at the edge of the Hibiya inlet. This changed quickly. Equally divided between military and townspeople, the population grew dramatically before levelling off in the early 18th century at around 1.2 million. In an age when London still had under one million people, Edo was probably the world's biggest metropolis. Fifteen successive Tokugawa shoguns ruled for more than 250 years. All roads led to Edo: five highways radiated from the city, communications aided by regular post stations, including Shinagawa, Shinjuku, Itabashi and Senju.

The regional feudal lords retained local autonomy, but a system of alternate annual residence forced them to divide their time between their own lands and the capital. *Daimyo* finances were drained by the regular journeys with retinues and the need to maintain large residences in Edo. There was little chance to foment trouble in the provinces and, as a further inducement to loyalty, family members were kept in Edo as permanent hostages.

Although Tokugawa Ieyasu's advisers had included Englishman Will Adams (whose story is fictionalised in the novel *Shogun*), a policy of national seclusion was introduced in 1639. Contact with Western countries was restricted to a small Dutch trade mission on the island of Dejima, near Nagasaki in Kyushu, far from Edo. This policy didn't change for more than 200 years, resulting in Japan's culture remaining remarkably self-contained and untouched.

The layout of Edo reflected the social order, with the high ground of central Tokyo (the *yamanote*) the preserve of the military classes, and the *shitamachi* ('low city') area outside the castle walls occupied by the townspeople. There was also an attempt to conform to Chinese principles of geomancy by having the two temples that would hold the Tokugawa family tombs – Kanei-ji (*see p122*) and Zojo-ji (*see p106*) – in the auspicious north-east and south-west of the city. More problematically, since Mt Fuji lay west rather than north (the traditionally favoured direction for a mountain), Edo Castle's main gate (Otemon) was placed on its east side, instead of the usual south.

Completed in 1638, Edo Castle was the world's largest. Its outer defences extended 16 kilometres (ten miles). The most important of the four sets of fortifications, the *hon-maru* or principal fortress, contained the shogun's residence, the inner chambers for his wife and concubines, and the halls of state. The keep stood on an adjacent hill, overlooking the city. Between the double set of moats, regional *daimyo* had their mansions arranged in a strict hierarchy of 'dependent' and 'outside' lords.

East of the castle walls, the low-lying *shitamachi* districts were home to merchants, craftsmen, labourers and others attracted to Edo's wealth and power. Less than one-fifth of the land, much of it reclaimed, held around half the population. The curving wooden bridge, Nihonbashi, was the hub of the nation's highways and the spot from which all distances were measured.

Nearby were wealthy merchants' residences and grand shops such as Echigoya (forerunner of today's Mitsukoshi department store), the city's prison and the fish market. Behind grand thoroughfares, the crowded backstreet tenements of Nihonbashi and Kanda were a breeding ground for disease and in constant danger of flooding. Fires were also common in the largely wooden city.

The worst conflagration was the 'Long Sleeves Fire' of 1657, in which the original castle buildings were destroyed and more than 100,000 people died, around a quarter of Edo's total population. The flames began at a temple, Hommyo-ji in Hongo, where monks had been burning two long-sleeved kimono belonging to young women who had recently died. The fire raged for three days; by the morning of the fourth day, three-quarters of Edo had gone up in smoke.

Reconstruction work was soon under way. Roads were widened and new fire breaks introduced. Many had perished because they couldn't escape across the Sumida river, which, for military reasons, had no bridges; opening up Fukagawa and Honjo for development, a bridge was now erected at Ryogoku. There was also a general dispersal of temples and shrines to outlying areas such as Yanaka and reclaimed land in Tsukiji. The Yoshiwara 'pleasure quarters' (licensed prostitution area) were moved out too – from Ningyocho to beyond Asakusa and the newly extended city limits.

New residences for *daimyo* were established outside the castle walls, leading to a more patchwork mix of nobles' estates and townspeoples' districts, although the basic pattern of *shitamachi* areas in the east was retained. *Daimyo* mansions inside the castle were rebuilt in a more restrained style. The

Suicidal samurai

Literary celebration of suicide is not exclusively Japanese, but in a country where around 30,000 people a year take their own life, it's tackled with unique fervour. Ritualised samurai suicide was most famously romanticised by novelist and nationalist revolutionary Mishima Yukio, who disembowelled himself after a failed coup in 1970.

Mishima's suicide highlights the strong literary heritage of the act. Suicides – honourable and tragic – resonate throughout the stories that make up Japan's national narrative. During the 19th-century Boshin Wars the *Byakkotai* (White Tiger Brigade), a group of Fukushima schoolboys, killed themselves after seeing smoke rise over a hill – they mistakenly believed their lord's castle had been burned to the ground. Their errant self-sacrifice won the admiration of Mussolini, who sent a bronze eagle that still stands in the grounds of the castle in Aizu-Wakamatsu City. But these impetuous kids play second fiddle to the tale of the 47 *ronin* (masterless samurai), or *Chushingura*, as it is commonly known. Adapted, played, retold and viewable in almost every art form, it wins prize billing for its fatally attractive combination of honour besmirched, time bided, revenge taken and thus honour restored.

The tale begins with 18th-century lord Naganori Asano, who had been summoned to Edo Castle to arrange a reception for imperial envoys. According to the story, his protocol instructor, Kira Yoshinaka, called him a bumpkin and refused to teach him the rituals. Asano bore the insults until the day of the visit, when he attacked Kira in the palace grounds. For this breach of etiquette Asano was ordered to commit *seppuku*, ritual suicide.

However, 47 of Asano's samurai, shorn of their lord, their status and their means of survival, swore vengeance. On the morning of 14 December 1702, they reunited in Edo and attacked Kira's estate, eventually finding and beheading the object of their vengeance.

They then took the head to **Sengaku-ji** temple (*see p136*) in Takanawa, where they placed it on Asano's tomb and turned themselves in, knowing they faced execution for their actions. In the face of public pressure, the shogun ordered 44 of them to commit *seppuku* – rather than be executed as common criminals (one had died en route, while two were not samurai rank and thus not permitted the dubious honour of committing *seppuku* – write your own 'gutted' jokes.)

Those wishing to relive the experience can follow the route of the *ronin* using the map at www.tokyo-kurenaidan.com/chushingura.htm.

innermost section of the reconstructed castle was more subdued, lacking the high tower of its predecessor.

One byproduct of the stability of the Tokugawa regime was that the large number of military personnel stationed in Edo found themselves with relatively little to do. Complex bureaucracy developed, and there were ceremonial duties, but members of the top strata of the feudal system soon found themselves outstripped economically by the city's wealthy merchants. In these circumstances, a daring vendetta attack staged by the band of masterless samurai known later as the 47 *ronin* caused a sensation (*see p15* **Suicidal samurai**).

A vibrant new urban culture grew up in Edo's *shitamachi* districts. During the long years of peace and relative prosperity, the pursuit of pleasure provided the populace, particularly the city's wealthy merchants, with welcome relief from the feudal system's stifling social confines. Landscape artists such as Hiroshige (1797-1868) depicted a city of theatres, temples, scenic bridges, festivals and fairs. There were numerous seasonal celebrations, including big firework displays (still held) to celebrate the summer opening of the Sumida river, as well as cherry-blossom viewing along its banks in spring.

Kabuki, an Edo favourite, didn't always have the approval of the high city. In 1842 a government edict banished theatres up the Sumida river to Asakusa, where they stayed until after the fall of the shogunate. As the district already boasted the temple of Senso-ji, with its fairs and festivals, and the Yoshiwara pleasure quarters lay only a short distance away, the act merely cemented Asakusa's position as Edo's favoured relaxation centre.

THE AMERICANS ARRIVE

Notice that Japan could no longer isolate itself from the outside world arrived in Edo Bay in 1853 in the shape of four US 'black ships' under the command of Commodore Matthew Perry. Hastily prepared defences were helpless, and the Treaty of Kanagawa signed with Perry the following year proved to be the thin end of the wedge, as Western powers forced further concessions. In 1855 Edo suffered a major quake that killed over 7,000 people and destroyed large parts of the lower city. In 1859 Townsend Harris, the first US consul-general, arrived to set up a mission at Zenpuku-ji temple in Azabu.

Voices of discontent had already been raised against the government: there were increasingly frequent famines, and proponents of 'National Learning' called for a return to some purer form of Shinto (the native religion). The foreign

War crimes tribunal, November 1948. *See p19.*

threat now polarised opinion. In 1860 the senior councillor of the shogunate government, Ii Naosuke, was assassinated outside Edo Castle. Under the slogan 'expel the barbarian, revere the emperor', a series of incidents took place against foreigners. Power drained from Edo as the government looked to build a unified national policy by securing imperial backing in Kyoto. *Daimyo* residences in Edo were abandoned after the old alternate residence requirement was abolished in 1862.

The Tokugawa regime was finally overthrown early in 1868, when a coalition of forces from the south declared an imperial 'restoration' in Kyoto in the name of the 15-year-old emperor Meiji, and then won a military victory at Toba-Fushimi. Edo's population fell to around half its former level as remaining residents of the *yamanote* areas departed. A last stand by shogunate loyalists at the Battle of Ueno was hopeless, and left in ruins large parts of the Kanei-ji temple complex, which housed the tombs of several Tokugawa shoguns.

MEIJI ERA (1868-1912)

Following the restoration of imperial rule, the emperor's residence was swiftly transferred from Kyoto to Edo, which was renamed Tokyo ('Eastern Capital'). The city now became both the political and imperial capital, with the inner section of Edo Castle serving as the new Imperial Palace. By the mid 1880s the population had reverted to its earlier level, but the *shitamachi* area lost much of its cultural distinctiveness as many wealthier residents moved to smarter locations. Industrialisation continued to bring newcomers from the countryside. By the end of the Meiji era in 1912, Tokyo housed a total of nearly two million people.

To the south-west of the palace, the districts of Nagatacho and Kasumigaseki became the heart of the nation's new government and bureaucratic establishment. 'Rich country, strong army' was the rallying cry, but learning from abroad was recognised to be essential: government missions were dispatched overseas, foreign experts brought in, and radical reforms initiated in everything from education to land ownership.

Laying the foundations of a modern state meant sweeping away much of the old feudal structure. Government was centralised and the *daimyo* pensioned off. The introduction of conscription in 1873 ended the exclusive role of the warrior class. Disaffected elements led by Saigo Takamori rebelled in Satsuma in 1877, but were defeated by government forces. The following year, six former samurai from Satsuma staged a revenge attack and murdered Meiji government leader Okubo Toshimichi.

Ending old social restrictions fuelled economic development. The Bank of Japan was established in 1882, bringing greater fiscal and monetary stability. Industrialisation proceeded apace and factories sprang up near the Sumida river and in areas overlooking Tokyo Bay. After 1894 Marunouchi became the site of a business district called 'London Town' because of its blocks of Victorian-style office buildings. In 1889 a written constitution declared the emperor 'sacred and inviolable'. Real power remained with existing government leaders, but there was a nod to greater popular representation. Elections were held among the top 1.5 per cent of taxpayers, and the first session of the Imperial Diet (parliament) took place in 1890.

By the early 1890s the government was making progress on ending the much-hated 'unequal treaties' earlier conceded to the West. Taking a leaf from the imperialists' book, Japan seized Taiwan in 1895 after a war with China. Ten years later its forces defeated the Russians in Manchuria and Korea during the Russo-Japanese War. This was the first victory over a Western power by an Asian country, but there were riots in Hibiya Park at the peace treaty's perceived leniency towards Russia. In 1910 Japan annexed Korea.

> ## 'At 12 storeys, the Ryounkaku brick tower was Tokyo's tallest building and contained the city's first elevator.'

New goods and ideas from overseas started to pour into Tokyo, especially after Japan's first train line started services between Yokohama and Shinbashi station in 1872. Men abandoned their traditional topknots; married women followed the lead of the empress and stopped blackening their teeth. There were gas lights, beer halls, the first department stores and public parks, and even ballroom dancing at Hibiya's glittering Rokumeikan reception hall (designed by British architect Josiah Conder), where the elite gathered in their best foreign finery to display their mastery of the advanced new ways.

After a major fire in 1872 the former artisan district of Ginza was redeveloped with around 900 brick buildings; newspaper offices were the first to flock to what would become Tokyo's most fashionable area. Asakusa kept in touch with popular tastes through attractions such as the Ryounkaku brick tower: at 12 storeys, it was Tokyo's tallest building and contained the city's first elevator. Asakusa was also home to Japan's first permanent cinema, which opened in 1903, and the cinemas, theatres and music halls of the Rokku district remained popular throughout the early decades of the 20th century.

TAISHO ERA (1912-26)

The funeral of Emperor Meiji in 1912 was accompanied by the ritual suicide of General Nogi, a hero of the Russo-Japanese War (the house where he killed himself can be seen at Nogi Jinja; *see p106*). The new emperor, Taisho, was in constant poor health, and his son, Hirohito, became regent in 1921.

There was a brief flowering of 'Taisho Democracy': in 1918 Hara Takashi became the first prime minister from a political party, an appointment that came after a sudden rise in rice prices prompted national disturbances, including five days of rioting in the capital. Hara was assassinated in 1921 by a right-wing extremist, but universal male suffrage was finally introduced in 1925.

Tokyo was beginning to spill over its boundaries, and part of Shinjuku was brought inside the city limits in 1920, an early indication of the capital's tendency to drift further westwards following the expansion of suburban train lines. Ginza was enjoying its heyday as a strolling spot for fashionable youth. In nearby Hibiya, a new Imperial Hotel, designed by world-famous American architect Frank Lloyd Wright, opened in 1923.

Such modernisation could not quell the forces of nature, however. Shortly before noon on 1 September 1923, the Kanto region was hit by a devastating earthquake. High winds fanned the flames of cooking fires and two days of terrible conflagrations swept through Tokyo and the surrounding area, including Yokohama, leaving more than 140,000 dead and large areas devastated. Around 63 per cent of Tokyo homes were destroyed in the Great Kanto Earthquake, with the traditional wooden buildings of the old *shitamachi* areas hardest hit. Rumours of well-poisoning and other misdeeds led vigilante groups to massacre several thousand Koreans before martial law was imposed.

Temporary structures were quickly in place and there was a short building boom. The destruction in eastern areas accelerated the population movement to the western suburbs, but plans to remodel the city were largely laid aside because of cost.

SHOWA ERA (1926-89)

Hirohito became emperor in 1926, ushering in the Showa era. His 63-year reign – the longest of any Japanese emperor – coincided with a period of extraordinary change and turbulence. Tokyo recovered gradually from the effects of the 1923 earthquake and continued growing. Post-quake reconstruction was declared officially over in 1930.

In 1932 Tokyo's boundaries underwent major revision to take account of changing population patterns, with growing western districts such as Shibuya and Ikebukuro, and the remaining parts of Shinjuku, coming within the city limits. The total number of wards jumped from 15 to 35 (later simplified to the 23 of today), and the city's land area increased sevenfold. At a stroke, the population doubled to over five million, making Tokyo the world's second most populous city after New York.

The early 20th-century era of parliamentary government was not to last. Political stability fell victim to the economic depression that followed a domestic banking collapse in 1927 and the Wall Street crash two years later. Extremist nationalist groups saw expansion overseas as the answer to the nation's problems. In November 1930, after signing a naval disarmament treaty, prime minister Hamaguchi Osachi was killed by a right-wing extremist in Tokyo station.

In 1931 dissident army officers staged a Japanese military takeover of Manchuria, bringing conflict with world opinion. Pre-war party government ended after a short-lived rebellion of younger officers on 15 May 1932; the prime minister, Inukai Tsuyoshi, and other cabinet members were assassinated, and a series of national unity governments took over, dependent on military support. A puppet state, Manchukuo, was declared in Manchuria, and Japan left the League of Nations. On 26 February 1936 the army's First Division mutinied and attempted a coup in the name of 'Showa Restoration'. Strategic points were seized in central Tokyo, but the rebellion was put down.

In an atmosphere of increasing nationalist fervour and militarism, Japan became involved in widening international conflict. Full-scale hostilities with China broke out in July 1937 (imperial troops killed 300,000 in the Chinese capital in the infamous Rape of Nanking), but Japanese forces got bogged down after early advances. In 1940 Japan signed a tripartite pact with Germany and Italy. Western powers, led by the US, declared a total embargo of Japan in summer 1941. Negotiations between the two sides reached an impasse, and on 7 December 1941 Japan attacked the US Pacific fleet at Pearl Harbor.

After a series of quick successes in the Pacific and South-east Asia, Japanese forces began to be pushed back after the Battle of Midway in June 1942. By late 1944 Tokyo lay within the range of American bombers. A series of incendiary attacks devastated the capital; the pre-dawn raid by 300 bombers on 10 March 1945 is estimated to have left 100,000 dead, a million people homeless and a quarter of the city obliterated. On 6 August an atomic bomb was dropped on Hiroshima, followed by another on Nagasaki three days later. Cabinet deadlock left the casting vote to the emperor, whose radio broadcast to the nation on 15 August announced Japan's surrender.

Much of Tokyo lay in ruins; food and shelter posed immediate problems. As many as one in ten slept in temporary shelters during the first post-war winter.

On 1 September 1923 the **Great Kanto Earthquake** devastated Tokyo. *See p18*.

POST-WAR PROSPERITY

Following surrender, Japan was occupied by Allied forces under the leadership of General Douglas MacArthur, who set about demilitarising the country and promoting democratic reform. The emperor kept his throne but renounced his divine status. Article nine of the new constitution of 1946 included strict pacifist provisions, and the armed forces were disbanded. In 1948 seven 'Class A' war criminals, including wartime prime minister Tojo Hideki, were executed.

The outbreak of the Korean War in 1950 provided a tremendous boost to the Japanese economy, with large contracts to supply US forces. Under MacArthur's orders, a limited rearmament took place, leading to the eventual founding of the Self-Defence Forces (as Japan's military is called). A new security treaty with the US was signed in 1951, and the occupation ended in 1952.

With national defence left largely in US hands, economic growth was the priority under the long rule of the pro-business Liberal Democratic Party (LDP), formed in 1955. Prosperity started to manifest itself in the shape of large new office buildings in central Tokyo. In 1960 prime minister Ikeda Hayato announced a plan to double national income over a decade – a target achieved with ease in the economic miracle years that followed.

The Olympics were held in Tokyo in 1964, the same year *shinkansen* (bullet trains) started running between the capital and Osaka. Improvements to Tokyo's infrastructure were made in preparation for the Olymics; after the Games were over, redevelopment continued apace. Frank Lloyd Wright's Imperial Hotel, amazingly a survivor of both the 1923 earthquake and the war, was demolished in 1967, the year the city's inner 23 wards achieved their peak population of almost nine million. To the west of Shinjuku station, Tokyo's first concentration of skyscrapers started to take shape during the early 1970s.

Despite the economic progress, there was an undercurrent of social discontent. Hundreds of thousands demonstrated against renewal of the US-Japan Security Treaty in 1960 (which allowed American military bases on Japanese soil), and the end of the decade saw students in violent revolt. In 1970 novelist Mishima Yukio dramatically ended his life after failing to spark a nationalist uprising at the city's Ichigaya barracks. In Chiba, radical groups from the other end of the political spectrum joined local farmers to battle with riot police, delaying completion of Tokyo's new international airport at Narita from 1971 to 1975 and its opening until 1978.

The post-war fixed exchange rate ended in 1971, and growth came to a temporary halt with the oil crisis of 1974, but the Japanese economy continued to outperform its Western competitors. Trade friction developed, particularly with the US. After the Plaza Accord financial agreement of 1985, the yen jumped to new highs, inflating the value of Japanese financial assets. Shoppers switched to designer labels as a building frenzy gripped Tokyo, which was deemed the world's most expensive city. Land values soared and feverish speculation fuelled a 'Bubble economy'.

HEISEI ERA (1989-)

The death of Hirohito in 1989 at the age of 87 came at the beginning of the sweeping global changes marking the end of the Cold War. Hirihito's son, Akihito, took over, becoming Japan's 125th emperor and introducing the Heisei period.

As the 1990s wore on, the system that had served Japan so well in the post-war era stumbled. A collapse in land and stock-market prices brought the Bubble economy to an end in 1990 and left Japanese banks with a mountain of bad debt. An economy that had been the envy of the world became mired in its deepest recession since the end of World War II.

> ## 'The 1995 Kobe earthquake reminded Tokyo residents of their vulnerability to natural disaster.'

Tokyo ushered in a new era in 1991, when the metropolitan government moved to a thrusting new skyscraper in Shinjuku (Tange Kenzo's twin-towered Tokyo Metropolitan Government Building; see p120), symbolising the capital's shift away from its traditional centre.

Long-standing demands for an end to 'money politics' finally proved irresistible in 1993, when the LDP lost power for the first time in 38 years. A short-lived nine-party coalition enacted a programme of political reform, but the LDP clawed its way back to power in 1994 through an unlikely partnership with its erstwhile foe, the rapidly declining Japan Socialist Party, and remained at the heart of subsequent coalitions.

In January 1995 the Kobe earthquake reminded Tokyo residents of their vulnerability to natural disaster. In March a sarin-gas attack on city subways by members of the Aum Shinrikyo doomsday cult provoked more horror and much agonised debate. Discussions about moving the national government to a less quake-prone location continued. Special events to mark the opening of the Odaiba waterfront development were cancelled on cost grounds.

In a new climate of job insecurity and fragile consumer confidence, the 'Heisei recession' proved resilient to the traditional stimulus of public works programmes. In April 1999, attracted by the promise of strong leadership, Tokyo voted hawkish former-LDP independent, Ishihara Shintaro, as their new governor. Two years later, LDP outsider Koizumi Junichiro took over as prime minister from Mori Yoshiro, boasting record popularity ratings and promising reform with 'no sacred cows'. Nevertheless, the slow pace of political and economic change in Japan continued to frustrate observers.

Tokyo sat out Japan's co-hosting of the 2002 football World Cup, with the final held in nearby Yokohama, but the event improved the nation's ties with neighbouring South Korea. Relations with China, however, stayed in the deep freeze, bedevilled by Koizumi's controversial annual visits to Yasukuni Shrine (see p98), which honours Japan's war dead, including convicted war criminals. At the same time, revelations about North Korea's nuclear arms programme and its abduction of Japanese citizens in the 1970s and 1980s worsened relations between the two countries.

In contrast to the fortunes of other Iraq War allies, Koizumi voluntarily stepped down in late 2006 with his popularity intact. His successor, Abe Shinzo, is seen as a more conservative and far less charismatic leader. His lack of flair may not be the political hindrance it would be in other nations, since Japan is well used to grey leaders, and Abe takes control of a country on an economic upturn. But more nuclear posturing from Japan's unruly neighbour, and pressures from his political base to strengthen Japan's global position, mean he'll need all the leadership skills he can find. Among his first acts have been meetings to mollify China and South Korea, as well as parliamentary acts to bring more patriotism to the classroom and strengthen the role of the Defense Agency.

Key events

c10,000-300 BC Jomon period.
c300 BC-AD 300 Yayoi period; introduction
of wet-rice cultivation, bronze and ironware
into Japan from continental Asia.
1st century Japan ('land of Wa') first
mentioned in Chinese chronicles.
4th century Yamato court exists in Nara area.
6th century Buddhism introduced from Korea.
710 Nara becomes imperial capital.
794 Capital moves to Heian (Kyoto).
1019 Murasaki Shikibu writes *Tale of Genji*.
1180 First recorded use of the name Edo.
1185-1333 Kamakura is site of military
government.
1274, 1281 Attempted Mongol invasions.
1457 Ota Dokan builds first castle at Edo.
1590 Edo becomes headquarters of
Tokugawa Ieyasu. Construction of Edo Castle.
1592 Toyotomi Hideyoshi invades Korea.
1598 Withdrawal from Korea.
1603 Ieyasu named shogun; Edo becomes
seat of national government.
1635 Edicts formalise system of alternate
residence in Edo for feudal lords.
1639 National seclusion policy established.
1657 'Long Sleeves Fire' decimates Edo.
1688-1704 *Genroku* period of cultural flowering.
1703 47 *ronin* vendetta carried out.
1707 Mt Fuji erupts, ash falls on Edo.
1720 Ban on import of foreign books lifted.
1742 Floods and storms kill 4,000 in Edo.
1787-93 Kansei reforms; rice granaries
set up in Edo after famine and riots.
1804-29 Bunka-Bunsei period; peak of
Edo merchant culture.
1825 Government issues 'Order for
Repelling of Foreign Ships'.
1841-3 Reforms to strengthen economy.
1853 Arrival of US 'black ships' at Uraga.
1854 Treaty of Kanagawa signed with US
Commodore Perry.
1855 Earthquake kills over 7,000 in Edo.
1860 Ii Naosuke assassinated.
1862 End of alternate residence system.
1868 Tokugawa shogunate overthrown in
Meiji Restoration. Imperial residence
moved from Kyoto; Edo renamed Tokyo.
1869 Yasukuni Shrine established to Japan's
war dead. Rickshaws appear in Tokyo.
1871-3 Meiji leaders tour US and Europe.
1872 Shinbashi to Yokohama train service.
1874 Tokyo's first gas lights appear in Ginza.
1877 Satsuma rebellion.
1889 New Meiji constitution promulgated.

1894-5 Sino-Japanese War.
1902 Anglo-Japanese alliance signed.
1904-5 Russo-Japanese war.
1910 Korea brought into Japanese Empire.
1912 Emperor Meiji dies; Taisho era begins.
1923 Great Kanto Earthquake; 140,000 died
and Tokyo devastated.
1925 Universal male suffrage introduced.
1926 Hirohito becomes emperor.
1927 Asia's first subway line opens
between Asakusa and Ueno.
1930 Post-earthquake reconstruction
declared officially complete.
1931 Military takeover of Manchuria.
1932 Prime minister Inukai Tsuyoshi
assassinated. Extension of Tokyo boundaries
means city's population is doubled.
1933 Japan leaves League of Nations.
1936 Army rebellion in central Tokyo.
1937 Hostilities in China; Rape of Nanking.
1940 Tripartite pact with Germany and Italy.
1941 Pearl Harbor attack begins Pacific War.
1945 Incendiary bombing of Tokyo. Atomic
bombs dropped on Hiroshima and Nagasaki.
Japan surrenders; occupation begins.
1946 Emperor renounces divinity.
New constitution promulgated.
1951 Security Treaty signed with US.
1952 Occupation ends.
1954 Release of first *Godzilla* film.
1955 Liberal Democratic Party (LDP) formed,
along with Japan Socialist Party.
1960 Demonstrations against renewal of
US-Japan security treaty.
1964 Tokyo Olympic Games. First *shinkansen*
bullet train runs between Tokyo and Osaka.
1968-9 Student unrest.
1971 Yen revalued from US$360 to $308.
1989 Death of Hirohito; Heisei era begins.
1990 End of 'Bubble economy'.
1993 LDP loses power after 38 years.
1994 Socialist Party's Murayama Tomiichi
becomes prime minister in coalition with LDP.
1995 Kobe earthquake. Sarin gas attack
on Tokyo subway.
1998 Asian economic crisis spreads.
2001 Koizumi Junichiro replaces Mori Yoshiro.
2002 Japan co-hosts football World Cup;
Koizumi visits North Korea.
2003 400th anniversary of government
move to Edo.
2004 Japanese troops deployed in Iraq.
2006 Koizumi Junichiro relinquishes office,
replaced by Abe Shinzo.

Tokyo Today

As the economy rebounds, the capital is glittering again.

Tokyo, capital of Japan since 1869, sits at the centre of the most populated metropolitan area on the planet, but unlike many other cities that impress by size alone, this city bristles with superlatives, offering residents and visitors alike the safest streets, cleanest taxis, most timely trains and, usually, most courteous citizens. The city's history and culture have seen it become something of a capital of the New Grand Tour – surpassing the European capitals as a place one visits to see one's own mores in a new light.

Taking in Tokyo for the first time, it appears to have no recognisable structure. Raised concrete expressways and electric cables twist like Lilith's locks over old wooden houses, across rivers and between gleaming skyscrapers, while below, narrow lanes criss-cross the Kanto alluvial plain in a shattered-glass pattern.

Despite its size, this is not a city that shouts about its greatness. Tokyo plays hard to get and it is only when you discover its quiet corners, such as the camphor-populated grove of the Yushima Seido Confucian Shrine in Ochanomizu (1-4-5 Yushima, Bunkyo-ku) or the *nomiya* (diminutive bars) of Yanaka's Hatsunei Komichi, that you really discover its essence.

Picturesque old buildings such as Yushima Seido are, however, an increasingly rare find in Tokyo. Many blame the war and earthquakes for the lack of heritage structures, but the truth is, most ageing shops and dwellings fall to the rapacious demand for land that has turned much of this city into a vast concrete jungle.

> ### 'Constant knocking down and rebuilding mean Tokyo is a city where architects are allowed to have fun.'

But constant knocking down and rebuilding mean Tokyo is a city where architects are allowed to have some fun. Ludicrous land prices combined with corporate one-upmanship have seen developers dot Tokyo with prize-winning designs built at improbable angles and with cutting-edge technology. Amid the sea of grey stand creations by some of the world's most sought-after architects: Philippe Starck's flame-topped La Flamme d'Or in Asakusa; Pritzker Prize-winner Kevin Roche's Shiodome City Center; Ito Toyo's tree-like Tod's headquarters on Omotesando, a few doors down from SANAA's acrylic-covered design for Christian Dior; and Tange Kenzo's Park Hyatt.

THE BOUNCE-BACK

Shaken by the collapse of the economy in the 1990s, Tokyoites a decade or so ago were beginning to question whether their skyscraper-filled city mattered globally. Today many of the city's inhabitants have more than overcome those doubts, having emerged from years of financial strife and introspection more confident and capable than ever.

Major retail and leisure firms are counting on the heavily predicted consumer spending boom said to be just around the corner – a host of commercial redevelopments have sprung up, including Omotesando Hills and the huge LaLaport, while a former Defense Agency site in Roppongi has been transformed by New York Freedom Tower architects Skidmore, Owings & Merrill (SOM) into Tokyo Midtown – a virtual city within a city. The complex includes the new Ritz-Carlton, which is joined in the suddenly crowded luxury-hotel market by a new Cesar Pelli-designed Mandarin Oriental, a stone's throw from Tokyo Station, and über-chic chain Peninsula, set to open a hotel in the city in September 2007.

> ### 'Maverick right-winger Ishihara Shintaro is bigger than Godzilla in this city.'

Yet those who were uprooted by the last fiscal free fall, and can't afford a bed of any description, have formed a homeless underclass conservatively estimated by the government to number 5,000. These destitute citizens live under blue tarpaulins in Tokyo's parks and along its riverbanks. While Osaka's homeless men and women have become a political force, fighting 'evictions' – and winning a court battle to officially register their homes – Tokyo's outcasts, by contrast, continue to face regular harassment and have been pushed to the margins of this supposedly classless society.

A magnet for the young, Tokyo has, however, managed to escape the worst of the problems linked to Japan's rapidly ageing population. (By 2030, more than a third of the nation's population could be aged 65 or over.) Young Tokyoites know, though, that, come retirement, it will be every man and woman for themselves. Hoping the problem will go away, the government is refusing to raise taxes to pay for pensions, causing workers to push back their planned retirement ages.

A WOMAN'S PLACE

Tokyo's economy may be hit hard in the future by the lack of skilled young workers, but skilled young women still believe they must choose between motherhood and their career, and men still don't view fatherhood as a practical responsibility, with less than two per cent of new dads taking the paltry paternity leave available. Tokyo's economy soldiers on, staffed by overworked middle-aged men, while women who do choose to work find themselves trapped under a very low glass ceiling, and criticised by conservatives for not staying at home and procreating. Of course, not all women who work have chosen to do so. After Tokyoite women reach the age of 31, they may find themselves referred to as *makeinu* – literally, 'loser dog'. But instead of being insulted by this tag, Tokyo's thirtysomething female workers have taken the term and given it a new twist, wearing it as a badge of pride. It's finally considered plausible that a woman might choose not to marry, and these independently wealthy single women appear to be having fun buying bijou properties, travelling abroad (business class, of course) and climbing the more accessible ladders of foreign companies. The rise of girl power in Tokyo is being helped by key writers such as Hasegawa Junko, Itoyama Akiko and Shimamoto Rio, who are set on redefining the role of women in Japanese society.

Omotesando Hills.

Tokyo's youth also seem to be enjoying themselves – flooding on to the streets at weekends and on weeknights. While Tokyoite teens once had a herd mentality, slavishly following the latest trends until it was time to don a grey suit, more and more young people are putting off joining the rat race – a shift that has given birth to original and taboo-breaking ideas. Of course, taboos are not hard to break in this conservative city – one Japanese university bars students with pierced ears (a sign of self-abuse) and dyed hair (showing a lack of self-respect).

Tokyo's teens and twentysomethings are shocking even their older siblings by dabbling in recreational drugs. While drugs have always been available on the dingier inner-city streets, they are now becoming common among some subcultures, with amphetamines (*tama*, or 'balls') and cocaine (*shiroi kona*, literally 'white powder') the drugs of choice. Ultra-nationalist Tokyo governor Ishihara Shintaro's answer to the problem is the 'just say no' approach – meaning saying no to foreign immigrants; apparently they are the ones bringing in all the illicit substances.

A tale of two princesses

Masako and Kiko are the two commoners who have married Japan's imperial heirs. Before they began charming the crowds with their princessly hand waves, both were daughters of middle-class families. Owada Masako completed studies at Harvard, Oxford and Tokyo University before using her linguistic skills to follow in her father's footsteps as a diplomat. Kawashima Kiko also had her share of worldly exposure, growing up in Austria and the US, with her university-professor father.

But the similarities end there. Kiko met her Prince – Akishino – as an undergraduate at Gakushuin University, and the two tied the knot in 1988. Masako is also speculated to have met her heir at Tokyo University, but found her globe-trotting career harder to sacrifice. She finally consented to the love-struck Crown prince Naruhito in 1993.

After her wedding, Princess Kiko popped out two baby girls in quick succession: Mako in 1991 and Kako in 1994. Princess Masako, on the other hand, had to face the mounting expectation of a royal family that needed a male heir, and hadn't seen one in 41 years. The pressure of being viewed for only one purpose – bearing a boy – is said to be the primary cause of the Crown princess's alleged depression, which led to her seclusion from the public. Princess Masako eventually gave birth to a girl – Aiko – in 2001. The nation's succession laws apply only to males.

Princess Masako's withdrawal from official duties, and inability to bear an heir, led to divisions in the usually inscrutable imperial household. As criticism mounted, Masako's hubbie stepped in with unprecedented bravado. The Crown prince openly criticised the Imperial Household Agency for its treatment of his wife. This, in turn, caused the normally low-profile Prince Akishino, during his own 39th-birthday speech, to disparage his older brother for not consulting the emperor before speaking so candidly. The brothers' verbal exchange was a sign of strife inside Japan's most impervious household.

Faced with the succession crisis, Japan's former prime minister, Koizumi Junichiro, together with a government-appointed advisory panel, began to back a contentious initiative that would allow a female to ascend the Chrysanthemum Throne.

In what can only be described as a well-timed miracle, however, Princess Kiko ended the long dearth of imperial boys in 2006. While most Japanese celebrated the news, Prince Hisahito's arrival nipped any talk of reform in the bud, and perceptive career women saw it as another affirmation of the virtues of the dutiful wife and mother in Japan.

Marunouchi: Tokyo's financial centre.

POLITICAL DYNAMITE

Maverick right-winger Ishihara Shintaro is bigger than Godzilla in this city, and a man who people either love or loathe. The Kobe-born governor has played off his enemies and called in favours from his friends throughout his seven years in power. Always ready with an insensitive and bellicose soundbite, Ishihara recently won himself a few more enemies by saying that bullying can make schoolchildren stronger, by admitting that he had shot a whale, and by saying that a Falklands-style war with China would be a good way to settle a dispute over a group of small islands claimed by both nations. He's also a man of contradictions: a public intellectual who has cut the education budget (although he found the money to fund lectures for teachers who refuse to honour national symbols); a believer in hard work who frequently absents himself from his office; and a supporter of US President George W Bush who nevertheless remains resolutely anti-American. His Prince Philip sense of diplomacy has seen him offend China, France (resulting in a lawsuit), both Koreas and much of the rest of Asia during his two terms, but overall he remains popular in this city, with Tokyoites admiring his strength and charisma.

Of course, up until September 2006, there was a figure much bigger than Ishihara on Tokyo's political landscape – Prime Minister Koizumi Junichiro. Known as 'Lion Heart' for his shaggy mane, the maverick leader oversaw a revolutionary change in Japanese politics during his five years in charge. It is thought that current PM Abe Shinzo, the first prime minister to be born after the war, will struggle to maintain the authority he needs to tackle Japan's high level of national debt, crumbling health and social-security systems and lack of foreign capital. While Abe has a reputation for being a hawk, he has hinted, in a move designed to shore up damaged relations with Beijing and Seoul, that he may not visit Tokyo's controversial Yasukuni Shrine, which is home to the nation's war dead, but also to over 1,000 war criminals, including Kimura Heitaro, who oversaw the brutal killings of thousands on Burma's Death Railway.

Fears provoked by missile and nuclear tests in North Korea – it's Kim Jong Il, not Osama bin Laden, who is seen as a national security threat here – have, however, given Abe the chance to revise the constitution, push nationalism in schools and even allow some of his cabinet to flirt with the idea of Japan itself going nuclear. But while debate rages over whether Japan should equip itself with nuclear arms or give its soldiers the right to shoot people, no major public debate has taken place about basic anti-terrorism measures for the rail system, such as removing bins from platforms. However, Tokyo's emergency services are well prepared to act should a major disaster – be it natural or man-made – occur.

For now, the biggest man-made disasters are limited to Tokyo's sports teams. In football, first-division FC Tokyo has played well enough in recent seasons to avoid relegation but not to impress, while Greater Tokyo-area teams Kawasaki Frontale and Yokohama F Marinos have fared little better. But Yokohama-born former Marinos player Nakamura Shunsuke has been noted in Europe. In baseball, Tokyo's once all-conquering Giants have suffered a two-year run of bad form, dropping below the city's unfashionable Yakult Swallows in the pecking order, while the Yokohama BayStars remain less than stellar. Yokohama-born right-handed pitcher Matsuzaka Daisuke, however, signed a $52 million deal with the Boston Red Sox in November 2006, after being voted most valuable player at the inaugural World Baseball Classic, won by Japan. And in the unlikely event that Tokyo is successful in its bid for the 2016 Olympics, the failings of its sports teams will be soon forgotten.

While the likes of Abe and Ishihara, Matsuzaka and Nakamura make headlines, it's the thinkers – the *makeinu* women and urban teens who have jumped off the school-university-company conveyor belt – who will ensure that their city remains the capital of the New Grand Tour. But it is the middle-aged, grey-suited men and women who eat their bento-box lunches in the quiet corners of this city who one must get to know to truly understand Tokyo today.

Tokyo Metropolitan Government Building. *See p28.*

Architecture

A metropolis designed by disaster and inspiration alike.

Architecturally, the jumbled cityscape of Tokyo isn't as immediately striking as those of New York, Paris or London. It lacks grand boulevards, historic monuments and a sense of ordered urban planning. Instead, the visitor's initial impression is usually one of a very contemporary kind of confusion, with nondescript high-rises jostling gleaming space-age designs, one-storey dwellings beneath looming skyscrapers, giant video screens and banks of neon, throngs of pedestrians below websof tangled overhead cables.

Without the ancient temples of Kyoto and Nara, historic or traditional-style buildings are relatively few and far between in the present-day Japanese capital. This is partly a result of nature: a history of fires and terrible earthquakes has stripped the city of much of its architectural heritage. It is also partly a consequence of man-made forces: heavy wartime bombing, compounded by breakneck post-war economic development and an unsentimental lack of attachment to the old. The metropolis is in a constant state of reinvention.

Tokyo has been a laboratory for the meeting and synthesis of local and Western styles ever

since it first flung its doors open to the wider world, back in 1868. This drive to embrace the future continues to inform the development of the city's architecture today.

TRADITIONAL STYLES

Japanese architecture has traditionally been based on the use of wooden materials. Very few original structures remain from the city's former incarnation as Edo, capital of the Tokugawa shoguns, although parts of the imposing pre-modern fortifications of the 17th-century Edo Castle can still be seen when walking around the moat and gardens of the Imperial Palace, built on part of the castle site.

The original wooden houses and shops of Edo-era *shitamachi* ('low city') districts have now almost completely disappeared. Outside the very heart of the city, some recognisably traditional features, such as eaves and tiled roofs, are still widely used on modern suburban housing, while tatami mats and sliding doors are common inside even more Western-style apartment blocks.

The city's shrines and temples are overwhelmingly traditional in form, though not often old. The **Meiji Shrine** (*see p85*) is an impressive example of the austere style and restrained colours typical of Shinto architecture, which is quite distinctive from that of Buddhist temples, where the greater influence of Chinese and Korean styles is usually apparent. Many present-day buildings of older religious institutions are reconstructions of earlier incarnations; the well-known temples of **Senso-ji** and **Zojo-ji** are both examples, although in these cases some remnants of earlier structures also survive. The Sanmon Gate of Zojo-ji, which dates from 1605, and **Gokoku-ji**, which dates from 1681, are rare, unreconstructed survivors.

In contrast, when the wooden building of **Hongan-ji** temple in Tsukiji burned down for the ninth time in the temple's long history after the 1923 earthquake, it was rebuilt in sturdier stone. The design by architect Ito Chuta, also responsible for the earlier Meiji Shrine, was also quite different: an eye-catching affair recalling Buddhism's roots in ancient India.

WESTERNISATION AND REACTION

After the Meiji Restoration of 1868, the twin influences of Westernisation and modernisation quickly made themselves felt in Tokyo, the new national capital. Early attempts to combine Western and traditional elements by local architects resulted in extraordinary hybrids featuring Japanese-style sloping roofs rising above wooden constructions, with ornate front façades of a distinctly Western style. Kisuke Shimizu's Hoterukan (1868) at the Foreign Settlement in Tsukiji and his First National Bank (1872) in Nihonbashi were two notable Tokyo examples. Neither survives today.

Tokyo's earliest buildings of a purely Western design were chiefly the work of overseas architects brought to Japan by the new Meiji government. Englishman Thomas Waters oversaw the post-1872 redevelopment of Ginza with around 900 red-brick buildings, thought to be more resilient than wooden Japanese houses. Ironically, none of them made it through the 1923 earthquake.

Waters's fellow countryman Josiah Conder, who taught at Tokyo Imperial University, was the most influential Western architect of the early Meiji period, with important projects in the capital including ministry buildings, the original Imperial Museum (1881) at Ueno and Hibiya's Rokumeikan reception hall (1883). His **Furukawa Mansion** (1914) in Komagome and **Nikolai Cathedral** (1891) in Ochanomizu still exist, although the latter was badly damaged in the 1923 earthquake.

Later Meiji official architecture was often a close reflection of Western styles, although it was Japanese architects who increasingly handled the prestige projects. Remaining red-brick structures of the period include the **Ministry of Justice** (1895), constructed in Kasumigaseki by the German firm of Ende & Bockman, and the **Crafts Gallery** of the National Museum of Modern Art (1910), which once housed the administrative headquarters of the Imperial Guard. The imposing **Bank of Japan** building (1896) was designed by one of Conder's former students, Tatsuno Kingo, who was also responsible for the Marunouchi wing of **Tokyo Station** (1914), modelled on Centraal Station in Amsterdam. A far more grandiose overseas inspiration, that of Versailles, is said to have been used for the **Akasaka Detached Palace** (1909), created by Katayama Tokuma, whose other work includes the **Hyokeikan** building (1909) of the renowned Tokyo National Museum in Ueno Park.

The era after World War I saw the completion of Frank Lloyd Wright's highly distinctive Imperial Hotel (1922), which famously survived the Tokyo earthquake shortly after its opening, but was demolished in the 1960s. The period after the earthquake saw the spread of social housing, and a prominent example, finally knocked down in 2003, was the Dojunkai Aoyama tenement apartment blocks (1926) on Omotesando. Another post-quake innovation was the *kanban* (signboard) style, designed to

Tokyo International Forum. *See p28.*

protect buildings against fire by a cloaking of sheet copper, and often still seen today in the heavily oxidised green mantles of pre-war shops.

The influence of overseas trends can be discerned in the modernism of Yoshida Tetsuro's **Tokyo Central Post Office** (1931) and the art deco of the **Tokyo Metropolitan Teien Art Museum** (1933), built originally as a mansion for Prince Asaka and planned mainly by French designer Henri Rapin. The present-day **Diet Building** (1936) also shows a strong art deco influence, but its design became a source of heated debate in the increasingly nationalist climate of the period when it was completed.

A reaction against Westernisation had already been apparent in the work of Ito Chuta, who had looked towards Asian models. Demands for a distinctive national look led to the so-called 'Imperial Crown' style, exemplified by the main building of the **Tokyo National Museum** (1938) in Ueno. This was the design of Watanabe Hitoshi, an architect of unusual versatility whose other works include the **Hattori Building** (1932) of Wako department store at Ginza Yon-chome crossing, and the **Daiichi Insurance Building** (1938). The latter was used by General MacArthur as his Tokyo headquarters after the war, and is now the shorter, older part of the DN Tower 21 complex in Hibiya.

POST-WAR TOKYO

The priority in the early post-war period was often to provide either extra office space for companies trying to cope with the demands of an economy hurtling along at double-digit growth rates, or a rapid answer to the housing needs of the city's growing population. Seismic instability meant that tall buildings were not initially an option, and anonymous, box-like structures proliferated.

Even as architects gained confidence in new construction techniques designed to provide greater protection against earthquakes, many of the initial results were strangely undistinguished. The city's first cluster of skyscrapers, built in West Shinjuku from the early 1970s, has been described as resembling a set of urban tombstones. Even so, a later addition, the imposing, twin-towered **Tokyo Metropolitan Government Building** (1991; **photo** *p26*) by Tange Kenzo, is now among the capital's best-known landmarks.

The dominant figure of post-war Japanese architecture, Tange has managed to combine both Western and traditional Japanese elements in an astonishing variety of high-profile Tokyo projects, which stretch right back to the now-demolished metropolitan offices in Yurakucho (1957). Well-known works include **St Mary's Cathedral** (1963) in Edogawabashi, **Yoyogi National Stadium** (1964), the **Hanae Mori Building** (1978) on Omotesando, the **Akasaka Prince Hotel** (1983) and the **UN University** (1992) in Aoyama.

Tange's long career connects generations of Japanese architects. One collaborator was Maekawa Kunio, a pre-war student of Le Corbusier in Europe, who became one of Japan's foremost modern architects, with works such as the **Tokyo Metropolitan Festival Hall** (1961) and the **Tokyo Metropolitan Art Museum** (1975). Another was postmodernist Isozaki Arata, the man responsible for the **Ochanomizu Square Building** (1987), as well as the Museum of Contemporary Art (1986) in Los Angeles.

Tokyo ordered itself something of a postmodernist makeover as the Bubble economy took hold in the 1980s, and the resultant splurge of 'trophy architecture' left the city with a string of enjoyably arresting landmarks. The **Spiral Building** (1985) in Aoyama is one contribution to the new city look by Maki Fumihiko; another is the strange, low-level **Tokyo Metropolitan Gymnasium** (1990) in Sendagaya. Also hard to ignore is the **Super Dry Hall** in Asakusa by Philippe Starck, one of an number of foreign architects to have worked on projects in Tokyo in recent years. These include Rafael Vinoly, the creator of the stunning **Tokyo International Forum** (1996, *see p252;* **photo** *p27*) on the site of the old Tokyo government building in Yurakucho; Norman Foster, whose **Century Tower** (1991) is located near Ochanomizu; and Renzo Piano with his **Maison Hermès**, designed for the fashion store, (2001) in Ginza.

National Arts Center. *See p29.*

Don't miss **Buildings**

In a city that doesn't do uniformity, here are the places you shouldn't miss:

For that sci-fi look
Edo-Tokyo Museum
The alien-spacecraft style of Kikutake Kiyonori's 1992 creation is made up of traditional elements recalling the city's past. Its height, 62m (203ft), exactly matches that of the old Edo Castle. *See p68.*

The Catholic contribution
St. Mary's Cathedral
3-16-15 Sekiguchi, Bunkyo-ku (3941 3029/ www.tsukijihongwanji.jp). Edogawabashi station (Yurakucho line), exit 1a.
Striking religious constructions in Tokyo are usually the preserve of Shintoism or Buddhism, but this towering concrete crucifix by Tange Kenzo in 1964 is spectacular inside and out, giving the temples and shrines a run for their money.

If bigger is better
Tokyo Metropolitan Building
The twin-towered Gotham City epic from Tange Kenzo, built in 1991, was eclipsed height-wise by the five-metres taller Tokyo Midtown (*see p107*), but this 243m (797ft) giant still looks the best.

For a funky façade
Mikimoto Ginza 2
2-4-12 Ginza, Chuo-ku (3562 3130). Ginza station (Ginza, Hibiya, Marunouchi lines), exit A13. **Map** Ginza p75.
It's cultivated pearls galore inside, but the irregular blobby windows of Ito Toyo's façade looks like someone has taken potshots with a bazooka.

The traditional look
Kabuki-za
Grandly meets preconceptions of what a *kabuki* theatre should look like. The original 1925 design harked back to the medieval Momoyama era, a style that was retained when it was rebuilt in 1951. *See p264.*

Only in Tokyo
Aoyama Technical College
7-9 Uguisudanicho, Shibuya-ku. Shibuya station (Yamanote, Ginza, Hanzomon lines), south exit.
Outlandish 1991 postmodernism from Watanabe Sei that throws together strangely haphazard angles, insect-like protrusions and blocks of spectacular red on metal. It is also widely known as *Gundam*, after the incredibly popular, and long-running, science-fiction *anime* series.

The reclamation of Tokyo Bay also opened up land for a wide range of projects. On Odaiba, designated as a futuristic showcase back in the Bubble era, Tange's **Fuji TV Building** (1996), Watanabe Sei's **K-Museum** (1996) and Sato Sogokeikau's extraordinary **Tokyo Big Sight** (1994) all vie for attention, while the interior of the **Venus Fort** shopping mall (1999) offers a bizarre Vegas-style take on Ancient Rome. Nearby, on the city side of Rainbow Bridge, an imposing new generation of high-rise offices in Odaiba thrusts upwards on the waterfront skyline.

In the first decade of the 21st century, as the long-stagnant economy rebounds, architects are being asked to create ever more eye-catching creations to lure consumers. First to arrive was the **Marunouchi Building** (2002; *see p191*), on the site of the city's first modern office block, which cheerfully cast aside an old taboo prohibiting buildings that look down on the emperor's residence. The following year brought lifestyle super-complex **Roppongi Hills** and the acclaimed **Prada store** (both by Herzog

& de Meuron), then some striking high-rises for **Chanel** (Peter Marino, 2004) in Ginza, **Tod's** in Aoyama and **Mikimoto Ginza 2**, both by Ito Toyo in 2005. In the same year, Ando Tadao brought his concrete visions to fashion boulevard Omotesando with low-rise retail and restaurant complex **Omotesando Hills**, which replaced a much-loved set of ivy-covered, Bauhaus-inspired apartments that had stood since 1927. The very latest contribution to the consumer frenzy is the **Tokyo Midtown** (*see p107*), a towering complex of shops, restaurants and apartments. And the latest must-see is Kurokawa Kisho's **National Arts Center** (2007; *photo p28*). This 30 billion yen construction features four storeys of undulating glass set in generous grounds.

Tokyo continues to reinvent, rebuild and redesign itself, and the revitalised economy, combined with the city's laissez-faire planning regulations, means a fast-changing, eye-popping cityscape. If the buildings today aren't to your taste, come back in ten years, and there'll be a whole new set to enjoy.

Otaku

Patrick Macias reports on the revenge of the Tokyo nerds.

Japan has a centuries-long history of visual culture and a globally respected pop culture that thrives on animation and comics. At the very centre of this *anime*, manga and video-game boom are *otaku,* Japan's obsessive nerds who have colonised the area of Akihabara, Tokyo's 'Electric Town'. This breed of obsessives derive their name from a peculiarly polite use of the Japanese language. The word '*otaku*' (literally, 'your house' or 'household') is used as an exceptionally formal second-person pronoun. Tokyo's obsessive collector types began using the word to refer to each other as it enabled them – linguistically at least – to maintain a certain level of privacy and distance. Despite openly expressing their passions for manga, *anime* and all manner of obscure fetishes, *otaku* tend to be painfully shy about their personal lives.

Today's male *otaku* have made the back alleys of Akihabara (Akiba to the locals) their

home. Here they go on the prowl for local delicacies, including *anime*, manga, video games, electronics and 'idol goods' (products devoted to cutesy nubile young girls). If you come across guys in well-worn jeans, buttoned up shirts and tatty trainers, rummaging in their backpacks for gadgets, DVDs and girlfriend-simulator video games, you have almost certainly found Tokyo's *otaku*.

Their tastes have transformed Akiba, which began life as a post-war black market for electronics, into the ultimate geek playground. And when they're not devouring manga or perfecting their gaming skills, what geeks like most are maids.

The *otaku* maid trend started with a café (*see p32* **Maid in Japan**) where boys were served by costumed young ladies with extra squeaky voices. The concept took off, and there are now around 50 such establishments in the area. Not only this – there's a whole world of maid-related services on offer in Akiba. There are maid masseuses (Moema, Soto-Kanda Daini Nagashima Bldg 2F, 3-2-3 Soto-Kanda, 5294 0025), maid beauticians (Maid Beauty Salon Oave, 4-8-3 Soto-Kanda, 5296 2006) and maid tour guides to help you navigate the whole Akiba fantasy land (http://akiba-guide.com). Even **Candy Fruit Optical** (3-16-3 Soto-Kanda, 3252 4902), an optician that's been in the same location for over five decades, now requires its staff to dress as maids.

'There are silicone-doll rental stores and costume shops selling schoolgirls' uniforms in sizes up to Male XL.'

And *otaku* obsessions don't stop here. Elsewhere, there are silicone-doll rental stores, costume shops selling schoolgirls' uniforms in sizes up to 'Male XL', arcades devoted entirely to *gashapon* – the gumball machines that dispense plastic toys ranging from the saccharin to the sickening – and for the more committed figurine fan, there are life-size characters costing up to ¥600,000 that you can purchase in 60 easy instalments.

More fleshy fantasies are on offer at the **Yamagiwa Softkan** (3-13-12 Soto-Kanda, 5256 3300), ostensibly a music and software store, but with an entire floor devoted to idol DVDs, where customers purchasing the DVDs flagged at the counter receive tickets to a meet 'n' greet with the star herself. Meanwhile, **Comic Toranoana** (4-3-1 Soto-Kanda, 5294 0123), which stocks a massive range of *dojinshi* – small-run underground comics penned by fans – caters for the *anime* and manga side of things.

Akiba is full to bursting with geek goods, and many elements of the *otaku*'s obsessive collector culture have crossed over to the mainstream. Akiba is fast becoming an area that attracts a diverse crowd of visitors, rather than just being the fanatical geek sanctuary it once was. Even the government-sponsored Japanese National Tourist Organization (*see p314*) now offers free tours of Akihabara and information on how to 'immerse yourself in Japanese *anime* and comics'.

GENERATION GEEK
The first real generation of *otaku* came of age during the 1960s, nursed by early *anime* hits like *Astro Boy* and superhero shows such as *Ultraman*. By the early 1970s there were

millions of young adults in Japan reading comics, watching animation and dedicating themselves to what many in the West would write off as kids' stuff. The arrival of *Star Wars*, robot *anime Gundam*, and the first video games later in the decade added even more fuel to the fire.

By the 1980s, it was clear that a new kind of culture was evolving out of *anime*, manga, games and science fiction. In 1983 Nakamori Akio wrote an essay entitled *A Study of Otaku*, which sought to make sense of it all. He is credited with coining the name '*otaku*' after observing the unusually common usage of the word among this group.

In 1989, however, the word took on sinister overtones that still linger today. A 27-year-old man named Miyazaki Tsutomu kidnapped and murdered three young girls. When the police stormed his home, they found it full of *anime* and manga. The only term available on hand to describe such a person was *otaku,* and a full-scale backlash ensued. It was then that *otaku* really needed a haven to call their own, where

Otaku culture: Does my head look big in this?

they could be safe from the suspicious eyes of the public at large. They found it in Akihabara.

The area had long been Tokyo's designated hub for discount consumer electronics. But by the 1980s, there were plenty of chain stores offering such fare throughout the city. However, Akihabara's stores were still often the first to offer new releases of hardware, software and peripherals. *Otaku*, lured in by all this tech, began to slowly take over the area. And they brought with them their ravenous hunger for *anime*, manga, action figures, video games and pornography.

In the late '90s, the science fiction *anime* series *Neon Genesis Evangelion* became a massive hit in Japan, playing to mainstream and *otaku* audiences alike. Suddenly it was almost fashionable to have a vast knowledge of *anime* and manga. And more importantly, the huge sums of money the series generated

Maid in Japan

Call it geisha culture for the *otaku* age. Maid cafés far outnumber standard cafés on the streets and alleys of Akihabara, such is the demand for coffee and cakes presented by costumed young ladies who shriek 'Welcome home, master!' as you enter. Whether it's your idea of heaven or hell, the maid café is now an essential stop on any Tokyo itinerary. With around 50 such establishments in this small patch of the city, finding a café is a breeze, but the most memorable maid action awaits you at one of these two scene veterans:

Café Mai:lish

FH Kyowa Square Bldg 2F, 3-6-2 Soto-Kanda, Chiyoda-ku (5289 7310/www.mailish.jp). Akihabara station (Yamanote, Sobu lines), Electric Town exit; (Hibiya line), exit 3. **Open** 11am-10pm daily. **Credit** AmEx, JCB, MC, V.
One of Akihabara's oldest maid cafés, Mai:lish is the genre's archetype. Although it is pricier than some of the newer maid establishments (¥1,000 will get you a glass of Coke and a blob of ice-cream), your investment pays off in the details. The Victorian maid uniform is a faultless re-creation, and the soda fountain looks like something straight out of the '50s. The mood between the maids and their masters (that is, customers) can be a bit chilly, but that's part of the appeal for the regulars who are big on 'unfulfilled longing'. Check the website for special events, such as 'Glasses Day' or 'Mini-Skirt Policewoman Day'. Foreign nerds are welcome and there's an English menu.

@home Café

Mitsuwa Bldg 7F, 1-11-4 Soto-Kanda, Chiyoda-ku (5294 7707/www.cafe-athome. com). Akihabara station (Yamanote, Sobu lines), Electric Town exit; (Hibiya line), exit 3. **Open** 11.30am-10pm (last order 9pm) daily. **No credit cards**.

Here's a maid-café that offers an over-the-top maid café experience worthy of Las Vegas. The girls here aren't so much maids as performers in a kind of Hooters-style theme restaurant. Along with serving cute little bunny-wunny ice-cream cakes and heart-shaped hamburgers, the squeaky maids will (for an additional fee) play games with the customers, including such timeless pursuits as Paper, Scissors, Stone and Pop-Up Pirate. Don't even think of trying to come here on a weekend: the wait to get in often exceeds an hour.
Other location: Don Quixote Akihabara 5F, 4-3-3 Soto-Kanda, Chiyoda-ku (3254 7878).

showed that there was plenty of money in geeks. The spending habits and psychology of the *otaku* came under the scrutiny of leading academics, the media and even the government. Together they wondered if the cure to Japan's economic woes could be found within the hyper-consumerist lifestyle of the *otaku*. (Current estimates of the *otaku* industry value it at around $3 billion.)

The next big turning point for *otaku* came in 2004 with the arrival of the book *Densha Otoko* (Train Man). It concerned a typical Akihabara dweller who finds love after rescuing a beautiful woman from harassment on a commuter train. Allegedly based on real events chronicled on an internet thread (a claim now largely believed to be false), the tale was embellished with much comedy and drama, becoming a hit TV series and then a feature film. All eyes began to peer once again at Akihabara and its nerd culture.

A TOURIST ATTRACTION

With the buzz about Akihabara and *otaku* at fever pitch, the area has seen plenty of redevelopment. Among the several glitzy new skyscrapers is the UDX Center, which houses the **Tokyo Anime Center** (4-14-1 Soto-Kanda, 5298 1188). There's also been a massive influx of tourists, both domestic and foreign. Needless to say, not all *otaku* are delighted with the attention being lavished upon their once-private clubhouse.

Luckily for them, there are plenty of other geek retreats in the city. Foremost is the **Nakano Broadway** shopping arcade (*see p194*). Located in the rear of this otherwise unspectacular mall is a maze of collector stores. The numerous rare goods all command huge prices, but some good deals can be found. Collectors scouring for a specific toy or *anime* video will likely find it here.

'There are butler cafés, staffed by women cross-dressing as impossibly beautiful men.'

And lest it seem that cultural obsessions are the preserve of Tokyo's male population, there's also Ikebukuro's Otome Road – a small strip of comic shops and *anime* stores frequented by female *otaku*. The big draw here is the *anime* and manga genre known as 'boys' love', which depicts same-sex liaisons between gorgeous guys. There are also butler cafés, staffed by women cross-dressing as impossibly beautiful men.

In Tokyo anyone with even the slightest interest in *anime*, manga, maids, or even just the obscure, is sure to have a blast.

Patrick Macias is the author of Otaku in USA *(Ohta Shuppan, 2006) and the co-author of* Cruising the Anime City: An Otaku Guide to Neo-Tokyo *(Stone Bridge Press, 2004).*

Tokyo's tribes

The *otaku* aren't the only urban tribe to prowl the streets of Tokyo. Here are four more of the current crop.

Illustration by Neil Cameron, www.neilcameron.com

Gothloli

Who: Teenage girls from the suburbs who mix and match eternal darkness with 19th-century innocence and then take the express train to Tokyo. Their collective handle, 'Gothloli', is a typically Japanese mash-up of the words 'Gothic' and 'Lolita'.

What they wear: Expensive designer brands with names like Baby, The Stars Shine Bright and Moi-même-Moitié. Also known to create their clothes from scratch.

Where to find them: On the bridge near Harajuku station. Shopping at the Marui Young department store in Shinjuku.

Role models: Alice in Wonderland, Marie Antoinette, Dracula, Victoriana.

Hime Gal

Who: *Hime* means 'princess' in Japanese, a term also synonymous with 'filthy rich' and 'spoiled rotten' in most other languages. *Hime* Gals tend to look more like Stepford Wives than real royals, but in their minds, they are the spitting image of Cinderella at the ball.
What they wear: Elegant pink-and-white dresses, tea-coloured bouffant hairdos, enormous fake flowers and floppy pink bows.
Where to find them: Shopping at stores such as Jesus Diamante and Liz Lisa. Holding court in cafés and restaurants around the Shibuya-Harajuku-Omotesando axis.
Role models: Paris Hilton, Disney princesses.

Choi Waru Oyaji

Who: Middle-aged men (*oyaji*) who enjoy (or aspire to) a stylish, epicurean lifestyle. They're trendy in a *choi* (little bit) *waru* (bad boy) kind of way and hang out in flashy night spots to play the ladies. Their style bible is popular men's mag *Leon*.
What they wear: Crisp white shirts and brand-name watches are staples. Luxury Italian brands are dressed down for wild-man appeal.
Where to find them: Restaurants and lounge bars in Ginza, Roppongi and Aoyama. They also make frequent appearances at Japan's surf beaches.
Role models: Chiselled Italians – especially Girolamo Panzetta, an Italian-born TV personality and *Leon* cover-star.

Center Guy

Who: In an attempt to woo the girls once and for all, the boys have gone all bling-bling in Shibuya. The results resemble a cross between a biker, a cowboy and the frontman of an '80s hair-metal band.
What they wear: Frayed jeans and fur-lined collars, pointy-toed boots, a big, old belt buckle, and colossal sunglasses. The entire look can be bought off the rack at Jackrose stores throughout Tokyo.
Where to find them: Shibuya, naturally, on namesake boulevard Center-*gai* (English: Centre Street) and in Shibuya clubs such as Atom or Club Asia.
Role models: DJs, pro-fighters and male models.

THE SHORTLIST

WHAT'S NEW | WHAT'S ON | WHAT'S BEST

 Barcelona
WHAT'S NEW | WHAT'S ON | WHAT'S NEXT

 **Berlin**
WHAT'S NEW | WHAT'S ON | WHAT'S NEXT

 **London**
WHAT'S NEW | WHAT'S ON | WHAT'S NEXT

 Manchester
WHAT'S NEW | WHAT'S ON | WHAT'S BEST

  New York
WHAT'S NEW | WHAT'S ON | WHAT'S NEXT

  Paris
WHAT'S NEW | WHAT'S ON | WHAT'S NEXT

  Prague
WHAT'S NEW | WHAT'S ON | WHAT'S NEXT

 **Rome**
WHAT'S NEW | WHAT'S ON | WHAT'S NEXT

Coming soon…

 **Amsterdam**
2008
WHAT'S NEW | WHAT'S ON | WHAT'S NEXT

 **Dubrovnik**
WHAT'S NEW | WHAT'S ON | WHAT'S NEXT

 **Las Vegas**
WHAT'S NEW | WHAT'S ON | WHAT'S NEXT

 **Tokyo**
WHAT'S NEW | WHAT'S ON | WHAT'S NEXT

 Venice
WHAT'S NEW | WHAT'S ON | WHAT'S NEXT

- **POCKET–SIZE GUIDES**
- **WRITTEN BY LOCAL EXPERTS**
- **KEY VENUES PINPOINTED ON MAPS**

le at all major bookshops at only
and from timeout.com/shop

Time
SHOR

Where to Stay

Where to Stay

The luxury groups have arrived in force, but there are still affordable options.

Indulge in some old-fashioned Japanese hospitality at **Kimi Ryokan**. *See p43.*

For around a decade the **Park Hyatt** (*see p49*) was the undisputed champion of five-star slumber in Tokyo. There were rivals – the **Westin** (*see p40*), the **Four Seasons** (*see p54*) at Chinzan-so – but the celeb set always picked Shinjuku's towering paragon of luxury. The **Grand Hyatt** (*see p51*) stole some of its thunder in 2003, with more stylish rooms and an arguably better location. But now the gloves are off. By the end of 2007 Tokyo will add a **Ritz-Carlton** (www.ritzcarlton.com/hotels/tokyo/) and a **Peninsula** (www.peninsula.com/tokyo.html) to its suddenly impressive array of luxury hotels. Whether this city actually needs so much top-end accommodation remains to be seen, but if there is a glut, we can look forward to the chains competing to prove themselves the most luxurious. The **Mandarin Oriental** *(see p45)* has already set the bar high with a first-anniversary weekend package that included a return flight on a private jet to their Hong Kong hotel and cost an impressive ¥18 million for three nights.

At the other end of the spectrum, Tokyo's budget options are more limited. The city's famous capsule hotels are the last resort of the drunk, desperate and male (most are men-only). They offer cheap accommodation in a small tube that's barely big enough to swing a room key. It's something to try for the experience, but extended stays are unheard of. For couples, love hotels (*see pp42-3*) are a more comfortable and kitsch option, although you'll be kicked out with all your luggage each morning. But while Tokyo offers few beds for the shoestring-budget backpack set (*see p121* **Hey big spender**), there are plenty of affordable places to stay. *Minshuku* are Japan's version of the B&B and usually a friendly, no-frills option. Business hotels are designed with commercial travellers primarily in mind. They are a step down in quality and service from the top-end spots, and rooms are often on the small side, but they offer decent value for money.

Most hotels offer Western-style rooms, although some of the top-end places also have slightly pricier Japanese-style rooms. For the full tatami-and-futon experience, you'll need a *ryokan* – the Japanese-style inns that can be pricey but usually include a sumptuous Japanese meal.

Tokyo is a massive, sprawling metropolis, so where you stay will have a big impact on your enjoyment of the city. If nightlife rocks your boat, then think about Shibuya or Roppongi. Culture? Try Asakusa or Ueno. Or for easy access to anywhere in the city, Shinjuku is hard to beat.

SALES TAX
All room rates are subject to Japan's usual five per cent sales tax, but if your bill climbs to the equivalent of over ¥15,000 per night (including service charges), you will be liable to pay an additional three per cent tax. Then there's a flat-rate surcharge of ¥100 per night for rooms costing ¥10,000-¥14,999, rising to ¥200 for rooms costing ¥15,000 or over. This money goes to help the metropolitan government promote Tokyo as a tourist destination.

No tipping is expected in any Tokyo hotel, although most high-end places include a standard service charge of 10-15 per cent in their room rates. Ask when booking.

Asakusa

Expensive

Asakusa View Hotel
3-17-1 Nishi-Asakusa, Taito-ku (3847 1111/fax 3842 2117/www.viewhotels.co.jp/asakusa). Tawaramachi station (Ginza line), exit 3. **Rooms** 338. **Rates** ¥13,000-¥18,000 single; ¥19,000-¥34,000 double/twin; ¥50,000-¥300,000 suite. *Japanese* ¥40,000-¥63,000. **Credit** AmEx, DC, JCB, MC, V. **Map** Asakusa p63.
With its uniformed staff and marble lobby somewhat incongruent with this downtown, working-class neighbourhood, the Asakusa View boasts a

The best Hotels

For luxury with convenience
Grand Hyatt Tokyo. *See p51.*

For a stylish room that won't break the bank
Granbell Hotel. *See p47.*

For hanging with the hipsters
Claska. *See p54.*

For the Japanese experience
Sukeroku No Yado Sadachiyo. *See right.*

For fun
P&A Plaza. *See p43.*

fairly high standard of accommodation, and its rates reflect its status as the only luxury hotel in the area. If you want to make the hotel live up to its name, go for a room as high up as you can: the view from the top over Asakusa and the Sumida river is worth catching. Non-visitors can also pop in for a drink to the Belvedere lounge on the 28th floor. A nice touch is that the sixth floor is given over to Japanese-style rooms, complete with their own garden.
Bars (3). Concierge. Disabled-adapted rooms. Japanese & Western rooms. No-smoking rooms. Parking (¥1,000/night). Pool (indoor). Restaurants (3). Room service (7am-11pm).

Moderate

Hotel Sunroute Asakusa
1-8-5 Kaminarimon, Taito-ku (3847 1511/fax 3847 1509/www.sunroute-asakusa.co.jp). Tawaramachi station (Ginza line), exit 3. **Rates** ¥8,925-¥11,025 single; ¥17,325-¥19,950 twin; ¥15,225 double; ¥13,860 disabled-adapted room. **Credit** AmEx, DC, MC, V. **Map** Asakusa p63.
Small rooms and lack of facilities notwithstanding, this business hotel offers reasonable value for money for those determined to sleep in beds rather than on futons. The building is simple and clean, with a vaguely European ambience. US diner-style chain restaurant Jonathan's is situated on the second floor.
Disabled-adapted room. Internet (shared terminal). No-smoking rooms. Parking (¥1,500/night). Restaurant.

Ryokan Shigetsu
1-31-11 Asakusa, Taito-ku (3843 2345/fax 3843 2348/www.shigetsu.com). Asakusa station (Asakusa line), exit A4; (Ginza line), exits 1, 6. **Rates** ¥7,665 single; ¥14,700 twin. *Japanese* ¥9,450 single; ¥16,800-¥26,250 double. **Credit** AmEx, MC, V. **Map** Asakusa p63.
Barely 30 seconds from Asakusa's market and temple complex, yet surprisingly peaceful, the Shigetsu offers a choice of comfortable rooms in Japanese and Western styles in an elegant downtown setting. All rooms have their own bathrooms, although there is also a Japanese-style communal bath on the top floor. Recent years have seen a shift back to Japanese-style rooms, with 15 of the 23 now featuring traditional tatami and futon furnishings. Booking is recommended and can be made through the Japan Inn Group (www.jpinn.com).
Internet (shared terminal). Japanese & Western rooms. No-smoking rooms. Restaurant.

Sukeroku No Yado Sadachiyo
2-20-1 Asakusa, Taito-ku (3842 6431/fax 3842 6433/ www.sadachiyo.co.jp). Asakusa station (Asakusa line), exit A4; (Ginza line), exits 1, 6 or Tawaramachi station (Ginza line), exit 3. **Rooms** 20. **Rates** ¥15,000 single; ¥19,000-¥28,000 double; ¥28,500-¥42,000 triple. **Credit** MC, V. **Map** Asakusa p63.
This smart, modern *ryokan* is wonderfully situated five minutes' walk from Asakusa's temple. From the outside, the building resembles a cross between a

European chalet and a Japanese castle, but inside it's pure Japanese, with receptionists shuffling around the desk area dressed in kimonos. Staff are obliging, but speak only minimal English. All rooms are Japanese-style and come in a variety of sizes, the smallest being just five mats. The communal Japanese baths should help make a stay here a memorable and incredibly relaxing experience.
Internet (shared terminal). Japanese rooms only. Room service (7.30am-10pm).

Budget

Sakura Ryokan
2-6-2 Iriya, Taito-ku (3876 8118/fax 3873 9456/ www.sakura-ryokan.com). Iriya station (Hibiya line), exit 1. **Rooms** 18. **Rates** ¥5,500-¥6,600 single; ¥10,000-¥11,000 double/twin. *Japanese* ¥5,500-¥6,600 single; ¥10,000-¥11,000 double; ¥13,200-¥13,800 triple. **Credit** AmEx, DC, JCB, MC, V.
Ten minutes' walk north from Asakusa's temple complex, in the traditional downtown area of Iriya, the Sakura is a friendly, traditional, family-run *ryokan*. Of the Japanese-style rooms, only two have their own bathrooms, while seven of the Western-style rooms have baths. There's also a communal bath on each floor.
Internet (shared terminal). Japanese & Western rooms. Parking (¥1,000/night).

Ebisu

Deluxe

The Westin Tokyo
1-4-1 Mita, Meguro-ku (5423 7000/fax 5423 7600/ www.westin-tokyo.co.jp). Ebisu station (Yamanote, Hibiya lines), east exit. **Rooms** 445. **Rates** ¥53,200-¥68,200 single; ¥58,400-¥74,400 double/twin; ¥120,200-¥465,500 suite. **Credit** AmEx, DC, JCB, MC, V.
The Westin, at the far end of Ebisu's giant Garden Place development, opened in 1994. Its spacious lobby attempts to recreate the feeling of a European palace, while all guest rooms are palatial in size and feature soft lighting and antique-style furniture. A good view is pretty much guaranteed.
Bars (3). Business centre. Concierge. Disabled-adapted rooms. Internet (high-speed). No-smoking rooms. Parking (¥1,000/night). Restaurants (6). Room service (24hr).

Moderate

Hotel Excellent
1-9-5 Ebisu-Nishi, Shibuya-ku (5458 0087/fax 5458 8787/www.soeikikaku.co.jp). Ebisu station (Yamanote line), west exit; (Hibiya line), exit 3. **Rooms** 127. **Rates** ¥9,150 single; ¥11,550 double; ¥13,100 twin. **Credit** DC, MC, V.
A thoroughly basic but phenomenally popular business hotel offering no-frills accommodation in small, functional and bland rooms. The main reason

for its success is its location, one stop away from Shibuya on the Yamanote line and in the heart of the lively Ebisu area.
Bar. Internet (high-speed). No-smoking rooms. Restaurants (2).

Ginza & around

Deluxe

Conrad Tokyo
Tokyo Shiodome Bldg, 1-9-1 Higashi-Shinbashi, Minato-ku (6388 8000/fax 6388 8001/www. conradtokyo.co.jp). (Ginza line), exit 2; Shinbashi station (Yamanote, Asakusa lines), exit 1; Shiodome station (Oedo, Yurikamome lines), exit 9. **Rooms** 290. **Rates** ¥52,000-¥62,000 single; ¥57,000-¥67,000 double; ¥79,000-¥500,000 suite. **Credit** AmEx, DC, JCB, MC, V.
One of several luxury hotels to set up shop in Tokyo in recent years, the Conrad opened in July 2005 high above the glimmering Shiodome complex. Its 290 rooms – said to be the largest in Tokyo at 48sq m (517sq ft) – feature modern Japanese design and occupy the top ten floors of the 37-storey Tokyo Shiodome Building. No expense has been spared; extras include a 25m swimming pool, ten-room spa, floor-to-ceiling windows, plasma-screen TVs and wireless internet. The Conrad is also home to provocative British chef Gordon Ramsay's first restaurant in Japan.
Bar. Business centre. Concierge. Gym. Internet (high-speed/wireless). No-smoking rooms. Parking. Pool (indoor). Restaurants (3). Room service (24hr). Spa.

Dai-ichi Hotel Tokyo
1-2-6 Shinbashi, Minato-ku (3501 4411/fax 3595 2634/www.daiichihotels.com/hotel/tokyo). Shinbashi station (Yamanote, Asakusa, Ginza lines), Hibiya exit. **Rooms** 277. **Rates** ¥31,000-¥48,000 double; ¥80,000-¥350,000 suite. **Credit** AmEx, DC, JCB, MC, V. **Map** Ginza p75.
This 1993 tower, a ten-minute walk from Ginza, appears to be losing out to the increasing number of new hotels in nearby mini metropolis Shiodome City. The interior is a strange mix of styles: the entrance hall is a self-conscious echo of the grandeur of old European luxury hotels; the restaurants are a tribute to the designers' ability to cram many different styles of interior decor into one building. Rooms, however, are immaculate, of a good size and beautifully furnished and decorated. A sleek swimming pool and fitness centre are available in the annex.
Bars (2). Business centre. Concierge. Gym. Internet (high-speed). No-smoking rooms. Parking (¥1,000/night). Pool (indoor). Restaurants (10). Room service (24hr). Spa.

Hotel Seiyo Ginza
1-11-2 Ginza, Chuo-ku (3535 1111/fax 3535 1110/ www.seiyo-ginza.com). Ginza-Itchome station (Yurakucho line), exits 7, 10. **Rooms** 77. **Rates** ¥45,000-¥60,000 single/double; ¥65,000-¥220,000 suite. **Credit** AmEx, DC, JCB, MC, V. **Map** Ginza p75.

It's location, location, location that matters at the **Keio Plaza Hotel**. *See p48.*

Calling itself an 'ultra-luxury hotel management company', Rosewood Hotels & Resorts took over the Seiyo in 2000 and has since elevated the already upscale boutique property to unrivalled heights of fancy. The 77 rooms have all been refurbished, each in its own distinct style, to recreate a 'personal residence' away from home. Winner of *Travel & Leisure* magazine's award for the best hotel in Asia in 2004, the Seiyo offers the added luxury of a round-the-clock butler and concierge service, and twice-daily housekeeping. It also enjoyed the distinction of hosting the world's most expensive dinner, created by chef Joel Robuchon and wine expert Robert Parker, at $13,000 per person, including a three-night stay.

Bars (2). Business centre. Concierge. Gym. Internet (high-speed). No-smoking floors (2). Parking (free). Restaurants (3). Room service (24hr).

Imperial Hotel

1-1-1 Uchisaiwaicho, Chiyoda-ku (3504 1111/fax 3581 9146/www.imperialhotel.co.jp). Hibiya station (Chiyoda, Hibiya, Mita lines), exits A5, A13 or Yurakucho station (Yamanote, Yurakucho lines), Hibiya exit. **Rooms** 1,052. **Rates** ¥36,000-¥60,000 single; ¥41,000-¥90,000 double; ¥60,000-¥1,000,000 suite. **Credit** AmEx, DC, JCB, MC, V. **Map** Ginza p75.

There has been an Imperial Hotel on this site overlooking Hibiya Park since 1890. This 1970 tower block-style building replaced the glorious 1923 Frank Lloyd Wright creation that famously survived the Great Kanto Earthquake on its opening day. It's currently nearing the end of a five-year renovation plan that will conclude with the overhaul of the lobby and all guest rooms by 2008.

Bars (3). Business centre. Concierge. Disabled-adapted room. Gym. Internet (high-speed). No-smoking rooms. Parking (free). Pool (indoor). Restaurants (14). Room service (24hr).

Expensive

Ginza Mercure

2-9-4 Ginza, Chuo-ku (4335 1111/fax 4335 1222/ www.mercureginza.com). Ginza-Itchome station (Yurakucho line), exit 11. **Rooms** 209. **Rates** ¥20,790 single; ¥32,340 double; ¥47,250 suite. **Credit** AmEx, DC, JCB, MC, V. **Map** Ginza p75.

This French-owned hotel opened in autumn 2004 in a great central location, just behind Matsuya department store. Niftily converted from an existing office building, it has the feel of a European boutique hotel, featuring smart cherry-wood furniture, stylish wallpaper and black-and-white photos of old Paris. All the rooms vary in size (numbers 16 and 18 are the biggest), and there are 18 special 'ladies' rooms' on the eight, ninth and tenth floors. The breakfast room doubles as a French bistro, and staff speak English. A good choice for both business and independent travellers.

Bar. Business centre. Concierge. Disabled-adapted room. Internet (high-speed). No-smoking rooms. Parking (¥1,500/night). Restaurant.

Other locations: Mercure Hotel Narita, 818-1 Hanazaki-cho, Narita, Chiba-ken (0476 23 7000).

Mitsui Urban Hotel

8-6-15 Ginza, Chuo-ku (3572 4131/fax 3572 4254/ www.mitsuikanko.co.jp/urban/ginza). Shinbashi station (Yamanote, Asakusa, Ginza lines), Ginza exit. **Rooms** 265. **Rates** ¥14,500-¥20,500 single; ¥25,000-¥34,800 twin; ¥25,000-¥28,800 double. **Credit** AmEx, DC, JCB, MC, V. **Map** Ginza p75.

The Mitsui is an unassuming, practical choice on the edge of Ginza. Rooms are quite small and basically furnished, and the relative lack of facilities is reflected in the price. The lobby looks somewhat dated but the hotel's proximity to Ginza's nightlife quarter

Love hotels

Japan's chronic lack of privacy – and the thinness of its rice-paper walls – has helped create a thriving tradition of 'love hotels'. These short-stay establishments (usually rented in two-hour blocks) are ubiquitous, with entire sections of the capital's neighbourhoods devoted to them. And while slightly risqué, the use of such places has much in common with sex in general in Japan – not talked about openly, but widely indulged. Love hotels offer such a quintessentially Japanese experience that any couple travelling to Tokyo should try one out, if only for the afternoon.

The system for using a love hotel varies from place to place, but the basics are simple enough. Open around the clock, they offer rates for different blocks of time. Overnight rates are relatively cheap compared to other hotels (so they can be used as emergency accommodation), but most will not admit overnight guests until after 11pm at the earliest, so as to maximise profit from the day trade.

On entering a hotel, you are typically faced with pictures of each room with their prices listed beneath – the cheaper is for a short 'rest', the higher for an overnight stay. Only the illuminated rooms are unoccupied. Push the button on the room of your choice, then go to the front desk to collect the key. In cheaper love hotels, all rooms may be the same, and you simply go to the service window (you are usually unable to see the clerk and vice versa) and pay for the required time. Some hotels are fully automatic, with machines printing out room numbers so that

guests can avoid the potential embarrassment of interacting with another human. Go to your room, lock the door, and the rest is up to you.

As with any hotel, the more you pay, the more you're likely to get. Prices for a two-hour visit range from around ¥3,500 for a room with a bed, TV, bathroom and nothing more, to ¥15,000-plus for a room with its own swimming pool, swings or bondage paraphernalia. All love hotels have immaculate

means it's often filled with Japanese businessmen and kimono-clad hostesses on their way to or from work. *Bar. Internet (high-speed). No-smoking floor. Parking (¥1,500/night). Restaurants (4). Room service (10pm-midnight).*

Moderate

Hotel Ginza Daiei

3-12-1 Ginza, Chuo-ku (3545 1111/fax 3545 1177). Higashi-Ginza station (Asakusa line), exits A7, A8; (Hibiya line), exit 3. **Rooms** 106. **Rates** ¥11,965-¥13,960 single; ¥16,000 double; ¥18,000-¥21,800 twin; ¥23,000 triple. **Credit** AmEx, DC, JCB, MC, V. **Map** Ginza p75.

A well-situated, no-frills hotel that's well past its prime, the Ginza Daiei does at least offer decent-sized

rooms with plain, functional pine furniture and inoffensive decor. Services are minimal, but high-speed internet has been installed in recent years. If you opt for the top-price 'Healthy Twin' room, you'll get the added bonus of a jet bath. *Internet (high-speed). No-smoking rooms. Parking (¥1,000/night).*

Hotel Villa Fontaine Shiodome

1-9-2 Higashi-Shinbashi, Minato-ku (3569 2220/fax 3569 2111/www.villa-fontaine.co.jp). Shiodome station (Oedo line), exit 10; (Yurikamome line), Shiodome Sumitomo Bldg exit. **Rooms** 497. **Rates** ¥12,000-¥16,000 single; ¥16,000-¥18,000 double; ¥21,000 triple. **Credit** AmEx, DC, JCB, MC, V.

The Villa Fontaine chain has mushroomed across the city in the last few years. Prices are surprisingly low, and many of its hotels offer unique options such bathrooms, some with jacuzzi or sauna, since the Japanese like to wash before jumping in the sack. When you leave, pay the person at the desk; in automatic hotels, simply feed your money into the talking machine by the door.

The highest concentrations of love hotels in Tokyo are to be found in the Kabuki-cho district in Shinjuku, Dogenzaka in Shibuya and by the railway tracks near Ikebukuro station, although there are clusters in many other areas too. You'll even find a sprinkling in swankier neighbourhoods, such as Ebisu.

Bron Mode

2-29-7 Kabuki-cho, Shinjuku-ku (3208 6211/ www.hotel-guide.jp). Shinjuku station (Yamanote, Chuo, Sobu lines), east exit; (Marunouchi line), exit B7; (Shinjuku line), exit 1 or Shinjuku-Nishiguchi station (Oedo line), exit D3. **Rates** ¥6,000-¥10,290 rest; ¥11,000-¥20,790 stay. **Credit** AmEx, DC, JCB, MC, V.

Flashy and futuristic-looking, the Bron Mode fancies itself as a little bit upmarket. Rooms have karaoke, jet bath/jacuzzi and sauna, and gay and lesbian couples are welcome.

Hotel Listo

2-36-1 Kabuki-cho, Shinjuku-ku (5155 9255). Shinjuku station (Yamanote, Chuo, Sobu lines), east exit; (Marunouchi line), exit B7; (Shinjuku line), exit 1 or Shinjuku-Nishiguchi station (Oedo line), exit D3. **Rates** ¥5,200-¥14,700 rest; ¥9,500-¥28,000 stay. **Credit** AmEx, JCB, MC, V.

A love hotel in Kabuki-cho, surrounded by fir trees so a certain level of clandestine discretion is assured.

Meguro Club Sekitei

2-1-6 Shimo-Meguro, Meguro-ku (3494 1211). Meguro station (Yamanote, Mita, Nanboku lines), west exit. **Rates** ¥9,000-¥13,000 rest; ¥13,000-¥19,000 stay. **Credit** AmEx, MC, V. **Map** Meguro p71.

A famous Tokyo love hotel, standing on its own like a fairytale palace. Check in and pay via a machine in the foyer. Rooms are huge and well furnished. Karaoke, jet bath/sauna and free drinks are standard, as are microwave ovens. Don't ask.

P&A Plaza

1-17-9 Dogenzaka, Shibuya-ku (3780 5211/ www.p-aplaza.com). Shibuya station (Yamanote, Ginza lines), south exit; (Hanzomon line), exit 5. **Rates** ¥5,500-¥15,800 rest; ¥9,800-¥29,300 stay. **Credit** AmEx, DC, JCB, MC, V. **Map** Shibuya p109.

One of the most famous love hotels in the capital, located in Dogenzaka near Shibuya station. The P&A's top-priced suite contains a swimming pool. A jet bath or jacuzzi comes as standard in all rooms.

Villa Giulia

2-27-8 Dogenzaka, Shibuya-ku (3770 7781). Shibuya station (Yamanote, Ginza lines), Hachiko exit; (Hanzomon line), exit 1. **Rates** ¥5,500-¥9,500 rest; ¥12,000-¥18,000 stay. **Credit** AmEx, JCB, MC, V. **Map** Shibuya p109.

From the outside, Villa Giulia looks rather like an Italian restaurant. Inside, it's clean and fully automatic. Push a button, take a slip for your room, then follow the spoken (Japanese) instructions for payment.

as women-only floors. This branch, opened in 2004, sits in the gleaming Shidome complex. A funky approach to interior design has resulted in, for example, a striking atrium/lobby area with cone-shaped lights and unusual artworks by the lifts. The well-designed rooms make the most of their small size, using discreetly patterned luxury fabrics and nifty shutter/blind combinations. Free, always-on broadband internet access is a bonus. Shame about the disappointing buffet breakfast. This is the smartest of the hotel's ever-increasing locations, which include Roppongi, Ueno and Nihonbashi. *Business centre. Disabled-adapted room. Internet (high-speed). No-smoking rooms. Parking (¥2,100/night).*
Other locations: throughout the city (central reservations 5339 1200).

Ikebukuro

Budget

Kimi Ryokan

2-36-8 Ikebukuro, Toshima-ku (3971 3766/www. kimi-ryokan.jp). Ikebukuro station (Yamanote, Marunouchi, Yurakucho lines), exits west, C6. **Rooms** 38. **Rates** ¥4,500 single; ¥6,500-¥7,500 double. **No credit cards. Map** Ikebukuro p87.

A *ryokan* that caters almost exclusively to foreign visitors, Kimi offers simple, small, Japanese-style rooms. Bathing and toilet facilities are communal but very clean; there's even a Japanese bath for use at set times. Downstairs in the communal lounge, backpackers and travellers exchange gossip. Kimi also runs an information and accommodation service for foreigners apartment-hunting in Tokyo (3986 1604), and a telephone answering service for businesspeople (3986 1895). Booking is advised. **Photo** *p38.* *Japanese rooms only.*

Marunouchi & around

Deluxe

Four Seasons Hotel Tokyo at Marunouchi

Pacific Century Place, 1-11-1 Marunouchi, Chiyoda-ku (5222 7222/fax 5222 1255/www.fourseasons.com/ marunouchi). Tokyo station (Yamanote, Marunouchi lines), Yaesu south exit. **Rooms** 57. **Rates** ¥58,000-¥84,000 single/double; ¥98,000-¥400,000 suite. **Credit** AmEx, DC, JCB, MC, V. **Map** Marunouchi p93.
The Four Seasons offers unparalleled luxury and style in the heart of the city's business district. It's decorated in cool, modern timber and is beautifully lit. The rooms are among the biggest in any Tokyo hotel, and some boast great views. Service is multilingual and utterly impeccable, as you're entitled to expect for the price. Each room comes with high-speed internet access, a 42in plasma-screen TV with surround sound and a DVD player.

Bar. Business centre. Concierge. Gym. Internet (high-speed). No-smoking rooms. Parking (¥5,000/ night). Restaurant. Room service (24hr). Spa.

Expensive

Hilltop Hotel

1-1 Kanda-Surugadai, Chiyoda-ku (3293 2311/fax 3233 4567/www.yamanoue-hotel.co.jp). Ochanomizu station (Chuo, Marunouchi lines), Ochanomizubashi exit. **Rooms** 74. **Rates** ¥13,960-¥21,000 single; ¥23,100-¥33,600 double/twin; ¥42,000-¥58,150 suite. **Credit** AmEx, DC, JCB, MC, V.
Map Marunouchi p93.
Not many hotels in Tokyo can be said to exude genuine charm, so the Hilltop deserves some credit for retaining its old-fashioned traditions, with antique writing desks and small private gardens for the more expensive suites. That said, its seventh storey, called the Art Septo Floor, offers funky furniture and decor, plus large-screen TVs and enhanced stereos. Known throughout Tokyo as a literary hangout, the Hilltop tries to boost the concentration of blocked writers by pumping ionised air into every room.
Bars (3). Internet (high-speed). Japanese & Western rooms. Parking (¥1,000/night). Restaurants (7). Room service (7am-2am).

Sisters are doing it by themselves

Only a society as patriarchal as Japan's could create a word to describe women who venture to restaurants, cinemas or hotels on their own. The term *ohitorisama* derives from the question asked of anyone entering a hotel or restaurant alone: '*ohitorisama desuka?*' ('Just one person?'). And since the turn of the century this has been used to describe the emerging breed of independent women who see no stigma in enjoying companion-free trips.

The most vocal champion of the *ohitorisama* trend was the late journalist Iwashita Kumiko, previously best known as an expert on stalkers. According to Iwashita, staying alone in hotels is one of the accomplishments of a true lady. She even laid out five rules for the perfect solo stay:
1. Research carefully
2. Sell yourself when making the reservation
3. Be open-minded
4. Pay enough to buy security
5. Maintain a sense of urgency throughout
With these rules in mind, said Iwashita, Tokyo's women could visit the most formal of settings without the need for a companion. The hotel industry seems to agree and has

jumped on the *ohitorisama* boom with special packages tailored to Japan's single women.

The **ANA Intercontinental Tokyo** (*see p51*) offers an 'Angel Holiday Plan' (from ¥43,000). The *ohitorisama* gets a double room to herself, an in-room massage, herbal teas and a late check-out. She can also enjoy a room-service macrobiotic breakfast.

The **Rihga Royal Hotel Tokyo** (1-104-19, Totsukamachi, Shinjuku-ku, 5285 1121) ties up with various companies from different industries to pamper the ladies, before teasing marketing information from them. Special bedding and beauty appliances are provided in the rooms, as is a questionnaire that feeds straight back to the companies to help them with their product development. The ¥19,500-¥22,500 package includes a night in a twin room and a ¥1,000 taxi coupon for the ride home.

Anyone looking for further *ohitorisama* treats in the city can check http://ohitorisama. hershe.co.jp – the official website of the Iwashita-established Committee for the Advancement of Ohitorisama, which details appropriate hotels, spas, restaurants, holidays and consumer goods.

Mandarin Oriental Tokyo

2-1-1 Nihonbashi-Muromachi, Chuo-ku (3270 8800/ fax 3270 8828/www.mandarinoriental.com/tokyo). Mitsukoshimae station (Ginza line), exit A7. **Rooms** 157. **Rates** ¥65,000-¥72,000 double/twin; ¥120,00- ¥800,000 suite. **Credit** AmEx, DC, JCB, MC, V.

Focusing not just on Tokyo, but on the historic Nihonbashi area in which it sits, the Mandarin is the antidote to that feeling that luxury hotels are the same the world over. Many of the materials are sourced from local artisans. The lobby and rooms all hint at traditional Japanese motifs, from the *torii* shrine gates and *washi* paper lanterns to the woven fabrics that hang in place of paintings. The view from the rooms trumps most of its top-end rivals, with a mosaic of lights from the business district in the foreground, and Mt Fuji straight ahead. **Photo** *p47*.

Bar. Business centre. Concierge. Disabled-adapted room. Gym. Internet (high-speed). Non-smoking floors. Parking (¥3,000/night). Restaurants (5). Spa.

Marunouchi Hotel

1-6-3 Marunouchi, Chiyoda-ku (3217 1111/fax 3217 1115/www.marunouchi-hotel.co.jp). Tokyo station (Yamanote line), Marunouchi north exit; (Marunouchi line), exit 12. **Rooms** 205. **Rates** ¥23,300 single; ¥26,765-¥44,290 double/twin; ¥115,700-¥115,900 suite. **Credit** AmEx, DC, JCB, MC, V. **Map** Marunouchi p93.

There's been a Marunouchi Hotel since 1924; its latest incarnation opened in the Oazo Building (*see p191*) in autumn 2004. The lobby is on the seventh floor, from where a truly spectacular atrium soars through the centre of the hotel. Rooms (which vary considerably in size) are on the ninth to 17th floors – hence some fantastic views over the train tracks of neighbouring Tokyo station – and major in sumptuous materials in a palette of browns and golds. Restaurants include Japanese and French ones, and business facilities are good. A classy joint.

Bar. Disabled-adapted rooms. Internet (high-speed). No-smoking rooms. Parking (¥1,500/night). Restaurants (5). Room service (7am-10pm).

Moderate

Hotel Kazusaya

4-7-15 Nihonbashi-Honcho, Chuo-ku (3241 1045/fax 3241 1077/www.h-kazusaya.co.jp). Kanda station (Yamanote, Ginza lines), east exit; Mitsukoshimae station (Ginza, Hanzomon lines), exit A10 or Shin-Nihonbashi station (Sobu Kaisoku line), exit 8. **Rooms** 71. **Rates** ¥8,925-¥9,975 single; ¥10,500-¥12,600 double; ¥14,700 twin; ¥18,900 triple. *Japanese* (3-4 people) ¥22,050-¥25,200. **Credit** AmEx, DC, JCB, MC, V. **Map** Marunouchi p93.

There has been a Hotel Kazusaya in Nihonbashi since 1891, but you'd be hard pushed to know it from the modern exterior of the current building, in one of the last *shitamachi* areas in the heart of Tokyo's business district. Inside, you'll find good-sized, functionally furnished rooms, including one

Japanese-style tatami room for three to four guests. Service is obliging, although only minimal English is spoken by most staff.

Internet (high-speed). Japanese & Western rooms. No-smoking rooms. Parking (¥2,100/night). Restaurant.

Kayabacho Pearl Hotel

1-2-5 Shinkawa, Chuo-ku (3553 8080/fax 3555 1849/ www.pearlhotel.co.jp/kayabacho). Kayabacho station (Hibiya, Tozai lines), exit 4B. **Rooms** 268. **Rates** ¥8,295-¥9,345 single; ¥15,960-¥21,000 twin; ¥18,585-¥23,625 triple. **Credit** AmEx, DC, JCB, MC, V. **Map** Marunouchi p93.

An upmarket business hotel in the heart of the business district, the Pearl has good-sized, well-furnished rooms and reasonable service. Staff speak some English. An unexpected plus is the canalside location.

Business centre. No-smoking rooms. Parking (¥1,500/night). Restaurant.

Ryokan Ryumeikan Honten

3-4 Kanda-Surugadai, Chiyoda-ku (3251 1135/fax 3251 0270/www.ryumeikan.co.jp/honten.html). Ochanomizu station (Chuo, Marunouchi lines), Hijiribashi exit. **Rooms** 12. **Rates** ¥10,000-¥13,100 single; ¥17,000-¥18,000 double; ¥22,500-¥24,000 triple. **Credit** AmEx, DC, JCB, MC, V. **Map** Marunouchi p93.

Just south of Ochanomizu's Russian Nikolai Cathedral, this *ryokan* is modern and clean, with helpful staff and good-sized Japanese rooms. In an architectural sense, though, it's a nightmare, occupying part of a modern office block that blends completely into the surrounding skyscrapers. The interior is a testament to how ingeniously the Japanese can disguise the shortcomings of a building to produce a pleasant atmosphere, but you still might find yourself wishing you'd stayed somewhere a little more traditional. The branch in Nihonbashi is slightly cheaper and more imposing.

Internet (high-speed). Japanese rooms only. Parking (free). Restaurant. Room service (7.30am-10pm).

Other locations: Hotel Yaesu Ryumeikan 1-3-22 Yaesu, Chuo-ku (3271 0971/fax 3271 0977).

Sumisho Hotel

9-14 Nihonbashi-Kobunacho, Chuo-ku (3661 4603/fax 3661 4639/www.sumisho-hotel.co.jp). Ningyocho station (Asakusa, Hibiya lines), exit A5. **Rooms** 86. **Rates** ¥8,820 single; ¥11,000 double; ¥12,600-¥19,500 twin. *Japanese* ¥13,860-¥19,500. **Credit** AmEx, DC, JCB, MC, V. **Map** Marunouchi p93.

A little tricky to find, this charming Japanese-style hotel manages to take an ugly modern Tokyo building and imbue it with something quintessentially Japanese; in this case a small pond, which you need to cross to get to the foyer. It's a pleasant enough place to stay, with good facilities and a high level of service, although non-Japanese speakers may find it hard to make themselves understood. The first floor contains a communal bath, although all rooms are equipped with their own bathrooms.

Internet. Japanese & Western rooms. Restaurant.

Budget

Hotel Nihonbashi Saibo

3-3-16 Nihonbashi-Ningyocho, Chuo-ku (3668 2323/ fax 3668 1669/www.hotel-saibo.co.jp). Ningyocho station (Asakusa, Hibiya lines), exit A4. **Rooms** 126. **Rates** ¥8,190-¥9,900 single; ¥10,920 double; ¥13,230 twin. **Credit** AmEx, DC, JCB, V. **Map** Marunouchi p93.

The good news for anyone looking to stay in this quiet area not far from Tokyo station is that while the Saibo has remodelled its interior and guest rooms – rooms are still small and services sparse, however – the bargain rates have been retained. A good bet for solo travellers looking for functional and relatively modern accommodation.
Internet (high-speed/shared terminal). Restaurants (2).

Sakura Hotel

2-21-4 Kanda-Jinbocho, Chiyoda-ku (3261 3939/fax 3264 2777/www.sakura-hotel.co.jp). Jinbocho station (Hanzomon, Mita, Shinjuku lines), exits A1, A6. **Rooms** 43. **Rates** ¥3,780 dorm; ¥6,090-¥7,140 single; ¥8,300 double; ¥8,400 twin. **Credit** AmEx, DC, JCB, MC, V. **Map** Marunouchi p93.

Of all the budget hotels and *ryokan* in Tokyo, this is the most central, located in the Jinbocho district just a mile or so north of the Imperial Palace. Small groups can use the dorm rooms, which sleep six. Rooms are tiny but clean, and all are no-smoking. Staff are on duty 24 hours a day and speak good English. Book well in advance.
Internet (shared). No smoking. Restaurant.

YMCA Asia Youth Centre

2-5-5 Sarugakucho, Chiyoda-ku (3233 0611/fax 3233 0633/www.ymcajapan.org/ayc). Suidobashi station (Chuo line), east exit; (Mita line), exit A1. **Rooms** 55. **Rates** ¥5,040-¥6,300 single; ¥9,240-¥11,550 twin; ¥11,592-¥14,490 triple. **Credit** JCB, MC, V.

Part of the Korean YMCA in Japan, this centre offers many of the same facilities and services you'd expect at a regular hotel, a fact reflected in its relatively high prices. In terms of location, it shares many advantages with the nearby Hilltop Hotel (*see p44*). The smallish rooms are Western in style, with their own bathrooms.
Internet (shared terminals). Restaurant.

Odaiba

Deluxe

Le Meridien Grand Pacific Tokyo

2-6-1 Daiba, Minato-ku (5500 6711/fax 5500 4507/www.grandpacific.lemeridien.com). Daiba station (Yurikamome line). **Rooms** 884. **Rates** ¥26,000-¥37,000 single; ¥31,000-¥42,000 double/twin; ¥39,000-¥45,345 triple; ¥80,000-¥130,000 suite. **Credit** AmEx, DC, JCB, MC, V. **Map** Odaiba p101.

Luxury hotels don't come much more luxurious than this. Le Meridien opened in 1998 on the island area of Odaiba and has spectacular views over Rainbow Bridge and the Tokyo skyline. The only real drawback is its location: Odaiba is great for a day out, but as a base for touring Tokyo it's rather inconvenient. Perhaps appreciating the lack of any real local character, the hotel supplies some of its own through a third-floor art gallery and, more bizarrely, a museum of music boxes one floor down. Even if you don't stay here, it's worth visiting the Sky Lounge on the 30th floor for the great views.
Bars (3). Business centre. Concierge. Disabled-adapted rooms. Gym. No-smoking rooms. Parking (¥1,000/night). Pools (indoor/outdoor). Restaurants (7). Room service (6am-1am). Spa.

Shibuya

Deluxe

Cerulean Tower Tokyu Hotel

26-1 Sakuragaokacho, Shibuya-ku (3476 3000/fax 3476 3001/www.ceruleantower-hotel.com). Shibuya station (Yamanote line), south exit; (Ginza, Hanzomon lines), Hachiko exit. **Rooms** 414. **Rates** ¥27,720-¥39,270 single; ¥36,960-¥66,990 double/twin; ¥93,400-¥438,900 suite. *Japanese* ¥75,075-¥77,385. **Credit** AmEx, MC, V. **Map** Shibuya p109.

It may be outshone in the luxury market by the myriad new entrants, but the Cerulean is Shibuya's lone top-end establishment, and with rooms on the 19th to 37th floors of the area's tallest building, it offers grandstand views. In addition to the usual restaurants and bars, it also has a *Noh* theatre (*see p264*) and a jazz club, JZ Brat (*see p254*). Room furnishings may be a step down from the likes of the Grand Hyatt, as may be the price. Except, that is, for the 35th to 37th Executive Floors, which offer free access to the gym, daily newspapers, web TV and refreshments in the salon.
Bars (2). Business centre. Concierge. Disabled-adapted rooms. Gym. Internet (high-speed). Japanese & Western rooms. No-smoking rooms. Parking (free). Pool (indoor). Restaurants (6). Room service (24hr). Spa.

Expensive

Arimax Hotel Shibuya

11-15 Kamiyamacho, Shibuya-ku (5454 1122/fax 3460 6513/www.arimaxhotelshibuya.co.jp). Shibuya station (Yamanote, Ginza, Hanzomon lines), Hachiko exit. **Rooms** 23. **Rates** ¥22,145-¥33,695 single; ¥27,920-¥39,670 double; ¥75,475 suite. **Credit** AmEx, DC, JCB, MC, V. **Map** Shibuya p109.

Modelled on European boutique hotels, the Arimax Hotel Shibuya offers a choice of English or neo-classical room styles and exudes the atmosphere of a long-established gentlemen's club, with warm, dim lighting and dark wood panelling the dominant decorative themes. All guest rooms include business amenities. The only drawback may be the location, about 15 minutes' walk from the buzzing centre of Shibuya.

Bar. Internet (high-speed). Parking (free). Restaurant. Room service (drinks 5pm-midnight Mon-Fri, 5-11pm Sat, Sun; food 5-9.30pm daily).

Excel Hotel Tokyu

Shibuya Mark City, 1-12-2 Dogenzaka, Shibuya-ku (5457 0109/fax 5457 0309/www.tokyuhotels.co.jp/ en/TE/TE_SHIBU). Inside Shibuya station (Yamanote, Ginza, Hanzomon lines). **Rooms** 408. **Rates** ¥20,790-¥27,720 single; ¥24,255-¥28,875 double; ¥26,565-¥41,580 twin; ¥34,650 triple; ¥41,580 quadruple; ¥115,500 suite. **Credit** AmEx, DC, JCB, MC, V. **Map** Shibuya p109.

Situated in the Mark City complex attached to Shibuya station, the Excel is very popular with domestic visitors wanting to spend their stay in the capital in the heart of Shibuya. Pleasant and clean, with spacious rooms and nice views, it's one of few good-quality hotels in this part of town. There are six special floors: two for women only, with added security; three for business travellers; and a 'Healing Floor', with aromatherapy, soothing music and relaxation programmes.

Bar. Concierge. Disabled-adapted rooms. Internet. No-smoking floors. Parking (¥1,500/night). Restaurants (2). Room service (7-10am; 9pm-midnight). Spa.

Moderate

Granbell Hotel

15-17 Sakuragaoka-cho, Shibuya-ku (5457 2681/ fax 5457 2682/www.granbellhotel.jp). Shibuya station (Yamanote line), south exit; (Ginza, Hanzomon lines), Hachiko exit. **Rooms** 55. **Rates** ¥13,000 single; ¥26,000-¥28,000 double/twin; ¥45,000-¥65,000 suite. **Credit** AmEx, JCB, MC, V. **Map** Shibuya p109.

Tokyo has been surpirsingly slow to join the boutique-hotel boom. For a few years now, the Claska (*see p54*) has been the only choice in town for those seeking a quirky, personalised place to stay. Now there's the Granbell too. Not nearly as fancy as the Claska, but a lot more convenient, the Granbell is located just a couple of blocks from Shibuya station. The 55 rooms are minimalist, with a big splash of pop art, and the service is friendly and attentive. The single rooms are small, but for this price, there's no better place to stay. **Photo** *p50*.

Bar. Internet (LAN). No smoking rooms. Restaurant. Room service (24hr).

Shinagawa

Deluxe

The Strings Hotel Tokyo

Shinagawa East One Tower 26F-32F, 2-16-1 Konan, Minato-ku (4562 1111/fax 4562 1112/www. stringshotel.com). Shinagawa station (Yamanote line), Konan exit. **Rooms** 206. **Rates** ¥37,000-¥56,000 single; ¥45,000-¥62,000 double; ¥140,000-¥200,000 suite. **Credit** AmEx, DC, JCB, MC, V.

Mandarin Oriental Tokyo. *See p45.*

Opened in 2003, ANA's Strings Hotel brings a new level of class and service to the revitalised Shinagawa district. Its rooms occupy the top floors of a gleaming new skyscraper and are decked out in soothing earth tones. The 59 higher-end Club Rooms offer sparkling views over Tokyo Bay, as well as extra amenities, including one complimentary meal per day. The hotel's convenient location just off the JR Tokaido *shinkansen* tracks also makes it a great base for travelling between cities.

Bar. Business centre. Concierge. Disabled-adapted rooms. Gym. Internet. No-smoking rooms. Parking (¥1,500/night). Restaurants (2). Room service (24hr).

Expensive

Le Meridien Hotel Pacific Tokyo

3-13-3 Takanawa, Minato-ku (3445 6711/fax 3445 5137/www.pacific-tokyo.com). Shinagawa station (Yamanote line), Takanawa exit. **Rooms** 954. **Rates** ¥25,610 single; ¥33,895-¥38,550 double/twin; ¥58,150-¥150,900 suite. **Credit** AmEx, DC, JCB, MC, V.

This 1971 monolith benefits from a pleasant garden that gives it a sense of space that many Tokyo hotels lack. The hotel might look its age from the outside, and the decor is a mix of bland and garish, but there's no faulting the facilities. Rooms are of a good size and kept bang up to date thanks to what appears to be a constant process of renovation and redecoration. The Shinagawa area hasn't got much to recommend it, though it's a short hop into the centre via the Yamanote line, and the bullet train line makes it a popular choice for business travellers. This is another of the hotels frequently used by travel companies for package tours and stopovers.

Bars (3). Business centre. Concierge. Disabled-adapted rooms. Internet (high-speed). No-smoking rooms. Parking (free). Pool (outdoor). Restaurants (6). Room service (6am-midnight). Spa.

Takanawa Prince Hotel, New Takanawa Prince Hotel & Sakura Tower

3-13-1 Takanawa, Minato-ku (3442 1111/fax 3444 1234/www.princehotels.co.jp/english). Shinagawa station (Yamanote line), Takanawa exit then free shuttle bus. **Rooms** New Takanawa Prince 946; Sakura Tower 309; Takanawa Prince 414. **Rates** ¥20,000 single; ¥24,200 double/twin; ¥75,000 suite. **Credit** AmEx, DC, JCB, MC, V.

The Takanawa Prince, the New Takanawa Prince and the Sakura Tower – all part of the same chain – operate as separate hotels, with separate tariffs, but are linked by glorious landscaped grounds. Guests can also use the facilities of all three. The oldest, the Takanawa Prince, recently remodelled its rooms with new wallpaper, carpeting and furniture, as well as air-con units and liquid-crystal TVs. It has also added a number of rooms specially for women. The New Takanawa Prince is gaudy from the outside but impressive within, while the Sakura Tower, a pink monster of a building, offers the most up-to-date facilities and

the priciest accommodation. The services listed below are for all three hotels combined.

Bars (5). Business centre. Concierge. Disabled-adapted rooms. Gym. Internet (high-speed). Japanese & Western rooms. No-smoking rooms. Parking (free). Pools (2, outdoor). Restaurants (18). Room service (24hr). Spa.

Deluxe

Hilton Tokyo

6-6-2 Nishi-Shinjuku, Shinjuku-ku (3344 5111/fax 3342 6094/www.hilton.com/hotels/TYOHITW). Nishi-Shinjuku station (Marunouchi line), exit C8 or Tochomae station (Oedo line), exit C8. Free bus from Keio department store (bus stop 21), Shinjuku station, west exit. **Rooms** 806. **Rates** ¥20,700-¥34,000 single; ¥23,700-¥37,000 double; ¥32,200-¥120,000 suite. **Credit** AmEx, DC, JCB, MC, V. **Map** Shinjuku p117.

A luxury hotel in west Shinjuku, the Hilton opened in 1984 after vacating its previous premises in Akasaka. Rooms are of a good size, although the views, often blocked by other towers in the area, can be disappointing. As you'd expect, the standard of service is high. For business travellers, the hotel offers five executive floors, with separate check-in, a fax machine in each room and their own guest relations officers on hand to help out and advise. The Hilton is also one of few Tokyo hotels to have its own tennis courts.

Bar. Business centre. Concierge. Disabled-adapted rooms. Gym. Internet (high-speed). Japanese & Western rooms. No-smoking rooms. Parking (¥1,500/night). Pool (indoor). Restaurants (6). Room service (24hr).

Other locations: Hilton Tokyo Bay, 1-8 Maihama, Urayasu-shi, Chiba-ken (047 355 5000).

Keio Plaza Hotel

2-2-1 Nishi-Shinjuku, Shinjuku-ku (3344 0111/fax 3345 8269/www.keioplaza.com). Shinjuku station (Yamanote line), west exit; (Marunouchi line), exit A17; (Shinjuku line), exit B1 or Tochomae station (Oedo line), exits A1, B1. **Rooms** 1,450. **Rates** ¥21,567 single; ¥30,230 double/twin; ¥41,880 triple. **Credit** AmEx, DC, JCB, MC, V. **Map** Shinjuku p117.

The lavish decor that once made this Tokyo's most prestigious hotel now looks seriously dated compared to its new luxury rivals. The location, however, is still pretty tough to beat: a stone's throw from the world's busiest train station, with upper floors offering superlative views of the metropolis. In spring 2005 the hotel opened three floors of 'Plaza Premier' rooms: spacious, elegant spaces with all the electronics and business support expected of a luxury hotel. The Plaza plans to continue its renovations until all floors have been updated. **Photo** *p41*.

Bars (4). Business centre. Disabled-adapted rooms. Gym. Internet (high-speed). No-smoking rooms. Parking (¥1,000/night). Pool (outdoor). Restaurants (13). Room service (24hr).

Park Hyatt Tokyo

*3-7-1-2 Nishi-Shinjuku, Shinjuku-ku (5322 1234/
fax 5322 1288/http://tokyo.park.hyatt.com).
Shinjuku station (Yamanote, Marunouchi
lines), west exit; (Shinjuku line), exit 6 or
Tochomae station (Oedo line), exit A4. Free
shuttle bus from in front of Shinjuku L Tower,
Shinjuku station, west exit.* **Rooms** 178. **Rates**
¥53,000-¥65,000 double/twin; ¥120,000-¥300,000
suite. **Credit** AmEx, DC, JCB, MC, V.
Map Shinjuku p117.

Despite being Tokyo's most decorated hotel, the Park
Hyatt is perhaps now best known for its starring role
in Sofia Coppola's 2003 hit *Lost in Translation*. By
Tokyo standards, it's a small, intimate establishment, a feeling emphasised by the well-lit decor and
artworks on display. The reception is on the glass-
walled 41st floor, with stunning views over the
whole of the city. Service is attentive but not overly
fussy, and the immaculately equipped rooms are
among the largest in any Tokyo hotel. The celebrated

Tatami treats

If you can bear to forgo a few home comforts,
then staying in a *ryokan* (traditional Japanese
inn) is a great choice, particularly since they
tend to be cheaper than Western-style hotels.
Ryokan also make excellent lodgings for
groups: you can have as many futons as you
can fit on the tatami (straw mat) floor, for an
extra charge that is significantly less than the
price of another room.

There are a few matters of *ryokan* etiquette.
First, remove your shoes when entering. Staff
will show you to your room, and introduce you
to the waiting flask of hot water and green
tea. Decor will include a *shoji* (sliding paper
screen) and a *tokonoma* (alcove), which is
for decoration, not for storing luggage. Inside
the cupboard you will find a *yukata* (dressing
gown) and *tanzen* (bed jacket), which can be

worn inside the inn and double as pyjamas.
When putting on a *yukata*, put the left side
over the right.

By day the futons are folded away in a
cupboard. Staff will make up the futons at
around 8pm. They'll be back the following
morning at about 8am with breakfast. More
expensive *ryokan* usually have private
bathrooms, but at the cheaper end of the
scale you will be expected to bathe Japanese-
style in a communal bath. For tips on bathing
etiquette, *see p64*.

Most *ryokan* are family-run businesses,
so many impose a curfew of 11pm. If you're
going to be out later, be sure to tell your
hosts. If a curfew doesn't suit you, check with
the individual *ryokan* in advance. We've listed
some of the best choices in this chapter.

Granbell Hotel.
See p47.

Club on The Park aesthetic and fitness centre includes a luxurious spa with Vichy shower.
Bars (2). Business centre. Concierge. Disabled-adapted rooms. Gym. Internet (high-speed). No-smoking rooms. Parking (free). Pool (indoor). Restaurants (4). Room service (24hr). Spa.

Moderate

Shinjuku Washington Hotel

3-2-9 Nishi-Shinjuku, Shinjuku-ku (3343 3111/fax 3342 2575/www.wh-rsv.com/english/shinjuku). Shinjuku station (Yamanote, Marunouchi lines), south exit; (Oedo, Shinjuku lines), exits 6, 7. **Rooms** 1,296. **Rates** ¥10,000-¥12,500 single;

¥15,000-¥19,200 double/twin. **Credit** AmEx, DC, JCB, MC, V. **Map** Shinjuku p117.

A step down in price and luxury from other west Shinjuku hotels, the Washington nonetheless offers a high standard of accommodation and service. Its main target market is business travellers, so rooms tend to be small and blandly furnished. Also, there is now a women-only floor, and a business floor with upgraded amenities. The newer annex (containing 337 rooms) offers roughly the same level of service, with more modern decor.
Bar. Disabled-adapted rooms. Internet (high-speed). No-smoking rooms. Parking (¥100-¥250/30mins). Restaurants (4). Room service (main bldg 6-11pm; annex 6-10pm).
Other locations: Akihabara Washington Hotel, 1-8-3 Sakuma-machi, Kanda, Chiyoda-ku (3255 3311/fax 3255 7343); Tokyo Bay Ariake Washington Hotel, 3-1-28 Ariake, Koto-ku (5564 0111/fax 5564 0525).

Star Hotel Tokyo

7-10-5 Nishi-Shinjuku, Shinjuku-ku (3361 1111/fax 3369 4216/www.starhotel.co.jp/city/tokyo.html). Shinjuku station (Yamanote line), west exit; (Marunouchi, Shinjuku lines), exit D4 or Shinjuku-Nishiguchi station (Oedo line), exit D4. **Rooms** 214. **Rates** ¥9,450-¥12,100 single; ¥17,850-¥18,900 double; ¥17,850-¥27,300 twin. **Credit** AmEx, JCB, MC, V. **Map** Shinjuku p117.

In terms of position, the Star offers everything its more expensive west Shinjuku rivals do. Tucked among all-night restaurants on a noisy main road, it's a great location from which to base your Tokyo explorations, with the red-light district of Kabuki-cho on one side and access to the rest of the city via Shinjuku station on the other. Rooms are tiny and frill-free, but the Star has made some cosmetic upgrades and remains one of the best options on its side of Shinjuku.
Bar. Internet (high-speed). No-smoking rooms. Parking (¥1,500/night). Restaurants (3). Room service (5-10pm).

Budget

Shinjuku Palace Hotel

2-8-12 Kabuki-cho, Shinjuku-ku (3209 1231).
Shinjuku station (Yamanote line), east exit; Shinjuku-
Sanchome station (Marunouchi, Shinjuku lines),
exit C7. **Rooms** 34. **Rates** ¥6,700-¥6,800 single;
¥9,800 double; ¥10,500 twin. *Japanese* ¥9,800.
No credit cards.
A palace in name only, this hotel in the heart of
Kabuki-cho offers basic, no-frills accommodation
aimed primarily at local businessmen or salarymen
who've stayed one drink too long and missed the
last train home. Surrounded by late-night noodle
joints and love hotels, the Palace is clean and
friendly; just don't expect to be able to make much
meaningful communication in English. Rooms are
small, but how much time are you really going to
spend here?
Japanese & Western rooms.

Roppongi & Akasaka

Deluxe

Akasaka Prince Hotel

1-2 Kioi-cho, Chiyoda-ku (3234 1111/fax 3262
5163/www.princehotelsjapan.com/akasakaprince
hotel). Akasaka-Mitsuke station (Ginza, Marunouchi
lines), exit D or Nagatacho station (Hanzomon,
Nanboku, Yurakucho lines), exits 7, 9A, 9B.
Rooms 761. **Rates** ¥28,900-¥42,800 single;
¥38,200-¥48,600 twin; ¥42,800-¥52,000 double;
¥42,800-¥150,200 suite/Japanese. **Credit** AmEx,
DC, JCB, MC, V.
Situated to the west of the Imperial Palace complex
and designed by award-winning architect Tange
Kenzo, the 40-storey Akasaka Prince is part of a
complex that includes a convention centre,
European-style guesthouse, banqueting building
and numerous restaurants. Inside the main tower
it's all glittering marble and bright lights. The
building's clean lines extend to the furnishings in
the rooms, which are elegantly simple.
Bars (3). Business centre. Concierge. Disabled-
adapted room. Gym. Japanese & Western rooms.
No-smoking rooms. Parking (free). Pool (outdoor).
Restaurants (10). Room service (24hr).

ANA Intercontinental Tokyo

1-12-33 Akasaka, Minato-ku (3505 1111/fax 3505
1155/www.anahoteltokyo.jp/e). Tameike-Sanno
station (Ginza, Nanboku lines), exit 13. **Rooms** 901.
Rates ¥31,185-¥34,650 single; ¥40,425-¥51,975
twin; ¥40,425-¥75,075 double; ¥48,510-¥51,975
triple; ¥80,850-¥323,400 suite. **Credit** AmEx, DC,
JCB, MC, V. **Map** Roppongi p103.
In 2007 owners All Nippon Airways joined forces
with the Intercontinental chain and rebranded this
29-storey hotel. Its airy lobby has been redone in
gleaming marble and cherry wood, with the
modern space broken up by cascading waterfalls
and artworks. Spacious, well-equipped rooms have

all been recently renovated. The hotel provides
stunning views on a clear day – you can see Mt Fuji
from the open-air rooftop pool.
Bars (3). Business centre. Concierge. Disabled-adapted
room. Gym. Internet (high-speed). No-smoking rooms.
Parking (¥1,000/night). Pool (outdoor). Restaurants
(8). Room service (6am-2am). Spa.

Grand Hyatt Tokyo

6-10-3 Roppongi, Minato-ku (4333 1234/fax 4333
8123/www.tokyo.grand.hyatt.com). Roppongi station
(Hibiya line), exit 1C; (Oedo line), exit 3. **Rooms**
390. **Rates** ¥43,000-¥58,000 single/double; ¥80,000-
¥500,000 suite. **Credit** AmEx, DC, MC, V.
Map Roppongi p103.
Though it shares a celebrity buzz with its sister
hotel the Park Hyatt, the effortlessly sleek Grand
is pleasingly low-key. Its location in the upmarket
Roppongi Hills complex might not suit those who
like their Tokyo served straight up, but by the same
token it provides a restful retreat. And having high-
end shops and restaurants, a 53-floor panorama
and world-class art on your doorstep can be considered quite an amenity. As is the Nagomi spa
(though there's a charge for guests) which, in addition to the usual list of artful treatments, has a lap
pool, steam and sauna and a luminous white
jacuzzi. Its palette is taupe and cream, marble and
wood, as it is in the relatively modest number of
guest rooms. Though not flashy, these are extremely
comfortable and well thought out, with dimmable
lights, Bose stereos and free high-speed internet,
and a tub you could park your car in. **Photo** *p55.*
Bars (3). Business centre. Gym. Internet
(high-speed). No-smoking rooms. Parking
(¥2,000/night). Pool (indoor). Restaurants (7).
Room service (24hr). Spa.

Hotel New Otani Tokyo

4-1 Kioi-cho, Chiyoda-ku (3265 1111/fax 3221
2619/www1.newotani.co.jp/en/tokyo). Akasaka-
Mitsuke station (Ginza, Marunouchi lines), exit D or
Nagatacho station (Hanzomon, Nanboku, Yurakucho
lines), exit 7. **Rooms** 1,600. **Rates** ¥29,000-¥52,000
single; ¥34,000-¥57,000 double; ¥80,000-¥850,000
suite. *Japanese* ¥55,000-¥74,000. **Credit** AmEx, DC,
JCB, MC, V.
The New Otani sprawls like a mini metropolis over
a vast area ten minutes' walk west of the Imperial
Palace. From the outside, the building bears the
unattractive hallmarks of its 1969 construction, but
inside, the dim lighting and spacious foyers produce
the feeling of a luxury cruise ship. To the rear of the
hotel is a beautifully laid-out and tended Japanese
garden. Within the garden stand several of the
hotel's numerous restaurants, which include the
only branch of the legendary Parisian eaterie La
Tour d'Argent. Capacity was increased in 1979 by
the addition of a 40-storey tower block.
Bars (4). Business centre. Concierge. Disabled-
adapted rooms. Gym. Internet (high-speed). Japanese
& Western rooms. No-smoking rooms. Parking (free).
Pools (indoor/outdoor). Restaurants (26). Room
service (6am-1am). Spa.

Hotel Okura Tokyo

2-10-4 Toranomon, Minato-ku (3582 0111/fax 3582 3707/www.okura.com/tokyo). Roppongi-Itchome station (Nanboku line), exit 3 or Tameike-Sanno station (Ginza, Nanboku lines), exit 13. **Rooms** 858. **Rates** ¥30,450 single; ¥31,125-¥126,000 double; ¥89,250-¥525,000 suite. **Credit** AmEx, DC, JCB, MC, V. **Map** Roppongi p103.

The Okura, next door to the US Embassy, doesn't appear to have changed much in the last half century. The huge wooden lobby's gold-and-beige decor evokes a bygone era's understated hipness, while the guest rooms offer an antiquated fusion of European and Japanese styles. But the Okura is taking steps to modernise itself, beginning with two 'Relaxation Floors' that feature jet baths, saunas and massage services in plush new rooms. *Bars (3). Business centre. Concierge. Disabled-adapted rooms. Gym. Internet (high-speed). No-smoking rooms. Parking (free). Pools (indoor/outdoor). Restaurants (9). Room service (24hr). Spa.*

Tokyo Prince Hotel Park Tower

3-3-1 Shibakoen, Minato-ku (3432 1111/fax 3434 5551/www.princehotels.co.jp/parktower-e). Akabanebashi station (Oedo line), Akabanebashi exit. **Rooms** 673. **Rates** ¥34,000-¥70,000 double/twin; ¥104,000-¥980,000 suite. *Japanese* ¥115,000-¥230,000 suite. **Credit** AmEx, DC, JCB, MC, V.

Occupying the corner of Shiba Park next to the Tokyo Tower, this 33-storey luxury hotel opened in spring 2005, offering everything from a jazz bar to a natural hot-spring spa. All rooms have internet service, jet baths and balconies with views across the park and as far as Mt Fuji, plus all the amenities you'd expect for the price. The Royal Suite even comes with a full-time butler. *Bars (2). Business centre. Concierge. Disabled-adapted rooms. Gym. Internet (high-speed). Japanese & Western rooms. No-smoking rooms. Parking (¥500/30mins). Pool (indoor). Restaurants (2). Room service (24hr). Spa.*

Expensive

Hotel Arca Torre Roppongi

6-1-23 Roppongi, Minato-ku (3404 5111/fax 3404 5115/www.arktower.co.jp). Roppongi station (Hibiya, Oedo lines), exit 3. **Rates** ¥11,000-¥13,000 single; ¥14,000-¥17,000 double; ¥21,000 twin. **Credit** AmEx, DC, JCB, MC, V. **Map** Roppongi p103.

Arca Torre is a smart, bright, high(ish)-rise business hotel sandwiched between the adults' playground of Roppongi and the Roppongi Hills complex. Rooms are small and functional; if you want a bigger room, go for a twin. The vibe is vaguely Italian, with lots of marble flourishes and a first-floor café. For nightlife lovers, the hotel's location is hard to beat, but light sleepers will bemoan the noisy streets. *Disabled-adapted room. No-smoking rooms. Restaurants (2).*

Hotel Avanshell

2-14-4 Akasaka, Minato-ku (3568 3456/fax 3568 3599/www.avanshell.com). Akasaka station (Chiyoda line), exit 2 or Tameike-Sanno station (Ginza, Nanboku lines), exit 10. **Rooms** 71. **Rates** ¥15,750-¥23,625 single; ¥19,950-¥31,500 double; ¥34,650 triple; ¥25,988-¥40,952 suite. **Credit** AmEx, DC, JCB, MC, V.

The Avanshell is the latest incarnation of a one-time serviced apartment building on a side street in Akasaka, a fact that's reflected in the mini kitchens and other apartment-style touches. Long-term stays are encouraged, with a range of electronics and other items available to rent. Rooms are designed around five themes, with names like Zen, Primo and Ultimo, and are pleasingly spacious, with large living and work areas in addition to separate bedrooms. *Internet (high-speed). Japanese & Western rooms. No-smoking floors. Parking (¥1,575/night). Restaurant. Room service (5.30-10pm).*

Moderate

Hotel Ibis

7-14-4 Roppongi, Minato-ku (3403 4411/fax 3479 0609/www.ibis-hotel.com). Roppongi station (Hibiya, Oedo lines), exit 4A. **Rooms** 182. **Rates** ¥13,382-¥15,461 single; ¥16,285-¥26,765 double; ¥22,145-¥26,675 twin; ¥27,720 triple; ¥41,980 suite. **Credit** AmEx, DC, JCB, MC. **Map** Roppongi p103.

It seems hard to believe, given the recent burst of building activity in the area, but just half a decade ago, this was the closest hotel to the centre of Roppongi. Now, with all the new competition, Hotel Ibis is looking a little worn, and customers may well be enticed elsewhere. That said, it's always clean, functional and good value. And perhaps no other can claim to embody Roppongi more effectively, with a gentlemen's club off the front desk, a karaoke lounge downstairs, plus Italian and Vietnamese restaurants thrown into the mix. *Bar. Disabled-adapted rooms. Internet (shared terminal). No-smoking rooms. Parking (¥2,100/night). Restaurants (3).*

Budget

Asia Center of Japan

8-10-32 Akasaka, Minato-ku (3402 6111/fax 3402 0738/www.asiacenter.or.jp). Nogizaka station (Chiyoda line), exit 3. **Rooms** 173. **Rates** ¥8,610 single; ¥10,290 semi-double; ¥12,390-¥14,490 double; ¥16,590 twin; ¥45,150 suite. **Credit** AmEx, JCB, MC, V.

Founded by the Ministry of Foreign Affairs in the 1950s as a cheap place for visiting students to stay, this has long since outgrown its origins and offers comfortable, no-frills accommodation to all visitors on a budget. A new building was added in 2003, presenting a greater variety of Western-style rooms, with clean if unexciting furnishings. The in-house dining hall offers a gathering place and a decent breakfast buffet for a reasonable ¥945. A good

choice for those who don't want to sacrifice location in favour of price, the Asia Center of Japan is conveniently situated for the Aoyama area.
Disabled-adapted rooms. Internet (high-speed). No-smoking floor. Parking (¥1,500/night). Restaurant.

Ueno & around

Moderate

Homeikan Honkan/ Daimachibekkan

5-10-5 Hongo, Bunkyo-ku (Honkan 3811 1181/ Daimachibekkan 3811 1186/fax 3811 1764). Hongo-Sanchome station (Marunouchi line), Hongo-Nichome exit; (Oedo line), exit 2 or Kasuga station (Mita line), exits A5, A6. **Rooms** *Honkan* 24; *Daimachibekkan* 30. **Rates** ¥6,500-¥7,500 single; ¥11,000-¥13,000 double; ¥13,500-¥16,500 triple. Special long-stay rate available. **Credit** AmEx, DC, JCB, MC, V.

This wonderful old *ryokan* in the sleepy streets of Hongo looks just like a Japanese inn ought to: wooden, glass-fronted and with an ornamental garden at the front. And its owners plan to keep it that way following the *ryokan's* designation as an important cultural property by the Ministry of Education. Be sure to have a word with Homeikan's cordial, English-speaking manager Koike Kunio when making a reservation – he can help you choose a room and, if need be, direct you away from the rowdy Japanese students who often lodge here. The inn is divided into two buildings, which face each other, with another branch a five-minute walk away. The only drawback is its location, around 20 minutes' walk from the nearest real action around Ueno or Ochanomizu stations.
Internet (shared terminal). Parking (free). Room service (7am-10pm).
Other locations: Morikawabekkan, 6-23-5 Hongo, Bunkyo-ku (3811 8171/fax 3811 1764).

Ueno First City Hotel

1-14-8 Ueno, Taito-ku (3831 8215/fax 3837 8469/ www.uenocity-hotel.com), exit 6. **Rooms** 77. **Rates** ¥8,000-¥8,500 single; ¥11,000-¥16,000 double/twin. *Japanese* (1-6 people) ¥8,400-¥24,000. **Credit** AmEx, DC, JCB, MC, V. **Map** Ueno & Yanaka p123.

A cut above the normal business hotel, this place offers comfortable Western- and Japanese-style accommodation in a modern, red-brick block not far from Ueno Park and its myriad attractions.
Bar. Internet (shared terminal). Japanese & Western rooms. No-smoking rooms. Restaurant.

Budget

Hotel Edoya

3-20-3 Yushima, Bunkyo-ku (3833 8751/fax 3833 8759/www.hoteledoya.com). Yushima station (Chiyoda line), exit 5. **Rooms** 49. **Rates** ¥4,960-¥7,850 single. *Japanese* ¥6,930-¥8,950 single;

¥7,960-¥12,930 double/twin; ¥11,550-¥17,670 triple/quadruple. **Credit** AmEx, DC, JCB, MC, V. **Map** Ueno & Yanaka p123.

This mainly Japanese-style *ryokan*, not far from Ueno Park, offers a good standard of accommodation at reasonable prices. There's a small Japanese tearoom and garden on the first floor, and the roof has an open-air hot bath for both men and women.
Japanese & Western rooms. Parking (free). Restaurant.

Ryokan Katsutaro

4-16-8 Ikenohata, Taito-ku (3821 9808/fax 3821 4789/www.katsutaro.com). Nezu station (Chiyoda line), exit 2. **Rooms** 7. **Rates** ¥5,200 single (no bath); ¥8,400-¥16,000 2-4 people (no bath); ¥9,600-¥17,200 2-4 people (with bath). **Credit** AmEx, MC, V. **Map** Ueno & Yanaka p123.

In a backstreet on the northern side of Ueno Park, Katsutaro is a small, friendly *ryokan* with good-sized rooms and the atmosphere of a real family home (which it is). Rooms can be occupied by up to four people, at an extra charge of roughly ¥4,000 per person. The owner speaks a little English, but have a phrasebook handy if you want the conversation to progress. Just a short walk away is the Annex (¥6,000 single, ¥10,000-¥12,000 double), which is more modern and has more facilities.
Internet (high-speed/shared terminal). Japanese rooms only. Parking (free).
Other locations: Annex, 3-8-4 Yanaka, Taito-ku (3828 2500/fax 3821 5400).

Ueno Tsukuba Hotel

2-7-8 Moto-Asakusa, Taito-ku (3834 2556/fax 3839 1785/www.hotelink.co.jp). Inaricho station (Ginza line), exit 2. **Rooms** 111. **Rates** ¥5,000-¥5,500 single; ¥7,000 semi-double; ¥8,000 twin; ¥12,000 triple. *Japanese* ¥4,725 single; ¥4,200 per person 2-5 people. **No credit cards. Map** Ueno & Yanaka p123.

A basic business hotel in Ueno, the Tsukuba is clean and good value for money. Rooms are tiny, so opt for a Japanese-style room, where the futon is cleared away in the morning. Western-style rooms have baths, but if you stay in a Japanese room you'll be expected to bathe Japanese-style in the communal bath on the ground floor. The hotel is two minutes' walk from Inaricho station on the Ginza line.
Internet (high-speed/wireless). Japanese & Western rooms. Parking (¥2,100/night).
Other locations: Iriya Station Hotel, 1-25-1 Iriya, Taito-ku (3872 7111/fax 3872 7113).

Yanaka

Budget

Ryokan Sawanoya

2-3-11 Yanaka, Taito-ku (3822 2251/fax 3822 2252/www.tctv.ne.jp/members/sawanoya). Nezu station (Chiyoda line), exit 1. **Rooms** 12. **Rates** ¥4,700-¥5,000 single (no bath); ¥9,240 double (no bath); ¥9,870 double (with bath); ¥12,600 triple (no bath); ¥14,175 triple (with bath). **Credit** AmEx, MC, V. **Map** Ueno & Yanaka p123.

One of the few *ryokan* to cater almost exclusively for foreign visitors, Sawanoya has a small library of English-language guidebooks and provides its own map of the old-style Yanaka area. Rooms are small but comfortable, and there are signs in English reminding you how to behave and how to use the bath. More expensive rooms have their own bath; cheaper ones have access to the communal bath and shower. There's also a small coffee lounge. The couple who own the place will do everything possible to make your stay enjoyable.

Internet (high-speed/shared terminal). Japanese rooms only.

Elsewhere

Deluxe

Four Seasons Hotel Tokyo at Chinzan-so

2-10-8 Sekiguchi, Bunkyo-ku (3943 2222/fax 3943 2300/www.fourseasons.com/tokyo). Mejiro station (Yamanote line), then 61 bus or Edogawabashi station (Yurakucho line), exit 1A. **Rooms** 283. **Rates** ¥43,000-¥50,000 single; ¥48,000-¥55,000 double; ¥68,000-¥500,000 suite. **Credit** AmEx, DC, JCB, V.

Inconveniently located in the wilds of northern Tokyo, this is a breathtakingly opulent and beautiful hotel popular with locals on weekend escapes and celebrities seeking privacy away from the bright lights of the city. Take a stroll around the Japanese garden – with its own firefly population, as well as ancient statues from Nara and Kamakura – then enjoy the wide open spaces of the lobby area. Everything is immaculate, from the service to the decor of the rooms, a mixture of old Japanese and European styles.

Bars (2). Business centre. Concierge. Disabled-adapted rooms. Gym. Internet (high-speed). No-smoking rooms. Parking (free). Pool (indoor). Restaurants (4). Room service (24hr). Spa.

InterContinental Tokyo Bay

1-16-2 Kaigan, Minato-ku (5404 2222/fax 5404 2111/www.interconti-tokyo.com). Hamamatsucho station (Yamanote line), south exit or Takeshiba (Tokyo monorail) station. **Rooms** 339. **Rates** ¥36,000-¥62,000 double; ¥100,000-¥300,000 suite. **Credit** AmEx, DC, JCB, MC, V.

The InterContinental opened in the mid 1990s in the hitherto little-explored area that fronts Tokyo's Sumida river. Amid the grim industrial surroundings, the luxurious hotel and the adjoining New Pier Takeshiba shopping and dining complex stand out like a diamond in a cowpat. If its location is the hotel's main shortcoming, then its prime selling point is certainly the view over the river and spectacular Rainbow Bridge to the island of Odaiba. All rooms, and their bathrooms, have a river prospect.

Bars (2). Business centre. Concierge. Internet (high-speed). No-smoking rooms. Parking (¥1,500/night). Restaurants (6). Room service (24hr). Spa.

Expensive

Claska

1-3-18 Chuo-cho, Meguro-ku (3719 8121/fax 3719 8122/www.claska.com). Gakugei-Daigaku station (Tokyu Toyoko line) then 10mins walk. **Rooms** 9. **Rates** ¥10,500-¥12,600 single; ¥18,900-¥84,000 double. **Credit** AmEx, DC, JCB, MC, V.

Nine rooms occupying two floors: hotels don't get any more exclusive than the Claska. Add the funky designer vibe, and you have one of the most sought-after spots in the city. Having opened in 2003 in a refurbished business hotel, the Claska prides itself on offering a new style of living. Each room is set up and styled differently, with the most expensive boasting a 41sq m (441sq ft) terrace. The rest of the building is taken up by a hip bar/restaurant, gallery, dog-grooming salon, bookshop, open-plan workspace and residential hotel. It's a little far from the action but manages to draw its share of bright young things with nightly DJ sets in the lobby.

Bar. Internet (high-speed). Parking (free). Restaurant. Room service.

Hotel Monterey Hanzomon

23-1 Ichibancho, Chiyoda-ku (3556 7111/fax 3556 7199/www.hotelmonterey.co.jp/hanzomon/index.html. Hanzomon station (Hanzomon line), exit 5. **Rooms** 340. **Rates** ¥15,800-¥17,000 single; ¥18,000-¥31,000 double/twin. **Credit** AmEx, DC, JCB, MC, V.

Opened in mid 2006 a stone's throw from the British Embassy and Imperial Gardens, the latest Monterey is a stylish place with rooms tastefully decorated in what they describe as 'Edo taste'. In practice, this means colourful rooms of pinks and yellows, with touches of classic Japanese design. This isn't designer living to the degree offered at Claska, Grand Hyatt Tokyo or the Mandarin Oriental, but it's a comfortable, peaceful option.

Internet (high-speed). No-smoking rooms. Parking (¥1,500). Restaurant.

Other locations: Hotel Monterey Ginza, 2-10-2 Ginza, Chuo-ku (3544 7111/fax 3544 1600); Hotel Monterey Lasouer Ginza, 1-10-18 Ginza, Chuo-ku (3562 7111/fax 3562 6328).

Moderate

Hotel Bellegrande

2-19-1 Ryogoku, Sumida-ku (3631 8111/fax 3631 8112/www.hotel-bellegrande.co.jp). Ryogoku station (Oedo line), west exit. **Rooms** 150. **Rates** ¥9,450 single; ¥12,700-¥16,800 double; ¥13,750-¥42,400 twin; ¥84,800 suite. **Credit** AmEx, DC, JCB, V.

A modern, business-style hotel barely a wrestler's stride from the sumo stadium in Ryogoku – a quiet, traditional area that comes alive during the city's three annual sumo tournaments. The unglamorous location is reflected in the prices of the rooms, which are small but comfortable. There are ten designated rooms for women with a few added amenities.

Bar. No-smoking rooms. Parking (¥1,500/night). Restaurants (5).

Grand Hyatt Tokyo.
See p51.

Budget

Hotel New Koyo

2-26-13 Nihonzutumi, Taito-ku (3873 0343/fax 3873 1358/www.newkoyo.jp). Minowa station (Hibiya line), exit 3. **Rooms** 75. **Rates** ¥2,500-¥2,700 single; ¥4,800 double. **Credit** AmEx, MC, V.
Clean and friendly, with facilities that put more expensive places to shame (kitchens on each floor, laundry machines, a Japanese-style bath), the New Koyo may offer the cheapest overnight stay in Tokyo. Rooms are tiny, however, and the place is slightly out of the way, although central Tokyo is easily accessible from the nearby Hibiya line station. The owners also run a more traditional and upmarket Japanese-style inn, the Andon (www.andon.co. jp), in the same area. *Internet (shared terminal). Japanese & Western rooms.*

Juyoh Hotel

2-15-3 Kiyokawa, Taito-ku (3875 5362/fax 5603 5775/www.juyoh.co.jp). Minami-Senju station (Hibiya line), south exit. **Rooms** 76. **Rates** ¥3,200 single; ¥6,400 double. **No credit cards.**

Another cheap option in Taito-ku, the Juyoh caters almost exclusively for foreign visitors. The rooms really are minuscule, and since only three of them are doubles, early booking is essential, via the well-designed and easy-to-use website. The second floor is reserved for female guests only. Bath and shower facilities are shared. Doors close at 1am and reopen again at 5am.
Internet (wireless/shared terminals). No-smoking rooms.

Tokyo International Youth Hostel

Central Plaza 18F, 1-1 Kaguragashi, Shinjuku-ku (3235 1107/fax 3267 4000/www.tokyo-yh.jp). Iidabashi station (Sobu line), west exit; (Nanboku, Oedo, Tozai, Yurakucho lines), exit 2B. **Rooms** 33. **Rates** ¥3,860 per person; ¥2,000 children. **No credit cards.**
Shared rooms (men and women sleep separately here) are the order of the day at this hostel, which occupies the 18th and 19th floors of a skyscraper above Iidabashi station. All rooms are perfectly spotless, and the entire place is no-smoking. Guests are not allowed into the building between 10am and 3pm. The excellent website is regularly updated with room availability information; weekends tend to be booked up ages in advance. Watch out for the 11pm curfew.
Disabled-adapted rooms. Japanese & Western rooms. No smoking.

Other options

Minshuku

Expect to pay around ¥5,000 per night. You should book at least two days in advance.

Japan Minshuku Centre

103 Toka Bldg, 3-11-8 Hirai, Edogawa-ku (3683 3396/www.minshuju.jp). Hirai station (JR Sobu line), south exit. **Open** 11am-9pm Mon-Sat.

Minshuku Association of Japan

KS Axe Bldg 3F, 27-6 Haraikatamachi, Shinjuku-ku (5225 9577/fax 5225 9578/www.minshuku.or.jp). Ushigome Kagurazaka station (Oedo line), exit A1. **Open** noon-5pm Mon-Fri.

Capsule hotels

Capsule Hotel Azuma

3-15-1 Higashi-Ueno, Taito-ku (3831 4047/fax 3831 7103/www2.famille.ne.jp/~uenoyado/ azuma.html). Ueno station (Yamanote line), Asakusa or Hirokoji exits; (Ginza, Hibiya lines), exit 1. **Capsules** 144. **Rates** ¥3,500. **No credit cards.** **Map** Ueno & Yanaka p123.

Central Land Shibuya

1-19-14 Dogenzaka, Shibuya-ku (3464 1777/3464 7771/www.shibuyadogenzaka.com/capsule). Shibuya station (Yamanote, Ginza, Hanzomon lines), Hachiko exit. **Capsules** 140. **Rates** ¥3,700. **Credit** MC, V. **Map** Shibuya p109.

Shinjuku Kuyakusyo-Mae Capsule Hotel

1-2-5 Kabuki-cho, Shinjuku-ku (3232 1110/www. toyo-bldg.ne.jp/hotel). Shinjuku station (Yamanote line), east exit; (Marunouchi line), exit B7; (Oedo, Shinjuku lines), exit 1. **Capsules** 460. **Rates** from ¥4,200. **No credit cards. Map** Shinjuku p117.

Long-term accommodation

Finding long-term accommodation in Tokyo can be a nightmare for foreigners. Many Japanese landlords refuse to deal with the non-Japanese, so specialist companies have stepped into the breach to let to foreigners, sometimes by the week. If you do find something suitable, it probably won't be cheap. You will be required to pay a damage deposit (*shikikin*), usually equivalent to between one and three months' rent, a brokerage fee (*chukairyo*) to the agent, usually another month's rent, and finally key money (*reikin*), usually one or two months' rent – a non-refundable way of saying thank you to the landlord for having you. You then have to find a month's rent in advance.

Understandably deterred by the cost of finding a place of their own, many foreigners fall back on so-called *gaijin* houses – apartment buildings full of foreigners sharing bathrooms, cooking facilities and, in some cases, rooms. All the operations listed below are used to dealing with foreigners and offer a full range of accommodation.

Asahi Homes

3-2-19 Roppongi, Minato-ku (3583 7544/fax 3583 7587/www.asahihomes.co.jp). Roppongi-Itchome station (Nanboku line), exit 1. **Credit** AmEx, DC, MC, V.

Upmarket agency offering fully serviced apartments in well-chosen locations, with a minimum stay of one week. Weekly rent starts from ¥66,150 for a studio, rising to ¥310,800 for a three-bedroom apartment, including internet access and a weekly maid service.

Bamboo House

Office Bamboo Nippori 1F, 2-5-4 Nishi-Nippori, Ararkawa-ku (3645 4028/fax 4400 3008/ www.bamboo-house.com). Mikawashima station (Joban line). **Credit** AmEx, MC, V.

A chain of serviced apartments and guesthouses scattered across the less fashionable parts of Tokyo and Chiba. Rooms are 9-12sq m (32-43sq ft), with shared facilities. Daily rates start from ¥3,500; monthly rates from ¥58,000.

Cozy House

3-15-11 Ichikawa, Ichikawa City, Chiba-ken (047 379 1539/www.cozyhouse.net). Konodai station (Keisei

line) then 10mins walk. **Rooms** 7. **Rates** ¥2,940-¥4,725 daily shared; ¥4,725 daily private; ¥30,450-¥52,500 monthly shared; ¥77,700-¥80,850 monthly private. **Credit** (deposit only) MC, V.

Cozy House has two locations: a cheaper one in more central Kita-ku, and this main branch, slightly out of the way in Chiba. Its aim is to bring foreigners in Japan together, to which end the incredibly friendly owner lays on demos of Japanese crafts and traditions. Cozy House is just a 15-minute train ride from Tokyo station.

Other locations: 15-1 Sakae-cho, Kita-ku (090 8176 0764).

Hoyo Tokyo

4-19-7 Kita-Shinjuku, Shinjuku (3362 0658/fax 3362 9438/www.hoyotokyo.jp). Okubo station (Chuo, Sobu lines), north exit. **Open** 9.30am-6.30pm Mon-Fri. **No credit cards.**

An agency with around 1,000 units, Hoyo offers studio apartments from ¥42,000 per week (plus a deposit of ¥50,000) or ¥135,000 per month. Family apartments cost from ¥300,000 a month (¥100,000 deposit). There is an English website as well as one in Japanese.

Oak House

4-30-3 Takashimadaira, Itabashi-ku (3780 1660/fax 5784 3370/www.oakhouse.jp). Shin-Takashimadaira station (Mita line). **No credit cards.**

This guesthouse agency offers private rooms for ¥53,000 per week in this location, as well as dorm-style accommodation, shared rooms and private apartments around the city.

Sakura House

K1 Bldg 2F, 7-2-6 Nishi-Shinjuku, Shinjuku-ku (5330 5250/fax 5330 5251/www.sakura-house.com). Shinjuku station (Yamanote line), west exit; (Marunouchi line), exit D5; (Oedo, Shinjuku lines), exit 3. **Open** 8.50am-5.50pm Mon-Sat. **Credit** DC, MC, V.

Owned by the people who operate the Sakura Hotel (*see p46*), which is in itself a guarantee of quality, this agency offers guesthouses and apartments in 83 locations around the city.

Tokyo Apartment

3-2-24 Roppongi, Minato-ku (5575 7575/fax 5575 7117/www.tokyoapt.com). Roppongi-Itchome station (Nanboku line), exit 2. **Open** 9am-6pm Mon-Fri. **Credit** DC, MC, V.

An agency that deals exclusively with foreigners, and offers everything from one-night backpacker deals to fully fledged, long-term apartment contracts. Apartments start at ¥100,000 per month.

Weekly Center

Central reservations 5950 1111/www.weeklycenter. co.jp. **Rates** ¥25,000-¥60,000/wk. **No credit cards.**

This budget chain has a dozen locations dotted around Tokyo, offering weekly stays for around the same price as top hotels charge for one night. Monthly rates are also available. The cheapest central branch is in Ochanomizu.

Sightseeing

Features

Maps

Introduction

There's a megalopolis waiting to be discovered.

Most of the clichés are true. Tokyo is a neon-wrapped, hectic playground where Hello Kitty is a deity, trains are never late, vending machines are everywhere, and food doesn't always lie still on your plate. Ancient and pop culture vie for space (pop culture usually wins), and there's an insatiable thirst for innovation, which means the Japanese capital always seems a step or two ahead of your imagination.

The first time you set foot in the great entertainment and shopping hubs of Ginza, Roppongi, Shibuya or Shinjuku, you'll be wide-eyed and overwhelmed. Huge liquid-crystal screens blast a cacophony of sounds; bright signs and adverts fill your vision. But there are also oases of high culture and Zen-like calm, often just a few steps from the chaos. In Ginza you'll find the Kabuki-za, Shibuya is a stone's throw from the capital's largest Shinto shrine. There are also areas that run at a more sedate pace, such as Yanaka, and the Chuo line stops.

GETTING AROUND

The first thing you need to know is that Tokyo isn't a walking city. The city's key districts and sights are spread wide apart, with vast tracts of grey city in between. The good news is that the transport system's reputation for efficiency is well founded.

Japan Railways' Yamanote train line is the best way to orientate yourself. It connects many of the city's major districts, including Shinjuku, Shibuya, Ikebukuro, Harajuku and Ueno. The other areas are a quick metro ride from one of the big Yamanote line hubs.

Most stations have bilingual signs and rail maps, but the metro has also idiot-proofed its routes by colour-coding its lines and numbering stations. Hiroo station, for example, is the third stop on the grey Hibiya line, and thus is marked on maps as H-3. We've included a subway map, in English, on *pp334-5* to make life even easier. A Yamanote line map appears on *p336*.

Guided tours

Official tour guides in Tokyo have to pass rigorous examinations in the finer points of the city's history and culture. No matter how much you've been reading, you'll learn more from one of these human encyclopaedias.

By bus

Hato Bus

3435 6081/www.hatobus.co.jp/english.
Bookings 9am-7pm daily. **Credit** AmEx, DC, MC, V.
The nation's largest tour-bus operator offers a wide variety of tours, including half-day, full-day and night trips with English-speaking guides. Prices start at around ¥4,000. Buses depart from Hamamatsucho.

SkyBus Tokyo

3215 0008/www.skybus.jp. **Bookings** 10am-6pm daily. **Credit** AmEx, DC, MC, V.
Launched in autumn 2004, this open-top red double-decker takes 45 minutes to tour the Marunouchi and Imperial Palace area. The

ticket office is on the ground floor of the Mitsubishi Building, next to the Marunouchi Building (*see p191*). Tours run on the hour and cost ¥1,200 (¥600 under-12s).

Sunrise Tours

5796 5454/www.jtbgmt.com/sunrisetour.
Bookings 9am-6pm Mon-Fri. **Credit** AmEx, DC, MC, V.
Run by Japan Travel Bureau, Sunrise provides the widest range of English-language tours in Tokyo, and also offers trips to out-of-town destinations as far afield as Kyoto.

On foot

Mr Oka's Walking Tours of Tokyo

0422 51 7673/www.homestead.com/mroka.
Bookings 7-10pm daily. **No credit cards**.
Retired historian Oka offers introductory walking tours of Tokyo in English, ranging from ¥2,000 to ¥4,000. Private tours can be arranged for parties of up to ten. The fee does not include any transport costs.

Tokyo's Suijo river buses (3457 7830/www.suijobus.co.jp) can't compete with the trains for speed or price, but in good weather they're a much more pleasurable way to cross the city. Boats vary in style from paddle-steamer lookalikes to something that would be more at home in a *Star Trek* movie. All leave from Hinode Pier, a short walk from Hamamatsucho station on the Yamanote line.

SIGHTSEEING AREAS

We've divided the Sightseeing section by area, introducing each alphabetically. The tour kicks off with **Asakusa**, the historic district with an olde-worlde flavour that makes a delightful contrast to the chaos and hubbub elsewhere. Next stop is **Ebisu**, one of the city's more decorous nightlife areas, and its neighbouring fashion destination **Daikanyama**. Top-end shopping and gallery roaming are the main pursuits in **Ginza**, while **Harajuku** and adjacent **Aoyama** offer more fashion – funky, urban threads in the former, luxury gear in the latter.

Ikebukuro is the dowdy but rowdy northern hub. **Maranouchi**, site of the Imperial Palace and the geographical heart of Tokyo, is moving ever further upmarket and becoming yet another destination for brand-name spending. Over by Tokyo Bay is **Odaiba**, a man-made leisure zone and popular dating area. We then head to

A **Suijo** river bus.

Roppongi for the dual lure of sleazy expat nightlife, and a pair of self-contained mini cities. Nightlife, shopping and government share **Shinjuku** – Tokyo's biggest sub-centre – while a short ride south is the youthful playground of **Shibuya**.

In the north-east, **Ueno** offers the museum-packed Ueno Park; and adjoining it to the north, the tight-knit communities of low-rise **Yanaka** are another respite from the congested hotspots.

In the **Further Afield** chapter, we've also introduced the best destinations outside the Yamanote line loop, such as **Shimo-Kitazawa**, **Naka-Meguro** and stations along the **Chuo line**. Out here, on the city's suburban commuter railway lines, life is more relaxed, locals are friendlier, and entertainment is usually cheaper. For excursions well beyond the city limits, see **Trips Out of Town**, starting on *p277*.

MUSEUM TIPS

The general rules for visiting museums and galleries are as follows: many are closed on Monday, entrance fees are paid in cash, ID is required for discount admission, admission ends 30 minutes before the museum closes, lockers are free (with a refundable key deposit of ¥100), photography is forbidden, and there is little disabled access. Many museums offer little or no explanation in English, and places that hold temporary exhibitions are often only open sporadically. Some museums close on national holidays. Nearly all museums close over the New Year's holiday, from 28 December to 4 January.

Museum-hoppers should get a **Grutt Pass** (the name sounds far better in Japanese), which offers free or reduced admission to 56 of the city's most important spots. Costing ¥2,000, it's valid for two months and is available from major ticket outlets and participating museums.

Don't miss sights

Tsukiji fish market
The inner sanctum is by appointment only, but the outer market is still a fishy sensation. *See p77.*

Meiji Jingu
The beauty of this grand Shinto shrine belies its location behind Harajuku station. *See p85.*

Tokyo City View
The best place to view the city is from this stylish 52nd-floor observation deck, with a world-class art museum in its centre. *See p105.*

Golden Gai
Over 200 tiny drinking dens of myriad styles packed into five alleyways in Shinjuku. *See p179.*

Akihabara
Geek paradise, with everything from manga superstores to maid masseuses. *See p195.*

ITABASHI-KU

TOSHIMA
-KU

Seibu - Ikebukuro Line

Ikebukuro

See p87

BUNKYO-KU

Yanaka

Ueno
Park

Ueno

See p123

Seibu-Shinjuku Line

Chuo
Line

SHINJUKU
-KU

See p93

NAKANO
-KU

Shinjuku

CHIYODA
-KU

Imperial
Palace

Marunouchi

See p117

Shinjuku
Gyoen

Yotsuya

Yoyogi

Yoyogi
Park

See p82

Ginza

See p75

SHIBUYA
-KU

Harajuku

Aoyama

See p103

Shibuya

Roppongi

Tokyo
Tower

See p109

MINATO-KU

Daikanyama

Naka-Meguro

Rainbow
Bridge

See p71

Tokaido Line

MEGURO
-KU

Meguro

Tokyu Toyoko Line

Central Tokyo

SHINAGAWA
-KU

ARAKAWA
-KU

Sumida River

TAITO-KU

SUMIDA
-KU

Asakusa

See p63

KOTO-KU

EDOGAWA
-KU

CHUO-
KU

See p101

Odaiba

Yurikamome Line

Tokyo
Disneyland

Tokyo Bay

OTA-KU

South-east Asia

Beijing

Pyongyang NORTH
KOREA *Sea of
Japan*

Seoul SOUTH
KOREA TOKYO JAPAN

CHINA Yellow
Sea

*East China
Sea*

Shanghai

Taipei
TAIWAN

LAOS Hanoi Macau Hong Kong

*South
China Sea* PACIFIC OCEAN

THAILAND Vientiane

Bangkok VIETNAM

CAMBODIA
Phnom Penh Ho Chi Minh City Manila

PHILIPPINES

MALAYSIA BRUNEI SABAH
SARAWAK

Kuala
Lumpur

Singapore

0   2 miles

0   3 km

© Copyright Time Out Group 2007

Asakusa

A lively old section of town that's loved by locals and tourists alike.

Kaminarimon's giant red lantern is one of Tokyo's most distinctive sights. *See p65.*

Map p63

Long before Roppongi and Shibuya figured on anybody's radar of interest, Asakusa (pronounced 'a-sak-sa') was *the* place for entertainment in Tokyo. For a couple of centuries up until around 1940, this area adjacent to the eastern bank of the Sumida river was far and away the most exciting and dynamic part of town. It's a fine example of *shitamachi*, the low-lying districts of the city where the commoners lived cheek by jowl until Tokyo's population began drifting westwards in the aftermath of the Great Earthquake of 1923 and fire bombing in World War II. With this westward shift, Asakusa became increasingly peripheral to mainstream city life.

Today a sense of faded grandeur still hangs over the area. For the visitor the greatest appeal lies in the **Asakusa Kannon** temple. It is this temple complex and its environs that have helped make Asakusa into one of Tokyo's prime tourist attractions.

Also known as **Senso-ji**, Asakusa Kannon is Tokyo's oldest temple, with origins, so the remarkably precise story has it, dating to 18 March 628. That was when two brothers fishing on the Sumida river caught a five-centimetre (two-inch) golden statue in their net. Clearly lacking wisdom, they threw the statue back in the river twice, only for it to reappear both times. At this point they twigged that something out of the ordinary was happening, and took the statue to the village chief. He enshrined it in his house, and in 645 a hall was built for this image of Kannon, the Buddhist goddess of mercy, on the spot where today's temple stands. The complex also houses a Shinto shrine, **Asakusa Jinja**, which was established in 1649 to honour the two fishermen and the village headman.

In later years, Asakusa flourished because of its proximity to Yoshiwara, the biggest area of licensed prostitution in Edo (as Tokyo was known from 1600 to 1868). Seeking a little

Sightseeing

Asakusa

© Copyright Time Out Group 2005

Old soaks

The global spa boom hasn't neglected Japan. Slick modern complexes are popping up across the capital – try Roppongi's **Zaboo** (8770 8100, www.zaboo.jp) for a fancy soak. But a more authentically Japanese experience awaits you at one of the traditional *onsen* or *sento*. *Onsen* are Japan's hot springs, taking advantage of the nation's volcanic geology for piping-hot, mineral-rich water that is renowned for its healing effects. *Sento* (literally, 'penny baths') are the artifical equivalent – using heated tap water – and there are around 1,000 of them in Tokyo (look for short curtains with a sign that resembles flames emerging from a frying pan). Both baths are throwbacks to an era when the local public tub was the only place to wash, and while some places look as though they haven't had a facelift since that time, there are some great spots in the city to soak your stresses away.

The baths are communal, and segregated by sex, so you'll likely be bathing with a handful of naked locals. Most *sento* also have a cashier who sits in a stall with a perfect view of both changing rooms, but dutifully avoids gazing into either.

If you're heading for Hakone (*see pp284-7*), you'll find myriad *onsen*, many of them boasting spectacular views. High-end traditional inns often have private hot springs (*kashikiri onsen*), which can make the communal bathing experience more fun.

BATHING ETIQUETTE

Having paid and entered the relevant changing room – signs are written only in *kanji*, but often colour-coded red and blue – strip off completely and put your clothes in a locker. Proceed into the bathing area and start showering. This being communal bathing, it's considered essential to be spotlessly clean before you enter the bath, so be visibly diligent in scrubbing yourself. Then climb into the tub, relax, and always keep your head above water.

Be warned that the water temperature can, for the uninitiated, be extremely hot. Sluice yourself first to get acclimatised, then ease yourself into the bath. Lie back and enjoy.

Onsen

Asakusa Kannon Onsen

2-7-26 Asakusa, Taito-ku (3844 4141). Asakusa station (Asakusa, Ginza lines), Kannosamma exit. **Open** 6.30am-6pm Mon, Tue, Thur-Sun. **Admission** ¥700. **No credit cards**.
This classic bathhouse's waters are reportedly good for rheumatism and nervous disorders.

Azabu Juban Onsen

1-5-22 Azabu-Juban, Minato-ku (3404 2610). Azabu-Juban station (Nanboku line), exit 4. **Open** *Sento* 3-11pm Mon, Wed-Sun. *Onsen* 11am-9pm Mon, Wed-Sun. **Admission** *Onsen* ¥1,260. *Sento* ¥430. **No credit cards**.
Tokyo's most central natural hot spring is either a nostalgia trip or a crumbling little bathhouse, depending on your taste. Either way, it's the antithesis of the new super-spas. Gents take the blue curtain, ladies

refreshment before the evening's main activities, Yoshiwara's clientele could find that and plenty of other diversions in Asakusa – from acrobats and magicians to comedians and performing monkeys. In particular, the area flourished as the centre of *kabuki* theatre, a vastly popular form of entertainment whose leading actors were idolised like rock stars.

Nowadays, Asakusa is home to numerous festivals, both old and new. Tokyo's oldest and biggest festival, in May, is the **Sanja Matsuri** (*see p213*), a frenzied procession of more than a hundred *mikoshi* (portable shrines). The most modern is the **Asakusa Samba Carnival** (*see p214*) in late August, when hundreds of Brazilian and Japanese dancers parade through the streets. The **Sumida River Fireworks**

(*see p214*), Japan's biggest annual summertime fireworks display, is held at the end of July and broadcast on national TV.

The Asakusa subway line station sits adjacent to the Sumida river at the end of Asakusa Dori; a few hundred metres north, next to Azumabashi (Azuma Bridge), is the Ginza line station, at the end of Kaminarimon Dori. Across the road, next to the Tobu Isesaki line station, stands Tokyo's oldest Western-style hostelry, **Kamiya Bar** (*see p172*). Built in 1880, it is renowned as the home of 'Denki-Bran' (Electric Brandy), an unusual alcoholic concoction that produces truly spectacular hangovers.

The alcoholic vein continues when you look over Azumabashi to the Bubble-era **Asahi Building**, home of one of Japan's four main take the red, and you'll find a small bath with brown water (of natural origin), plus an even smaller, half-hearted jacuzzi. There are also a *sento* (Koshi no Yu) and a steam sauna.

Seta Onsen

4-15-30 Seta, Setagaya-ku (3707 8228/ www.setaonsen.co.jp). Futako Tamagawa station (Tokyu Denentoshi, Tokyu Oimachi, Tokyu Shin-Tamagawa lines) then 10mins walk or shuttle bus. **Open** *10am-11pm daily.* **Admission** *¥2,300.* **No credit cards**.
A large-scale, family-friendly *onsen* in a lovely garden setting. There are communal outdoor pools (these are the only baths in town that demand swimwear) and best of all, an outdoor bar. The view isn't great, but when you're sipping cocktails in the open-air hot spring, you won't care.

Sento

The price of all *sento* baths is set at a standard ¥430.

Aqua

4-9-22 Higashi-Nakano, Nakano-ku (5330 1126). Higashi-Nakano station (Chuo, Oedo lines), east exit. **Open** *3pm-midnight Tue-Sun.* **No credit cards**.
A modern *sento* with a variety of baths, including a *rotenburo* and sauna. Usefully, it stocks cold beers.

Daikoku-yu

32-6 Senju Kotobuki-cho, Adachi-ku (3881 3001). Kita-Senju station (Chiyoda, Hibiya lines), west exit then 15mins walk. **Open** *3pm-midnight Tue-Sun.* **No credit cards**.
This majestic, temple-like building is probably the most attractive *sento* in Tokyo. Cleaner than most of its peers and boasting its own *rotenburo* (outdoor *sento*), it also has cold beer in stock.

Komparu-yu

8-7-5 Ginza, Chuo-ku (3571 5469). Ginza station (Ginza, Hibiya lines), exit A2. **Open** *2-11pm Mon-Fri; 2-10pm Sat.* **Map** *Ginza p75.* **No credit cards**.
A few doors from Kyubei – one of Tokyo's most famous (and famously expensive) sushi restaurants – in ritzy Ginza is this tiny old bathhouse, which dates back to Edo days. There are two baths: *atatakai* (hot) and *nurui* (lukewarm) – lukewarm is hot enough for most.

Shimizu-yu

3-12-3 Minami-Aoyama, Minato-ku (3401 4404). Omotesando station (Chiyoda, Ginza, Hanzomon lines), exit A4. **Open** *4pm-midnight Tue-Sun.* **No credit cards**.
A soak in the heart of Omotesando. Stash your shopping and unwind with a bath.

Tamano-yu

1-13-7 Asagaya-Kita, Suginami-ku (3338 7860). Asagaya station (Chuo line), north exit. **Open** *3.30pm-1am Tue-Sun.* **No credit cards**.
A recently renovated, traditional *sento* with a number of novelty tubs, including one that ignores all sane advice and pumps electricity into the bath water for a tingling sensation.

brewing companies and the **Flamme d'Or** bar (*see p172*). Designed by Philippe Starck, this odd building is surmounted by a large golden sculpture whose distinct shape causes many locals to refer to it as the *unchi-biru* ('turd building'). In the face of such architectural extravagance, the local constabulary clearly didn't want to be left out, so the police box near the bridge sports a pagoda-style roof. North of the pier is **Sumida Koen**, a riverside park that is popular during cherry-blossom season.

The approach to Asakusa Kannon temple begins about 100 metres up Kaminarimon Dori from the bridge. It's impossible to miss the main gate to the temple, the **Kaminarimon** (Thunder Gate; **photo** *p62*), with its gigantic red paper lantern. Even in Edo days, this lantern was one

of the city's most distinctive sights. Between 1856 and 1858 the great *ukiyo-e* woodblock artist Hiroshige published a set of prints called *One Hundred Views of Edo*. Among those evocative depictions of the old city, the Kaminarimon lantern is about the only one that could be identified by a modern-day Tokyoite. Black-garbed rickshaw drivers cruise the entrance looking for tourists to ferry around. Across the road is the **Asakusa Culture & Sightseeing Centre** (3842 5566, open 9.30am-8pm daily), which has maps and information, and runs free one-hour tours on Sundays (at 11am and 2pm).

From the gate stretches the lively thoroughfare of **Nakamise Dori** (*see p192*). For centuries this street was lined with stalls catering to the crowds on their way to and from the temple.

Sightseeing

Kappabashi Dogu-gai Dori.
See p67.

Today there are about 150 stalls along its 300-metre (984-foot) length, selling such traditional goods as combs, fans, dolls, kimono, paper crafts, clothing, toys and snacks, many of which would be instantly recognisable to any resident of old Edo. Absent from the scene are the former archery galleries. These were presided over by attractive young women, whose make-up and manner made it clear that when they escorted a male customer into their back room it wasn't with a view to stringing up his bow.

The temple is the main attraction in Asakusa, but there are plenty of other sights of interest. Heading north through the temple precincts will lead you to Kototoi Dori; turn left and you'll walk past the **Goro-Goro Taiken Theatre**, famous for displays of highly stylised swordsmanship. Turning left again at a small shopping street called Hisagao Dori brings you to the entrance of Japan's oldest amusement park, **Hanayashiki**. Nearby is the small **Edo-Shitamachi Traditional Crafts Museum** (2-22-13 Asakusa, 3842 1990, open 10am-8pm daily, admission free), which displays traditional crafts made by local artists.

Just to the west beyond Hanayashiki is the small district of Rokku, centred on Rokku Eigagai. This was Edo and Tokyo's prime entertainment area, though, today, sadly, it's a pale imitation of its former self. Japanese folk music drifts from the open doorways of **Asakusa Engei Hall**, the home of *rakugo* – traditional comic storytelling. Garish posters of 1960s yakuza gangster films are pasted outside the Shin-Gekijo, Meiga-za and Toho cinemas. Further south, on Kokusai Dori opposite the police box, is the delightful **Drum Museum**, located on the second floor of a shop selling musical instruments and Buddhist shrines.

Aside from the temple grounds and brash culture of Rokku, Asakusa's busy shopping streets are great places for an idle wander to see a slice of traditional life. You might chance upon a kimono shop owner kneeling at his counter in front of variegated bolts of cloth; or a half-dozen *sembei* (rice cracker) makers chatting as they toast crackers on a charcoal grill; or a tea merchant, with jade-green wares displayed in woven baskets and the delicious smell of roasting fresh tea wafting from his shop.

Shopping of a more specialised kind can be found by walking west (away from the river) to **Kappabashi Dogu-gai Dori** (*see p192; photo p66*), Tokyo's main wholesale district for the restaurant industry. This is far more interesting than it sounds: it's where caterers come to buy all those (surprisingly expensive) plastic models of foodstuffs that you see in restaurant windows. All manner of kitchen hardware is on sale, from ceramic bowls to small fish knives to cauldron-sized pots. Shops line either side of Kappabashi Dori; look for the 12-metre (39-foot) high chef's head atop the Niimi Building.

Further south and back towards the river are other wholesale districts, specialising in dolls, stationery and fashion accessories – the nearest stations are Kuramae and Asakusabashi. Near the latter is the **Japanese Stationery Museum**, where you can explore the history of writing and calculating implements.

ON THE RIVER

Asakusa can also be the starting point for a cruise on the Sumida river. One option is to take the water bus (*suijo*) bus, which leaves every 20-45 minutes from the pier next to Azumabashi, heading south under 13 bridges en route to beautiful **Hama-Rikyu Detached Garden** (*see p79*). There's a network of five water-bus lines; for more details, *see p59*.

Or you could take a *yakata-bune* boat tour. These are leisurely cruises around Tokyo Bay on floating restaurants – and nicest at night. Several companies operate tours; try **Amisei** (3844 1869). Tickets are ¥10,000-¥20,000, but include as much food (tempura, sushi, yakitori) and drink (beer, sake, juice) as you can consume. Reservations are advisable.

RYOGOKU

Just across the Sumida river is Ryogoku, where sumo tournaments have been held for 300 years. You'll spot a few small statues of wrestlers outside the Ryogoku JR station and maybe a couple of souvenir stalls, but it's generally a nondescript area. It's home to the **Ryogoku Kokugikan** (*see p273*), the stadium where three of sumo's Grand Tournaments are held, in January, May and September, and various stables (*heya*), where the wrestlers live and train. Restaurants specialising in *chanko-nabe*, the stews the wrestlers eat, also cluster here; a good one to visit is **Yoshiba** (*see p141*).

If you're in town when no tournaments are in progress, it's possible to visit a stable to see the wrestlers in their daily morning practice sessions. There are over 40 stables in Tokyo, most situated close to the Kokugikan. Most allow visitors, on condition that they remain quiet – call ahead (in Japanese) to ask for permission. The stables let you in for free, but take along a small gift – such as a bottle of sake – for the stable master to show your appreciation. Photos are usually permitted, but don't point your feet towards the ring. Be warned: the day starts early. Junior wrestlers are up and about at 4am, and gruelling practice

Sightseeing

sessions start at around 5am. The higher-ranked wrestlers start to appear at around 8am.

Recommended stables are **Azumazeki** (4-6-4 Higashi Komagata, Sumida-ku, 3625 0033), **Dewanoumi** (2-3-15 Ryogoku, Sumida-ku, 3633 4920), **Musashigawa** (4-27-1 Higashi-Nippori, Arakawa-ku, 3801 6343) and **Oshiogawa** (2-17-7 Kiba, Koto-ku, 3643 8156). There's also an up-to-date list of addresses at www.accesscom.com/~abe/03haruheya.html.

If you couldn't care less about sumo, the excellent **Edo-Tokyo Museum** is located next door to the Kokugikan. There's also the **Tokyo Metropolitan Memorial & Tokyo Reconstruction Museum**.

FURTHER AFIELD

Asakusa thrived in the Edo era because of its proximity to Yoshiwara, but little survives of the red-light district today. What was once a huge, walled pleasure area is now the home of massage parlours, 'soaplands' and love hotels. What does remain, though, is the sad structure of the **Jokan-ji** temple, close to Minowa station (from Asakusa station, take the Ginza line to Ueno station, then the Hibiya line two stops to Minowa). The image of Yoshiwara may have a rakish, exotic appeal, but Jokan-ji presents the other side of the coin: this is where more than 11,000 prostitutes, mostly in their early 20s, were buried in a common grave.

From Minowa it is possible to get another experience of old Tokyo in the form of the **Arakawa Streetcar Line** (*see p88*). Old-fashioned green-and-cream trams trundle westwards along a 12-kilometre (eight-mile) route from Minowabashi station to Waseda, not far from Ikebukuro.

Asakusa Kannon Temple (Senso-ji) & Asakusa Jinja

2-3-1 Asakusa, Taito-ku (temple 3842 0181/shrine 3844 1575). Asakusa station (Asakusa, Ginza lines), exits 1, 3, 6, A4. **Open** *Temple & Shrine* 6.30am-5pm daily. *Grounds* 24hrs daily. **Admission** free. **Map** Asakusa p63.

The lively focus of traditional life in Tokyo, Asakusa Kannon is the city's most vivid reminder of the Edo era. Although the current buildings are constructed in a distinctly un-Edo-like ferro-concrete, they do offer an indication of the older city that lurks beneath the modern jacket of Tokyo. Most people enter from the south, through the main gate, Kaminarimon, past the stalls of Nakamise Dori and then through the two-storey Hozomon gate into the temple grounds proper. To the left stands a five-storey, 55m (180ft) pagoda, the second-highest in Japan; ahead are the magnificent sweeping roofs of the Main Hall, with the gold-plated Gokuden shrine inside. Behind and to the right is Asakusa Jinja, the starting point of the Sanja

Matsuri. A huge bronze incense burner stands in front of the Main Hall. The smoke is believed to have curative powers, and visitors usually stop to 'bathe' in it, often directing the smoke towards a troubled part of the body. You can make a wish, pick your fortune or buy good-luck charms from stalls. Other buildings and gardens occupy the extensive grounds.

Drum Museum (Taiko-kan)

Miyamoto Unosuke Shoten, Nishi-Asakusa Bldg 4F, 2-1-1 Nishi-Asakusa, Taito-ku (3842 5622/ www.tctv.ne.jp/members/taikokan). Tawaramachi station (Ginza line). **Open** 10am-5pm Wed-Sun. **Admission** ¥300; ¥150 concessions; free under-6s. **No credit cards**. **Map** Asakusa p63.

With a clay drum from Mexico, an *udekki* from Sri Lanka and hundreds of other drums from around the world, this interactive museum is a fine place to visit. Find your own rhythm by banging on many of them (a blue dot means it's allowed, a red one means it's not).

Edo-Tokyo Museum

1-4-1 Yokoami, Sumida-ku (3626 9974/www.edo-tokyo-museum.or.jp). Ryogoku station (Oedo line), exits A3, A4; (Sobu line), west exit. **Open** 9.30am-5.30pm Tue, Wed, Fri-Sun; 9.30am-7.30pm Thur. **Admission** ¥600; free under-15s; additional fee for special exhibitions. **No credit cards**.

This large museum's outlandish architectural style may not appeal to everyone, but the building houses

Thrills and spills at **Hanayashiki**.

the city's best collection of displays dealing with the history of Tokyo. Highlights include large-scale reconstructions of Nihonbashi bridge and a *kabuki* theatre, as well as detailed models of quarters of the city at different eras. Exhibits outline lifestyles and show how disasters, natural and man-made, altered the city's landscape. The English labelling is good.

Hanayashiki

2-28-1 Asakusa, Taito-ku (3842 8780/ www.hanayashiki.net/first.html). Asakusa station (Asakusa, Ginza lines), exit 3. **Open** 10am-6pm Mon, Wed-Sun. **Admission** ¥900; ¥400 concessions. **No credit cards. Map** Asakusa p63.
Hanayashiki has been in business since 1885 and still draws crowds. There are around 20 rides, more appealing for nostalgia than thrills – including Japan's oldest steel-track rollercoaster and a haunted house. Most have been upgraded over the years, but their scope is limited due to the park's small size.

Japan Stationery Museum

1-1-15 Yanagibashi, Taito-ku (3861 4905). Asakusabashi station (Asakusa, Sobu lines), east exit. **Open** 10am-4pm Mon-Fri. **Admission** free.
Exhibits range from flints and a tablet from Mesopotamia through Egyptian papyrus to abacuses and typewriters with interchangeable *kanji* keys. One highlight is a 14kg (31lb) brush made from the hair of over 50 horses. Descriptions are in Japanese.

Tokyo Metropolitan Memorial & Tokyo Reconstruction Museum

2-3-25 Yokoami, Sumida-ku (3623 1200). Ryogoku station (Oedo line), exits A3, A4; (Sobu line), west exit. **Open** 9am-4.30pm daily. Memorial museum closed Mon. **Admission** free.
Following the Great Kanto Earthquake of 1923, some 40,000 people who had fled their homes perished on this site when sparks set clothing and bedding alight. The fire raged for nearly a day and a half, destroying three-quarters of the city and killing 140,000 people. Seven years later, a three-storey pagoda-topped memorial building was erected; after World War II, the memorial's name was changed to include the 100,000 people who died in Tokyo's air raids. The Reconstruction Museum in a nearby building in the park contains wartime mementos. Both buildings are pretty run down and receive little attention. Most of what they do receive is concentrated on the controversial Yasukuni Shrine (*see p98*), which honours the war dead. Memorial services are held on 10 March and 1 September at 10am.

Getting there

Asakusa is on the Ginza and Asakusa subway lines and the Tobu Isesaki railway line. Water buses arrive at/depart from the pier next to Azumabashi.

Ebisu & Daikanyama

Cool cafés and funky fashion await you.

Map p71

Dining destination **Ebisu** (sometimes also spelled Yebisu) and shopping haven **Daikanyama** form an upmarket patch of Tokyo within a stone's throw of Shibuya. Ebisu proper comes alive at night, when hordes of young Tokyoites flock to eat, drink and be merry in the area's myriad restaurants, while the self-contained plaza of Ebisu Garden Place is liveliest on weekends, when shoppers and daytrippers crowd its stores, galleries and museums.

The weekend is also Daikanyama's appointed hour, as thousands of young – predominantly female – shoppers descend upon its scores of boutiques for essential wardrobe updates. A short walk from the west exit of Ebisu station, this prim neighbourhood is, refreshingly, one of the few districts in Japan that has managed to resist the rise of McDonald's, Starbucks, Wendy's and the like. One station down the tracks from Daikanyama is the increasingly hip and vibrant neighbourhood of **Naka-Meguro** (*see p130*).

Just to the south of Ebisu and one stop further on the Yamanote line is **Meguro** station – the starting point for some unusual and entertaining diversions.

Ebisu

In 1887 Japanese Beer Brewing Ltd established a brewery for its first product: a beer named after endomorphic deity Ebisu, one of the seven gods of good fortune. The enormous success of the beverage – it is still one of the nation's bestselling lagers – led to the area taking its celestial name.

The connection with beer is appropriate – this area is renowned for its wealth of restaurants and bars, and is regarded as Tokyo's number one spot for rowdy *go-kon* (group blind dates). In fact, local ties with the liquid gold business are still strong – Ebisu's biggest attraction is **Ebisu Garden Place**, a mall development backed by Sapporo beer that serves as the location for the company's headquarters, a Sapporo Beer Hall and the

Nature Study Institute & Park.
See p73.

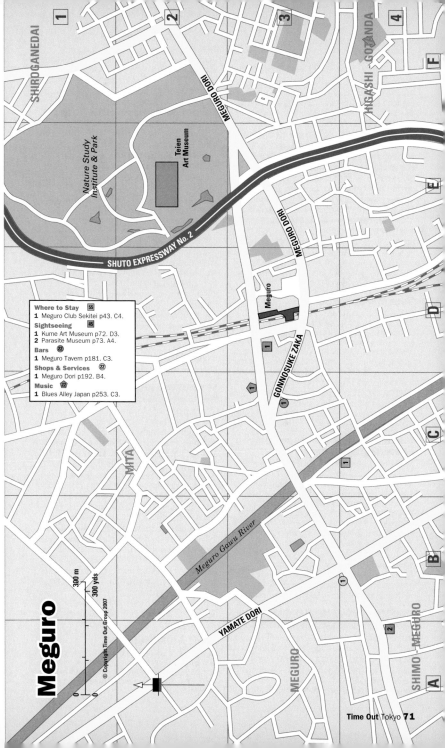

Meguro

Where to Stay [55]
1 Meguro Club Sekitei p43. C4.

Sightseeing [46]
1 Kume Art Museum p72. D3.
2 Parasite Museum p73. A4.

Bars [22]
1 Meguro Tavern p181. C3.

Shops & Services [22]
1 Meguro Dori p192. B4.

Music [22]
1 Blues Alley Japan p253. C3.

© Copyright Time Out Group 2007

Beer Museum Yebisu. A five-minute 'Skywalk' via a moving sidewalk from Ebisu station, the mall is a well-heeled mini city, housing dozens of shops, including a small branch of Mitsukoshi department store. It's also home to a host of restaurants, foremost among which is chef extraordinaire Joel Robuchon's palatial **Taillevent Robuchon** (5424 1338, www.taillevent.com/japon/), housed in a bright-yellow, mock-French château complete with wine shop and pâtisserie. Also figured into the development are the **Westin Tokyo** hotel (see p40), office towers, apartment buildings and the **Tokyo Metropolitan Museum of Photography**.

Venture out of the station through either the east or west exits, and you are plunged into a buzzing mélange of restaurants, cafés, bars, pubs (including **What the Dickens**; see p173) and nightclubs (including **Milk**; see p224) and, underlining the area's suitability as a dating spot, even a couple of love hotels.

Beer Museum Yebisu

B1F 4-20-1 Ebisu Garden Place, Shibuya-ku (5423 7255/www.sapporobeer.jp/brewery/y_museum/). Ebisu station (Yamanote line), east exit; (Hibiya line), exit 1. **Open** 10am-6pm Tue-Sun. **Admission** free; beer additional ¥200. **No credit cards**.
Commemorating the brewery that stood on the space it now occupies, Sapporo built this museum along with the sprawling prim-and-proper mall in which it sits. Past the historical photographs, beer labels, old posters and video displays, there's a virtual reality tour of the brewing process and, at last, a lounge. Alas, the beer's not free.

Tokyo Metropolitan Museum of Photography

Ebisu Garden Place, 1-13-3 Mita, Meguro-ku (3280 0099/www.syabi.com/). Ebisu station (Yamanote line), east exit; (Hibiya line), exit 1. **Open** 10am-6pm Tue, Wed, Sat, Sun (last entry 5.30pm); 10am-8pm Thur, Fri (last entry 7.30pm). **Admission** free. **No credit cards**.
Occupying a four-floor building in one corner of Ebisu Garden Place, this is Tokyo's premier photography showcase. It boasts a large permanent collection and brings in leading lights of the photography world for regular star-studded shows. The small Images & Technology Gallery in the basement presents a multimedia history of optics, featuring tricks such as morphing, and the occasional media art exhibition.

Daikanyama

Daikanyama is one of Tokyo's busiest shopping districts, with almost every available square metre devoted to clothing, mostly for girls in their late teens to early 20s. There are no big overseas brands here – Daikanyama kids prefer cutesy home-grown designer labels to logo-laden merchandise. The area offers many opportunities for observing the often risible outfits of Japan's most deeply afflicted fashion victims from the comfort of one of the numerous open-air cafés. Although the alfresco seats are limited, the area's hippest café, and a good place to check out Tokyo's beau monde, is **Frames** (Hikawa Bldg 1F, 2-11 Sarugakucho, 5784 3384, www.frames-tokyo.info, open 11.30am-4.30am/5am daily), located above nightclub **Air** (see p224).

If you're not shopping for young fashion, Daikanyama will have limited appeal, but there are several good places for picking up souvenirs. Anyone who appreciates the Japanese aesthetic will find something of interest at **Okura** (20-11 Sarugakucho, 3461 8511, open 11am/11.30am-8.30pm daily), where indigo-dyed T-shirts with traditional patterns are lined up alongside carefully crafted accessories in traditional materials like bamboo, hemp and silk.

Daikanyama fashionistas love to express themselves through headgear, and the area's number one hat emporium **CA4LA** (17-5 Daikanyamacho, 5459 0085, open 11am-8pm daily; also see p200) is constantly packed with funky youngsters. The creations on display might be too extravagant for some tastes – but come on, live a little.

Meguro

The area around Meguro station isn't rich in tourist attractions, but there are a couple of interesting museums in the area: the **Kume Art Museum**, next to the station's west exit, and the **Tokyo Metropolitan Teien Art Museum**, a short walk from the east exit. The latter is a 1930s French art deco house, once a prince's residence and now a beautiful blend of architectural showpiece, art museum and landscaped garden. Adjacent to the museum you'll find the botanical wonders of the **Nature Study Institute & Park**. Hungry folk should note that Tokyo's best doughnut shop, **Doughnut Plant** (La Residence de Shiroganedai 1F, 5-18-7 Shirokanedai, 5447 1095, www.doughnutplant.jp, open 9am-8pm daily), is just 100 metres (328 feet) down the road from the museum.

Further away to the east of the station is the unmissable **Parasite Museum**, the world's only museum dedicated to parasites.

Kume Art Museum

Kume Bldg 8F, 2-25-5 Kami-Osaki, Shinagawa-ku (3491 1510). Meguro station (Yamanote line), west exit. **Open** 10am-5pm Tue-Sun. **Admission** ¥500; ¥200-¥300 concessions. **No credit cards**. **Map** Meguro p71.

Life's a catwalk in fashion-focused **Daikanyama**. See p72.

Kume Kuchiro was one of the first Japanese artists to embrace the Impressionist style. This museum has changing displays of his paintings, with themes taken from his 1871-2 trek across the globe.

Nature Study Institute & Park

5-21-5 Shirokanedai, Minato-ku (3441 7176/www. ins.kahaku.go.jp). Meguro station (Yamanote line), east exit or Shiroganedai station (Mita, Nanboku lines), exit 1. **Open** *May-Aug* 9am-5pm Tue-Sun. *Sept-Apr* 9am-4.30pm Tue-Sun. **Admission** ¥300; free concessions. **No credit cards. Map** Meguro p71.

A primeval forest in central Tokyo? Yes, it's a remnant of the ancient Musashino plain. Established as a scientific study area in 1949, the park contains myriad plants, birds and insects. Admission is limited to a few hundred people at a time, so that visitors can enjoy the turtle-filled ponds and forested hills in peace. The one-room museum at the entrance is hardly a destination in itself, but it has a couple of interesting points, such as a map showing how the greenery in Tokyo has decreased since 1677, largely as a result of dwindling temple grounds. **Photo** *p70.*

Parasite Museum

4-1-1 Shimo-Meguro, Meguro-ku (3716 1264). Meguro station (Yamanote line), west exit. **Open** 10am-5pm Tue-Sun. **Admission** free. **Map** Meguro p71.

This unusual venture was opened in 1953 by Kamegai Satoru, a doctor whose practice was overwhelmed by patients afflicted by parasites (caused by the poor sanitary conditions that were widespread in post-war Japan). The museum displays some 300 samples of 45,000 parasites he collected, 20 of which were discovered by his foundation. The second floor has a display of an 8.8m (29ft) tapeworm taken from the body of a 40-year-old man, with a ribbon next to it showing you just how long 8.8m really is. Ugh. The shop sells parasites preserved in plastic keyrings: ideal gifts for your nearest and dearest.

Tokyo Metropolitan Teien Art Museum

5-21-9 Shirokanedai, Minato-ku (3443 0201/www. teien-art-museum.ne.jp). Meguro station (Yamanote line), east exit or Shiroganedai station (Mita, Nanboku lines), exit 1. **Open** 10am-6pm daily. Closed 2nd & 4th Wed of mth. **Admission** *Exhbitions* vary. *Garden* ¥200; free-¥100 concessions. **No credit cards. Map** Meguro p71.

This 1933 art deco mansion, fronted by both a Western-style rose garden and a Japanese stroll garden, was once the home of Prince Asaka Yasuhiko – the uncle of Emperor Hirohito – and his wife, Princess Nobuko – the eighth daughter of Emperor Meiji. The prince returned from a three-year stint in 1920s Paris enamoured of art deco and decided to build a modern residence. Henri Rapin designed most of the interior, while René Lalique added his touch to the crystal chandeliers and the doors. The actual house was completed by architects of the Imperial Household Department, foremost among them Yokichi Gondo. Regularly changing temporary shows are spread through the museum and double as house tours.

Getting there

Ebisu station is on the Yamanote line and the Hibiya subway line; Meguro is also on the Yamanote line. Daikanyama is on the Tokyu Toyoko line.

Ginza

Wide streets and flashy façades mark Tokyo's most upmarket neighbourhood.

Map p75

Throughout the recent economic slump, when all around were tightening their purse strings, Tokyo's fanciest district carried on regardless. Ginza is, was and always will be the epitome of Tokyo extravagance. Other areas, notably Marunouchi and Aoyama, have raised their game in the last few years, but it's still in Ginza that ladies saunter the wide streets dressed head to toe in luxury brands, shopping for more of the same. Likewise, Ginza is where you'll find politicians and businessmen on bottomless expense accounts quaffing overpriced drinks in the company of kimono-clad bar staff. Less affluent types simply come to dream.

Crammed into Ginza's eight main blocks (*chome*) are over 10,000 shops, many of them selling goods at Bubble-era prices. The area's reputation for exclusivity stretches right back to the 19th-century Meiji period, when Ginza became the first part of Tokyo to be rebuilt in red brick rather than wood. Red brick was thought to offer greater protection from natural disasters, a theory disproved in 1923 when the area was razed by the Great Kanto Earthquake. Unfortunately, not one single red brick from Ginza's first golden era survives today.

What does survive, though, is the Tokyo pastime of 'Ginbura', or Ginza strolling. The area has unusually wide pavements, which lend themselves perfectly to window-shopping and aimless wandering. From noon at weekends cars are banned from the main street, **Ginza**

Dori (also called **Chuo Dori**; photo *p76*), creating what is known as *hokousha tengoku* (pedestrian heaven). Cafés spill out on to the road, lending the area a relaxed, almost European feel.

Tiny shops selling traditional items such as kimonos, *wagashi* (Japanese sweets) and *go*-boards sit side by side with brand giants such as Gucci and Cartier. Foreign retail chains tend to choose to have their first Japanese outlets in prestigious Ginza before opening up elsewhere. And the need to stand out amid all this flashy competition has led the biggest names to commission stores with spectacular façades. Star architects have even made tourist attractions of stores for **Mikimoto** (photo *p78*), Hermès, Louis Vuitton and Chanel, whose building boasts top French chef Alain Ducasse's restaurant **Beige Tokyo** (5159 5500, www.beige-tokyo.com) on the tenth floor.

The reputation of the area for elegance and class is fiercely guarded by local shopkeepers. After the closure of the Sogo department store near Yurakucho station in 2001, they mounted strong resistance to the arrival of discount electronics superstore Bic Camera – which took over the Sogo building, giving the company its first presence in designer-label land.

While boutiques and restaurants with fearsome prices are the norm in Ginza, there are bargains to be had. As elsewhere in Tokyo, most restaurants offer special set-lunch deals,

Ginza

Time Out Tokyo **75**

Ginza Dori. *See p74.*

the difference here being that you have a chance to eat food for around ¥1,500 that might cost ten times as much in the evening. Most restaurants are off the main drag, many of them in basements, so take a walk around the backstreets and check out the prices, which are usually posted on boards outside (if they're not, don't go in – unless you want to terrify your bank manager). For fashion, **RagTag** (3-3-15 Ginza, 3535 4100, www.ragtag.jp/shop/ginza. html, open 11am-8pm daily; also *see p197*) is a six-storey second-hand clothing shop that deals only in the biggest brands. Ginza's fickle fashionistas keep the store stocked with barely worn garments from the latest catwalk collections.

There are many ways to explore Ginza on foot – setting off from Yurakucho station is a good option. The **Tokyo TIC** tourist office (*see p313*) is here too. Take the exit for Ginza and walk down a narrow street, then straight through the arcade running inside the Mullion complex – home to the Hankyu and Seibu department stores and several cinemas. You come out at the multi-directional zebra crossings of Sukiyabashi (Sukiya Bridge). Confusingly, there is no actual bridge. There used to be one going from the present-day Sukiyabashi Hankyu department store towards Hibiya, across the old outer moat of Edo Castle (now the Imperial Palace), but both bridge and waterway were casualties of 1960s road construction. Today a small monument marks the spot where the bridge once stood.

Standing with Sukiyabashi Hankyu department store on your right, you will see a Sony sign on the other side of the crossing. The electronic giant's eight-storey showcase, the **Sony Building** (*see p196*), will appeal to technology and gaming fans alike. All the latest Sony models are on display, with staff eager to

talk you through them. The sixth floor is a free PlayStation arcade where you can try the latest games; it's packed with kids at weekends, so visit during the week. The basement holds two floors of Sony Plaza, a chain that stocks import snacks, cosmetics and other colourful goodies. The narrow tower next door, made of semi-translucent gold glass bricks that seem to glow from within at night, is the **Hermès** flagship, designed by Renzo Piano.

Walk down Sotobori Dori (Outer Moat Avenue, once part of Edo Castle's waterway defences), towards Ginza Ha-chome and Shinbashi. Ginza streets are named and laid out in a grid, so it's difficult to get lost. Stop off at some of the small art galleries, most of which are free to enter. When you reach the boundary of Ginza at Gomon Dori, turn left towards Ginza Dori and the narrower streets of Sony Dori, Namiki Dori, Nishi Gobangai Dori and Suzuran Dori. Whichever route you take back to **Harumi Dori** (the other major thoroughfare), the atmospheric streets between Ginza Dori and Sotobori Dori are the best pottering area in Ginza. Zigzag towards the main crossroads in the district: the intersection of Ginza Dori and Harumi Dori – known as Yon-chome crossing because it's in on the edge of the Ginza-four sub-district (*yon* means four).

When you reach the crossing, you will see **Le Café Doutor Ginza** (*see p182*) at the base of the cylindrical **San-ai Building** (**photo** *p78*). The large green frog on top of the police box is to provide good luck for drivers. On the other side of Harumi Dori is **Wako** (*see p190*), a watch and jewellery department store famous for its window displays and clocktower. In Ozu's classic film *Tokyo Story* (1953), two women are driven past Wako, the store representing the high-class, modern face of Tokyo. 'Outside Wako at Yon-chome crossing' is a common meeting spot.

Facing Wako, on the other side of Ginza Dori, is upscale department store **Mitsukoshi** (*see p189*; the bronze lion at its entrance is another popular meeting point). And on the fourth corner is yet another rendezvous spot, the **Nissan Gallery**, where the latest models are exhibited on the ground floor. The famous paper specialist **Kyukyodo** (*see p204*) is also here, next door to the San-ai Building.

From the Yon-chome crossing, with your back to Wako, heading left along Ginza Dori will take you past more high-class stores – spectacular at night when the neon signs are switched on – and, eventually, into Kyobashi, where you'll find the

Metropolitan Police Department Museum, the **National Film Centre** and one of Tokyo's best Indian restaurants, **Dhaba India** (*see p154*).

Heading straight down Harumi Dori, meanwhile, will take you to the traditional-style **Kabuki-za** theatre (*see p264*), home of *kabuki*. Reserved seats are pricey, but a single act of the day-long programme can be enjoyed for around ¥1,000. You'll have to queue for tickets, and opera glasses are essential, but it's a good way to get a taste of Japan's traditional performing arts.

Continue walking down Harumi Dori, turn right on to Shinohashi Dori, and you'll eventually reach **Tsukiji Fish Market**, one of the world's

Something fishy

Take advantage of your jet lag and pay an early morning visit to one of Tokyo's most memorable sights, the wholesale fish market at Tsukiji. Colourful, cacophonous and chaotic – it's a fascinating spectacle. Some 50,000 workers and 14,000 retailers come daily to do business here. Over 1,600 stalls sell 450 varieties of seafood – fresh, frozen, smoked, dried, pickled – and much of it is totally unfamiliar. If it lives in water, you'll find it here.

There's been a fish market in Tokyo since 1590, but Tsukiji's current location is much younger, established in 1935. It comprises an inner and an outer market. The inner section, strictly wholesale, is where the auction (and the action) happens, though since 2005 visitors have had to obtain a special permit to enter. The best way to circumvent this hassle is to join a guided tour (try the Seiyo Ginza Hotel; *see p40*).

The tuna auction is the one to watch: it starts at around 5am and is finished by 6.30am. Auctions of vegetables and fruit follow, and the bulk of the market's business is done by midday. It's worth noting that flash photography is not permitted during auctions. You should also wear clothes that you don't mind getting dirty, and remember to watch out for (and give way to) the numerous moving vehicles and vendors.

After the auction, visit the outer market, which has wider, quieter alleys and is easier to navigate. It's open to all and offers a wide range of foodstuffs and kitchen goods. Don't miss breakfast at one of the restaurants near the main gate – noodles, curry, tempura and *tonkatsu* are all available, but sushi is the thing: it's the freshest in Tokyo.

Tsukiji is open six days a week (closed Sundays, national holidays, two Wednesdays per month, New Year and Obon in August). Tsjukijishijo station (exit A2) on the Oedo subway line is on the doorstep; to find the auction area, walk straight through the market from the main gate to the end. You can pick up a useful map from the tourist offices (*see p313*) or visit the website www.tsukiji-market.or.jp/tukiji_e.htm.

With the current location getting rather crowded and outdated, the inner market will be moving two kilometres (1.25 miles) south to Toyosu in 2012.

Bright lights: the **San-ai Building**. See p76.

largest wholesale markets and one of the city's unmissable sights (*see p77* **Something fishy**).

On the northern side of the Yamanote line tracks, opposite the **Imperial Hotel** (*see p41*), is the **Takarazuka** theatre (*see p266*), home to an all-female musical revue. *Takarazuka* is imbued with less tradition and history than *kabuki*, but it's an equally unique experience. Next door is a large park, **Hibiya Koen**. Once the parade ground for the Japanese army, it was turned into the country's first Western-style park in 1903, complete with rose gardens, a bandstand and open-air theatre. It's a great spot for an impromptu picnic or romantic late-night stroll. At the northern end of the park is a moat, which surrounds the expansive grounds of the **Imperial Palace** (*see p92*).

SHINBASHI AND SHIODOME

At the southern limits of Ginza, towards the area around Shinbashi station, you'll see a collection of skyscrapers gleaming in the distance. This complex, known as **Shiodome**, opened in mid 2003 on the site of a former Japan Railways goods yard. In clement weather the wide-open plazas often host buskers and performance artists. The commercial and cultural impact of Shiodome, however, was muted somewhat by the almost simultaneous opening of **Roppongi Hills** (*see p191*), a larger, ritzier rival. Shiodome hasn't attracted the upmarket restaurants or designer boutiques, and thus doesn't draw the crowds its competitor across town does. Still, it's worth a visit for the ultra-modern Tokyo vibe.

One of the skyscrapers is home to Dentsu, Japan's largest advertising agency; in the

basement lies the **ADMT Advertising Museum Tokyo**, a great, interactive look at over 300 years of ads in Japan. The museum is at the rear of **Caretta Shiodome** (*see p190*), a shopping and dining arcade that also houses **Shochu Authority** (Caretta Shiodome B2F, 1-8-2 Higashi-Shimbashi, 5537 2105, open 11am-10pm daily), a spacious shop with over 3,200 varieties of sake and knowledgeable staff on hand. Sitting quietly between the skyscrapers of Shiodome is a fascinating glimpse at the area's past. The **Old Shinbashi Station** is a reconstruction of one of Tokyo's first railway stations, the foundations of which are now visible through the glass floor.

After shopping and eating your way around all this gleaming modernity, take a five-minute walk to **Hama-Rikyu Detached Garden**, a one-time duck hunting ground and the most picturesque spot in the Ginza area.

ADMT Advertising Museum Tokyo

Caretta Shiodome B1F-B2F, 1-8-2 Higashi-Shinbashi, Minato-ku (6218 2500/www.admt.jp). Shinbashi station (Yamanote line), Shiodome exit; (Asakusa, Ginza lines), exit 6 or Shiodome station (Oedo, Yurikamome lines), exit 6. **Open** 11am-6.30pm Tue-Fri; 11am-4.30pm Sat. **Admission** free.
This fab museum is devoted to Japanese advertising, from fascinating 17th-century woodblock prints to

Mikimoto. See p74.

modern product-placement techniques. Although English explanations are limited, the images largely speak for themselves. Inspired technology allows touch-screen browsing of historic ads, and on-demand viewing of award-winning commercials from the past three decades. The museum also contains a library of over 100,000 digitised images.

Hama-Rikyu Detached Garden (Hama-Rikyu Onshi Teien)

1-1 Hama-Rikyu Teien, Chuo-ku (3541 0200). Shiodome station (Oedo, Yurikamome lines), exit 10 or Suijo water bus. **Open** 9am-5pm daily. **Admission** ¥300; ¥150 concessions. **No credit cards.**
This tranquil garden, once a hunting ground for the Tokugawa shogunate, now cowers in the shadow of the new Shiodome development. The garden's main appeal lies in the abundance of water in and around it and the fact that it feels deceptively spacious, thanks to beautiful landscaping. Situated on an island, it is surrounded by an ancient walled moat with only one entrance, over the Nanmon Bridge (it's also possible to reach Hama-Rikyu by boat from Asakusa (*see p59*). The focal points are the huge pond, which contains two islands (one with a tea-house) connected to the shore by charming wooden bridges, and a photogenic 300-year-old pine tree.

Metropolitan Police Department Museum

Matsushita Denko Tokyo Honsha Bldg B2-2F, 3-5-1 Kyobashi, Chuo-ku (3581 4321/www.keishicho.metro. tokyo.jp/index.htm). Kyobashi station (Ginza line), exit 2. **Open** 10am-6pm Tue-Sun. **Admission** free. **Map** Ginza p75.
With a reputation lying somewhere between inept and corrupt, Japan's police force needs a little more than this drab collection of artefacts to turn things around. The absence of anything relating to modern crime-fighting might alarm more than reassure visitors, and the most exciting-looking exhibit is an arcade-style gaming machine that, disappointingly, turns out to be a safe-driving simulator. Still, if you've been dragging your kids around designer boutiques all day, you might redeem yourself here: diminutive visitors can dress as mini officers, sit on a Kawasaki police motorcycle with flashing lights, peer into a helicopter and meet force mascot Pipo-kun.

National Film Centre

3-7-6 Kyobashi, Chuo-ku (3561 0823/www.momat. go.jp/english/index.html). Kyobashi station (Ginza line), exit 1. **Open** 11am-6.30pm Tue-Fri. **Library** 10am-6.30pm Tue-Fri. **Admission** ¥500; ¥100-¥300 concessions; free under-6s; additional charge for special exhibitions. **No credit cards. Map** Ginza p75.
Japanese and foreign films – 19,000 of them – star at the country's only national facility devoted to the preservation and study of cinema. Fans throng to its two cinemas for series focusing on, for example, DW Griffith or Korean films from the 1960s. Visitors can also check out the library of film books on the fourth

Hama-Rikyu Detached Garden.

floor or exhibitions of photos, graphic design and film-related items (often drawn from its own collection) in the gallery on the seventh floor.

Old Shinbashi Station

1-5-3 Higashi-Shinbashi, Minato-ku (3572 1872). Shinbashi station (Yamanote line), Shiodome exit; (Asakusa, Ginza lines), exits 3, 4 or Shiodome station (Oedo, Yurikamome lines), exits 3, 4. **Open** 11am-6pm Tue-Sun. **Admission** free.
A reconstruction of the Shinbashi passenger terminus, part of the first railway in Japan, which opened in 1872. The current structure (opened in 2003) stands on the foundations of the original. These were uncovered during excavations, and can be viewed through a glass floor in the basement. Those of ironic bent may notice that Londoners still use stations every day that would be considered archaeological treasures in Tokyo, but quibbles aside, this is a great project, with a permanent railway history exhibition hall and English labelling. There's also a pleasant café.

Getting there

The Ginza area is well served by trains. There's Yurakucho station (JR Yamanote and Yurakucho subway lines), Hibiya station (Chiyoda, Hibiya and Mita subway lines), and Ginza station (Ginza, Hibiya and Marunouchi subway lines). Shinbashi is on the Yamanote, Asakusa and Ginza lines, while Shiodome is on the Oedo subway and Yurikamome monorail.

Sightseeing

Harajuku & Aoyama

Trendsetting teens, big-brand boutiques and a spectacular Shinto shrine.

Map p82

Harajuku and Aoyama are two of Tokyo's biggest fashion districts. The former is arguably the heart of the city's vibrant youth fashion scene, and it's the best place to shop for the latest urban brands. The adjacent area of Aoyama, meanwhile, appeals to a moneyed and upmarket crowd who favour international mega-brands.

The tree-lined boulevard of Omotesando runs through both districts. The Aoyama end, running either side of Aoyama Dori and Omotesando subway station, is where you'll find the fanciest stores, some eye-catching architecture and the new **Omotesando Hills** retail complex. The street stretches downhill to the junction with Meiji Dori and on to Meiji-Jingumae subway station and nearby Harajuku JR station. These lower regions offer more affordable shopping – Puma and Gap rather than Prada and Gucci.

And just a little further is the green expanse of **Yoyogi Park** and the **Meiji Jingu** complex, Tokyo's largest Shinto shrine.

Aoyama

After Ginza, this is where all the big-name global brands want to be. **Christian Dior**, **Ralph Lauren**, **Louis Vuitton** and **Tod's** are all represented, but **Prada**, with its bubble-glass high-rise, is still the highlight of the area. And things just got better, or worse, depending on your point of view, since the opening of the Ando Tadao-designed **Omotesando Hills** (*see p190*) in 2005. The brainchild of the corporation behind multi-use mini-city Roppongi Hills (*see p190*), the far smaller Omotesando version is almost entirely devoted to retail, with flashy fashion brands such as

Gotta have faith

Japanese adherents of Shinto number around 106 million, while those regarding themselves as Buddhists amount to 95 million. This tally of over 200 million is not bad for a country with a population of less than 130 million. Clearly, when it comes to religion, the Japanese believe there's no harm in hedging one's bets. It's common for people to have their rites-of-passage ceremonies in a Shinto shrine, their marriage in a Christian chapel and their funeral in a Buddhist temple.

Though the majority of Japanese people happily embrace both native Shinto and imported Buddhism, these are about as different as two faiths could be. Shinto is unconcerned with matters of afterlife, which is a major concern in Buddhism, for example.

Shinto is a primitive faith: it imparts no ethical doctrine and possesses no holy scriptures. It is at heart a system of animistic belief in natural spirits (*kami*) – the religious system of an ancient nation of rice farmers that has survived into the modern age.

Some of Shinto's most visible features are its numerous festivals, many of which are fertility rites, supplicating the deities to bestow a good rice crop on the community.

Purity has long been a major feature of Shinto, and this is evident at the place of worship (conventionally termed 'shrine' in English, to distinguish it from Buddhist temples). After passing through the shrine's distinctive *torii* (gate), worshippers often ritually wash their hands and mouth with water from a stone basin before offering their prayers at the main hall.

Talismans play an important role too, so stalls at the shrine sell amulets for luck in health, love, exams and even driving. You'll also see collections of small wooden plaques (*ema*) on which people write wishes, white fortune-telling slips of paper (*omikuji*) tied around trees in the grounds, and sometimes colourful strings of 1,000 origami cranes (*senbazuru*).

By the time Buddhism arrived in Japan from Korea in the sixth century AD, it was already 1,000 years old, and in its long journey across Asia from India had picked up rituals, symbols and tenets that would have seemed utterly alien to its original founders. Mahayana Buddhism, as practised in Japan, introduced the notion

Sightseeing

YSL and Dolce & Gabbana hogging the bulk of the floorspace. Unless you're heading to one of the posh eateries inside, this monument to Mammon is best experienced from the other side of the street, preferably after dark when the glass panels of its façade emit their chameleon-like ambient glow.

Head uphill from Omotesando Hills and you'll find **Anniversaire** (3-5-30 Kita-Aoyama, Minato-ku), with three floors of upscale shopping, a fancy French restaurant and a Parisian-style café. The cafe's outdoor seats are prime people-watching territory, but beware: you'll pay through the nose for a cup of coffee.

Head downhill and, on the opposite side of the road, is the traditional façade of **Oriental Bazaar** (*see p204*). A godsend for souvenir hunters, the store's three floors are stuffed with all manner of Japanese goods. Best of all, everything is quite cheap, probably less than half the price you'd pay at an average department store. Nearby is toy megastore **Kiddyland** (*see p209*). The centre of cute, cuddly, crazy and comical Japan, it offers myriad toys, games and dolls; be prepared for sensory overload.

The side streets that lie in between Omotesando and Aoyama Dori are worth exploring; you'll come across narrow winding alleys, old-fashioned homes, tiny art galleries and foreigner-friendly **Las Chicas** (*see p161*), a complex of eating, drinking and art spaces set around a pretty courtyard.

Back at the Omotesando/Aoyama Dori crossing, there's much to explore along Aoyama Dori itself. Head south (towards Shibuya), and you'll soon pass, on the left, the white exterior of **Spiral** (*see p239*), one of Tokyo's key art and design spaces. Just beyond is a turning into another key shopping street, **Kotto Dori**, which runs down to join Roppongi Dori. It has upmarket fashion houses next to effete French restaurants, plus some posh clubs and bars. A stroll along here at night should reveal a mix of well-to-do partiers, hard-core ravers and average folk out for a good time. For a healthy dose of whimsy, pop into the **Okamoto Taro Memorial Museum**, about halfway down Kotto Dori and one block to the left. Not far away is Aoyama's prime art oasis, the **Nezu Institute of Fine Arts**, set in tranquil woods complete with ponds, stone trails and teahouses.

Further along Aoyama Dori is the massive **United Nations University Centre** and, next door, the **National Children's Castle**

of *bodhisattvas*, who put off their own salvation in order to bring enlightenment to others. Kannon is a popular *bodhisattva*, as is Jizo, often seen by roadsides and in temples as a small stone figure wearing a red bib.

Temples are often very ornate and brightly coloured, while shrines tend to be more muted. At both, people make offerings, often with a ¥5 coin, which is considered lucky. Temples also sell good-luck charms, and commonly feature incense burners; you'll see people directing the smoke, which is deemed to have beneficial powers, over themselves.

You can't enter the main buildings at temples or shrines, but otherwise there are no off-limit areas, and locals won't be offended by sightseers. Photography is widely permitted, though it may be forbidden indoors at some temples – look for signs. You may be required to take off your shoes before entering some buildings.

Must-see religious sites in Tokyo are the **Meiji Shrine** (*see p85*) and the **Asakusa Kannon (Senso-ji) Temple** (*see p68*); if you're really keen, head to the temple towns of Kamakura (*see pp288-291*) or Nikko (*pp292-294*).

Harajuku & Aoyama

© Copyright Time Out Group 2007

200 m
200 yds

To Aoyama Cemetery

MINAMI-AOYAMA

GAIEN-NISHI DORI

AOYAMA DORI

Omotesando Station

Anniversaire Building

Mizuho Bank

OMOTESANDO

Omotesando Hills

Oriental Bazaar

Gap

MEIJI DORI

Togo Shrine

TAKESHITA DORI

JINGUMAE

Meiji-Jingumae Station

Harajuku Station

MEIJI DORI

Yamanote Line

SHIBUYA-KU

Meiji Shrine Inner Garden

Yoyogi Park

INOKASHIRA DORI

National Gymnasium

JINNAN

KOEN DORI

NHK Hall

NHK Broadcasting Centre

(*see p220*), a great resource for local parents. Among other attractions here are a video library, fine-arts studio, computer playroom and a very popular rooftop playport.

Heading in the opposite direction along Aoyama Dori (towards Akasaka) leads to the giant necropolis of **Aoyama Cemetery**, to the south of Gaienmae subway station. Occupying some of the most expensive land in Tokyo, it was once part of the local *daimyo*'s estate and became a cemetery in 1872 after a brief stint as a silk farm. It contains more than 100,000 graves and is a good spot for cherry-blossom viewing in April. On the other side of the main road is **Meiji Shrine Outer Garden** and various sports facilities built for the 1964 Olympics, including the **National Stadium** (*see p270*) and **Jingu Baseball Stadium** (*see p269*). Also in the vicinity is the **Watari-Um Museum of Contemporary Art**.

Nezu Institute of Fine Arts

6-5-1 Minami-Aoyama, Minato-ku (3400 2536/ www.nezu-muse.or.jp). Omotesando station (Chiyoda, Ginza, Hanzomon lines), exit A5. **Open** 9.30am-4.30pm Tue-Sun. **Admission** ¥1,000; ¥700 concessions. **No credit cards.**
Tobu Railway founder Kaichiro Nezu had a penchant for Chinese art and collected Shang and Zhou bronzes. Over the years, the museum's collection of over 7,000 objects has grown through donations of Korean ceramics and Japanese ink paintings from private collectors. Some of the most famous works are on permanent display, while others rotate in temporary exhibitions.

Okamoto Taro Memorial Museum

6-1-19 Minami-Aoyama, Minato-ku (3406 0801/ http://taro-okamoto.or.jp). Omotesando station (Chiyoda, Ginza, Hanzomon lines), exit B1. **Open** 10am-6pm Mon, Wed-Sun. **Admission** ¥600; ¥300 concessions. **No credit cards.**
This two-storey museum just off Kotto Dori was once the studio of artist Taro Okamoto, who died in

1996. The adjoining café looks into a lovely tropical garden packed with his wacky sculptures.

United Nations University Centre

United Nations University Bldg, 5-53-70 Jingumae, Shibuya-ku (3499 2811/library 5467 1359/www.unu. edu/ctr.html). Omotesando station (Chiyoda, Ginza, Hanzomon lines), exit B2. **Open** 10am-1pm, 2-5.30pm Mon-Fri. **Admission** free. **Map** Shibuya p109.
The UNU Centre houses a permanent UN staff, hosts international conferences on global problems and offers classes. On the eighth floor is a good library for exploring human-rights issues and global concerns. The galleries on the first and second floors are also worth checking out.

Watari-Um Museum of Contemporary Art

3-7-6 Jingumae, Shibuya-ku (3402 3001/www. watarium.co.jp). Gaienmae station (Ginza line), exit 3. **Open** 11am-7pm Tue, Thur-Sun; 11am-9pm Wed. **Admission** ¥1,000; ¥800 concessions. **No credit cards. Map** Harajuku & Aoyama p82.
Mario Botta designed this small art museum for the Watari family in 1990. It holds four exhibitions a year, some of which originate at the museum, while others are brought in from abroad. There's a good art bookshop and a pleasant café in the basement.

Harajuku

It's rammed, noisy, lurid and often obnoxious, but **Takeshita Dori** (*see p194*) is Harajuku's iconic thoroughfare. This narrow pedestrianised lane of small clothes shops and crêpe stands is teen heaven. It's a solid mass of humanity at weekends, and a shuffle through this awe-inspiring sight is a must. Takeshita Dori starts on the opposite side of the road from quaintly old-fashioned Harajuku station and stretches to Meiji Dori; halfway along are some steps leading up to the **Togo Shrine**, the setting for a great flea market on the first and fourth Sundays of the month. The surrounding side streets are crammed with one-off clothing shops, quirky jewellery stores and eateries, and well worth a wander.

Key stores include **Laforet** (*see p197*), on the corner of Meiji Dori and Omotesando, opposite a huge branch of Gap. A popular meeting spot, it offers five floors of teeny-bopper shopping heaven with an art museum/event space as the cherry on top. Behind Laforet lies another universe – the 'floating world' of *ukiyo-e* woodblock prints in the small, dimly lit and *tatami*-floored **Ukiyo-e Ota Memorial Museum of Art**. Leave your shoes in a locker at the entrance, and don't miss the basement gift shop. Fans of contemporary architecture should visit the **GA Gallery**, located north of Harajuku station, between the railway tracks and Meiji Dori.

Harajuku is also justly famous for the largest Shinto shrine in the city. The entrance to the **Meiji Shrine** is through an 11-metre (36-foot) *torii* (gate), the largest in the country, built from 1,600-year-old Japanese cypress trees imported from Taiwan. A wide gravel path winds through the thickly wooded Inner Garden, with various smaller paths leading off into the dense overhanging foliage, before reaching the shrine's buildings. As with the Imperial Palace and its grounds, this huge patch of green is instantly recognisable from observation decks across the city. The serene atmosphere, punctuated by birdsong, is a world away from the mayhem of Harajuku's shops.

Each Sunday the bridge beside Harajuku station, in front of the entrance to the Meiji Shrine's Inner Garden, a collection of garishly dressed 'cosplay' (costume play) aficionados display themselves. Don't be shy to take their photo – that's the highest form of flattery for cosplay queens.

The costumes range from cool to inventive to bizarre. A favourite outfit over the past few years has been the 19th-century French maid's kit. Black and white, frilly and provocative, it's not your typical 14-year-old's attire – but the look is more comic book than anything shocking. Another eye-catching offering is the nurse's uniform, with a twist. Not content to splatter their smocks with a bit of blood from supposed patients (in vogue a while back), the girls now complete the outfit with their own delicately arranged fake blood and bandages.

Adjoining the Inner Garden are the lush expanses of **Yoyogi Park**, a favourite with couples and families, who spend warm afternoons lounging on the grass. Formerly a residential area for US military, then the site of the Olympic Village in 1964, it became a park in 1967. It's known for its autumn foliage, especially the golden gingko trees. At the southern end of the park, across Inokashira Dori, lie the headquarters of state broadcaster NHK and architect Tange Kenzo's **Yoyogi National Stadium** (*see p272*), also built for the Olympics and still one of Tokyo's most famous modern landmarks.

GA Gallery

3-12-14 Sendagaya, Shibuya-ku (3403 1581/ www.ga-ada.co.jp). Yoyogi station (Yamanote line), east exit; (Oedo line), exit A1. **Open** 10am-6.30pm Tue-Fri; noon-6.30pm Sat, Sun. **Admission** ¥500; free concessions. **No credit cards**.

Takeshita Dori.

Go for a jog in **Yoyogi park** (rockabilly outfit not obligatory). *See p84.*

Global Architecture's annual 'GA Houses' and 'GA Japan' exhibitions make it one of Tokyo's best places for modern and contemporary Japanese and international architecture. The building also houses an excellent architecture bookshop.

Meiji Shrine & Inner Garden

1-1 Yoyogi-Kamizonocho, Shibuya-ku (3379 5511/ www.meijijingu.or.jp). Harajuku station (Yamanote line), Omotesando exit or Meiji-Jingumae station (Chiyoda line), exit 2. **Open** *Shrine & Inner Garden Spring, autumn 5.10am-5.50pm daily. Summer 5am-6.30pm daily. Winter 6am-4.10pm daily. Meiji Shrine Garden Mar-Oct 9am-5pm daily. Nov-Feb 9am-4pm daily.* **Admission** *Shrine & Inner Garden free. Meiji Shrine Garden ¥500. Treasure house ¥200.* **No credit cards. Map** Harajuku & Aoyama p82.

Opened in 1920, the shrine is dedicated to Emperor Meiji – whose reign (1868-1912) coincided with Japan's modernisation – and his consort, Empress Shoken. Exceedingly popular, especially at New Year, when it draws crowds of a million-plus, the shrine hosts numerous annual festivals, including two sumo dedicatory ceremonies in early January and at the end of September. Shinto weddings take place here regularly. The current main building dates from 1958, a reconstruction after the original was destroyed during World War II. It is an impressive example of the austere style and restrained colours typical of Shinto architecture. Just off the main path to the shrine,

through the wooded Inner Garden, are two entrances to another garden, the little-visited Meiji Jingu Gyoen. It's neither large nor especially beautiful, but it is quiet – except in June, when the iris field attracts many admirers. Vegetation is dense, limiting access to the few trails, which lead to a pond and teahouse.

Ukiyo-e Ota Memorial Museum of Art (Ota Kinen Bijutsukan)

1-10-10 Jingumae, Shibuya-ku (3403 0880/www. ukiyoe-ota-muse.jp). Harajuku station (Yamanote line), Omotesando exit or Meiji-Jingumae station (Chiyoda line), exit 5. **Open** *10.30am-5.30pm Tue-Sun. Closed 27-end of mth.* **Admission** *¥700; ¥500 concessions.* **No credit cards. Map** Harajuku & Aoyama p82.

The late Seizo Ota, chairman of Toho Mutual Life Insurance, began collecting *ukiyo-e* prints after he saw that Japan was losing its traditional art to Western museums and collectors. Temporary exhibitions drawn from his 12,000-strong collection often include works by popular masters like Hiroshige and Hokusai.

Getting there

Omotesando station is on the Chiyoda, Ginza and Hanzomon subway lines. Harajuku station is on the Yamanote line and nearby Meiji-Jingumae is on the Chiyoda line.

Ikebukuro

Despite its frumpy image, there's lots going on.

Tokyo Metropolitan Art Space. *See p88.*

Map p87

Ikebukuro, which ranks third behind Shinjuku and Shibuya as one of the main sub-centres of Tokyo, has a resolutely uncool reputation. But this actually works in its favour, as the resulting lack of pretension gives the whole area a freer, more laid-back atmosphere. Indeed, since few people head for Ikebukuro as they would for one of its more glamorous counterparts, most of the people you'll find here live nearby, giving it a community vibe comparable to that found in Japan's provincial cities. But laid-back doesn't mean quiet: every available square inch is crammed with shops, bars, restaurants, karaoke rooms, cinemas, love hotels and other 'entertainment' establishments.

The nerve centre of Ikebukuro is one of Tokyo's largest train stations, served by two subway lines, two private railways and numerous JR lines. While this makes it an easy place to reach, it can be a difficult place to get around, as the station is devoid of significant landmarks. Among more than 40 exits, the most popular meeting spot is the Ike Fukuro ('Lake Owl') statue at the bottom of the stairs inside exit 22. That a statue the size of a beer barrel should be the most distinctive feature of a station sprawling over many city blocks is damning proof of its poor design.

Once you escape the station, though, navigation gets easier. Look north to spot the 30-storey phallic cement chimney of the local garbage incineration plant, and use this as your guide to the **Ikebukuro Sports Centre** (*see p276*), in the building immediately next door to the plant. The centre's tenth-floor gym and 11th-floor swimming pool provide a bird's-eye impression of how Ikebukuro is laid out while you work out.

Since most of the above-ground railway lines run north–south, Ikebukuro itself divides into east and west. Each side is dominated by a gigantic department store half next to, and half on top of, the train station. This is the result of a feud between wealthy arch-rival half-brothers Tsutsumi Yasujiro and Nezu Kaichiro, who developed the two private rail lines – the Seibu Ikebukuro and Tobu Tojo lines, respectively – that serve the area. Each encouraged local growth by building a department store at the station. Both stores grew to be among the largest in the world.

Confusingly, the **Seibu** department store (*see p189* – whose name originates from 'west area railway line' – is located on the east side of the station, and **Tobu** (*see p190*) – the 'east area railway line' – has the west side covered. It's advisable to pick up a store map for each, as there's a danger of getting very lost. Outside these two overwhelming stores, east and west Ikebukuro remain distinct.

WEST SIDE

Before World War II, the area west of Ikebukuro station was known in some circles as 'the Montparnasse of Tokyo'. Its cheap homes were occupied by artists and writers, including Edogawa Rampo (1894-1965), the revered detective novelist whose name is a Japanised pronunciation of Edgar Allan Poe.

Even today, much of western Ikebukuro consists of quiet residential neighbourhoods, though few pre-war buildings remain. One survivor is **Jiyu Gakuen Myonichikan**, a school building designed by Frank Lloyd

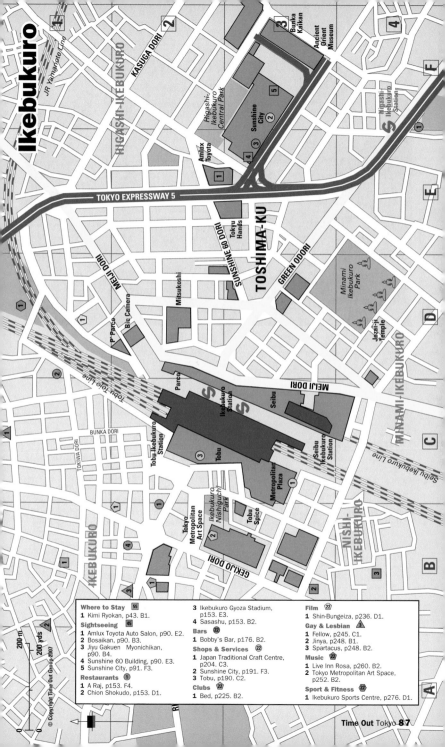

Ikebukuro

JR Yamanote Line

KASUGA DORI

HIGASHI-IKEBUKURO

Higashi-Ikebukuro Central Park

Amlux Toyota

Sunshine City

Bunka Kaikan

Ancient Orient Museum

Higashi-Ikebukuro Station

TOKYO EXPRESSWAY 5

TOSHIMA-KU

MEIJI DORI

SUNSHINE 60 DORI

Tokyu Hands

GREEN ODORI

Minami Ikebukuro Park

Mitsukoshi

Jōzai-ji Temple

MINAMI-IKEBUKURO

Bic Camera

P'Parco

Tobu Tojo Line

Parco

Ikebukuro Station

Seibu

MEIJI DORI

Seibu Ikebukuro Station

BUNKA DORI

Tobu Ikebukuro Station

Tobu

Metropolitan Plaza

NISHI-IKEBUKURO

Seibu Ikebukuro Line

TOKIWA DORI

Ikebukuro Nishiguchi Park

Tobu Spice

IKEBUKURO

Tokyo Metropolitan Art Space

GEKIJO DORI

200 m
200 yds

© Copyright Time Out Group 2007

Where to Stay 55
1 Kimi Ryokan, p43. B1.

Sightseeing 45
1 Amlux Toyota Auto Salon, p90. E2.
2 Bosaikan, p90. B3.
3 Jiyu Gakuen Myonichikan, p90. B4.
4 Sunshine 60 Building, p90. E3.
5 Sunshine City, p91. F3.

Restaurants 1
1 A Raj, p153. F4.
2 Chion Shokudo, p153. D1.
3 Ikebukuro Gyoza Stadium, p153. E3.
4 Sasashu, p153. B2.

Bars 22
1 Bobby's Bar, p176. B2.

Shops & Services 22
1 Japan Traditional Craft Centre, p204. C3.
2 Sunshine City, p191. F3.
3 Tobu, p190. C2.

Clubs 22
1 Bed, p225. B2.

Film 22
1 Shin-Bungeiza, p236. D1.

Gay & Lesbian 3
1 Fellow, p245. C1.
2 Jinya, p248. B1.
3 Spartacus, p248. B2.

Music 22
1 Live Inn Rosa, p260. B2.
2 Tokyo Metropolitan Art Space, p252. B2.

Sport & Fitness 22
1 Ikebukuro Sports Centre, p276. D1.

Time Out Tokyo **87**

Sunshine 60 Dori.

Wright in 1921. It and the nearby **Mejiro Teien** garden provide an oasis of tranquillity that makes a welcome contrast to the bustle of Ikebukuro station. Contributing to that bustle are thousands of students from Rikkyo University, also located to the west of the station. The campus is unremarkable most of the year, but around Christmas its red-brick buildings are decked out with festive lights.

The other major department store on this side is **Marui**, directly down the street perpendicular to the station's main west exit. Metropolitan Plaza, home to the **Japan Traditional Craft Centre** (*see p204*) – a good place for learning more about Japanese arts and crafts – is right next to Tobu.

Directly opposite the Metropolitan exit is **Tobu Spice**, a building full of restaurants. In the basement of the next building behind that is the **Dubliners** (*see p180*) – one of Tokyo's ever-expanding number of Irish pubs; it attracts long-time foreign residents and Japanese regulars, as well as musicians keen on Celtic music. The Dubliners' entrance faces a broad stone plaza that is the only significant car-free open space in the area. You're likely to find old men hunched over *shogi* and *go*-boards, as well as musicians. On the west side of the plaza stands the airy, glass-enclosed **Tokyo Metropolitan Art Space** (*see p252; photo p86*), used for classical concerts, plays and ballets. A block south of the plaza is the **Bosaikan**, an earthquake simulation centre designed to teach citizens how to survive the impending Big One.

EAST SIDE

There are two main exits on this side of the station – the east exit and the Seibu exit. Turn left out of either, and you will come to **Parco**, which is part of the Seibu complex. **P' Parco**, slightly along, is one source of the wild fashions worn in the trendier parts of Tokyo. One block further up the main street, Meiji Dori, is the Ikebukuro branch of **Bic Camera**, an electronics megastore so big it occupies more than one building.

If you think this area is mobbed, just try making your way to the main centre of Ikebukuro – **Sunshine 60 Dori**, the wide tree-lined street that heads due east. The thoroughfare is packed with tiny shops, many selling discount clothing, as well as restaurants and cinemas. The **Sanrio** shop is worth a giggle – two whole floors offering Hello Kitty goods, cooed over by seemingly grown women.

Sunshine 60 Dori is so called because it ultimately leads to the **Sunshine 60 Building**, part of the **Sunshine City** complex. In the building's massive mall are all kinds of fashion shops and restaurants, and within the complex, an observatory, an aquarium, a planetarium, a theme park and the Ancient Orient Museum (among other attractions). To check out other aspects of modern-day Japan, visit the **Amlux Toyota** car showroom and the **Animate** manga emporium just next door.

A few blocks further to the east a more old-fashioned experience awaits, in the form of the **Arakawa Streetcar Line** – one of Tokyo's last two surviving tram lines. Small, one-car trams – *chin-chin densha* ('ding-ding trains') – trundle through picturesque residential areas, sometimes slipping behind rows of houses or joining cars and buses on the streets. Hop aboard for an unhurried look at non-tourist Tokyo – it's possible to stand behind the driver and look over his shoulder for the best view. There's a standard fare of ¥160, and stops along the 12-kilometre (eight-mile) route include **Asukayama Park**

and its three small museums, **Zoshigaya Cemetery** and the nearby **Zoshigaya Missionary Museum**, and Waseda University. The tram connects with the JR lines at Oji and Otsuka stations, while Sunshine City is only a few blocks' walk from Mukohara station.

FURTHER AFIELD
Thanks to its profusion of railway lines, Ikebukuro is a good staging point for excursions

How to play pachinko

Pachinko sets little alarm bells ringing in polite society. Nobody will admit to playing, but the sheer number of parlours proves that plenty of people are. And some people make a good living as a result.

A *pachinko* machine resembles a cross between a pinball and a slot machine, and uses zillions of mini steel balls. Gaudily decorated, ear-splittingly noisy parlours are scattered all over Tokyo, from the bustling shopping areas to the hushed suburbs.

If you stand in Shinjuku's Kabuki-cho, surrounded by palatial parlours blasting a cacophony of bleeps and whirrs, it will be hard to believe that *pachinko* is, technically, illegal. But it is. So there are a few hoops to jump through to circumvent the law. First, you need to buy a prepaid card from a machine near the entrance (so you'll be gambling points rather than money). Slip your card into the slot, push the ball-eject button, turn the handle to flick the balls, and you're rolling.

Now comes the tricky part. The balls have to land in the centre hole to start the numbers on the screen revolving. This is done by inching the handle back and forth to find the optimum setting. Once you're satisfied the balls are going in (aim for at least ten hits every ¥500), wedge a coin into the handle to hold it in place and wait to win. In the meantime, you're free to read a book, call a friend or write a short story. Any sudden ejaculation of steel balls means you're a winner: cash them in or continue playing.

In the unlikely event that your machine pays out, you'll have to carry your little balls to a desk where you can exchange them for a variety of prizes. The least enticing ones may look like taped-up lumps of rock, or fake gold bars. Opt for these 'special prizes' anyway, and take them to a small window somewhere off-premises (look on the counter for a map), where someone will repurchase them for yen.

Winning at *pachinko* is largely a matter of luck, but there are some pointers. First, you don't just plonk yourself at any old machine. No, you reconnoitre, you suss out the parlour; you see who's winning, which machines haven't paid out. Once you've picked, throw a pack of cigarettes into the trough to mark your spot – smoking is compulsory.

Most serious players believe the machines are rigged, sometimes in the player's favour. You'll notice that the people seated by the entrance are on incredible winning streaks. The battle for a door seat explains why you'll see long lines of people waiting up to two hours each morning for the parlours to open.

Sightseeing

to other areas. Two of Tokyo's main amusement parks are accessible from here: **Toshimaen** (*see p91*) and **Tokyo Dome City** (*see p219*). A more peaceful option lies next door to Tokyo Dome: **Koishikawa Korakuen**, the oldest garden in the city, laid out in the 17th century.

Amlux Toyota Auto Salon

3-3-5 Higashi-Ikebukuro, Toshima-ku (5391 5900/ www.amlux.jp/english/floor/f1_f.shtml). Ikebukuro station (Yamanote line), east exit; (Marunouchi, Yurakucho lines), exit 35. **Open** *B1F & 1F* 11am-9pm Tue-Sun. *2F-4F* 11am-7pm Tue-Sun. **Admission** free. **Map** Ikebukuro p87.

Toyota claimed this was the world's biggest car showroom until it opened an even bigger one in Mega Web (*see p100*) in Odaiba. But Amlux still echoes with the sound of slamming doors as scores of petrolheads gleefully hop in and out of the 70 or so vehicles on display – essentially Toyota's entire consumer line. More amazing is that you can test drive any vehicle as long as you have a valid driving licence (Japanese or international). Rates start at the absurdly low price of ¥250 for 30 minutes.

Asukayama Park

1-1-3 Oji, Kita-ku (3916 1133). Asukayama station (Toden Arakawa line) or Oji station (Keihin Tohoku line), south exit; (Namboku line), exit 1. **Open** *Museums* 10am-5pm Tue-Sun. **Admission** *Individual museum* ¥300; ¥100 concessions. *All museums* ¥720; ¥240 concessions. **No credit cards.**

This wooded hilltop park was once the estate of Shibusawa Eiichi (1840-1931), president of Japan's first modern bank. Former US President Ulysses Grant was treated to a ju-jitsu demonstration here in 1879 while staying as Shibusawa's guest. The towering mansion is long gone, but a few outbuildings remain. The park's main attractions are the 'Asukayama Three Museums', which stand in a row at the park's eastern edge.

The Paper Museum (www.papermuseum.jp) displays items related to paper art, papermaking technology and the history of paper, and sometimes holds participatory workshops. The Kita City Asukayama Museum (3916 1133) focuses on local archaeological finds, including a dugout canoe from the Jomon period, Japan's Stone Age. English signage is minimal, but the displays are largely self-explanatory. The Shibusawa Memorial Museum (3910 0005, www.shibusawa.or.jp) praises the achievements of Shibusawa Eiichi. Most of the exhibits are old documents, some in English – including a signed letter from Thomas Edison.

Bosaikan

2-37-8 Nishi-Ikebukuro, Toshima-ku (3590 6565/www.tfd.metro.tokyo.jp/ts/ik/ikeb.htm). Ikebukuro station (Yamanote line), Metropolitan exit; (Marunouchi, Yurakucho lines), exit 3. **Open** 9am-5pm Mon, Wed-Fri. Closed 3rd Wed of mth. **Admission** free.

This earthquake-prone city is long overdue for a devastating trembler, so the Tokyo Fire Department has created this 'life safety learning centre' in its HQ to simulate a real emergency. There's first-aid training and survival tips, but the real fun is the shaking room, the smoke maze and the only chance you'll ever have to play with fire extinguishers without getting reprimanded. The whole thing takes around two hours, and while you can just drop in and take part, it's advisable to reserve a place.

Jiyu Gakuen Myonichikan

2-31-3 Nishi-Ikebukuro, Toshima-ku (3971 7535/www.jiyu.jp/index-e.html). Ikebukuro station (Yamanote line), exit 3. **Open** 10am-4pm Tue-Sun. **Admission** ¥600. **No credit cards. Map** Ikebukuro p87.

Architect Frank Lloyd Wright's Imperial Hotel in Tokyo was famously demolished in 1968, but few people realise that a smaller Wright building – a private school – still stands in Ikebukuro. Now used as an alumni meeting hall rather than for classes, it is open for tours (but it's wise to call ahead first, especially at weekends, when it's regularly booked for weddings). Viewed from the outside, the unusual geometry of the window frames is the clearest indication of Wright's signature.

Koishikawa Korakuen

1-6-6 Koraku, Bunkyo-ku (3811 3015). Iidabashi station (Namboku, Oedo lines), exit C3 or Korakuen station (Marunouchi line), exit 2. **Open** 9am-5pm daily. **Admission** ¥300. **No credit cards.**

Koishikawa Korakuen was first laid out in 1629. It's now only a quarter of its original size, but it's still beautiful, with a range of walks, bridges, hills and vistas (often the miniatures of more famous originals) that encourage quiet contemplation. The entrance, tucked away down a side street, can be a little difficult to find.

Mejiro Teien

3-20-18 Mejiro, Toshima-ku (5996 4810). Ikebukuro station (Yamanote line), south exit; Marunouchi, Yurakucho lines), exit 39 or Mejiro station (Yamanote line). **Open** *Jan-June, Sept-Dec* 9am-5pm daily. *July, Aug* 9am-7pm daily. Closed 2nd & 4th Mon of mth. **Admission** free.

This small garden a short walk from Wright's school building creates the illusion of greater space by way of a deep artificial valley with a pond at the bottom. The gazebo over the pond and a grassy area behind some trees are good spots for a picnic lunch.

Sunshine 60 Building

3-1-1 Higashi-Ikebukuro, Toshima-ku (3989 3331/ www.sunshinecity.co.jp). Ikebukuro station (Yamanote line), east exit; (Marunouchi, Yurakucho lines), exit 35 or Higashi-Ikebukuro station (Yurakucho line), exit 2. **Open** *Observatory* 10am-9pm daily. *Namjatown* 10am-10pm daily. **Admission** *Observatory* ¥620; ¥310 concessions. *Namjatown* ¥300; ¥200 concessions; 1-day passport ¥3,900; ¥3,300 concessions. **No credit cards. Map** Ikebukuro p87.

One of the fastest lifts in the world will whisk you to the observatory on the top floor of this 60-storey

Ikebukuro's **Otome Road** is packed with manga shops.

skyscraper in around 35 seconds. The building's lower floors house the World Import Mart shopping mall and Namjatown, an unbelievably tacky indoor amusement park.

Sunshine City

3-1-3 Higashi-Ikebukuro, Toshima-ku (3989 3466/ www.sunshinecity.co.jp). Ikebukuro station (Yamanote line), east exit; (Marunouchi, Yurakucho lines), exit 35 or Higashi-Ikebukuro station (Yurakucho line), exit 2. **Open** *Aquarium 10am-6pm daily. Planetarium 11am-6pm daily. Ancient Orient Museum 10am-5pm (last entry 4pm) daily.* **Admission** *Aquarium* ¥1,800. *Planetarium* ¥800. *Museum* ¥500. **No credit cards**. **Map** Ikebukuro p87.

Sunshine City occupies the former site of Sugamo Prison, where General Tojo Hideki, Japan's wartime prime minister, was hanged in 1948 (a small monument on the northern corner of the block marks where the gallows stood). As well as the Sunshine 60 Building (*see above*), the complex contains the world's first aquarium in a high-rise building, with more than 20,000 fish and shows by performing seals. There's also a planetarium. The Ancient Orient Museum in the Bunka Kaikan building focuses on western Asia, especially Iran and Pakistan – check out the Parthian-era bull-shaped ceremonial drinking vessel, with nipple-spouts on its chest.

Toshimaen

3-25-1 Koyama, Nerima-ku (3990 8800/www. toshimaen.co.jp/index.html). Toshimaen station (Oedo line), exit A2. **Open** *Mid July-Aug* 10am-8pm daily. *Sept-mid July* 10am-5pm Fri-Sun. *Toshimaen Garden Spa* 10am-11pm daily. **Admission** *Entry only* ¥1,000. *Entry & ride pass* ¥3,800. *Toshimaen Garden Spa* ¥2,000; ¥1,200 after 9pm. **Credit** AmEx, DC, JCB, MC, V.

Every summer this old, uninspiring amusement park turns spectacular with the opening of Hydropolis, a waterpark that includes a surf pool and a very elaborate set of waterslides. A year-round attraction next door is an *onsen* mineral water spa.

Zoshigaya Cemetery

4-25-1 Minami-Ikebukuro, Toshima-ku (3971 6868). Zoshigaya station (Toden Arakawa line). **Open** 24hrs daily. **Admission** free.

This tree-shaded cemetery is the final resting place of such notables as John Manjiro (1827-98), the legendary Edo-era link between East and West, in plot 1-2-10-1, and writer Lafcadio Hearn (1850-1904), who is buried in plot 1-1-8-35 under his Japanese name, Koizumi Yakumo. In plot 1-14-1-3 lies Natsume Soseki (1867-1916), one of Japan's best-loved novelists. Disgraced general Tojo Hideki is in plot 1-1-12-6.

Zoshigaya Missionary Museum

1-25-5 Zoshigaya, Toshima-ku (3985 4081/http:// humsum.cool.ne.jp/cho-41.html). Higashi-Ikebukuro station (Yurakucho line), exit 5 or Zoshigaya station (Toden Arakawa line). **Open** 9am-4.30pm Tue-Sun. Closed 3rd Sun of mth. **Admission** free.

Few homes of early foreign Tokyo residents have escaped the ravages of time. This one, built in 1907, belonged to American missionary JM McCaleb. When it was threatened with demolition a few years ago, residents campaigned to save it. The white clapboard building is strangely displaced, time-warped from old America to the hubbub of modern Tokyo.

Getting there

Ikebukuro station is on the Yamanote line and the Marunouchi and Yurakucho subway lines, as well as the JR Saikyo, Seibu Ikebukuro and Tobu Tojo train lines. The Toden Arakawa tram line does not serve the station directly, but makes stops in eastern Ikebukuro, including Higashi-Ikebukuro Yonchome, outside Higashi-Ikebukuro station on the Yurakucho line.

Marunouchi

Even the financial sector is a shopaholic's paradise.

Map p93

Nothing of what is currently known as Marunouchi really lives up to its name, which means 'within the moat or castle walls'. But the world that was once within the walls was the most influential in Japan. Tokyo has been home to the Japanese royal family since 1868, and the Imperial Palace occupies a chunk of prime real estate in the geographical centre of the city, on part of the former site of Edo Castle, seat of the Tokugawa shogun.

Edo came to life in 1457 as Ota Dokan settled where the palace now stands. Once the shogun decided to rule from here too, his castle became the centre of the city. The Marunouchi area was created as he decreed that all *daimyo* (feudal lords) must live in Edo for half the year. Even today, Marunouchi remains the centre of Tokyo in many senses – political, imperial, economic and geographical.

Although it's increasingly gaining a reputation for shopping and dining, many Marunouchi visitors make a beeline for the **Imperial Palace**. It's directly in front of Tokyo station's central exit, across from Hibiya Dori. The moat, stone walls and outer gardens still divide it from the city, as they did long ago. The palace itself is out of bounds, except on 2 January and 23 December (the emperor's birthday), when the non-imperial masses are graciously allowed into part of the grounds to wave national flags and listen to a brief speech. On the other 363 days, the closest visitors can get is to take photos of the scenic Nijubashi (Double Bridge), with part of the palace buildings in the background. You can also stroll around the landscaped **Imperial Palace East Gardens**, which house a few historical remains and a Japanese-style garden.

At the top end of the gardens, across the main road, is another park, **Kitanomaru Koen**. This slightly unkempt section of the imperial grounds is home to the delights of the **Nippon Budokan** (*see p257 and p272*), **Japan Science Foundation Science Museum** and the **National Museum of Modern Art**. The park's cherry trees make a popular, postcard-perfect sight at blossom time in April.

Marunouchi went through a second heyday in the Meiji era (1868-1912), when it became the economic centre of the country and famous for its buildings. This showcase of foreign architecture was then dubbed 'London Town'. It was not only the pride of the city, but also a sign that Japan had opened up to the world. The main remaining example is **Tokyo station** (**photo** *p92*), built to resemble Amsterdam's Centraal station. This is the traditional starting point for a Marunouchi tour and also contains a small art gallery. Other cultural outposts include the **Idemitsu Museum of Arts**, opposite the bottom corner of the Imperial Palace site;

Where to Stay 55

1 Four Seasons Hotel Tokyo, p44. D4.
2 Hilltop Hotel, p44. D1.
3 Hotel Kazusaya, p45. E2.
4 Hotel Moneterey Hanzomon, p54. A2.
5 Hotel Nihonbashi Saibo, p46. F3.
6 Kayabacho Pearl Hotel, p45. F4.
7 Mandarin Oriental Tokyo, p45. F4.
8 Marunouchi Hotel, p45. D3.
9 Ryokan Ryumeikan Honten, p45. D1.
10 Sakura Hotel, p46. C1.
11 Sumisho Hotel, p45. F3.

Sightseeing

1 Bank of Japan, p96. E3.
2 Bridgestone Museum of Art, p96. E4.
3 Communications Museum, p97. D2.
4 Currency Museum, p97. E3.

5 Idemitsu Museum of Arts, p97. D4.
6 Imperial Palace East Gardens, p97. C3.
7 Japan Science Foundation Science Museum, p97. B2.
8 Kite Museum, p97. F3.
9 National Museum of Modern Art, p98. C2.
10 National Museum of Modern Art, Crafts Gallery, p98. B2.
11 Tokyo Station Gallery, p98. D3.
12 Tokyo Stock Exchange, p98. F3.
13 Transportation Museum, p98. E1.
14 Yasukuni Shrine & Japanese War-Dead Memorial Museum, p98. A1

Restaurants

1 Aroyna Tabeta, p154. D4.
2 Bar de España Muy, p154. D3.
3 Botan, p153. E1.

4 Brasserie aux Amis, p154. D4.
5 Isegen, p153. E1.
6 Izumo Soba Honke, p154. C1.
7 Kanda Yabu Soba, p154. E1.
8 Shisen Hanten, p155. A4.
9 Takara, p154. D4.
10 Tapas Molecular Bar, p155. E2.

Bars

1 Ieyasu Hon-jin, p174. C1.
2 Mandarin Bar, p176. E2.

Coffee Shops

1 Marunouchi Café, p183. D4.
2 Mironga, p184. C1.

Shopping

1 American Pharmacy, p207. D3.
2 Daimaru, p187. E3.
3 Ebisu-Do Gallery, p203. C1.
4 Hara Shobo, p204. C1.
5 Marunouchi Building, p191. D4.

6 Maruzen, p194. D3.
7 Oazo, p191. D3.
8 Pokemon Centre, p209. E4.
9 Takashimaya, p189. E4.
10 Yamamoto Yama, p203. E3.

Film

1 Institut Franco-Japonais, p234. A1.
2 Iwanami Hall, p234. C1.
3 National Film Centre, p236. E4.

Galleries

1 Base Gallery, p239. F3.
2 Zeit-Foto Salon, p240. E4.

Music

1 Casals Hall, p252. D1.
2 Cotton Club, p260. D4.
3 Nippon Budokan, p257. B1.
4 Tokyo TUC, p255. F1.

Performing Arts

1 National Theatre, p265. A3.

Sport & Fitness

1 Chiyoda Kuritsu Sogo Taiikukan Pool, p276. E2.

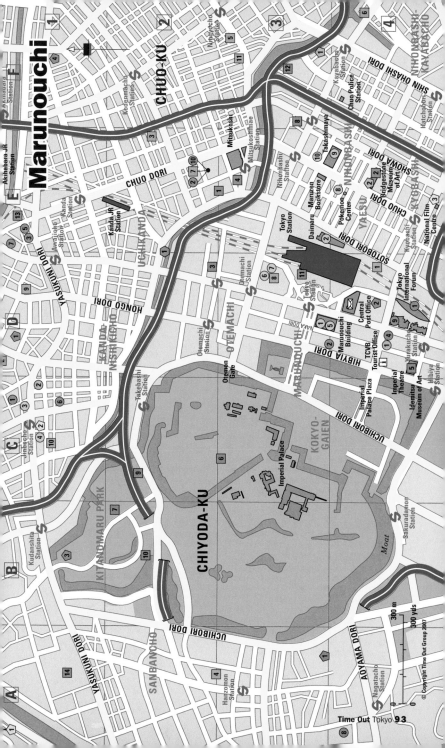

Walk on Old Tokyo

Time: Three to four hours.

Leaving Kudanshita station from exit one, walk up the hill (a prime cherry-blossom area) until you reach the bridge over the moat that is below on your left. From here, either continue up the slope and cross the road for the **Yasukuni Shrine** (and the Yushukan, its controversial museum; *see p98*), or turn left over the bridge, head past the guard and through the impressive Edo-era gates into **Kitanomaru Park**.

The park, once a part of the Imperial Palace, is home to two museums and the **Nippon Budokan** (*see p257 and p272*) – built for the 1964 Olympics and now a multi-use venue that regularly hosts big-name foreign music stars. Kitanomaru Park also contains plenty of picnic spots, and is a popular place for joggers trying to avoid exhaust fumes.

Following the road past the Budokan, you eventually come to the Soviet-style **Japan Science Foundation Science Museum** (*see p97*), just north of which is a bronze statue of post-war prime minister Shigeru Yoshida. The museum itself has an underwhelming concrete exterior, while the lobby could be that of an East German hotel circa 1970. However, inside, there are plenty of interactive treats and displays, perfect for killing an hour or two.

Carrying on down the road takes you over an expressway and to the perimeter of the Imperial Palace. On your left is the **National Museum of Modern Art** (*see p98*). On your right, you should be able to spot the red-brick **Crafts Gallery**, which has revolving exhibits of Japanese and foreign handicrafts.

To continue into the **Imperial Palace East Gardens** (*see p97*), use the footbridge to cross the road and walk straight up through the Kita-Hanebashimon gate. Past the policeman, just inside the gate, is a booth, at which you will be given a returnable coupon.

The gardens are large and well designed for meandering. In addition to a large number of stone bases that used to support *donjons* (towers), the gardens also house the **Museum of Imperial Collections**, a small concert hall and hundreds of trees that are at their most picturesque in autumn.

Leaving the gardens via the Otemon gate brings you right back to the present. The skyscrapers of the Otemachi and Marunouchi business districts looming large. The

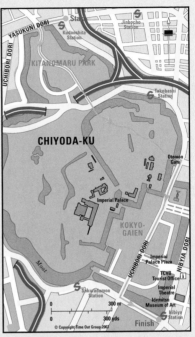

Exchange (open 8am-9pm Mon-Fri), across Uchibori Dori on the ground floor of the **Palace Hotel** (1-1-1, Chiyoda-ku, 3211 5211, www.palacehotelstokyo.com), does passable sandwiches for those in need of sustenance. Otherwise, turn right and walk along the front of the palace until you hit its Outer Gardens. Here, the combination of enthusiastically trimmed pine trees and a vast, empty plaza looks a cross between London's Horseguard's Parade and a giant bonsai collection.

Continuing south along Uchibori Dori across the plaza, the Imperial Palace moat finally turns right, at which point you can cross into **Hibiya Park**. Entering the park through the north entrance, you should see on your left an outdoor café, which among other things serves decent fish 'n' chips at prices comparable to Tokyo's British pubs. But from here it's only a hop, a step and a jump through the garden's main east exit towards Yurakucho and Ginza for countless other drinking, eating and entertainment options.

Oazo.

the **Bridgestone Museum of Art**, east of Tokyo station; and also the **Communications Museum**, just to the north of the station.

In a similar vein to Wall Street or the City of London, Tokyo's central business district has traditionally been a sedate area, especially at weekends, but the last few years have seen a major transformation. With heavyweight financing provided by Mitsubishi Real Estate, Marunouchi has been reinvented as a consumer hotspot. The focal point of the area's renewal is the 36-storey **Marunouchi Building** (*see p191*). Known locally as the 'Marubiru', it's an impeccably clean and modern-looking shopping, restaurant and office complex. It was the first construction that was ever allowed to overlook the grounds of the Imperial Palace, an indication that commercialism trumps tradition in 21st-century Japan. The restaurants on the top two floors offer superlative views.

Marubiru's newest neighbour is the aptly named and Sir Michael Hopkins-designed **Shin Marunouchi Building** (New Marunouchi Building) – set to open as this guide goes to press – situated directly across the street from the similarly monikered original. The building's motto is 'all in one for the office worker', and

the format follows the Marunouchi Building closely: shopping on the first five floors, dining on the next two and many more levels of offices on top.

Nearby, yet another new shopping, dining and office centre, **Oazo** (*see p191*), offers more of the same, but is notable for book retailer Maruzen's vast flagship store, as well as the smart **Marunouchi Hotel** (*see p45*).

The most dramatic transformation of all has occurred on **Naka Dori** (Centre Street), which runs from the Marunouchi Building to Yurakucho station. Once a quiet street of office buildings, it has been repaved, lined with trees and now has the exclusive feel of a Bond Street or Fifth Avenue. Baccarat, Hermès and Emporio Armani are just some of the high-end retailers to have opened here. The street also boasts a listed building, **Meiji Seimeikan**, although you might have trouble spotting it now that it's been cocooned within **My Plaza**, yet another high-end shopping/dining/office complex.

For fans of modern architecture, one of the most striking constructions is the **Tokyo International Forum** (*see p252*), close to Yurakucho station. It is divided into two buildings, the most eye-catching being the ship-shaped Glass Hall Building, designed by Rafael

Lost in the shadow of an elevated highway is the **Nihonbashi bridge**.

Vinoly, which has a glass roof and 60-metre (197-foot) glass wall. The adjacent building is far less impressive but hides an interior bustling with people attending conventions and other social events. The three main halls are increasingly used for concerts, film premières and festivals.

To the east – go under the train tracks – is Pacific Century Place, opened in 2001, which contains Tokyo's second **Four Seasons** hotel (*see p44*) and plenty of restaurants and coffee bars. From here it's easy walking distance to Kyobashi and Nihonbashi, two areas that give a taste of the way Tokyo was before the swanky new consumer complexes hit town.

Nihonbashi has an important place in the history of Tokyo, as depicted by several *ukiyo-e* artists of the 19th century. There's not much left now, though. The renowned Nihonbashi bridge (a wooden structure from which all distances to and from Tokyo used to be calculated) was rebuilt in stone in the Meiji era and now lies in the shadow of an elevated highway, retaining none of the character it once had. For sightseers, there's the **Tokyo Stock Exchange**, **Kite Museum**, the **Bank of Japan** and its adjacent **Currency Museum**.

FURTHER AFIELD

Within easy reach of Marunouchi are a couple of worthwhile sights. In **Akihabara** – devoted to electronic goods (*see p195*) and geek culture (*see pp30-3*) – lies the **Transportation Museum**.

Its three floors of air, sea and land vehicles include Emperor Meiji's imperial carriage and Japan's first locomotive. Two stops from Tokyo station on the Chuo line is **Ochanomizu**, an area famous for sports shops and universities, which also boasts **Nikolai Cathedral** (4-1 Kanda-Surugadai, Chiyoda-ku, 3291 1885, open to visitors 1-3.30pm Tue-Fri, Japanese service 10am Sun). This cruciform Russian Orthodox church, complete with an onion dome, was designed by British architect Josiah Conder and completed in 1891. The original, larger dome was destroyed in the 1923 Great Kanto Earthquake. The cathedral occupies the site of a former Edo-era watchtower and offers visitors a commanding view of the area.

Bank of Japan

2-1-1 Nihonbashi-Hongokucho, Chuo-ku (English tours 3279 1111/www.boj.or.jp). Mitsukoshimae station (Ginza, Hanzomon lines), exits A8, B1. **Tours** (1hr; book 1wk ahead) 9.45am, 11am, 1.30pm, 3pm Mon-Fri. **Admission** free. **Map** Marunouchi p93.
The Bank of Japan has two buildings, descriptively named Old and New. The New Building is where all the banking activities occur, and the Old Building… well, it just looks nice. The first Western-style construction by Japanese builders, the Old Building is said to be modelled on London's Bank of England.

Bridgestone Museum of Art

1-10-1 Kyobashi, Chuo-ku (3563 0241/www. bridgestone-museum.gr.jp). Tokyo station (Yamanote, Chuo, Marunouchi, Sobu lines), Yaesu (central) exit.

Open 10am-8pm Tue-Sat; 10am-6pm Sun.
Admission ¥800; ¥500-¥600 concessions;
free under-12s. **Credit** AmEx, JCB, MC, V.
Map Marunouchi p93.
Ishibashi Shojiro, founder of the giant Bridgestone
Corporation, wheeled his private collection into this
museum back in 1952. Impressionism, European
modernism and Japanese Western-style paintings
form the core holdings, but exhibitions can cover
genres ranging from Ancient Greek to 20th-century
abstraction. For a taste of what's inside, stroll past
the artworks displayed in the street-level front
windows. There's a tearoom on the first floor.

Communications Museum

*2-3-1 Otemachi, Chiyoda-ku (3244 6811). Otemachi
station (Chiyoda, Hanzomon, Marunouchi, Mita,
Tozai lines), exit A5.* **Open** 9am-4.30pm Tue-Sun.
Admission ¥110; ¥50 concessions. **Credit**
(shop, over ¥3,000 only) AmEx, JCB, MC, V.
Map Marunouchi p93.
This massive museum relays the stories and tech-
nological histories of national public broadcasting
company NHK, telecoms giant NTT and the now-
defunct Post & Telecommunications Ministry.
Philatelists can peruse 280,000 old and new stamps
from everywhere from Afghanistan to Zimbabwe
(including an 1840 English penny black). Kids can
race post-office motorbikes in a video game, compare international postboxes and ogle a room-sized
mail sorter. On the telecommunications floor,
ample interactive displays teach how the telephone
works. A full range of historic public payphones –
from pink to yellow to green – is sealed behind
glass. The gift shop sells vintage postcards and
collectable stamps.

Currency Museum

*1-3-1 Nihonbashi-Hongokucho, Chuo-ku (3277 3037/
www.imes.boj.or.jp/cm/english_htmls/index.htm).
Mitsukoshimae station (Ginza, Hanzomon lines),
exits A5, B1.* **Open** 9.30am-4.30pm Tue-Sun.
Closed 5, 6 Mar. **Tours** (1hr) 1.30pm Tue, Thur.
Admission free. **Map** Marunouchi p93.
Run by the Bank of Japan, this museum traces the
long history of money in the country, from the use
of imported Chinese coins in the late Heian period
(12th century) to the creation of the yen and the central bank in the second half of the 19th century. See
beautiful, Edo-era, calligraphy-inscribed gold
oblongs, occupation-era notes from Indonesia and
the Philippines, Siberian leather money and Thai
leech coins. Or get the feel for some serious dosh by
lifting ¥100 million (about the size of two phone
books), safely stored inside a perspex box.

Idemitsu Museum of Arts

*Tei Geki Bldg 9F, 3-1-1 Marunouchi, Chiyoda-ku
(3213 9404/www.idemitsu.co.jp/museum). Hibiya
station (Chiyoda, Hibiya, Mita lines), exit B3.*
Open 10am-5pm Thur, Sat, Sun; 10am-7pm
Fri. **Admission** ¥800; free-¥500 concessions;
free under-15s. **Credit** (shop only) MC, V.
Map Marunouchi p93.

Idemitsu Sazo, founder of Idemitsu Kosan Co, collected traditional Chinese and Japanese art for more
than 70 years. This museum (opened in 1966) features
displays drawn from a respected permanent collection
of ceramics, calligraphy and painting (for example,
Rimpa-style irises painted by Sakai Hoitsu on a six-
fold screen). There's a good view of the Imperial Palace.

Imperial Palace East Gardens (Kokyo Higashi Gyoen)

*Chiyoda, Chiyoda-ku. Otemachi station (Chiyoda,
Hanzomon, Marunouchi, Mita, Tozai lines), exits
C10, C13B.* **Open** 9am-4.30pm daily. **Admission**
free; token collected at gate to be submitted on
leaving. **Map** Marunouchi p93.
This is the main park of the Imperial Palace, accessible through three old gates: Otemon (five minutes
from Tokyo station), Hirakawamon (close to
Takebashi bridge) and Kita-Hanebashimon (near
Kitanomaru Park).There are few historical features
in the manicured park, except for two old watch-
houses, the remains of the old dungeon at the northern
end (near Kita-Hanebashimon) and, at the exit into
the next area, a wall of hand-carved stones dropping
a great height into the water. There's also the small
Museum of Imperial Collections.

Japan Science Foundation Science Museum (Kagaku Gijutsukan)

*2-1 Kitanomaru Koen, Chiyoda-ku (3212 8544/
www.jsf.or.jp). Kudanshita station (Hanzomon,
Shinjuku, Tozai lines), exit 2 or Takebashi station
(Tozai line), exit 1A.* **Open** 9.30am-4.50pm daily.
Admission ¥600; ¥250-¥400 concessions.
No credit cards. Map Marunouchi p93.
This museum takes to extremes the maxim 'learning by doing'. The unique five-spoke building, in a
corner of Kitanomaru Park, consists of five floors of
interactive exhibits. Its drab, dated entrance belies
the fun displays inside. Children can learn the rudi-
ments of scientific principles while standing inside
a huge soap bubble, lifting a small car using pulleys
and generating electricity by shouting. There's not
a lot of English used, but much of the interaction
does not need translation.

Kite Museum

*Taimeiken 5F, 1-12-10 Nihonbashi, Chuo-ku (3275
2704/www.tako.gr.jp). Nihonbashi station (Asakusa,
Ginza, Tozai lines), exit A4, C5.* **Open** 11am-5pm
Mon-Sat. **Admission** ¥200; ¥100 concessions.
No credit cards. Map Marunouchi p93.
This uplifting museum is a cornucopia of kites,
including Indonesian dried leaves, giant woodblock-
print samurai and a huge styrofoam iron. The former
owner of the first-floor restaurant (one of Tokyo's earliest forays into Western-style dining) spent a lifetime
collecting the 2,000 kites now layering the walls, pack-
ing display cases and crowding the ceiling. Don't
expect detailed explanations of the exhibits; this is
more of a private hobby on public display – as often
happens in Tokyo. The museum is not clearly marked
– look for the long white sign on the building.

Sightseeing

National Museum of Modern Art

3-1 Kitanomaru Koen, Chiyoda-ku (5777 8600/ www.momat.go.jp/english/index.html). Takebashi station (Tozai line), exits 1A, 1B. **Open** *Art Museum* 10am-5pm Tue-Thur, Sat, Sun; 10am-8pm Fri. *Crafts Gallery* 10am-5pm Tue-Sun. **Admission** ¥420; ¥70-¥130 concessions; free seniors, under-16s; additional charge for special exhibitions. Free 3 Nov, 1st Sun of mth. **Credit** (shop only) AmEx, JCB, MC, V. **Map** Marunouchi p93.

This is an alternative-history MoMA, one consisting mostly of Japanese art from the turn of the 20th century onwards. Noteworthy features of the permanent collection are portraits by early Japanese modernist Kishida Ryusei and grim wartime paintings by Fujita Tsuguharu. The 1969 building, designed by Taniguchi Yoshiro (father of architect Taniguchi Yoshio) was renovated to the tune of ¥7.8 billion in 2001. Its location next to the moat and walls of the Imperial Palace makes it a prime stop for viewing springtime cherry blossoms and autumn foliage. Nearby is the Crafts Gallery, an impressive 1910 European-style brick building, once the base for the legions of guards who patrolled the Imperial Palace.

Tokyo Station Gallery

Inside Tokyo station, 1-9-1 Marunouchi, Chiyoda-ku (3212 2485/www.ejrcf.or.jp). Tokyo station (Yamanote, Chuo, Marunouchi, Sobu lines). **Open** 10am-7pm Tue-Fri; 10am-6pm Sat, Sun. **Admission** ¥600; |¥400 concessions; free children Sat. **No credit cards**. **Map** Marunouchi p93.

Your JR train ticket helps to support this small museum, run by East Japan Railways and located inside sprawling Tokyo station, near the Marunouchi central entrance. Though the station's aged brick walls may not be the best backdrop for paintings, they do offer a look into the past. The museum has no permanent holdings, but brings in shows from around Japan and the rest of the world.

Tokyo Stock Exchange (Tokyo Shoken Torihiki Sho)

2-1 Nihonbashi-Kabutocho, Chuo-ku (3665 1881/ www.tse.or.jp). Kayabacho station (Hibiya, Tozai lines), exit 11. **Open** 9am-4.30pm Mon-Fri. **Tour** (English) 1.30pm daily. **Admission** free. **Map** Marunouchi p93.

Sadly, you won't be able to witness much wailing and gnashing of teeth here, since the TSE, home to global giants such as Toyota and Sony, abolished its trading floor in 1999. The stock market of the world's second-largest economy is now run almost entirely by sophisticated computers, which means the building is eerily quiet, the former trading floor taken over by a huge glass cylinder with the names and real-time stock prices of listed companies revolving at the top. If you want to catch what little action is left, visit on a weekday during trading hours (9-11am, 12.30-3pm). The guided tour lasts approximately 40 minutes and includes a 20-minute video explaining the history and function of the TSE. On the way out, don't forget to invest in a souvenir T-shirt, mug or some golf balls.

Transportation Museum (Kotsu Hakubutsukan)

1-25 Kanda-Sudacho, Chiyoda-ku (3251 8481/ www.kouhaku.or.jp). Akihabara station (Yamanote, Hibiya lines), Electric Town exit. **Open** 9.30am-5pm Tue-Sun. **Admission** ¥310; ¥150 concessions. **No credit cards**. **Map** Marunouchi p93.

From rickshaws to rockets, this large museum is a compendium of land, sea, air and space transport. It began life as a railway museum in 1921, and the exhaustive and exhausting train section is where you'll still find the kids. See how Tokyo's JR lines start their day in a massive model railway set-up. Virtually drive a Yamanote-line train through Tokyo in a real conductor car, or change antique switching lights from red to green. The museum has the first train used in Japan – an 1872 steam locomotive made in England that travelled between Shinbashi and Yokohama – and the latest, an experimental mag-lev system. The gift shop is stocked with every conceivable Japanese model train, unique transportation paraphernalia and unusual souvenirs.

Yasukuni Shrine & Yushukan War-Dead Memorial Museum

3-1-1 Kudankita, Chiyoda-ku (3261 8326/www. yasukuni.or.jp). Kudanshita station (Hanzomon, Shinjuku, Tozai lines), exits 1, 3 or Ichigaya station (Chuo, Nanboku, Shinjuku, Sobu, Yurakucho lines), exits A3, A4. **Open** *Grounds* 6am-5pm daily. *Museum* 9am-5pm daily. **Admission** *Shrine* free. *Museum* ¥800; ¥300-¥500 concessions. **No credit cards**. **Map** Marunouchi p93.

Yasukuni is one of Tokyo's grandest shrines, conceived by Emperor Meiji to commemorate those who died defending him against the shogun. It is also the nation's most controversial landmark. It houses the souls of almost 2.5 million war dead, but 14 in particular have brought the shrine notoriety. World War II leaders such as Matsui Iwane, the general who ordered the destruction of Nanking, are enshrined here, with the reasoning that their Class A war criminal status is a Western construct and irrelevant to the Shinto religion. The neighbouring Yushukan war museum stokes the flames with an intriguing take on historic events, arguing, for example, that the Russo-Japanese War (1904-5) inspired Mahatma Gandhi, and suggesting that the Pearl Harbor attack saved the US economy. Former PM Koizumi Junichiro became the first premier to make annual visits to the shrine, delighting his nationalist supporters but provoking anger from Japan's neighbours and wartime victims. All eyes are now on his successor, Abe Shinzo, a noted nationalist who made several low-key visits to the shrine before assuming the top spot.

Getting there

Tokyo station is the terminus of the JR Chuo line and is on the JR Yamanote and Keihin Tohoku lines, as well as the Marunouchi subway line. It is also the main terminus for *shinkansen* bullet trains. Other subways stations dot the area too.

Odaiba

Oh, they do like to play beside the seaside.

Map p101

You'll either love or hate Odaiba. Its wide avenues give a spacious feel, and with entertainment galore and the water of Tokyo Bay just a couple of streets away, it's a much-loved dating spot for young Tokyoites. But this pristine playground will disappoint anyone looking for traditional Tokyo. The area started out as a Bubble-era project to develop Tokyo Bay on reclaimed land, with the name being taken from the cannons placed offshore by the Tokugawa shogunate in the late Edo period to protect Japan from invasion. Over the past decade it's turned into something of a community apart from the rest of Tokyo, at its busiest on summer weekends.

A trip to Odaiba begins by taking the elevated, driverless Yurikamome monorail from Shinbashi or Shiodome stations and watching the view unfold. The gateway to Odaiba is **Rainbow Bridge**, named after the illuminations that light it up after dark. It's become one of the most impressive additions to Tokyo's skyline, along with the ever-changing psychedelic patterns of the enormous Ferris wheel in the distance behind it. If you want to take things slower, you can also walk across the bridge in about 30 minutes.

Coming over the bridge, the first sight that hits you is the extravagant 25-storey structure

Statue of Liberty.

of the **Fuji TV** headquarters (*see p100*), designed by acclaimed Japanese architect Tange Kenzo and crowned by a 1,200-tonne glittering metal sphere. Inside the sphere is an observation deck that, on clear days, gives breathtaking views.

Get off at Odaiba Kaihin-Koen station if you want to visit the Fuji TV building, or to explore the nearby shopping and entertainment centre of **Decks** (www.odaiba-decks.com). Inside this nautical-themed centre, you'll find the Island and Seaside Malls, the Joypolis Game Centre and several restaurants. The Decks Tokyo Brewery, on the fifth floor, is notable for the Daiba brand micro-beer brewed on site.

Follow the signs to 'Daiba-Itchome Shotengai', on the fourth floor, and you'll find one of Odaiba's most intriguing attractions: a loving re-creation of 1960s Japan. Wander down dark and twisty corridors, and visit shops covered in old movie posters and selling food and toys from the post-war days. On the floor above is Little Hong Kong, a cluster of Chinese restaurants surrounded by mock-ups of 1940s railway stations.

Next to Decks is another mall, **Aqua City** (www.aquacity.co.jp). Here you'll find yet more shops, cafés and restaurants and the 13-screen Mediage cinema. In front of Aqua City, next to the water, is – oddly enough – a small-scale replica of the **Statue of Liberty**, built in France and erected in 2000.

From here you can walk (or jump back on the monorail to Aomi station) to **Palette Town**, home of the **Mega Web** amusement park (*see p100*), and the huge Stream of Starlight Ferris wheel. If you're thinking of taking a ride, however, be prepared for a wait – the queues can be huge. This area is also home to **Venus Fort** (*see p192*) – an unusual shopping mall aimed at women, with an Italianate interior and a fake sky that changes according to the time of day – and rock venue **Zepp Tokyo** (*see p259*).

There are also several museums worth seeing in Odaiba. The **Museum of Maritime Science**, **National Museum of Emerging Science & Innovation** and **Tokyo Metropolitan Waterworks Science Museum** (for all, *see p100*) all have plenty on offer.

Beyond the science museum stands the imposing blue-glass arch of the **Telecom Center**, a major satellite and telecommunications hub with an observation deck (2-38 Aomi, Koto-ku,

The accurately named **Tokyo Big Sight**.

11.30am-9.30pm daily, admission ¥600). And next to this lies the **Oedo Onsen Monogatari**, a hot-spring theme park with customers in *yukata* (dressing gowns) strolling around.

Odaiba is also home to **Tokyo Big Sight**, Japan's largest exhibition and convention centre. There's a scattering of parks; the most pleasant is **Odaiba Seaside Park** in front of Decks and Aqua City, which includes a man-made sand beach. This is also where the Suijo Bus boats stop (*see p59*).

Fuji TV Building
2-4-8 Daiba, Minato-ku (5500 8888/www.fujitv. co.jp). Odaiba Kaihin-Koen station (Yurikamome line). **Open** 10am-8pm Tue-Sun. **Admission** *Studios & observation deck* ¥500. **Credit** (gift shop only) AmEx, DC, JCB, MC, V. **Map** Odaiba p101.
The headquarters of the Fuji TV corporation, one of Japan's nationwide commercial channels, has exhibitions (mostly in Japanese with occasional English subtitles) on popular programmes and guided tours around studios in use. Entrance is free, but you have to pay to get into the studios and observation deck.

Mega Web
1 Aomi, Koto-ku (3599 0808/test drive reservations 0070 800 489 000/www.megaweb.gr.jp/english/index.html). Aomi station (Yurikamome line) or Tokyo Teleport station (Rinkai line). **Open** *Toyota City Showcase* 11am-9pm daily. *History Garage* 11am-9pm Mon-Fri, Sun; 11am-10pm Sat. **Admission** free. **Map** Odaiba p101.
Part of the huge Palette Town development that opened in 1999, Mega Web certainly lives up to its name. Its giant Ferris wheel – at 115m (383ft) one of the tallest in the world – is visible for miles, and lit with amazing kaleidoscopic patterns at night. Beneath it is the world's largest car showroom, the

Toyota City Showcase. Here you can sit in the newest models, take a test drive (¥300) on the two-lap track (Japanese or international driver's licence required) or be ferried around in the company's self-driving electric town-car prototypes (¥200). Expect a queue for tickets, especially at weekends.

Museum of Maritime Science (Funeno Kagakukan)
3-1 Higashi-Yashio (Odaiba), Shinagawa-ku (5500 1111/www.funenokagakukan.or.jp). Funeno-Kagakukan station (Yurikamome line). **Open** 10am-5pm daily. **Admission** ¥700; ¥400 concessions. **Credit** (restaurant only) V. **Map** Odaiba p101.
Attractions include displays on marine exploration and replicas of ancient Japanese ships.

National Museum of Emerging Science & Innovation (Nihon Kagaku Miraikan)
2-41 Aomi (Odaiba), Koto-ku (3570 9151/www. miraikan.jst.go.jp). Funeno-Kagakukan station or Telecom Center station (Yurikamome line). **Open** 10am-5pm Mon, Wed-Sun. **Admission** ¥500; ¥200 concessions; free under-6s. **No credit cards.** **Map** Odaiba p101.
Upon entering, the visitor beholds a globe 6.5m (22ft) in diameter above the lobby, with 851,000 LEDs on its surface showing real-time global climatic changes. The museum holds interactive displays on robots, genetic discoveries and space travel and, perhaps most bizarre of all, a model using springs and ball bearings to explain the operating principle of the internet. There are ample explanations in English, and a good gift shop.

Oedo Onsen Monogatari
2-57 Omi, Koto-ku (5500 1126/www.ooedoonsen.jp). Telecom Center station (Yurikamome line). **Open** 11am-9am daily (last entry 2am). **Admission** *11am-6pm* ¥2,800; *after 6pm* ¥1,900; *extra charge after 2am* ¥1,500. **Map** Odaiba p101.
This hot-spring theme park does a pretty good job of recreating an Edo-period bathhouse, with numerous bathing areas, indoor and out, plus hot-sand baths and saunas. The admission fee includes *yukata* and towels.

Tokyo Metropolitan Waterworks Science Museum
2-4-1 Ariake, Koto-ku (3528 2366/www. waterworks.metro.tokyo.jp/pp/kagakukan/kagaku. htm). Kokusai Tenjijo-Seimon station (Yurikamome line). **Open** 9.30am-5pm Tue-Sun. **Admission** free. **Map** Odaiba p101.
This museum channels a fundamental ingredient of life, water, into exciting displays and interactive games. Take a virtual ride down a river or chill out watching big bubbles pass through huge tubes.

Getting there

Odaiba is on the Yurikamome monorail line (a one-day travel pass costs ¥800) and the Rinkai line. You can also get there by water bus (*see p59*).

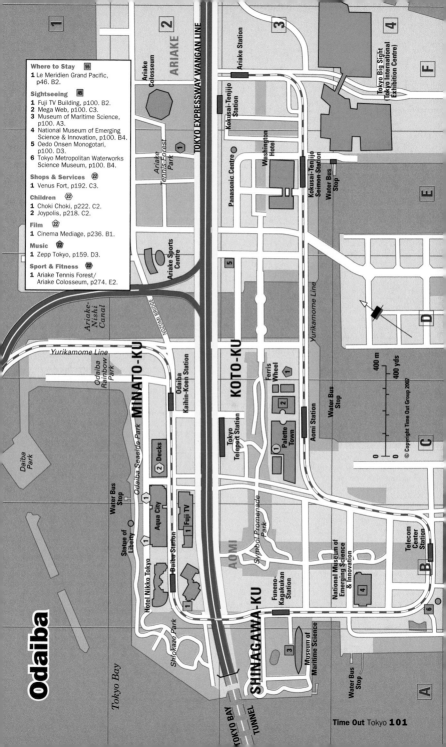

Odaiba

Where to Stay 55
1 Le Meridien Grand Pacific, p46. B2.

Sightseeing 45
1 Fuji TV Building, p100. B2.
2 Mega Web, p100. C3.
3 Museum of Maritime Science, p100. A3.
4 National Museum of Emerging Science & Innovation, p100. B4.
5 Oedo Onsen Monogatari, p100. D3.
6 Tokyo Metropolitan Waterworks Science Museum, p100. B4.

Shops & Services 22
1 Venus Fort, p192. C3.

Children 22
1 Choki Choki, p222. C2.
2 Joypolis, p218. C2.

Film 22
1 Cinema Mediage, p236. B1.

Music 22
1 Zepp Tokyo, p159. D3.

Sport & Fitness 22
1 Ariake Tennis Forest/ Ariake Colosseum, p274. E2.

ARIAKE

Ariake Colosseum

Ariake Tennis Forest Park

TOKYO EXPRESSWAY WANGAN LINE

Ariake Station

Kokusai-Tenjio Station

Tokyo Big Sight Tokyo International Exhibition Centre

Panasonic Centre

Washington Hotel

Kokusai-Tenjio Seimon Station

Water Bus Stop

Ariake Sports Centre

Ariake-Nishi Canal

NOZOMI BRIDGE

Yurikamome Line

Odaiba Rainbow Park

MINATO-KU

Yurikamome Line

KOTO-KU

Ferris Wheel

Odaiba Kaihin-Koen Station

Palette Town

Aomi Station

Water Bus Stop

400 m
400 yds
© Copyright Time Out Group 2007

Daiba Park

Water Bus Stop

Odaiba Seaside Park

2 Decks

Tokyo Teleport Station

Symbol Promenade Park

Telecom Center Station

Statue of Liberty

Aqua City

Fuji TV

Daiba Station

Hotel Nikko Tokyo

AOMI

Funeno-Kagakukan Station

National Museum of Emerging Science & Innovation

Tokyo Bay

Shiokaze Park

SHINAGAWA-KU

Museum of Maritime Science

TOKYO BAY TUNNEL

Water Bus Stop

Time Out Tokyo **101**

Roppongi

Moving on up – Tokyo's sleaziest area gets another facelift.

Map p103

This is the traditional heart of Tokyo's hedonism. With over half a century of building a reputation as the place to go for sleazy revelry, deafening music and drink-till-you-hurl tomfoolery, Roppongi is the place you don't let your daughter anywhere near.

As a result, Tokyo's leading property magnate Mori Minoru raised a few eyebrows when, in 1995, he announced plans to build a huge, multibillion-yen, upmarket urban development right next to the bedlam. **Roppongi Hills** opened to great fanfare in April 2003, and its popularity has yet to wane. Official figures claim 100,000 visitors each weekday, rising to 300,000 each weekend. The complex is designed as a 'city within a city', housing more than 200 cafés, restaurants and shops, hundreds of Conran-designed serviced apartments, a major art museum, the nine-screen **Virgin Toho Cinemas** (see p236), the Ashahi TV studio, several parks and the sumptuous **Grand Hyatt Tokyo** (see p51). With an emphasis on the luxury side of life, Roppongi Hills has only one thing in common with the Old Roppongi – the distinctly foreign feel; anyone looking for traditional Japan won't find it here.

Reaching Roppongi Hills is easy – the Hibiya and Oedo subway lines are on its doorstep – but navigating the complex is close to impossible, even with the official map. The layout swirls with corridors, escalators and floor plans so complex that you could almost believe the

architects (who also designed Las Vegas's Bellagio casino-hotel) were instructed to disorientate visitors. In the middle is Mori's eponymous 54-storey tower – the top supposedly modelled on a samurai helmet – home to the world-class **Mori Art Museum** and an observation deck, **Tokyo City View** (both on the 52nd floor; see p105), and a wallet-busting private members' club. Louise Bourgeois's huge spider sculpture, *Maman*, crouches benignly in front of the tower. For more details of what the complex contains, visit www.roppongihills.com.

The arrival of Mori's mini city drove the area's image dramatically upmarket, and its success hasn't gone unnoticed. In March 2007 a rival complex opened on the doorstep of Roppongi Hills. **Tokyo Midtown** (see p107) faithfully replicates Mori's vision, incorporating a landmark tower, a luxury hotel and an art centre, while eschewing the navigational nightmare. Midtown looks set to tip the area's balance towards New Roppongi and its well-heeled patrons.

But for now, just blocks from the high-end consumption, carnal pleasures continue unabated. To experience the flesh fest, head to the main crossing near Roppongi station. Take exit 3 from the station, head right along Roppongi Dori, and you'll see a crowd milling in front of the **Almond** pastry shop (see p184), immediately recognisable by its pink-and-white striped awnings. This is a conventional meeting spot, where you'll encounter the first of many strip-club or karaoke touts.

Roppongi

© Copyright Time Out Group 2007

Gaien-Higashi Dori. *See p105.*

The road immediately next to Almond is a neglected street of crumbling buildings and the occasional restaurant, which leads down to the Roppongi Hills complex. But take the main street just beside it – with the illuminated spire of **Tokyo Tower** gleaming in the distance – and you're in the heart of the action. Street vendors, more strip-show touts and gaudy bar signs provide the ambience. At the weekend each of the bars and clubs will be rammed with party people in various states of intoxication. The best known, and rowdiest, of the bars is **Gas Panic** (see p177), a legendary meat market that likes its music loud and its customers drunk. But explore the side streets off this main strip, and you'll find many similar establishments (see pp171-81 for more bars in the area). Bigger, marginally more sophisticated nightclubs include **Alife** (see p226) and **Vanilla** (see p227), but there are plenty of other options (see pp225-7).

Even if a night of debauchery doesn't appeal, Roppongi has plenty to offer on a culinary level. The area is short on Michelin stars, but the international crowds bring their international palates, and Roppongi boasts a greater variety of food than any other part of the city (see pp155-160 for recommended restaurants).

Roppongi today betrays little of its roots. Until the 17th century, the area was no more than a thoroughfare for Shibuya's residents, but things changed in 1626, when shogun Hidetaka chose Roppongi for his wife's burial ground. The four Buddhist priests who oversaw her funeral were each handed generous rewards by the grateful leader. All four spent their riches building new temples in the area, giving Roppongi its first image – as a centre of spirituality.

In the mid-18th century the area's official population was 454. It wasn't until the late 19th century that modern Roppongi began to take shape. The government decided to relocate a division of the Imperial Guard to the area, thus heralding the start of a long military association. Following World War II, the US occupiers also picked Roppongi as a base, and it developed to serve the various visceral needs of military men.

Sights are few and far between, though contemporary art lovers will enjoy **Complex**, an old building on the slope leading to Roppongi Hills that contains a cluster of diminutive galleries, including **Ota Fine Arts** (see p240). Further afield are a couple of small private art museums, both housed in upmarket hotels – the **New Otani Museum** near Akasaka-Mitsuke station, and the **Okura Shukokan Museum of Fine Art** near Roppongi-Itchome station.

South-east from the Roppongi intersection lies **Tokyo Tower**; it may have been trumped by taller buildings with better views, but it's still an iconic structure. The best spot for souvenir photos is adjoining **Shiba Koen**, with the tower and **Zojo-ji Temple** next door framed in a classic Tokyo shot. In the summer several pools in the park are open to the public and there are playgrounds and other attractions within walking distance. North of the tower is the **NHK Broadcast Museum**, which tunes you into the history of radio and TV in Japan.

In the other direction from the Roppongi crossing, up **Gaien-Higashi Dori** (photo p104), lies **Nogi Jinja**, dedicated to the memory of General Nogi Maresuke and an example of the key role that ritual suicide played in Japan's past.

NISHI-AZABU, AZABU-JUBAN AND HIROO

Before Roppongi Hills came along, **Nishi-Azabu** was the chalk to Roppongi's cheese. Loaded with stylish bars, restaurants and clubs, it pulls a sophisticated crowd. Like Roppongi, Nishi-Azabu lights up at sundown; unlike Roppongi, there's always an atmosphere of calm about the place. It's the perfect location for dates or entertaining clients. Nishi-Azabu has no station, so access is via Roppongi station. Take exit 1 and walk down Roppongi Dori towards Shibuya. When you reach a crossroads with Hobson's ice-cream shop opposite you, that's the heart of Nishi-Azabu.

Further east is **Azabu-Juban**, another district rich in restaurants, though with a more traditional feel. This Azabu has a station on the Nanboku and Oedo subway lines, and it comes alive each August for the Azabu-Juban Noryo Festival (see p214), featuring *taiko* drumming and traditional dancing. It's also home to an *onsen* (see p64 **Old soaks**) and a large import food store, **Nissin** (see p203). Also in the area, although not within walking distance, is **Hiroo**, an expat haven thanks to the numerous embassies nearby. Its shops, cafés and restaurants betray strong Western influences, and most employ English-speaking staff.

Mori Art Museum & Tokyo City View

Mori Tower 52F-53F, 6-10-1 Roppongi, Minato-ku (6406 6100/www.mori.art.museum/html/eng/index. html). Roppongi station (Hibiya, Oedo lines), exit 1. **Open** 10am-10pm Mon, Wed, Thur; 10am-5pm Tue; 10am-midnight Fri-Sun. **Admission** ¥1,500. **Credit** AmEx, DC, JCB, MC, V. **Map** Roppongi p103. The exhibitions are world-class, focused mainly on contemporary culture, but the secrets of the Mori Art Museum's success are location (part of the phenomenally popular Roppongi Hills), location (on the 52nd and 53rd floors of the Mori Tower, offering spectacular views) and location (within a two-floor 'experience' that includes a bar, café, shop and panoramic observation deck). One ticket allows access to all areas, and the late opening hours maximise accessibility. Exhibitions are deliberately varied – with past shows including Bill Viola's video art and an exhibiition about humour in contemporary art. The vista from Tokyo City View isn't quite 360°, and it's expensive compared to the free Tokyo Metropolitan Government building observatory (*see p120*), but the views are arguably better, especially at night with a drink in your hand from Mado Lounge (*see p177*).

New Otani Museum

Hotel New Otani, Garden Court 6F, 4-1 Kioicho, Chiyoda-ku (3221 4111/www.newotani.co.jp/group/museum/index.html). Akasaka-Mitsuke station (Ginza, Marunouchi lines), exit D or Nagatacho station (Hanzomon, Nanboku, Yurakucho lines), exit 7. **Open** 10am-6pm Tue-Sun. **Admission** ¥500; ¥200 concessions; free hotel guests. **No credit cards.**
The museum inside the New Otani houses a collection of Japanese and Japanese-inspired woodblock prints, plus a selection of traditional Japanese and modern European paintings (including works by Vlaminck and School of Paris artists). The place is small, consisting of two rooms near the hotel reception, but often has shows not seen elsewhere.

NHK Broadcast Museum

2-1-1 Atago, Minato-ku (5400 6900/www.nhk.or.jp/museum/index-e.html). Kamiyacho station (Hibiya line), exit 3 or Onarimon station (Mita line), exit 2. **Open** 9.30am-4.30pm Tue-Sun. **Admission** free.
This museum is run by the national public broadcasting company. The nation's first radio station began broadcasting in July 1925 from this location (NHK has since moved to bigger digs in Shibuya). There are two floors of early equipment, and vintage TV shows and news broadcasts play throughout the museum and can also be viewed in the video library.

Nogi Jinja

8-11-27 Akasaka, Minato-ku (3478 3001/house enquiries 3583 4151/www.nogijinja.or.jp). Nogizaka station (Chiyoda line), exit 1 or Roppongi station (Hibiya, Oedo lines), exit 7. **Open** *Walkway* 8.30am-5pm daily. *House* 9.30am-5pm 12, 13 Sept. **Admission** free. **Map** Roppongi p103.
When Emperor Meiji died, on 13 September 1912, General Nogi Maresuke and his wife proved their loyalty by joining him in death; he killed himself by *seppuku* (disembowelment), she by slitting her throat with a knife. The house in which they died is adjacent to the Nogi Shrine, which is dedicated to his memory. The house is open only two days a year, on the eve and anniversary of their deaths, but an elevated walkway allows you to peek in through the windows, one of which provides a glimpse of Nogi's bloodstained shirt.

Okura Shukokan Museum of Fine Art

Hotel Okura, 2-10-4 Toranomon, Minato-ku (3583 0781/www.okura.com/tokyo/info/shukokan.html). Roppongi-Itchome station (Nanboku line), exits 2, 3. **Open** 10am-4.30pm Tue-Sun. **Admission** ¥800; ¥400-¥500 concessions; free hotel guests. **No credit cards. Map** Roppongi p103.

This two-storey Chinese-style building sits in front of the retro-modern Hotel Okura (*see p52*), one of Tokyo's finest. Inside there's a small mix of Asian antiquities: paintings, calligraphy, Buddhist sculpture, textiles, ceramics, swords, archaeological artefacts, lacquerware and metalwork. The exhibitions change five or six times a year.

Tokyo Tower

4-2-8 Shiba-Koen, Minato-ku (3433 5111/2/www.tokyotower.co.jp). Kamiyacho station (Hibiya line), exit 1 or Onarimon station (Mita line), exit A1 or Akabanebashi station (Oedo line), Akabanebashi exit. **Open** *Tower* 9am-10pm daily. *Other attractions* 10am-9pm daily. **Admission** *Main Observatory* ¥820; ¥310-¥460 concessions. *Special Observatory* ¥600; ¥350-¥400 concessions. *Waxwork Museum* ¥870; ¥460 concessions. *Trick Art Gallery* ¥400; ¥300 concessions. *Mysterious Walking Zone* ¥410; ¥300 concessions. *Combined ticket* ¥1,900; ¥950-¥1,100 concessions. **No credit cards. Map** Roppongi p103.
The resemblance to the Eiffel Tower is deliberate, as is the superior height – 13m (43ft) taller than the Parisian structure. Back in 1958, when it was built, it must have been impressive. Nowadays, though, constructions such as the Mori Tower and Shinjuku's Tocho both offer more impressive views. The tower still functions as a radio and TV mast, but its days as the observation deck of choice are long gone. The attractions inside, including a wax museum and trick art gallery, only serve to highlight how dated the tower has become. But it remains Tokyo's most recognisable structure and, ironically, its most striking attraction when viewed at night from any of the other observation decks.

Zojo-ji Temple

4-7-35 Shiba Koen, Minato-ku (3432 1431/www.zojoji.or.jp/en/). Shiba-Koen station (Mita line), exit A4 or Daimon station (Asakusa, Oedo lines), exit A6. **Open** *Temple* 6am-5.30pm daily. *Grounds* 24hrs daily. **Admission** free.
The main temple of the Buddhist Jodo sect in the Kanto area, Zojo-ji was built in 1393 and moved to its present location in 1598. In the 17th century 48 temples stood on this site. The main hall has been destroyed three times by fire in the last century, the current building being a 1970s reconstruction. The most historic element is the Sangedatsumon main gate – dating back to 1605, it's the oldest wooden structure in Tokyo. Each of its three sections represents three of the stages that are necessary to attain nirvana. A mausoleum in the grounds contains the tombs of six Tokugawa shoguns. There's also a cemetery, with row upon row of small statues of Jizo, guardian of (among other things) stillborn, aborted or miscarried babies.

Getting there

Roppongi station is on the Hibiya and Oedo subway lines. A concourse from exit 1C of the Hibiya line takes you direct to the heart of Roppongi Hills, in front of the Mori Tower. Azabu-Juban is on the Oedo and Nanboku lines, and Hiroo on the Hibiya line.

Tokyo Midtown

Given that it has one of the highest population densities in the world, Tokyo is home to surprisingly few skyscrapers. That's gradually changing, though, as civil engineers find ways to build higher structures that can withstand the powerful earthquakes that hit Japan.

Following hot on the heels of Roppongi Hills (*pictured*) 238m (780-foot) Mori Tower is Tokyo's latest giant urban regeneration project, Tokyo Midtown (www.tokyo-midtown.com), with a 248m (813-foot) monolith named, rather perfunctorily, the Midtown Tower. Although it's unlikely to trouble the judging panels of architectural prizes, the tower is currently the tallest building in the city.

The complex it sits in is, like its local rival, loosely based on the vertical cities proposed by Le Corbusier and others in the inter-war years. Midtown is a city within a city, featuring offices, apartments, shops and restaurants, as well as the Ritz-Carlton Tokyo hotel, the Suntory Museum of Art and 21_21 Design

Sight, a design gallery housed in a futuristic building inspired by the fabrics of fashion maestro Issey Miyake.

What distinguishes Midtown from its rivals, though, is the four hectares of greenery in which all these amenities are housed. Roppongi Hills has its greenery, but not on the scale of the beautifully landscaped Hinokicho Park, which covers 40 per cent of the grounds and separates Midtown from the hustle and bustle of the rest of Roppongi. This is Tokyo's most upmarket mega-mall experience, with jewellery from Harry Winstone and fashion from Savile Row's Richard James and Madison Avenue's Aaron Basha. Only those itching to splash the cash should venture into the shopping area or risk suffering some serious bling envy. The 12 restaurants and 30 or so cafés, though, are some of Tokyo's best and well worth a visit. To access it, take the Nanboku line to Roppongi-Itchome station and look for the 248m (813-foot) tower.

Shibuya

Teenage kicks right through the day and night.

Map p109

Shibuya is best known as the bright, brash centre of Tokyo's teen culture. Tokyo's youths have made Shibuya their playground, and the area's innumerable shops, cafés, clubs, bars and restaurants largely cater to their tastes. This is a fast, fun and affordable part of town.

The entire nation's youth culture stems from Shibuya and, whether they know it or not, these kids also supply the rest of the world with fashion cues. The English footballers' WAG look? Very late '90s Shibuya. Car-crash mismatching of colours and styles? It happened here first. During the day, the area is all about shopping, with music and fashion dominating its stores. But when darkness falls and the neon is switched on, myriad clubs, bars, cinemas, live venues and less salubrious establishments keep the area throbbing till dawn.

Traditionally, the action has been limited to the wedge of land west of the Yamanote line train tracks, but thanks to the economic and cultural triumph of Tokyo's youth, and ongoing improvements in transport links, the fun is expanding in all directions. The JR station's Hachiko exit is still the gateway to most of the area's attractions, but it's now worth wandering elsewhere for some great gems of nightlife or independent stores.

In the paved square outside the exit is a small bronze statue of the eponymous **Hachiko**, a dog of legendary loyalty who walked to Shibuya to meet his owner at the end of each day, then travelled in vain to the station for a further seven years after the old man's death. He too passed on in 1935, earning obituaries in national newspapers and the honour of his statue becoming Shibuya's most popular – and thus overcrowded – meeting spot.

Next to the square is the world's busiest pedestrian crossing, also named Hachiko (**photo p111**), across which a scuttling horde pours every three minutes. To a backdrop of blaring video screens and neon-clad buildings, this is the Tokyo of popular imagination, the first choice for foreign TV crews looking for an instant symbol of the manic city. You can watch it all from the second floor of Starbucks.

Beside Starbucks, on the far side of Hachiko crossing is the entrance to **Center Gai** (**photo p112**), a pedestrian street lined with cheap chain restaurants, mobile-phone vendors and trainer shops. It's also the catwalk for Tokyo's teen trendsetters, who mill around in the latest garish fashions. The likely source of their threads is **109** (*see p196*; **photo p114**). This

Shibuya

To Aoyama

JINGUMAE

United Nations University

National Children's Castle

SHIBUYA-KU

Mitake Park

SHIBUYA

Mitake Shrine

MIYAMASUSAKA

AOYAMA DORI

ROPPONGI DORI

YAHATAZAKA

Tofuku-ji Temple

Konno Shrine

MEIJI DORI

Tokyu Toyoko Line

JR & Tokyu Shibuya Station

Tokyu

MEIJI DORI

Miyashita Park

Shibuya Station

Yamanote Line

Hachiko Statue

KOEN DORI

Seibu

JINNAN

Parco

CENTER GAI

109 Building

Inokashira Line Shibuya Station

Mark City

Cerulean Tower Tokyu Hotel

TAMAGAWA DORI

BUNKAMURA DORI

Shibuya BEAM Building

UDAGAWACHO

Tokyu Honten

Bunkamura

DOGENZAKA

DOGENZAKA

300 m

300 yds

© Copyright Time Out Group 2007

Walk on People watching

Time: three hours

Save this walk for a sunny Sunday when the city's youths come out in force – and in costume. Dive in at the deep end by taking the Hachiko exit from Shibuya station. With luck you'll find local kids squatting on the street hawking all manner of wares and services, from artistic calligraphy to 'listening to your story for five minutes'.

Facing you on the far side of the world's busiest pedestrian crossing is the **Q-Front** building, with its four-storey projection of pop videos and high-tempo ads. Directly to the left is **Centre Gai**, the pedestrianised mecca for tarted-up teens, including the 'Centre Guys' (*see p34-5*, **Tokyo tribes**) and perhaps their super-tanned, brightly dressed female counterparts – the *mamba*.

Once past the congested street entrance, the human traffic eases, and you can stroll along perusing the latest fashions. Turn right at the far end of the street and immediately on your right is **Hiki Café** (32-8 Udagawacho, 3770 1345). In clement months, Hiki's terrace is a cosy spot to take a break and watch Shibuya scuttling past.

Heading back into the action, continue to the end of the street and turn left. Ahead of you is the city's DJ district. The spacious **DMR** store on the left draws the DJs, while the tiny cubby-holes in the Noa building above offer rarer, pricier treats for collectors.

Turn right at the **Tokyu Hands** shop and walk to the main intersection with Koen Dori ('Park Street'). Straight ahead is the **Tokyo Wonder Site** (*see p240*) for a cultural diversion. Take a left; as you walk up the hill, a detour a block to the right leads to numerous outlets for urban and vintage fashion, including **RagTag** (*see p197*). Cross the street at the top of Koen Dori and you'll find yourself on a pedestrianised avenue. On weekends it's lined with performers and their audiences. Most of the acts are unsigned bands looking to pick up new fans. You might also spot some stand-up comedians, puppeteers or, more disturbingly, wannabe 'idols' offering their cuteness to admiring huddles of middle-aged men.

At the end of the avenue lies a plaza. There are frequent festivals held here, often with regional themes. The best of the lot is the massive **Thai Festival** that takes place each May (*see p213*).

From the plaza, take the footbridge into Yoyogi Park. This spacious, verdant spot is a great place to relax after the bustle of Shibuya, but there's more fun to be had by veering right, to the park entrance. Each Sunday afternoon a dozen or so rockabillies in greaser gear and pompadours descend on the area, crank out stripped-down 1950's rock 'n' roll from their sound systems, and spend the afternoon twisting and spinning for the crowd of onlookers.

The fun continues just around the corner towards Harajuku station, where the 'cosplay' (costume play) kids hold court. The bridge just south of the station is the main venue or masquerading the elaborate, often handmade costumes. The 'gothloli' look (*see p34-5*, **Tokyo tribes**) is a favourite. Most cosplayers are delighted to pose for the cameras.

If your people-watching urge is sated, head to Harajuku station. If not, the backstreets of Harajuku offer a take on urban fashion that's a shade less brassy than that of Shibuya.

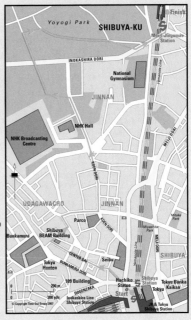

Hachiko crossing. *See p108.*

ten-storey cylindrical collection of boutiques, a block to the left of Center Gai, is not so much a store as a way of life for the area's flamboyantly attired teenage girls. The store's most accessorised ambassadors are known as '*gyaru*' – an approximation of the English 'gal'. Blurring the line between vendor and consumer, staff here – who are sounded out for design ideas and often used as models – tend to be sourced from the store's regular customers. These shopper/sellers are encouraged to constantly suggest new ideas and trends (and some trends have a lifespan of just a fortnight here). It's a retailing phenomenon lubricated by just-in-time production, cheap Chinese manufacturing and the hard-earned yen of their elders and betters. Whether or not such clothing is to your taste, a visit to see the young shoppers in action is an essential experience.

The street that forks to the right of 109 leads to **Bunkamura**, a massive arts centre owned by the same corporation (Tokyu) as the fashion superstore, but catering to a very different crowd. It's an oasis of calm that contains, among other things, **Le Cinema** (*see p233*), performance spaces **Theatre Cocoon** (*see p268*) and **Orchard Hall** (*see p251*) and a good museum.

Just before reaching Bunkamura you'll notice the six-storey, bright-yellow emporium known as Don Quixote. In a two-fingered salute to the traditional retail format, the layout is deliberately bewildering, with sex toys sitting beside shoes, and 'mini-skirt police' costumes mixed in with travel bags. Food, jewellery, electronics, furniture and toys are just some of the products piled high and sold cheap here. The shop assistants double as buyers and have remarkably free reign to order anything they think might sell, so the selections are eclectic and fast-changing.

A right turn at Bunkamura will lead you back to the bustle. The Shibuya BEAM building on the right-hand side is home to **Equus Plaza**, a must for horse-racing fans, and a large basement branch of manga/*anime* specialist **Mandarake** (*see p209*). Catering to fans of all incomes, here teens can browse old comics while high-rolling geeks can, at the time of writing, snap up a *Princess Mononoke anime* cell for a mere ¥472,000. The staff have been known to perform song and dance routines in full *anime* costume to celebrate particularly big purchases. None of the customers would ever find this weird.

Continue to the next T-junction, head left and you'll find yet another Tokyu-run institution – **Tokyu Hands** (*see p208*). Often misleadingly termed a stationery or hardware store, it hawks everything from hi-fis to Halloween masks, and is the best place to find the latest, only-in-Japan novelties. Vinyl enthusiasts should explore the surrounding streets, where dozens of vinyl-only music stores, some little larger than a cupboard, offer 'Shibuya taste' discs: mainly hip hop, house

Teen magnet **Center Gai.** *See p108.*

and reggae. DJing is an enduring craze among Tokyo's youth, and Shibuya supplies the vinyl.

Between Tokyu Hands and the next main street, Koen Dori, is another teen haven, **Parco** (*see p197*). The hip division of Seibu department store, Parco takes up three separate buildings (Part 1, Part 2 and Part 3). At the top of Part 3 is the **Parco Museum of Art & Beyond**, which hosts an eclectic mix of trendsetting shows.

The rest of Shibuya is a winding maze of streets best approached with a casual wander. It can be a disorientating experience – but that's half the fun – and with each of the main roads leading downhill to the station, it's hard to become seriously lost.

If you tire of consumerism, Shibuya also houses some quirky museums, including the **Tobacco & Salt Museum**, the **TEPCO Electric Energy Museum** (both north of Parco) and the **Eyeglass Museum** (on Dogenzaka). Further west in the Shoto area, quiet contemplation is the order of the day at two small art museums: the **Toguri Museum** and the **Shoto Museum**. Nearby is the unusual **Gallery Tom** (2-11-1 Shoto, 3467 8102, open 10.30am-5.30pm Tue-Sun, admission ¥600), which has been catering for the visually impaired for two decades. It's the only gallery in town where visitors are encouraged to get touchy-feely with the sculptures and 3-D art.

Further out, a couple of stops from Shibuya on the Keio Inokashira line, is the low-key **Japan Folk Crafts Museum**.

When the shops close, head back towards Bunkamura and turn left. This takes you uphill to the hub of Shibuya's nightlife, home to several of Tokyo's best-known clubs (**Womb**, **Vuenos**, **Club Asia**, **Ruby Room**, **Neo**; *see p223-31* for details), as well as a great many of its love hotels. At these, from around ¥3,000, you can 'rest' with a friend for a couple of hours. Alternatively, you might choose to fork out ¥30,000 for a night at the luxurious **P&A Plaza**, where the suite boasts a private swimming pool (*see p42* **Love hotels**).

After a long period of looking like its main function is as an after-hours schoolyard, Shibuya has started to push its image upmarket. First, a trio of train operators joined forces to tack **Mark City** (*see p190*) on to the side of the existing station. This shopping and dining complex currently houses stores and restaurants designed to attract a (slightly) more moneyed crowd. Next came the grand **Cerulean Tower Tokyu Hotel** (*see p46*). The newest arrival is Meiji Dori's **Picasso 347** (1-23-16 Shibuya, Shibuya-ku) shopping tower, which houses spacious FCUK and Hilfiger stores as well as a cinema, sports complex and café terrace.

Some complain that these shiny additions detract from the area's downbeat charm. But the same protests have been heard since the original Tokyu department store rose up beside the station in 1934 (some of the original shops displaced by Tokyu still operate underneath Hachiko), and Shibuya has never been a place to stand still.

Bunkamura The Museum

Bunkamura B1, 2-24-1 Dogenzaka, Shibuya-ku (3477 9111/www.bunkamura.co.jp). Shibuya station (Yamanote, Ginza lines), Hachiko exit; (Hanzomon line), exit 3A. **Open** 10am-7pm Mon-Thur, Sun; 10am-9pm Fri, Sat. **Admission** usually ¥1,000. **Credit** (shop only) AmEx, JCB, MC, V. **Map** Shibuya p109.
One of the best museums in Tokyo is run by a department-store chain (it's owned and operated by the Tokyu corporation, which also runs 109, Tokyu Hands and part of Mark City). Bunkamura hosts international art blockbusters featuring subjects and artists ranging from Tintin to Picasso. Elsewhere in this major shopping and cultural centre are boutiques, an art-house cinema, two theatre/music spaces, an art bookshop and various restaurants.

Eyeglass Museum

Iris Optical 6F-7F, 2-29-18 Dogenzaka, Shibuya-ku (3496 3315). Shibuya station (Yamanote, Ginza lines), Hachiko exit; (Hanzomon line), exits 1, 3A. **Open** 11am-5pm Tue-Sun. **Admission** free. **Map** Shibuya p109.

Not the flashiest of Tokyo's museums, this slightly dilapidated spot above an optician's is nevertheless an interesting diversion from a shopping trip in Shibuya. Glasses galore sit quietly, with very few annotations, for the viewing pleasure of spectacle fanatics. A 19th-century eyeglass workshop specially imported from France is complemented by a chipped mannequin.

Japan Folk Crafts Museum (Mingei-kan)

4-3-33 Komaba, Meguro-ku (3467 4527/ www.mingeikan.or.jp). Komaba-Todaimae station (Keio Inokashira line), west exit.

Open 10am-5pm Tue-Sun. **Admission** ¥1,000; ¥200-¥500 concessions. **Credit** MC, V.

Kyoto University professor Yanagi Soetsu created this museum in 1936 to spotlight *mingei*, literally 'arts of the people'. The criteria for inclusion in the collection were that objects should be made anonymously, by hand, and in large quantities. Yanagi collected ceramics, metalwork, woodwork, textiles, paintings and other everyday items from Japan, China, Korea and Taiwan at a time when their beauty wasn't always recognised. Handwritten labels (in Japanese) and simple wooden display cases complement the rustic feel.

Animania

Take a look at the pink creatures frolicking in the field. Although they might look like the bastard offspring of children's telly and a porn channel, their mission is far more mundane. The ten-year-old **Noppon brothers** are the official mascots of the Tokyo Tower.

If you're wondering why the city's most instantly recognisable structure might need mascots, let alone ones resembling cuddly phalluses, it's all thanks to Tokyo's mania for cartoon characters.

The toothy cuboid enjoying a ski jump below is **Domo-kun**, the inexplicably grizzly face of national broadcaster NHK, who we're told shares a cave with an elderly rabbit and can't eat apples because of a quirk in his DNA.

And NHK isn't the only company getting in on the mascot act. Daikin, one of the nation's leading manufacturers of air conditioners, uses a cheerful water droplet called **Pichon-kun**. The cartoon face of the NTT Docomo mobile-phone company, meanwhile, is a beady-eyed fungus called **Docomodake**. Even the police are in on the character craze with a little smurf-like creature called

Pipo-kun (after the onomatopoeia for a police siren), who reminds citizens how to behave themselves.

And not to be outdone, the fire department has **Kyuta-kun**, a wide-eyed young firefighter with an oversized helmet and horns.

The most successful characters, such as Japan Railway's **Suica Penguin** (the cutesy public face of its magnetised travel card), develop fan bases who buy branded merchandise and parade the corporate symbol around the streets.

At the other end of the spectrum are the *yuru chara* (loose characters), whose tenuous existence bring more ridicule than affection. These Z-list beasts are often the creations of local towns or minor-league bureaucratic enterprises. Contenders for the *yuru chara* crown include **Earth-kun,** the smiling face of the Tokyo Bureau of Sewage, and the truly bizarre mascot of neighbouring Chiba prefecture's Environmental Regeneration Foundation: a yellow dog named **Chiba-Ken,** whose prefecture-shaped head looks like the result of a horrible environmental tragedy.

So when the marketing minds behind the Tokyo Tower suggested that the 332-metre (1090-foot) structure needed a pointy-headed pink icon, they were only following the lead of hundreds of other companies and government ventures in giving Tokyoites what they crave: a cute, comforting face to deal with. Nothing this cute could ever let you down.

Put your hands in the air for teen-shopping mecca **109**. See p108.

Parco Museum of Art & Beyond

Parco Part 3 7F, 15-1 Udagawacho, Shibuya-ku (3464 5111/www.parco-art.com). Shibuya station (Yamanote, Ginza lines), Hachiko exit; (Hanzomon line), exits 3A, 6, 7. **Open** 10am-8.30pm during exhibitions. **Admission** ¥500; ¥400 concessions. **Credit** AmEx, DC, JCB, MC, V. **Map** Shibuya p109.
This top-floor gallery's programming policy perfectly fits the Shibuya demographic, with regularly changing exhibitions on pop-culture themes, plus work by only the trendiest photographers and designers from Japan and overseas. Past shows have featured photos by the dog-loving William Wegman, and that enduring pop icon, Che Guevara.

Shoto Museum of Art

2-14-14 Shoto, Shibuya-ku (3465 9421). Shinsen station (Keio Inokashira line), north exit. **Open** 9am-5pm Tue-Sun. **Admission** ¥300; ¥100 concessions; free children Sat. **No credit cards.**
The Shoto's rough stone exterior gives way to curved walls encircling a central fountain. It's no Guggenheim, but this odd bit of ageing architecture (owned by Shibuya ward) sometimes hosts inspired shows. It's also inexpensive and quiet.

TEPCO Electric Energy Museum (Denryoku-kan)

1-12-10 Jinnan, Shibuya-ku (3477 1191/www5. mediagalaxy.co.jp/Denryokukan). Shibuya station (Yamanote, Ginza lines), Hachiko exit; (Hanzomon line), exits 6, 7. **Open** 10am-6pm Mon, Tue, Thur-Sun. **Admission** free. **Map** Shibuya p109.
'Let's make friends with electricity' is the slogan of this energy giant's six-storey homage to the joy of electrons and protons. Adults might tire quickly of the corporate message, but it's a great place to keep the kids busy. Teaching your offspring to play with electricity might not seem the sagest of lessons, but the innovative games and multimedia activities will keep them genuinely entertained.

Tobacco & Salt Museum

1-16-8 Jinnan, Shibuya-ku (3476 2041/www.jti.co.jp/ Culture/museum). Shibuya station (Yamanote, Ginza lines), Hachiko exit; (Hanzomon line), exits 6, 7. **Open** 10am-6pm Tue-Sun. **Admission** ¥100; ¥50 concessions. **No credit cards. Map** Shibuya p109.
The tenuous rationale for this pairing of themes is that both were once nationalised commodities. Tobacco gets the most exposure, with two of the four floors devoted to the history, manufacture and culture of the killer leaf. Besides the gallery of packet designs, collection of pipes and videos of cigarette production, one of the most fascinating aspects of the museum is the number of families that bring their kids to learn about the marvel of smoking. On the third floor a 1.2-tonne block of Polish salt and a model *Cutty Sark* crafted from crystals are among the sodium-based exhibits. The top floor is often the best, with an ever-changing exhibition that has, in the past, ranged from tequila production to 19th-century prostitutes' wigs. If you're inspired to spark up, the gift shop sells a range of cigarettes.

Toguri Museum of Art

1-11-3 Shoto, Shibuya-ku (3465 0070/www.toguri-museum.or.jp). Shibuya station (Yamanote, Ginza lines), Hachiko exit; (Hanzomon line), exit 3A or Shinsen station (Keio Inokashira line). **Open** 9.30am-5.30pm Tue-Sun. **Admission** ¥1,030; ¥420-¥730 concessions. **Credit** AmEx, DC, JCB, MC, V.
The art of porcelain is the focus of this quiet museum. Its 11,000 antique Chinese and Japanese pieces rotate through four shows a year. All displays are accompanied by captions in Japanese and English.

Getting there

Shibuya is on the Yamanote train line and the Ginza and Hanzomon subway lines, as well as various suburban rail lines, including the JR Saikyo, Keio Inokashira, and Tokyu Toyoko and Denentoshi lines.

Shinjuku

The neon-lit Tokyo you've seen in the movies.

Live life in neon on the cosmopolitan strip of **Shinjuku Dori**.

Map p117

Shinjuku is Tokyo's largest sub-centre and easily the most cosmopolitan area, with luxurious department stores, sleazy strip clubs, smoky jazz bars and gay porn shops all just a few blocks from each other. The area is divided into two distinct east and west sections by the JR Yamanote and Chuo train lines. The clean-cut west is home to the city government, corporate skyscrapers and the luxurious **Park Hyatt Tokyo** (*see p49*), while the cacophonous east offers everything from big-brand shopping to neon-lit sex parlours.

It is also a major transportation hub. In fact, Shinjuku station is the busiest in the world. Those photos you've seen of commuters being pushed on to crowded trains by uniformed guards in rush hour? Shinjuku station, every morning of the week, from 7.30am onwards. Get up early and take a camera, but don't expect there to be much room on the platform. And with over 50 exits, miles of tunnels and several different levels, it's also the station you're most likely to get lost in. This is the one station where it's essential to know which exit you need.

EAST AND SOUTH SIDES

Head out of the east exit from the Yamanote line station, and you'll see the main street of **Shinjuku Dori**. Facing you will be the large video screen of **Studio Alta** – a multi-storey shopping centre specialising in young girls' fashion, but more popular as Shinjuku's meeting spot. The east side is where all the action is. It houses the glitzy neon and dodgy hostess bars of **Kabuki-cho** (**photo** *p116*), Japan's largest red-light area, as well as the gay district of Ni-chome (two-chome) and the colourful bars of San-chome (three-chome). Numerous music venues and nightclubs are scattered throughout.

Kabuki-cho lies north of Yasukuni Dori and contains hundreds of restaurants, bars, sex clubs, *pachinko* parlours and love hotels – if you're male, you won't get five yards before some strip-club tout tries to lure you into their premises. It's not a particularly dangerous area, but explore with caution and don't flash your wallet too openly. Adjoining it is **Golden Gai**, a collection of tiny watering holes that are a throwback to earlier days. Not all welcome foreigners; *see p179* **Golden Gai** for those that do.

Kabuki-cho. *See p115.*

Sightseeing

surrounding streets. The grandaddy of them all, and the expat's fave for its larger-than-usual clothes, is **Isetan** (*see p187*).

Consumption is definitely the name of the game here. In fact, the city planners (although that's a vague notion in Japan) clearly thought there wasn't enough spending going on in Shinjuku, so in the early 1990s they built a huge shopping complex, **Takashimaya Times Square** (*see 190*), to the south of the station. At one end is the 240-metre (787-foot) shaft of the **NTT DoCoMo Yoyogi Building**, resembling a cross between the Empire State Building and a Venetian clocktower. The complex occupies old train-switching grounds; now Shinjuku's revitalised south exit has taken its place as a destination for shoppers, restaurant-hunters and party-goers.

It may surprise some that for all Shinjuku's consumerist dazzle, the area is also steeped in counter-culture. **Ni-chome** is the most active and open gay and lesbian district in the country, with queer literature, ads and goods openly displayed (something unusual for Japan) on airy side streets (*see pp243-9*). The little alleyways between Kabuki-cho and Golden Gai are home to avant-garde performance houses, as well as intellectual denizens set up as tiny bars. Indeed, Shinjuku was the explosive epicentre of Japan's active and demonstrative youth movement in the 1960s (something that can be viewed in director Oshima Nagisa's 1968 classic *Diary of a Shinjuku Thief*). This feeling has never left some of the smaller byways of the east side.

Further east and south of Shinjuku Dori is the vast green lung of **Shinjuku Gyoen**, one of Tokyo's largest parks. It's a spectacular sight at *hanami* (cherry-blossom viewing), and with its 1,500 trees paint the whole place pink. And to the north of Kabuki-cho, centred on Shin-Okubo station, is Tokyo's 'Koreatown', a district that

Occupying a substantial plot between Golden Gai and Meiji Dori is the large **Hanazono Shrine**. Erected in the 16th century, the shrine has been rebuilt many times but still retains the gripping presence of a historical monument that is very active. With striking orange pillars, railings and *torii* (gates), it holds numerous lively festivals, notably a three-day event at the end of May and a pre-New Year's fest in November.

Shinjuku is also a big shopping zone. Department store **Lumine Est** (*see p189*), notable mainly for the Shunkan restaurant area on the seventh and eighth floors, perches above the east side of the station. Modern art lines the walls, and restaurants include Wolfgang Puck, the Gumbo & Oyster Bar and Okinawan specialist Nabbie & Kamado. Numerous other department stores, including Mitsukoshi, Marui and Keio, line Shinjuku Dori and the

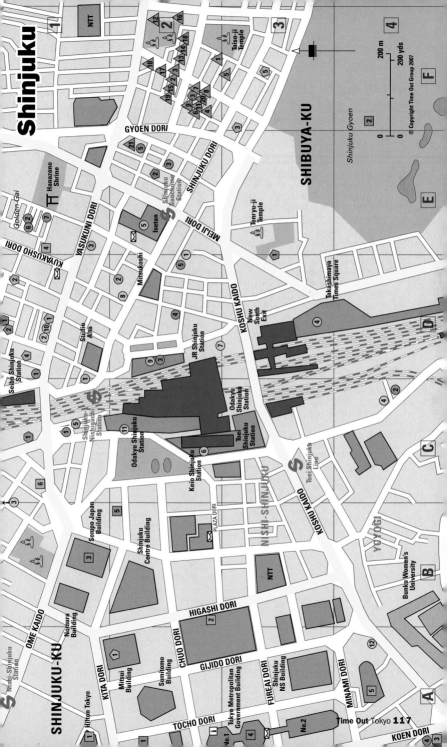

Shinjuku

SHINJUKU-KU

SHIBUYA-KU

YOYOGI

Golden Gai

Hanazono Shrine

Taiso-ji Temple

NTT

GYOEN DORI

YASUKUNI DORI

KUYAKUSHO DORI

OME KAIDO

Isetan

Mitsukoshi

Studio Alta

Shinjuku Sanchome Station

SHINJUKU DORI

MEIJI DORI

JR Shinjuku Station

Shinjuku-Nishiguchi Station

Seibu Shinjuku Station

Nishi-Shinjuku Station

Odakyu Shinjuku Station

Keio Shinjuku Station

Toei Shinjuku Station

Odakyu Shinjuku Station

Tenryu-ji Temple

Shinjuku Gyoen

KOSHU KAIDO

New South Exit

Takashimaya Times Square

Toei Shinjuku Line

PLAZA DORI

Sompo Japan Building

Shinjuku Centre Building

Nomura Building

NTT

NISHI-SHINJUKU

HIGASHI DORI

CHUO DORI

GIJIDO DORI

FUREAI DORI

Shinjuku NS Building

Tokyo Metropolitan Government Building

Sumitomo Building

Mitsui Building

KITA DORI

TOCHO DORI

Hilton Tokyo

No.1

No.2

Bunka Women's University

MINAMI DORI

KOEN DORI

Shinjuku Gyoen

200 m
200 yds

© Copyright Time Out Group 2007

Time Out Tokyo 117

Manga mania

The Japanese love their comics. Known as manga (a term coined by Hokusai in 1814 and meaning 'crazy drawings'), they account for almost 40 per cent of everything published in Japan. You can find manga magazines as thick as phone directories, and epic stories that take numerous volumes to complete. The 400-page *Shonen Jump* magazine, costing a mere ¥240, shifts three million copies a week. Manga cover every subject under the sun, from child-rearing to porn.

While manga have clearly been influenced by Western comics and animation, they also draw on Japan's long tradition of visual entertainments, such as *ukiyo-e* ('floating world' prints) and erotic *shunga* prints.

The man principally responsible for starting this all-consuming love affair is Tezuka Osamu (1928-89), creator of Tetsuwan Atomu (aka Astro Boy) and founder of the post-war manga and *anime* (animated cartoons) industries. Since the war, manga have evolved into Japan's unique mass literary form with their own iconic vocabulary; they are the sources of many of the country's most successful films and TV series, both animated and live-action. Much of this success stems from the dizzying diversity of their stories, styles and subjects, and their appeal to both sexes and every age group and taste.

Traditionally, the biggest sellers have been the *shonen* titles for boys and the more adult *seinen* ranges for men, but there are some 40 *shojo* magazines for girls and, more recently, over 50 *redikomi* aimed at women. Written and drawn mainly by women, these cover everything from 'Office Lady' lifestyles, pregancy advice and sex therapy to raunchy erotica and the gloriously titled 'Truly Horrifying Mother-in-Law and Daughter-in-Law Comics', which tackle the trials of newly-wed wives.

That's not counting niche titles covering such subjects as golf, *pachinko*, military history or the unique genre of *shonen ai* – stories about gay boys that are hugely popular with teenage girls. And don't forget *dojinshi* (self-published fanzines); Tokyo's twice-yearly Comiket fairs for *dojinshi* attract nearly half a million visitors.

Most manga are printed in black or one-colour ink on white or tinted newsprint, with perhaps a small full-colour section. They are read from what Westerners consider the 'back', and from right to left across the page.

Most casual readers discard the magazines or leave them for others on trains or in cafés. What the Japanese prefer to buy and put on their shelves are the compact, usually paperback books that compile several episodes of a story in one volume.

Manga are widely available in most of Tokyo's bookshops, and department stores often dedicate large areas, sometimes entire floors, to them. Devoted readers may prefer specialist or second-hand outlets such as **Tora no Ana** (*see p195*) and **Mandarake** (*see p209*), while whole boutiques are dedicated to specific creators like Tezuka or characters like Doraemon. Myriad spin-off products range from figurines to clothes emblazoned with manga heroes and heroines. There are also numerous 24-hour manga cafés, such as **GeraGera** (*see p186*), where you can read from a vast quantity of manga books, both old and new, for a modest charge.

You will struggle to find English-language editions in Japan, but they are increasingly available in the West – manga has been the fastest-growing book category in the US for a number of years.

Paul Gravett wrote Manga: Sixty Years of Japanese Comics (*Laurence King, 2004*).

has seen a resurgence in recent years, as Korean culture becomes increasingly fashionable in Tokyo. For good restaurants in the area, *see p156* **Seoul food**.

WEST SIDE

The west side offers a clutch of skyscrapers (Tokyo's only such neighbourhood), a plethora of banking, insurance and other company headquarters, and some smart hotels. Among the corporate high-rises are the **Sompo Japan Museum**, worth a look for some of its famous (and famously expensive) paintings, and the **Toto Super Space**, where you can view the latest in Japan's celebrated toilet technology.

The Tokyo government's headquarters, known as Tocho and designed by Tange Kenzo, are also here. Completed in 1991, the twin-towered centrepiece of this impressive complex is the **Tokyo Metropolitan Government Building No.1**: a must-visit, both architecturally and for the great – and free – views from its two observation decks. Directly behind the TMG site is **Shinjuku Central Park**, better known for its homeless community than its scenery.

In stark contrast to the gleaming high-rises is **Omoide Yokocho**, just outside the station's north-west exit. This narrow alleyway lined with ramshackle yakitori stalls, each with seating for no more than a handful of customers, is the last remnant of a vanished world. It dates from the post-war years, when Shinjuku was the site of a thriving black market; whatever you needed, you could find it in the area's teeming and seamy side streets. Atmospheric, intimate and distinctly out of step with modern-day Tokyo, Omoide Yokocho occupies prime real estate and may not defy the developers for much longer.

South of the main road of Koshu Kaido is women's fashion college Bunka Gakuen, which founded the small **Bunka Gakuen Costume Museum** on its 60th anniversary in 1979. Further west lies the **Tokyo Opera City** complex, containing halls for classical music (*see p251*), one of the city's best-funded private contemporary art galleries (*see p241*) and the **NTT Inter Communication Centre**, a museum of media arts. Adjacent is the **New National Theatre, Tokyo** (*see p251*).

ELSEWHERE

Shinjuku is also a good jumping-off point for other neighbourhoods. To the south, Yoyogi is a large area that abuts Yoyogi Park and the **Meiji Shrine** complex (*see p85*) and contains the **Sword Museum**.

Heading east, back towards Chiyoda-ku, is Yotsuya, home to one of Tokyo's more surprising buildings. The **Akasaka Detached Palace** (aka Geihinkan, 2-1-1 Moto-Akasaka,

Minato-ku) is a hybrid of Versailles and Buckingham Palace. Its construction, in the early years of the 20th century, was intended to prove that Japan could do anything the West could. The late Emperor Hirohito lived here when he was crown prince, but the only people allowed in these days are visiting dignitaries – a great pity. Nearby is the Tokyo Fire Department-owned **Fire Museum**, which offers an insight into the key role fire has played in the development of the city.

Bunka Gakuen Costume Museum

3-22-7 Yoyogi, Shibuya-ku (3299 2387/www.bunka. ac.jp/museum/hakubutsu.htm). Shinjuku station (Yamanote, Chuo, Sobu lines), south exit; (Oedo, Shinjuku lines), exit 6. **Open** 10am-4.30pm Mon-Sat. **Admission** ¥500; ¥200-¥300 concessions. **No credit cards**. **Map** Shinjuku p117.

The small collection includes examples of historical Japanese clothing, such as an Edo-era fire-fighting coat and a brightly coloured, 12-layer *karaginumo* outfit. Kamakura-period scrolls illustrate the types of dress worn by different classes of people. The displays change four or five times a year.

Fire Museum

3-10 Yotsuya, Shinjuku-ku (3353 9119/www.tfd. metro.tokyo.jp/ts/museum.htm). Yotsuya-Sanchome station (Marunouchi line), exit 2. **Open** 9.30am-5pm Tue-Sun. **Admission** free.

This museum traces the cultural history of fire-fighting, from decorative uniforms to vintage ladder trucks to the elaborate pompoms used to identify neighbourhood brigades. Between 1603 and 1868, 97 major conflagrations swept through Tokyo. Scale models, sound and lights recreate an Edo-period blaze in miniature. Video monitors show footage of the fires that destroyed the city after the 1923 Great Kanto Earthquake and World War II fire bombing. Elsewhere, cartoon stories (in Japanese) teach children what to do in case fire breaks out at home. Kids also love climbing into the rooftop helicopter.

NTT Inter Communication Centre

Tokyo Opera City Tower 4F, 3-20-2 Nishi-Shinjuku, Shinjuku-ku (0120 144 199/www.ntticc.or.jp). Hatsudai station (Keio New line), east exit. **Open** 10am-6pm Tue-Sun. Closed 2nd Sun Feb, 1st Sun Aug. **Admission** free; additional charge for special exhibitions. **Credit** (shop) AmEx, DC, JCB, MC, V.

Opened by telecoms giant NTT in 1996, this museum is at the leading edge of media design and arts. The permanent collection includes a timeline of art videos and interactive installations.

Shinjuku Gyoen

11 Naito-cho, Shinjuku-ku (3350 0151/www. shinjukugyoen.go.jp). Shinjuku-Gyoenmae station (Marunouchi line), exit 1. **Open** *Park* 9am-4.30pm Tue-Sun; daily during cherry blossom (early Apr) and chrysanthemum (early Nov) seasons. *Greenhouse* 11am-3pm Tue-Sun. **Admission** ¥200; ¥50 concessions. **No credit cards**. **Map** Shinjuku p117.

Shinjuku Gyoen opened as an imperial garden in 1906, during Japan's push for Westernisation, and was the first place in the country where many non-indigenous species were planted. The fascination with the West is evident in the garden's layout: there are both English- and French-style sections, as well as a traditional Japanese garden.

Sompo Japan Museum

Sompo Japan Bldg 42F, 1-26-1 Nishi-Shinjuku, Shinjuku-ku (3349 3081/www.sompo-japan.co. jp/museum). Shinjuku station (Yamanote, Chuo, Sobu lines), west exit; (Marunouchi line), exits A16, A17; (Shinjuku line), exit 3 or Shinjuku-Nishiguchi station (Oedo line), exit D1. **Open** 10am-6pm Tue-Sun. **Admission** ¥500; ¥300 concessions; free under-15s; additional charge for special exhibitions. **No credit cards. Map** Shinjuku p117.

The views from this 42nd-floor museum are spectacular. Perhaps to compete, the owner, insurance company Yasuda (as the firm was previously called), purchased Van Gogh's 1889 *Sunflowers* in 1987 for the then record-breaking price of over ¥5 billion (£24 million). There is now some concern that it may not be authentic, but no one is certain. This symbol of Japan's go-go Bubble years hangs alongside Cézanne's *Pommes et Serviette* (bought in 1990) in a dim glass box. The museum's core work is by Japanese artists, specifically Togo Seiji (1897-1978), who donated 200 of his own pieces and 250 items from his art collection.

Sword Museum

4-25-10 Yoyogi, Shibuya-ku (3379 1386). Sangubashi station (Odakyu line). **Open** 10am-4.30pm Tue-Sun. **Admission** ¥525; free concessions. **No credit cards.**

The confiscation of swords as offensive weapons during the American occupation after World War II threatened the traditional Japanese craft of sword-making. To safeguard it, the Society for the Preservation of Japanese Art Swords was established in 1948. Twenty years later, it opened this museum to display its collection of centuries-old swords and fittings. Even non-enthusiasts may find themselves mesmerised.

Tokyo Metropolitan Government Building No.1

2-8-1 Nishi-Shinjuku, Shinjuku-ku (5321 1111/ observatory 5320 7890/www.yokoso.metro. tokyo.jp). Tochomae station (Oedo line), exit 4. **Open** *North Observatory* 9.30am-11pm Tue-Sun. *South Observatory* 9.30am-5pm Mon, Wed-Sun. **Admission** free. **Map** Shinjuku p117.

Two of the best views over Tokyo have the added bonus of being free (unlike the Mori Tower's City View; *see p105*). Each of the TMG twin towers (243m/797ft tall) has an observation deck on the 45th floor, affording a 360° panorama interrupted only by the other tower – on a clear day you can see Mt Fuji. Admire the cityscape while sipping a coffee from the cafeteria in the centre of the vast floor. The south observatory is the best choice by day; after dark, the view from the north deck is preferable. The easiest way to get to the TMG complex from Shinjuku station is by underground tunnel; it's well signposted. Other buildings in west Shinjuku with free viewing areas include the Shinjuku Centre Building (53F) and the Nomura Building (49F).

Toto Super Space

L-Tower Bldg 26F-27F, 1-6-1 Nishi-Shinjuku (3345 1010). Shinjuku station (Yamanote, Chuo, Sobu lines), west exit; (Marunouchi line), exits A16, A17; (Shinjuku line), exit 3 or Shinjuku-Nishiguchi station (Oedo line), exit D1. **Open** 10am-6pm daily. Closed 1st & 3rd Wed of mth. **Admission** free. **Map** Shinjuku p117.

It may be a dubious honour, but Japan leads the world in toilet technology. This showroom has something to intrigue even the most jaded loo user. As well as the now-standard bidet toilets, Toto also makes baths that fill themselves automatically and can be switched on via the internet. And for the health-conscious user, there's a toilet that analyses what's deposited in there. No, really.

Getting there

Shinjuku is served by about a dozen railway lines, including the JR Yamanote, Chuo, Saikyo and Sobu lines, and the Keio line, the Odakyu line and the Seibu Shinjuku line. It's also on the Marunouchi, Oedo and Shinjuku subway lines. Tochomae (on the Oedo line) is the closest station to the TMG headquarters, while Shinjuku-Sanchome (Marunouchi and Shinjuku lines) is convenient for Kabuki-cho and Ni-chome.

Tokyo Metropolitan Government Building No.1.

Hey, big spender?

Tokyo has officially lost its title of 'most expensive city in the world' to Moscow, but the Japanese haven't given up their love affair with luxury. Still, there are plenty of options for the traveller on a budget. The **Tokyo Metropolitan Government** offers reasonably priced volunteer-guided tours (up to ¥3,540 per person, depending on numbers) of the major tourist areas (www.tourism.metro. tokyo.jp). At the other end of the spectrum, for ¥200,000 a day, **Bespoke Tokyo** (www. bespoketokyo.jp) looks after businesspeople, celebrities and money-no-object tourists.

Luxury

The ¥5,000 loaf. Baked in Paris on Thursday, flown to Tokyo at the weekend, and on the shelf at **Takashimaya** in Nihonbashi (*see p190*) by Wednesday; the Poilâne loaf is pricier than a bottle of Veuve Clicquot, but only five of them make the 9,600-kilometre (6,000-mile) trip to Tokyo each week. And, yes, it tastes like a six-day-old loaf.

The ¥2,000,000 hotel room. The new **Ritz Carlton** at Tokyo Midtown in Roppongi (*see p107* **Tokyo Midtown**) is the city's highest hotel and boasts its loftiest prices. A 24-hour stay in the 300-square-metre (3,229-square-foot) Ritz Carlton Suite on the 53rd floor will set you back ¥1,388 a minute.

The ¥18.9 million Hello Kitty. For the girl who has everything, the ultimate souvenir from the Capital of Cute is a limited-edition, 590-gram platinum figurine of the feline superstar, which went on sale at **Mitsukoshi** in Nihonbashi (*see p189*) in December 2006.

The ¥80,000 steak. **Aragawa** in Shinbashi (3-3-9 Shinbashi, Minato-ku, 3591 8765) topped the *Forbes* list of the world's most expensive restaurants. It dishes up steaks cut from pampered, beer-fed Japanese cattle, served with pepper and mustard. The top price is for prize-winning meat; 'regular' steaks start at ¥50,000.

The ¥90,000 city view. Charter a helicopter from **Excel Air** (www.excel-air.com) and fly up to five people over the metropolis by day or night. As the chopper tilts from side to side, you can look straight down on the chaos below. The tours leave from Urayasu Heliport near Maihama station on the JR Keiyou line.

Budget

The ¥150 loaf. The six- or eight-slice Pasco loaf sells at every major convenience store. It's soft, fluffy and moist when you buy it; and virtually the same a week later. Don't ask why.

The ¥1,500 bed for the night. Bangkok this isn't, but that doesn't mean you can't find cheap digs. A bunk in a 12-person shared dormitory at the **Khaosan Tokyo Asakusa Annex** (www.khaosan-tokyo.com, 3842 8286) near the Sumida river is cheap enough to make the stingiest backpacker smile.

The ¥150 souvenir. Japanese potters spend a lifetime mastering skills to create world-famous plates, cups and sake flasks, but you can get replicas and other bargain gifts at **Outlet** in Daikanyama (1-34-17 Ebisu-Nishi, Shibuya-ku, 5489 5404).

The ¥120 meal in a can. In the geek wonderland of **Akihabara** (*see p195*), where the boys spend every yen on manga and maids, there are few restaurants. Instead, there is canned *oden* (boiled fish and veg) from vending machines.

The free city view. The observatories on the 45th floors of the **Tokyo Metropolitan Government Building No.1** (*see p120*) offer near-panoramic views of the city and don't cost a yen.

Ueno

A touch of Old Tokyo, with a bustling street market and picturesque park.

Map p123

Long before feng shui gained a foothold in the West, China's ancient rules of geomancy were being strictly applied in feudal Japan. And it is thanks to feng shui that Ueno, one of Tokyo's main sub-centres, came into being. Around the start of the 17th century, shogun Tokugawa Ieyasu began assiduously building a new administrative capital out of the fishing village in a swamp that came to be known as Tokyo. His successor, Hidetada, was advised that he ought to build a great temple north-east of Edo Castle to guard against the evil spirits that were apt to enter from that inauspicious direction. So, in 1625, he duly installed a massive complex of 36 temples in Ueno.

Only a hint of his complex remains today, but the land that the temples occupied is home to the feature for which Ueno is now best known – its park. **Ueno Koen** (Ueno Park) was Tokyo's first public park when it opened in 1873, but just five years earlier it had been the site of the bloody Battle of Ueno between supporters of the new Meiji government and warriors still loyal to the Tokugawa shogun. The government won, but in the process **Kanei-ji**, the centre of the temple complex where six of Japan's 15 shoguns are buried, was destroyed. Today the site holds a temple and three cemeteries.

The park contains a slew of attractions – from museums to shrines and temples to a zoo. It lacks lawns and picnic areas, but is famed for its collection of cherry trees. Enormous throngs of Tokyoites gather here every spring in blossom season, though these raucous affairs tend to focus more on portable karaoke machines than flowers. The groundsheets that the partygoers sometimes leave behind get reused for shelters by the homeless people who live in the park.

If you arrive at the JR station, head to the main (above-ground) hall, one of the few station buildings in Tokyo to have largely survived Japan's decades of redevelopment. The high ceilings and grandiose architectural style recall a time when this was one of the city's main transport hubs, ferrying people in from the north before the *shinkansen* dragged most passengers away to the main terminus at Tokyo station. That was when the east side of Tokyo was king, and Asakusa and Ueno were the city's playgrounds, before the action started

Ameyoko Market. See p125.

Sightseeing

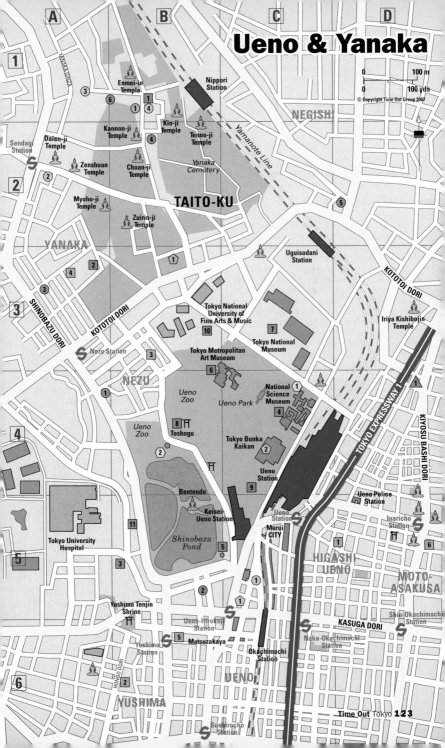

Ueno & Yanaka

to drift westwards, to Shibuya and Shinjuku. The first subway line in Asia opened in 1927 to link Asakusa to Ueno and is now part of the Ginza line.

There's more to Ueno than its park, though. Near the station is the area's other great attraction: a lively, exciting street market that offers a real flavour of the Tokyo of yesteryear. To the north of Ueno, across Kototoi Dori, is **Yanaka** (*see p127*), another of Tokyo's *shitamachi* ('low city') districts; it's a short walk from the northern end of Ueno Park into Yanaka Cemetery and its environs.

INSIDE THE PARK

Take the park exit from the station, cross the road and pick up an English map from the information booth. Ueno Koen is home to some of Japan's greatest cultural assets and Tokyo's best collection of museums. The first you come to is the Le Corbusier-designed **National Museum of Western Art**. Next door is the **National Science Museum** (*see p221*) and, north of that, the **Tokyo National Museum**, the grandest museum in the park. All the other museums – the **Tokyo Metropolitan Art Museum**, the **University Art Museum** and **Ueno Royal Museum** – are within easy striking distance. For more information, see the individual entries below.

Shitamachi Museum. *See p125*.

The park also contains **Ueno Zoo** (*see p220*), the most famous in the country, with a diverse selection of critters, from a giant panda and Asian lions to wolf-like *dholes* and bison, alongside more familiar animals. The zoo occupies the western section of the park. Near to its main entrance, just around from the kiddies' amusement park, is the approach to **Toshogu Shrine**, the finest of the park's historical monuments.

The most attractive part of Ueno Park is the southern area around **Shinobazu Pond** (Shinobazunoike). Given its present inland position, it may be difficult to imagine that this large pond was once part of an inlet of Tokyo Bay. Causeways divide the pond, which is now freshwater, into three: one section is part of Ueno Zoo and has a large colony of cormorants, one is a boating pond, and the third is home to a great diversity of waterfowl and comes alive with pink lotus flowers in summer. At the centre of the three causeways is an island on which sits **Bentendo**, a strong contender for the title of most charming temple in Tokyo. It is dedicated to Benten (also called Benzaiten), the goddess of music and feminine beauty and the only female among the Seven Deities of Good Fortune (these auspicious figures are especially evident at New Year). You can nourish more earthy parts at the food stalls that line the approach to the temple.

From Bentendo, cross over Dobutsuen Dori (the main path that bisects the park) to reach the red **Kiyomizu Kannondo** temple. It is dedicated to Kannon and modelled on the famous Kiyomizu-dera temple in Kyoto. This was completed in 1631, and is one of the few temple buildings to have survived the destruction of the Battle of Ueno.

Nearby, in the south-east corner of this side of the park, stands the bronze statue of **Saigo Takamori**, a fascinating figure and the person on whom Katsumoto, the warrior played by Ken Watanabe in *The Last Samurai*, is based. Saigo played an instrumental role in the Meiji restoration of 1868, which ended the reign of the shoguns and brought into power a new imperial government. Later, Saigo became disenchanted with the government he had done so much to create, and got mixed up with an ill-fated rebellion, which ended with Saigo and his supporters committing *hara-kiri*. It is this rebellion that formed the basis for the Tom Cruise film. Of course, Hollywood presents Katsumoto as a virile warrior, whereas in actual fact, by the time of his rebellion, Saigo was so obese he had to be carried around in a chair. His statue in Ueno Park (unveiled in 1898) depicts him in a deliberately unmilitary mode, in a kimono taking his dog for a walk.

Toshogu Shrine. *See p126.*

At a fork in the road about 90 metres (295 feet) into the market is a dubious-looking building with an amazing basement food hall selling whole frogs, durian fruit and other difficult-to-get delicacies from around the world. Meanwhile, under the railway tracks, cheap watches and electronic goods are the order of the day, along with bootleg CDs.

A couple of additional attractions are located across the western side of the park. Beyond the pond's boating area, on the other side of the main road, is **Yokoyama Taikan Memorial Hall**, dedicated to the life and work of one of Japan's greatest painters of the modern era. Following the road above the hall in a southerly direction will bring you to **Kyu Iwasaki-tei House & Gardens**, which was built by influential British architect Josiah Conder, one of many Westerners to bring Western learning to Japan in the 19th century.

Kyu Iwasaki-tei House & Gardens

1-3-45 Ikenohata, Taito-ku (3823 8033/www.tokyo-park.or.jp/english/park/detail_06.html#kyuiwasakitei). Yushima station (Chiyoda line), exit 1. **Open** 9am-5pm daily. **Admission** ¥400; free concessions. **No credit cards. Map** Ueno & Yanaka p123.

Built in 1896 for Iwasaki Hisaya, son of the founder of the Mitsubishi conglomerate, this compound reveals the fin-de-siècle sheen beneath Ueno's grimy surface. Josiah Conder designed the recently renovated main residence – a two-storey wooden structure with Jacobean and Pennsylvanian country-house elements (and the first Western-style toilet in Japan) – and the adjacent billiards room in the form of a log cabin. In the large tatami rooms, visitors can sip green tea and admire *fusuma* (sliding doors) painted with seasonal motifs by Hashimoto Gaho.

National Museum of Western Art (Kokuritsu Seiyo Bijutsukan)

7-7 Ueno Koen, Taito-ku (3828 5131/www.nmwa.go.jp). Ueno station (Yamanote line), park exit; (Ginza, Hibiya lines), Shinobazu exit. **Open** 9.30am-5.30pm Tue-Thur, Sat, Sun; 9.30am-8pm Fri. **Admission** ¥420; free-¥130 concessions; additional charge for special exhibitions. Free 2nd & 4th Sat of mth. **No credit cards. Map** Ueno & Yanaka p123.

The core collection housed in this 1959 Le Corbusier-designed building, Japan's only national museum devoted to Western art, was assembled by Kawasaki shipping magnate Matsukata Kojiro in the early 1900s. Considering that the collection was begun so recently, it is surprisingly good, ranging from 15th-century icons to Monet to Pollock.

Shitamachi Museum (Shitamachi Fuzoku Shiryokan)

2-1 Ueno Koen, Taito-ku (3823 7451/www.taitocity.net/taito/shitamachi). Ueno station (Yamanote, Ginza, Hibiya lines), Shinobazu exit. **Open** 9.30am-4.30pm Tue-Sun. **Admission** ¥300; ¥100 concessions. **No credit cards. Map** Ueno & Yanaka p123.

Further south, at the corner of the pond next to the main road, stands the **Shitamachi Museum**. *Shitamachi* refers to the low-lying areas of Tokyo inhabited by the hoi polloi, and this small gem of a place recreates the city as it was in the 19th and early 20th centuries.

OUTSIDE THE PARK

History of a very different kind is to be found in the area around **Ameyoko** (*see p192*), which begins close by Ueno station on the other side of the main road from the park. The name hints at the place's history: the 'Ame' in Ameyoko originally referred to 'sweets', and the name meant 'confectioner's alley'. But during the occupation following World War II this became a major area for black-market goods, many of which came from the US military. Thus the 'American' aspect to the name took on significance.

Ameyoko is home to Tokyo's liveliest market, with more than 500 stalls shoehorned into a 400-metre (quarter-mile) stretch that leads south to Okachimachi station. The weekend crowds can be so thick that progress is at a snail's pace (watch your valuables: this is a popular spot for pickpockets). As well as myriad fishmongers and fruit and vegetable stalls, there are scores of small shops selling cheap jeans, T-shirts and goods 'inspired' by international designers. It is also a reliable source of hard-to-find foods and spices. Families from south and south-east Asia stock up on chillies, basmati rice and coriander, while homesick Americans seek solace in Milky Way bars or Hershey's chocolate imported from their homeland.

This museum presents the living environment of ordinary Tokyoites between the pivotal Meiji restoration of 1868 and the Great Earthquake of 1923. It's a small counterpart to the large-scale Edo-Tokyo Museum (*see p68*) in Ryogoku. Take off your shoes and step into re-creations of a merchant's shop, a coppersmith's workshop and a sweet shop. Everything has a hands-on intimacy: open up a drawer and you'll find a sewing kit or a children's colouring book. Upstairs are traditional toys that even today's kids still delight in. **Photo** *p124.*

Tokyo Metropolitan Art Museum

8-36 Ueno Koen, Taito-ku (3823 6921/www.tobikan. jp). Ueno station (Yamanote line), park exit; (Ginza, Hibiya lines), Shinobazu exit. **Open** *Main Gallery* 9am-5pm Tue-Sun. *Library* 9am-5pm daily (closed 1st & 3rd Mon of mth). **Admission** *Galleries* vary: free-¥1,500; free-¥500 concessions. *Library* free. **Credit** (gift shop only, over ¥3,000) JCB, MC, V. **Map** Ueno & Yanaka p123.

Designed by Maekawa Kunio, this brick-faced art museum was largely constructed underground to remain unobtrusive, with limited success. Temporary shows in the main hall feature everything from traditional Japanese art to art nouveau.

Tokyo National Museum (Tokyo Kokuritsu Hakubutsukan)

13-9 Ueno Koen, Taito-ku (3822 1111/www.tnm. go.jp). Ueno station (Yamanote line), park exit; (Ginza, Hibiya lines), Shinobazu exit. **Open** 9.30am-5pm Tue-Sun. **Admission** ¥500; free-¥420 concessions; additional charge for special exhibitions. **Credit** (gift shop only) JCB, MC, V. **Map** Ueno & Yanaka p123.

If you have just one day to devote to museum-going in Tokyo and are interested in Japanese art and artefacts, this is the place to visit. Japan's oldest and largest museum houses over 89,000 items. Past the ornate gateway, there's a wide courtyard and fountain surrounded by three main buildings. Directly in front is the Honkan, or main gallery, dating from 1937, which displays the permanent collection of Japanese arts and antiquities. The 25 rooms regularly rotate their exhibitions of paintings, ceramics, swords, kimonos, sculptures and the like. The Toyokan building to the right features three floors of artworks from other parts of Asia. The Hyokeikan, the 1909 European-style building to the left, is only open for special events. Behind the Hyokeikan is the Gallery of Horyu-ji Treasures, which houses some of Japanese Buddhism's most important and ancient artefacts, from the seventh-century Horyu-ji temple in Nara. The Heiseikan, behind the Honkan, holds month-long temporary blockbuster exhibitions of Japanese and Asian art. There are also plenty of places to eat around the complex, and a good gift shop.

Toshogu Shrine

9-88 Ueno Koen, Taito-ku (3822 3455). Ueno station (Yamanote line), park exit; (Ginza, Hibiya lines), Shinobazu exit. **Open** 9am-sunset daily. **Admission** ¥200; ¥100 concessions. *Garden* ¥600. **No credit cards. Map** Ueno & Yanaka p123.

Toshogu is dedicated to the first Tokugawa shogun, Ieyasu, and its style is similar to the shrine in Nikko (also called Toshogu; *see p292*) where he is buried. The Ueno Toshogu was built in 1627, then remodelled in 1651. It has withstood earthquakes and fires, as well as the Battle of Ueno, and is one of Tokyo's oldest buildings. The huge lantern on the left before the first gate is one of the largest in Japan. Karamon, the front gate of the temple, is famous for its dragon carvings. **Photo** *p125.*

Ueno Royal Museum (Ueno no Mori Bijutsukan)

1-2 Ueno Koen, Taito-ku (3833 4195/www.ueno-mori.org). Ueno station (Yamanote line), park exit; (Ginza, Hibiya lines), Shinobazu exit. **Open** 10am-5pm daily (until 6pm during special exhibitions). **Admission** varies; usually free. **No credit cards. Map** Ueno & Yanaka p123.

This medium-sized *Kunsthalle* in the woods of Ueno Park holds the annual VOCA exhibition of emerging Japanese artists, as well as touring shows from the likes of New York's MoMA and Barcelona's Picasso Museum. It has no permanent collection, and its temporary exhibitions are sporadic.

University Art Museum

12-8 Ueno Koen (5685 7755/www.geidai.ac.jp/ museum). Ueno station (Yamanote line), park exit; (Ginza, Hibiya lines), Shinobazu exit. **Open** 10am-5pm Tue-Sun. **Admission** ¥300; ¥100 concessions; additional charge for special exhibitions. **No credit cards. Map** Ueno & Yanaka p123.

The museum connected to Japan's most prestigious national art and music school has an impressive collection of over 40,000 objects, ranging from Japanese traditional art to Western paintings and photos. The large new building, opened in 1999, holds both permanent collections and some temporary exhibitions.

Yokoyama Taikan Memorial Hall

1-4-24 Ikenohata, Taito-ku (3821 1017/www.tctv. ne.jp/members/taikan). Yushima station (Chiyoda line), exit 1. **Open** 10am-4pm Thur-Sun. **Admission** ¥500; ¥200 concessions. **No credit cards. Map** Ueno & Yanaka p123.

Regarded as one of Japan's great modern painters, Yokoyama Taikan was born at the beginning of the Meiji restoration and lived through 89 years of change. In his house overlooking Shinobazu Pond, Yokoyama practised *nihonga* (traditional Japanese painting), taking images from nature as his inspiration. If his paintings don't impress, his gardens will. The house closes in bad weather and occasionally during the summer.

Getting there

Ueno is on the Yamanote line and Ginza and Hibiya subway lines; if you're heading for the park, arriving via the Yamanote line is the best option. At the northern end of the park is Uguisudani station, also on the Yamanote line; and at the southern end, Keisei-Ueno station, on the Kesei line. Yushima and Nezu stations, on the Chiyoda line, are not far away.

Yanaka

Tokyo's slow lane.

Map p123

When the frantic pace of Tokyo starts to wear you down, come to Yanaka. On the other sideof town from the concrete canyons of Shinjuku and Shibuya, this picturesque spot has somehow managed to survive many of the upheavals of the past century.

Low-key, low-rise Yanaka, together with the neighbouring districts of Nezu and Sendagi, forms a rough-shaped lozenge north-west of Ueno Park, between Nezu and Nishi-Nippori stations. But it's a world away from the grand museums and huge, brash street market of Ueno. Yanaka survives as an endearing place where life seems to potter along more or less just as it did a century ago.

The area is also home to Tokyo's highest concentration of temples, ranging from the grand to the humble. The temples were moved here from elsewhere in Tokyo following the 1657 Long Sleeves Fire, which destroyed much of the city. Yanaka has led something of a charmed life ever since. First it became a playground for the wealthy, and then almost a living museum of old Tokyo, escaping destruction in both the Kanto Earthquake of 1923 and the air raids in World War II.

The best way to see Yanaka is on foot; the route described below takes in many of the area's most famous sights. If you're prepared to risk getting lost, there's a lot more to be discovered in its steep, winding backstreets.

A WALKING TOUR OF YANAKA

First, take the Yamanote line to Nippori station. Leave by the west exit, which will bring you to a narrow footpath at the foot of a flight of steps. In front of you at the top of the steps is the main street through Yanaka Cemetery, but before heading there take a look at **Tenno-ji** temple at the start of the road. The temple was founded over 500 years ago and once covered a far larger area. Its star attraction is the bronze Buddha, cast in 1690, that overlooks the temple gate. The temple gained notoriety in the early 19th century, when it was one of the few places where people could buy lottery tickets. Naturally, it became a very popular spot – until the government spoiled all the fun and closed the business down. Tenno-ji is also dedicated to Bishamonten, one of the Seven Deities of Good Fortune.

Leave the temple grounds and head down the central avenue of **Yanaka Cemetery** (opened 1874), one of Tokyo's largest graveyards and, along with Aoyama Cemetery, one of its most picturesque. These days the avenue is usually quiet, but over 150 years ago it was a den of iniquity, lined with tea shops that doubled as brothels and illegal gambling dens. However, the cemetery does become rather popular during cherry-blossom time. The Japanese are oddly fond of holding blossom-viewing parties in the grounds of the city's cemeteries, and Yanaka is noted for its blooming cherry trees.

The cemetery contains the remains of many prominent figures, including Natsume Soseki (1867-1916), usually regarded by the Japanese as their finest modern writer. Before new banknotes went into circulation in 2004, all the ¥1,000 notes bore his image. Yanaka Cemetery is also the resting place of the last Tokugawa shogun, Yoshinobu (1837-1913), who surrendered power to the emperor in 1868.

Continue down the path until the *koban* (police box). To the left and slightly behind the *koban* is a small fenced-off area. The rubble inside is all that's left of Yanaka's five-storey pagoda, once the tallest building in Edo. Constructed in 1644, it burned down in 1772 and was rebuilt. It burned down for the last time in 1957, part of a macabre lovers' suicide pact. Turn right at the police box; the path you are on ends in a T-junction just past some modern houses. Facing you at the end of the street is **Choan-ji** temple, dedicated to Jurojin, a god of long life.

Turn right at the junction and on your left, down a side street, you will catch a glimpse of a traditional Japanese slate wall, part of the complex surrounding **Kannon-ji** temple, where two of the famous 47 *ronin* (*see p15* **Suicidal samurai**) studied. Inside the grounds on the right is a small pagoda dedicated to their memory.

Turn left out of the temple and continue along the main road. Shortly afterwards, on a corner on the right, is **Saboh Hanahenro** (7-17-11 Yanaka, 3822 6387, open 11am-6pm Wed-Sun, map Ueno & Yanaka p123), a friendly corner restaurant/teahouse, and then **Sandara** (7-18-6 Yanaka, 5814 8618, open 10.30am-6pm Tue-Sun, map Ueno & Yanaka p123), a charming little shop that sells traditional Japanese pottery. On the other side of the road, a little further on, is **Ryusen-ji**, a minor but picturesque temple with bending trees and sloping roofs. An alternative refuelling stop is **Jinenjiyo** (5-9-25 Yanaka, 3824 3162, open 11.30am-9.30pm Tue, Fri, Sat; 11.30am-5.30pm Wed, Thur, Sun, map Ueno & Yanaka p123), a quaint little coffee shop further up the road on your left. Its speciality is *'yakuzen* curry', which contains traditional Chinese medicines thought to be good for the circulation.

Further down, on the right, is the **Asakura Choso Museum**, situated in the black concrete building that was at one point the house and studio of sculptor Asakura Fumio. Despite its unprepossessing façade, it's a fascinating dwelling well worth a visit. From the museum, turn right and continue along the street, passing on your right an alleyway lined with small drinking dens, or *nomiya*. This is **Hatsunei Komichi**, one of the last wooden-roofed arcades in Tokyo.

At the end of the street, turn left (to return to Nippori station, turn right) and follow the road to the right, down a flight of steps. On the way, you'll pass eccentric Persian/Turkish restaurant **Zakuro** (Nishi-Nippori Konishi Bldg B1F, 3-14-13 Nishi-Nippori, 5685 5313, http://zakuro.oops.jp, open 11am-11pm Mon, Tue, Thur-Sun, map Ueno & Yanaka p123). Turn right at the bottom of the steps, and 50 metres down the road stands **Midori-ya** (3-13-5 Nishi-Nippori, 3828 1746, open 10am-6.30pm (6pm in winter) Mon, Tue, Thur-Sun, map Ueno & Yanaka p123), which is a traditional maker of hand-woven basketware. Prices range from ¥500 for trinkets to over ¥30,000 for handbags. Return to the foot of the steps and turn right, into the incongruously named **Yanaka Ginza**, the area's main (pedestrianised) shopping street. A surprising number of traditional businesses still survive; notable among these is **Goto no Ame** (3-15-1 Nishi-Nippori, 3821 0880, open 10.30am-8pm Mon, Tue, Thur-Sat, 10.30am-7pm Sun), which sells traditional sweets, many made on the premises. Other shops offer such wares as *geta* (Japanese wooden shoes), green tea, rice crackers, pottery or tofu.

Turn left at the bottom of Yanaka Ginza, and walk straight on, past the **Ryokan Katsutaro** (*see p53*), until you reach the traffic lights at the end of the street. Turn left at the lights and walk up the hill to **Daien-ji** temple, established in 1591. This is a highly unusual building in that it consists of two symmetrical halves. The left half was intended to serve as a Shinto shrine, the right as a Buddhist temple, but such plans were rejected by the shogunate, which enforced the separation of Buddhism and

Shinto. The temple is famous for its colourful chrysanthemum festival in mid October.

Leave the temple, turn left, cross the road at the pedestrian crossing and turn right by the large white school building with a pagoda. Continue straight down this road, bearing left when it forks, to reach the **Daimyo Clock Museum**, which showcases the Japanese-style clocks made for Edo-era *daimyo* feudal lords.

Return to the main street from the museum, turn left and then next left, down a slope with a wonderful Japanese inn, **Ryokan Sawanoya** (*see p53*), close by a crossroads. Take the road to the right at this junction and follow the small street for about 500 metres (a third of a mile). This brings you out to Sansaki-zaka, and just to the left is **Isetatsu** (2-18-9 Yanaka, 3823 1453, open 10am-6pm daily, map Ueno & Yanaka p123). This shop sells fine decorated papers, whose patterns are made from intricately carved wooden blocks.

Following Sansaki-zaka down brings you to Sendagi station (on the Chiyoda line). The walk can be ended here, or you can go on to **Nezu Shrine**, which is about 400 metres (a quarter of a mile) away: turn left on to the main road, Shinobazu Dori, and then right at the first main junction. Dating from 1706, the shrine is a colourful spot with a giant painted gate and landscaped gardens stretching up a hillside. For most of the year it's an attractive peaceful spot, but in April, when the hillside azalea bushes bloom, the whole place swarms with camera-toting visitors. An interesting time to visit throughout the year is 6.30am, when scores of locals gather to go through their daily communal exercises, all directed by a voice on a crackly radio.

Three art museums are also located nearby. Return to Shinobazu Dori, turn right and then continue as far as the big junction with Kototoi Dori. Turn right and walk for 300 metres until you reach a largish junction; take the road to the left, and you will soon see the **Tachihara Michizo Memorial Museum**, followed by the **Takeshisa Yumeji Museum of Art** and **Yayoi Museum of Art**.

It's best to avoid Yanaka on Mondays and Wednesdays, when this sleepy corner gets even sleepier as many of its cafés and museums close.

Asakura Choso Museum

7-18-10 Yanaka, Taito-ku (3821 4549/www.taitocity. net/taito/asakura/). Nippori station (Yamanote line), west exit. **Open** 9.30am-4.30pm Tue-Thur, Sat, Sun. **Admission** ¥400; ¥150 concessions. **No credit cards. Map** Ueno & Yanaka p123.
This museum is the former house and atelier of Asakura Fumio (1883-1964), who was a leading figure in modern Japanese sculpture. The three-level building – designed by the artist in 1936 – melds

Take it easy with a stroll through the streets of low-key **Yanaka**.

modernism and traditional Japanese architecture. The centrepiece is a delightful rock and water garden, also designed by the artist. From the rooftop garden you can see just how low-rise Yanaka is compared with the rest of Tokyo.

Daimyo Clock Museum

2-1-27 Yanaka, Taito-ku (3821 6913). Nezu station (Chiyoda line), exit 1. **Open** 10am-4pm Tue-Sun. Closed July-Sept. **Admission** ¥300; ¥100-¥200 concessions. **No credit cards.** **Map** Ueno & Yanaka p123.
Daimyo feudal lords were the only people who could afford the clocks displayed here. Before Japan adopted the solar calendar in 1870, there was a set number of hours between sunrise and sunset, with the result that the length of an hour was longer in summer than in winter. Times were named after the animals of the Chinese zodiac. This one-room museum displays dozens of other timepieces, from alarm clocks to watches worn with a kimono.

Tachihara Michizo Memorial Museum

2-4-5 Yayoi, Bunkyo-ku (5684 8780/www.tachihara.jp). Nezu station (Chiyoda line), exit 1. **Open** 10am-5pm Tue-Sun. **Admission** ¥400; ¥200-¥300 concessions. **No credit cards.**
One of three small museums facing a historic gate of Tokyo University. This one is dedicated to Tachihara Michizo, an artist noted for his pastels. Unfortunately the museum does not supply English translations, though it is still worth a look.

Takeshisa Yumeji Museum of Art & Yayoi Museum of Art

2-4-3 Yayoi, Bunkyo-ku (Takeshisa Yumeji Museum 5689 0462/Yayoi Museum 3812 0012/www.yayoi-yumeji-museum.jp). Nezu station (Chiyoda line), exit 1. **Open** 10am-4.30pm Tue-Sun. **Admission** ¥800; ¥400-¥700 concessions. **No credit cards.**
This building houses two museums, both of them dedicated to the history of Japanese manga (comics) and illustrations.

Getting there

Nippori station is on the Yamanote line. Other stations in the area include Sendagi and Nezu, both on the Chiyoda line, and Nishi-Nippori, on both lines.

Further Afield

Step outside the main loop for some of the city's funkiest neighbourhoods.

Just off the tourist radar sit several lively, characterful neighbourhoods that are well worth checking out. **Naka-Meguro** – arguably Tokyo's coolest area right now – is the spiritual home of its design-conscious twentysomethings. **Shimo-Kitazawa** meanwhile, is young, vibrant and one of the cheapest places for a decent night out. And the first handful of stations along the **Chuo line**, one of the city's longest and most crowded commuter lines, also offer pockets of interest. We've included a selection of attractions dotted about the metropolitan area below too.

Naka-Meguro

To the uninitiated, Naka-Meguro – which lies to the south of Shibuya and east of Ebisu – might seem to be a wholly unremarkable corner of the city. But the generic veneer is part of the appeal: this area doesn't like to advertise the fact that it has recently emerged as Tokyo's hippest hang-out. Relatively cheap rents – for central Tokyo – have attracted a hip crowd of young artists, designers and musicians, and, crucially for a land in which shopkeeping is considered an art form, upcoming retailers.

The Meguro river, which defines this funky district, is lined with small cafés, boutiques and interior outfitters catering to image-conscious locals and curious visitors, many of whom wander in from neighbouring shopping haven Daikanyama. These establishments are almost all owned and run by entrepreneurs rather than big corporations – rare for Japan – and the cool spaces they have created are what fuels the hype surrounding this trendy tract.

Naka-Meguro retains a sleepy feel, and places of interest are not clustered enough for it ever to seem crowded, except during *sakura* (cherry-blossom) season, and even then, the riverside festivities are a relatively understated affair.

Art fans visit at all times of year to view the **Museum of Contemporary Sculpture**. Fans of café culture, meanwhile, should head for **Chano-ma** (Kangyo Bldg 6F, 1-22-4 Kami-Meguro, 3792 9898, open noon-2am Mon-Thur, Sun, noon-4am Fri, Sat). Located just across from the train station, with a nondescript lift door at ground level, this urban haven has clever lighting, Eames chairs and elevated mattress-seating for socks-off sprawling.

For hearty dining, several rowdy *izakaya* are situated by the river, close to the station. **Aguri** (*see p166*) and pizza specialist **Salvatore** (1-22-4 Kami-Meguro, 3719 3680, open noon-2pm, 6pm-10pm daily) are both worth a visit. But to sample the local speciality *nabe* (hotpot), follow the train tracks away from the river to the famed *motsu nabe* (offal hotpot) restaurant **Torigoya** (3-5-22 Kami-Meguro, 3710 6762, open 5pm-midnight Mon-Sat, noon-midnight Sun), run by a camp amateur *enka* singer. On the other side of the tracks is a metalworking factory turned pork *nabe* restaurant, **Butanabe Kenkyushitsu** (3-5-19 Kami-Meguro, 3713 7250, open 6pm-2am Tue-Sat, 6pm-midnight Sun). Following the tracks a couple of blocks further on the Torigoya side brings you to the unadvertised entrance of **Depot** (*see p242*), a restaurant with a cavernous gallery displaying edgy street art.

Chano-ma.

Mizuma Art Gallery (*see p242*), whose well-connected curator brings in a steady stream of Tokyo's hottest upcoming artists, is the only venue in this locale that doesn't double up as a shop or eaterie. Visit **Cow Books** (1-14-11 Aobadai, 5459 1747, www.cowbooks.jp, open 2pm-pm Tue-Sun) – facing the river – for out-of-print books and vintage magazines, and **Buro-stil** (1-6-19 Higashiyama, 3794 9955, open 1-10pm daily, closed 2nd and 3rd Tue of mth) for wacky retro furniture.

Fashion shopping is what the vast majority of visitors come to Naka-Meguro for. In addition to a dozen or so second-hand stores and a handful of posh boutiques pushing upmarket European prêt-à-porter, there are some excellent home-grown labels that are worth a browse. Check out the eye-opening oufits on offer at the flagship store of geeky teen favourite **Frapbois** (1-20-4 Aobadai, 6415 4688, www.frapbois.jp, open 11am-8pm daily) and, behind it, **Metal Burger** (MS Bldg B1F, 1-19-7 Aobadai, 5728 4765, www.metalburger.com, open noon-8pm daily), which supplies punk looks to jovial anarchists. The out-there vintage selection at hole-in-the-wall **Waingman Wassa** (1-23-5, Aobadai, 5773 5586, open 1-9pm daily) perfectly encapsulates the area's irreverent style.

Museum of Contemporary Sculpture

4-12-18 Naka-Meguro, Meguro-ku (3792 5858/ www.museum-of-sculpture.org). Naka-Meguro station (Hibiya, Tokyu Toyoko lines), central exit. **Open** 10am-5pm Tue-Sun. **Admission** free.
The Watanabe Collection includes more than 200 pieces by 56 contemporary Japanese artists. Three outdoor areas filled with large, mostly conceptual works complement two storeys of figurative studies. The marble tombstones in the adjacent graveyard provide an interesting counterpoint.

Getting there

Naka-Meguro station is the first stop on the Hibiya subway line and two stops from Shibuya on the Tokyu Toyoko line.

Shimo-Kitazawa

Shimo-Kitazawa, a short train ride from both Shibuya and Shinjuku, is a favourite among young Tokyoites looking for something a little less trashy than Shibuya. It's loaded with cool shops, cafés and bars, though the odd faceless chain has muscled in.

The award-winning novelist Ekuni Kaori, author of the recently translated tale of tangled Tokyo relationships *Twinkle, Twinkle*, and film actor Takenaka Naoto (*Shall We Dance*, *Trick*) have their homes here. The office of the late Itami Juzo, one of Japan's ground-breaking movie directors, is nearby, and legendary theatre directors such as Ninagawa Yukio and Mori Hajime have staged productions on the area's illustrious boards.

The creative impetus behind the area's growth came from the *sho-gekijou* (small theatre) movement of the 1960s, which was born of frustration with the way theatres were dominated by either Western realism or tradition-bound *kabuki* and *Noh*. Its theatres gave younger actors and directors the freedom to express themselves, and a large number of them came to be concentrated here.

As well as theatre, the neighbourhood has become famous for its 'live houses' – the dark, dynamic, box-like venues where Tokyo's aspiring bands hone their skills. At weekends, these places – particularly the well-known ones, such as **Shelter** (*see p261*), **Club Que** (*see p260*) and **Club 251** (*see p259*) – are rammed full with a body-pierced, leather-wearing crowd moshing politely in front of a tiny stage.

The station has two exits, north and south, both of which lead to areas of interest. From the north exit, turn right and after about 200 metres, you'll come to the first set of crossroads. The street that stretches away to both sides takes you past boutiques selling new and second-hand clothes ranging from cute to bizarre, with everything in-between. There's been in influx of mainstream and chain shops in the past few years, but the area's essential character remains one of quirky individuality.

Keep walking, and you'll get to another crossroads. Turning right leads back to the train tracks, and straight-ahead down a small alleyway will take you past **fxg** (*see p207*) – the shop that spearheaded the current wave of cheap, stylish opticians – to Ichibangai Dori.

Over on the other side of the station you'll find plenty of life after dark, as this where local residents and visitors come to eat, drink and mosh themselves into a happy, eardrum-ringing haze. Directly opposite the station's south exit is the area's main street, Minami Shotengai, which is packed full of fast-food shops, *pachinko* parlours and cheap boutiques. Half-way down the street the area's distinctive character starts to reveal itself, with its second-hand book, game and CD shops. A road branching off to the right, with Mr Donuts on the corner, points the way to a quiet, leafy street with one of the best *izakaya* in the area – the stately **Shirube** (3413 3785, open 5.30pm-midnight Sun-Thur; 5.30pm-2am Fri, Sat). Right opposite Shirube is English pub **Heaven's Door** (*see p181*), a haven for those looking for a decent pint and the UK football.

Sightseeing

Going back to the main street and walking right to the bottom, you'll find a knot of streets leading off in five directions. These streets contain numerous little bars and restaurants, many of them serving ethnic food and drink.

Back at the south exit, turn left and head down the nameless street that has a Starbucks on the corner. Halfway down is the basement venue Club Que, while at the end is Chazawa Dori, with Shelter off to the left and Club 251 about ten minutes' walk to the right. The streets between the Minami Shotengai and Chazawa Dori are well worth a wander, as they host several 'natural-food' *izakaya* and the most famous *sho-gekijou* in the area, the **Honda Theatre** (2-10-15 Kitazawa, Setagaya-ku, 3468 0030, www.honda-geki.com).

Arty, lively and occasionally pretentious, Shimo-Kitazawa has the power to restore the faith of those who say Tokyo is losing its soul.

Getting there

Shimo-Kitazawa station is on the Keio Inokashira line (from Shibuya station) and the Odakyu line (from Shinjuku station).

The Chuo line

The JR Chuo line heads west in the evening from its first station, Tokyo, stopping at the key business hubs of Ochanomizu, Yotsuya and Shinjuku before trekking out to the 'bedtowns' and suburbs of western Tokyo and the cities beyond. Its cargo is a mass of sleeping, occasionally drunk, always exhausted commuters heading home. In the morning it all happens in reverse: the Chuo line picks up the same crew of wage slaves and spits them out again in the bowl of central Tokyo for another day's Japan Inc.

The Chuo line is one of the most important train lines in the capital, and one of the most crowded in all of Japan, with commuters jammed in so tightly it's – almost – worth joining in for the experience. Wise travellers, however, avoid it between 7.30am and 9.30am (into the city) and 6pm and 9pm (out of the city). The last train of the night from Shinjuku station, at around 12.30am, is a great way to come face to face – literally – with the locals, and redefine your concept of personal space .

Living on the government-run Chuo line is more expensive than on the privately owned lines, because services run every three minutes at peak times and stop at all the major commercial centres. The line is given a high priority by JR, second only to the Yamanote line. Only the occasional platform jumper affects its solid punctuality. It's also famous

for gropers (although this is now changing, following publicity and increasing prosecution by JR), drunks and cattle-truck conditions at the times outlined above.

The first two stations out of Shinjuku – Okubo and Higashi-Nakano – contain little of note. The most interesting locales are between Nakano and Kichijoji stations; below we describe the highlights of each area.

These stations are served by two types of train: the yellow-coloured local (Sobu line) and the orange-coloured express (Chuo line). The Sobu line starts in Chiba prefecture and stops at all stations (including Shinjuku), but goes no further west than Mitaka. From Shinjuku, the Chuo line plonks down first at Nakano before going station by station out to various termination points, the furthest located deep in the suburbs of west Tokyo. Trains run between roughly 6am and midnight, and their frequency makes it easy to hop from one destination to another; stations are only a few minutes apart. If you're exploring at the weekend, take the Sobu line – because Chuo trains stop only at Ogikubo, rather than at every station between Nakano and Mitaka. After hours, take a taxi.

Further along the line are more delights, such as the historic buildings held at the open-air branch of the **Edo-Tokyo Open-Air Architecture Museum** in Musashi-Koganei.

Nakano

Although best known these days for its cheap shopping, Nakano was once home to 80,000 dogs. The fifth shogun, Tokugawa Tsunaiyasho, was particularly fond of mutts, and in 1695 built an *inuyashiki* (dog castle) across the whole of Nakano to keep his tens of thousands of canine mates in comfort. Dogs can still be seen today, wandering the streets, unaware of their providence.

A must-see for fans of manga, *anime* and 'cosplay' (costume play) is the sprawling empire of **Mandarake**. What was once one shop selling recycled manga comics has slowly spread its Akira-like tentacles across **Nakano Broadway** (*see p194*), the town's main shopping mall next to the station's north exit. Now, 14 shops on three floors of the four-storey centre sell comics, figurines, vintage toys, animation cells, CDs, video games, posters, cosplay costumes – in fact, anything related to Japan's *otaku* phenomenon (*see pp30-3*). Start on the third floor at comic HQ, and lose an afternoon wandering around. Key rings and tiny figurines sell from ¥100, and make cheap and unique souvenirs. Japanese schoolgirl dresses can be had for a bigger outlay. Broadway is also

Hip area **Shimo-Kitazawa** is packed with cool shops. *See p131*.

home to a host of discount shoe and fashion
shops, with prices far below those charged a
five-minute tain ride away in Shinjuku.

The warren of streets around the Broadway
complex has scores of restaurants, bars and
izakaya, many offering food at bargain prices.

Slightly out of Nakano centre are quirky
Tetsugakudo Park and the **Toy Museum**.

Tetsugakudo Park

*1-34-28 Matsugaoka, Nakano-ku (3954 4881). Arai
Yakushi-mae station (Seibu Shinjuku line), north exit
then 12mins walk or Nakano station (Chuo line), north
exit then bus to Tetsugakudo.* **Open** 9am-5pm daily.
A hillside park founded by philosopher Inoue Enryo,
who wanted to enshrine philosophical theory in
physical form. The park contains 77 spots that sym-
bolise different doctrines. On the top of the hill are
six Meiji-era buildings that are open to the public
during *hanami* (cherry-blossom viewing) and in
October on public holidays and at weekends.

Toy Museum

*2-12-10 Arai, Nakano-ku (3387 5461/www.toy-art.
co.jp/museum.html). Nakano station (Chuo line),
north exit.* **Open** 10.30am-4pm Mon, Wed, Thur,
Sat, Sun. **Admission** ¥500; free under-2s.
No credit cards.
This hands-on, crafts-oriented place has no shortage
of local kids busy playing. And there's not a video
game or TV in sight.

Koenji

Koenji is home to a youthful live music scene
and plenty of students. A cluster of bars around
both sides of the station exit provide a window
into a selection of musical styles – mainly
punk/grunge, but also jazz, country and
western, and soul. The best of these, **Inaoiza**
(2F Sunny Mansion, 2-38-16 Koenjikita, 3336
4480, open 8pm-2am daily), is a decades-old bar
that serves up many a random treat. Local
talent plays most evenings from 8pm, and entry
is ¥1,500, or free if no one is jamming.

Also worth a visit is **Las Meninas** (*see
p181*), run by affable Geordie Johnny Miller.
Enjoy seasonal dishes with a Mediterranean/
tapas focus, supported by of 30 outstanding
Spanish wines and 15 sherries. Prices are half
what you would pay in central Tokyo. Ask for a
map at the police box just outside the north exit
– staff are used to directing foreigners.

Koenji also has a reputation as Tokyo's centre
for all things associated with the southern
Japanese island of Okinawa. Tuck into some
Okinawan food at the Tokyo-famous **Dachibin**
(3-2-13 Koenji-Kita, 3337 1352, open 5pm-5am
daily). Most of the cooking is *chanpuri* (mixed
fried things) and many dishes feature the bitter
flavours of the Okinawan vegetable *goya* –

Inokashira Park.

chanpuri goya is a good start. If you tire of the
pedestrian flavours of Orion, the island's own
beer, then ask for *awamori* – Okinawan sake. It
comes in two strengths: five-year-old 35 per cent
and the older 45 per cent. Drink with respect.

Asagaya

Seeing itself as the prince among the kissed
toads of the Chuo line, Asagaya strives to match
the urbanity of inner Tokyo. This self-confidence
is based on both slight and solid cultural
connections. The area's well-founded reputation
for jazz grows every year as its Jazz Street
festival, held in October, continues to mutate
both in size and composition. A number of bars
showcase local jazz players throughout the year.

Scribblers of all types laid the foundations
for Asagaya's self-important world view. The
Asagaya-kai was a group of prominent Japanese
authors who spent much of their time in the area
from 1910 to the early 1950s. The group's leader,
Masuji Ibuse, gained international fame with
his novel *Black Rain*, the story of a Hiroshima
woman's struggle with radiation poisoning.
From the 1970s the area enjoyed an art
renaissance when it became a draw for Japan's
best manga artists. These days, though, its
wealthy residents spend rather than create, and
a little ambulatory effort will unearth good
restaurants and cramped but homely bars.

It's worth seeing the aged trees lining Nakasugi Dori, the main street under the railway tracks, which are at their most gloriously green from May to June. Film buffs note: the square on the south side of the station was a backdrop in the original version of horror movie *The Ring*.

Ogikubo

Key word: ramen. One of Tokyo's best-known ramen shops is in Ogikubo, and people travel from all over Japan to eat there. **Harukiya** (1-4-6 Kami-Ogi, 3391 4868, open 11am-9pm daily) seats only 16 people, and there's usually a small queue. Ask for *chuka soba* or, for extra slices of pork, *chashumen*. Harukiya was established in 1952, on the heels of a black market that sprang up after World War II. There's also a good daily fish, meat and veg market in the area, sprawling over the basement of the Ogikubo Town 7 shopping centre.

Although not a particularly pretty place, Ogikubo retains a bustling, working-class feel and, more than at most stations on the Chuo line, a sense of history.

Nishi-Ogikubo

In the 1960s peaceful 'Nishi Ogi' rose to heights of civil disobedience as a gathering point for organic, veggie-loving hippies. Two cults have also risen from these nondescript surroundings – the most notorious was Aum Shinrikyo, the religious sect responsible for the 1995 subway sarin gas attacks that killed 12 people.

Now, fortunately, the area is best known for its antiques and bric-a-brac shops – around 75 of them, in fact. Take the north exit from the station and head for the *koban* (police box). Boldly stride up to the policeman, make no sudden moves, and say 'aAtiku mapu onegai shimasu'. He'll pull one from his desk, and you'll be on your way to a pleasant day strolling the backstreets. You'll find both Western and Japanese antiquities on sale, but don't expect bargains. The north-west section of the walk has the best furniture, lighting and antiques shops, and there are also a few eccentric second-hand bookshops that may reward your browsing.

Kichijoji

On the edge of Tokyo's 23 wards, Kichijoji is slowly emerging as west Tokyo's own Shibuya. Although lacking the latter's urbane tribalism, the area attracts large numbers of school and university students, giving a youthful vibe and freshness that other destinations on the Chuo line lack. At weekends, the shopping malls and department stores teem with life, and many people also visit spacious **Inokashira Park**.

Jazz venues and ethnic restaurants are something of a speciality, while digging deep among the streets outside the station's north exit will turn up numerous bars and eateries. This plethora of choice makes Kichijoji an excellent night-time excursion.

An early lunch at **Superbacco** (Frente Kichijoji Bldg B1, 2-1-31 Kichijoji Minami-cho, 0422 49 2005, open 11am-9.30pm daily) makes a good start to the day. This restaurant is Venetian-themed right down to its menu (Italian and Japanese) and the standing room-only wine bar by the entrance. Unusually for Tokyo, an intelligent range of wines is available from ¥200 upwards, accompanied by cheap, tapas-style snacks. Great pasta, fish, seafood and meat dishes in the restaurant are also good value. Superbacco is in the basement of the building complex housing Kichijoji station.

The under-lit black interiors of the **Outback Kitchen & Bar** (2-8-1 Kichijoji-honcho, 0422 21 1548, www.sometime.co.jp, open 6pm-2am daily) are popular with couples. This groovy two-storey basement bar has a long cocktail menu, a clued-in selection of wines, and a solid range of spirits and Cuban cigars. Eclectic jazz floats out of two huge speakers, and a sit-down meal can be had on the small second floor. It's a little expensive, but worth the outlay.

Another good choice is upmarket **Kin no Saru** ('The Golden Monkey', Inokashira Parkside Bldg, 1-21-1 Kichijoji, 0422 72 8757, open noon-3.30pm, 5.30-11.30pm Mon-Sat; 5.30-11pm Sun), which serves up modern Japanese with flair. Traditional floor seating and tables signpost its trim Japanese aesthetics, while Inokashira Park views create a romantic ambience. There are no English menus, but staff are young and helpful.

Inside the park itself, funky café **Pepecafe Forest** (4-1-5 Inokashira-Koen, 0422 42 7081, open noon-10pm Mon, Wed-Sun) lies across from the central bridge over the lake. Its plastic walls roll up in summer, making it the ideal place for evening beers.

In between the park and Mitaka (further up the Chuo line) lies the **Ghibli Museum**, a showcase for the Oscar-winning animation studio of the same name.

Ghibli Museum

1-1-83 Shimo-Renjaku, Mitaka-shi (0570 05 5777/ www.ghibli-museum.jp). Kichijoji station (Chuo line), north exit then 15mins walk or Mitaka station (Chuo line), south exit then community bus. **Open** (tours only) 10am, noon, 2pm, 4pm Mon, Wed-Sun. **Admission** ¥1,000; ¥400-¥700 concessions. **Credit cards** (gift shop only) AmEx, DC, JCB, MC, V.

Sightseeing

Miyazaki Hayao's studio has produced some of Japan's most popular and complex animation classics, from *My Neighbour Totoro* to *Princess Mononoke* and *Spirited Away*. If you want to learn more about the studio's work, be warned that gaining access to this museum is tougher than getting into the Kremlin. You need to purchase tickets in advance (which can be done from overseas; check the website), then show up at the prescribed day and time with your ticket and some ID. You will be escorted into another world: you can view original prints, play in rooms with painted ceilings and walls, and watch short animations in the cinema. The gift shop sells original animation cells.

Inokashira Park

1-18-31 Gotenyama, Musashino-shi (0422 47 6900). Kichijoji station (Chuo line), park exit then 10mins walk. **Open** 24hrs daily.

Located just 15 minutes from the centre of Tokyo, this park has more than enough to occupy you for an afternoon, including a zoo (not the greatest in the world; *see p219*), a pond with amusingly shaped rental boats, and enough playground facilities to keep the little ones happy. At weekends the park comes alive with street traders, musicians and artists. In late March and early April it fills with people enjoying *hanami* (cherry-blossom viewing) and it's worth making the trip to join them.

Other sights

Edo-Tokyo Open-Air Architectural Museum (Edo-Tokyo Tatemono-en)

3-7-1 Sakuracho, Koganei Ishi (042 388 3300/ www.tatemonoen.jp). Musashi Koganei station (Chuo line), north exit then any bus from bus stops 2 or 3 to Koganei Koen Nishi-Guchi. **Open** *Apr-Sept* 9.30am-5.30pm Tue-Sun. *Oct-Mar* 9.30am-4.30pm Tue-Sun. **Admission** ¥400; free-¥200 concessions. **No credit cards**.

Tokyo's façade may be in a never-ending cycle of renewal, but its architectural heritage is well preserved in an unexpectedly rich hoard of buildings at this picturesque branch of the Edo-Tokyo Museum (*see p68*). As well as swanky private residences and quaint old town shops, there's a host of one-offs, such as an ornate bathhouse and a mausoleum built for a shogun's wife. Even the visitors' centre once served as a ceremonial pavilion in front of the Imperial Palace. Be prepared for lots of slipping in and out of shoes if you want to visit the interiors.

Kasai Seaside Park

6-2 Rinkai-cho, Edogawa-ku (3686 6911/www. senyo.co.jp/kasai). Kasai-Rinkai Koen station (Keiyo line) or by Suijo water bus. **Open** *Park* 24hrs daily. *Birdwatching centre & visitors' centre* 9.30am-4.30pm daily. *Beach* 9am-5pm daily. *Big wheel* 10am-7.40pm Mon-Fri; 10am-8.40pm Sat, Sun. *Tokyo Sea Life Park* 9.30am-5pm Tue-Sun. **Admission** free. *Big wheel* ¥700. *Tokyo Sea Life Park* ¥700. **No credit cards**.

Located by the water at the eastern edge of the city, close to the Tokyo Disney Resort (*see below*), this is one of Tokyo's biggest parks and was built to re-create a natural seashore environment. Inside are the Tokyo Sea Life Park, two small beaches, a Japanese garden and a lotus pond. The birdwatching area includes two ponds and tidal flats.

Museum of Contemporary Art, Tokyo (MoT)

4-1-1 Miyoshi, Koto-ku (5245 4111/www.mot-art-museum.jp). Kiba station (Tozai line), exit 3 then 15mins walk. **Open** 10am-6pm Tue-Sun. **Admission** ¥500; ¥250-¥400 concessions; free under-12s; additional charge for special exhibitions. **Credit** (shop only) JCB, MC, V.

This huge, city-owned showpiece opened in 1995 on reclaimed swampland in a distant part of Tokyo. Its collection of 3,500 international and Japanese artworks has its moments, but the temporary exhibitions are the main reason to visit. Visitors can access the database, extensive video library, and magazine and catalogue collection (all available in English).

Sengaku-ji Temple

2-11-1 Takanawa, Minato-ku (3441 5560/www. sengakuji.or.jp). Sengaku-ji station (Asakusa line), exit A2. **Open** *Temple Apr-Sept* 7am-6pm daily. *Oct-Mar* 7am-5pm daily. *Museum* 9am-4pm daily. **Admission** free.

The most interesting thing about this temple is its connection with one of Japan's most famous stories – that of the 47 samurai attached to Lord Ako (*see p15* **Suicidal samurai**). After he drew his sword on a rival, Kira Yoshinaka, in Edo Castle, Ako was ordered to commit *seppuku* (death by ritual disembowelment). He was buried here. His 47 loyal followers then became *ronin*, or samurai without a master, bent on avenging his death. They killed Kira and were then themselves permitted to die in the same manner as their master, and to be buried close to him, also at Sengaku-ji. Their tombs are at the top of a flight of steps. Follow the smoke trails from the incense left by well-wishers.

Tokyo Disney Resort

1-1 Maihama, Urayasu-shi, Chiba (English information 045 683 3333/www.tokyodisneyresort. co.jp/tdr/index_e.html). Maihama station (Keiyo, Musashino lines), south exit. **Open** varies. **Admission** (per park) *1-day passport* ¥5,500; ¥3,700-¥4,800 concessions. Off-peak, 2-day passports also available. **Credit** AmEx, DC, JCB, MC, V.

Sitting on a huge tract of land in Tokyo Bay, the Tokyo Disney Resort comprises two adjacent but separate theme parks: Disneyland and DisneySea. The latter, opened in 2001, has given the whole enterprise a massive shot in the arm, since the rest of the park was starting to show its age in parts. Disneyland's seven main zones boast 43 attractions, while DisneySea has 23 water-based attractions. Disney has a special place in the hearts of many Japanese people, so the queues can be horrendous. Go early, and preferably on a weekday.

Eat, Drink, Shop

Restaurants

So fresh it wriggles.

Stiletto-worthy **Stellato**. *See p145.*

Tokyo's gourmet obsession continues unabated. The city is one of the best dining destinations in the world, and boasts more than 300,000 places to eat, with Michelin-starred establishments at one end of the spectrum and street-side ramen stalls at the other.

The economic upturn has given restaurateurs the confidence to invest in dazzling designer settings (the aptly named **Dazzle**, *see p147*, is a good example), and foreign superstar chefs (Ramsay, Ducasse, Robuchon) have all turned up for a slice of the action.

But dining in the capital isn't all about big-name, high-end dining. Tiny ramen or sushi shops attract long queues of punters with their renowned signature dishes. If you have time, join one of the lunchtime lines and find out what the locals deem worth the wait.

Unlike Japanese dining in the West, most restaurants pick one type of food to specialise in. Which is why this is the place to try the world's best sushi, sashimi, tempura or sukiyaki.

It's also the place to discover less internationally famous foods, such as the rarefied multi-course banquets known as *kaiseki*, or the anything-goes *chanko-nabe* stews that give sumo wrestlers their physiques. If you want a wider choice, try the top floors of department stores for more generalised menus.

There's plenty of international dining too, some of it every bit as good as you'd find in New York or London. And appropriately for a population that enjoys one of the longest life expectancies in the world, the health and sustainable living boom has hit Tokyo – great news for vegetarians and organic food fans.

In the evenings, look out for *izakaya* (literally, 'sake places'), a catch-all term covering the gamut from raucous, crowded taverns to discreet drinking holes of greater refinement. What they all have in common is their suitability as places to unwind at the end of the day. As in tapas bars, you need only order a couple of dishes at a time with your beer, sake or *shochu*. Some serve food of memorable quality; others are basic yakitori joints. Those with lanterns outside (usually red, sometimes white) are likely to be less expensive.

Dining in Tokyo can be staggeringly expensive – even with the yen's recent dip. But eating out needn't require taking out a loan. One strategy is to have your main meal in the middle of the day. Many restaurants offer special lunch discounts and set meals, while noodle shops provide affordable, filling fare. In student areas such as **Koenji** and **Shimo-Kitazawa** (for both *see pp130-136*), there are plenty of low-priced eateries, family restaurants and fast-food chains, both Japanese and Western. And if all else fails, drop into one of the ubiquitous convenience stores and pick up a lunch box, sushi roll or *onigiri* rice ball.

ETIQUETTE

You don't have to worry too much about etiquette when dining out, but there are a few no-nos. Don't stick your chopsticks vertically into your rice or use them to pass food directly to another person's chopsticks (both are funerary customs). Don't spear food with your chopsticks or wave them around in the air. Remember to remove your shoes in a Japanese-style restaurant. When leaving, it is polite to say *gochiso sama deshita* ('thank you for the meal'). Tipping will cause more confusion than delight.

The essential element of any *izakaya*, and good food to boot, at **Shunju Tsugihagi**. *See p147*.

TIMES AND PRICES

Lunch is usually served between 11am and 2.30pm, but most workers dine from noon to 1pm, so it gets crowded then. Dinner is typically from about 6pm to 11pm, with last orders at around 10.30pm – though things run much later in Roppongi and other major nightlife areas.

Prices listed below are for an average dinner with one drink. We've noted if you can get a menu in English; some (usually cheaper) restaurants also display realistic plastic models of dishes in their windows, so you can point at what you want. All our selections have been checked at the time of writing, but Tokyo's restaurant scene is fast changing, so call ahead to confirm before making a long trek.

Asakusa

Japanese

Hatsuogawa

2-8-4 Kaminarimon, Taito-ku (3844 2723). Asakusa station (Asakusa, Ginza lines), exits 1, 2, 3, A3, A4. **Open** noon-2pm, 5-8pm Mon-Sat; 5-8pm Sun. **Average** ¥3,000. **No credit cards. Map** Asakusa p63.
Stones, plants, bamboo latticework and a white *noren* (shop curtain) mark the entrance to this venerable eel shop. The *unaju* box set is delicious; or try *kabaya-ki* – skewered eel with the rice served separately.

Komagata Dojo

1-7-12 Komagata, Taito-ku (3842 4001/www. dozeu.co.jp). Asakusa station (Asakusa, Ginza lines), exit A1. **Open** 11am-9pm daily. **Average** ¥2,500. **Credit** AmEx, DC, JCB, MC, V. **English menu. Map** Asakusa p63.
You dine here much as you would have done a century ago – sitting on thin cushions at low tables that are little more than polished planks on the rush-matting floor. The menu revolves around *dojo* – small, plump, eel-like fish served (in ascending order of delectability) as *nabe* hot-pots; *yanagawa* (in a runny omelette); or *kabayaki* (grilled, like eel). Not a gourmet delicacy, perhaps, but an absolute Asakusa institution.

Mugitoro

2-2-4 Kaminarimon, Taito-ku (3842 1066/www. mugitoro.co.jp). Asakusa station (Asakusa, Ginza lines), exits A1, A3, A4. **Open** 11.30am-10.30pm daily (last orders 9pm). **Average** ¥3,000. **Credit** AmEx, DC, JCB, MC, V. **Map** Asakusa p63.
The speciality at this Japanese restaurant is rice cooked with barley and served with a bowl of grated yam (so gooey it must be healthy). There are lots of other options too, ranging from simple lunches to full evening meals.

Otafuku

1-6-2 Senzoku, Taito-ku (3871 2521/www. otafuku.ne.jp). Iriya station (Hibiya line), exits 1, 3. **Open** *Feb-Sept* 5-11pm Tue-Sat; 5-10pm Sun.

Oct-Jan 5-11pm Mon-Sat; 4-10pm Sun.
Average ¥3,500. **Credit** AmEx, DC, JCB,
MC, V. **English menu.**
This place has been serving *oden* since the Meiji era.
The chef takes great pride in his special Kansai-style
version (with a much lighter broth than the Tokyo
version). Otafuku also specialises in sake, which
complements the delicate flavour of the vegetables
and fish cakes that make up *oden*.

Sometaro
2-2-2 Nishi-Asakusa, Taito-ku (3844 9502).
Tawaramachi station (Ginza line), exit 3. **Open**
noon-10pm daily. **Average** ¥2,500. **No credit**
cards. English menu. Map Asakusa p63.
Comfort food in a funky wooden shack, within easy
walking distance of Asakusa's tourist sights. It can
get incredibly sweaty in summer, but when you're
sitting round the *okonomiyaki* pan, the intimate
atmosphere is wonderfully authentic.

Yoshiba
2-14-5 Yokoami, Sumida-ku (3623 4480). Ryogoku
station (Oedo line), exit A1; (Sobu line), east exit.
Open 11.30am-1.30pm, 5-10pm Mon-Sat; also 5-10pm
Sun during sumo tournaments. **Average** ¥4,000.
No credit cards.
Chanko-nabe is the legendary food of sumo
wrestlers, said to help them put on those extra
tonnes – but only if eaten in huge amounts late at
night. For the rest of us, it's just a warming, mixed
casserole. Nowhere makes a more atmospheric sam-
pling spot than Yoshiba, a former sumo stable where
you sit around the hard-packed mud of the ring
where wrestlers used to practise.

Non-Japanese

Vin Chou
2-2-13 Nishi-Asakusa, Taito-ku (3845 4430).
Tawaramachi station (Ginza line), exit 3. **Open**
5-10.30pm Mon, Tue, Thur-Sat; 4-9.30pm Sun.
Average ¥4,500. **Credit** MC, V. **Map** Asakusa p63.
This five-star yakitori shop is an offshoot of the
nearby French bistro La Chèvre. This explains why
it offers charcoal-grilled Bresse chicken, quail and a
fine range of wines and cheese. Casual and simple,
this is some of the best food in the neighbourhood.

Ebisu & Daikanyama

Japanese

Chibo
Yebisu Garden Place Tower 38F, 4-20-3 Ebisu,
Shibuya-ku (5424 1011/www.chibo.com). Ebisu
station (Yamanote line), east exit; (Hibiya line), exit 1.
Open 11.30am-3pm, 5-10pm Mon-Fri; 11.30am-10pm
Sat, Sun. **Average** ¥4,000. **Credit** AmEx, DC, JCB,
MC, V. **English menu.**
This branch of one of Osaka's top *okonomiyaki*
restaurants replicates the original Kansai-style
recipes. In addition to the usual meats and seafood,

stuffings include asparagus, *mochi* (rice cakes),
cheese and, of course, mayonnaise. Friendly staff,
reasonable prices, a large menu and a gorgeous view
make this a popular place.
Other locations: 108-7 Ginza, Chuo-ku (5537 5900);
BIC Camera 6F, 1-11-1 Yurakucho, Chiyoda-ku (5288
8570); Seibu department store 8F, 1-28-1 Minami-
Ikebukuro, Toshima-ku (3980 3351).

Ippudo
1-3-13 Hiroo, Shibuya-ku (5420 2225/www.ippudo.
com). Ebisu station (Yamanote line), west exit;
(Hibiya line), exit 1. **Open** 11am-4am daily.
Average ¥2,000. **No credit cards.**
Once you get past all the ordering choices – red or
white pork broth; noodles soft-cooked, medium or
al dente; with or without *chashu* pork – you can settle in and appreciate all the little touches that make
Ippudo different from other ramen shops. The layout is simple and open, with lots of plain wood; you
can add your own condiments (spicy beansprouts,
sesame seeds and garlic that you grind yourself);
and there are unlimited pots of *rooibos* (red bush)
tea to quench your thirst.
Other locations: throughout the city.

The best Restaurants

Eat, Drink, Shop

For contemporary Japanese cuisine
Traditional artistry meets the modern
aesthetic at **Banrekiryukodo** (*see p155*).

For designer dining
There's nowhere more dazzling than **Dazzle**
(*see p147*).

For power-dining North American-style
A steak and wine dinner at **Beacon**
(*see p161*).

For sushi you can trust
You'll get no MSG or additives at **Sushi**
Ouchi (*see p161*).

For when you've got a teenager in tow
The theatrical setting and masked waiters
at **Ninja** (*see p165*) will entertain even the
bolshiest adolescent.

For the ultimate grilled chicken
The yakitori at **Bird Land** (*see p145*) has
to be tasted to be believed.

For your soul
Bon's (*see p148*) Zen veggie menu offers
a karmic boost.

A guide to Japanese cuisine

The staple food in Japan, around which everything else revolves, is rice. Indeed, the word for meal (*gohan*) literally means 'cooked rice'. In farming communities rice is still eaten three times a day (sometimes noodles are substituted), along with a simple side dish, a bowl of miso soup and some pickles. This is a Japanese meal at its most basic.

Until 150 years ago, meat-eating (especially from four-legged animals) was shunned, and Japanese cooking is still heavily weighted towards seafood and products made from protein-rich soya beans, such as tofu, *yuba* (soya milk skin), *natto* (fermented beans), soy sauce and miso.

There is a strong emphasis on using fresh ingredients, so the varieties of seafood, vegetables and mushrooms will vary throughout the year, reflecting the season. In addition, each region of the country, from Hokkaido down to Okinawa, has its own specialities – both food and drink; all are available in Tokyo. Even at the humblest eateries and street stalls, food quality is invariably high and hygiene standards impeccable.

Below is a guide to the most common elements of Japan's amazingly diverse cuisine. For a menu glossary, *see p168*.

Kaiseki ryori

Japan's haute cuisine developed from the highly formalised light meals that were served with the tea ceremony. Kaieski consists of a sequence of small dishes, apparently simple but always immaculately prepared and presented to reflect the seasons. Courses follow each other at a slow pace: a one-hour meal would be considered hurried.

The order of the meal is: starter (often highly elaborate); sashimi; clear soup; then a series of dishes prepared in different styles (grilled; steamed; served with a thick dressing; deep-fried; a 'salad' with a vinegar dressing); and finally rice and miso soup, with a light dessert to clear the palate at the end. *Kaiseki* can be very pricey, though some restaurants serve simplified versions for around ¥5,000.

Kushi-age

Pieces of meat, seafood or vegetables are skewered and deep-fried till golden brown in a coating of fine breadcrumbs. Usually eaten with a sweetened soy-based sauce, salt or even a dab of curry powder, washed down with beer, and rounded off with rice and miso soup.

Nabemono & one-pot cooking

One-pot stews cooked at the table in casseroles (*nabe*) of iron or heavy earthenware are delicious and warming in winter. Everyone is served (or helps themselves) from the one pot: you just pluck out what you want using long chopsticks, and dip into the sauce provided. Favourite *nabe* styles include chicken *mizutaki*; duck meat; *yose* (mixed seafood and vegetables); and *chanko*, the sumo wrestlers' stew into which anything goes.

Noodles: soba, udon & ramen

There are two main indigenous varieties of noodle: soba (thin, grey, made from buckwheat mixed with wheat flour) and udon (chunkier wheat noodles, usually white). These are eaten chilled, served on a bamboo tray with a soy-based dipping sauce; or hot, usually in a soy-flavoured broth. Either way, accompaniments can include tempura, grated *daikon* (radish) or sweetened tofu. Chinese-style ramen noodles are even more popular. These crinkly, yellowish noodles are served in a rich, meat-based soup flavoured with miso, soy sauce or salt, and topped with vegetables or *cha-shu* (sliced, barbecued pork).

Oden

Fish cakes, tofu, vegetables, whole eggs and *konnyaku* (devil's tongue) are simmered long and slowly in a shoyu-flavoured broth and eaten with a dash of hot mustard. This simple wintertime dish goes wonderfully with sake, and is often served at outdoor *yatai* (street stalls). Cheap versions can smell chokingly pungent, but the subtle flavour of *oden* in fine restaurants can be a revelation.

Sashimi

Raw fish, delicately sliced and artfully arranged, is an essential course in most Japanese meals. It is usually served with a dip of soy sauce, plus a dab of pungent green wasabi (or sometimes grated ginger). Best appreciated with a few sips of good sake.

Shojin ryori

Japan's long tradition of vegetarian cooking lives on in *shojin ryori* – Buddhist temple cuisine that generally follows the same lines as mainstream *kaiseki*, except that no fish is used in the cooking stocks (shiitake mushrooms and *konbu* seaweed are used instead); garlic and onion are also banned. Tofu and *yuba* (soya milk skin) feature prominently in *shojin* meals and also in *fucha ryori*, a variant style with more Chinese influence. See p148 **Shojin ryori**.

Sukiyaki & *shabu-shabu*

These meat dishes, both cooked at the table, have evolved over the last century to become key parts of Japanese cuisine. Sukiyaki combines tender cuts of meat (usually beef, but sometimes pork, horse or chicken) with vegetables, tofu and other ingredients, such as *shirataki* (jelly-like *konnyaku* noodles), which are lightly cooked in a sweetened soy-sauce broth. As they cook, you fish them out and dip them into beaten raw egg.

Shabu-shabu is paper-thin slices of beef quickly dipped into a boiling cooking stock, usually in a special copper pot. The name derives from the sound made as the meat is swished to and fro in the broth.

Sushi

The classic style of arranging raw fish or other delicacies on patties of vinegared rice dates back to the 18th century, when sushi became a popular street food in Edo. Top sushi shops can be daunting, as they don't post their prices, and customers are expected to know their *uni* (sea urchin) from their *ikura* (salmon roe). The easiest (and cheapest) way to learn your way around the etiquette and vocabulary is to explore the many *kaiten* (conveyor belt) sushi shops, where prices are fixed and you can take what you want without having to order. Another style of sushi popular in Osaka and western Japan is *chirashi-zushi* – large bowls of sushi rice with morsels of fish, egg and vegetables scattered on top.

Tempura

The Portuguese are credited with introducing the idea of deep-frying seafood and vegetables in a light, crisp batter – and also with the name itself. But in Japan the technique has been elevated to a fine art. Premium tempura, cooked one morsel at a time in top-quality sesame oil, should never taste too oily.

Teppanyaki, *okonomiyaki & monja*

Beef is never cheap in Japan, but Japanese beef (especially Kobe *wagyu* beef) is a luxury item. The marbled fat lends itself perfectly to being cooked on a flat *teppan* grill – Japan's contribution to the art of the steak. Seafood and vegetables are also cooked the same way in front of you.

Okonomiyaki ('grilled whatever you like') is a cross between a pancake and an omelette, stuffed with meat, beansprouts, chopped cabbage and other goodies. Many *okonomiyaki* restaurants also do *yaki-soba* (fried Chinese-style noodles). Originally from western Japan (Hiroshima and Osaka both lay claim to it), *okonomiyaki* is cheap, robust and satisfying. The Tokyo version is known as *monja*.

Tofu cuisine

Tofu and other soya-bean derivatives are celebrated for their protein content and versatility, and feature strongly in Japanese cooking. Tofu specialist restaurants tend to use small amounts of fish or chicken (often in the soup stocks), so they are classified separately from the strictly vegetarian *shojin* tradition.

Tonkatsu

The *katsu* in *tonkatsu* means 'cutlet', a very popular dish first introduced during the Meiji period, when meat-eating began to catch on. The *katsu* is now almost always pork, usually lean cuts of sirloin, dredged in flour, dipped in egg, rolled in breadcrumbs and deep-fried.

Unagi

Another of Japan's great delicacies. Fillets of freshwater eel are basted and very slowly grilled (often over charcoal). The delectably rich, fatty white meat is considered a restorative and is said to improve stamina, eyesight and even virility. That is why it is consumed with extra gusto during the debilitating heat of the summer months.

Yakitori & kushiyaki

Yakitori ('grilled bird') is the Japanese version of the kebab: skewered morsels of chicken cooked over a grill, seasoned either with salt or a slightly sweet soy-based glaze. Most yakitori shops also do wonderful things with vegetables.

Eat, Drink, Shop

Jinroku

*6-23-2 Shirokane, Minato-ku (3441 1436/www.
jinroku.jp). Hiroo station (Hibiya line), exits 1, 2.
Open 6pm-3am (last food order 1.30am) Tue-Sat;
6-11pm Sun.* **Average** *¥3,500.* **Credit** *AmEx, MC,
V.* **English menu.**

Okonomiyaki raised to a superior level, in gleaming upmarket surroundings. Besides the standard pancakes, the chefs at Jinroku also fry up great *gyoza* dumplings, teppanyaki seafood, tofu steaks and *yaki-soba* (fried noodles). Be sure to try the *negi-yaki*, which uses chopped green leeks in place of the usual Chinese cabbage. Help it all down with cheap Chilean cabernet.

Kookaï

*3-49-1 Ebisu, Shibuya-ku (3440 1272/www.
kookai-web.com). Hiroo station (Hibiya line), exits
1, 2.* **Open** *11am-11pm daily.* **Average** *¥2,000.*
No credit cards. English menu.

There's plenty of good ramen in Ebisu, but this branch of the reliable Kookaï chain is hip, clean and foreigner-friendly – albeit a hefty walk from any station. As a change from the usual soup-style noodles, try the *tsukemen*, served on a tray with various garnishes and a hot dipping broth on the side.

Non-Japanese

Bistrot des Arts

*4-9-5 Ebisu, Shibuya-ku (3447 0408). Ebisu station
(Yamanote line), east exit; (Hibiya line), exit 1.*
Open *11.30am-3am Mon-Sat; 11.30am-11pm Sun.*
Average *¥4,000.* **Credit** *AmEx, DC, JCB, MC, V.*

Forsaking the usual clichés of checked tablecloths and the like, Bistrot des Arts espouses a chic, modern look complemented with rotating exhibitions of contemporary art. The cuisine is well above the bistro norm, and the late-night hours make it a great stop-off for a glass of wine and a light meal – try their *confit de canard*, or a comforting bowl of classic French onion soup.

Cardenas Charcoal Grill

*1-12-14 Ebisu-Nishi, Shibuya-ku (5428 0779/www.
cardenas.co.jp/chacoal). Ebisu station (Yamanote
line), west exit; (Hibiya line), exit 4.* **Open** *6pm-2am
daily.* **Average** *¥5,000.* **Credit** *AmEx, JCB, MC,
V.* **English menu.**

This is the most stylish and satisfying of the three Californian-style restaurants that share the Cardenas name and its distinctive take on Pacific Rim fusion food. The centrepiece is the grill, which serves up chicken, steak, fish and seafood, backed up by a strong selection of US West Coast wines.
Other locations: Cardenas Ginza Kanematsu Bldg 7F, 6-9-9 Ginza, Chuo-ku (5537 5011); Cardenas Chinois 5-22-3 Hiroo, Shibuya-ku (5447 1287).

La Casita

*Selsa Daikanyama 2F, 13-4 Daikanyama,
Shibuya-ku (3496 1850/www.lacasita.co.jp).
Daikanyama station (Toyoko line).* **Open** *5-10pm
Mon; noon-10pm Tue-Sun.* **Average** *¥3,000.*
No credit cards. English menu.

Like most of Tokyo's south-of-the-border restaurants, La Casita isn't authentically Mexican. But the heady aroma of corn tortillas grabs you upon entering this airy 'little house' and won't let go until you've sampled the near-perfect *camarones al mojo de ajo* (grilled shrimp with garlic, Acapulco-style) or the *enchiladas rojas* bathed in spicy tomato sauce.

Isola

*Nishimura Bldg 1F, 6-17-2 Shirokane, Minato-ku
(5447 2733). Shirokanedai station (Nanboku line),
exit 1.* **Open** *6-10.30pm Mon-Fri; noon-1.30pm, 6-
11.30pm Sat, Sun.* **Average** *¥4,500.* **Credit** *AmEx,
DC, JCB, MC, V.* **English menu.**

Where pizza is concerned, Isola really means business. The space may be simple and the seats uncomfortable, but the pizzas – cooked to perfection in the hand-crafted, wood-fired Neapolitan-style oven that dominates the dining room – are second to none. The *quattro formaggi* (four cheeses) or the *shirasu* (whitebait) come particularly recommended. But whether they are worth the hefty price tag (up to ¥3,000 a pop) is definitely your call.
Other locations: throughout the city.

Khumbila

*1-9-11 Ebisu-Minami, Shibuya-ku (3719 6115/www.
khumbila.com). Ebisu station (Yamanote line), west exit;
(Hibiya line), exit 4.* **Open** *11.30am-2.30pm, 5-11.30pm
Mon-Sat; 11.30am-11.30pm Sun.* **Average** *¥3,500.*
Credit *AmEx, DC, JCB, MC, V.* **English menu.**

There are a number of Nepalese places around town, but none in the same league as Khumbila, housed in a quirky building by oddball local architect Horikawa Hideo. Whether you order the Indian-accented curries or the Tibetan-style *momo* dumplings, it's all carefully adapted to suit Japanese tastes. Non-smokers enjoy a floor to themselves, but the best seats in the house are at the top, sitting on the floor under the dome-like roof.

Lohotoi

*3-48-1 Ebisu, Shibuya-ku (3449 8899/www.long-
fu-fong.com). Hiroo station (Hibiya line), exits 1, 2.*
Open *11.30am-2.30pm, 6-11pm Mon, Tue, Thur-Sun.*
Average *¥5,000.* **Credit** *AmEx, DC, JCB, MC, V.*

Neither too funky nor too pristine, Lohotoi occupies a very welcome middle ground, producing flavourful, satisfying Hong Kong cuisine. The dim sum – all prepared in-house by the HK-born chefs – are excellent, as are the seafood dishes and sweet-sour spare ribs.

Luxor

*2F Barbizon 25, 5-4-7 Shirokanedai, Minato-ku
(3446 6900/www.luxor-r.com). Shirokanedai station
(Nanboku line), exit 1.* **Open** *11.30am-3pm, 5.30-
10.30pm Mon-Sat.* **Average** *¥11,000.* **Credit** *AmEx,
DC, JCB, MC, V.* **English menu.**

Mario Frittoli takes the *cucina* of his native Tuscany and dresses it up to match his ritzy premises in upmarket Shirokanedai. There is more than a whiff of celebrity here (from both Frittoli and his well-heeled clientele), but the cooking is creative and confident, and the own-made pasta is outstanding.

Dazzle. *See p147*.

Stellato combines a flair for the dramatic – huge chandeliers, a blazing log fire and an immodest faux-Moorish façade – with modern American cooking that is always interesting and frequently exceptional. The nicest touch is the rooftop lounge with a view of Tokyo Tower. **Photo** *p139*.

Tableaux
11-6 Sarugakucho, Shibuya-ku (5489 2201/ www.global-dining.com). Daikanyama station (Tokyu Toyoko line). **Open** 5.30pm-1am daily (last orders 11pm). **Average** ¥8,000. **Credit** AmEx, MC, V. **English menu**.
There is more than a touch of kitsch to the decor, but the eclectic Pac-Rim fusion food is entirely serious. Tableaux has become a favourite port of call with the well-heeled Daikanyama set, many of whom drop by for a Havana and cognac in the cigar bar.

Tio Danjo
2F Ogihara Bldg No.3, 1-12-5 Ebisu, Shibuya-ku (5420 0747). Ebisu station (Yamanote line), east exit; (Hibiya line), exit 1. **Open** 5.30pm-11pm Mon-Sat **Average** ¥6,000. **Credit** AmEx, DC, JCB, MC, V. Owner-chef 'Uncle' Keita Danjo is a dyed-in-the-wool Iberophile, and has assembled a great range of tapas recipes and wines from all over Spain. The second-floor restaurant is not particularly atmospheric, but his ground-floor tapas bar remains lively till late.

Ginza & around

Japanese

Azumitei
Ginza Inz 1 Bldg 2F, 3-1-saki Ginza-Nishi, Chuo-ku (5524 7890/www.azumi-food.com/ginza/index.html). Yurakucho station (Yamanote, Yurakucho lines), Sukiyabashi exit. **Open** 5-11pm daily. **Average** ¥6,000. **Credit** AmEx, DC, JCB, MC, V. **Map** Ginza p75.
This sleek, modern restaurant specialises in premium sukiyaki and *shabu-shabu*, prepared with finely marbled beef from Japanese *wagyu* steers. The full-course dinners (¥6,300 and up) make a great introduction to contemporary Japanese cuisine, but you can also order more simply from the à la carte menu. Try to nab one of the semi-private booths in the centre of the restaurant.

Bird Land
Tsukamoto Sozan Bldg B1F, 4-2-15 Ginza, Chuo-ku (5250 1081). Ginza station (Ginza, Hibiya, Marunouchi lines), exit C6. **Open** noon-1.30pm, 5-10pm Tue-Fri; 5-9pm Sat. **Average** ¥6,000. **Credit** AmEx, DC, JCB, MC, V. **English menu**. **Map** Ginza p75.
Bird Land was one of the first places to offer upmarket yakitori, served with imported beers and fine wines. Grill master Wada Toshihiro uses top-quality, free-range bantam chickens that are so tasty you can enjoy them raw as sashimi. Start off with the chicken-liver pâté and don't miss the

Ninniku-ya
1-26-12 Ebisu, Shibuya-ku (3446 5887). Ebisu station (Yamanote line), west exit; (Hibiya line), exit 1. **Open** 6pm-midnight Tue-Sun. **Average** ¥5,000. **Credit** AmEx, JCB, MC, V. **English menu**.
Ninniku is the Japanese word for garlic, and everything on the menu here, with the possible exception of the drinks, is laced with it. The odours of towering garlic bread, viciously flavourful curries and mouth-watering pasta and rice dishes, with Chinese, Thai, Indian and other ethnic twists, waft out on to the street.

Ricos Kitchen
4-23-7 Ebisu, Shibuya-ku (5791 4649). Ebisu station (Yamanote line), east exit; (Hibiya line), exit 1. **Open** 11.30am-3.30pm, 6-11pm Tue-Sun. **Average** ¥6,000. **Credit** AmEx, MC, V. **English menu**.
Chef Natsume Haruki produces a suave and satisfying 'cucina nueva americana', served in a chic, airy space. This, and the location close to Ebisu Garden Place, is why Ricos has been full virtually every day since it opened. Definitely one worth seeking out.
Other locations: 1-20-3 Higashi-Azabu, Minato-ku (3588 8777).

Stellato
4-19-17 Shirokanedai, Minato-ku (3442 5588/ www.global-dining.com). Shirokanedai station (Mita, Nanboku lines), exit 2. **Open** 11.30am-3pm Mon-Fri; 5.30pm-midnight daily. **Average** ¥7,000. **Credit** AmEx, DC, JCB, MC, V. **English menu**.

Eat, Drink, Shop

superb *sansai-yaki* (breast meat grilled with Japanese pepper). It's a small place – just a few tables and a U-shaped counter – and so popular that reservations are hard to get. But seats usually start freeing up by around 8pm, so it's always worth trying your luck.

Kondo

Sakaguchi Bldg 9F, 5-5-13 Ginza, Chuo-ku (5568 0923). Ginza station (Ginza, Hibiya, Marunouchi lines), exits A3, A4. **Open** noon-8.30pm Mon-Sat. **Average** ¥8,000. **Credit** AmEx, DC, JCB, MC, V. **English menu**. **Map** Ginza p75.

Sit at the counter and marvel as chef Fumio Kondo and his assistants deliver a succession of exquisite morsels of golden, batter-fried seafood and vegetables. A kimono-clad waitress hovers, constantly replacing the paper mats that absorb excess oil. Kondo is a tempura artist of the old school, but his restaurant is less formal (and more affordable) than other traditional tempura shops. The view over the Ginza rooftops is a further bonus.

Little Okinawa

8-7-10 Ginza, Chuo-ku (3572 2930/www.little-okinawa.co.jp). Shinbashi station (Yamanote line), Ginza exit; (Asakusa line), exit A3; (Ginza line), exit 3. **Open** noon-1.30pm, 5pm-3am Mon-Fri; noon-1.30pm, 4pm-midnight Sat, Sun. **Average** ¥3,500. **Credit** AmEx, DC, JCB, MC, V. **English menu**. **Map** Ginza p75.

This cheerful, busy hole-in-the-wall serves the foods of Japan's southernmost islands. The Chinese influence is strong, especially in the emphasis on noodles and pork. Among the more accessible dishes are deep-fried chips of *goya* (bitter gourd), *jimami-dofu* (a creamy peanut mousse) and *rafuti* (delectable, slow-simmered pork belly). Once you've had a few shots of *awamori*, the local rice-based, rocket-fuel hooch, you'll be ready for more exotic offerings such as *mimiga* (gelatinous pig's ear) or *umi-budo* (crunchy seaweed).

Ohmatsuya

Ail d'Or Bldg 2F, 6-5-8 Ginza, Chuo-ku (3571 7053). Ginza station (Ginza, Hibiya, Marunouchi lines), exit B9. **Open** 5-10pm Mon-Sat. **Average** ¥9,000. **Credit** AmEx, DC, JCB, MC, V. **English menu**. **Map** Ginza p75.

Ohmatsuya serves the foods of rural Yamagata prefecture, but it does so in swish Ginza style. The decor is faux rustic, with wooden beams and farmhouse furniture. Every table has a charcoal fireplace on which fish, vegetables, mushrooms and delicious *wagyu* beef are grilled as you watch. The rest of the menu features plenty of wild mountain herbs and fresh seafood from the Japan Sea coast, not to mention some of the best sake in the country.

Oshima

Ginza Core Bldg 9F, 5-8-20 Ginza, Chuo-ku (3574 8080). Ginza station (Ginza, Hibiya, Marunouchi lines), exits A3, A4. **Open** 11am-10pm daily. **Average** ¥6,000. **Credit** AmEx, DC, JCB, MC, V. **Map** Ginza p75.

Oshima offers traditional Japanese food from the Kaga (Kanazawa) area, expertly prepared and beautifully presented. There's a wide range of set meals, including tempura, *shabu-shabu* and *nabe* (hot-pot) courses. The 'ladies' afternoon lunch (*kaiseki*)', served after 2pm, is a bargain.

Other locations: Odakyu Halc Annex 8F, 1-5-1 Nishi-Shinjuku, Shinjuku-ku (3348 8080); Hotel Pacific Tokyo 3F, 3-13-3 Takanawa, Minato-ku (3441 8080).

Gonpachi. *See p157.*

Robata

1-3-8 Yurakucho, Chiyoda-ku (3591 1905). Hibiya station (Chiyoda, Hibiya, Mita lines), exit A4. **Open** 5-11pm daily. **Average** ¥5,000. **No credit cards.** **Map** Ginza p75.

This venerable *izakaya* provides one of the most charming dining experiences in central Tokyo. Perch yourself on one of the wooden seats and pick from the freshly prepared dishes arrayed in huge bowls on the giant counter. The food is a curious mix of Japanese and Western – salads, pork in cream sauce, tofu dishes and tomato-based veggie stews – which goes just as well with wine as with sake.

Shin-Hinomoto

2-4-4 Yurakucho, Chiyoda-ku (3214 8021). Yurakucho station (Yamanote, Yurakucho lines), Hibiya exit. **Open** 5pm-midnight daily. **Average** ¥4,000. **No credit cards.** **English menu.** **Map** Ginza p75.

Tucked under the Yamanote line tracks and shuddering every time a train passes overhead, Shin-Hinomoto delivers the classic *izakaya* experience. That means it's cramped, boisterous and smoky, and serves a good range of cheap, honest grub with plenty of sake and *shochu* to wash it down. What makes it unique is that the master of the house is an English expat.

Shunju Tsugihagi

Nihon Seimei Bldg B1F, 1-1-1 Yurakucho, Chiyoda-ku (3595 0511/www.shunju.com/ja/restaurants/ tsugihagi). Hibiya station (Chiyoda, Hibiya, Mita lines), exit A13. **Open** 11.30am-2.30pm, 5-11pm Mon-Sat; noon-2.30pm, 5-9.30pm Sun **Average** ¥7,000. **Credit** AmEx, DC, JCB, MC, V. **English menu.** **Map** Ginza p75.

The newest and largest member of the ever-reliable Shunju group conforms to a tried-and-tested modern-*izakaya* formula. On offer is everything from home-made tofu and country-style vegetable dishes to premium seafood and grilled meats. Be warned: it's pricier than other branches of Shunju, reflecting the upscale ambience/neighbourhood. **Photo** *p140.*

Sushi Bun

Chuo Shijo Bldg No.8, 5-2-1 Tsukiji, Chuo-ku (3541 3860/www.sushibun.com). Tsukiji station (Hibiya line), exit A1. **Open** 6.30am-3pm Mon-Sat. **Average** ¥3,000. **No credit cards.** **English menu.**

When the fish market finally moves out of Tsukiji (there are plans to move it to Koto ward, but not until after 2012), Sushi Bun and the other barrow boys' sushi shops will be lost – so go now before it's too late. Like the others, Bun is cramped (the counter seats just 12) and invariably full from first light until closing time. For fish this fresh, the set meal (¥3,500) is brilliant value.

Ten-Ichi

6-6-5 Ginza, Chuo-ku (3571 1949/www.tenichi.co. jp). Ginza station (Ginza, Hibiya, Marunouchi lines), exits C3, B6. **Open** 11.30am-9.30pm daily.

Average ¥10,000. **Credit** AmEx, DC, JCB, MC, V. **English menu.** **Map** Ginza p75.

Top-quality tempura, served direct from the wok to your plate, is one of the finest delicacies in Japan's cuisine. And you won't find it prepared better than at Ten-Ichi, Tokyo's best-known tempura house. The atmosphere is tranquil and pampering, the tempura light and aromatic. A full-course meal also includes sashimi, salad, rice and dessert. This Ginza flagship is the most refined member of the restaurant chain (it regularly hosts visiting dignitaries and film stars), but other branches all guarantee similar quality.

Other locations: Imperial Hotel, 1-1-1 Uchisaiwaicho, Chiyoda-ku (3503 1001); Sony Bldg B1F, 5-3-1 Ginza, Chuo-ku (3571 3837); CI Plaza B1F, 2-3-1 Kita-Aoyama, Minato-ku (3497 8465); Mitsui Bldg B1F, 2-1-1 Nishi-Shinjuku, Shinjuku-ku (3344 4706).

Ten-Ichi Deux

Nishi Ginza Depato 1F, 4-1 Ginza (3566 4188). Yurakucho station (Yamanote line), Ginza exit; (Yurakucho line), exit A7 or Ginza station (Ginza, Hibiya, Marunouchi lines), exits C5, C9. **Open** 11am-10pm daily. **Average** ¥2,000. **Credit** AmEx, DC, JCB, MC, V. **English menu.** **Map** Ginza p75.

This smart but casual offshoot of the reputable Ten-Ichi chain specialises in light (and more affordable) tempura-based meals with simple side dishes. The *ten-don* (tempura prawns on a rice bowl) makes a small but satisfying snack.

Non-Japanese

Bangkok Kitchen

Ginza Corridor, 8-2 Saki Ginza, Chuo-ku (5537 3886). Ginza station (Ginza, Hibiya, Marunouchi lines), exit C1 or Shinbashi station (Yamanote line), Ginza exit; (Asakusa line), exit A3; (Ginza line), exit 3. **Open** 11am-3pm, 5.30-11.15pm Mon-Fri; 5.30-11.30pm Sat, Sun. **Average** ¥3,500. **Credit** AmEx, DC, JCB, MC, V. **Map** Ginza p75.

Contemporary Bangkok touches down in the heart of Ginza. Besides the Thai noodles promised by the sign outside, you will find plenty of fiery curries, pungent soups and spicy Isaan specialities, prepared with finesse. The kitchen crew and most of the waiters are Thai, so the ambience is as authentic as the flavours.

Dazzle

Mikimoto Ginza 2 8/9F, 2-4-12 Ginza, Chuo-ku (5159 0991/www.huge.co.jp). Ginza station (Ginza, Hibiya, Marunouchi lines), exit C8. **Open** *restaurant* 5.30-10.30pm daily; *bar* 5.30pm-1am daily. **Average** ¥8,000. **Credit** AmEx, DC, JCB, MC, V. **Map** Ginza p75.

Dazzle's remarkable interior lives up to its immodest name. This eaterie in the Mikimoto 2 building is a glittering, cavernous space dominated by a massive, glass-fronted wine cellar. So what if the fusion food – think oysters, foie gras and grilled fish – is overambitious and overpriced? This is currently the most glamorous eating in town. **Photo** *p145.*

Eat, Drink, Shop

Gordon Ramsay at Conrad Tokyo

The Conrad Tokyo, Tokyo Shiodome Bldg 28F, 1-9-1 Higashi-Shinbashi, Minato-ku (6388 8657/www. conradtokyo.co.jp/restaurants/grdnrms). Shinbashi station (Yamanote, Asakusa lines), exit 1; (Ginza line), exit 2 or Shiodome station (Oedo line) exit 9. **Open** 11.30am-2.30pm, 5.30-10pm daily. **Average** ¥10,000. **Credit** AmEx, DC, JCB, MC, V.

The setting for Ramsay's first venture in Asia is a high-rise hotel in the futuristic Shiodome district. Mosaique of foie gras, lobster ravioli, cannon of lamb: the signature dishes are all present and correct, expertly recreated by chef-in-residence Andy Cook, a long-time Ramsay protégé. His chef's table, in front of the open kitchen, is superlative. On the down side, the high ceilings make the room feel somewhat sterile, and to see the view you have to adjourn to the hotel lounge.

Les Saisons

Imperial Hotel 2F, 1-1-1 Uchisaiwaicho, Chiyoda-ku (3539 8087). Hibiya station (Chiyoda, Hibiya, Mita lines), exits A5, A13 or Yurakucho station (Yamanote, Yurakucho lines), Hibiya exit. **Open** 7-10am, 11.30am-3pm, 5.30-10pm daily. **Average** ¥16,000. **Credit** AmEx, DC, JCB, MC, V. **Map** Ginza p75.

Always one of Tokyo's top French restaurants, Les Saisons – the Imperial Hotel's flagship restaurant – has hit a peak with the arrival of brilliant young chef Thierry Voisin (formerly of Les Creyères in Reims). The dining room is ample and luxurious, the service supremely professional, the wine cellar extensive, and Voisin's haute cuisine outstanding (especially his autumn *gibiers*). It all adds up to classic heavy-weight dining.

Shojin ryori

You'd never believe it from a glance at today's menus, but Japan was once a vegetarian country. In the 7th and 8th centuries AD, shortly after Buddhism arrived in Japan, no fewer than four emperors issued decrees banning the consumption of flesh.

Needless to say, things are different today, and the veggie visitor is likely to encounter bemusement at best when describing their diet. But there is one legacy of the nation's more ardently Zen past that the modern herbivore can enjoy: *shojin ryori*. Devised almost 800 years ago by a monk named Dogen, this ceremonial Zen dining is based on a multitude of precepts that govern colour, taste, texture and nutrition, as well as more ethical concerns. Meat and fish are, of course, strictly forbidden, but so are onions and garlic, which are considered an assault on the senses and a threat to the Zen disciple's command of his or her desires.

As in *kaiseki* dining, the food is served in a procession of around a dozen small dishes, each an elegantly presented bite-size course. Expect the whole meal to take a couple of hours.

Since wasting food is a serious transgression in Zen thinking, most *shojin ryori* restaurants demand that bookings are made at least two days ahead to avoid over purchasing. And leaving food on your plate is unthinkable.

Bon

1-2-11 Ryusen, Taito-ku (3872 0375/ www.fuchabon.co.jp). Iriya station (Hibiya line), exit 3. **Open** noon-3pm, 5.30-9pm Mon-Fri; noon-9pm Sat; noon-8pm Sun. **Average** ¥7,000. **Credit** MC, V. **English menu.**

Bon (*pictured*) serves *fucha ryori*, a strand of *shojin* that gives a more obvious tip of the hat to its Chinese origins. The feel is almost rustic in its simplicity, and the meals are beautifully presented. The interior of this restaurant is stunning, with a cobbled stone corridor linking immaculate tatami rooms.

Daigo

Forest Tower 2F, 2-3-1 Atago, Minato-ku (3431 0811/www.shiba-daigo.com). Kamiyacho station (Hibiya line), exit 3 or Onarimon station (Mita line), exit A5. **Open** noon-3pm, 5-9pm daily. **Average** ¥18,000. **Credit** AmEx, DC, JCB, MC, V. **English menu.** The priciest *shojin* spot in Tokyo serves dishes as complex and subtle as the finest *kaiseki* cusine. Each meal comprises a dozen or more exquisite dishes, like edible brush paintings to be savoured with your eyes as much as your mouth. A meal here will linger in your memory for months – as will the bill.

Gesshinkyo

4-24-12 Jingumae, Shibuya-ku (3796 6575/ www.bs-n.co.jp/men/15.html). Harajuku station (Yamanote line), Omotesando exit or Meiji-Jingumae station (Chiyoda line), exit 5. **Open** 6-10pm Mon-Sat. Closed 2nd Sat of the mth. **Average** ¥13,000. **No credit cards. Map** Harajuku p82.

Tanahashi-san, the master of Gesshinkyo, studied *shojin ryori* with Zen nuns in Kyoto, but has gone on to develop his own unorthodox, vegetable-intense version of the

WaZa

Mikimoto Ginza 2 7F, 2-4-12 Ginza, Chuo-ku (5524 5965/www.dynac-japan.com/waza). Ginza station (Ginza, Hibiya, Marunouchi lines), exit C8. **Open** 11.30am-2.30pm, 5-11.30pm daily. **Average** ¥6,000. **Credit** AmEx, DC, JCB, MC, V. **Map** Ginza p75.

One floor below the glamorous Dazzle (*see p147*), in the landmark Ito Toyo-designed Mikimoto Ginza 2 building, WaZa serves confident, contemporary dishes in a sleek and intimate setting. The menu focuses on charcoal-grilled meat and chicken, pot-au-feu, cheese fondue and lots of fresh vegetables, and there is also pasta, Western-style salads and Iberico salami. The set lunches, with self-service salad, soup and coffee, are especially good value. The place is sometimes hired out for parties.

Harajuku & Aoyama

Japanese

Crayon House Hiroba

3-8-15 Kita-Aoyama, Minato-ku (3406 6409/ www.crayonhouse.co.jp). Omotesando station (Chiyoda line), exit A1; (Ginza, Hanzomon lines), exit B2. **Open** 11am-10pm daily. **Average** ¥2,500. **Credit** AmEx, DC, JCB, MC, V. **Map** Harajuku & Aoyama p82.

Sitting next to a natural food shop, Crayon House is not exclusively vegetarian, but serves up a good selection of wholesome, well-prepared dishes, many with organic ingredients. It consists of two mini restaurants: Hiroba, offering Japanese food, and Home, offering Western dishes.

genre. The interior is classy and intimate, but the food is rough-hewn, intense on the palate (try the green *sansho* pepper sorbet) and very satisfying.

Itosho

3-4-7 Azabu-Juban, Minato-ku (3454 6538). Azabu-Juban station (Nanboku, Oedo lines), *exit 1.* **Open** 5.30-9.30pm Mon-Sat. **Average** ¥8,000. **No credit cards.**

This central Tokyo spot has been run for over three decades by a genial chef who happily describes each of the dishes being presented. The menu is a mix of orthodox and inventive, with the rice-grain tempura a particular highlight.

T. See p157.

Kyushu Jangara Ramen

Shanzeru Harajuku Ni-go-kan 1F-2F, 1-13-21
Jingumae, Shibuya-ku (3404 5572/www.kyushu
jangara.co.jp). Harajuku station (Yamanote
line), Omotesando exit or Meiji-Jingumae station
(Chiyoda line), exit 3. **Open** 11am-2am Mon-
Thur, Sun; 11am-3.30am Fri, Sat. **Average**
¥1,500. **No credit cards**.
Kyushu ramen from Fukuoka City is the speciality
here, and how you have it is entirely up to you. At
this bright and breezy noodle house customers can
specify particular broths (lighter or heavier), types
of noodles (thin, thick or in between), quantities and
toppings. There are always queues snaking down
the stairs, but don't worry – with 73 seats, an opening will soon appear.
Other locations: 3-11-6 Soto Kanda, Chiyoda-ku
(3512 4059); 7-11-10 Ginza, Chuo-ku (3289 2307);
2-12-8 Nagata-cho, Chiyoda-ku (3595 2130); 1-1-7
Nihonbashi, Chuo-ku (3281 0701).

Maisen

4-8-5 Jingumae, Shibuya-ku (3470 0071/http://
members.aol.com/maisenpr). Omotesando station
(Chiyoda, Ginza, Hanzomon lines), exit A2. **Open**
11am-10pm daily. **Average** ¥3,000. **Credit** DC,
JCB, MC, V. **English menu**. **Map** Harajuku &
Aoyama p82.
The main branch of this *tonkatsu* chain is built
around a converted bathhouse. If you're able to get
a seat in the huge and airy dining room in the back,
you'll notice several telltale signs of the building's
origins: very high ceilings and a small garden pond.
You can't go wrong with any of the set meals
offered here; standard *rosu katsu* or lean *hire katsu*
are both good choices, and each comes with rice,
soup and pickled radish.
Other locations: 1-1-5 Yurakucho, Chiyoda-ku
(3503 1886).

Natural Harmony Angolo

3-38-12 Jingumae, Shibuya-ku (3405 8393).
Gaienmae station (Ginza line), exits 2, 3. **Open**
11.30am-2.30pm, 6-10pm Tue-Sun. **Average** ¥1,200-
¥1,500. **No credit cards**. **English menu**. **Map**
Harajuku & Aoyama p82.
Still Tokyo's best natural-food restaurant, this no-
smoking venue boasts a simple, wood-clad interior
and an additive-free menu. The food, mostly in a
Japanese vein, is tasty, and although some fish is
served, the ethos is strongly vegetarian. The baked
aubergine is fantastic; the wholewheat pizzas
somewhat less so.

Tama

CI Plaza 2F, 2-3-1 Kita-Aoyama, Minato-ku
(5772 3933/http://r.gnavi.co.jp/a611800). Gaienmae
station (Ginza line), exit 4. **Open** 11.30am-2pm, 5.30-
11pm Mon-Thur; 11.30am-2pm, 6pm-midnight Fri;
noon-3pm, 6-11pm Sat; noon-3pm, 5-11pm Sun.
Average ¥3,500. **Credit** AmEx, DC, JCB, MC, V.
English menu.
Tama serves inventive *izakaya* food rejigged for the
new century and backed up with an exemplary

selection of sake and *shochu*. Unlike so many similar sake-centric spots, Tama is hip enough to appeal to design-conscious Aoyama types while also remaining refreshingly affordable.

Non-Japanese

adding:blue
6-3-16 Minami-Aoyama, Minato-ku (5485 2266/www.addingblue.com). Omotesando station (Chiyoda, Ginza, Hanzomon lines), exit B1. **Open** 5.30-11pm Mon-Fri; 3-10pm Sat. **Average** ¥5,000. **Credit** AmEx, DC, JCB, MC, V. **English menu.**
One part casual café-wine bar, two parts sleek, contemporary restaurant, adding:blue is run by, and located a stone's throw from, the Blue Note jazz club (*see p253*), hence the name and the hip typography. Chef Takahisa Nagasawa's modern Mediterranean cuisine really excels. But it's the refreshing lack of attitude and relaxed open terrace that keep people constantly coming back for more.

L'Artémis
2-31-7 Jingumae, Shibuya-ku (5786 0220/http://r. gnavi.co.jp/g853800). Harajuku station (Yamanote line), Omotesando exit or Meiji-Jingumae station (Chiyoda line) exit 5. **Average** ¥5,000. **Credit** AmEx, DC, JCB, MC, V. **Map** Harajuku & Aoyama p82.
L'Artémis showcases the excellent skills of Yusuke Nakada, one Tokyo's most able young chefs (and a protégé of Regis Marcon). His ¥3,990 Menu Pétillant includes his signature smoked-salmon salad (with poached egg and caviar) and superb scrambled egg with *uni* (urchin). The tables are a bit cramped, but at these prices who cares?

Benoit
La Porte Aoyama 10F, 5-51-8 Jingumae, Shibuya-ku (5468 0881/www.benoit-tokyo.com). Omotesando station (Chiyoda, Ginza, Hanzomon lines), exit B2. **Open** 11.30am-2.30pm, 5.30-10pm daily. **Average** ¥9,000. **Credit** AmEx, DC, JCB, MC, V. **English menu.**
Alain Ducasse's second Tokyo restaurant presents a fine example of his inventive take on Mediterranean bistro cuisine. Benoit is relaxed and informal, but everything runs like precision clockwork. To sample the food and atmosphere, drop in during the afternoon for a salad or a bowl of the delectable *soupe de poisson*. It's also worth keeping an eye out for the special monthly Wine Days, when all bottles are discounted.

Le Bretagne
4-9-8 Jingumae, Shibuya-ku, Shibuya-ku (3478 7855/ www.le-bretagne.com). Omotesando station (Chiyoda, Ginza, Hanzomon lines), exit A2. **Open** 11am-11pm Mon-Sat; 11am-10pm Sun. **Average** ¥4,000. **Credit** AmEx, DC, JCB, MC, V. **English menu.** **Map** Harajuku & Aoyama p82.
Owner Bertrand Larcher is a native Breton, so it's no surprise that his buckwheat *galettes* are authentically tasty. The sweet crêpes are excellent too. So

close to swanky Omotesando, Le Bretagne's homely wood-clad interior makes a welcome break from fashion-store façades.

Fonda de la Madrugada
Villa Bianca B1, 2-33-12 Jingumae, Shibuya-ku (5410 6288/www.fonda-m.com). Harajuku station (Yamanote line), Omotesando exit or Meiji-Jingumae station (Chiyoda line), exit 5. **Open** 5.30pm-2am Mon-Thur, Sun; 5.30pm-5am Fri, Sat. **Average** ¥4,500. **Credit** AmEx, DC, JCB, MC, V. **English menu.** Map Harajuku & Aoyama p82.
This basement hacienda has some of the best Mexican food in Tokyo, and the most authentic atmosphere too. Chugging on a bottle of Dos Equis, serenaded by mariachi singers, with tortillas and chicken in mole sauce cooked and served by Latinos… you could almost be in Cancún.

Fujimamas
6-3-2 Jingumae, Shibuya-ku (5485 2262/www. fujimamas.com). Harajuku station (Yamanote line), Omotesando exit or Meiji-Jingumae station (Chiyoda line), exit 4. **Open** 11am-11pm daily. **Average** ¥4,000. **Credit** AmEx, DC, JCB, MC, V. **English menu.** Map Harajuku & Aoyama p82.
Chef Mark Vann and his polyglot crew produce confident, accessible East-West fusion cuisine in a converted two-storey wooden Japanese house (once used as a tatami workshop). The servings here are large and the prices reasonable, given the swanky address. The well-stocked bar draws a gregarious mix of locals and expats.

Fumin
Aoyama Ohara Bldg B1F, 5-7-17 Minami-Aoyama, Minato-ku (3498 4466). Omotesando station (Chiyoda, Ginza, Hanzomon lines), exit B1. **Open** 11.45am-2.30pm, 6-9.30pm Mon-Fri; 11.45am-2.30pm, 6-9pm Sat, Sun. Closed 1st Mon of mth. **Average** ¥4,000. **No credit cards.** Map Harajuku & Aoyama p82.
This well-loved Chinese restaurant serves full-flavoured home-style cooking, in generous servings. The *negi* (spring onion) wonton, *kaisen gyoza* (seafood dumplings) and house special Fumin noodles are so popular you'll inevitably have to wait in line.

Ghungroo
Seinan Bldg 2F, 5-6-19 Minami-Aoyama, Minato-ku (3406 0464/www.ghungroo-jp.com). Omotesando station (Chiyoda, Ginza, Hanzomon lines), exit B1. **Open** 11.30am-10.30pm Mon-Thur; 11.30am-11pm Fri; noon-11pm Sat; noon-9.30pm Sun. **Average** ¥3,500. **Credit** AmEx, DC, JCB, MC, V. **English menu.** Map Harajuku & Aoyama p82.
The closest you can get in Tokyo to an upscale British-style Indian curry house, Ghungroo is divided into two rooms, the inner chamber being the more inviting. The menu contains few surprises, but the chicken dishes and okra curry are especially good. As with most Indian cooking in Japan, the rice is Japanese-style short grain – best to stick with the naan, fresh from the tandoor.

Hannibal Deux

Harajuku Miwa Bldg B1F, 3-53-3 Sendagaya, Shibuya-ku (3479 3710/www.hannibal.cc). Harajuku station (Yamanote line), Omotesando exit or Meiji-Jingumae station (Chiyoda line), exit 5. **Open** 5.30-11pm daily. **Average** ¥4,500. **Credit** AmEx, DC, JCB, MC, V. **Map** Harajuku & Aoyama p82.

Chef Mondher Gheribi's Tunisian home cooking adds another dimension to this colourfully cosmopolitan area. He draws on influences from around the Mediterranean, but his best dishes are the ones that hail from his homeland – *mechoui* salad, excellent roast chicken stuffed with banana and herbs, and home-made *khobz* bread served with red-hot harissa sauce. The recent move from Okubo to Harajuku is a definite plus.

Harem

CI Plaza B1, 2-3-1 Kita-Aoyama, Minato-ku (5786 2929/www.harem.co.jp). Gaienmae station (Ginza line), exit 4. **Open** 11.30am-2.30pm, 5.30-11pm daily. **Average** ¥5,000. **Credit** AmEx, DC, JCB, MC, V. **English menu. Map** Harajuku & Aoyama p82.

After a gap of a year, Harem has made a welcome return, now in the CI Plaza. The atmosphere here is more refined than at most of Tokyo's mom-and-pop Turkish eateries, and so is the cuisine. Among the standouts: the excellent meze, *imam bayildi* (aubergine) and *hunkar gebendi* ('His Majesty's favourite') lamb. Food fit for a sultan.

Kaikatei

7-8-1 Minami-Aoyama, Minato-ku (3499 5872). Omotesando station (Chiyoda, Ginza, Hanzomon lines), exit B1. **Open** 11am-2pm, 6-11pm Mon-Sat. **Average** ¥3,500. **No credit cards.**

Visiting Kaikatei is like stepping back in time to 1930s Shanghai: old beer posters, wooden clocks, dated LPs and odd murals of barbarian foreigners lend an air of wartime mystery. Shrimp in crab sauce is delicately flavoured, and a good match for mildly spicy Peking-style chicken with cashew nuts and rich black-bean sauce.

Kurkku Kitchen

2-18-21 Jingumae, Shibuya-ku (5414-0944/www.kurkku.jp/english/kitchen.html). Harajuku station (Yamanote line), Omotesando exit or Meiji-Jingumae station (Chiyoda line), exit 5. **Open** 11.30am-2pm, 6-10pm Tue-Sun. **Average** ¥4,500. **Credit** AmEx, DC, JCB, MC, V. **English menu. Map** Harajuku & Aoyama p82.

The centrepiece of an ambitious project marrying quality food, contemporary architecture and green thinking, Kurkku Kitchen bases its French-Japanese hybrid cuisine on organic produce and meat. Most of the food is cooked over a charcoal grill, and it's all delectable.

Lauburu

6-8-18 Minami-Aoyama, Minato-ku (3498 1314). Omotesando station (Chiyoda, Ginza, Hanzomon lines), exit B3. **Open** 6-11pm Mon-Sat. **Average** ¥5,000. **Credit** AmEx, DC, JCB, MC, V.

Chef Shinichiro Sakurai has mastered the sturdy, heart-warming cuisine of France's Basque country in all its glory. His intimate restaurant is simple and rustic, much like his cooking. Look no further to find the heartiest cassoulet in all of Asia, and back it up with the sturdy wines of Madiran and south-west France.

Nataraj

Sanwa-Aoyama Bldg B1F, 2-22-19 Minami-Aoyama, Minato-ku (5474 0510/www.nataraj.co.jp/en/aoyama). Gaienmae station (Ginza line), exit 1B. **Open** 11.30am-3pm, 5-11pm Mon-Fri; 11.30am-11pm Sat, Sun. **Average** ¥3,500. **Credit** AmEx, DC, JCB, MC, V.

Chef Sadananda and his team prepare sophisticated, vegetarian Indian delicacies that are so good you'll never ask where the meat went. The original restaurant in Ogikubo may be funkier and more casual, but this newer branch near Gaienmae is far more accessible. The Ginza outlet is suitably glitzy. **Other locations:** Ginza Kosaka Bldg 7F-9F, 6-9-4 Ginza, Chuo-ku (5537 1515); Hukumura-Sangyou Bldg B1F, 5-30-6 Ogikubo, Suginami-ku (3398 5108).

Local view Joi Ito

I love the little eateries inside the Toyokawa Inari shrine in Akasaka. They serve *oden* and soba, are very quaint and kitsch and are a pretty mellow way to feel very rural in the middle of Akasaka.

There's a trio of stores just inside the main entrance (watch out for pigeon droppings). The middle one is my favourite. Order *oden* and *kitsune soba* (buckwheat noodles with deep-fried tofu). They also sell all kinds of weird little trinkets, and you can grab some traditional Japanese junk food on the way out.

Toyokawa Inari Shrine

1-4-7 Moto-Akasaka, Minato-ku (3408 3414). Akasaka-Mitsuke station (Ginza, Marunouchi lines), exit D. **Open** dawn-dusk daily; *shop and cafés* 11am-5pm daily.

Cousin of Cornelius (see p207) and godson of Timothy Leary, Ito is a renowned technophile, entrepreneur and networker extraordinaire. He's a board member of the Mozilla Foundation, Creative Commons and the Open Source Initiative, and runs a popular blog at http://joi.ito.com.

Pure Café
5-5-21 Minami-Aoyama, Minato-ku (5466 2611/ www.pure-cafe.com). Omotesando station (Chiyoda, Ginza, Hanzomon lines), exit B3. **Open** 8.30am-10pm daily. **Average** ¥2,000. **No credit cards.** **English menu. Map** Harajuku & Aoyama p82.
Set in the heart of Tokyo's fashionable Aoyama district, Pure Café melds its health-conscious, near-vegan principles with a bright, contemporary interior (it's part of the glass-fronted Aveda holistic spa complex). The menu offers a mix of East and West, along with organic wines and beer. Pure Café's early opening hours make it just the place for a healthy breakfast.

Ikebukuro

Japanese

Ikebukuro Gyoza Stadium
2-3F Namjatown, World Importmart, 3 Higashi-Ikebukuro, Toshima-ku (5950 0765/www. teamnamja.com/ftp/ikebukuro_gyoza). Ikebukuro station (Yamanote, Marunouchi, Yurakucho lines), east exit. **Open** 10am-10pm daily. **Average** ¥2,000. **No credit cards. Map** Ikebukuro p87.
One of Tokyo's most bizarre experiences. Inside a Japanese ghost theme park lies this arcade of booths serving *gyoza* – Japan's take on Chinese-style dumplings (mostly pan-fried). Upstairs you'll find Dessert Republic and Ice Cream City, both serving frozen desserts from all over Japan in weird and wonderful local flavours (grilled chicken-wing ice-cream, anyone?)

Sasashu
2-2-2 Ikebukuro, Toshima-ku (3971 9363). Ikebukuro station (JR, Marunouchi, Seibu, Tobu, Yurakucho lines), east exit. **Open** 5pm-10pm Mon-Sat. **Average** ¥5,000. **No credit cards. Map** Ikebukuro p87.
This classic *izakaya* is the only reason for entering the mildly seamy backstreets of Ikebukuro. Settle in at a low table and sample good, simple *izakaya* food and a superb range of regional sake.

Non-Japanese

A Raj
2-42-7 Minami-Ikebukuro, Toshima-ku (3981 9688). Higashi-Ikebukuro station (Yurakucho line), exit 3. **Open** 11.30am-11pm Mon, Wed-Sun. **Average** ¥2,500. **Credit** AmEx, DC, JCB, MC, V. **English menu. Map** Ikebukuro p87.
With its colourful wall hangings of Ganesha, Hanuman and Shiva, this modest Indian diner is a welcome find in a barren location (it's situated underneath an expressway overpass). Besides the fine range of well-priced curries, chef A Raj also delivers good *dosas, idli, uppama* and other South Indian exotica. Not worth crossing town for, but a gem if you're nearby.

Chion Shokudo
1-24-1 Ikebukuro, Toshima-ku (5951 8288). Ikebukuro station (Yamanote, Marunouchi, Yurakucho lines), east exit. **Open** 11am-2pm, 6pm-2.30am Mon-Fri; 6pm-2.30am Sat, Sun. **Average** ¥3,000. **No credit cards. Map** Ikebukuro p87.
Specialising in the fiery cuisine of Sichuan, this basement eaterie is run by and for the local Chinese community. Watch live Chinese satellite TV as you tuck into spicy *tantan-men* noodles. Prices are as low as you'd expect, with Tsingtao beer just ¥280 per bottle.

Shilingol
4-11-9 Sengoku, Bunkyo-ku (5978 3837). Sugamo station (Yamanote line), south exit; (Mita line), exit A2 or Sengoku station (Mita line), exit A4. **Open** 6-10.30pm daily. **Average** ¥3,500. **No credit cards. English menu.**
As much a Mongolian cultural centre as a restaurant, this converted coffee shop serves little that isn't made with mutton. You can have it stuffed in dumplings, skewered on kebabs, stewed with spuds, swished in *shabu-shabu* style or simply boiled on the bone. To help it down, there's Genghis Khan vodka and live performances of folk music on the two-stringed 'horse-head' cello. Totally transporting.

Marunouchi & around

Japanese

Botan
1-15 Kanda-Sudacho, Chiyoda-ku (3251 0577). Kanda station (Yamanote line), east exit; (Ginza line), exits 5, 6 or Awajicho station (Marunouchi line), exit A3 or Ogawamachi station (Shinjuku line), exit A3. **Open** 11.30am-8pm Mon-Sat. **Average** ¥7,000. **No credit cards. Map** Marunouchi p93.
Botan's charm lies in its history and classic wooden premises as much as its food. There's only one thing on the menu, chicken sukiyaki, served in the old style. You will be well taken care of by matrons in kimonos, who bring glowing charcoal to the grill atop your low table, set a small iron dish on top, then begin cooking: chicken, onion, tofu and vegetables, all simmering in the rich, sweet house sauce.

Isegen
1-11-1 Kanda-Sudacho, Chiyoda-ku (3251 1229). Kanda station (Yamanote line), east exit; (Ginza line), exits 5, 6 or Awajicho station (Marunouchi line), exit A3 or Ogawamachi station (Shinjuku line), exit A3. **Open** 11.30am-2pm, 4-9pm Mon-Sat; 11.30am-2pm, 4-8pm Sun. **Average** ¥5,000. **No credit cards. Map** Marunouchi p93.
Isegen's legendary *anko nabe* (monkfish casserole) is basic but warming – just like the sprawling wooden premises, which are just round the corner from Botan (*see above*) and the same vintage. The *anko* season runs from September to April – the best time of year for a hearty hot-pot. The rest of the year the menu revolves around *ayu* (a trout-like sweetfish) and other freshwater fish.

Eat, Drink, Shop

Izumo Soba Honke

1-31 Kanda-Jinbocho, Chiyoda-ku (3291 3005/ www.izumosoba.jp). Jinbocho station (Hanzomon, Mita, Shinjuku lines), exit A7. **Open** 11.30am-8.30pm Mon-Fri; 11.30am-6.30pm Sat. **Average** ¥3,000. **Credit** AmEx, DC, JCB, MC, V. **Map** Marunouchi p93.

The hand-chopped soba noodles here are some of the best in town: wholesome and robust, prepared in the country style popular in Shimane (western Japan). The classic way to eat them is cold, served in stacks of five small trays with a variety of condiments. A good range of hot soba in broth is also available.

Kandagawa Honten

2-5-11 Soto-Kanda, Chiyoda-ku (3251 5031/ www.unagidaisuki.com/mkandagawa.html). Ochanomizu station (Chuo, Marunouchi lines), Hijiribashi exit or Suehirocho station (Ginza line). **Open** 11.30am-1.30pm, 5-9.30pm Mon-Sat. Closed 2nd Sat of mth. **Average** ¥5,000. **Credit** DC, MC, V.

In this splendid old townhouse kimono-clad waitresses serve succulent, tender eel grilled over charcoal and basted with thick, sweet soy sauce. Don't miss the *unaju*: eel served on a bed of white rice inside an ornate lacquered box. A classic dish of old Tokyo, in a setting to match. Kandagawa is just steps from the electronic frazzle of Akihabara, but a world away in atmosphere. Advance reservations are essential here.

Kanda Yabu Soba

2-10 Kanda-Awajicho, Chiyoda-ku (3251 0287). Kanda station (Yamanote line), east exit; (Ginza line), exits 5, 6 or Ogawamachi station (Shinjuku line), exit A3 or Awajicho station (Marunouchi line), exit A3. **Open** 11.30am-8pm daily. **Average** ¥2,500. **No credit cards. English menu.** **Map** Marunouchi p93.

Like a living museum dedicated to the traditional art of the buckwheat noodle, Kanda Yabu Soba is housed in a low Japanese house with a small garden, decorated inside with *shoji* screens, tatami and woodblock prints. Besides its excellent soba, Yabu serves tasty side dishes if you fancy joining the locals in some beer or sake.

Takara

Tokyo International Forum B1 Concourse, 3-5-1 Marunouchi, Chiyoda-ku (5223 9888/www.t-i-forum.co.jp/general/guide/shops/takara/index.php). Tokyo station (Yamanote, Marunouchi lines), Tokyo Forum exit. **Open** 11.30am-2.30pm, 5-11pm Mon-Fri; 11.30am-3pm, 5-10pm Sat, Sun. **Average** ¥4,500. **Credit** AmEx, DC, JCB, MC, V. **English menu.** **Map** Marunouchi p93.

Takara offers welcome sanctuary in the echoing concrete of the International Forum's basement. The food is reliable – standard modern *izakaya* fare, bolstered with a few Spanish-style tapas – but the main draw here is the brilliant selection of sake from throughout Japan, plus fine microbrewed ales and a better-than-expected wine list. The place also serves good set lunches.

Non-Japanese

Aroyna Tabeta

3-7-11 Marunouchi, Chiyoda-ku (5219 6099/www. tabeta.com/yurakucho). Tokyo station (Yamanote, Marunouchi lines), Tokyo Forum exit. **Open** 11am-10.30pm Mon-Sat; 11am-10pm Sun. **Average** ¥1,500. **No credit cards. English menu.** **Map** Marunouchi p93.

Nowhere in Tokyo makes Thai street food that's as authentic and cheap as at this funky little diner that's located under the train tracks near the International Forum (*see p252*). Simple set meals (including curries, fried noodles and the house speciality, braised pork) are just ¥630 each: a veritable bargain, especially for this upwardly mobile stretch of the city.

Bar de España Muy

Tokyo Bldg Tokia 2F, 2-3-3 Marunouchi, Chiyoda-ku (5224 6161/http://r.gnavi.co.jp/a634205). Tokyo station (Yamanote, Marunouchi lines), Marunouchi South exit. **Open** 11.30am-2.30pm, 5.30-11pm Mon-Fri; 11.30am-4pm, 5.30-11pm Sat, Sun. **Average** ¥4,000. **Credit** AmEx, DC, JCB, MC, V. **Map** Marunouchi p93.

Chic and contemporary Barcelona-style tapas served in a setting of steel, glass and polished wood. The bar runs half the length of the building, giving brilliant views over the passing trains as you sip cava and nibble *albondigas*, fresh-made mini-tortillas or ink-black paella. There's even a small outside terrace looking up at the dramatic International Forum (*see p252*).

Brasserie aux Amis

Shin-Tokyo Bldg 1F, 3-3-1 Marunouchi, Chiyoda-ku (6212 1566/www.auxamis.com/ brasserie). Tokyo station (Yamanote, Marunouchi lines), Marunouchi exit or Yurakucho station (Yamanote, Yurakucho lines), International Forum exit. **Open** 11am-2pm, 6-10.30pm Mon-Fri; 11am-2pm, 5.30-9.30pm Sat, Sun. **Average** ¥4,500. **Credit** AmEx, DC, JCB, MC, V. **Map** Marunouchi p93.

A slice of Paris in Marunouchi, right down to the red banquettes, brass fittings and menu chalked on the large wall mirrors. There's a small bar by the door, for a quick espresso or a glass of *vin ordinaire*, as well as a top-notch wine list to go with the authentically hearty brasserie food.

Dhaba India

2-7-9 Yaesu, Chuo-ku (3272 7160/www.dhaba india.com). Kyobashi station (Ginza line), exit 5. **Open** 11.15am-3pm, 5-11pm Mon-Fri; noon-3pm, 5-10pm Sat, Sun. **Average** ¥3,000. **Credit** AmEx, DC, JCB, MC, V. **English menu.** **Map** Ginza p75.

The best Indian food in town. Modest and unpretentious, this is one of the few places where you can find South Indian specialities. Delicious masala dosas, curries and thali meals, served with real basmati rice (evenings only), prepared by ever-friendly staff from the subcontinent.

Ukai Tofuya is overlooked – but not overshadowed – by the Tokyo Tower. *See p158.*

Shisen Hanten
Zenkoku Ryokan Kaikan 5F-6F, 2-5-5 Hirakawa-cho, Chiyoda-ku (3263 9371/http://szechwan.jp). Nagatacho station (Hanzomon, Nanboku, Yurakucho lines), exit 5. **Open** 11.30am-2pm, 5-10pm daily. **Average** ¥5,000. **Credit** AmEx, DC, MC, V. **English menu. Map** Marunouchi p93.
Good Szechuan cuisine, albeit with the spices toned down for Japanese palates, from chef Shin Kenichi, best known for his appearances in the Iron Chef TV cooking shows. His classic dish is *mapo-dofu* (spicy minced meat with tofu), but in summer, queues form for his *hiyashi chuka*, chilled Chinese-style noodles and chopped vegetables topped with sesame or vinegar sauce.
Other locations: throughout the city.

Tapas Molecular Bar
Mandarin Oriental Hotel 38F, 2-1-1 Nihonbashi-Muromachi, Chuo-ku (3270 8800/www.mandarinoriental.com/hotel/558000169.asp). Mitsukoshimae station (Ginza, Hanzomon lines), exit A8. **Open** 6pm, 8pm (reservations only). **Average** ¥12,000. **Credit** AmEx, DC, JCB, MC, V. **English menu. Map** Marunouchi p93.
Tokyo's first outpost of molecular gastronomy, high up in the Mandarin Oriental tower. It's no rival to Spain's El Bulli or the UK's Fat Duck in either scale or creativity, but it's still remarkable culinary theatre, watching as your food – 25 courses or more – emerges from syringes or super-chilled distilling retorts. With only seven seats and two sittings per night, reservations in this bar are hard to snare.

Roppongi & Nishi-Azabu

Japanese

Banrekiryukodo
2-33-5 Higashi-Azabu, Minato-ku (3505 5686/www.banreki.com). Azabu-Juban station (Nanboku, Oedo lines), exit 3. **Open** noon-1.30pm, 6-9.30pm Mon-Sat. **Average** ¥9,000. **Credit** AmEx, DC, JCB, MC, V. **English menu.**
Banreki (as it's known to its many admirers) offers an excellent, contemporary take on Japanese cuisine. Its interior melds traditional craftsmanship with cutting-edge design, and its *kaiseki*-style meals are multi-course gourmet taste adventures that go just as well with wine as premium sake. The ground-floor dining area consists of a single huge wooden counter. If you want more privacy, try to book the beautiful tea ceremony-style tatami room downstairs. Reservations are essential.

Bincho
Marina Bldg 2F, 3-10-5 Roppongi, Minato-ku (5474 0755). Roppongi station (Hibiya, Oedo lines), exit 5. **Open** 5.30-11.30pm Mon-Sat; 5.30-11pm Sun. **Average** ¥6,000. **Credit** AmEx, DC, JCB, MC, V. **English menu. Map** Roppongi p103.
Settle back in Bincho's dark, romantic and typically Japanese-style interior and enjoy the heady aroma of premium yakitori chicken and seasonal vegetables – grilled over top-quality Bincho charcoal, of course – complemented with a large array of side

Seoul food

Compared to the subtleties of Japanese cuisine, the food of its nearest neighbour packs much more of a punch. Meat plays a central role in the Korean diet, especially beef – usually grilled over charcoal. Garlic finds its way into just about every dish, as does fiery red chilli. And no meal is complete without a serving of pungent *kimchi* pickles.

Korean food has been a big favourite in Tokyo for years now, and its popularity shows no signs of waning. The best place to find it is around Shin-Okubo station on the Yamanote line – an area dubbed Koreatown. **Matsuya** (*see p164*) and **Kankoku Shokudo** are our current favourites. We've also picked out a trio of more central places to enjoy the fiery flavours.

Jap Cho Ok

4-1-15 Minami-Aoyama, Minato-ku (5410 3408/www.1999group.com/zassouya). Gaienmae station (Ginza line), exit 1B. **Open** *5.30pm-2am Mon-Sat; 5.30pm-11pm Sun.* **Average** *¥4,500.* **Credit** *AmEx, DC, JCB, MC, V.*

Not only did Jap Cho Ok prove to Tokyoites that *kalbi* and *bibinbap* could be designer-stylish, it was also the first place to introduce vegetarian dishes from Korea's Buddhist tradition. Settle in for a full meal in one of the alcove areas or perch on a stool at the tables in the centre of the room for a drink and a bite. Either way, reservations are advised.

Kankoku Shokudo

1-12-3 Okubo, Shinjuku-ku (3208 0209). Shin-Okubo station (Yamanote line) or Higashi-Shinjuku station (Oedo Line), exit A1. **Open** *9am-2am daily.* **Average** *¥2,000.* **No credit cards.**

Even before this area became known as Koreatown, Kankoku Shokudo (*pictured*) was the place to go to for full-blown Korean fare. It's a funky eaterie in the *izakaya* style – that is, you're there for the beer and *makkoli* rice wine as much as for the extremely spicy food. Staff speak even less English than Japanese.

Nabi

Accordy Jingumae B1, 2-31-20, Jingumae, Shibuya-ku (5771 0071/www.nabi-tokyo. com). Harajuku station (Yamanote line), Takeshita exit or Meiji-Jingumae station (Chiyoda line), exit 5. **Open** *11.30am-1am Mon-Sat; 6pm-midnight Sun.* **Average** *¥3,000.* **Credit** *AmEx, DC, JCB, MC, V.* **Map** *Harajuku p82.*

The chic interior was designed by the Idée group. The menu has a strong emphasis on organic vegetables and medicinal herbs, and the seasonings are applied with a light hand. This is modern Korean cooking for the hip, late-night Harajuku crowd.

Saikabo

3-10-25 Yotsuya, Shinjuku-ku (3354 0100). Yotsuya-Sanchome station (Marunouchi line), exit 2. **Open** *11.30am-11pm daily.* **Average** *¥4,500.* **Credit** *JCB, MC, V.*

The Saikabo chain dishes up some of the best Korean food in Tokyo. Some of the other branches are sleeker and more refined, but here at the original branch they don't pull any punches. Settle in with *kalbi* (grilled meats), *chige* (stew) and *ishiyaki-bibimbap* (rice cooked in sizzling-hot stone pots). Local aficionados rate the *chijimi* pancakes among the best in Tokyo.

Other locations: throughout the city.

dishes, as well as sake from all over the country. **Other locations**: Jyuko Bldg, 8-12-12 Ginza, Chuo-ku (5537 6870).

Fukuzushi

5-7-8 Roppongi, Minato-ku (3402 4116/www. roppongifukuzushi.com). Roppongi station (Hibiya, Oedo lines), exit 3. **Open** 11.30am-2pm, 5.30-11pm Mon-Sat; 5.30-10pm Sun. **Average** ¥7,000. **Credit** AmEx, DC, JCB, MC, V. **English menu**. **Map** Roppongi p103.

Tokyo may have more exclusive (and even pricier) sushi shops than Fukuzushi, but few are as welcoming or accessible. Superlative seafood in an elegant yet casual setting that feels miles away from the gritty hubbub of Roppongi.

Gonpachi

1-13-11 Nishi-Azabu, Minato-ku (5771 0170/ www.global-dining.com). Roppongi station (Hibiya, Oedo lines), exit 1. **Open** 11.30am-5am daily. **Average** ¥5,500. **Credit** AmEx, DC, JCB, MC, V. **English menu**. **Map** Roppongi p103.

Dominating the Nishi-Azabu crossing like a feudal Japanese castle, Gonpachi was supposedly an inspiration for the film *Kill Bill*. Sit at rustic wooden tables or in private booths and sup on simple country-style cooking, such as yakitori, grilled pork or soba noodles. The waiters dress in folksy *happi* coats and traditional festival music plays over the speakers. The separate third-floor sushi restaurant is more sophisticated, in both atmosphere and food, and has an open-air terrace. When George W Bush was in town, this is where then-Prime Minister Koizumi Junichiro took him. **Photo** *p146*. **Other locations**: Mediage 4F, 1-7-1 Daiba, Minato-ku (3599 4807); E Spacetower 14F, 3-6 Maruyamacho, Shibuya-ku (5784 2011); 1-23 Ginza, Chuo-ku (5524 3641).

Hinokiya

6-19-45 Akasaka, Minato-ku (6808 6815/ www.pjgroup.jp/hinokiya). Akasaka station (Chiyoda line), exit 6 or Roppongi station (Hibiya line), exit 6; (Oedo line), exit 7. **Average** ¥6,000. **Credit** AmEx, DC, JCB, MC, V. **English menu**. **Map** Roppongi p103.

Hidden behind the brand-new Midtown complex, Hinokiya offers an upmarket version of a *robata-yaki* grill. Pick out whichever ingredients you fancy – seafood, meat, tofu or vegetables – and the kitchen staff cook them over charcoal in front of you, passing it to you across the counter on long wooden paddles. It's theatrical, fun and remarkably tasty.

Maimon

3-17-29 Nishi-Azabu, Minato-ku (3408 2600/ www.maimon.jp). Roppongi station (Hibiya, Oedo lines), exit 1. **Open** 6pm-4am Mon-Thur; 6pm-5am Fri, Sat; 6pm-midnight Sun. **Average** ¥8,000. **Credit** AmEx, DC, JCB, MC, V. **English menu**. **Map** Roppongi p103.

This über-stylish oyster bar (run by the same company behind New York's oh-so-hot Megu) offers an astounding 40 varieties of the mollusc, served either raw in the shell or cooked in numerous ways. Alternatives include yakitori and other charcoal-grilled delicacies (beef tongue, pork, shellfish and more), with a great range of sake and *shochu*. **Other locations**: 1-1-10 Ebisu-Minami, Shibuya-ku (3715 0303); 8-3-saki Ginza, Chuo-ku (3569 7733).

Nodaiwa

1-5-4 Higashi-Azabu, Minato-ku (3583 7852/ www.geocities.co.jp/Milkyway/8859/nodaiwa). Akabanebashi station (Oedo line), Akabanebashi exit or Kamiyacho station (Hibiya line), exit 1. **Open** 11am-1.30pm, 5-8pm Mon-Sat. **Average** ¥4,000. **Credit** MC, V. **English menu**. **Map** Roppongi p103.

Housed in a converted *kura* storehouse transported from the mountains, Nodaiwa is the most refined *unagi* shop in the city. It only uses eels that have been caught in the wild, and the difference is noticeable in the texture, especially if you try the *shirayaki* (grilled without any added sauce and eaten with a dip of shoyu and wasabi).

Pintokona

Hollywood Plaza B2F, 6-4-1 Roppongi, Minato-ku (5771 1133). Roppongi station (Hibiya, Oedo lines), exit 1. **Open** 11am-11pm daily. **Average** ¥4,500. **Credit** AmEx, DC, JCB, MC, V. **Map** Roppongi p103.

A conveyor-belt sushi bar with a difference. Here, you can either help yourself to whatever's going past, or peruse the menu, sing out your order and wait for it to be prepared and delivered straight to you. Quality and freshness are definitely superior, but so too are the prices.

Shunju

House 530 B1, 5-16-47 Roppongi, Minato-ku (3583 2611/www.shunju.com/ja/restaurants/ toriizaka). Roppongi station (Hibiya, Oedo lines), exit 3. **Open** 6-11.30pm daily. **Average** ¥6,000. **Credit** AmEx, DC, JCB, MC, V. **English menu**. **Map** Roppongi p103.

Shunju is a typical modern *izakaya* – a sophisticated blend of modern and traditional, farmhouse and urban, Japanese and imported. You'll find good food with many creative touches, a stylish design sense and a young (but not too young) and casual crowd. It can get smoky and noisy, but never boisterous or out of hand. It's part of the same group that owns Kitchen Shunju (*see p161*) in Shinjuku. **Other locations**: throughout the city.

T

Atago Shrine, 1-5-3 Atago, Minato-ku (5777 5557/www.tasaki-shinya.com/restaurant/ts.html). Kamiyacho station (Hibiya Line), exit 3 or Toranomon station (Ginza Line), exit A1. **Open** 11.30am-2pm, 5-10pm Tue-Sun. **Average** ¥5,000. **Credit** AmEx, DC, JCB, MC, V.

Just about everything you eat and drink at T (pronounced 'Tay') is grown, netted or brewed inside Greater Tokyo, mostly in the rural area to the west of the city or the Izu islands to the south. The menu offers simple but beautifully prepared dishes,

Eat, Drink, Shop

with plenty of fresh seafood. The location makes it even more special – a low building on top of a wooded knoll in the middle of the city, in the precincts of a Shinto shrine. **Photo** *p150*.

Ukai Tofuya

4-4-13 Shiba Koen, Minato-ku (3436 1028/www. ukai.co.jp/shiba). Shiba-Koen station (Mita line), exit A4. **Open** 11am-8pm daily. **Average** ¥8,000. **Credit** AmEx, DC, JCB, MC, V.

With its wooden architecture, miniature gardens and koi-filled ponds, Ukai Tofuya evokes the spirit of traditional Japan. The illusion is broken when you look up and see Tokyo Tower right over you. But if you don't have time to get out to Ukai Toriyama (*see* p167), the original restaurant in the Ukai group, this makes a very worthy second-best. **Photo** *p155*.

Non-Japanese

L'Atelier de Joel Robuchon

Roppongi Hills Hillside 2F, 6-10-1 Roppongi, Minato-ku (5772 7500/www.robuchon.com). Roppongi station (Hibiya, Oedo lines), exit 1. **Open** 11.30am-2pm, 6-10pm daily. **Average** ¥8,000. **Credit** AmEx, DC, JCB, MC, V. **Map** Roppongi p103.

Robuchon now has his 'casual' (a relative term, here) counter-style Atelier restaurants on three continents, and the Tokyo operation is a perfect match with upmarket Roppongi Hills. You sit at the plush counter looking in at the open kitchen, ordering one or two dishes at a time as if it were a sushi counter or a tapas bar (the Spanish influence is also strong in the cuisine). Set dinners start from ¥8,400. Reservations are accepted, but only for the first sitting at 6pm; after that, it's first come, first served.

Bangkok

Woo Bldg 2F, 3-8-8 Roppongi, Minato-ku (3408 7353). Roppongi station (Hibiya, Oedo lines), exit 1. **Open** 11.30am-2pm Mon-Fri; 5-11pm Mon-Sat; 11.30am-9pm Sun. Closed 3rd Sun of mth. **Average** ¥2,500. **No credit cards**. **English menu**. **Map** Roppongi p103.

This funky second-floor diner is worth tracking down, as it produces good Thai street food without fuss or delay. Among the highlights are *tom kha kai* soup in traditional clay pots, and the minced-meat *larb* 'salads', generously spiked with chillies, lemongrass, mint and onion.

China Café Eight

3-2-13 Nishi Azabu, Minato-ku (5414 5708/www. cceight.com). Roppongi station (Hibiya, Oedo lines), exit 3. **Open** 24 hours daily. **Average** ¥3,500. **Credit** AmEx, DC, JCB, MC, V. **English menu**. **Map** Roppongi p103.

The staff can be surly and the seating cramped, but you won't find cheaper Peking duck in town. The suggestive decor has novelty value and the location – right across from the sumptuous Grand Hyatt makes it feel even more surreal, especially in the wee hours, when it fills up with clubbers.

Cicada

5-2-40 Minami-Azabu, Minato-ku (5447 5522/ www.cicada.co.jp). Hiroo station (Hibiya line), exit 3. **Open** 6-11pm Mon, Sun; noon-3pm, 6pm-3am Tue-Sat. **Average** ¥7,000. **Credit** AmEx, DC, JCB, MC, V. **English menu**.

Spain is the inspiration, but the whole Mediterranean is reflected in the excellent modern cooking of American chef David Chiddo and his crew. Hugely popular with the expat community (and deservedly so), Cicada always generates a great atmosphere. The large dining room is smoke-free, though the bar is anything but. Booking is highly recommended.

Citabria

2-27-4 Nishi-Azabu, Minato-ku (5766 9500/ www.citabria.co.jp). Omotesando station (Chiyoda, Ginza, Hanzomon lines), exit B1. **Open** noon-2pm, 5.30-11.30pm daily. **Credit** AmEx, DC, JCB, MC, V. **English menu**.

Tucked away in a residential Azabu backstreet, Citabria feels as polished and exclusive as a private club. And chef Endo Tsutomu's modern French cuisine is equally accomplished. This lovely restaurant is the perfect place to spend those evenings that call for something a little bit special.

Coriander

B1F, 1-10-6 Nishi-Azabu, Minato-ku (3475 5720/ www.simc-jp.com/coriander). Roppongi station (Hibiya, Oedo lines), exit 2. **Open** 11.30am-2pm Mon-Fri; 6-11pm Mon-Sat. **Average** ¥5,000. **Credit** AmEx, DC, JCB, MC, V. **English menu**. **Map** Roppongi p103.

A cosy basement restaurant that markets itself as 'new Thai', Coriander serves tasty dishes that are lighter than its more authentic cousins and often contain unusual ingredients, as with the carrot *tom yam* soup. The decor is pleasant, heavy on the cushions, greenery and incense, and service is keen if not always efficient.

Erawan

Roi Bldg 13F, 5-5-1 Roppongi, Minato-ku (3404 5741/www.gnavi.co.jp/gn/en/g038502h. htm). Roppongi station (Hibiya, Oedo lines), exit 3. **Open** 5.30-11.30pm Mon-Fri; 5-10.30pm Sat, Sun. **Average** ¥6,000. **Credit** AmEx, DC, JCB, MC, V. **English menu**. **Map** Roppongi p103.

The teak-wood interior and tropical artefacts make Erawan one of the classiest Thai restaurants in town. The chefs don't stint on the spices, and the Thai waitresses serve it all up with customary grace. A great choice for something a bit different. **Other locations**: 1-1-39 Hiroo, Shibuya-ku (3409 8001); 3-28-10 Shinjuku, Shinjuku-ku (3341 5127).

Garçon de la Vigne

5-17-11 Hiroo, Shibuya-ka (3445 6626/www. le-garcon.jp). Hiroo station (Hibiya line). **Open** noon-2pm, 6-10.30pm Mon-Sat. **Average** ¥6,000. **Credit** AmEx, DC, JCB, MC, V.

As the name suggests, this upmarket bistro (which opened in September 2005) focuses on the wine list

A beacon of hedonism, in the form of prime steaks and fine wine: **Beacon**. *See p161.*

as much as it does the food, but unusually (for Tokyo), it shuns Bordeaux in favour of Burgundy and the Loire Valley. Dinner menus start from just ¥3,800, and the food is good enough to warrant splurging on a decent bottle.

Hainan Jeefan Shokudo

6-11-16 Roppongi, Minato-ku (5474 3200/www.route9g.com). Azabu-Juban station (Nanboku, Oedo lines), exit 7. **Open** 11.30am-2pm, 6-11pm Mon-Sat. **Average** ¥3,500. **Credit** AmEx, DC, JCB, MC, V. **Map** Roppongi p103.

The lunchtime speciality at this friendly little Singapore-style diner is Hainan-style soft-simmered chicken served with rice. At dinner, the place also knocks out an extensive range of Singapore-style street-stall staples, including curries, stir-fries and spicy *laksa lemak* noodles. The small outdoor terrace is popular in summer.

Harmonie

4-2-15 Nishi-Azabu, Minato-ku (5466 6655). Hiroo station (Hibiya line) or Roppongi station (Hibiya, Oedo lines), exit 1. **Open** noon-3pm, 6pm-2am Mon-Sat. **Average** ¥6,000. **Credit** AmEx, DC, JCB, MC, V. **English menu. Map** Roppongi p103.

Chef Yamada Jitsuhiro was a pioneer in matching casual bistro food with top wine (he has an astounding cellar of Burgundies). His winter menu features *gibiers* (boar, venison and wild fowl), much of which

he hunts himself. The cosy, wood-clad second-floor dining room is entirely no-smoking, but you can head to his intimate stand-up bar downstairs for your Cohiba and rare Armagnac.

J's Kitchen

5-15-22 Minami-Azabu, Minato-ku (5475 2727/www.js-kitchen.com/jpindex.htm). Hiroo station (Hibiya line), exit 1. **Open** 11am-10pm Mon-Sat; 11am-4.30pm Sun. **Average** ¥3,000. **Credit** AmEx, DC, JCB, MC, V. **English menu.**

Owner Ueki Kumiko set up this casual deli-restaurant to provide the kind of wholesome food she wanted to serve her young son Jerome (after whom the place is named). Organic, additive-free and entirely vegan, the macrobiotic fare here speaks with a pronounced southern California accent.

Oak Door

Grand Hyatt Hotel 6F, 6-10-3 Roppongi, Minato-ku (4333 8784/www.grandhyatttokyo.com/cuisine/oakdoor.htm). Roppongi station (Hibiya, Oedo lines), exit 1. **Open** 11.30am-4pm (last orders 2.30pm), 6-11.30pm (last orders 10.30pm) daily. **Average** ¥8,000. **Credit** AmEx, DC, JCB, MC, V. **English menu. Map** Roppongi p103.

A huge selection of premium steaks (each *wagyu* steer individually identified), cooked to order in wood-burning ovens, and a gleaming cellar of New World wines: no wonder Oak Door is so popular with the expense-account expat community.

Porterhouse Steaks

1-15-4 Nishi-Azabu, Minato-ku (5771 5788/www.
chanto.com/restauranto/porterhouse/index.html).
Nogizaka station (Chiyoda line), exit 5. **Open** 6pm-
midnight Mon-Sat; 5-9.30pm Sun. **Average** ¥8,000.
Credit AmEx, DC, JCB, MC, V. **English menu.**
Map Roppongi p103.
Taking over from the now-defunct Ken's Chanto
Dining, Porterhouse Steaks is a temple devoted to
the pleasures of premium beef, grilled perfectly and
served in style. Top of the line is the eponymous
porterhouse – a 21oz offering for just ¥11,000. A red-
meat fan must.

Roti

Piramide Bldg 1F, 6-6-9 Roppongi, Minato-ku
(5785 3761/www.rotico.com). Roppongi station
(Hibiya, Oedo lines), exit 1. **Open** 11.30am-5pm,
6-10pm Mon-Fri; 11.30am-5pm, 6-11pm Sat;
11am-5pm, 6-10pm Sun. **Average** ¥4,000. **Credit**
AmEx, DC, JCB, MC, V. **English menu.** **Map**
Roppongi p103.
The speciality at this casual, self-styled 'modern
American brasserie' is the rotisserie chicken. There's
a good selection of New World wines and American
microbrews to provide appropriate lubrication.

Roy's

West Walk 5F, 6-10-1 Roppongi, Minato-ku
(5413 9571/www.soho-s.co.jp/roys/index_fs.html).
Roppongi station (Hibiya, Oedo lines), exit 1.
Open 11am-4pm, 5.30-11.30pm daily. **Average**
¥6,000. **Credit** AmEx, DC, JCB, MC, V. **English
menu.** **Map** Roppongi p103.
Hawaii-based Roy Yamaguchi's Euro-Asian-Pacific
cuisine is fusion food at its best. His simple and stylish menu incorporates Japanese and other Asian
flavours into dishes such as seared shrimp with
spicy miso butter sauce or Mediterranean-style
seafood frittata with pickled ginger and spicy
sprouts. The evening views from the luxurious new
premises in Roppongi Hills are fabulous.

Vietnamese Cyclo

Piramide Bldg 1F, 6-6-9 Roppongi, Minato-ku
(3478 4964/http://r.gnavi.co.jp/g222004). Roppongi
station (Hibiya, Oedo lines), exit 3. **Open** 11.30am-
3pm, 5-9.30pm Mon-Sat; noon-9.30pm Sun. **Average**
¥5,000 **Credit** AmEx, DC, JCB, MC, V. **English
menu.** **Map** Roppongi p103.
There's more style than content to this Saigon
eaterie, down to the cyclo trishaw parked at the
door. Vietnamese flavours have been toned down
for Japanese tastes, but the *goi cuon* spring rolls are
still undeniably tasty.

Les Vinum

4-5-8 Nishi-Azabu, Minato-ku (5466 8607/
www.corri-corri.com/vinum). Hiroo station (Hibiya
line), exit 3. **Open** 6pm-2am, 5.30pm-midnight
Tue-Sun and holidays. **Average** ¥5,000. **Credit**
AmEx, DC, JCB, MC, V. **English menu.**
Les Vinum proves that good wine can go brilliantly with Japanese cuisine. The charcoal-grilled
seafood and meat served here are both excellent

(especially the venison and wild fowl in autumn)
and the wine list includes a wide selection at just
¥4,400. The place even has a BYOB policy. For
this area, that's unheard of.

Shibuya & around

Japanese

Kaikaya

23-7 Maruyama-cho, Shibuya-ku (3770 0878/
www.kaikaya.com). Shinsen station (Inokashira
line). **Open** 11.30am-2pm, 6-11.30pm Mon-Fri;
6-11.30pm Sat, Sun (weekends reservations only).
Average ¥5,000. **Credit** AmEx, DC, JCB, MC, V.
English menu.
There's always a friendly welcome at this laid-back
Japanese-style diner on the fringes of Shibuya.
Owner-chef Tange Teruyuki combines his love of
the ocean (that's his surfboard on the wall) and
cooking to offer an excellent seafood menu, plentiful sake and reasonable prices.

Kanetanaka-so

Cerulean Tower Tokyu Hotel 2F, 26-1 Sakuragaoka-
cho, Shibuya-ku (3476 3420/www.kanetanaka.co.jp/
so/index.html). Shibuya station (Yamanote, Ginza
lines), west exit; (Hanzomon line), exit 8. **Open**
11.30am-3pm, 5.30-11pm daily. **Average** ¥11,000.
Credit AmEx, DC, JCB, MC, V. **Map** Shibuya p109.
Kanetanaka is one of Tokyo's most exclusive *ryotei*
(traditional restaurants), but this sleek, chic offshoot
is thoroughly modern and totally accessible. Instead
of tatami mats and *washi* paper screens, it's furnished with tables and chairs, and blinds of silvery
metal. The multi-course *kaiseki* meals give Japan's
traditional haute cuisine an inventive contemporary
slant. The restaurant is housed in the Cerulean
Tower Hotel, which also contains a *Noh* theatre and
a jazz club.

Negiya Heikichi

36-18 Udagawa, Shibuya-ku (3780 1505/www.
kiwa-group.co.jp/restaurant/a100118.html). Shibuya
station (Yamanote, Ginza lines), Hachiko exit;
(Hanzomon line), exits 6, 7. **Open** 11.30am-2.30pm,
5-11pm Mon-Sat; 11.30am-2.30pm, 5-10.30pm Sun.
Average ¥5,000. **Credit** AmEx, DC, JCB, MC, V.
English menu. **Map** Shibuya p109.
A welcome retreat from Shibuya's brash Center-gai,
Heikichi has a rustic, retro feel. The menu is typical
of a modern *izakaya*, with one major difference – just
about everything features *negi* (Japanese leeks).
Unless you're a big fan of the vegetable, then the
¥4,000 set dinner may be overkill. But don't miss
the *negi-no-kuroyaki*, charcoal-charred leek.

Soranoniwa

4-17 Sakuragaoka-cho, Shibuya-ku (5728 5191).
Shibuya station (Yamanote, Ginza lines), east exit;
(Hanzomon line), exit 8. **Open** 5pm-11.45pm Mon-
Sat; 5pm-11.30pm Sun. **Average** ¥6,000. **No credit
cards. English menu.**

Presenting one of Japan's most traditional foods with a modern twist, Soranoniwa specialises in tofu and other soy foods. The highlight of the menu is the tofu cooked in a wooden box at your table. Tofu never tastes better than when it's freshly set, and this smart restaurant is definitely the best place to try it.

Sushi Ouchi

2-8-4 Shibuya, Shibuya-ku (3407 3543). Shibuya station (Yamanote, Ginza lines), east exit; (Hanzomon line), exit 11. **Open** *noon-1.30pm, 5-11.30pm daily.* **Average** ¥7,000. **No credit cards.** **Map** Shibuya p109.

Owner-chef Hisashi Ouchi ensures all his seafood is wild, adds no sugar or MSG to his rice, uses only free-range eggs and shuns all artificial additives. This is no gimmick. Ouchi's sushi is wonderful, and so are the premises, a homely room with wooden beams and antique furniture.

Non-Japanese

Ankara

Social Dogenzaka B1F, 1-14-9 Dogenzaka, Shibuya-ku (3780 1366/www.ankara.jp). Shibuya station (Yamanote, Ginza lines), Hachiko exit; (Hanzomon line), exit 1. **Open** *5-11.30pm Mon-Sat; 5-10pm Sun.* **Average** ¥3,000. **Credit** MC, V. **English menu.** **Map** Shibuya p109.

Tucked away in the backstreets of Shibuya, this cheerful little Turkish restaurant serves up an array of delicious meze and other Turkish delicacies.

Beacon

1-2-5 Shibuya, Shibuya-ku (6418 0077/www.ty harborbrewing.co.jp/home/restaurants/beacon_e.html). Omotesando station (Chiyoda, Ginza, Hanzomon lines), exit B2. **Open** *11.30am-3pm; 6-10pm daily.* **Average** ¥9,000. **Credit** AmEx, DC, JCB, MC, V. **English menu.** **Map** Shibuya p109.

The latest venture by David Chiddo (the man behind Cicada, *see p158* and TY Harbor, *see p167*) is described as an 'urban chop-house'. That means prime steaks from grain-fed Aussie Angus cattle, free-range chicken, Loch Fyne salmon and more, all grilled expertly over charcoal. The look at Beacon is sleek and understated, the cellar is stocked with New World wines and the adjoining bar pours killer cocktails. Just the place for celebrating or entertaining. **Photo** *p159.*

Las Chicas

5-47-6 Jingumae, Shibuya-ku (3407 6865/www.vision.co.jp/2004/h_lc.html). Omotesando station (Chiyoda, Ginza, Hanzomon lines), exit B2. **Open** *11am-11pm Mon-Thur, Sun; 11am-11.30pm Fri, Sat.* **Average** ¥4,000. **Credit** AmEx, DC, JCB, MC, V. **English menu.** **Map** Shibuya p109.

Las Chicas comprises a restaurant, bar, café, DJ lounge and exhibition space, but most of all it's an arty, *gaijin*-friendly space in which to hang out. The cuisine has a strong Aussie influence and the cooking is always more than competent – good seafood and grills, as well as simpler bar-type snacks such as potato wedges with sour cream and Thai chilli sauce. In summer, the open patio is just perfect for chilling with a bottle of crisp Aussie chardonnay.

Don Ciccio

2-3-6 Shibuya, Shibuya-ku (3498 1828). Shibuya station (Yamanote, Ginza lines), east exit; (Hanzomon line), exit 11. **Open** *6pm-midnight Mon-Sat.* **Average** ¥7,500. **Credit** AmEx, DC, JCB, MC, V. **Map** Shibuya p109.

Friendly and casual, this new mid-market trattoria specialises in the *cucina* and *vini* of Sicily. The pastas and hearty main dishes (both seafood and meat) are excellent, though desserts are not so special. There may be cheaper Italian places in town, but few can match the quality of the ingredients or the enthusiasm of the staff here.

Legato

E Space Tower 15F, 3-6 Maruyama-cho, Shibuya-ku (5784 2121/www.legato-tokyo.jp). Shibuya station (Yamanote, Ginza lines), Hachiko exit; (Hanzomon line), exit 1. **Open** *11.30am-2pm, 5.30-10.30pm daily.* **Average** ¥7,000. **Credit** AmEx, DC, JCB, MC, V. **English menu.** **Map** Shibuya p109.

Trust the Global Dining Group – also behind Tableaux and Stellato (for both, *see p145*) – to do things in style. Legato occupies the top floor of a tower at the top of Dogenzaka hill, and its food is as theatrical as the lavish decor. The menu mixes Asian and Western influences, in accordance with Tokyo's current vogue, and features Vietnamese spring rolls and Chinese noodles alongside lamb chops and pizza. There's also a bar/lounge open until 4am on Friday and Saturday nights.

Underground Mr Zoogunzoo

Aoyama City Bldg B1, 2-9-11 Shibuya, Shibuya-ku (3400 1496/www.unitedf.com/zoogunzoo). Shibuya station (Yamanote, Ginza lines), east exit; (Hanzomon line), exit 11. **Open** *6pm-2am (restaurant 6pm-11pm) Mon-Sat.* **Average** ¥5,000. **Credit** AmEx, DC, JCB, MC, V. **English menu.** **Map** Shibuya p109.

This cosy basement wine bar boasts a decor every bit as eccentric as its name. The cuisine is modern (meaning here a Japanese take on Italian), and portions are modest, but there's a great cellar, focusing exclusively on Antipodean wines, with half a dozen always available by the glass. The lights stay dimmed, the welcome is friendly, and hectic Tokyo always feels a long way away.

Shinjuku & around

Japanese

Kitchen Shunju

Lumine Est 8F, 3-38-1 Shinjuku, Shinjuku-ku (5369 0377/www.shunju.com/ja/restaurants/shinjuku). Shinjuku station (Yamanote, Marunouchi, Oedo, Shinjuku lines). Lumine Est is located above the station's east exit. **Open** *11am-3pm, 5-11.30pm*

Stand bars

The practice of eating and drinking on your feet has been a blue-collar prerogative for centuries. But only in the past few years has it suddenly become fashionable in Tokyo. Known in Japanese as *tachinomi* or (from the English) 'sutando baaru', these drinking holes provide surprisingly good food, and many are now serving wine, as well as beer and sake. Wherever you end up, though, you can be sure it will be crowded, convivial and cheap.

Akitaya

2-1-2 Hamamatsucho, Minato-ku (3432 0020). Hamamatsucho station (Yamanote line), north exit. **Open** *3.30-9pm Mon-Fri; 3.30-8.30pm Sat.* **No credit cards.**
Standing on the main drag in Hamamatsucho, Akitaya is a landmark – a classic old-school *tachinomi* serving cheap beer, sake and *shochu* to go with the charcoal-grilled organ meats. The building was redeveloped recently, with Akitaya losing its retro patina but none of its popularity.

Buchi

9-7 Shinsen-cho, Shibuya-ku (5728 2085). Shinsen station (Inokashira line). **Open** *5pm-3am daily.* **Credit** *AmEx, DC, JCB, MC, V.*
An artsy, well-dressed crowd props up the counters and spills out on to the street at this chic, contemporary bar. They come to drink – wine as much as sake – but also because the food menu is so vast. Raw oysters, sashimi, terrines, pappardelle, steaks and more: this is the opposite of slumming it. The location could be more convenient, though.

Buri

1-14-1 Ebisu-Nishi, Shibuya-ku (3496 7744). Ebisu station (Yamanote, Hibiya lines), west exit. **Open** *5pm-3am daily.* **Credit** *AmEx, JCB, MC, V.*
Before Buchi, there was Buri in Ebisu. Here, the focus is on yakitori and good *izakaya*-style snacks, with a great range of sake to wash it down. There are scores of brews to choose from, from all corners of Japan. The sake theme extends to the interior decoration with brilliant effect.

Ebisu 18-Ban

2-3-13 Ebisu-Minami, Shibuya-ku (3794 1894/ www.18-ban.com). Ebisu station (Yamanote, Hibiya lines), west exit. **Open** *6pm-5am daily.* **No credit cards.**
The *tachinomi* boom intersects with Tokyo's new infatuation with tapas at this hip, cramped little hideout. Ebisu 18-Ban is invariably buzzing and packed to the rafters. There are a few bar stools, but even if you have to cradle your sherry standing up, it's always good fun.

daily. **Average** ¥5,000. **Credit** AmEx, DC, JCB, MC, V. **English menu.** **Map** Shinjuku p117.
The Shunju ethos – light, creative, modern Japanese food served in a stylish, casual setting – dovetails perfectly with the decor in the stylishly revamped Lumine Est mini mall. Sit at the long open kitchen to watch the chefs at work, or relax in cosy private alcoves.
Other locations: throughout the city.

Tsunahachi

3-31-8 Shinjuku, Shinjuku-ku (3352 1012/ www.tsunahachi.co.jp). Shinjuku station (Yamanote line), east exit; (Marunouchi line), exit A6; (Oedo, Shinjuku lines), exit 1 or Shinjuku-Sanchome station (Marunouchi, Shinjuku lines), exits A1-A5. **Open** *11am-10.30pm daily.* **Average** ¥5,000. **Credit** AmEx, DC, JCB, MC, V. **English menu.** **Map** Shinjuku p117.
Who says tempura has to be expensive? Surviving amid the gleaming modern buildings of Shinjuku, Tsunahachi's battered wooden premises are a throwback to the early post-war era – as are the prices. The whole place is filled with the whiff of cooking oil, but the food is perfectly good enough for everyday fare.
Other locations: throughout the city.

Yukun-tei

3-26 Arakicho, Shinjuku-ku (3356 3351/ www.akasakayukun.com). Yotsuya-Sanchome station (Marunouchi line), exit A4. **Open** *11.30am-1.30pm, 5-10.30pm Mon-Sat (Sat reservations only).* **Average** ¥7,500. **Credit** AmEx, DC, JCB, MC, V.
This friendly *izakaya* serves Kyushu and southern Japanese cuisine (which revolves around seafood, pork and *shochu* spirits). The lunch sets are fantastic: *onigiri teishoku* features two enormous *onigiri* (rice balls), while *inaka udon teishoku* is a very generous bowl of udon noodles with rice and tasty side dishes. In the evening, the place does good sashimi, and grilled and simmered dishes, and offers a good range of sake. Don't miss out on the succulent *kakuni* pork.

Maru

*3-22-10 Hatchobori,
Chuo-ku (3552 9210).
Hatchobori station
(Hibiya line), exit B1.*
Open 5-11pm Mon-Fri.
No credit cards.
Maru has grown from a
simple counter inside
a modest sake shop
into a vibrant, friendly
neighbourhood bar.
Whatever your poison –
beer, sake, *shochu*, sherry
or wine – the prices are
low, and they have an
eclectic selection of food
to match it. If your legs
give out, you can retreat to
the tables upstairs, or the smarter restaurant
on the third floor.

through an evening. It draws a well-dressed,
young crowd who sip *shochu* and wine.

Q

*4-4-2 Ebisu, Shibuya-ku (5793 5591). Ebisu
station (Yamanote line), east exit; (Hibiya
line), exit 1.* **Open** 5pm-4am Mon-Sat.
No credit cards.
Ebisu boasts more than its share of
interesting stand bars, and this chic little
place is one of the latest and the best.
Hidden away down a backstreet, it serves
up fare that's solid enough to last you

Uogashi Nippon-ichi

*25-6 Udagawacho, Shibuya-ku (5728 5451/
www.uogashi.jp). Shibuya station (Yamanote,
Ginza lines), Hachiko exit; (Hanzomon line),
exits 6, 7.* **Open** 11am-11pm daily. **No credit
cards. Map** Shibuya p109.
Sushi is the draw here, and it's surprisingly
good for the rock-bottom prices. There are
branches of this sushi chain in many parts of
Tokyo, but this one makes a welcome change
to all the Center-gai fast-food joints.
Other locations: Seio Bldg B1F, 2-2-18 Ginza
Chuo-ku (3561 6672); Tokyo Tatemono Dai 5 Yaesu
Bldg B1F, 1-4-14 Yaesu, Chuo-ku (3271 8231);
Akasaka Tokyu Plaza 3F, 2-14-3 Nagatacho,
Chiyoda-ku (3592 0393).

Non-Japanese

Angkor Wat

*1-38-13 Yoyogi, Shibuya-ku (3370 3019). Yoyogi
station (Yamanote line), west exit; (Oedo line), exit
A1.* **Open** 11am-2pm, 5-10pm daily. **Average**
¥2,500. **No credit cards.**
What this bustling little restaurant lacks in ambience it makes up for in tasty Cambodian-Chinese
cooking. It can feel a bit like a diner (indeed, the food
is served with amazing speed), and there are queues
outside at lunch. Start with the spring rolls and
chicken salad, then ask the cheerful Cambodian
waitresses (most of them relatives of the proprietor)
to help you navigate the menu further.

Ban Thai

*Dai-ichi Metro Bldg 3F, 1-23-14 Kabuki-cho,
Shinjuku-ku (3207 0068/jp.ban-thai.jp). Shinjuku
station (Yamanote line), east exit; (Marunouchi line),
exits B12, B13; (Oedo, Shinjuku lines), exit 1.* **Open**
11.30am-3pm, 5pm-midnight Mon-Fri; 11.30am-
midnight Sat, Sun.* **Average** ¥3,000. **Credit** AmEx,
DC, JCB, MC, V. **English menu. Map** Shinjuku p117.
After two decades in this convenient location, Ban
Thai has become a Tokyo fixture. But it's still very
reliable, with especially good curries.

China Grill – Xenlon

*Odakyu Hotel Century Southern Tower 19F, 2-2-1
Yoyogi, Shibuya-ku (3374 2080/www.xenlon.com/
Shinjuku.index.html). Shinjuku station (Yamanote
line), south exit; (Marunouchi, Oedo lines), exit A1;
(Shinjuku line), exit 6.* **Open** 11.30am-11pm daily.
Average ¥8,000. **Credit** AmEx, DC, JCB, MC, V.
English menu. Map Shinjuku p117.
Impeccable service and impressive views of the neon
skyline make this stylish Chinese restaurant well

worth the splurge. The Cantonese menu, which nods toward Western rather than Japanese influences, includes excellent dim sum at lunchtime. **Other locations**: throughout the city.

Hyakunincho Yataimura

2-20-25 Hyakunincho, Shinjuku-ku (5386 3320/ www.yataimura.jp). Shin-Okubo station (Yamanote line). **Open** 11.30am-2.30pm, 5pm-2am Mon-Thur; 11.30am-4am Fri-Sun. **Average** ¥2,500. **Credit** AmEx, DC, JCB, MC, V. **English menu** (some stands).
The cheerfully chaotic *Yataimura* ('food-stall village') provides a one-stop culinary tour of Asian street food. A score of small stands set around a large central eating area supply a choice of cuisines (Malaysian, Chinese, Thai, Vietnamese and Indian). The proprietors vie aggressively for your custom, so quickly order beer and snacks while you consider the rest of your meal. Fun, funky and, best of all, cheap.

Matsuya

1-1-17 Okubo, Shinjuku-ku (3200 5733). Shin-Okubo station (Yamanote line). **Open** 11am-5am daily. **Average** ¥3,000. **No credit cards**.
The name may sound Japanese, but the food is 100 per cent Korean home-style cooking. Kick off your shoes, sit on the floor and tuck into Matsuya's rugged *kamjatang* hot-pot, a delectable chilli-rich stew of potatoes and massive pork backbones. Subtle fare this is not, but it's great for keeping out the winter chill. Wash it all down with the milky (but potent) *makkoli* rice wine.

New York Grill

Park Hyatt Tokyo 52F, 3-7-1-2 Nishi-Shinjuku, Shinjuku-ku (5323 3458/www.parkhyatttokyo.com). Shinjuku station (Yamanote line), west exit; (Marunouchi line), exit A13; (Oedo, Shinjuku lines), exit 6. **Open** 11.30am-2.30pm, 5.30-10.30pm daily. **Average** ¥14,000. **Credit** AmEx, DC, JCB, MC, V. **English menu**. **Map** Shinjuku p117.
The New York Grill offers sky-high power dining (and brilliant views) at the apex of the Park Hyatt hotel. The food – great seafood and meat dishes prepared in modern New World style – is consistently excellent, service is polished, and the well thought out selection of North American wines unrivalled in Japan. Sunday brunch is an expat institution, as are evening cocktails in the adjoining New York Bar.

Thien Phuoc

Kotoku Bldg 2F, 3-11 Yotsuya, Shinjuku-ku (3358 6617). Yotsuya-Sanchome station (Marunouchi line), exit 2. **Open** 11am-3pm, 5-11pm Mon-Fri; noon-11pm Sat, Sun. **Average** ¥4,000. **No credit cards**.
Despite the humble location, tucked well back from the street, Thien Phuoc is worth searching out for its excellent Saigon street-stall food. Try the crisp *banh xeo* pancakes, spicy Hue-style beef *pho* noodles and memorable *cha gio* (spring rolls). Reasonable prices are another reason to make a beeline for this popular, but low-key, joint.

Ueno

Japanese

Goemon

1-1-26 Hon-Komagome, Bunkyo-ku (3811 2015/ www.tcn-catv.ne.jp/~goemon). Hakusan station (Mita line), exit A2 or Hon-Komagome station (Nanboku line), exit 2. **Open** noon-2pm, 5-10pm Tue-Fri; noon-8pm Sat, Sun. **Average** ¥6,000. **No credit cards**.
Hidden away in Hakusan, this Kyoto-style tofu restaurant is one of Tokyo's best-kept secrets. The entrance is lined with bamboo and the garden has a waterfall, carp ponds and a couple of rustic bowers where you can sit in clement weather. The winter speciality is *yudofu* (piping hot tofu in broth); in summer, try the *hiya yakko* (chilled tofu). This is not the place for a rushed meal; last orders are taken two hours before closing time.

Hantei

2-12-15 Nezu, Bunkyo-ku (3828 1440/www.hantei. co.jp). Nezu station (Chiyoda line), exit 2. **Open** noon-2.30pm, 5-10pm Tue-Sat; 4-9.30pm Sun. **Average** ¥4,500. **No credit cards**. **English menu**. **Map** Ueno & Yanaka p123.
Kushi-age (skewers of meat, fish or vegetables) is not gourmet fare, but Hantei makes it refined. This is partly due to the care that goes into the preparation, but mostly because of the beautiful old wooden building. There's no need to order: staff will bring course after course, stopping after every six to ask if you want to continue.

Ikenohata Yabu Soba

3-44-7 Yushima, Bunkyo-ku (3831 8977/www. yabu-soba.com). Yushima station (Chiyoda line), exit 2. **Open** 11.30am-2pm, 4.30-8pm Mon, Tue, Thur-Sat; 11.30am-8pm Sun. **Average** ¥3,000. **No credit cards**. **English menu**. **Map** Ueno & Yanaka p123.
Kanda Yabu Soba (*see p154*) has spawned numerous shops run by former apprentices. This one does predictably good noodles at reasonable prices in a simple Japanese setting. The menu also includes a range of snacks, and, in winter, offers suitably warming *nabe* hot-pots.

Yanaka

Japanese

Nezu Club

2-30-2 Nezu, Bunkyo-ku (3828 4004/www.nezuclub. com). Nezu station (Chiyoda line), exit 1. **Open** 6-10pm Wed-Sat. **Average** ¥6,500. **Credit** AmEx, DC, JCB, MC, V. **Map** Ueno & Yanaka p123.
Chef Yamada Etsuko's stylish Japanese cuisine is not as formal as *kaiseki*, but it is far more sophisticated than regular home cooking. She has a very creative modern touch that reflects the restaurant's

innovative setting: a converted 30-year-old, metal-frame workshop tucked away down a narrow alley in this very traditional neighbourhood.

Sasanoyuki

2-15-10 Negishi, Taito-ku (3873 1145). Uguisudani station (Yamanote line), north exit. **Open** 11am-9.30pm Tue-Sun. **Average** ¥5,000. **Credit** AmEx, DC, JCB, MC, V. **English menu**. **Map** Ueno & Yanaka p123.

Tokyo's most famous tofu restaurant was founded way back in the Edo period by a tofu-maker lured from Kyoto by the Kanei-ji temple's imperial abbot. Despite its illustrious past, Sasanoyuki is as down to earth as the Nippori neighbourhood it sits in, with very reasonable prices.

Elsewhere in central Tokyo

Japanese

Buri

3-13-12 Akasaka, Minato-ku (3560 6322). Akasaka station (Chiyoda line), exit 1. **Open** 11.30am-2pm, 5pm-midnight Mon-Fri; 5pm-midnight Sat. **Average** ¥4,000. **Credit** AmEx, DC, JCB, MC, V. **English menu**.

You won't find a friendlier place in Akasaka than this upscale *izakaya*, a grander relative of the Ebisu bar of the same name. Sit at the counter and watch the chefs at work. Or just relax and enjoy the excellent seafood and other traditional dishes. There's a great selection of sake too, with tasting sets so you can compare different styles.

Jidaiya

Naritaya Bldg 1F, 3-14-3 Akasaka, Minato-ku (3588 0489). Akasaka station (Chiyoda line), exit 1. **Open** 11.30am-2.30pm, 5pm-4am Mon-Fri; 5-11pm Sat, Sun. **Average** ¥5,000. **Credit** AmEx, DC, JCB, MC, V.

Jidaiya recreates a rustic Japanese farmhouse, complete with tatami mats, dried ears of corn, fish-shaped hanging fireplace fixtures and heaps of old-looking wooden furniture. The atmosphere is contrived but fun, and large shared tables contribute to the conviviality. The food is all Japanese, with an emphasis on seafood, meat and vegetables cooked at the table.

Ninja

Akasaka Tokyu Plaza 1F, 2-14-3 Nagatacho, Chiyoda-ku (5157 3936/www.ninja.tv). Akasaka-Mitsuke station (Ginza, Marunouchi lines), Sotobori Dori exit. **Open** 5.30pm-4am Mon-Sat; 5-11pm Sun. **Average** ¥5,000. **Credit** AmEx, DC, JCB, MC, V. **English menu**.

Waiters dressed as ninjas usher you through a series of winding wooden corridors designed to evoke the interior of an ancient Japanese castle. Others sneak up with menus and food, and there's also an itinerant magician. It's good, harmless fun and very popular. Food is Japanese with plenty of Western tweaks. **Photo** *p166*.

Sakura Sakura

5-15-10 Shirokanedai, Minato-ku (3440 7316/www.sakura2.co.jp). Shirokanedai station (Nanbokui line). **Open** 11.30am-11pm Tue-Sun. **Average** ¥7,000. **Credit** AmEx, DC, JCB, MC, V.

The multi-course meals (from ¥5,520) of Kyoto-style *obanzai* cuisine are light and flavourful, emphasising tofu, *yuba* and seasonal vegetables. It's a beautiful setting too: a small three-storey wooden house decorated with vermilion walls, black woodwork and kimono fabric over the windows.

Seigetsu

Kamiya Bldg 2F, 6-77 Kagurazaka, Shinjuku-ku (3269 4320/www.teshigoto.net). Kagurazaka station (Tozai line), Kagurazaka exit or Ushigome-Kagurazaka station (Oedo line), exit A3. **Open** 5-11.30pm Mon-Fri; 5-11pm Sat, Sun. **Average** ¥4,000. **Credit** AmEx, DC, JCB, MC, V. **English menu**.

The open kitchen in this bustling, wood-clad *izakaya* produces a good range of seafood and side dishes – the charcoal-grilled fish and chicken are notable. Not only is there a fine selection of sake and *shochu*, but the place can also provide a list in English. There's even a (cramped) no-smoking section.

Torijaya

4-2 Kagurazaka, Shinjuku-ku (3260 6661/www.bolanet.ne.jp/torijaya). Iidabashi station (Chuo, Sobu lines), west exit; (Nanboku, Yurakucho lines), exit B3 or Kagurazaka station (Tozai line), Kagurazaka exit or Ushigome-Kagurazaka station (Oedo line), exit A3. **Open** 11.30am-2pm, 5-9.30pm Mon-Sat; 11.30am-3pm, 4-9pm Sun. **Average** ¥6,000. **Credit** AmEx, JCB, MC, V.

Kyoto-style cuisine is the focus of this traditional restaurant. It's referred to as *udon kaiseki*, but things never get too formal. The centrepiece of any meal here is *udon-suki* – a hearty hot-pot of chicken, vegetables and thick-cut wheat noodles.

Non-Japanese

Calabash

Hamamatsucho Bldg B1, 2-10-1 Hamamatsucho, Minato-ku (3433 0884/www.calabash.co.jp). Hamamatsucho station (Yamanote line), exit S5 or Daimon station (Asakusa, Oedo lines), exit B2. **Open** 11.30am-2pm, 6-11pm Mon-Sat. **Average** ¥4,000. **Credit** AmEx, DC, JCB, MC, V.

More than just a friendly little diner, Calabash serves as the focus for Tokyo's small francophone West African community. Proprietor Eddie Harouna Dabo hails from Mali, but his menu spans virtually the whole continent (as does his drinks cabinet). There's often live music.

Manuel Churrascaria

2-3-22 Takanawa, Minato-ku (3443 5002/www.pjgroup.jp/manuel/takanawa/index.html). Takanawadai station (Asakusa line), exit A1. **Open** noon-2.30pm, 6-11pm Tue-Sun. **Average** ¥5,000. **Credit** AmEx, DC, JCB, MC, V.

Catch the waiter if you can, at **Ninja**. *See p165*.

The third and smallest of the three Manuel restaurants is a cosy, bistro-scale North Portuguese-style-grillhouse. The spicy African chicken is highly recommended, as are the spare ribs and sardines. There are wines from Douro and Dao to wash it all down with, and vintage port if you feel like lingering.

Stefano

Terui Bldg 1F, 6-47 Kagurazaka, Shinjuku-ku (5228 7515/www.stefano-jp.com). Kagurazaka station (Tozai line), exit 1 or Ushigome-Kagurazaka station (Oedo line), exit A3. **Open** 11.30am-2pm, 6-11pm Tue-Sat; noon-3pm, 5.30-9pm Sun. **Average** ¥6,000. **Credit** AmEx, DC, JCB, MC, V. **English menu**.

Chef Stefano Fastro hails from the Veneto, and his culinary repertoire ranges from Venetian seafood to the meaty, almost Austrian fare of the mountains. It's a modest place and rather off the beaten track, but many rate Stefano among their favourite Italian restaurants in Tokyo. The gnocchi alone make it worth seeking out.

Tribes

10-7 Wakamiyacho, Shinjuku-ku (3235 9966/ www.tribes.jp). Kagurazaka station (Tozai line), Kagurazaka exit or Ushigome-Kagurazaka station (Oedo line), exit A3. **Open** 6pm-midnight Mon-Sat. **Average** ¥5,000. **Credit** AmEx, DC, JCB, MC, V. **English menu**.

African inspiration meets French cuisine meets Tokyo style in the alleys of Kagurazaka. The

result is an original and chic little bar-restaurant with a menu (and wine list) that ranges from Morocco down to South Africa. Among the standouts: *pepe*, a Nigerian stew seasoned with plenty of pepper, and ostrich meat (raised in Japan) served as kebabs or in rich sausages.

Wine Cellar Davis

2-5-6 Takanawa, Minato-ku (3440 6045). Takanawadai station (Asakusa line), exit A1. **Open** 5.30pm-midnight Tue-Sat; 5-9pm Sun. Closed 1st, 3rd Sun of mth. **Average** ¥4,000. **Credit** AmEx, DC, JCB, MC, V. **English menu**.

Owner Shoko Davis has amassed a considerable wine cellar over the years, and her kitchen turns out robust French-Italian cuisine. This place is excellent value and a perennial favourite with the local expat community. The obscure location ensures they don't have to share it.

Further afield

Japanese

Aguri

1-6-7 Kami-Meguro, Meguro-ku (3792 3792/www. agurimeguri.com/nakameguro/index.html). Naka-Meguro station (Hibiya, Toyoko lines). **Open** 5pm-4am Mon-Sat; 5pm-1am Sun. **Average** ¥4,000. **Credit** AmEx, MC, V.

Friendly, casual and inexpensive, this large *izakaya* close to the river has just enough style to raise it above the average. Platters of prepared foods line the counter in tapas style, while short-order cooks stand ready to rustle up grilled fish and teppanyaki meat or vegetables.
Other locations: Dogenzaka Center Bldg 6F, 2-29-8 Dogenzaka, Shibuya-ku (3780 3788).

Higashi-yama

1-21-25 Higashiyama, Meguro-ku (5720 1300). Naka-Meguro station (Hibiya, Toyoko lines). **Open** 6pm-1am Mon-Sat. **Average** ¥6,000. **Credit** AmEx, MC, V.
Inventive traditional cuisine from a team of gifted chefs, matched by a beautifully sleek, modern interior (the creation of Ogata Shinichiro): this is Japanese contemporary designer dining at its best. The staff are friendly and reservations essential.

Ukai Toriyama

Minami-Asakawa 3426, Hachioji-shi (0426 61 0739/www.ukai.co.jp/toriyama). Takaosan-Guchi station (Keio line) then free shuttle bus. **Open** 11am-9.30pm Mon-Sat; 11am-8.30pm Sun. **Average** ¥6,000. **Credit** AmEx, DC, JCB, MC, V. **English menu.**
Here you sit in quaint teahouse-style cottages in a manicured, pond-filled garden, grilling your own *jidori* chicken over charcoal, or dining on other seasonal Japanese delicacies. Anyone visiting Mt Takao should make a special detour for a meal here. In fact, it's worth making a special trip, despite the long journey (50 minutes from Shinjuku by train, then ten minutes by bus). Reservations are highly recommended. Note that last orders is 90 minutes before closing time.

Non-Japanese

Café Eight

3-17-7 Aobadai, Meguro-ku (5458 5262/http:// cafe8.exblog.jp/i10). Ikejiri-Ohashi (Denentoshi line). **Open** 11am-10pm Tue-Sun. **Average** ¥3,000. **Credit** AmEx, DC, JCB, MC, V. **English menu.**
The original vegetarian Café Eight in Aoyama was sorely missed when it closed down, and its new incarnation is neither as vibrant nor as convenient. But the laid-back 'Eat Your Vegetables' philosophy and good vibe remains unchanged.

Izmir

2F Passage Asagaya, 2-13-2 Asagaya-Kita, Suginami-ku (3310 4666/www.asagaya-izmir.com) Asagaya station (JR Chuo Line), north exit. **Open** 5.30pm-midnight Tue-Sun. Closed 3rd Tue of mth. **Average** ¥3,000. **Credit** AmEx, JCB, MC, V. **English menu.**
An anonymous mini mall out on the Chuo Line is an unlikely venue for such excellent, down-to-earth Turkish cuisine. Chef Süleyman Özeri produces all the standards with aplomb (the Adana kebabs are great), while his partner Elif greets customers with all the warmth of the Aegean.

Jiang's

3F Kurokawa Bldg, 3-5-7 Tamagawa, Setagaya-ku (3700 2475/www.giangs.com). Futako-Tamagawa station (Denentoshi line). **Open** 5-10pm Tue-Sun. **Average** ¥3,500. **Credit** AmEx, JCB, MC, V. **English menu.**
Nguyen Thi Giang was born in Hanoi and raised in south Vietnam, and the menu in her spotless little restaurant in a suburban mall reflects both influences. The hearty *cha gio* rolls full of tasty pork are cooked in northern style, while the delicate *banh xeo* pancakes are as sweet and satisfying as you'd find in Hue. The best home-style Vietnamese food in Tokyo, and worth the train ride (six stops) from Shibuya.

Junkadelic

4-10-4 Kami-Meguro, Meguro-ku (5725 5020/http:// junkadelic.jp). Naka-Meguro station (Hibiya, Toyoko lines). **Open** 6pm-2am daily. **Average** ¥4,000. **No credit cards. English menu.**
Day of the Dead figurines, primitive murals and battered, junk-shop furniture set the scene at Junkadelic. The frozen Margaritas are large and lurid. The kitchen turns out a strange Japanese hybrid of Tex-Mex cantina food that's never less than tasty. Later in the evening it segues into a DJ bar.

Makani & Lanai

2-16-11 Aobadai, Meguro-ku (5428 4222/www .zetton.co.jp/aloha/ml/index.htm). **Open** 11.30am-3am Mon-Sat; 11.30am-midnight Sun. **Average** ¥3,000. **Credit** AmEx, DC, JCB, MC, V. **English menu.**
The food here, which with names like *pupu* and *ahi poke* won't mean much unless just you flew in from Hawaii, is distinctly lightweight. But it's the river location, right on cherry-lined Megurogawa, that establishes M&L's credentials. An ideal spot for chilling with a Kona beer or three.

Osteria La Luna Rossa

2-5-23 Naka-Meguro, Meguro-ku (3793 4310). Naka-Meguro station (Hibiya, Toyoko lines). **Open** 11.30am-2pm, 6-10pm Mon, Wed-Sun. **Average** ¥6,000. **Credit** AmEx, DC, JCB, MC, V.
The gentrification of the Meguro River banks continues apace, with La Luna Rossa a prime example. Sleek tranquil decor, a massive subterranean wine cellar and outstanding *cucina* from the gifted young chef, Yagi Kosuke. Taste his delicate *fritti* or *pastella di scampi* and swoon. In central Tokyo you'd pay twice as much for food of this calibre.

TY Harbor Brewery

2-1-3 Higashi-Shinagawa, Shinagawa-ku (5479 4555/www.tyharborbrewing.co.jp). Tennozu Isle station (Tokyo monorail), central exit. **Open** 11.30am-2pm, 5.30-10 pm Mon-Fri; 11.30am-3pm, 5.30-9pm Sat, Sun. **Average** ¥4,000. **Credit** AmEx, DC, JCB, V. **English menu.**
Tokyo's best brewpub produces a range of Californian-style ales and porters, and the attached restaurant serves up straightforward, if uninspired, diner fare. The canalside location is one of the few places where you can sit outside on the waterfront.

Eat, Drink, Shop

Menu reader

MAIN TYPES OF RESTAURANT

寿司屋   ***sushi-ya***
sushi restaurants

イクラ	*ikura*	salmon roe
タコ	*tako*	octopus
マグロ	*maguro*	tuna
こはだ	*kohada*	punctatus
トロ	*toro*	belly of tuna
ホタテ	*hotate*	scallop
ウニ	*uni*	sea urchin roe
エビ	*ebi*	prawn
ヒラメ	*hirame*	flounder
アナゴ	*anago*	conger eel
イカ	*ika*	squid
玉子焼き	*tamago-yaki*	sweet egg omelette
かっぱ巻き	*kappa maki*	rolled cucumber
鉄火巻き	*tekka maki*	rolled tuna
お新香巻き	*oshinko maki*	rolled pickles

蕎麦屋（そば屋）   ***soba-ya***
Japanese noodle restaurants

天ぷらそば うどん   *tempura soba, udon*
noodles in hot broth with prawn tempura

ざるそば うどん   *zaru soba, udon*
noodles served on a bamboo rack in a lacquer box

きつねそば うどん   *kitsune soba, udon*
noodles in hot broth topped with spring onion and fried tofu

たぬきそば うどん   *tanuki soba, udon*
noodles in hot broth with fried tempura batter

月見そば うどん   *tsukimi soba, udon*
raw egg broken over noodles in hot broth

あんかけうどん   *ankake udon*
wheat noodles in a thick fish bouillon/soy sauce soup with fishcake slices and vegetables

鍋焼きうどん   *nabeyaki udon*
noodles boiled in an earthenware pot with other ingredients and stock. Mainly eaten in winter.

居酒屋   ***izakaya***
Japanese-style bars

日本酒	*nihon-shu*	sake
冷酒	*rei-shu*	cold sake
焼酎	*shoochuu*	barley or potato spirit

チュウハイ   *chuuhai*
shoochuu with juice or tea

生ビール	*nama-biiru*	draught beer
黒ビール	*kuro-biiru*	dark beer
梅酒	*ume-shu*	plum wine

ひれ酒   *hirezake*
hot sake flavoured with blowfish fins

焼き魚   *yaki zakana*   grilled fish

煮魚   *ni zakana*
fish cooked in various sauces

刺し身   *sashimi*
raw fish in bite-sized pieces, served with soy sauce and wasabi

揚げ出し豆腐   *agedashi doofu*
deep fried plain tofu served with savoury sauce

枝豆   *edamame*
boiled green soybeans in the pod

おにぎり   *onigiri*
rice parcel with savoury filling

焼きおにぎり   *yaki onigiri*
grilled rice balls

フグ刺し   *fugusashi*
thinly sliced sashimi, usually spectacularly arranged and served with ponzu sauce

フグちり *fuguchiri*
chunks of fugu in a vegetable stew

雑炊 *zosui*
rice porridge cooked in fuguchiri broth

焼き鳥屋 *yakitori-ya*
yakitori restaurants

焼き鳥 *yakitori*
barbecued chicken pieces seasoned with
sweet soy sauce

つくね *tsukune* minced chicken balls

タン *tan* tongue

ハツ *hatsu* heart

シロ *shiro* tripe

レバー *reba* liver

ガツ *gatsu* intestines

鳥皮 *tori-kawa* skin

ネギ間 *negima* chicken with leek

おでん屋 *oden-ya*
oden restaurants or street stalls

さつま揚げ *satsuma-age* fish cake

昆布 *konbu* kelp rolls

大根 *daikon* radish

厚揚げ *atsu-age* fried tofu

OTHER TYPES OF RESTAURANT

料亭 *ryotei*
high-class, traditional restaurants

ラーメン屋 *ramen-ya*
ramen noodle shop

天ぷら屋 *tempura-ya* tempura restaurants

すき焼き屋 *sukiyaki-ya*
sukiyaki restaurants

トンカツ屋 *tonkatsu-ya*
tonkatsu restaurants

お好み焼き屋 *okonomi yaki-ya*
okonomiyaki restaurants

ESSENTIAL VOCABULARY

A table for..., please **...onegai shimasu**

one/two/three/four
hitori/futari/san-nin/yo-nin

Is this seat free? **kono seki aite masu ka**

Could we sit...? **...ni suware masu ka**

over there **asoko**

outside **soto**

in a non-smoking area **kin-en-seki**

by the window **madogiwa**

Excuse me
sumimasen/onegai shimasu

May I see the menu, please
menyuu o onegai shimasu

Do you have a set menu?
setto menyuu/teishoku wa arimasu ka

I'd like... **...o kudasai**

I'll have... **...ni shimasu**

a bottle/glass...
...o ippon/ippai kudasai

I can't eat food containing...
...ga haitte iru mono wa taberare masen

Do you have vegetarian meals?
bejitarian no shokuji wa arimasu ka

Do you have a children's menu?
kodomo-yoo no menyuu wa arimasu ka

The bill, please
o-kanjyoo onegai shimasu

That was delicious, thank you
gochisou sama deshita

We'd like to pay separately
betsubetsu ni onegai shimasu

It's all together, please
issho ni onegai shimasu

Is service included?
saabisu-ryoo komi desu ka

Can I pay with a credit card?
kurejitto caado o tsukae masu ka

Could I have a receipt, please?
reshiito onegai shimasu

Eat, Drink, Shop

SAPPORO

TOKYO LION GINZA

SAPPORO BEER STATION EBISU GARDEN PLACE

Bars

We raise a glass to a city that really likes a drink.

The near-legendary **Kamiya Bar**. *See p172.*

If you like beer, whisky or sake, you're in for a treat in Tokyo. It's not just the quality and ranges on offer of these three favourites that impress, it's also the extraordinary number of opportunities you'll have to indulge your taste buds. You won't look out of place sinking a drink in a cinema, bowling alley, temple grounds or hot spring.

Tokyoites pursue their alcoholic passions with such vigour that it's easy to find fellow drinkers in the wee hours of a weekday, and just as easy to find some top-quality booze to toast them with. If you're looking for the finest malts, rums, tequilas or wines, you'll find them in this metropolis. And you'll pay through the nose for them.

For the cost-conscious drinker, there is the curious option of *happoushu* and the drinks known locally as 'third beers'. To circumvent the tax on beer, these brews are created with lower levels of malt. As the government attempts to catch up by lowering the percentage of malt in its definition of beer, the breweries reply with ever less malty brews. Currently,

the malt content of these cheaper options lies between zero and 25 per cent. The drinks have their fans, but only the dullest of taste buds would mistake them for real beer.

Despite the vast number of drinking spots, defining a 'bar' is quite a challenge. Drinking and eating are such inseparable activities for Tokyoites that some of the best boozing spots are technically restaurants – such as the **TY Harbor Brewery** (*see p167*) – and many of the places listed below have impressive food menus. Even venues that consider themselves strictly bars will probably serve a mandatory snack called *otoshi*. This could be a handful of peanuts, a bowl of potato salad or something far less identifiable. Expect to pay ¥500-¥1,500 depending on the area and style of bar. The same dish is served to every customer – a service that is considered more sophisticated than demanding an entrance fee. This system can make bar-hopping an expensive pursuit unless you look for the 'no charge' signs (in English) posted outside most free bars.

The quintessential eating and drinking experience is the *izakaya*. Ranging from rowdy dives to designer settings, these bars offer giant jugs of beer and a wide selection of reasonably priced Japanese fare. Other popular options include the ever-increasing number of Irish and English pubs (the best of which include **What the Dickens**, *see p173*, and the **Meguro Tavern**, *see p181*), most of which serve Guinness on tap and have no *otoshi* charge.

The best Bars

The classiest
Mandarin Bar (*see p176*).

The friendliest
African Bar Esogie (*see p180*).

The nuttiest
Kagaya (*see p175*).

The best view
Mado Lounge (*see p177*).

The tastiest
Las Meninas (*see p181*).

Eat, Drink, Shop

Dagashi – a sweet place to eat candy (with an alcohol chaser). *See p173.*

Tokyoites love their tiny, crumbling drinking dens too. Top of the list are the venues in the Golden Gai area (*see p179* **Golden Gai**); but **Nonbei Yokocho** (Drinking Alley) – a row of tiny bars under the train tracks just opposite Shibuya station's Hachiko exit – and the **Albatross** (*see p180*) in Shinjuku's **Omoide Yokocho** (which is more colloquially known as Shonben Yokocho, or 'Piss Alley') are also well worth a try.

Each area of the city has a discernible character reflected in its bars. Harajuku, Aoyama and Nishi-Azabu are the best places for sleek lounges and designer interiors. Roppongi, meanwhile, offers the complete opposite: tatty, noisy joints with drinks as cheap as the pick-up lines you'll hear within. In Shibuya and outlying Shimo-Kitazawa you'll find quaint, affordable bars, while Ginza is the place to test your credit limit.

Take care if you see the words 'pub' or 'snack' outside a small Japanese bar; these two words are misleading for foreigners in search of a drink. Such places often turn out to be tamer versions of hostess bars, where the staff will drink away merrily on your bar tab. Prices are rarely displayed, so if you are not the guest of a regular customer you can expect to pay an arbitrary and sky-high sum at the end of the night.

But this is an exception. In general, you'll find Tokyo's bars welcoming, even if you don't speak the language. Generous licensing laws mean that many places don't close until the trains begin running at 5am – which means the first few trains of the day often carry a jumble of sleepy-eyed salarymen heading for work, and baggy-eyed soaks (who may or may not also be office-bound). Fortunately, public drunkenness is treated with tolerance.

Asakusa

Flamme d'Or

Asahi Super Dry Hall 1F-2F, 1-23-16 Azumabashi, Sumida-ku (5608 5381/ www.asahibeer.co.jp/restaurant/azuma/ flamdoll1.html). Asakusa station (Asakusa line) exit A5; (Ginza line), exits 4, 5. **Open** *June-Aug* 11.30am-11pm daily. *Sept-May* 11.30am-10pm daily. **Credit** AmEx, MC, V. **Map** Asakusa p63.

One of Tokyo's quirkier landmarks, the enormous golden object atop Philippe Starck's ultra-modern building across the river from the temples of Asakusa is most often compared to an undiscovered root vegetable. Or a golden turd. The beer hall inside is also distinctive: oddly shaped pillars, tiny port-hole windows and sweeping curved walls covered in soft grey cushioning. But for all the fancy design, the atmosphere is somewhat sterile. English menus are available, as is a choice of German-style bar snacks and Asahi draught beers. On the 22nd floor of the building next door is another bar, the Asahi Sky Room, which serves beer and soft drinks from 10am to 9pm daily.

Kamiya Bar

1-1-1 Asakusa, Taito-ku (3841 5400/ www.kamiya-bar.com). Asakusa station (Asakusa line), exit A5; (Ginza line), exit 3. **Open** 11.30am-10pm Mon, Wed-Sun. **No credit cards. Map** Asakusa p63.

Established in the late 1800s, Kamiya is something of a legend. It's the oldest western-style bar in Tokyo and one of the friendliest to boot. The crowds certainly don't come here for the decor (think Formica tables and too-bright lighting), but the atmosphere – loud, smoky and occasionally raucous – is typical of this working-class neighbourhood. Try the house Denki Bran (Electric Brandy) – a sweet blend of wine, gin and brandy that's a lot nicer than it sounds. **Photo** *p171.*

Ebisu & Daikanyama

Bar

*1-9-11 Ebisu-Minami, Shibuya-ku (5704 0186).
Ebisu station (Yamanote, Hibiya lines), west
exit.* **Open** 5pm-5am daily. **Credit** AmEx, DC,
JCB, MC, V.

Perhaps the owners couldn't think of a better name
for this ethereal drinking den, or perhaps they used
up all their imagination on the interior, where glass
beads on the pillars twinkle like distant stars amid
the orange glow of Japanese paper lanterns, all to a
backdrop of space-like sounds. The speciality is
Scotch, with a staggering 200 single malts on offer
at around ¥600 a throw.

Bar Kitsune

*Chatolet Shibuya B1F, 2-20-13 Higashi, Shibuya-ku
(5766 5911/www.usen.com/tenpo/kitsune/shibuya.
html). Ebisu station (Yamanote, Hibiya lines),
west exit.* **Open** 7pm-midnight Mon; 7pm-3am
Tue-Thur, Sun; 7pm-5am Fri, Sat. **Credit** AmEx,
DC, JCB, MC, V.

Situated on Meiji Dori between Ebisu and Shibuya,
this vast bar pushes back the boundaries between
restaurant, DJ bar and club, but stops short of providing a dancefloor. It's rare to see a foreign face
here, as Kitsune hasn't been colonised by bar- and
club-hoppers. The numerous semi-private areas are
great to relax in.

Dagashi

*1-13-7 Ebisu-Nishi, Shibuya-ku (5458 5150). Ebisu
station (Yamanote, Hibiya lines), west exit.* **Open**
6.30pm-4.30am Mon-Sat; 6pm-1am Sun. **Credit**
AmEx, DC, MC, V.

A beautiful *izakaya* serving standard drinks alongside steaming dishes of Asian favourites. The
twist is the all-you-can-eat candy (*dagashi*), which
is offered free to every customer. Sweet-toothed
boozers can plunge their hand into the numerous
buckets of trad Japanese candies and crispy snacks.
For an extra ¥500 you can take a bag home. The
name outside is only in Japanese, so look for the
blazing orange signs. **Photo** *p172*.

Kissa Ginza

*1-3-9 Ebisu-Minami, Shibuya-ku (3710 7320/www8.
plala.or.jp/dj/index.html). Ebisu station (Yamanote,
Hibiya lines), west exit.* **Open** 10am-2am Mon-Sat.
Credit AmEx, DC, JCB, MC, V.

Here's a recipe for postmodern kitsch, Tokyo-style.
Take a 40-year-old coffee shop that hasn't seen a dec-
orator in 30 years, install a glitter ball, two turntables and… absolutely nothing else. Result: the
blue-rinse set still come for coffee in the daytime, but
the evening brings lounge-loving urban hipsters
who love the laid-back grooves. The draft beers are
served in narrow sundae glasses – not great value
but good fun the first few times.

What the Dickens

*Roob 6 Bldg 4F, 1-13-3 Ebisu-Nishi, Shibuya-ku
(3780 2099). Ebisu station (Yamanote, Hibiya lines),
west exit.* **Open** 5pm-1am Mon-Thur; 5pm-2am Fri,
Sat; 3pm-midnight Sun. **No credit cards.**

At the top of the building that houses nightclub Milk
(*see p224*) is this popular British-style pub. The
walls are decorated with Dickens manuscripts
(which have been liberally recaptioned in the gents'
toilets). Unfortunately, food is of genuine British pub
standard. Local bands play nightly.

Office. *See p175.*

Eat, Drink, Shop

Local potions

Japan has three key indigenous alcoholic drinks: *nihonshu*, *shochu* and *awamori*. The famous 'sake' is a synonym of *nihonshu*, but can also be a catch-all for booze in general, so *nihonshu* is the unambiguous way to order.

Nihonshu is brewed from rice, and fermented with an enzyme that converts the starches to sugar – a step that parallels malting barley in beer-making. This allows sake to rise to as high as 20 per cent alcohol – though it's almost always watered down again to around 16 per cent. *Nihonshu* can be served hot or cold, but in general it's the cheap stuff that's heated and the premium stuff that's best enjoyed chilled. For the really good stuff, look for the word *daiginjo*; but be prepared to pay for it.

Shochu and *awamori* are distinct in that both are distilled rather than brewed. Thus they're significantly more potent, usually at least 50 per cent proof. *Shochu* can be made from one of several raw materials, including barley, rice or the popular purple Satsuma

sweet potato. If it's distilled only once, it's termed *honkaku shochu* ('the real thing') and can wonderfully bear the fragrance of the source produce. But it can also be distilled multiple times into a clear liquor that's great for mixing with fruit juices. Japan's convenience store shelves are loaded with canned versions of just such a potion – called *chu-hai*. Premium *shochu* can be enjoyed in a number of ways: on the rocks, mixed with a little hot water, or perhaps with a pickled plum thrown in the glass.

Awamori is also distilled but is made only with imported Thai long-grain rice, and it hails from the southern islands of Okinawa. It has a significantly more earthy flavour than *shochu* thanks to the special mould that's used in the distilling process. *Awamori* can be drunk on the rocks, mixed with hot or cold water, or even straight (in small doses), but Okinawans drink it with ice and water. Look for the *kuusu*, a premium version aged for at least three years.

Xex Daikanyama

La Fuente Daikanyama 3F, 11-1 Sarugakucho, Shibuya-ku (3476 0065/www.ystable.co.jp/ restaurant/xexdaikanyama/bar.html). Daikanyama station (Tokyu Toyoko line). **Open** 6pm-3am daily. **Credit** AmEx, DC, JCB, MC, V.

This restaurant/bar complex offers two great spots for red-blooded romantics. The bar is all sultry jazz ambience and quality cocktails, while outside on the terrace a reflecting pool and flickering lanterns create a Balinese-style look. Take note: while anyone is welcome to enter, Xex operates a membership system that reserves many of the best seats for those willing to shell out a ¥30,000 joining fee plus ¥7,350 per month.

Ginza

Cabaret

Ginzazetton Bldg B1F, 5-14-15 Ginza, Chuo-ku (5148 3601/www.zetton.co.jp/j/ restaurant/cabaret/cabaret.htm). Higashi-Ginza station (Asakusa, Hibiya lines), exit 4. **Open** 8pm-5am Mon-Sat. **Credit** AmEx, DC, JCB, MC, V. **Map** Ginza p75

Descend the red velvet-draped spiral staircase and… that's pretty much where the cabaret theme ends. But you'll find yourself in the sleek basement of Zetton, a Korean/Japanese restaurant in the backstreets of Ginza. Be warned, though: a seat at the bar costs ¥500, and a spot on the sofa carries a hefty ¥1,500 charge.

Hajime

Iraka Ginza Bldg B1F, 6-4-7 Ginza, Chuo-ku (5568 4552/www.ginza-hajime.com). Ginza station (Ginza, Hibiya, Marunouchi lines), Sotobori Dori exit. **Open** 6pm-3am Mon-Fri; 6-11pm Sat. **Credit** AmEx, DC, JCB, MC, V. **Map** Ginza p75.

Hajime looks like an old apartment from the outside but is actually a sleek, modern designer bar. Yellow light gives the tiny basement space a warm glow. The menu focuses on wines – both grape and rice varieties. This being Ginza, there's a predictable ¥1,000 seating charge.

Hibiki

Caretta Shiodome 46F, 1-8-1 Higashi-Shinbashi, Minato-ku (6215 8051). Shiodome station (Oedo line), exit A1; (Yurikamome line), Dentsu exit. **Open** 11am-4pm, 5-11.30pm daily. **Credit** AmEx, DC, JCB, MC, V.

A pleasantly upmarket *izakaya* with great Japanese food and even better views, near the top of one of the towers in the Shiodome complex. The food is freshly prepared Japanese grill fare, at around ¥800 a dish, while drinks cost around ¥700. The view over the river towards Odaiba is spectacular, taking in both the Rainbow Bridge and Odaiba Ferris wheel, but window tables should be reserved in advance.

Ieyasu Hon-jin

1-30 Kanda-Jinbocho, Chiyoda-ku (3291 6228). Jinbocho station (Hanzomon, Mita, Shinjuku lines), exit A7. **Open** 5-10pm Mon-Fri. **No credit cards.** **Map** Marunouchi p93.

Amiable host Taisho bangs the drum behind the bar to greet each new customer to this cosy, top-class *yakitori* bar named after the first of the Tokugawa shoguns. There are only a dozen seats, so everyone crowds around the counter, where a wide choice of food lies in glass cases, already on sticks, ready to be popped on the coals and grilled. The food is excellent, as is the beer and sake, which Taisho dispenses with natural flair, pouring into small cups from a great height. Not cheap (expect around ¥4,000-¥7,000 for a couple of hours' eating and drinking), but still good value. Avoid the 6-8pm after-work rush and don't go in a group of more than three.

Kagaya

B1F, 2-15-12 Shinbashi, Minato-ku (3591 2347/ www1.ocn.ne.jp/~kagayayy). Shinbashi station (Yamanote, Asakusa lines), Karasumori exit; (Ginza line), exit 8; (Yurikamome line), exit 6. **Open** 6pm-midnight Mon-Sat; by appointment only Sun. **No credit cards.**

If you're looking for the goofy side of Tokyo, this should be your first stop. It's run entirely by 'Mark', the Japanese equivalent of Robin Williams, whose crackpot behaviour has made Kagaya famous. The drinks menu features beverages and country names.

Quons.

Choose one of each and Mark will disappear into his magic cupboard to re-emerge in a costume that reflects your choice. Drinks come in glasses that move, shake or make noises, and serve as the prelude to games such as table football or Jenga. You can also, if you wish, dress as a frog or giant teddy bear. Mark also dishes up home-style Japanese grub, with a billing system that's explained by mime. It's a small place, so reservations are recommended.

Lion Beer Hall

7-9-20 Ginza, Chuo-ku (3571 2590/www.ginzalion. jp). Ginza station (Ginza, Hibiya, Marunouchi lines), exit A4. **Open** 11.30am-11pm Mon-Sat; 11.30am-10.30pm Sun. **Credit** AmEx, MC, V. **Map** Ginza p75.

This 1930s beer hall, part of the Sapporo Lion chain, is a tourist attraction in itself. The tiled and wood-panelled interior looks as if it's been transplanted from Bavaria, and a menu laden with sausages adds to the effect. Friday night sessions have been known to descend into mass karaoke demonstrations. There is also a cheap and cheerful restaurant upstairs serving both Japanese and Western dishes.

Harajuku & Aoyama

Den Aquaroom

FIK Bldg B1F, 5-13-3 Minami-Aoyama, Minato-ku (5778 2090). Omotesando station (Chiyoda, Ginza, Hanzomon lines), exit B1. **Open** 6pm-2am Mon-Thur, Sat; 6pm-4am Fri; 6-11pm Sun. **Credit** AmEx, DC, JCB, MC, V.

Fish tanks, and lots of them, are the defining feature of this fashionable yet comfortable bar. There's a wide selection of cocktails and an intriguing menu (in English) of good-value Asian-influenced food.

Office

Yamazaki Bldg 5F, 2-7-18 Kita-Aoyama, Minato-ku (5786 1052). Gaienmae station (Ginza line), exit 2. **Open** 7pm-3am daily. **No credit cards.**

You'll find that theme bars of all description abound in Tokyo, but none has quite the same bizarrely unattractive concept as Office. With a photocopier by the window, power points for workaholics and bookshelves against the wall, the management seems not to have noticed that its bar offers the best view in the area. DJs play mellow tunes most nights, and the crowd are young, urban trendies. **Photo** *p173.*

Quons

2F 5-51-6 Jingumae, Shibuya-ku (5468 0633/ www.quons.jp). Omotesando station (Chiyoda, Ginza, Hanzomon lines), exit B2. **Open** 6pm-5am Mon-Sat; 6pm-2am Sun. **Credit** AmEx, DC, JCB, MC, V. **Map** Shibuya p109

The interior is by-the-numbers trendy bar, with designer sofas, hip music and artsy projections on the wall. But it's the roof that offers the best reason to spend an evening at Quons, if the weather allows. The cosy wooden top deck falls a bit short of the Balinese effect it seems to be aiming for, but it's still a great place to sip cocktails with a breeze on your cheeks.

Eat, Drink, Shop

Sekirei

Meiji Kinenkan, 2-2-23 Moto-Akasaka, Minato-ku (3746 7723/www.meijikinenkan.gr.jp/sekirei). Shinanomachi station (Chuo, Sobu lines). **Open** *June-Aug* 4.30-10.30pm Mon-Fri; 5.30-10.30pm Sat, Sun. Closed Sept-May. **Credit** AmEx, DC, JCB, MC, V.

For a summer-time drink there's nowhere that beats Sekirei. Kimono-clad traditional *buyou* dancers perform nightly on the spot where Emperor Meiji once signed the Japanese constitution. Meanwhile, a predominantly suit-wearing crowd sinks beers and wine while lounging in grand wicker chairs skirting the immaculate lawn. Any place this beautiful ought to be prohibitively expensive. Luckily, it's not. Beer clocks in at just ¥700 a jug, and the *izakaya*-style food is equally reasonable. Shinanomachi is a few stops east from Shinjuku.

Sign

2-7-18 Kita-Aoyama, Minato-ku (5474 5040). Gaienmae station (Ginza line), exit 3. **Open** 10am-3am Mon-Fri; 11am-midnight Sat, Sun. **No credit cards.**

An unashamedly artistic and artsy bar-cum-restaurant-cum-gallery a stone's throw from the station, Sign manages the difficult trick of being all things to all punters. While nearby office workers drop in and treat it as their local, creative types flock to the basement gallery, and clubbers come to listen to the occasional shows by local DJs.

Ikebukuro

Bobby's Bar

Milano Bldg 3F, 1-18-10 Nishi-Ikebukuro, Toshima-ku (3980 8875/http://plaza.rakuten.co.jp/bobbysbar). Ikebukuro station (Yamanote, Marunouchi, Yurakucho lines), west exit. **Open** 6pm-2am/3am Mon, Tue, Thur-Sat; 6pm-midnight Sun. **No credit cards.** **Map** Ikebukuro p87.

A small, foreigner-friendly bar on the west side of Ikebukuro station, offering a fine selection of imported beers with live music most nights. It shares a building with the New Delhi Indian restaurant, which offers good food at reasonable prices, and is a conveniently placed bolt-hole after a few lagers.

Marunouchi

Mandarin Bar

37F Mandarin Oriental Hotel, 2-1-1 Nihonbashi-Muromachi, Chuo-ku (3270 8800/www. mandarinoriental.com/hotel/558000168.asp). Mitsukoshimae station (Ginza line), exit A7. **Open** 11.30am-midnight daily. **Credit** AmEx, DC, JCB, MC, V. **Map** Marunouchi p93.

Superb cocktails, impeccable design, faultless service: what else are you looking for? Local design hotshot Kosaka Ryu was asked to create 'something sexy, but like nothing you've seen before'. His spacious layout incorporating a Zen pool and an array of designer furnishings succeeds on both counts. The view of Nihonbashi's business district is impressive, but you might not even notice.

The best, with zest: **Mandarin Bar**.

Roppongi

Agave

Clover Bldg B1F, 7-15-10 Roppongi (3497 0229/ www.lead-off-japan.co.jp/tempo/agave/index.html). Roppongi station (Hibiya, Oedo lines), exit 4B. **Open** 6.30pm-2am Mon-Thur; 6.30pm-4am Fri, Sat. **Credit** AmEx, DC. **Map** Roppongi p103.

From the orange stone walls to the snifters and sangritas, Agave is a perfect replica of an upmarket Mexican cantina in all ways but two: few cantinas stock 400 varieties of tequila and mescal, and no joint in Mexico would charge so much for them. With single measures costing from ¥800 to an impressive ¥9,400, this is the only place in Roppongi where customers don't hurl their cactus juice straight down their throats. **Photo** *p177.*

Bauhaus

Reine Roppongi Bldg 2F, 5-3-4 Roppongi (3403 0092/www.e-bauhaus.jp). Roppongi station (Hibiya, Oedo lines), exit 3. **Open** 8pm-1am Mon-Sat. **Credit** AmEx, DC, JCB, MC, V. **Map** Roppongi p103.

One of those 'only in Japan' experiences, this is a music venue that has featured the same band for over 20 years. Nowhere else in the world can you listen to flawless covers of the Rolling Stones, Pink Floyd or Madonna performed by men and women who can't speak three words of English, and then have them serve you food and drink between sets. It's on the pricey side, though, with a ¥2,700 music charge. Sets every hour.

Bernd's Bar
*Pure 2F, 5-18-1 Roppongi, Minato-ku (5563 9232/
www.berndsbar.com). Roppongi station (Hibiya, Oedo
lines), exit 3.* **Open** 5-11pm/empty Mon-Sat. **Credit**
AmEx, MC. **Map** Roppongi p103.
A small corner of Germany, with fresh pretzels on
the tables, and Bitburger and Erdinger on tap for
washing down your Wiener schnitzel. Try to get a
window table for the view of Roppongi's nightlife.
If you happen to meet owner Bernd Haag, you'll find
he can chat with you in English, German and
Spanish, as well as Japanese.

Cavern Club
*Saito Bldg 1F, 5-3-2 Roppongi (3405 5207/www.
kentos-group.co.jp/cavern). Roppongi station (Hibiya,
Oedo lines), exit 3.* **Open** 6pm-2.30am Mon-Sat;
6pm-midnight Sun. **Credit** AmEx, DC, JCB, MC, V.
Map Roppongi p103.
Tokyo's famous Beatles imitators play here most
nights – look for the Silver Beats on the schedule.
Some say they sound better live than the originals.
In low light, if you're very drunk and wearing dark
enough glasses, you might even convince yourself
you're back in '60s Liverpool. Music fee is ¥1,500.

Gas Panic
*2F-3F, 3-15-24 Roppongi, Minato-ku (3405 0633/
www.gaspanic.co.jp). Roppongi station (Hibiya, Oedo
lines), exit 3.* **Open** 6pm-5am daily. **No credit
cards. Map** Roppongi p103.
Gas Panic is a Roppongi institution, where young
people go to grope other young people. The chart
classics and Eurobeat play at such high volume that
your mating ritual needs to be physical rather than
verbal. To give an idea of what it's like, note that
you must have a drink in your hand at all times, and
drinking water is not in evidence. Every drink costs
¥400 at happy hour (6-9.30pm daily) and all night
on Thursday. There are three other Gas Panic outfits in Roppongi, two in Shibuya and another in
Yokohama; check the website for details.

Heartland
*West Walk Roppongi Hills, 6-10-1 Roppongi, Minato-
ku (5772 7600/www.heartland.jp). Roppongi station
(Hibiya line), exit A1; (Oedo line), exit 3.* **Open**
11am-5am daily. **Credit** AmEx, DC, JCB, MC, V.
Map Roppongi p103.
A recent addition to the Roppongi drinking stable,
Heartland is a chrome and glass, standing-room-
only DJ bar serving the eponymous Heartland beer.
It's also a meat market for rather upmarket meat.
There's an open-air courtyard for warm weather.

High Tide
*1-10-14 Nishi-Azabu, Minato-ku (5785 3684/
www.bar-hightide.com). Roppongi station (Hibiya,
Oedo lines), exit 2.* **Open** 6pm-5am Mon-Sat; 6pm-
3am Sun. **Credit** AmEx, DC, JCB, MC, V. **Map**
Roppongi p103.
High Tide is a small, dimly lit back-alley bar with
smartly dressed, rather aloof staff – just like countless other joints in this area. What sets it apart is the
semi-private room, where customers lounge on the
floor cushions, prop their drinks on a polished slice
of tree trunk and make the most of the ultra low-key
service. It's a place for dates, not mates. **Photo** *p178.*

Mado Lounge
*Mori Tower 52F, 6-10-1 Roppongi, Minato-ku
(6406 6652/www.tokyocityview.com/en/index.html).
Roppongi station (Hibiya line), exit 1C; (Oedo line),
exit 3.* **Open** 10am-11pm Mon-Thur, Sun; 10am-
midnight Fri, Sat. **Credit** AmEx, DC, JCB, MC, V.
Map Roppongi p103.
Part of Roppongi Hills' Tokyo City View observation deck, Mado Lounge opened in 2006, supple-
menting the great view with booze and quality local
DJs. The elevator to the 52nd floor costs ¥1,500, but
also gets you entrance to the Mori Art Museum,
which resides in the centre (*see p106*).

Maduro
*Grand Hyatt Tokyo 4F, 6-10-3 Roppongi,
Minato-ku (4333 1234/freephone 0120 588 288/
www.grandhyatttokyo.com). Roppongi station
(Hibiya line), exit 1C; (Oedo line), exit 3.* **Open**
6pm-2am Mon-Thur, Sun; 6pm-3am Fri, Sat. **Credit**
AmEx, DC, JCB, MC, V. **Map** Shibuya p109.
The luxurious bar of the five-star Grand Hyatt
Tokyo, Maduro is the place to go once that business
deal is sealed. The jet-set clientele don't mind the
¥1,575 seating charge; they come for the spacious
lounge setting and superior drinks menus. If you
know your Speysides from your Islays and your
Krugs from your cavas, this is your spot.

Agave. *See p176.*

Paddy Foley's Irish Pub

Roi Bldg B1F, 5-5-1 Roppongi, Minato-ku (3423 2250/www.paddyfoleystokyo.com). Roppongi station (Hibiya, Oedo lines), exit 3. **Open** 5pm-1am daily. **Credit** AmEx, MC, V. **Map** Roppongi p103.

One of Tokyo's first Irish pubs, Paddy Foley's still offers the best craic, despite increasing competition. Guinness, naturally, is the house speciality, and the food is good. It can get as crowded as a London pub at weekends, something the locals (who always sit down to drink) regard with mild bemusement.

Super-deluxe

B1F, 3-1-25 Nishi-Azabu, Minato-ku (5412 0515/ www.super-deluxe.com). Roppongi station (Hibiya, Oedo lines), exit 1B. **Open** 6pm-2am Mon-Sat. **Credit** V. **Map** Roppongi p103.

Picked up by *Time* magazine as Asia's best spot for 'avant-garde idling', Super-deluxe is the brainchild of a pair of architects who envisaged the spot as 'a bar, a gallery, a kitchen, a jazz club, a cinema, a library, a school…' and so on. Closer in atmosphere to an artists' salon than a bar, Super-deluxe offers something different every night, from slide shows to club nights. If you want to meet the creative cream of Tokyo, this is the place. Also the home of Tokyo Ale – the city's finest microbrew. **Photo** *p180*.

These

2F, 2-13-19 Nishi-Azabu, Minato-ku (5466 7331/ www.these-jp.com). Roppongi station (Hibiya, Oedo lines), exit 1. **Open** 7pm-4am daily. **Credit** MC, V. **Map** Roppongi p103.

As much library as bar – and pronounced 'tay-zay' – this strange spot exudes the feel of a British gentlemen's club, but with superior service. The bar has shelves and shelves of magazines and books for browsing, both foreign and Japanese, as well as a large central room where you are free to chat while indulging in one of the long list of whiskies. Harry Potter fans should watch out for the secret room.

Tokyo Sports Café

Fusion Bldg 2F, 7-13-8 Roppongi, Minato-ku (5411 8939/www.tokyo-sportscafe.com). Roppongi station (Hibiya, Oedo lines), exits 2, 4. **Open** 6pm-5am Mon-Sat (closing time varies depending on matches). **Credit** DC, JCB, MC, V. **Map** Roppongi p103.

One of the longest-established and largest sports bars in Tokyo, this place screens all major sporting events from around the world, with space to show two things at once. It offers an extensive range of beers – both domestic and imported – and cocktails. Happy hour lasts from 6pm to 8pm daily.

Shibuya

Bello Visto

Cerulean Tower Tokyu Hotel 40F, 26-1 Sakuragaoka-cho, Shibuya-ku (3476 3000/www.ceruleantower-hotel.com). Shibuya station (Yamanote, Ginza, Hanzomon lines), south exit. **Open** 4pm-midnight Mon-Fri; 3pm-midnight Sat, Sun. **Credit** AmEx, DC, JCB, MC, V. **Map** Shibuya p109.

There are more luxurious hotel bars in town, but the enormous glass windows of the 40th floor Bello Visto make this a spot worth checking out. The menu focuses on wine, with a frankly terrifying list of expensive tipples from all over the world. Prices start at ¥900 a glass, and a 10% service charge will be added to your bill. To ensure a seat by the window, booking is advisable.

Chandelier Bar/Red Bar

1-12-24 Shibuya, Shibuya-ku. Shibuya station (Yamanote, Ginza, Hanzomon lines), east exit. **Open** 8pm-5am Mon-Thur, Sun; 8pm-11am Fri, Sat. **Map** Shibuya p109.

Once the pick of Tokyo's late-night/early morning bars, this spot has lost some of its popularity due to the snooty staff and the fickle whims of Tokyo's trendies. But thanks to the generous opening times, it's still the best place in Shibuya to hit when everywhere else shuts. The dual-named bar is, appropriately, red and stuffed with chandeliers, adding a touch of surreality and superficial class. From Shibuya station, walk up the Miyamasuzaka hill towards the post office, turn left at the first corner past the lights and then take the first right; it's on the left past the Concombre restaurant.

Insomnia Lounge

Ikuma Bldg B1F, 26-5 Udagawacho, Shibuya-ku (3476 2735/www.gnavi.co.jp/miwa). Shibuya station (Yamanote, Ginza, Hanzomon lines), Hachiko exit. **Open** 6pm-5am daily. **Credit** AmEx, DC, JCB, MC, V. **Map** Shibuya p109.

High Tide. *See p177.*

Golden Gai

While the skyline all around rises ever higher, this tiny section of east Shinjuku between Kuyakusho Dori and Hanazono shrine remains resolutely stuck in the 1950s. The four ramshackle streets of Golden Gai host some 200 tiny drinking dens, most of which can accommodate only around ten customers. The area was long renowned for the frosty reception that awaited strangers and tourists, but many of the leases changed hands at the start of the decade, and there are now a number of places, including those listed below, that welcome all comers. Most Golden Gai bars charge a seating fee of around ¥1,000, but this can rise to a staggering ¥4,000 at those wishing to discourage strangers.

Albatross G

2F 5th Avenue, 1-1 Kabukicho, Shinjuku-ku (3202 3699/www.alba-s.com). Shinjuku station (Yamanote, Chuo lines), east exit; (Marunouchi line), exits B6, B7; (Oedo, Shinjuku lines), exit 1. **Open** 8pm-5am Mon-Sat. **No credit cards. Map** Shinjuku p117.
Sister bar of the ever-popular Albatross (*see p180*), this version is spacious by Golden Gai standards, with a long counter and a cute upper-tier lounge that we suspect was originally designed as a storage space. The ¥300 seating charge is about the cheapest in Golden Gai.

La Jetée

1-1-8 Kabuki-cho, Shinjuku-ku (3208 9645). Shinjuku station (Yamanote, Chuo lines), east exit; (Marunouchi line), exits B6, B7; (Oedo, Shinjuku lines), exit 1. **Open** 7pm-empty Mon-Sat. **No credit cards. Map** Shinjuku p117.
A tiny Golden Gai institution, owned by a film fanatic (the place gets its name from the Chris Marker classic) who speaks fluent French but little English. Popular with French expatriates and creative types, it's also a favourite haunt of many visiting filmmakers, from Wim Wenders to Quentin Tarantino.

Shot Bar Shadow

1-1-8 Kabuki-cho, Shinjuku-ku (3209 9530). Shinjuku station (Yamanote, Chuo lines), east exit; (Marunouchi line), exits B6, B7; (Oedo, Shinjuku lines), exit 1. **Open** 5pm-midnight Mon-Fri; 6pm-midnight Sat (members only after midnight). **No credit cards. Map** Shinjuku p117.
The master of this tiny bar speaks Arabic, German, Russian and French, thanks to his time in the Foreign Legion. For you to become a member, and get in after midnight, he must be able to remember your name. A friendly place where six is a crowd, typical in Golden Gai.

This womb-like basement bar is covered from floor to ceiling in soft red fabric. For the ultimate queasy experience, try sitting at the bar and gazing into the mirrored lights above it. There's an extensive food and cocktail menu, and a cover charge of ¥525. Remove your shoes when you enter.

Pink Cow

Villa Moderna B1F, 1-3-18 Shibuya, Shibuya-ku (3406 5597/www.thepinkcow.com). Shibuya station (Yamanote, Ginza, Hanzomon lines), Hachiko exit. **Open** 5pm-late Tue-Thur, Sun; 5pm-3am Fri, Sat. **Credit** (over ¥5,000) AmEx, DC, JCB, MC, V. **Map** Shibuya p109.

With an interior that's either garish or funky, depending on your taste, the Pink Cow is not the low-key venue its backstreet location would suggest. It's popular with artistic expats, and the regular events are as quirky and diverse as a knitting salon and a short-film festival. The grub is good; the Friday and Saturday buffet is a reasonable ¥2,500.

Tantra

Ichimainoe Bldg B1F, 3-5-5 Shibuya, Shibuya-ku (5485 8414). Shibuya station (Yamanote, Ginza, Hanzomon lines), east, new south exits. **Open** 8pm-5am daily. **Credit** AmEx, DC, JCB, MC, V. **Map** Shibuya p109.

Super-stylish creative hub **Super-deluxe**. See p178.

Blink and you'll miss the entrance to Tantra– the only sign is a small, dimly lit 'T' above a nondescript stairwell on the corner of a nondescript office building on the south side of Roppongi Dori, near Shibuya. But heave open the imposing metal door and you'll find yourself in what resembles a secret, subterranean drinking club, decorated with stone pillars, veiled alcoves, flickering candles and statues depicting scenes from the *Kama Sutra*. On your first visit you'll feel like you've gatecrashed a very private party, but have courage and don't be put off by the ice-cool staff. The ¥1,000 cover charge is a warning not to enter without a substantial wad waiting in your wallet.

Shinjuku

African Bar Esogie

3F Muraki Bldg, 3-11-2 Shinjuku, Shinjuku-ku (3353 3334/www4.point.ne.jp/~esogie). Shinjuku San-chome station (Marunouchi, Shinjuku lines), exit C3. **Open** 6pm-midnight Mon, Tue, Thur; 6pm-4am Fri, Sat; 6-11pm Sun. **No credit cards.** **Map** Shinjuku p117.

Shinjuku's San-chome district is crammed with tiny bars, most of them musically themed, and Esogie is arguably the pick of the bunch. Nigerian owner Lucky might just be the friendliest bartender in town, and the Afrobeat and highlife tunes make it easy to forget you're in a narrow black bar with minimal furnishings. Lucky gives djembe performances most nights, and invites customers to try their hand. The imported African beers aren't cheap, but unusually for this area there's no seating charge, and the range of authentic African dishes is reasonable.

Albatross

1-2-11 Nishi-Shinjuku, Shinjuku-ku (3342 5758). Shinjuku station (Yamanote, Shinjuku lines), west exit; (Marunouchi, Oedo lines), exit B16. **Open** 5pm-2am daily. **No credit cards.** **Map** Shinjuku p117.

Hidden among the tiny, time-worn *yakitori* stalls of Omoide Yokocho, by Shinjuku station, Albatross is a tiny three-storey salon that seats, in total, around 30 people. The floor above is officially a gallery, more accurately a Japanese-style room with a few pictures on the walls. Upper-floor customers place their orders and receive their drinks through a hole in the floor; an operation that becomes increasingly perilous as the night progresses and senses diminish. Up top, in lenient weather, a rickety roof accommodates half a dozen more drinkers. The crowd is a genuinely eclectic mix of suits, artists, expats and students.

Clubhouse Tokyo

Marunaka Bldg 3F, 3-7-3 Shinjuku, Shinjuku-ku (3359 7785/www.clubhouse-tokyo.com). Shinjuku-Sanchome station (Marunouchi, Shinjuku lines), exits C3, C4. **Open** 5pm-midnight Mon-Fri; 3pm-late Sat, Sun. **No credit cards.** **Map** Shinjuku p117.

Clubhouse is the only specialist sports bar in Shinjuku and can get phenomenally crowded on big game nights. Premiership football is screened, but the true passion here is rugby. Monday night is darts night. There are British and Irish beers on tap.

The Dubliners

Shinjuku Lion Hall 2F, 3-28-9 Shinjuku, Shinjuku-ku (3352 6606/www.gnavi.co.jp/lion/05.html). Shinjuku station (Yamanote line), east exit; (Marunouchi, Oedo, Shinjuku lines), exit A8. **Open** noon-1am Mon-Sat; noon-11pm Sun. **Credit** AmEx, MC, V. **Map** Shinjuku p117.

The oldest and scruffiest of the growing chain of Irish pubs owned by Sapporo, one of Japan's largest brewers and also its Guinness importer. Draught Guinness and cider (little known in Japan) accompany standard domestic beers, while the menu offers semi-authentic fish and chips. The Shibuya branch is the cosiest, the Ikebukuro branch the most raucous, and the Sanno Park Tower branch the quietest.

Eat, Drink, Shop

Other locations: 2-29-8 Dogenzaka, Shibuya-ku (5459 1736); Sun Grow Bldg B1F, 1-10-8 Nishi-Ikebukuro, Toshima-ku (5951 3614); Sanno Park Tower B1F, 2-11-1, Nagatacho, Chiyoda-ku (3539 3615); 1-1-18 Toranomon, Minato-ku (5501 1536); Imonnishi Azabu Bldg 1F, 1-14-1 Nishi-Azabu, Minato-ku (3479 0345).

The Ghetto
1-1-10 Hyakunincho, Shinjuku-ku (5287 6213/ www.theghettotokyo.com). Shin Okubo station (Yamanote line). **Open** 6pm-midnight daily. **No credit cards.**
It's an apt name for a bar located in Tokyo's grottiest love-hotel district, but the Ghetto gets its name from its graffiti covered façade and B-boy theme. As you enter the building there's a skate ramp to your right, and one of Tokyo's quirkiest new bars to your left. Although the shambolic interior suggests it was created an hour or two before your arrival, the mishmash of fluffy sofas, plastic chairs, tatami mats and tall stools makes it a fun and funky bar that's refreshingly free from pretension.

Elsewhere in central Tokyo

Artist's Café
Tokyo Dome Hotel 43F, 1-3-61 Koraku, Bunkyo-ku (5805 2243/www.tokyodome-hotels.co.jp). Kasuga station (Mita, Oedo line), exit A1 or Korakuen station (Marunouchi, Nanboku line), exit 2 or Suidobashi station (Chuo line), west exit; (Mita line), exits A3, A4. **Open** 11.30am-2.30pm, 6-11pm daily. **Credit** AmEx, DC, JCB, MC, V.
A pleasant jazz-themed bar and restaurant on the 43rd floor of a swanky hotel. The nice feature is that the two main windows to the left and right of the lift offer totally different views. To the right, you tower over houses and small local businesses, while to the left the monoliths of Shinjuku heave into view.

Shunju
Sanno Park Tower 27F, 2-11-1 Nagatacho, Chiyoda-ku (3592 5288/www.shunju.com/top.html). Tameike-Sanno station (Ginza, Nanboku lines), exit 7. **Open** 11.30am-2pm, 5-11pm Mon-Fri; 5-11pm Sat. **Credit** AmEx, DC, JCB, MC, V.
From this upmarket whisky and cigar bar high in the Sanno Park Tower you get a good view of the jumbled cityscape towards Shibuya. The illuminated glass wine cellar and shelves of whisky (from ¥1,200 a glass) stand out amid the bar's dark elegance, and you feel a world away from the buzzing chaos 27 floors below. Staff also serve a mean Martini and good seasonal cocktails.

Further afield

Combine
103 Riverside Terrace, 1-10-23 Naka-Meguro, Meguro-ku (3760 3939). Naka Meguro station (Toyoko line). **Open** noon-4am Mon-Sat; noon-2am Sun. **Credit** AmEx, DC, JCB, MC, V.

Naka-Meguro has no shortage of fashionable hangouts, but this one is a great spot day or night. Art is the chosen theme, with a wall of hundreds of art books in English and Japanese. There are also turntables that get an occasional airing. But the best things about Combine are its airy interior, riverside location and lack of affectation.

Heaven's Door
Takimoto Bldg 2F, 2-17-10 Kitazawa, Setagaya-ku (3411 6774/http://heavensdoortokyo.fc2web.com). Shimo-Kitazawa station (Keio Inokashira, Odakyu lines), south exit. **Open** 6pm-2am Mon-Sat; 4pm-2am Sun. **No credit cards.**
An extremely comfortable bar near Shimo-Kitazawa station run by charismatic Brit expat Paul Davies. Comfy sofas, a Joe Orton-style approach to interior design, a crowd of friendly regulars and a complete absence of food mark this place out. Heaven's Door also hosts a monthly alternative politics salon with English-language films.

Meguro Tavern
Sunwood Meguro 2F, 1-3-28 Shimo-Meguro, Meguro-ku (3779 0280/www.themegurotavern.com). Meguro station (Yamanote line) west exit; (Mita, Nanboku lines), Chuo exit. **Open** 6pm-1am Mon-Fri; 5pm-1am Sat; noon-11pm Sun. **No credit cards.** **Map** Meguro p71.
An above-average English pub with a menu designed to reassure expats. The Sunday lunch roast beef and Yorkshire pud is a local institution. One of the best places too for traditional Christmas dinner.

Las Meninas
Plaza Koenji 2F, 3-22-7 Koenji-Kita, Suginami-ku (3338 0266). Koenji station (Chuo line), north exit. **Open** 6pm-late Tue-Sun. **Credit** AmEx, DC, JCB, MC, V.
Johnny the giant Geordie is the unlikely manager of this elegant, spotless tapas bar. Among the myriad late-night drinking spots of Koenji, Las Meninas stands out for both the banter of the big man and his cooking. A one-time chef, Johnny serves such reliably high-class, home-cooked fare that most customers ignore the menu and simply ask for 'food'. In an area known for cheap, friendly bars, this place is notable on both counts. The drink menu emphasises Spanish wines, sherries and beer.

Mother
5-36-14 Daizawa, Setagaya-ku (3421 9519). Shimo-Kitazawa station (Keio Inokashira, Odakyu lines), south exit. **Open** 6pm-2am Mon-Sat; 5pm-2am Sun. **No credit cards.**
The extreme kitsch of this Shimo-Kitazawa bar, which resembles a mix of gingerbread house, treehouse and pub, betrays what is in fact a classy establishment. There's a wide selection of bottled beers, as well as a high-quality menu of freshly made Okinawan and Thai dishes. The playlist consists mostly of legends such as Sly and the Family Stone, the Rolling Stones, Bob Dylan and the like, but you can bring your own CDs and staff will play them.

Coffee Shops

Or 'How to dodge Seattle's giants'.

For a nation of renowned tea-drinkers, the Japanese love their caffeine. The city's very first coffee shop opened in Ueno back in 1888, when beans arrived from Brazil as free gifts (to get the nation hooked on the brew). And as today's landscape shows, it worked like a charm. The jazz and counter-culture booms of the '60s and '70s, when the country's youth looked West for inspiration, helped cement the *kissaten* (coffee shop)'s role as the place to hang out.

The city's youth still look West for their coffee – but these days it's to Seattle, whose most famous chain is proliferating like frogspawn across the city. The local equivalent, **Doutor** (*see below*), is holding its own thanks to its superior coffee and smoker-friendly outlets. But it's a different story for the independents. The quaint, character-laden places that don't know their lattes from their mochaccinos are quietly departing the most modern districts, although the sheer number of *kissaten* (estimated at over 10,000) means that it's still easy to find a place that doesn't serve coffee with a plastic lid.

The 1990s saw the emergence of 24-hour manga *kissaten*, combining coffee with comic books, online access and a comfy chair to crash in when that last train has departed and you can't afford a hotel room. More recently the trend has been towards slick establishments with DJs and designer furniture, such as **Idée Caffè** (*see p184*) or **Café 246** (*see p183*).

Wherever you sip, it isn't going to be cheap. A cup of coffee in a non-franchise *kissaten* may average ¥500-¥600, but you're free to sit for hours on some of the world's most expensive real estate as the world rushes by outside.

Asakusa

Angelus
1-17-6 Asakusa, Taito-ku (3841 2208). Asakusa station (Asakusa, Ginza lines), exits 1, 3. **Open** 10am-9.30pm Tue-Sun. **No credit cards.** **Map** Asakusa p63.
Perhaps, at some point in the distant past, this was the way local upmarket operations got to grips with handling new-fangled foreign delicacies. Out front is a smart counter selling a fancy selection of Western-style cakes; further inside, the coffee shop section is a more spartan affair of plain walls and dark wood trimmings.

ef
2-19-18 Kaminarimon, Taito-ku (3841 0114/gallery 3841 0442/www.gallery-ef.com). Asakusa station (Asakusa line), exit A5; (Ginza line), exit 2. **Open** 11am-7pm (café & gallery), 6pm-midnight (bar) Mon, Wed, Thur, Sat; 11am-2am Fri; 11am-10pm Sun. **No credit cards. Map** Asakusa p63.
This retro-fitted hangout is a welcome attempt to inject a little Harajuku-style cool into musty Asakusa, but among its own more surprising attractions is a small art gallery (*see p237*) converted from a 130-year-old warehouse. Duck through the low entrance at the back, and suddenly you're out of 1950s Americana and into tatami territory, with admittance to the main exhibits up a steep set of traditional wooden steps. A place to try when you're tired of the local temples.

Ginza

Benisica
1-6-8 Yurakucho, Chiyoda-ku (3502 0848). Hibiya station (Chiyoda, Hibiya, Mita lines), exit A4. **Open** 9.30am-11.45pm daily. **No credit cards.** **Map** Ginza p75.
The traditional neighbourhood café is realised in ideal form just across the railway tracks from Ginza, with an extensive selection of meal-and-cake sets to boot. Benisica claims to be the original inventor of 'pizza toast' – a near cousin of Welsh rarebit – now featured on coffee-shop menus all over Japan.

Le Café Doutor Ginza
San'ai Bldg 1F, 5-7-2 Ginza, Chuo-ku (5537 8959). Ginza station (Ginza, Hibiya, Marunouchi lines), exits A1, A3. **Open** 7.30am-11pm Mon-Fri; 8am-11pm Sat; 8am-10pm Sun. **No credit cards.** **Map** Ginza p75.
The most impressive branch of the cheap 'n' cheerful chain that proliferated across Tokyo during the recession-hit 1990s is still conspicuously affordable despite its location on one of the city's most famous intersections – the Ginza Yon-chome crossing. Streetside tables or the highly prized upstairs window seats provide perfect views of the bustling Ginza crowds outside. The coffee is Doutor's standard fare, but the sandwiches are a slight step upmarket.
Other locations: throughout the city.

Café Fontana
Abe Bldg B1, 5-5-9 Ginza, Chuo-ku (3572 7320). Ginza station (Ginza, Hibiya, Marunouchi lines), exits B3, B5. **Open** noon-11pm Mon-Fri; 2-11pm Sat; 2-7pm Sun. **No credit cards. Map** Ginza p75.

A typically genteel Ginza basement establishment, but one where the individually served apple pies come in distinctly non-dainty proportions. Each steaming specimen contains a whole fruit, thinly covered in pastry, then doused thoroughly in cream.

Café Paulista
Nagasaki Centre, 8-9-16 Ginza, Chuo-ku (3572 6160/www.paulista.co.jp). Ginza station (Ginza, Hibiya, Marunouchi lines), exits A3, A4, A5. **Open** 8.30am-10pm Mon-Sat; noon-8pm Sun. **No credit cards**. **Map** Ginza p75.

This Brazilian-themed Ginza establishment was founded back in 1914. The all-natural beans are imported directly from Brazil, keeping blend coffee prices down to ¥498, a bargain for the area. Low leather seats, plants and wall engravings catch the eye amid a general brown-and-green motif.

Ki No Hana
4-13-1 Ginza, Chuo-ku (3543 5280). Higashi-Ginza station (Asakusa, Hibiya lines), exit 5. **Open** 10am-8pm Mon-Fri. **No credit cards**. **Map** Ginza p75.

The pair of signed John Lennon cartoons on the walls is the legacy of a chance visit by the former Beatle one afternoon in 1978. With its peaceful atmosphere, tasteful floral decorations, herbal teas and lunchtime vegetarian curries, it isn't too difficult to understand Lennon's appreciation of the place. Apparently, the overawed son of the former owner also preserved the great man's full ashtray, including butts. Alas, he kept this as a personal memento, so it isn't on display.

Harajuku & Aoyama

Café 246
1-2-6 Minami-Aoyama, Minato-ku (5771 6886/ www.246cafe-book.com). Aoyama Itchome station (Ginza, Hanzomon, Oedo lines), exit 3. **Open** 11am-2am Mon-Sat; 11.30am-11.30pm Sun. **Credit** AmEx, DC, JCB, MC, V.

Where the beautiful people come for caffeine. Designer retro furnishings, a club jazz soundtrack and a spacious layout mark Café 246 as both a hip hangout and a great place to relax. The broad terrace looks straight on to a grey street, but you didn't come to Tokyo for the view, did you?

Daibo
2F, 3-13-20 Minami-Aoyama, Minato-ku (3403 7155). Omotesando station (Chiyoda, Ginza, Hanzomon lines), exits A3, A4. **Open** 9am-10pm Mon-Sat; noon-8pm Sun. **No credit cards**. **Map** Harajuku & Aoyama p82.

The biggest treat at this cosy, wood-bedecked outpost is the excellent milk coffee, which comes lovingly hand-dripped into large pottery bowls. Even the regular blend coffee reveals a true craftsman's pride and is available in four separate varieties. There's just one long wooden counter plus a couple of tables, but the restrained decoration and the low-volume jazz soundtrack combine to create a soothing and restful vibe.

Volontaire
2F, 6-29-6 Jingumae, Shibuya-ku (3400 8629). Meiji-Jingumae station (Chiyoda line), exit 4. **Open** noon-7pm (bar 7pm-midnight) Mon-Sat. **No credit cards**. **Map** Harajuku & Aoyama p82.

A hole-in-the-wall, old-style coffee and jazz joint that's handily placed near the Omotesando crossing. There's only a single counter for seating, but the area behind the bar bulges with old vinyl. Volontaire switches to bar mode in the evening, with a hefty cover charge.

Marunouchi

Marunouchi Café
Shin Tokyo Bldg 1F, 3-3-1 Marunouchi, Chiyoda-ku (3212 5025/www.marunouchicafe.com). Yurakucho station (Yamanote line), Tokyo International Forum exit; (Yurakucho line), exit A1 or Nijubashimae station (Chiyoda line), exit B7. **Open** 8am-9pm Mon-Fri; 11am-8pm Sat, Sun. **No credit cards**. **Map** Marunouchi p93.

If the Japanese coffee shop is essentially a place to hang out, this popular innovator could be a glimpse

Ben's Café. *See p184.*

of a new, low-cost future. Connoisseurs may not care for canned coffee dispensed from vending machines, but it's difficult to argue with the price (¥120). While the surroundings are less spacious than the former premises across the street, internet access and magazines are still available.

Mironga

1-3 Kanda-Jinbocho, Chiyoda-ku (3295 1716). Jinbocho station (Hanzomon, Mita, Shinjuku lines), exit A7. **Open** *10.30am-10.30pm Mon-Fri; 11.30am-6.30pm Sat, Sun.* **No credit cards.** **Map** Marunouchi p93.

Probably the only place in Tokyo where non-stop (recorded) tango provides seductive old-style accompaniment to the liquid refreshments. Argentina's finest exponents of the dance feature in the impressive array of fading monochromes on the walls, and there's also a selection of printed works on related subjects lining the bookshelves. Of the two rooms, the larger and darker gets the nod for atmosphere. As well as a wide range of coffees, Mironga proffers a good selection of imported beers and reasonable food.

Roppongi

Roppongi's new **Midtown** complex (*see p102*) boasts a Dean & Deluca café, set to open as we go to print.

Almond Roppongi

6-1-26 Roppongi, Minato-ku (3402 1870/ www.roppongi-almond.jp). Roppongi station (Hibiya, Oedo lines), exit 3. **Open** *9am-5am Mon-Sat; 10am-3pm Sun.* **No credit cards.** **Map** Roppongi p103.

A pink-hued landmark at the main Roppongi intersection, Almond has provided an instantly recognisable meeting spot for generations of revellers, and it is possibly the single best-known coffee shop in Tokyo. Relatively few venture inside, however, where the coffee and cakes are pretty standard fare – it's part of an unremarkable coffee-shop chain. **Other locations**: throughout the city.

Idée Caffè

Roppongi Hills Hillside B1F, 6-10-2 Roppongi, Minato-ku (5770 5280/www.idee.co.jp/food/66caffe). Roppongi station (Hibiya line) exit 1C; (Oedo line) exit 3. **Open** *11am-midnight Mon-Fri; 10am-midnight Sat, Sun.* **Credit** AmEx, DC, JCB, M, V. **Map** Roppongi p103.

This popular café with a wide terrace is run by local interior brand Idée and draws a young crowd with its pristine look, wallet-friendly prices and in-store DJ playing jazzy house. It's a great place to relax after a trek around Roppongi Hills, but expect to wait for a seat at weekends.

Shibuya

Coffee 3.4 Sunsea

Takano Bldg 1F, 10-2 Udagawacho, Shibuya-ku (3496 2295/www.coffee-sunsea.com). Shibuya station (Yamanote, Ginza, Hanzomon lines), Hachiko

exit. **Open** *noon-11pm Tue-Sat; noon-midnight Sun.* **No credit cards.** **Map** Shibuya p109.

Kathmandu hippie chic and postmodern Shibuya cool meet in this laid-back retreat, with classical Indian sitar and tabla on the soundtrack. Cushion-strewn sofas, ethnic wood carvings and a large tank of hypnotic tropical fish all add to the dreamy effect. Self-indulgent sensory overload is guaranteed from the sensational coffee float. It's somehow in keeping with the mood of the place that the owners don't have fixed days off; they close whenever they feel like it, so be sure to call ahead before you visit.

Lion

2-19-13 Dogenzaka, Shibuya-ku (3461 6858/http:// lion.main.jp). Shibuya station (Yamanote, Ginza, Hanzomon lines), Hachiko exit. **Open** *11am-10.30pm daily.* **No credit cards.** **Map** Shibuya p109.

There's a church-like air of reverence at this sleepy shrine to classical music. A pamphlet listing stereophonic offerings is laid out before the customer, seating is in pew-style rows facing an enormous pair of speakers, and conversations are discouraged. If you must talk, then do so in whispers. The imposing grey building is an unexpected period piece amid the gaudy love hotels of Dogenzaka.

Satei Hato

1-15-19 Shibuya, Shibuya-ku (3400 9088). Shibuya station (Yamanote line), east exit; (Ginza line), Toyoko exit; (Hanzomon line), exit 9. **Open** *11am-11.30pm daily.* **No credit cards.** **Map** Shibuya p109.

Step through the marble-tiled entrance and into top-grade *kissaten* territory of a traditionalist bent. A huge collection of china cups stands behind the counter, while sweeping arrangements of seasonal blooms add colour to a dark wood interior that recalls an earlier age. The most expensive coffee on the menu is Blue Mountain at ¥1,000.

Shinjuku

Ben's Café

1-29-21 Takadanobaba, Shinjuku-ku (3202 2445/ www.benscafe.com/en). Takadanobaba station (Yamanote line), Waseda exit; (Tozai line), exit 3. **Open** *11.30am-11.30pm Mon-Thur, Sun; 11.30am-12.30am Fri, Sat.* **No credit cards.**

Great food, great coffee, friendly staff and Wi-Fi make this New York-style café a local favourite. Ben's also hosts occasional art shows, weekend poetry readings and live music. The friendly staff speak English and the coffee is great. **Photo** *p183.*

Bon

Toriichi Bldg B1, 3-23-1 Shinjuku, Shinjuku-ku (3341 0179). Shinjuku station (Yamanote, Chuo, Sobu lines), east exit; (Marunouchi line), exit A5; (Oedo, Shinjuku lines), exit 1. **Open** *12.30-11.30pm daily.* **No credit cards.** **Map** Shinjuku p117.

The search for true coffee excellence is pursued with surprising vigour at this pricey but popular Shinjuku basement. The cheapest choice from the

Drink your greens

Tea-drinking in Japan is both a daily routine and a highly ritualized art. Exquisite tearooms at the **Imperial Hotel** (3504 1111, www.imperialhotel.co.jp/index_e.html) and the **Hotel New Otani** (3265 1111, www.new otani.co.jp/en/group/index.html), or the Meiji-era teahouse at picturesque event venue **Happo-en** (3443 3775, www.happo-en.com/english/index.html) stage full, elaborate tea ceremonies (reservations essential). At the other end of the spectrum, the **Koots** chain (www.koots.co.jp) applies the Starbucks model to the classic drink, with quirky modern takes such as green-tea mocha or frozen tea shakes. For something in between, give one of the options below a try.

Cha Ginza (Uogashi-Meicha)
2F & 3F, 5-5-6 Ginza, Chuo-ku (3571 1211/ www.uogashi-meicha.co.jp/shop_01.html). Ginza station (Ginza, Hibiya, Marunouchi lines), exit B5. **Open** 11am-7pm Tue-Sun. **No credit cards.** **Map** Ginza p75.
Buy a ¥500 ticket at the street-level tea shop and head to the wine-bar-esque second floor for *sencha* (green leaf tea) served with a sip of sake. Alternatively, have *matcha* (powered green tea) on the glass-ceilinged third floor where staff whisk a thick, frothy tea in a simplified ceremony that begins with a sip of water to cleanse the palate. All tea is served with a seasonal Japanese sweet.

Nakajima no Ochaya (Hamarikyu Onshi Teien)
1-1 Hamarikyu Teien, Chuo-ku (3541 0200/ www.tokyo-park.or.jp/english/park/detail_ 04.html#hamarikyu). Shinbashi station (Yamanote line) Karasumori exit, (Ginza line) exit 2, (Asakusa line) exit 5 or Shiodome station (Oedo line) exit 5. **Open** 9am-4pm daily. Closed 29 Dec-1 Jan. **No credit cards.**
Located on a tidal pond in Hama-Rikyu Garden, (*see p79*), this teahouse with traditional tatami mats boasts the best view of our tea-shop picks. Remove your shoes, take a seat on the red felt and gaze out at the one-time falcony ground while you wait for your tray of *matcha* and a traditional sweet. Outdoor seating is available. Park admission: ¥300.

Sadeu
2F Shinjuku Takashimaya, 5-24-2 Sendagaya, Shibuya-ku (5361 1467/www.sadeu.jp). Shinjuku station (JR lines) South or New South exit, (Marunouchi line) exit A8, (Oedo, Shinjuku lines) exit A1. **Open** 10am-8pm Mon-Fri, Sun; 10am-8.30pm Sat. **Credit** AmEx, DC, JCB, MC, V. **Map** Shinjuku p117.
A hip young clientele, drawn by this café's minimalist design, mingles with an older crowd of traditional tea-drinkers fresh from shopping in the Takashimaya department store. Accordingly, Sadeu's menu includes innovative concoctions such as *matcha* banana shakes, as well as a variety of quality traditional teas. Sit at the counter if you want to watch the staff perform the café's quirky interpretation of the tea ceremony. Light Japanese meals are also available.

Saryo Tsujiri
B2F Caretta Shiodome, 1-8-2 Higashi-Shinbashi, Minato-ku (5537 2217/www.giontsujiri.co.jp/saryo/index.html). Shinbashi station (Yamanote line) Karasumori exit, (Ginza line) exit 4, (Asakusa line) Shiodome exit or Shiodome station (Oedo line) exit 6, (Yurikamome line). **Open** 11am-11pm Mon-Sat; 11am-10pm Sun and holidays. **Credit** AmEx, DC, JCB, MC, V.
And you thought green-tea ice cream was creative. Expect long lines for this café's wide range of green-tea desserts. Sorbet, mousse, jelly and cakes all come in vivid green tones, as do noodles and, if you still fancy it, tea.

menu will set you back a cool ¥1,000, but at least the cups will be bone china – selected from an enormous collection. Special tasting events are held periodically for connoisseurs.

GeraGera

B1 & B2, 3-17-4 Shinjuku, Shinjuku-ku (3350 5692/www.geragera.co.jp). Shinjuku station (Yamanote, Chuo, Sobu lines), east exit; (Marunouchi line), exit A5; (Oedo, Shinjuku lines), exit 1. **Open** 24hrs daily. **No credit cards.** **Map** Shinjuku p117.

Manga coffee shops spread rapidly after emerging in the mid 1990s with a winning formula of coffee and Japanese comic books. More recently, computer games and internet access have been added as regular features. This branch of one of the main chains has 250 seats, with facilities available at ¥200 per 30 minutes or ¥880 for three hours (or five hours between 10pm and 6am). The self-service hot and cold drinks cost ¥180.

Other locations: throughout the city.

New Dug

B1, 3-15-12 Shinjuku, Shinjuku-ku (3341 9339/ www.dug.co.jp). Shinjuku station (Yamanote, Chuo, Sobu lines), east exit; (Marunouchi line), exit B10; (Oedo, Shinjuku lines), exit 1. **Open** noon-2am Mon-Sat; noon-midnight Sun (bar from 6.30pm). **Credit** AmEx, DC, JCB, MC, V. **Map** Shinjuku p117.

Way back in the 1960s and early '70s, Shinjuku was sprinkled with jazz coffee shops. Celebrated names of that bygone era included Dug, an establishment whose present-day incarnation is a cramped brick-lined basement on Yasukuni Dori. Everything about the place speaks serious jazz credentials, with carefully crafted authenticity and assorted memorabilia. A basement bar annexe below the nearby KFC is used for live performances.

Tajimaya

1-2-6 Nishi-Shinjuku, Shinjuku-ku (3342 0881/ www.shinjuku.or.jp/tajimaya). Shinjuku station (Yamanote, Chuo, Sobu lines), west exit; (Marunouchi line), exit A17; (Oedo, Shinjuku lines), exit 3. **Open** 10am-11pm daily. **No credit cards.** **Map** Shinjuku p117.

Caught between the early post-war grunge of its immediate neighbours and the skyscraper bustle of the rest of west Shinjuku, Tajimaya responds with abundant bone china, coffees from all over the world, non-fetishist use of classical music, and milk in the best copperware. Scones on the menu provide further evidence of advanced sensibilities, but the deeply yellowed walls and battered wood could be smartened up for the sake of appearances.

Ueno

Miro

2-4-6 Kanda-Surugadai, Chiyoda-ku (3291 3088). Ochanomizu station (Chuo, Sobu lines), Ochanomizu exit; (Marunouchi line), exit 2. **Open** 9am-11pm Mon-Sat. **No credit cards.**

Named after Catalan surrealist artist Joan Miró, several of whose works adorn the walls. Both ambience and decor appear untouched by the passing decades. The location is pretty well hidden, down a tiny alley opposite Ochanomizu station.

Further afield

Café Bach

1-23-9 Nihonzutsumi, Taito-ku (3875 2669/ www.bach-kaffee.co.jp). Minami-Senju station (Hibiya line), south exit. **Open** 8.30am-9pm Mon-Thur, Sat, Sun. **No credit cards.**

All the beans are roasted on the premises of this dedicated coffee specialist in suburban Minami-Senju in northern Tokyo. Café Bach supplied the coffee for the G8 summit that took place in Okinawa in 2000, a meeting that is commemorated on the Japanese ¥2,000 note.

Jazz Coffee Masako

2-20-2 Kitazawa, Setagaya-ku (3410 7994). Shimo-Kitazawa station (Keio Inokashira, Odakyu lines), south exit. **Open** 11.30am-11pm daily. **No credit cards.**

This Shimo-Kitazawa spot has a really homely feel, in addition to all the jazz coffee-shop essentials such as an excellent sound system, an enormous stack of records and CDs behind the counter, and black walls (and a low ceiling) plastered with posters and pictures. The noticeboard at the flower-filled entrance proudly announces newly obtained recordings; inside, there are bookcases and sofas among the well-lived-in furnishings.

Mignon

2F, 4-31-3 Ogikubo, Suginami-ku (3398 1758/ http://members.jcom.home.ne.jp/stmera/mignon). Ogikubo station (Chuo line), south exit; (Marunouchi line), exit 2. **Open** 11am-10pm Mon-Tue, Thur-Sat; 11am-7pm Sun. **No credit cards.**

Classical music is the name of the game here, with a truly awesome collection of vinyl lining the shelves behind the counter. There's just one room, plus a small side gallery containing pottery items, but the space is comfortable and doesn't feel cramped. There's a good selection of coffee, plus teas and iced drinks.

Pow Wow

2-7 Kagurazaka, Shinjuku-ku (3267 8324). Iidabashi station (Chuo, Sobu lines), west exit; (Namboku, Oedo, Tozai, Yurakucho lines), exit B3. **Open** 10.30am-10.30pm Mon-Sat; 12.30-7pm Sun. **No credit cards.**

Heavy on the old-fashioned virtues of dark wood and tastefully chosen pottery, this spacious traditionalist coffee shop near the British Council showcases an extraordinary brewing performance in its narrow counter section. Large glass flasks bubble merrily away over tiny glass candles in the manner of some mysterious chemistry experiment. There's also an upstairs gallery space that's well worth checking out.

Shops & Services

If it exists, you can buy it here.

Japan's reputation for consumer culture is well deserved, and the crowded shops and streets of Ginza, Shibuya, Shinjuku, Omotesando, Ikebukuro, and other retail centres are a great place to gain an insight into this island nation. You'll find an extraordinary range of shops and products, from ritzy department stores and high-end international designer flagships to quirky boutiques and tiny outlets offering traditional crafts.

Long a city with luxury tastes, Tokyo has experienced an incredible change in shopping habits since the end of the Bubble era. Hundred-yen shops (where toiletries, household goods, toys and the like cost ¥100) have proliferated, as has 'pile 'em high, sell 'em cheap' chain **Don Quixote** (*see p208*). Budget clothing brand **Uniqlo** (*see p198*) is as popular as ever, and second-hand shops (just look for the word 'recycle') such as **RagTag** (*see p197*) have become more visible in a nation that had never previously taken to the idea of used goods. Yet none of this has affected the popularity of the top brands, whose fortunes have soared in parallel with the bargain-shopping boom. Since the economy began rebounding, the biggest names in fashion have been gobbling up retail space across the city.

OPENING HOURS, SALES AND TAX

With more money floating around, opening times are inching longer and longer. The standard is still 10am or 11am until 8pm, but many places now stay open until 9pm or 10pm, especially in areas such as Shinjuku and Shibuya. Independent shops may close for one day, usually Monday or Wednesday. Sunday trading is the norm in Tokyo, as the day has no religious significance – in fact, it's one of the busiest shopping days. The only day that many shops take off is New Year's Day.

Most shops (except the traditional, craft-oriented ones) are open on national holidays – but if you're heading for a specific place, it's wise to call ahead before you go. Christmas is not a holiday in Japan; 25 December is a normal working day with ordinary office hours. What's more, the Christmas decorations come down at the stroke of midnight on the 24th, to make space for the more traditional New Year celebrations – a practice that can be bemusing for foreign visitors. Sales are held seasonally, with the biggest at New Year and in early July.

Prices include a consumption tax of five per cent, which is levied on all goods and services. For information on tax refunds, *see p196* **Duty-free goods**.

One-stop shopping

Department stores

All Japanese *depato* share certain basic features. Food halls (*depachika*) – hectic places featuring branches of internationally famous pâtisseries, confectioners and delis – are always in the basement. The first few floors sell women's clothing and accessories, with menswear beginning directly above. The top levels include restaurants (*depa-resu*) that stay open at night after the main store has closed, and many of the rooftops are used as beer gardens in the summer. Most *depato* have Japanese craft and souvenir sections, and some offer worldwide delivery services. Almost all stores offer a tax-exemption service for purchases (mainly clothing, kitchenware and electrical goods) that total over ¥10,000 – you'll need your passport. Floor guides in English are available at the information desk.

Daimaru

1-9-1 Marunouchi, Chiyoda-ku (3212 8011/www. daimaru.co.jp/english/tokyo.html). Tokyo station (Yamanote, Chuo lines), Yaesu central exit; (Marunouchi line), exits 1, 2. **Open** 10am-9pm Mon-Fri; 10am-8pm Sat, Sun. **Credit** AmEx, DC, JCB, MC, V. **Map** Marunouchi p93.
The first six floors of this store located inside Tokyo station are devoted to fashion and accessories; Japanese souvenirs are on the seventh and tenth, restaurants on the eighth, and the Daimaru Museum on the 12th. 'Gochiso Paradise', on floor B1 by the Yaesu central exit, contains Japanese confectionery shop Shirotae, and Kihachi, a hugely popular cake outlet. The currency-exchange and tax-exemption counters are on the seventh floor. A shipping service is also available.

Isetan

3-14-1 Shinjuku, Shinjuku-ku (3352 1111/www. isetan.co.jp/iclub). Shinjuku-Sanchome station (Marunouchi, Shinjuku lines), exits B3, B4, B5 or Shinjuku station (Yamanote, Chuo lines), east exit; (Oedo line), exit 1. **Open** 10am-8pm daily. **Credit** AmEx, DC, JCB, MC, V. **Map** Shinjuku p117.
Tokyo's trendiest and friendliest department store is located in Shinjuku, spread out over eight buildings

Treats abound underground

The word *depachika* is a fusion of *depa*, meaning 'department store', and *chika*, the Japanese word for 'basement', and it's these nether regions of Tokyo's vast stores that cater to the nation's foodies. This is the place to come for glistening pieces of sushi, top-grade green tea, delicate Japanese *wagashi* confectionery and those famously overpriced melons.

Shops and stalls are grouped together by product, so wandering the *depachika* is a sensory treat as the yeasty bakery smell gives way to sweet pickle, fresh fish, a fruity tang or a subtle sugary whiff.

There's a dizzying array of seafood – raw, dried or cured – including slabs of the famous *otoro* (fatty tuna). In the meat section, look for the marbled cuts of beef from cows that have enjoyed a lifestyle of massages and, more bizarrely, beer. And if you're souvenir shopping, make sure you check out the exquisite Japanese confectioneries. They look like mini works of art and are usually studded with seasonal motifs.

For more immediate gratification, most stores have eat in-counters. In Shinjuku's **Takashimaya**, try Maisen's *tonkatsu* (deep-fried pork cutlets) or Tsunahachi's tempura. Elsewhere in Shinjuku, **Odakyu**'s food hall (*see p189*) houses Madame China, with its delicious handmade dim sum. For that marbled beef, head to **Takashimaya** in Nihonbashi (*see p190; photo right*), where Imahan offers a mini sukiyaki pot; in the same store, the more courageous diner will find fresh blowfish.

Some of Japan's most beloved brands, such as Toraya, renowned for its adzuki-bean *yokan* cakes, have been hawking their wares downstairs for generations. But they now compete with an increasing number of major international purveyors, including Fauchon, Harrods, Hediards and all the big-name chocolatiers.

The basement of **Tobu** in Ikebukuro (*see p190*) offers the widest selection, with well over 200 stalls, but more renowned destinations include **Isetan** in Shinjuku (*see p187*), **Mitsukoshi** in Ginza (*see p189*) and **Tokyu** at Shibuya station (*see p190*).

And when you've finished with the food, head upstairs, where most stores offer quality lacquerware, ceramics and tools.

very close to one another. The most noteworthy are the main building and men's building. The overseas shipping service is in the basement of the main building, and the tax-exemption counter is on the eighth floor of the annex. BPQC – an eclectic selection of Japanese and foreign concession shops selling cosmetics, perfumes, CDs and household goods – is on the B2 floor of the main building. Isetan also runs the I-Club, a free service for foreign residents in Japan. The club's monthly newsletter contains news of sales, discounts and special promotions, plus details of the Clover clothing range, available in larger sizes than the standard Japanese ones. Ask for membership details at the foreign customer desk on the eighth floor of the men's building.
Other locations: 1-11-5 Kichijoji Honcho, Musashino-shi (0422 211 111).

Keio

1-1-4 Nishi-Shinjuku, Shinjuku-ku (3342 2111/ www.keionet.com). Shinjuku station (Yamanote line), west exit; (Marunouchi line), exits A12-A14; (Oedo, Shinjuku lines), exit 3. **Open** 10am-8pm daily.
Credit AmEx, DC, JCB, MC, V. **Map** Shinjuku p117.
Keio has womenswear and accessories on the first four floors; menswear on the fifth; kimonos, jewellery and furniture on the sixth; children's clothes and sporting goods on the seventh; and office supplies on the eighth. The store also offers a range of clothing in Westerner-friendly larger sizes called Lilac. The tax-exemption counter is on the sixth floor.
Other locations: Keio Seiseki-Sakuragaoka, 1-10-1 Sekido, Tama-shi (042 337 2111).

Lumine Est

3-38-1 Shinjuku, Shinjuku-ku (5269 1111/www. lumine.ne.jp/est/index.html). Shinjuku station (Yamanote, Chuo, Marunouchi lines), above the east exit; (Oedo, Shinjuku lines), exit 1. **Open** 10.30am-9.30pm daily. **Credit** AmEx, DC, JCB, MC, V. **Map** Shinjuku p117.
Situated above the east exit of Shinjuku station, Lumine Est is chiefly notable for the Shunkan gourmet restaurant area, created by celebrated designer Sugimoto Takashi, on the seventh and eighth floors. The lower floors are laid out in a series of corridors that are fun for people-watching.

Matsuya

3-6-1 Ginza, Chuo-ku (3567 1211/www.matsuya. com). Ginza station (Ginza, Hibiya, Marunouchi lines), exits A12, A13. **Open** 10am-8pm daily (but closing time varies by month). **Credit** AmEx, DC, JCB, MC, V. **Map** Ginza p75.
Matsuya is notable for having in-store boutiques from the famous triumvirate of Japanese fashion revolutionaries: Issey Miyake, Yohji Yamamoto and Comme des Garçons, all of which are situated on the third floor. Traditional Japanese souvenirs are on the seventh, and shopping services for foreigners – tax exemption and overseas delivery – are on the third. The money-exchange counter is on the first floor.
Other locations: 1-4-1 Hanakawato, Taito-ku (3842 1111).

Matsuzakaya

10-1 Ginza, Chuo-ku (3572 1111/www.matsuzakaya. co.jp/ginza/index.html). Ginza station (Ginza, Hibiya, Marunouchi lines), exits A1-A4. **Open** 10.30am-7.30pm Mon-Wed, Sun; 10.30am-8pm Thur-Sat.
Credit AmEx, DC, JCB, MC, V. **Map** Ginza p75.
The main Matsuzakaya store is actually in Ueno, but the most convenient branch for shopaholics is this one, located in Ginza's main drag near Mitsukoshi and Matsuya. The tax-exemption and currency-exchange counters are on the basement second floor, and kimonos are sold on the sixth. The annex contains a beauty salon, art gallery and even a ladies' deportment school.
Other locations: 3-29-5 Ueno, Taito-ku (3832 1111).

Mitsukoshi

4-6-16 Ginza, Chuo-ku (3562 1111/www.mitsukoshi. co.jp). Ginza station (Ginza, Hibiya, Marunouchi lines), exits A7, A8, A11. **Open** 10am-8pm daily.
Credit AmEx, DC, JCB, MC, V. **Map** Ginza p75.
The oldest surviving department store chain in Japan (founded 1673), Mitsukoshi has its gargantuan flagship store in Nihonbashi. This Ginza branch (opposite Wako) has womenswear and accessories on the first five floors, menswear on the sixth, and household goods on the seventh. The B3 floor has toys, childrenswear and the tax-exemption counter. The bronze lion outside Mitsukoshi's main entrance is a popular meeting place.
Other locations: 1-4-1 Muromachi, Nihonbashi, Chuo-ku (3241 3311); 3-29-1 Shinjuku, Shinjuku-ku (3354 1111); 1-5-7 Higashi-Ikebukuro, Toshima-ku (3987 1111); 4-20-7 Ebisu, Shibuya-ku (5423 1111); 1-19-1 Honcho, Kichijoji, Musashino-shi (0422 29 1111).

Odakyu

1-1-3 Nishi-Shinjuku, Shinjuku-ku (3342 1111/ www.odakyu-dept.co.jp). Shinjuku station (Yamanote, Chuo lines), west exit; (Marunouchi line), exits A12-A14; (Oedo, Shinjuku lines), exit 3. **Open** 10am-8pm daily. **Credit** AmEx, DC, JCB, MC, V. **Map** Shinjuku p117.
Odakyu is split into two buildings connected by an elevated walkway and underground passageways. The main building has women's clothing on the first five floors, kimonos on the sixth, and furniture on the eighth, while the annex offers menswear, sportswear, four floors of the electronics retailer Bic Camera, and a Troisgros delicatessen in the basement food hall. The top three floors of the main building contain restaurants; the fifth holds the tax-exemption counter.

Seibu

21-1 Udagawa-cho, Shibuya-ku (3462 0111/www. seibu.co.jp). Shibuya station (Yamanote, Ginza lines), Hachiko exit; (Hanzomon line), exits 6, 7. **Open** 10am-8pm Mon-Wed, Sun; 10am-9pm Thur-Sat. **Credit** AmEx, DC, JCB, MC, V. **Map** Shibuya p109.
The Shibuya store is split into two buildings, Annexes A and B, which face each other across the street. Annex A sells mainly womenswear; Annex B menswear, children's clothes and accessories. The

tax-exemption counter is on the M2 (mezzanine) floor of Annex A. Seibu also runs retailers Loft and Movida, both of which are within easy walking distance of the store. Aimed at a young crowd, Loft sells interior decorations and various knick-knacks, while Movida houses top-end fashion store Via Bus Stop.
Other locations: 1-28-1 Minami-Ikebukuro, Toshima-ku (3981 0111); 2-5-1 Yurakucho, Chiyoda-ku (3286 0111); Shinjuku Loft, 4F-6F Mitsukoshi Bldg, 3-29-1 Shinjuku, Shinjuku-ku (5360 6210).

Takashimaya

2-4-1 Nihonbashi, Chuo-ku (3211 4111/www. takashimaya.co.jp). Nihonbashi station (Asakusa line), exit D3; (Ginza, Tozai lines), exits B1, B2. **Open** 10am-8pm daily. **Credit** AmEx, DC, JCB, MC, V. **Map** Marunouchi p93.
Here you'll find menswear on the first and second floors, womenswear on the third and fourth, children's clothing on the fifth, furniture on the sixth, and kimonos on the seventh. The tax-exemption counter is on the first floor and the overseas shipping service on floor B1. The massive Shinjuku branch – Takashimaya Times Square – contains a host of boutiques and restaurants, a branch of hardware shop Tokyu Hands, Kinokuniya International Bookshop in the annex and the Times Square Theatre on the 12th.
Other locations: Takashimaya Times Square, 5-24-2 Sendagaya, Shibuya-ku (5361 1111).

Tobu

1-1-25 Nishi-Ikebukuro, Toshima-ku (3981 2211/ www.tobu-dept.jp). Ikebukuro station (Yamanote line), west exit; (Marunouchi, Yurakucho lines), exits 4, 6. **Open** 10am-8pm daily. **Credit** AmEx, DC, JCB, MC, V. **Map** Ikebukuro p87.
The main building houses clothing for all occasions on the lower floors (including kimonos on the ninth), with an enormous selection of restaurants from the 11th to 17th floors. In the basement is Tokyo's largest food hall (*see p188* **Treats abound underground**). The central building sells clothing in larger sizes, plus a good range of interior goods and office supplies. The plaza building contains the designer collection. The currency-exchange and tax-exemption counters are on the basement first floor of the central building.

Tokyu Honten

2-24-1 Dogenzaka, Shibuya-ku (3477 3111/www. tokyu-dept.co.jp/honten). Shibuya station (Yamanote, Ginza lines), Hachiko exit; (Hanzomon line), exits 3, 3A. **Open** 11am-7pm daily. *Tokyu Food Show (B1F)* 11am-8pm daily. **Credit** AmEx, DC, JCB, MC, V. **Map** Shibuya p109.
Tokyu Honten sells designer fashions for men and women and high-end goods for the home. The gourmet food hall in the basement houses branches of the extremely popular delis Seijo Ishii and Dean & Deluca. The Tokyu Plaza store sells women's fashion, cosmetics and accessories, and has a CD shop and a branch of the Kinokuniya bookshop (but does not sell books in English).
Other locations: 2-3-1 Honcho, Kichijoji, Musashino-shi (0422 21 5111).

Wako

4-5-11 Ginza, Chuo-ku (3562 2111/www.wako.co.jp). Ginza station (Ginza, Hibiya, Marunouchi lines), exits A9, A10, B1. **Open** 10.30am-6pm Mon-Sat. **Credit** AmEx, DC, JCB, MC, V. **Map** Ginza p75.
This prestigious department store is located on the corner of Ginza Yon-chome, across from Mitsukoshi. The building's grand exterior – with its landmark clock tower – is matched only by the hushed ambience of the interior. As well as fine jewellery, porcelain and crystal, Wako sells designer apparel and accessories.
Other locations: 5-6-6 Hiro, Shibuya-ku (3473 0200).

Shopping malls

The urban landscape of Tokyo has changed considerably in the past few years thanks to a series of gargantuan multi-use constructions that serve not just as shopping malls, but also incorporate high-class office space, hotels, restaurants and even art galleries. They are theme parks of conspicuous consumption, with breathtaking exteriors designed by internationally renowned architects. The pioneer of this new movement is the Mori Corporation, which operates **Roppongi Hills** (incorporating the Grand Hyatt hotel, exclusive apartment buildings, restaurants and an art museum) and **Omotesando Hills**, a glorified mall designed by starchitect Ando Tadao. Both these developments, however, have been outshone by **Tokyo Midtown** – the tallest building in Tokyo at 248 metres (813 feet) – which occupies the former site of the Defense Agency, just a stone's throw from Roppongi Hills. This shopping, entertainment, residential and business concept has co-opted architects Ando Tadao, Kuma Kengo and Aoki Jun (*see p107* **Tokyo Midtown**).

Caretta Shiodome

1-8-2 Higashi-Shinbashi, Minato-ku (6218 2100/ www.caretta.jp). Shiodome station (Oedo line), exits 5, 6. **Open** hours vary.
Just across from the Conrad Tokyo, this 51-floor skyscraper offers a relatively uninspiring mix of more than 60 shops, cafés and restaurants as well as housing the head office of advertising giant Dentsu, the ADMT Advertising Museum (*see p78*) and the Dentsu Shiki Theatre (*see p265*).

Mark City

1-12-1 Dogenzaka, Shibuya-ku (3780 6503/www. s-markcity.co.jp). Shibuya station (Yamanote, Ginza lines), Hachiko exit; (Hanzomon line), exits 5, 8. **Open** *Shops* 10am-9pm daily. *Restaurants* 11am-11pm daily. **Map** Shibuya p109.
Shibuya's version of the multi-purpose mall is a relatively modest affair, housing a handful of boutiques and lifestyle stores in a building opposite Shibuya station. Restaurants and cafés are on the

Loveless. *See p197*.

fourth and third floors, women's clothing is on the second, accessories and cosmetics are on the first.

Marunouchi Building

2-4-1 Marunouchi, Chiyoda-ku (5218 5100/www. marubiru.jp/index2.html). Tokyo station (Yamanote, Chuo lines), Shin Marubiru exit; (Marunouchi line), exit 5. **Open** *Shops* 11am-9pm Mon-Sat; 11am-8pm Sun. *Restaurants* 11am-11pm Mon-Sat; 11am-10pm Sun. **Map** Marunouchi p93.

While essentially an office tower, 'Marubiru', as it is affectionately known by patrons, devotes its first four floors and basement to a 'Shopping Zone', while the fifth, sixth, 35th and 36th floors belong to the 'Restaurant Zone'. The basement food hall has an emphasis on big-name gourmet products, and there are also branches of American Pharmacy and upmarket grocery store Meidi-ya. Just across the street is the New Marunouchi Building, which opened in April 2007, whose first nine floors are dedicated to retail.

Oazo

1-6-4 Marunouchi, Chiyoda-ku (5218 5100/www. oazo.jp). Tokyo station (Yamanote, Chuo lines), Marunouchi north exit; (Marunouchi line), exits 10, 12, 14. **Open** *Shops* 11am-9pm daily. *Restaurants* 11am-11pm daily. **Map** Marunouchi p93.

This gleaming glass complex of shops, restaurants and offices opposite Tokyo station is affiliated to the nearby Marunouchi Building. Pride of place goes to Maruzen's flagship bookstore (with a good English-language section; *see p195*). You can also find the Japan Aerospace Exploration Agency's showroom.

Roppongi Hills

6-10 Roppongi, Minato-ku (6406 6000/www. roppongihills.com). Roppongi station (Hibiya line), exit 1C; (Oedo line), exit 3. **Open** hours vary. **Map** Roppongi p103.

Opened in 2003, Roppongi's mammoth shopping and entertainment development received more than 49-million visitors in its first year alone. The brainchild of Tokyo property magnate Mori Minoru, Roppongi Hills is an entire mini city – with 200 shops and restaurants, the Grand Hyatt hotel, many private apartment buildings, a multiplex cinema, a TV studio and the colossal Mori Tower, which is topped by the excellent Mori Art Museum and Tokyo City View observation deck. *See also p105*.

Sunshine City

3-1 Higashi-Ikebukuro, Toshima-ku (3989 3331/ www.sunshinecity.co.jp). Ikebukuro station (Yamanote line), east exit; (Marunouchi, Yurakucho lines), exits 43, 44 or Higashi-Ikebukuro station (Yurakucho line), exit 2. **Open** *Shops* 10am-8pm daily. *Restaurants* 11am-10pm daily. **Map** Ikebukuro p87.

The prototype for the huge malls that dominate Tokyo's retail scene, Sunshine City lacks much of the glossy glamour of its subsequent rivals. Most of its shops and restaurants are in the Alpa Shopping Centre. The complex also hosts the Ancient Orient Museum, an indoor theme park called Namja Town and the Gyoza Stadium (a collection of restaurants devoted to Japan's beloved dumplings). *See also p91*.

Urban Dock LaLaport Toyosu

2-4-9 Toyosu, Koto-ku (6910 1234). Toyosu station (Yurakucho Line), exit 2. **Open** *Shops* 10am-9pm daily. *Restaurants* 11am-11pm daily.

Officially Tokyo's largest shopping mall, covering almost 100,000sq m, LaLaport has little to excite in the shopping stakes, but it does have a few other attractions worth recommending. Top of the list is Kidzania (*see p218*), a career role-playing amusement park that offers children the chance to simulate a working day with pint-sized reproductions of grown-up jobs. It also boasts a Hello Kitty-themed amusement arcade and a cluster of shops for children, including Snoopy Town and Børnelund, as well as a cinema and a small gallery devoted to *ukiyo-e*. LaLaport's Tokyo Bay location offers impressive views of the city. To experience the full visual impact it has to offer, the mall is best visited by Himiko, the futuristic ferry designed by *anime* mastermind Leiji Matsumoto on the Tokyo Water Cruise from Asakusa to Toyosu along the Sumida River.

Venus Fort

Palette Town, 1 Aomi, Koto-ku (3599 0700/ www.venusfort.co.jp). Aomi station (Yurikamome line) or Tokyo Teleport station (Rinkai line). **Open** *Shops* 11am-9pm Mon-Fri, Sun; 11am-10pm Sat. *Restaurants* 11am-11pm daily. **Map** Odaiba p101.

Widely touted as the 'first theme park exclusively for women', this unusual mall is decorated in a faux-classic Graeco-Roman style designed to evoke the feeling of strolling through Florence or Milan (it even has an artificial sky that changes colour with the time of day outside). It contains mainly European-style boutiques and pâtisseries, and is part of the giant Odaiba bayfront complex (*see p99-101*).

Yebisu Garden Place

4-20 Ebisu, Shibuya-ku & 13-1/4-1 Mita, Meguro-ku (5423 7111/www.gardenplace.co.jp/english). Ebisu station (Yamanote line), east exit; (Hibiya line), exit 1. **Open** *Shops* 11am-8pm Mon-Sat; 11am-7.30pm Sun. *Restaurants* hours vary.

Within the spacious precincts of Yebisu Garden Place you'll find the Atre shopping arcade, Westin Hotel, Tokyo Metropolitan Museum of Photography and Yebisu Beer Museum. A large number of boutiques are located in the stylish, self-enclosed shopping centre, Glass Square, which also has an oyster bar.

Shopping streets

Shopping streets, or *shotengai*, exist in various forms around Tokyo. Often near railway stations, they are home to long-established shops and markets, and provide a less-sanitised retail experience than the super-shiny malls.

Ameyoko Plaza Food & Clothes Market

www.ameyoko.net. Ueno station (Yamanote, Ginza lines), Shinobazu exit; (Hibiya line), exits 6, 7 or Okachimachi station (Yamanote line), north exit. **Open** hours vary. **No credit cards**. **Map** Ueno & Yanaka p123.

This maze of streets next to the railway tracks between Ueno and Okachimachi stations comprises two markets: the covered Ueno Centre Mall and open-air Ameyoko itself. The mall sells an array of souvenirs and clothes, while the 500 stalls of jam-packed Ameyoko – one of Tokyo's greatest street markets – specialise in fresh food, especially fish. *See also p125*.

Cat Street

Harajuku station (Yamanote line), Omotesando exit or Meiji-Jingumae (Chiyoda line), exit 4. **Open & credit** varies. **Map** Harajuku & Aoyama p82.

Running for about half a mile perpendicular to each side of Omotesando, Cat Street is the spiritual home of Tokyo's vibrant street fashion culture. While the strip has been steadily heading upmarket over the past few years, it is still the main conduit for funkily dressed teens on shopping sprees in Tokyo. Highlights include the Tadao Ando-designed edifice housing the Armani Casa interior brand, and collectable figure store Pook et Koop.

Kappabashi Dori

Tawaramachi station (Ginza line), exit 1 or Asakusa station (Asakusa, Ginza lines), exits 1, 2, 3, A4. **Open & credit** varies. **Map** Asakusa p63.

If you're visiting Asakusa's Senso-ji temple (*see p68*) and Nakamise Dori, take a short detour to this area devoted to wholesale kitchenware shops. You'll find low-cost crockery, rice cookers, knives, grills, indeed everything you need to set up a restaurant, including the realistic-looking plastic models of dishes that are displayed in restaurant windows. The shops run along Shinbori Dori, from the corner of Asakusa Dori; look for the giant chef's head on the top of the Niimi store.

Meguro Dori

Toritsu Daigaku station (Tokyu Toyoko line). **Open & credit** varies. **Map** Meguro p71.

From its intersection with Yamate Dori, running about two miles south-west, Meguro Dori is dotted with dozens of quirky, independently run shops specialising in home furnishings. Nicknamed 'Interior Dori', the street offers every imaginable type of furnishing, from tatty antiques to fashionably minimalist Italian kitchens. Most of what's on offer is imported from Europe or the States, but there's still plenty of Made in Japan merchandise to be found. It's not the easiest area to access, but catch the Toyoko line to Toritsu Daigaku and walk towards Meguro.

Nakamise Dori

www.asakusa-nakamise.jp. Asakusa station (Asakusa, Ginza lines), exits 1, 3, A4. **Open** 8am-8pm daily. **No credit cards**. **Map** Asakusa p63.

This avenue of stalls and tiny shops leading up to the entrance to Senso-ji temple in Asakusa sells all sorts of Japanese souvenirs, some dating back to the Edo era. It also sells the kind of food that is

Present perfect

There's a vast range of gifts and souvenirs, both ancient and modern, classy and kitsch, available in Tokyo: here are a few ideas. For one-stop shopping, **department stores** (*see p187*) are a good bet. If you're short of time and/or money, **Oriental Bazaar** (*see p204*) on Omotesando stocks all the classic Japanese goodies. But Tokyo is a shopper's paradise, so a little digging will turn up something special.

Clothing

The obvious garment is a **kimono**, new or second-hand, which can range in price from ¥4,000 to ¥1,000,000. A cheaper and easier-to-wear option is the **yukata**, a cotton gown that is used by both sexes. Designs are highly detailed and use seasonal motifs such as cherry blossom, plum blossom, maple and pine. For men, the **happi** coat is a short tunic used in festivals, and for both sexes there are **tabi** (split-toed socks) and **tenugui** (a towel worn around the head at festivals, often decorated with some form of heraldic symbol). Accessories include the **netsuke**, a small carved pouch that is hung from the kimono belt.

Kitchenware

Ceramic and pottery **tableware** comes in all shapes and sizes, and at all price ranges; or there's (often expensive) **lacquerware** (*urushi-nuri*) and, of course, **chopsticks** – all vary according to their region of origin. Kappabashi Dori is the street to head for.

Cultural and traditional

Myriad antiques shops specialise in everything from **samurai swords** and **helmets** to **screens** – but you'll need a fat wallet, and they're difficult to transport. *Ukiyo-e* woodblock **prints** by Hiroshige, Hokusai or lesser-known artists are always popular; you can pay as little as ¥1,500 for a modern reproduction to many thousands for an original work. Head for a stationery/paper specialist for seasonal **greeting cards** and **calligraphy sets**; or for lanterns, fans, boxes and other ornamental goods made with colourful, handmade **washi** paper.

  Fuuring (wind chimes) are a reminder of the cooling, melodic sound heard in the heat of the Japanese summer, while **hagoita** (battledores), painted with decorative scenes from *kabuki* plays, are sold in November as household decorations for the New Year. Then there are the numerous implements used in the **tea ceremony**, and the *karuta* **card games** Hyakunin Isshu and Hanafuda (each has a long and fascinating history). Stalls near shrines and temples sell all sorts of small, cheap **good-luck charms**. Look for the omnipresent *maneki neko* (lucky cat); a raised left paw is for business success; a raised right paw is for money – or hedge your bets and get one with both paws raised.

Food and drink

There is a bewildering variety of edible/drinkable items to choose from, but **sake** and **green tea** are always reliable choices; go to a specialist for the best advice and largest range. Boxed **wagashi** (traditional Japanese sweets) are a thing of beauty, but they often have short shelf lives.

The quirky stuff

Japan is a world leader in bizarre inventions and offbeat novelties. The best place to shop is **RanKing RanQueen** (*see p209*), which stocks, and ranks, the hottest-selling goods. And this being Tokyo, the hottest-selling goods are usually highly entertaining. At time of writing, these include beauty products such as a mouth stretcher and a face shrinker, a snoring remedy that's a nicely designed sticky tape for the lips, and self-heating skin cream for winter. A more practical, and inexpensive, gift is the **hokaron** heat pads sold in pharmacies and most convenience stores.

Eat, Drink, Shop

associated with festivals, and traditional snacks such as *kaminari-okoshii* (toasted rice crackers) and *ningyo-yaki* (red bean-filled buns moulded into humorous shapes). *See also p65.*

Nakano Broadway

3387 1610/3388 7004/www.nbw.jp. Nakano station (Chuo, Tozai lines), north exit. **Open & credit** varies.
Walk down the cathedral-like *shotengai* and you'll reach the covered Broadway section. This contains numerous outlets of Mandarake (*see p209*), specialising in new and second-hand manga; branches of Fujiya Avic, the second-hand CD/DVD/*anime* store offering rarities and bootlegs; and a large number of shops selling collectable action figures.

Nishi-Ogikubo

www.sugishoren.com/street/400.htm. Nishi-Ogikubo station (Chuo, Sobu lines), north exit. **Open & credit** varies.
The area around the four main roads that cross at the Zenpukuji river is home to around 75 antiques, second-hand and 'recycle' shops. These sell everything from Japanese ceramics to 1950s American memorabilia. Take the station's north exit, stop at the *koban* (police box) and ask for a copy of the 'antikku mappu'.

Takeshita Dori

www.harajuku.jp/takeshita. Harajuku station (Yamanote line), Takeshita exit or Meiji-Jingumae station (Chiyoda line), exit 2. **Open & credit** varies. **Map** Harajuku & Aoyama p82.
Takeshita Dori stands as a symbol of Tokyo's collision of street cultures. Along this narrow sloping street (which runs from Harajuku station to Meiji Dori) you'll find stalls selling photos of fresh-faced 'idols' to star-struck schoolgirls, while the hip-hop boutique next door pumps out gangster rap. Shops specialising in 'Gothic Lolita' nurse and maid uniforms stand next to those selling retro-punk fashions and Beatles bootlegs. A must-see. Visit at the weekend for the full-on experience.

Undercover. *See p199.*

Books

The shops listed below are the best sources for books in English and other languages, on any subject. If you're looking for curiosities or bargains and have a day to spare, head for the **Kanda-Jinbocho** area (Jinbocho station) and the second-hand bookshops of Yasukuni Dori.

English-language newspapers are available from kiosks around train stations, as well as selected convenience stores.

Good Day Books

3F, 1-11-2 Ebisu, Shibuya-ku (5421 0957/www. gooddaybooks.com). Ebisu station (Yamanote line), east exit; (Hibiya line), exit 1. **Open** 11am-8pm Mon, Wed-Sat; 11am-6pm Sun. **No credit cards.**
Tokyo's oldest and best-known used English bookshop stocks more than 35,000 second-hand books

and 7,000 new ones. There's also an extensive selection of second-hand books on Japan and Japanese-language texts. You can sell/trade your second-hand books and DVDs here too.

The Intelligent Idiot

5-47-6 Jingumae, Shibuya-ku (5467 5866/www. vision.co.jp). Omotesando station (Chiyoda, Ginza, Hanzomon lines), exit B2. **Open** 2-8pm Mon, Wed-Fri; 12.30-7.30pm Sat, Sun. **No credit cards. Map** Shibuya p109.
Part of the eclectic Vision Network empire and located above the Las Chicas café (*see p161*), this shop sells new books in English at discount prices. It is also a showroom for furniture company Kyozon.

Kinokuniya Bookstore

3-17-7 Shinjuku, Shinjuku-ku (3354 0131/www. kinokuniya.co.jp). Shinjuku station (Yamanote, Chuo lines), east exit; (Marunouchi line), exits B7, B8;

(Oedo, Shinjuku lines), exit 1. **Open** 10am-9pm daily. **Credit** AmEx, DC, JCB, MC, V. **Map** Shinjuku p117. The best-known branch of this chain is on Shinjuku Dori, but the branch behind the nearby Takashimaya (on the south side of Shinjuku station) is bigger. Kinokuniya has perhaps the largest selection in Tokyo of new books in French and German, as well as English, with numerous specialised academic titles on offer too. It also carries numerous videos, audio-visual software and CD-Roms. Note that not all Kinokuniya branches sell English books.
Other locations: throughout the city.

Maruzen

Oazo 1F-4F, 1-6-4 Marunouchi, Chiyoda-ku (5288 8881/www.maruzen.co.jp). Tokyo station (Yamanote, Chuo lines), Marunouchi north exit; (Marunouchi line), exits 10, 12, 14. **Credit** AmEx, DC, JCB, MC, V. **Map** Marunouchi p93.
This flagship store inside the Oazo shopping complex (*see p191*) holds 200,000 books in English and other languages. There are bilingual book advisers on hand and a touch-screen computer search facility (available in English).
Other locations: throughout the city.

Nellie's English Books

Sunbridge Bldg 1F-2F, 1-26-6 Yanagibashi, Taito-ku (3865 6210/0120 071 329/www.nellies.jp). Asakusabashi station (Asakusa line), exit A3; (Sobu line), east exit. **Open** 10am-12.30pm, 1.15-6pm Mon-Fri. **Credit** AmEx, DC, JCB, MC, V.
Nellie's stocks a wide selection of materials useful for English-language teachers working in Japan. The range includes books, readers, videos, song-books and software.

Manga

Manga is an art form that has seeped into global consciousness – and is a valuable tool for understanding Japanese language and culture. The garish covers of the magazines and collected paperback volumes can be found anywhere, but there are a couple of specialist shops that are particularly worth a visit – as is Mandarake in **Nakano Broadway** (*see p194*) and Shibuya (*see pp108-114*). See also *p118* **Manga mania**.

Manga no mori

3-10-12 Takada, Toshima-ku (5292 7748/www.manganomori.net). Takadanobaba station (Yamanote, Tozai lines), Waseda exit. **Open** 11am-9pm daily. **Credit** AmEx, DC, JCB, MC, V.
The main branch of this chain sells a good range of classic Japanese manga, the latest imported titles from Marvel and DC, and a handful of action figures. The Ikebukuro branch specialises in manga for women.
Other locations: 1-28-1 Higashi-Ikebukuro, Toshima-ku (5396 1245); 6-16-16 Ueno, Taito-ku (3833 3411).

Tora no Ana

B1F-4F, 4-3-1 Soto-Kanda, Chiyoda-ku (5294 0123/www.toranoana.co.jp). Akihabara station (Yamanote, Sobu lines), Electric Town exit; (Hibiya line), exit 3. **Open** 11am-9pm Mon-Thur; 10am-9pm Fri-Sun. **Credit** DC, JCB, MC, V.
Look out for the giant cartoon mascot painted on the top of this flagship store in Akihabara. Inside the six-floor building it's a hive of activity as Japan's *otaku* (nerds) flip through the latest releases. In addition to the nation's bestselling new comics, the shop offers a selection of *dojinshi*, fanzines created by devoted manga amateurs, showcasing everything from Disney-esque fantasies to hard-core porn.
Other locations: 1-18-1 Nishi-Shinjuku, Shinjuku-ku (5908 1681); 1-13-4 Higashi-Ikebukuro, Toshima-ku (5957 7138); Akihabara Part 2, Kimura Bldg 2F-4F, 1-9-8 Soto-Kanda, Chiyoda-ku (5256 2055); Akihabara Part 3, Kyoeki Soto Kanda Bldg 4F-6F, 4-4-2 Soto-Kanda, Chiyoda-ku (3526 7211).

Electronics

For the visitor, the best place to buy electronics is **Akihabara**, the main area for duty-free shopping outside the airport. Tax exemption is available on purchases of ¥10,000 and over; take your passport, which needs to show that you've been in Japan for less than six months.
There are also some chain stores with prices that rival those of Akihabara. The most notable – with near-identical logos, layouts and products – are **Bic Camera** (1-41-5 Higashi-Ikebukuro, Toshima-ku, 5396 1111, www.biccamera.co.jp), **Sakuraya** (1-1-1 Nishi-Shinjuku, Shinjuku-ku, 5324 3636, www.sakuraya.co.jp), and **Yodobashi Camera** (1-11-1 Nishi-Shinjuku, Shinjuku-ku, 3346 1010, www.yodobashi.co.jp). They're geared to domestic consumption, so some knowledge of Japanese is useful. All have branches in major commercial districts throughout the city.
Photography enthusiasts should take a stroll around the backstreets east of Shinjuku station, where there's a host of second-hand camera shops.

Akky

1-12-1 Soto-Kanda, Chiyoda-ku (5207 5027). Akihabara station (Yamanote, Sobu lines), Electric Town exit; (Hibiya line), exit 3. **Open** 9.30am-8pm daily. **Credit** AmEx, DC, JCB, MC, V.
A well-presented store that sells all kinds of electrical appliances. All products are export models, sold with an international warranty and English instructions, at duty-free prices. An overseas delivery service is available. The staff speak a variety of languages.

Laox: Duty Free Akihabara

1-15-3 Soto-Kanda, Chiyoda-ku (3255 5301/www.laox.co.jp). Akihabara station (Yamanote, Sobu lines), Electric Town exit; (Hibiya line), exit 3. **Open** 10am-9pm daily. **Credit** AmEx, DC, JCB, MC, V.
One of Japan's biggest suppliers of duty-free overseas-model electronics and appliances. There

Eat, Drink, Shop

Duty-free goods

Foreign visitors can reclaim the five per cent sales tax at shops that have duty-free counters. These include most department stores and many electrical goods shops in **Akihabara** (see p195). Exempted items include food, beverages, tobacco, pharmaceuticals, cosmetics, film and batteries. To qualify, your total purchases must cost more than ¥10,000, and your passport must show that you have been in Japan for less than six months. Take the paid-for goods and receipts to the store's tax-refund counter, along with your passport; the refund will be paid on the spot. When you leave Japan, make sure you have your purchases with you (preferably in your carry-on bag – Customs may ask to see them).

are English-language catalogues and instruction manuals for most products. This branch is near the station, with a huge sign outside, so it's hard to miss.
Other locations: throughout the city.

Sony Building

5-3-1 Ginza, Chuo-ku (3573 2563/www.sonybuilding. jp). Ginza station (Ginza, Hibiya, Marunouchi lines), exit B9. **Open** 11am-7pm daily. **Credit** AmEx, DC, JCB, MC, V. **Map** Ginza p75.
This eight-floor building – a landmark in Ginza – contains showrooms for Sony's world-famous products, including the AIBO robot hound, PlayStation 3, VAIO, Cyber-Shot, Handycam and others. The building also contains a number of cafés and restaurants, and even an English pub. *See also p76.*

Takarada Musen

1-14-7 Soto-Kanda, Chiyoda-ku (3253 0101/www. takarada-musen.com). Akihabara station (Yamanote, Sobu lines), Electric Town exit; (Hibiya line), exit 3. **Open** 11am-8.30pm daily. **Credit** AmEx, DC, JCB, MC, V.
This small but busy shop has a number of bilingual staff to help you find what you want. Takarada specialises in overseas models of Sony products – digital cameras, video cameras, TVs, Walkmans and so on. English manuals are available.

Tokyo IT Services

Shinwa Bldg 5F, 2-6-8 Hamamatsucho, Minato-ku (5733 4279/www.tokyo-it.com). Hamamatsucho station (Yamanote line), south exit. **Open** 10am-6.30pm Mon-Fri; 11am-4pm Sat. **Credit** AmEx, DC, JCB, MC, V.
Tokyo IT Services offers English-language support to computer users in Tokyo, plus wireless network installation, laptop rental from ¥500 a day, and a computer repair service. For Macs and PCs.

User's Side 2

K&S Ebisu Bldg 2F-4F, 1-16-2 Hiroo, Shibuya-ku (5447 7011/www.users-side.co.jp/2/index.php). Ebisu station (Yamanote line), west exit; (Hibiya line), exit 1. **Open** 11am-7pm Mon-Sat. **Credit** AmEx, DC, JCB, MC, V.
User's Side 2 sells export models of Japanese technology, with English software. It also has an affordable repair and troubleshooting service, with English-language technical support and bilingual shop staff.
Other locations: 3-9-2 Sotokanda, Chiyoda-ku (5295 1011).

Fashion

Whether due to clearly defined seasons, racial homogeneity or the tiny homes that drive people outdoors, the Japanese take fashion very seriously indeed. Large tracts of the city are devoted to fashion retail, and each area has its own individual character. Upmarket luxury brands dominate the Ginza area and much of 'brand boulevard' Omotesando, which runs into the youth culture-oriented Harajuku. For the latest teen trends, head to Shibuya or neighbouring Daikanyama.

All Japanese clothing sizes are measured in centimetres. Western visitors often find Japanese sizes too small, though **Isetan** (*see p187*) in Shinjuku caters for larger frames.

Boutiques

10 Corso Como Comme des Garçons

Unimat Bleu Cinq Point Bldg, 5-3-18 Minami-Aoyama, Minato-ku (5774 7800). Omotesando station (Chiyoda, Ginza, Hanzomon lines), exit A5. **Open** 11am-8pm daily. **Credit** AmEx, DC, JCB, MC, V.
Located in the same building as Undercover and Y-3, this boutique is a collaboration between Comme des Garçons impresario Rei Kawakubo and Milanese fashion emporium 10 Corso Como. Spread over six floors, the store boasts a huge array of exclusive merchandise and is an essential destination for any fashion fan.

109

2-29-1 Dogenzaka, Shibuya-ku (3477 5111/ www.shibuya109.jp). Shibuya station (Yamanote, Ginza lines), Hachiko exit; (Hanzomon line), exit 3A. **Open** 10am-9pm daily. **Credit** varies. **Map** Shibuya p109.
This landmark Shibuya store is the domain of the *joshikousei* – the fashion-obsessed teenage girls who don't just follow trends but start them. Take a stroll around to see them in action and indulge in some amateur anthropology. Nearby 109-2 sells more of the same to pre-teens.
Other locations: 109-2 1-23-10 Dogenzaka, Shibuya-ku (3477 8111).

Follow the fash pack to Herzog & de Meuron's stunning **Prada** building. *See p200.*

Eat, Drink, Shop

Blackflag

5-4-24 Minami-aoyama, Minato-ku (5778 1999).
Omotesando station (Chiyoda, Ginza, Hanzomon
lines), exit A5. **Open** 11am-8pm daily. **Credit**
AmEx, DC, JCB, MC, V.
This hard-to-spot store is a collaboration between the
designers of popular street brands Neighborhood and
W)taps. The dark interior has a rustic 1930s
American Midwest look, contrasting with the com-
bat gear-inspired apparel and accessories on display.

Laforet Harajuku

1-11-6 Jingumae, Shibuya-ku (3475 0411/www.
laforet.ne.jp). Harajuku station (Yamanote line),
Takeshita exit, Meiji-Jingumae station (Chiyoda line),
exit 5. **Open** 11am-8pm daily. **Credit** AmEx, DC,
JCB, MC, V. **Map** Harajuku & Aoyama p82.
One of teenage Tokyo's hallowed sites, Laforet is
located in the heart of Harajuku, on the corner of
Omotesando and Meji Dori; look for the flower
sculptures outside. This multi-level emporium
contains numerous small boutiques selling clothes
and accessories aimed at young wearers of garish,
eccentric fashion. Exhibitions and multimedia
events are also held here.

Loveless

3-17-11 Minami-Aoyama, Minato-ku (3401 2301).
Omotesando station (Chiyoda, Ginza, Hanzomon
lines), exit A4. **Open** noon-10pm Mon-Sat; noon-8pm
Sun. **Credit** AmEx, DC, JCB, MC, V. **Map** Harajuku
& Aoyama p82.

Venture past French luggage-maker Goyard on the
ground level, down into the dungeon-like basement
floors to see an astounding assortment of wacky
fashions, including plenty of upcoming Japanese
labels that you won't find anywhere else. The sister
store Colour by Numbers (20-23 Daikanyamacho,
Shibuya-ku, 3770 1991), which stocks hot labels like
Mastermind Japan, Green and Mosslight, is also
worth a visit. **Photo** *p191.*

Parco

15-1 Udagawacho, Shibuya-ku (3464 5111/www.
parco.co.jp). Shibuya station (Yamanote, Ginza
lines), Hachiko exit; (Hanzomon line), exits 6, 7.
Open *Parts 1, 2, 3* 10am-9pm daily; *Quattro*
11am-9pm daily **Credit** AmEx, DC, JCB, MC, V.
Map Shibuya p109.
This mid-range clothing store occupies buildings in
Shibuya. Part 1 houses a theatre and an art bookshop,
Part 2 specialises in fashion, and Part 3 has an exhi-
bition space that hosts frequent shows by artists and
designers from Japan and abroad. Another branch is
the home of the concert hall Club Quattro (*see p260*).
Other locations: 1-28-2 Minami-Ikebukuro,
Toshima-ku (5391 8000); 1-5-1 Kichijoji-Honcho,
Musashino-shi (0422 218 111).

RagTag

1-17-7 Jinnan, Shibuya-ku (3476 6848/www.ragtag.
jp). Shibuya station (Yamanote, Ginza lines), Hachiko
exit; (Hanzomon line), exit 6. **Open** noon-9pm daily.
Credit AmEx, DC, JCB, MC, V. **Map** Shibuya p109.

Vending machines

The Japanese vending machine (*jidohanbaiki*) has acquired an almost legendary status. Locals take them very much for granted, but first-time visitors will be impressed by their ubiquity, the fact that they always work (and are never vandalised – unthinkable in most major cities elsewhere in the world), and the range of products sold.

The vast majority of vending machines in Tokyo sell soft drinks (hot and cold) or cigarettes, with a smaller number selling alcohol (usually beer or sake). Found on almost every street corner, singly or clustered in groups, most machines operate 24 hours, but those selling tobacco switch themselves off from 11pm until 7am (ostensibly to combat under-age smoking, although curiously porn machines operate opposite hours). The drinks machines tend to stop dispensing hot coffee or tea in the summer. ID (a driver's licence, usually) may be required to operate those carrying alcohol.

If you venture further afield, outside the main shopping areas, you may find machines that sell more esoteric products. Batteries, condoms, rice, tights, ice-cream, sex toys – all have vending machines devoted to them somewhere in Japan. The saucier machines selling 'used' schoolgirls' knickers are not an urban legend; they did exist, until the mayor ordered a crackdown on sleaze.

The *jidohanbaiki* arrived during the Tokyo Olympics in 1964; there are now over six million machines across Japan. All accept coins and ¥1,000 notes, and recently many began to take payment via mobile phone (placed against an electronic reader) or Suica (the Japan Railways magnetic travel card).

This Shibuya recycle shop is where fashion-obsessed types who have run out of closet space go to sell on their unwanted threads. An excellent browsing ground for those in search of designer labels at heavily discounted prices.
Other locations: 3-3-15 Ginza (3535 4100); 1-7-2 Jingumae (3478 0287); 3-32-8 Shinjuku (5366 6722); 2-34-12 Shimokitazawa (5790 5976)

Restir

4-2-2 Ginza, Chuo-ku (5159 0595/www.restir. com). Ginza station (Ginza, Hibiya, Marunouchi lines), exit C8. **Open** 11.30am-8.30pm Mon-Sat; 11am-8pm Sun. **Credit** AmEx, DC, JCB, MC, V. **Map** Ginza p75.
This mega-boutique offers one of the most luxurious fashion shopping experiences in Tokyo. Besides a VIP room and live DJ, it also offers high-quality customer service in reasonable English. The high-end brands include more than a few home-grown labels.

Uniqlo

5-7-7 Ginza, Chuo-ku. (3569-6781/www.uniqlo. co.jp). Ginza station (Ginza, Hibiya, Marunouchi lines), exit A2. **Open** 11am-9pm daily. **Credit** AmEx, DC, JCB, MC, V. **Map** Ginza p75.
UK residents will already be familiar with the name Uniqlo. This is the chain store that revolutionised retail in Japan with basic clothing at reasonable prices. But Uniqlo is in the process of going upmarket, and to that end it opened a huge flagship store in Ginza last year, designed by Tokyo resident architect duo Klein Dytham. The façade is a matrix of 1,000 illuminated cells, which form Tetris-style patterns.
Other locations: throughout the city.

Children

Casualwear chains such as Gap, Muji (*see p208*) and Uniqlo (*see p198*), have outlets throughout the city.

Familiar

*New Melsa Bldg B1F, 5-7-10 Ginza, Chuo-ku (3574
7111/www.familiar.co.jp). Ginza station (Ginza,
Hibiya, Marunouchi lines), exit A2.* **Open** 11am-8pm
Mon, Tue, Thur-Sun. **Credit** AmEx, DC, JCB, MC, V.
Map Ginza p75.

This upscale children's goods shop in Ginza handles
everything from clothes, shoes and umbrellas to
desks, beds, strollers and skincare. Prices are hefty,
but quality is high.

LIMI feu prankster

*6-7-12 Jingumae, Shibuya-ku (5464 2025/www.
limifeu.com). Harajuku station (Yamanote line),
Omotesando exit or Meiji-Jingumae (Chiyoda line),
exit 4.* **Open** noon-9pm daily. **Credit** AmEx, DC,
JCB, MC, V. **Map** Harajuku & Aoyama p82.

Tokyo's antidote to the frilly togs so often foisted on
toddlers comes courtesy of LIMI feu prankster, an
all-new store showcasing the children's line of Limi
Yamamoto, daughter of fashion paragon Yohji. The
whippersnappers can be left in a padded play area
while mum and dad rummage through the funky
threads. Mother-of-two Limi has a keen sense of
what trendy Tokyo moms want their kids to wear,
and this store is proving to be a big hit.

Sayegusa

*7-8-8 Ginza, Chuo-ku (3573 2441/www.sayegusa.
com). Ginza station (Ginza, Hibiya, Marunouchi
lines), exit A2.* **Open** 10.30am-7.30pm daily. **Credit**
AmEx, DC, JCB, MC, V. **Map** Ginza p75.

For the ultimate Tokyo children's clothing shopping
experience, visit Ginza's Sayegusa, purveyors of finery for small fry since 1869. Housed in a four-storey
Meiji-era building, this venerable establishment
offers top-of-the-range baby and children's clothing
and accessories on the first and second floors, party
dresses and suits in the first basement floor, and a
made-to-order clothing service on the floor beneath.
Expect impeccable service and gut-churning prices.

Designer: Japanese

A Bathing Ape

*5-5-8 Minami-Aoyama, Minato-ku (5464 0335/www.
bape.com). Omotesando station (Chiyoda, Ginza,
Hanzomon lines), exit A5.* **Open** 11am-7pm daily.
Credit JCB, MC, V. **Map** Harajuku & Aoyama p82.

Founded by stylist, DJ and entrepreneur Nigo in
1993, this pseudo-retro brand has evolved into the
epitome of Japanese cool. You'll have to search for
the entrance very carefully; the lack of sign is all part
of maintaining the brand's exclusivity.

Other locations: 4-28-22 B1F Jingumae, Shibuya-
ku (5464 0204).

Billionaire Boys Club/
The Ice Cream Store

*4-28-22 Jingumae, Shibuya-ku (5775 2633/www.
bbcicecream.com). Meiji-Jingumae station (Chiyoda
line) exit 5.* **Open** 11am-7pm daily. **Credit** JCB, MC,
V. **Map** Harajuku & Aoyama p82.

A collaboration between hip-hop artist and producer
Pharrell Williams and A Bathing Ape street-fash-
ion mogul Nigo, clothing label Billionaire Boys
Club and sneaker brand Ice Cream have side-by-
side shops on Propeller Street, one of Harajuku's
hippest strips. Head here for high-quality sneakers,
T-shirts, sweatshirts, parkas, shirts, jackets and
jeans in bold colours and designs.

Comme des Garçons

*5-2-1 Minami-Aoyama, Minato-ku (3406 3951).
Omotesando station (Chiyoda, Ginza, Hanzomon
lines), exit A5.* **Open** 11am-8pm daily. **Credit**
AmEx, DC, JCB, MC, V. **Map** Harajuku &
Aoyama p82.

Comme des Garçons' Rei Kawakubo is one of the
pioneers who put Japanese designers on the fashion
map. The extraordinary exterior of this flagship
store beckons the shopper into a maze of psychedelic
prints, classically themed suits and smart formal
wear. Tax-exemption service available.

Issey Miyake

*3-18-11 Minami-Aoyama, Minato-ku (3423 1407/
1408/www.isseymiyake.com). Omotesando station
(Chiyoda, Ginza, Hanzomon lines), exit A4.* **Open**
11am-8pm daily. **Credit** AmEx, DC, JCB, MC, V.
Map Harajuku & Aoyama p82.

Issey Miyake is one of the big three designers,
along with Yohji Yamamoto and Rei Kawakubo,
who transformed Japanese fashion back in the late
1980s. In his Tokyo store, you'll find original
creations and collaborations between designers
and artists that can't be seen anywhere else. Tax-
exemption service available.

Neighborhood

*4-32-5 Jingumae, Shibuya-ku (3401 1201). Harajuku
station (Yamanote line), Omotesando exit or Meiji-
Jingumae station (Chiyoda line), exit 4.* **Open** noon-
8pm daily. **Credit** AmEx, DC, JCB, MC, V. **Map**
Harajuku & Aoyama p82.

'Death from Above' declare the red neon signs outside this minimalist urban fashion shop. Inside are
men's jackets, shirts, jeans and accessories with a
biker or military influence.

Number (N)ine

*2-16-6 Ebisu, Shibuya-ku (5793 3799/www.
numberniners.com). Ebisu station (Yamanote line),
east exit.* **Open** noon-8pm Mon-Wed, Fri, Sat;
11am–7pm Sun. **Credit** AmEx, DC, JCB, MC, V.

This grunge rock-inspired menswear brand has
proven a huge hit in Europe and the States, with its
Paris catwalk collections receiving rave reviews.
The Tokyo store is generally host to an array of
shoe-gazing young men with Kurt Cobain fixations.
Worth an angst-ridden browse.

Undercover

*Unimat Bleu Cinq Point Bldg, 5-3-18 Minami-
Aoyama, Minato-ku (3407 1232). Omotesando
station (Chiyoda, Ginza, Hanzomon lines), exit A5.*
Open 11am-8pm daily. **Credit** AmEx, DC, JCB, MC,
V. **Map** Harajuku & Aoyama p82.

Undercover designer Jun Takahashi commands a fanatically loyal army of punk fashion rebels who adore his edgy clothes. Enter his unsettling world at this store and experience the artistic side of his dark fashion empire at gallery-cum-store Zamiang in the basement. **Photo** *p194*.

Yohji Yamamoto

5-3-6 Minami-Aoyama, Minato-ku (3409 6006/ www.yohjiyamamoto.co.jp). Omotesando station (Chiyoda, Ginza, Hanzomon lines), exit A5. **Open** 11am-8pm daily. **Credit** AmEx, DC, JCB, MC, V. **Map** Harajuku & Aoyama p82.

Paragon of conceptual fashion Yohji Yamamoto remains hugely respected by style commentators worldwide. This store not only stocks the dark, billowing creations on which his reputation was founded, but also his sportswear collaboration with Adidas Y-3.

Designer: international

Steadily tumbling real-estate prices have allowed many European luxury brands to build impressive flagship stores in central Tokyo, enhancing the urban landscape with cutting-edge architectural marvels. The Ginza district has seen the recent addition of a Renzo Piano-designed glass building for **Hermès**, a flagship store for **Chanel** that uses a façade composed of hundreds of thousands of LEDs, and an eight-story edifice by **Gucci**, which also houses a café and modest art gallery.

On the 'brand boulevard' of Omotesando, architect Aoki Jun designed a fabulous flagship for **Louis Vuitton**, while trendy Japanese duo SANAA created a glass building for **Dior**. Most popular with tourists, however, is the stunning **Prada** (photo *p197*) building in Omotesando, designed by Swiss duo du jour Herzog & de Meuron.

Fashion accessories

Hats

CA4LA

6-29-4 Jingumae, Shibuya-ku (3406 8271/www. ca4la.com). Harajuku station (Yamanote line), Omotesando exit or Meiji-Jingumae station (Chiyoda line), exit 4. **Open** 11am-8pm daily. **Credit** AmEx, DC, JCB, MC, V. **Map** Harajuku & Aoyama p82.

Tokyo youths looking to stand out from the crowd head straight for Japan's trendiest hat-maker CA4LA (pronounced 'ka-shi-la'). The Harajuku flagship offers a vast selection of funky headgear – from woolly bobble hats to pink panamas. Prices are very reasonable.
Other locations: 4-7-5 Ueno, Taito-ku (5807 7237); 2F Cinderella City, Isetan Main Building, 3-14-1

Shinjuku, Shinjuku-ku (3351 8138); 1-18-2 Jinnan, Shibuya-ku (3770 5051); 17-5 Daikanyamacho, Shibuya-ku (5459 0085).

Override 9999

5-17-25 Jingumae, Shibuya-ku (5766 0575/www.ovr. jp). Harajuku station (Yamanote line), Omotesando exit or Meiji-Jingumae station (Chiyoda line), exit 4. **Open** 11am-8pm daily. **Credit** AmEx, DC, JCB, MC, V. **Map** Harajuku & Aoyama p82.

Eye-catching headgear, as worn by the young bucks prowling Harajuku.
Other locations: 6-29-3 Jingumae, Shibuya-ku (5467 0047); 7-5 Daikanyama-cho, Shibuya-ku (5428 5085).

Jewellery

Atelier Shinji

5-6-24 Minami-Aoyama, Minato-ku (3400 5211/ www.ateliershinji.com). Omotesando station (Chiyoda, Ginza, Hanzomon lines), exit A5. **Open** 11am-8pm Mon-Fri. **Credit** AmEx, DC, JCB, MC, V. **Map** Harajuku & Aoyama p82.

This small Aoyama shop, located behind the Spiral building (*see p239*), sells the original creations of noted jeweller Naoi Shinji.
Other locations: (factory store) 2-2-2 Iriya, Taito-ku (3872 7201).

Mikimoto

2-4-12 Ginza, Chuo-ku (3562 3130/www.mikimoto. com). Ginza station (Ginza, Hibiya, Marunouchi lines), exit A9. **Open** 11am-7pm daily. **Credit** AmEx, DC, JCB, MC, V. **Map** Ginza p75.

This second flagship store for cultured pearl brand Mikimoto was designed by Ito Toyo. Its amazing pink façade is a favourite with tourists. The expensive creations inside aren't.
Other locations: 4-5-5 Ginza, Chuo-ku (3535 4611).

NIWAKA

2-8-18 Ginza, Chuo-ku. (3564 0707/www.niwaka. com). Ginza station (Ginza, Hibiya, Marunouchi lines), exit A13. **Open** 11am-8pm daily. **Credit** AmEx, DC, JCB, MC, V. **Map** Ginza p75.

This store's elegant nature-inspired designs are created by a team of artisans in workshops in Kyoto. The sleek jewellery comes in platinum or white, pink or yellow gold, and there is also a made-to-order service allowing customers to design their own sparkling creation.
Other locations: 3-13-8 Minami Aoyama, Minato-ku (3796 0803).

Tasaki Shinju

5-7-5 Ginza, Chuo-ku (3289 1111/www.tasaki.co.jp). Ginza station (Ginza, Hibiya, Marunouchi lines), exit A2. **Open** 10.30am-7.30pm daily. **Credit** AmEx, DC, JCB, MC, V. **Map** Ginza p75.

The flagship Ginza shop is known (with good reason) as the Jewellery Tower. Each floor of this huge building is devoted to a particular jewellery theme; the museum on the fifth floor is also worth a look.
Other locations: throughout the city.

Gallery Samurai. *See p203.*

Shoes

ABC Mart

1-11-5 Jinnan, Shibuya-ku (3477 0602/www.abc-mart.com). Shibuya station (Yamanote, Ginza lines), Hachiko exit; (Hanzomon line), exits 6, 7. **Open** 11am-9pm daily. **Credit** AmEx, DC, JCB, MC, V. **Map** Shibuya p109.

An incredibly cheap and busy chain of shops selling brand-name footwear and sportswear with heavy discounts.

Other locations: throughout the city.

Ginza Kanematsu

6-9-9 Ginza, Chuo-ku (3573 0077/www.ginza-kanematsu.co.jp). Ginza station (Ginza, Hibiya, Marunouchi lines), exit A4. **Open** 11am-9pm Mon-Sat; 11am-8pm Sun. **Credit** AmEx, DC, JCB, MC, V. **Map** Ginza p75.

Stylish shoes for both men and women, available in sizes larger than the usual Japanese ones.

Other locations: throughout the city.

Food & drink

Department store food halls (*see p187* **Treats abound underground**) are also worth a look.

Confectionery

Wagashi – traditional Japanese sweets – originated in Kyoto and are steeped in culture. The *wagashi* most palatable to the Westerner's sweet tooth are *yokan* (thick jellied candies made from gelatin, sugar and adzuki beans), *monaka* (adzuki-bean paste sandwiched between two crisp wafers), *zangetsu* (ginger-flavoured round pancakes folded in half) and *wasanbon* (a luxury powdery sugar pressed into tablets). Products vary according to the season and most are meant to be eaten quickly, so ask how long they'll keep.

Akebono

5-7-19 Ginza, Chuo-ku (3571 3640/www.ginza-akebono.co.jp/top.html). Ginza station (Ginza, Hibiya, Marunouchi lines), exit A1. **Open** 9am-9pm Mon-Sat; 9am-8pm Sun. **Credit** AmEx, DC, JCB, MC, V. **Map** Ginza p75.

This small but lively shop's variety of traditional Japanese sweets is also available in the basement food halls of all Tokyo's major department stores (*see p187* **Treats abound underground**).

Other locations: throughout the city.

Kihachi Patisserie

Flags Bldg 3F, 3-37-1 Shinjuku, Shinjuku-ku (5366 6384/www.kihachi.co.jp). Shinjuku station (Yamanote, Chuo lines), east-south exit; (Marunouchi line), exits A7, A8; (Oedo, Shinjuku lines), exit 1. **Open** 11am-9pm daily. **Credit** AmEx, DC, JCB, MC, V. **Map** Shinjuku p117.

This popular store makes and sells highly original cakes. They are often a fusion of Western and Japanese elements, using ingredients such as green tea or chestnuts.

Other locations: throughout the city.

Kimuraya

4-5-7 Ginza, Chuo-ku (3561 0091/www.kimuraya-sohonten.co.jp). Ginza station (Ginza, Hibiya, Marunouchi lines), exits A9, B1. **Open** 10am-9.30pm daily. **No credit cards. Map** Ginza p75.

This venerable shop one door away from Wako is historically and culturally significant for being the first in Tokyo to sell *anpan* – bread rolls filled with adzuki-bean paste. Break up a Ginza shopping or sightseeing trip with a visit to Kimuraya and try them for yourself.

Other locations: throughout the city.

Toraya

4-9-22 Akasaka, Minato-ku (3408 4121/www.toraya-group.co.jp). Akasaka-Mitsuke station (Ginza, Marunouchi lines), exit A. **Open** 8.30am-8pm Mon-Fri; 8.30am-6pm Sat, Sun. **Credit** AmEx, DC, JCB, MC, V.

Eat, Drink, Shop

Kimono Arts Sunaga. *See p204.*

This highly distinguished shop provides *wagashi* to the Imperial Family. It has 70 branches throughout Japan, and one in Paris.
Other locations: throughout the city.

Imported food

If you're pining for some tastes from home, the shops below probably have what you're looking for – at about twice the price you're used to paying.

Kinokuniya International

3-11-13 Minami-Aoyama, Minato-ku (3409 1231/ www.e-kinokuniya.com). Omotesando station (Chiyoda, Ginza, Hanzomon lines), exit A3. **Open** 9.30am-8pm daily. **Credit** AmEx, DC, JCB, MC, V. **Map** Harajuku & Aoyama p82.
No relation to the Shinjuku bookstore of the same name, this is the best-known and most prestigious of Tokyo's foreign-food specialists. It also sells English-language newspapers, magazines and cards. The store is scheduled to move in 2008 to a different Aoyama location.
Other locations: throughout the city.

Meidi-ya

2-6-7 Ginza, Chuo-ku (3563 0221/www.meidi-ya-store.com). Ginza-Itchome station (Yurakucho line), exit 8. **Open** 10am-9pm Mon-Sat; 10am-8pm Sun. **Credit** AmEx, DC, JCB, MC, V. **Map** Ginza p75.
Meidi-ya boasts an attractive array of imported foods from all over the world and an impressive wine cellar. The store also holds regular themed fairs at discount prices.
Other locations: throughout the city.

National Azabu

4-5-2 Minami-Azabu, Minato-ku (3442 3181). Hiroo station (Hibiya line), exit 1. **Open** 9.30am-8pm daily. **Credit** AmEx, DC, JCB, MC, V.
This Hiroo supermarket has a long history of serving the international community with imported groceries galore. It's known for its vast and impressive cheese selection. There's also a bookstore and stationery shop on the second floor.

Nissin

2-34-2 Higashi-Azabu, Minato-ku (3583 4586). Azabu-Juban station (Nanboku line), exit 3; (Oedo line), exit 6. **Open** 9am-9pm daily. **Credit** AmEx, DC, JCB, MC, V.
This huge outlet in Azabu-Juban specialises in imported meat – rabbit, kangaroo, pheasant and lots of sausages – but also sells a wide range of imported groceries. The third-floor wine department is very good.

Yamaya

3-2-7 Nishi-Shinjuku, Shinjuku-ku (3342 0601/ www.yamaya.jp). Shinjuku station (Yamanote, Chuo lines), south exit; (Marunouchi line), exits A16, A17; (Oedo, Shinjuku lines), exit 6. **Open** 10am-10pm daily. **Credit** AmEx, DC, JCB, MC, V. **Map** Shinjuku p117.

A medium-sized foreign-food and booze specialist with one unique feature for Tokyo: it's cheap. It has a vast selection of imported wines priced from a budget-beating ¥280, along with inexpensive cheeses and snack foods. Delivery of large orders within the 23 wards of central Tokyo costs ¥500. **Other locations**: throughout the city.

Japanese tea

Green tea is good for you. Catechin, the ingredient responsible for the bitter taste, is known to kill bacteria that can cause food poisoning. It's also thought to reduce the risk of cancer, prevent the build-up of cholesterol and even make your breath smell sweeter. For places to drink it, *see p185* **Drink your greens**.

Yamamoto Yama

2-5-2 Nihonbashi, Chuo-ku (3281 0010/www. yamamotoyama.co.jp). Nihonbashi station (Asakusa line), exit D3; (Ginza, Tozai lines), exit B4. **Open** 9.30am-7pm daily. **Credit** AmEx, DC, JCB, MC, V. **Map** Marunouchi p93.
Sells a wide selection of Japanese and Chinese teas and implements for *sado*, the tea ceremony.
Other locations: throughout the city.

Sake

There are many different types of Japan's rice spirit, depending on location, brewing method, amount of rice polished away and quantity of distilled alcohol added. The broad categories are *amakuchi* (sweet sake) and *karakuchi* (dry sake). In addition, some varieties are meant to be heated and served in a special ceramic jug (*tokkuri*). Premium brands of rice wine known as *jizake* are more expensive and highly sought after by connoisseurs. Sake shops can be found in the basements of most department stores. *See p188* **Treats abound underground**.

Shinanoya

1-12-9 Kabuki-cho, Shinjuku-ku (3204 2365/www. shinanoya.co.jp). Shinjuku station (Yamanote, Chuo lines), east exit; (Marunouchi line), exit B12; (Oedo, Shinjuku lines), exit 1. **Open** 11am-4am Mon-Sat; 11am-9pm Sun. **Credit** MC, V.
Sake and whisky from all over Japan, plus hundreds of single malt Scotches at prices cheaper than in the UK. There's also a small selection of foreign foods and snacks, and several imported beers.
Other locations: Daida Wine House, 1-42-1 Daida, Setagaya-ku (3412 2418); 8-6-22 Ginza, Chuo-ku (3571 3315).

Suzuden

1-10 Yotsuya, Shinjuku-ku (3351 1777). Yotsuya station (Chuo, Sobu lines), Yotsuya exit; (Marunouchi line), exit 1; (Nanboku line), exit 2. **Open** 9am-9pm Mon-Fri; 9am-6pm Sat. **Credit** AmEx, DC, JCB, MC, V.

A homely shop offering a wide selection of rare sake brands, with an area set aside for tasting.

Gift & craft shops

Many department stores sell kimonos, ceramics, chopsticks and other traditional souvenirs, while some of the shopping streets (*see pp192-194*) – notably **Nakamise Dori** and **Kappabashi**, both in Asakusa – are great for gifts. *See also p208* **Novelties & toys**.

Bingo-Ya

10-6 Wakamatsu-cho, Shinjuku-ku (3202 8778/ www.quasar.nu/bingoya). Wakamatsu-Kawada station (Oedo line), Kawada exit. **Open** 10am-7pm Tue-Sun. **Credit** AmEx, DC, JCB, MC, V.
Six floors of handmade traditional crafts, including pottery, fabrics, bamboo, lacquerware, glassware, dolls and folk art.

Ebisu-Do Gallery

Kamesawa Bldg 2F, 1-12 Kanda-Jinbocho, Chiyoda-ku (3219 7651/www.ebisu-do.com). Jinbocho station (Hanzomon, Mita, Shinjuku lines), exit A5. **Open** 11am-6.30pm Mon-Sat. **Credit** AmEx, DC, JCB, MC, V. **Map** Marunouchi p93.
Here you can buy original *ukiyo-e* prints (from around ¥20,000) and reproductions (from ¥3,000) by masters such as Hiroshige, Hokusai and Harunobu.

Fuji Torii

6-1-10 Jingumae, Shibuya-ku (3400 2777/www. fuji-torii.com). Harajuku station (Yamanote line), Omotesando exit or Meiji-Jingumae station (Chiyoda line), exit 4 or Omotesando station (Chiyoda, Ginza, Hanzomon lines), exit A1. **Open** 11am-6pm Mon, Wed-Sun. Closed 3rd Mon of mth. **Credit** AmEx, DC, JCB, MC, V. **Map** Harajuku & Aoyama p82.
Fuji Torii sells a wide variety of Japanese antiques (screens, ceramics, sculptures), as well as designing and selling its own original artwork and crafts.

Gallery Samurai

Aoyama TIM Bldg 3F, 3-13-20 Minami-Aoyama, Minato-ku (5474 6336/www.nihonto.co.jp). Omotesando station (Chiyoda, Ginza, Hanzomon lines), exits A3, A4. **Open** 11am-7pm daily. **Credit** AmEx, DC, JCB, MC, V. **Map** Harajuku & Aoyama p82.
A small shop in the heart of Aoyama, crowded with antique swords, guns, armour and helmets, not to mention screens, statues, woodblock prints and less classifiable curios. Staff speak fluent English. **Photo** *p201*.

Ginza Natsuno

6-7-4 Ginza, Chuo-ku (3569 0952/www.e-ohashi. com/natsuno/index.html). Ginza station (Ginza, Hibiya, Marunouchi lines), exit A5. **Open** 10am-8pm Mon-Sat; 10am-7pm Sun. **Credit** AmEx, DC, JCB, MC, V. **Map** Ginza p75.
Japanese chopsticks make affordable and easily portable souvenirs, so make a beeline for this shop and its amazing, eclectic collection. Ginza

Eat, Drink, Shop

Natsuno's premises are small, but there's a good array of stock and plenty to choose from.
Other locations: 4-2-17 Jingumae, Shibuya-ku (5785 4721).

Hara Shobo

2-3 Kanda-Jinbocho, Chiyoda-ku (5212 7801/www. harashobo.com). Jinbocho station (Hanzomon, Mita, Shinjuku lines), exit A6. **Open** 10am-6pm Tue-Sat. **Credit** AmEx, DC, JCB, MC, V. **Map** Marunouchi p93.

Hara Shobo sells all kinds of woodblock prints, both old and new. The company issues a catalogue, *Edo Geijitsu* ('Edo Art'), twice a year. The staff speak good English.

Ito-ya

2-7-15 Ginza, Chuo-ku (3561 8311/www.ito-ya.co.jp). Ginza station (Ginza, Hibiya, Marunouchi lines), exit A13. **Open** 10am-7pm Mon-Sat; 10.30am-7pm Sun. **Credit** AmEx, DC, JCB, MC, V. **Map** Ginza p75.

This huge, very busy store in Ginza specialises in Japanese paper. The main shop (Ito-ya 1 Bldg) sells conventional stationery and calligraphic tools, while the annex (Ito-ya 3 Bldg) – directly behind it and reached by walking through the main store – has origami, traditional handmade paper (*washi*), writing paper and ink.

Japan Traditional Craft Center

Metropolitan Plaza 1F-2F, 1-11-1 Nishi-Ikebukuro, Toshima-ku (5954 6066/www.kougei.or.jp/english/center.html). Ikebukuro station (Yamanote line), Metropolitan exit; (Marunouchi, Yurakucho lines), exit 3. **Open** 11am-7pm daily (11am-5pm every other Tue; closed occasional Wed). **Credit** AmEx, MC, V. **Map** Ikebukuro p87.

This organisation was founded with the aim of promoting awareness of Japan's traditional crafts. Learn about, then shop for, a broad cross-section of crafts (lacquer, ceramics, paper, kimonos, knives, textiles, stonework, household Buddhist altars and so on) at this showroom-cum-museum. There are permanent and temporary exhibitions, a reference library and even classes. The gift shop sells the work of craftspeople (who sometimes give demonstrations) from across the country.

Kimono Arts Sunaga

2-1-8 Azabu-Juban, Minato-ku (3457 0323). Azabu-Juban station (Oedo, Nanboku lines), exit 4. **Open** 11am-8pm Wed-Mon. **Credit** AmEx, DC, JCB, MC, V.

A friendly store offering tailor-made kimonos, as well as ready-to-wear versions, and a range of crafts and ornaments made from recycled kimono material. **Photo** *p202.*

Kyukyodo

5-7-4 Ginza (3571 4429/www.kyukyodo.co.jp). Ginza station (Ginza, Hibiya, Marunouchi lines), exit A2. **Open** 10am-7.30pm Mon-Sat; 11am-7pm Sun. **Credit** AmEx, DC, JCB, MC, V. **Map** Ginza p75.

Another Japanese paper specialist, Kyukyodo opened its first shop in Kyoto in 1663 and supplied incense to the Imperial Palace during the Edo period.

Still run by the Kumagai family that founded it, the shop moved to Ginza, with its distinctive arched brick entrance, in 1880. This branch in Ginza, with its distinctive arched brick entrance, still sells incense, alongside a selection of seasonal gift cards and lots of small, moderately priced items (boxes, notebooks, picture frames) made from colourful *washi*.
Other locations: 2-24-1 Shibuya, Shibuya-ku (3477 3111); 1-1-25 Nishi-Ikebukuro, Toshima-ku (3981 2211).

Noritake Shop Akasaka

7-8-5 Akasaka, Minato-ku (3586 0059/www. noritake.co.jp/tableware). Akasaka station (Chiyoda line), exit 7. **Open** 10am-6pm Mon-Fri. **Credit** AmEx, DC, JCB, MC, V.

Noritake is the name of one of Japan's oldest and most distinctive forms of pottery and china, and this is its flagship store.

Oriental Bazaar

5-9-13 Jingumae, Shibuya-ku (3400 3933). Harajuku station (Yamanote line), Omotesando exit or Meiji-Jingumae station (Chiyoda line), exit 4 or Omotesando station (Chiyoda, Ginza, Hanzomon lines), exit A1. **Open** 10am-7pm Mon-Wed, Fri-Sun. **Credit** (over ¥2,000) AmEx, DC, JCB, MC, V. **Map** Harajuku & Aoyama p82.

Probably the best-known gift shop in Tokyo, this is a useful one-stop outlet for almost everything: dolls, china, kimonos, *yukata*, woodblock prints, furniture, antiques and books on Japan. Ideal for stocking up on presents and souvenirs in one easy trip. Prices are generally moderate, and staff speak good English.
Other locations: No.1 Terminal Building 4F, Narita Airport (0476 329 333).

Sagemonoya

Palais Eternal Bldg 702 & 703, 4-28-20 Yotsuya, Shinjuku-ku (3352 6286/www.netsuke.com). Shinjuku-Gyoenmae station (Marunouchi line), Ookidomon exit or Yotsuya-Sanchome station (Marunouchi line), exits 1, 2. **Open** 1.30-6pm Wed-Sat or by appointment. **Credit** AmEx, DC, JCB, MC, V.

Sagemonoya specialises in *netsuke* and *sagemono* – the tiny, ornate accessories designed to hang from the belt of a kimono to hold tobacco, medicines and other small objects. This shop holds hundreds of collectibles, and staff can answer enquiries in English, French or German.

Tanagokoro

1-8-15 Ginza, Chuo-ku (3538 6555/www.tanagokoro. com). Ginza-Itchome station (Yurakucho line), exits 7, 9. **Open** 11am-8pm Mon-Fri; 11am-7pm Sat, Sun. **Credit** AmEx, DC, JCB, MC, V. **Map** Ginza p75.

Binchotan, a highly refined form of Japanese charcoal, has the power to purify, dehumidify and deodorise the air of a room it's placed in. This shop, whose name means 'palm of the hand', sells products made from *binchotan*. Shoppers can also indulge in the curative powers of *binchotan*'s fragrance in the basement healing room.

Find action figures, *anime* and kitsch galore at **Mandarake**. *See p209.*

See p209.

Health & beauty

Beauty salons

Boudoir

Mansion Kawai 101, 2-25-3 Jingumae, Shibuya-ku (3478 5898/www.boudoirtokyo.com). Harajuku station (Yamanote line), Takeshita exit or Meiji-Jingumae station (Chiyoda line), exit 5. **Open** 10am-8.30pm Mon-Fri; 10am-8pm Sat; 10am-6pm Sun. **Credit** AmEx, DC, JCB, MC, V. **Map** Harajuku & Aoyama p82.

Boudoir's mostly non-Japanese beauticians offer a full range of beauty treatments, including massages, facials, manicures, waxing and relaxation therapy.

Jennifer Hair & Beauty International

Roppongi Hills West Walk 6F, 6-10-1 Roppongi, Minato-ku (5770 3611). Roppongi station (Hibiya line), exit 1C; (Oedo line), exit 4. **Open** 10am-9pm daily. **Credit** AmEx, DC, JCB, MC, V. **Map** Roppongi p103.

Extensive hair, make-up and nail services, plus massages and relaxing treatments. The salon uses Kérastase products from Paris.

Nail Bee

Keitoku Bldg 3F, 3-3-14 Ginza, Chuo-ku (5250 0018/www.nailbee.com). Ginza station (Ginza, Hibiya, Marunouchi lines), exit C8. **Open** 11am-8pm daily. **Credit** AmEx, DC, JCB, MC, V. **Map** Ginza p75.

Tokyo's leading nail salon has been serving the international community's beauty needs for over a decade. In addition to manicures and nail art, Nail Bee offers facials, massages, waxing, pedicures and eyelash perms.

Other locations: Minochi Bldg 4F, 3-11-8 Roppongi, Minato-ku (3470 9665); Marui-City Shibuya Bldg 3F, 1-21-3 Jinnan, Shibuya-ku (5458 0026).

Cosmetics

Japan's three biggest cosmetics companies – **Kanebo** (www.kanebo.com), **Shiseido** (www.shiseido.co.jp) and **Shu Uemura** (www.shu-uemura.com) – are known and respected across the globe. Their products can be found in stand-alone shops as well as on the shelves of department stores throughout Tokyo and Japan.

Bizarre bazaar **ranKing ranQueen**. *See p209.*

Aizu Tulpe

1-13-14 Jingumae, Shibuya-ku (5775 0561).
Harajuku station (Yamanote line), Meiji-Jingumae
exit or Meiji-Jingumae station (Chiyoda line), exit 3.
Open 9am-11pm daily. **Credit** AmEx, DC, JCB, MC,
V. **Map** Harajuku & Aoyama p82.

Aizu is a boon for late-night shoppers and a bedazzling introduction to the fascinating world of Japanese cosmetics and medicine. The two floors are filled with every conceivable kind of beauty and health product.
Other locations: Seibu 7F, 1-28-1 Minami-Ikebukuro, Toshima-ku (5949 2745).

Kampo Boutique Aoyama

3-3-13 Minami-Aoyama, Minato-ku (5775 6932/
www.nihondo.co.jp). Omotesando station (Chiyoda,
Ginza, Hanzomon lines), exit A4. **Open** 10am-7pm
daily. **Credit** AmEx, DC, JCB, MC, V. **Map** Harajuku
& Aoyama p82.

This shop is the brainchild of the Nihondo corporation and employs the *kampo* (traditional Chinese medicine) method of product development. It sells a wide range of products, including natural cosmetics, health foods and herbal teas.
Other locations: throughout the city.

Hairdressers

Peek-a-Boo Ext

4-3-15 Jingumae, Shibuya-ku (5411 0848/www.peek-
a-boo.co.jp). Omotesando station (Chiyoda, Ginza,
Hanzomon lines), exit A2. **Open** 10am-10pm Tue-
Fri; 10am-9pm Sat; 10am-7.30pm Sun. **Credit** AmEx,
DC, JCB, MC, V. **Map** Harajuku & Aoyama p82.

This stylish chain of unisex salons has been an indispensable feature of Tokyo's style centre Aoyama since 1978. All forms of hair treatment are available here.
Other locations: throughout Harajuku and Aoyama.

Serendipity

Powerhouse Bldg B2F, 7-12-3 Roppongi, Minato-ku
(5414 1717). Nogizaka station (Chiyoda line), exit 3
or Roppongi station (Oedo line), exit 7; (Hibiya line),
exit 4A. **Open** noon-4am Mon-Sat; noon-8pm Sun.
Credit AmEx, DC, JCB, MC, V. **Map** Roppongi p103.

As well as reasonable prices, this hair salon near Roppongi has a unique selling point: it's open until 4am six days a week.

Who-Ga

Akasaka Kyo Bldg 1F, 2-16-13 Akasaka, Minato-ku
(5570 1773/www.who-ga-newyork.com). Akasaka
station (Chiyoda line), exits 5A, 5B. **Open** 11am-9pm
Mon, Wed-Fri; 10am-7pm Sat, Sun. **Credit** AmEx,
DC, JCB, MC, V.

The helpful, bilingual staff here all trained at Who-Ga's sister salon in New York. There's a popular membership system available for female customers; privileges include discounts for haircuts, perms and colouring services, along with further price reductions if reservations are made at least one week in advance.

Opticians

In recent years Tokyo has seen an increase
in shops/opticians that specialise in selling
stylish, up-to-the-minute eyewear at discount
prices. This development is due to a combination
of a deflationary economy and a self-conscious,
short-sighted nation keen to embrace
a new trend. Eye tests are often free.

fxg (Face By Glasses)

*2-35-14 Kitazawa, Setagaya-ku (5790 8027/www.
fxg.co.jp). Shimo-Kitazawa station (Keio Inokashira,
Odakyu lines), north exit.* **Open** 11am-8pm daily.
Credit AmEx, DC, JCB, MC, V.

Hatch

*2-5-8 Dogenzaka, Shibuya-ku (5784 3888/www.e-
hatch.jp). Shibuya station (Yamanote, Ginza lines),
Hachiko exit; (Hanzomon line), exits 2, 4.* **Open**
11am-8pm daily. **Credit** AmEx, DC, JCB, MC, V.
Map Shibuya p109.
Other locations: throughout the city.

Zoff

*Mark City 4F, 1-12-5 Dogenzaka, Shibuya-ku (5428
3961/www.zoff.co.jp). Shibuya station (Yamanote,
Ginza lines), Hachiko exit; (Hanzomon line), exits 5,
8.* **Open** 10am-9pm daily. **Credit** AmEx, DC, JCB,
MC, V. **Map** Shibuya p109.
Other locations: throughout the city.

Pharmacies

Basic items, such as sanitary towels, condoms
or sticking plasters can be purchased at any
convenience store (these are usually open
24 hours daily), however few are permitted
to sell pharmaceuticals.

The following pharmacies all have English-
speaking staff (except Roppongi Pharmacy,
which does, however, have a late-night service,
until 1am daily). Under Japanese law, Western
medicines are not generally available, but
pharmacy staff can help to find the best
possible Japanese equivalent. For emergency
medical information, *see p306.*

American Pharmacy

*Marunouchi Bldg B1F, 2-4-1 Marunouchi, Chiyoda-
ku (5220 7716/www.tomods.jp/). Tokyo station
(Yamanote, Chuo lines), Shin Marubiru, south
exits; (Marunouchi line), Marunouchi Bldg exit.*
Open 9am-9pm Mon-Fri; 10am-9pm Sat;
10am-8pm Sun. **Credit** AmEx, DC, JCB, MC, V.
Map Marunouchi p93.

Koyasu Drug Store Hotel Okura

*Hotel Okura Main Bldg B1F, 2-10-4 Toranomon,
Minato-ku (3583 7958). Roppongi-Itchome station
(Nanboku line), exit 3.* **Open** 8.30am-9pm Mon-Sat;
10am-9pm Sun. **Credit** AmEx, DC, MC, V. **Map**
Roppongi p103.

Eat, Drink, Shop

Local view Cornelius

In Setagaya ward, where I'm from, there's a
record shop called **Fujiyama**. The place is so
strange; it's open all hours, even if you go
there in the middle of the night. It's run by
just one person, and all that's on offer is
self-produced indie stuff. He's got so many
cassette tapes, but all just indie bands.

It's a place that looks like it should've
closed years ago, but it's been going since
the '80s and is just a weird shop that has
stuff you'd never find anywhere else. Whenever
someone comes to visit me, I think about
taking them there. It's so unique.

Fujiyama

*2-35-2 Shimouma, Setagaya-ku (3795 7595).
Sangenjaya station (Tokyu Denentoshi line).*
Open Tue-Sun (hours as per owner's whim).

*Tokyo native Keigo Oyamada found national
fame as a member of Shibuya-kei pop duo
Flipper's Guitar, before adopting the moniker
Cornelius and becoming one of Japan's most
eminent experimental musicians.*

Roppongi Pharmacy

6-8-8 Roppongi, Minato-ku (3403 8879). Roppongi station (Hibiya, Oedo lines), exit 3. **Open** 10am-1am daily. Closed 2nd Sun of mth. **No credit cards.** **Map** Roppongi p103.

Tattooing

Inkrat Tattoo

Linebuild Koenji 201, 4-27-7 Koenji-Minami, Suginami-ku (3317 0252/www.inkrattattoo.com). Koenji station (Chuo line), south exit. **Open** noon-8pm daily. **Credit** AmEx, DC, JCB, MC, V.

If you're after a tattoo and interested in traditional Japanese designs or *kanji* Chinese characters, try Inkrat. It has a number of expert Japanese artists available, and non-Japanese 'guest' artists frequently do shows and residencies at the studio.

Home & garden

The best place for interior shopping of all styles is the thoroughly inconvenient **Meguro Dori** (*see p192*). For more central options, see below.

Franc Franc

Shinjuku Southern Terrace, 2-2-1 Yoyogi, Shibuya-ku (5333 7701/www.francfranc.com). Shinjuku station (Yamanote, Chuo, Marunouchi lines), south exit; (Oedo, Shinjuku lines), exit A1. **Open** 11am-10pm daily. **Credit** AmEx, DC, JCB, MC, V. **Map** Shinjuku p117.

A popular and reasonably priced interiors shop, with a wide range of candles, incense, lamps, bathroom goods and furniture. It also has its own brand of compilation CDs, catering to the massive market for bossa nova music.

Other locations: throughout the city.

Mujirushi Ryohin

3-8-3 Marunouchi, Chiyoda-ku (5208 8241/www.muji.net). Yurakucho station (Yamanote line), Kyobashi exit; (Yurakucho line), exit A9. **Open** 10am-9pm daily. **Credit** AmEx, DC, JCB, MC, V. **Map** Ginza p75.

The shop better known as Muji – the original no-brand designer brand. This is the biggest Tokyo outlet of the all-purpose, one-stop store that went on to conquer London and Paris.

Other locations: throughout the city.

Three Minutes Happiness

3-5 Udagawa-cho, Shibuya-ku (5459 1851). Shibuya station (Yamanote, Ginza lines), Hachiko exit; (Hanzomon line), exits 6, 7. **Open** 11am-9pm daily. **Credit** AmEx, DC, JCB, MC, V. **Map** Shibuya p109.

Think of this as a high-class 100-yen shop, selling a large and eclectic mix of original household goods, most costing less than ¥1,000. It's owned by the Comme Ça fashion chain.

Tokyu Hands

12-18 Udagawa-cho, Shibuya-ku (5489 5111/www.tokyu-hands.co.jp). Shibuya station (Yamanote, Ginza lines), Hachiko exit; (Hanzomon line), exits 6, 7.

Open 10am-8.30pm daily. **Credit** AmEx, DC, JCB, MC, V. **Map** Shibuya p109.

From stationery to toilet-seat covers, this is the largest household goods store in Tokyo, packed with knick-knacks for the home. Particularly interesting is the party supplies section, which gives a unique glimpse into the Japanese sense of humour. It can be difficult to find your way around the multitude of floors.

Other locations: 1-28-10 Higashi-Ikebukuro, Toshima-ku (3980 6111).

Novelties & toys

BørneLund

Hara Bldg 1F, 6-10-9 Jingumae, Shibuya-ku (5485 3430/www.bornelund.co.jp). Harajuku station, (Yamanote line), Omotesando exit or Meiji-Jingumae station (Chiyoda line), exit 4. **Open** 11am-7.30pm daily. **Credit** AmEx, DC, JCB, MC, V. **Map** Harajuku & Aoyama p82.

No electric or 'character' toys are sold at this small shop near Omotesando, which specialises in imported wooden toys. You can touch and play with most of the items on display. Sofas and nursing/nappy-changing facilities are also provided.

Don Quixote

1-16-5 Kabuki-cho, Shinjuku-ku (5291 9211/www.donki.com). Shinjuku station (Yamanote, Chuo lines), east exit; (Marunouchi line), exits B12, B13; (Oedo, Shinjuku lines), exit B9. **Open** 24hrs daily. **No credit cards.** **Map** Shinjuku p117.

Pile 'em high, sell 'em cheap taken to the extreme. The aisles and shelves are cluttered, disorganized and disorientating. But you'll find everything from snacks to washing machines, if you look hard enough.

Other locations: throughout the city.

Hakuhinkan

8-8-11 Ginza, Chuo-ku (3571 8008/www.hakuhinkan.co.jp). Shinbashi station (Yamanote line), Ginza exit; (Asakusa line), exit A3; (Ginza line), exit 1. **Open** 11am-8pm daily. **Credit** AmEx, JCB, MC, V. **Map** Ginza p75.

This multi-storey emporium in Ginza, one of Tokyo's biggest toy shops, is a showcase for the wacky, the cuddly and the cute, all with a Japanese twist. The basement is the headquarters of the Licca-chan Club (the Japanese equivalent of Barbie). There is a tax-exemption counter on the fourth floor.

Kiddyland

6-1-9 Jingumae, Shibuya-ku (3409 3431/www.kiddyland.co.jp). Harajuku station (Yamanote line), Omotesando exit or Meiji-Jingumae station (Chiyoda line), exit 4. **Open** 10am-9pm daily. Closed 3rd Tue of mth. **Credit** AmEx, DC, JCB, MC, V. **Map** Harajuku & Aoyama p82.

Kiddyland is a Tokyo institution. The main Harajuku shop is a noisy, heaving maze of mascots, dolls, cuddly toys, furry toys, action figures, Disney, Kitty, Doraemon, Godzilla and more. Warning: this much cuteness can damage your mental health.

Other locations: throughout the city.

Hours of listening pleasure await at **Technique**. *See p210.*

Mandarake

5-52-15 Nakano, Nakano-ku (3228 0007/www.
mandarake.co.jp). Nakano station (Chuo, Tozai
lines), north exit. **Open** noon-8pm daily. **Credit**
AmEx, DC, JCB, MC, V.

Mandarake (pronounced 'Mandala-K') is the place
to go for action figures related to obscure Japanese
anime, retro US toys from the 1960s and '70s,
manga, *dojinshi* (fanzines) and any kind of kitsch
weirdness you care to name. It has numerous outlets in the Broadway shopping centre. The Shibuya
branch is almost as vast. **Photo** *p205.*
Other locations: throughout the city.

Pokemon Center

3-2-5 Nihonbashi, Chuo-ku (5200 0707/www.
pokemoncenter-online.com). Nihonbashi station
(Asakusa line), exit D3; (Ginza, Tozai lines), exits B1,
B2 or Tokyo station (Yamanote, Chuo, Marunouchi
lines), Yaesu (north) exit. **Open** 10am-7pm daily.
Credit AmEx, DC, JCB, MC, V. **Map** Marunouchi p93.
'Pocket Monster' may have lost ground to Yu-Gi-Oh!
and a variety of other games, but Pikachu's furry
yellow paw still has an iron grip on Japanese pop
culture. Come and see the monster-masters in their
central Tokyo stronghold.

ranKing ranQueen

West Bldg 2F, Tokyu Department Toyoko branch,
2-24-1 Shibuya, Shibuya-ku (3770 5480/www.
ranking-ranqueen.net). Shibuya station (Yamanote,
Ginza lines), Hachiko exit; (Hanzomon line), exits 3,
3A. **Open** 10am-11.30pm daily. **Credit** AmEx, DC,
JCB, MC, V. **Map** Shibuya p109.
The Japanese are obsessed with making lists and
charts of what's popular, which they call 'rankings'
– hence the puns in this shop's name. At ranKing,
ranQueen, a shop inside Shibuya JR station, you'll
find the top ten products for CDs, cosmetics, dieting aids, magazines and so on. It's an intriguing
insight into the mind of the Japanese consumer.
Photo *p210.*
Other locations: Shinjuku station, east exit (5919
1263); Jiyuugaoka station, central exit (3718 8890).

Records & CDs

HMV (www.hmv.co.jp) and **Tower Records**
(www.towerrecords.co.jp) have various
branches in Tokyo; the Shibuya outlet of
Tower (1-22-14 Jinnan, Shibuya-ku, 3496 3661)
is a favourite with expats, partly because it's
got one of the city's best foreign bookshops,
selling magazines and newspapers that are
unavailable elsewhere. Whatever your musical
preference, Tokyo has a shop, or shops, that
will cater to it. And the city is definitely a
vinyl lover's heaven. There are specialist
stores selling endless rarities, bootlegs and
classic discs, and all genres are represented.
Rock fans should head to the alleyways off
Otakibashi Dori, a short walk from Shinjuku

station's west exit. For hip hop, house or techno, try Shibuya; while, away from the centre, Shimo-Kitazawa is rich in quirky stores hawking more obscure offerings.

For new releases, domestic CDs are actually more expensive than foreign ones; thus it's possible to buy imported, big-name CDs for ¥1,500 to ¥2,500, while albums produced by Japanese artists usually sell for something in the region of ¥3,000.

Cisco

11-1 Udagawa-cho, Shibuya-ku (3462 0366/www. cisco-records.co.jp). Shibuya station (Yamanote, Ginza lines), Hachiko exit; (Hanzomon line), exits 3, 6. **Open** noon-10pm Mon-Sat; 11am-9pm Sun. **Credit** AmEx, DC, JCB, MC, V. **Map** Shibuya p109.
Cisco is at the cutting edge of dance music. Its Shibuya branch comprises five buildings close to one another, divided according to sub-genre. This is the place to come to see well-known DJs holding earnest discussions with shop owners across the in-store turntables.

Dance Music Record

36-2 Udagawa-cho, Shibuya-ku (3477 1556/ www.dmr.co.jp). Shibuya station (Yamanote, Ginza lines), Hachiko exit; (Hanzomon line), exits 3, 6. **Open** noon-10pm daily. **Credit** AmEx, DC, JCB, MC, V. **Map** Shibuya p109.
Dance Music Record is the name and dance-music records are the game. The first floor is a wide, open space with a comprehensive collection of the latest vinyl releases, both domestic and international. House and hip hop dominate the shelves, but it's also great for jazz re-releases, loungecore and R&B.

Disk Union

3-31-4 Shinjuku, Shinjuku-ku (3352 2691/www. diskunion.co.jp/top.html). Shinjuku station (Yamanote, Chuo lines), east, central exits; (Marunouchi line), exit A6; (Oedo, Shinjuku lines), exit 1. **Open** 11am-9pm Mon-Sat; 11am-8pm Sun. **Credit** AmEx, DC, JCB, MC, V. **Map** Shinjuku p117.
Stocking thousands of items, Disk Union deals mainly in second-hand CDs and vinyl. The Shinjuku main store is a tall, narrow building where each floor is devoted to a different genre, including world music, soundtracks and electronica. Branches nearby specialise in dance music, jazz, funk, punk and that much-maligned genre, progressive rock.
Other locations: throughout the city.

Dub Store

7-13-5 Nishi Shinjuku, Shinjuku-ku (5348 2180). Shinjuku station (Yamanote, Chuo lines), west exit; (Marunouchi line), exits A16, A17; (Shinjuku line), exit 3 or Shinjuku-Nishiguchi station (Oedo line), exit D1. **Open** noon-9pm daily. **Credit** AmEx, JCB, MC, V. **Map** Shinjuku p117.
This is Tokyo's best reggae store, with every conceivable genre of reggae and ska on original vinyl. The stock is expertly and meticulously categorised, and customers are welcome to listen to any of it.

Recofan

Shibuya Beam 4F, 31-2 Udagawa-cho, Shibuya-ku (3463 0090/www.recofan.co.jp). Shibuya station (Yamanote, Ginza lines), Hachiko exit; (Hanzomon line), exit 3A. **Open** 11.30am-9pm daily. **Credit** AmEx, DC, JCB, MC, V. **Map** Shibuya p109.
Recofan has a policy of selling new releases at bargain basement rates – in some cases, half the retail price. Each branch also has an extensive selection of second-hand CDs covering all genres. Regular shoppers receive a loyalty card that gives them even bigger discounts.
Other locations: throughout the city.

Technique

33-14 Udagawacho, Shibuya-ku (3464 7690/www. technique.co.jp). Shibuya station (Yamanote, Ginza lines), Hachiko exit; (Hanzomon line), exits 3, 6. **Open** 1-11pm daily. **Credit** AmEx, DC, JCB, MC, V. **Map** Shibuya p109.
Technique is the purveyor of all strands of dance-music vinyl – from progressive house to nu-jazz. Several listening decks and knowledgeable staff make this store of choice for many local DJs. **Photo** *p209.*

Sports

Tokyo's high-street shops and department stores are the places to head for most mainstream brands of sportswear and equipment. In addition, Yasukuni Dori, near Ochanomizu station on the Chuo line, is lined with outlets specialising in quality ski and snowboard gear.

Oshmans

1-14-29 Jingumae, Shibuya-ku (3478 4888/ www.oshmans.co.jp). Harajuku station (Yamanote line), Omotesando exit or Meiji-Jingumae station (Chiyoda line), exit 2. **Open** 10.30am-9.30pm daily. **Credit** AmEx, DC, JCB, MC. V. **Map** Harajuku & Aoyama p82.
Stockist of sports equipment galore, plus kit by Patagonia, Gramicci, Merrell, Maxim and many other brands.
Other locations: throughout the city.

Travel agents

No.1 Travel

Don Quixote Bldg 7F, 1-16-5 Kabuki-cho, Shinjuku-ku (3200 8871/www.no1-travel.com). Shinjuku station (Yamanote, Chuo lines), east exit; (Marunouchi line), exit B13 or Shinjuku-Nishiguchi station (Oedo line), exit D1. **Open** 10am-6.30pm Mon-Fri; 11am-4.30pm Sat. **Credit** AmEx, DC, JCB, MC. V. **Map** Shinjuku p117.
No.1 has been in business for 20 years and specialises in last-minute, discounted tickets. The helpful and knowledgeable staff speak a number of European and Asian languages.
Other locations: throughout the city.

Arts & Entertainment

Festivals & Events

Time to let your hair down.

Join the crowds for **Sanja**, Tokyo's largest annual festival. *See p213*.

With four distinct seasons, three religions, and three major breweries, Japan is awash with festivals. And Tokyo is no exception; in the capital barely a weekend goes by without some sort of cultural happening or celebration. Below we list the highlights of the annual calendar, but there are plenty of other festivities in between; contact the tourist offices (*see p313*) for more info on what's happening when you're in town.

The two big holiday periods are **Golden Week** (29 April to 5 May) and **New Year** (28 December to 4 January). The former contains three public holidays (Greenery Day, Constitution Day and Children's Day); people flee the city en masse, then all head home again at the same time. Tokyo remains relatively quiet, with many smaller shops and restaurants shut for the duration. Avoid travelling at this time, as prices increase and accommodation vacancies throughout Japan decrease. There's a similar problem at New Year, when many attractions, museums, shops and businesses shut until 5 January.

For information on Tokyo's climate and details of the dates of Japan's 14 official public holidays, *see p314*.

Spring

Fire-Walking Ceremony (Hi-watari)
0426 61 1115/www.takaotozan.co.jp. Kotsu Anzen Kitosho, near Takaosan-guchi station (Keio line).
Date 2nd Sun in Mar.
At the foot of Mt Takao, *yamabushi* (hard-core mountain monks) from Yakuoin Temple walk barefoot across burning coals while chanting incantations. Brave members of the public are then invited to test their own toughness of soul and sole by following in their footsteps (literally).

White Day
Date 14 Mar.
Invented by confectionery companies to make up for the fact that on Valentine's Day in Japan (*see p217*) only guys receive chocs, White Day is just for the ladies. And it also helps to sell more chocolate, of course.

St Patrick's Day Parade
www.inj.or.jp. **Date** 17 Mar or nearest Sun.
Enthusiastic local devotees of Gaelic culture demonstrate their baton-twirling, drumming, pipe-playing and dancing skills at this popular parade along Omotesando (*see p80*). The celebrations at Tokyo's many Irish pubs continue into the wee hours.

Geisai
www.geisai.net. **Date** Mar, Sept.
Started by artist Murakami Takashi, Geisai, like the older Design Festa (*see below*), is a twice-yearly art fair for little-known artists. A few of the major galleries appear, and it also runs a competition that gives its winners the chance to break into the commercial art market.

Cherry-Blossom Viewing (Hanami)
3201 3331. Ueno Park, Sumida Park, Yasukuni Shrine, Shinjuku Gyoen, Aoyama Cemetery & other locations. **Date** late Mar-early Apr.
The great outdoor event of the year sees popular viewing spots invaded by hordes of nature-loving locals. The ideal time to admire the blossoms is is at full bloom when petals start to fall off in the breeze like pink snow. It is also a big drinking occasion and by late afternoon many partygoers are no longer in a fit state to appreciate anything. Cases of alcohol poisoning are not unknown, and ambulance crews remain on alert. **Photo** *p214.*

Tokyo Motorcycle Show
www.motorcycleshow.org. **Date** late Mar-early Apr.
Plenty of stuff to set any biker's pulse racing, with the latest models from Japan and abroad, as well as some great classics. Held at the Tokyo Big Sight exhibition centre (*see p304*), the event celebrated its 33rd anniversary in 2006.

Art Fair Tokyo
5771 4520/www.artfairtokyo.com.
Tokyo International Forum, Hall B2, 3-5-1 Marunouchi, Chiyoda-ku. **Date** early Apr.
The largest art fair in Japan was launched in 2006 and features works from over 100 galleries, covering the art spectrum from *ukiyo-e* to avant-garde.

Start of the baseball season
Date early Apr.
The long road to the October play-offs usually starts with a three-game Central League series featuring the Giants, the city's perennial favourite. There's extra spice if the opposition is the Swallows – the capital's other big team – or the Giants' oldest rivals, the Hanshin Tigers. The games are held at either Tokyo Dome or Jingu Baseball Stadium (*see p269*).

Horseback Archery (Yabusame)
5246 1111. **Date** mid Apr.
Mounted riders in full medieval samurai gear fire their bows at three stationary targets while galloping at full speed. The event is held at Sumida Park in Asakusa. There's also a big *yabusame* festival at Tsurugaoka Hachiman-gu in Kamakura (*see p289*) in September, and the practice can be seen during the Meiji Shrine's autumn festival (*see p216*).

Meiji Jingu Spring Festival (Haru no Taisai)
3379 5511. **Date** 29 Apr-early May.
Free daily performances of traditional entertainment at the large Meiji Shrine complex (*see p85*) in Harajuku, including *gagaku* and *bugaku* imperial court music and dance, plus *Noh* and *kyogen* drama.

Design Festa
3479 1433/www.designfesta.com. **Date** May, Nov.
A twice-yearly showcase of hundreds of young artists, musicians and performers, turning the Tokyo Big Sight convention centre (*see p304*) into a big art fair.

Kanda Festival
Organised from Kanda Myojin Shrine (3254 0753/ www.kandamyoujin.or.jp). **Date** mid May.
Held in odd-numbered years, this is one of Tokyo's 'Big Three' festivals. In Edo days it was a local favourite thanks to the shrine's links with the popular tenth-century rebel Taira no Masakado. Events include *shinkosai* rites with participants parading in Heian costume, plus a gala procession that crosses the Kanda area with *mikoshi* portable shrines and floats.

Sanja Festival
Organised from Asakusa Shrine (see p68).
Date 3rd weekend in May.
Tokyo's largest annual festival, Sanja attracts huge crowds to Asakusa and honours the three seventh-century founders of Senso-ji temple. It climaxes after several days of events with three huge *mikoshi* portable shrines that carry the spirits of the three men as they are paraded around the streets. **Photo** *p212.*

Thai Festival
3447 2247/www.thaifestival.net.
Date Sat, Sun in mid May.
An annual festival of Thai food, drink, arts and culture in the southern part of Yoyogi Park (*see p84*), near the NHK Hall. The stage has demos of Muay Thai boxing, dancing and Thai bands

Summer

Iris Viewing
3201 3331. Meiji Shrine Inner Garden, Horikiri Iris Garden, Mizumoto Park & other locations. **Date** mid June.
The annual blooming of the beautiful purple and white flowers falls during the not-so-beautiful rainy season, but is no less popular for the bad timing.

Ground-Cherry Market (Hozuchi-ichi)
Date 9-10 July.
On these two days in July, prayers at Asakusa Kannon Temple (aka Senso-ji; *see p68*) are said to carry the equivalent of 46,000 days' worth of other times. Big crowds are attracted by this spiritual bargain. A ground-cherry market also takes place.

Tokyo International Lesbian & Gay Film Festival
www.tokyo-lgff.org. **Date** mid July.
Launched in 1992, the annual LGFF lasts around five days and offers a rare chance for locals to catch up on the best of gay cinema. The main venue is the Spiral building (*see p239*) in Harajuku.

Arts & Entertainment

Sumida River Fireworks

5246 1111. **Date** last Sat in July.
First held in 1733, this is the oldest, biggest and most crowded of Tokyo's summer firework events. Up to a million people pack the riverbank area in Asakusa (*see p64*) to see around 20,000 *hanabi* ('flower-fires') light up the night. The popular waterfront spots are not recommended for the claustrophobic.

Obon

Date 13-15 Aug.
The souls of the departed are said to return to the living world during this Buddhist festival honouring ancestral spirits. Observances include welcoming fires, Bon dances, night-time floating of lanterns on open water and the placing of horses made from vegetables on the doorsteps of rural homes to carry and sustain the ancestors' souls. It's not a public holiday, but many firms give workers time off to visit their relatives, leaving the capital unusually quiet.

War-End Anniversary

Date 15 Aug.
The annual anniversary of Japan's surrender to the Allied forces is still a source of diplomatic friction with neighbouring countries, as many leading Japanese politicians mark the day by visiting Yasukuni Shrine (*see p96*), where the souls of Japan's war dead, including those executed as war criminals, are honoured.

Azabu-Juban Noryo Festival

3451 5812/www.azabujuban.or.jp.
Date third weekend in August.
Azabu-Juban's shopping street becomes a slowly shuffling throng of people snaking past a multitude of food, games and antiques stalls as they make their way to or from a taiko drum performance with traditional Bon dancing.

Asakusa Samba Carnival

3842 5566. **Date** last Sat of Aug.
Thousands of brilliantly plumed dancers, some of whose costumes leave little to the imagination, shake their stuff in the streets of old Asakusa (*see p62*). It's a startling and colourful spectacle, with a competition for the parade's top troupe. The sidelines of the route can get very busy, so allow plenty of time; only tall latecomers can expect to get a good view of the action.

Awa Odori

3312 2728. **Date** last weekend in Aug.
Street carnival Japanese-style. This annual shindig in Koenji (*see p133*) features a form of traditional Tokushima folk dance known as the Fool's Dance. As the raucous refrain of its light-hearted song puts it: 'You're a fool whether you dance or not, so you may as well dance.'

Autumn

Tokyo Game Show

3591 1421/tgs.cesa.or.jp. **Date** late Sept.
A veritable mecca for gamers of every breed, the biggest computer and video-game show on the planet is held at the Makuhari Messe convention centre (*see p257*) and launches plenty of eagerly awaited new releases.

Moon Viewing (Tsukimi)

Date late Sept.
Parties to view the harvest moon have been held in the city since the Edo era, but light pollution in the city has proved problematic in the search for clear night skies, with less urban venues favoured nowadays. Those not wishing to travel may find solace in the annual *Tsukimi* burger promotion, recognising a distinctly lunar quality to the fried egg that comes as a seasonal extra.

Art-Link Ueno-Yanaka

http://artlink.jp.org. **Date** late Sept-mid Oct.
An annual art fair that includes exhibitions and events in galleries, shops and temples around the old cultural centre of Ueno and the artists' district of Yanaka. Keep an eye out for flyers or announcements in the media.

Takigi Noh

Date Sept-Oct.
Atmospheric outdoor performances of medieval *Noh* drama are staged at a number of shrines, temples and parks, illuminated by bonfires and torches.

Cherry-Blossom Viewing. *See p213.*

Arts & Entertainment

Superstitions

Tokyo's shrines do a roaring trade in protective amulets, fortune-telling papers, lucky wooden rakes and straight (often sizeable) cash donations to ward off bad luck – an indication of just how seriously many Japanese people take their superstitions. Some themes will be familiar – unlucky numbers, prophetic cups of tea and stepping on cracks – but they all get a local twist. Here are some of the most popular:

● The numbers four and nine are always unlucky, thanks to their phonetic similarity to the words for death and suffering, respectively. It's why few things come packaged in fours, and hospitals often omit those room numbers.
● Money is a common gift in Japan, especially at weddings. But the figure has to be an odd number, since anything divisible by two portends a future split in the relationship.
● Bodies are traditionally buried with the head pointing north, so it's considered unlucky to sleep this way. And while not quite a superstition, Japanese kids also learn that if they lie down directly after a meal they will become a cow.
● Stepping on the gaps between tatami mats is as unlucky in Japan as pavement cracks are in the West.
● To become wealthy you'll need either thick earlobes or to have a dream involving a snake.
● If a tea stem is floating upright in your tea, it means good luck.
● When you see a funeral car, quickly hide your thumbs. A dangling thumb will prevent you from being present at your parents' deaths. (This stems from the name for thumbs in Japanese: 'parent fingers'.)

● You'll also miss your parents' deaths if you cut your fingernails in the evening, rather than at any other time of day, although only if you are a Tokyoite. People in other regions incur alternative forms of bad luck by nocturnal trimming.
● And finally, a superstition that borders on plain common sense: don't eat eels and pickled plums at the same time or you'll get stomach cramps.

CEATEC Japan

5402 7603/www.ceatec.com/index.html.
Date early Oct.
Techie heaven. CEATEC Japan is the best place to see the latest consumer gadgets and communication technologies before they hit the shops. The fair is held at the Makuhari Messe convention centre (*see p257*) and attracts crowds keen to stay up to date with the latest digitial developments.

Japan Tennis Open

3481 2321. **Date** early Oct.
Early October sees the international tennis circus hit town for Japan's premier competitive event, held at Ariake Tennis Forest (*see p274*). Local interest tends to focus on the women's section of the tournament.

Tokyo Motor Show

www.tokyo-motorshow.com. **Date** late Oct-early Nov.
Held at the Makuhari Messe (*see p257*) and one of the major events in the automobile world's calendar, swish new products from both domestic and foreign manufacturers are showcased at the Tokyo Motor Show. Cars and motorbikes feature in odd-numbered years, while commercial vehicles feature in even ones.

Chrysanthemum Festival

3379 5511. **Date** late Oct-late Nov.
The start of autumn was traditionally marked by the Chrysanthemum Festival on the ninth day of the ninth month of the old lunar calendar. These delicate pale blooms are also represented on the crest of Japan's imperial family. You'll find many

blooms on display at the Meiji Shrine Inner Garden (*see p85*). If you're in town at this time of year they are well worth checking out.

Tokyo International Film Festival

www.tiff-jp.net. **Date** late Oct-early Nov.
The largest film fest in Japan screens over 300 films and attracts a glittering influx of international movie talent. The main venues are Roppongi Hills and Le Cinema (*see p233*) in the Bunkamura complex.

Meiji Jingu Grand Autumn Festival (Reisai)

3379 5511. **Date** 3 Nov.
This is the biggest annual festival at the Meiji Shrine (*see p85*) with performances of traditional music, theatre and *yabusame* (horseback archery).

Tori no Ichi Fair

www.torinoichi.jp. Chokoku-ji/Otori Jinja, Asakusa. **Date** Nov.
Kumade are expensive, gaudily decorated bamboo rakes, reputed to bring their owners prosperity and good fortune. Their power only lasts a year, and each November on the days of the rooster (*tori*) according to the Chinese calendar, people replace their old rakes with new ones. Asakusa's Chokoku temple and Otori Shrine occupy adjacent plots and host the largest Tori no Ichi Fair, with over 200 stalls.

Seven-Five-Three Festival (Shichi Go San)

3201 3331. **Date** 15 Nov.
During the Heian period (710-1185), children had their heads shaved from birth until they were three, when they could grow their hair. From the age of five boys could wear *hakama* and *haori* (traditional dress for men), and from seven girls could wear kimonos. These were special birthdays. Nowadays the third and seventh birthday are celebrated only by girls, the fifth by boys. Kids of these ages go to their local shrine on 15 November in their finest outfits, with important shrines besieged by junior hordes.

Autumn Leaves (Koyo)

3201 3331. Shinjuku Gyoen, Ueno Park, Meiji Shrine Inner Garden & other locations. **Date** 2nd half of Nov.
The spectacular golds and rusts of maple and gingko trees transform many of Tokyo's parks and gardens.

Japan Cup

0423 63 3141. Tokyo Racecourse, 1-1 Hiyoshi-cho, Fuchu-shi. Seimonmae station (Keio line). **Date** late Nov.
Top horses and jockeys from around the world race over 2.4km (1.5 miles) in Japan's most famous horse race, held about half an hour by train from Tokyo.

Winter

FIFA Club World Cup

www.fifa.com. **Date** mid Dec.
What was once the Toyota Cup, a one-off match between the winners of Europe's Champion's League

and South America's Copa Libertadores, has been replaced by a new tournament involving the club champions from all six continents.

47 Ronin Memorial Service (Ako Gishi-sai)

3441 5560. **Date** 14 Dec (also 1-7 Apr).
The famous revenge attack by the masterless samurai known as the 47 *ronin* (*see p15*) took place in the early hours of 31 January 1703, or 15 December 1702 by the old Japanese calendar. Two days of events, including dances, a parade in period costume and a Buddhist memorial ceremony, take place at Sengaku-ji temple (*see p136*), where the warriors are buried alongside their former master. There's also a parade in Ginza, with participants in samurai outfits.

Battledore Market (Hagoita Ichi)

3842 0181. **Date** 17-19 Dec.
Hagoita are paddle-shaped bats used to hit the shuttlecock in *hanetsuki*, the traditional New Year game. Ornamental versions come festooned with colourful pictures, and many temples hold markets selling them in December. The one at Asakusa Kannon Temple (*see p68*) is Tokyo's largest.

Emperor's Birthday (Tenno Tanjobi)

Date 23 Dec.
The only day, apart from 2 January, when the public is allowed to enter the inner grounds of the Imperial Palace (*see p97*).

Christmas Eve & Christmas Day

Date 24, 25 Dec.
Christmas Eve is the most romantic day of the year in Japan. Couples celebrate with extravagant dates involving fancy restaurants and love hotels. Few locals mark the following day, despite the battery of fairylights, decorated trees and piped carols deployed by department stores. Neither day is a public holiday.

Year End

Date 28-31 Dec.
The last official day of work is 28 December, but all through the month companies have *bonenkai*, work-organised drinking parties to celebrate the end of the year. After work on the 28th people begin a frantic round of last-minute house-cleaning, decoration-hanging and food preparation ready for the New Year's Eve festivities. Many stay at home to catch NHK's eternally popular TV show *Red & White Singing Contest*, although huge crowds also go out to shrines and temples for midnight, when bells are rung 108 times to dispel the 108 earthly desires that plague us all according to Buddhist teachings.

New Year's Day (Ganjitsu)

3201 3331. **Date** 1 Jan.
Japan's most important annual holiday sees large crowds fill temples and shrines for that all-important first visit of the year; some of the more famous spots are rammed from midnight onwards. Otherwise, New Year's Day tends to be a quiet family affair, except for postmen staggering under

enormous sacks of New Year cards (*nengajo*), which all Japanese people send to friends and colleagues. Only the first day of the year is an official holiday, but people stay away from work for longer, with most shops and businesses shut until 4 January.

Emperor's Cup Final

www.jfa.or.jp/eng/. **Date** 1 Jan.
The showpiece event of Japan's domestic football season is the climax of the main cup competition, at the National Stadium (*see p270*). It's become more popular since the 2002 World Cup was held in Japan.

New Year Congratulatory Visit (Ippan Sanga)

Date 2 Jan.
The public is allowed into the inner grounds of the Imperial Palace (*see p97*) on two days a year, and this is one of them (the emperor's birthday in December is the other; *see p216*). Seven times during the day, between 9.30am and 3pm, the public face of the state appears on the palace balcony with other members of the royal family to wave to the crowds from behind bulletproof glass.

Tokyo Metropolitan Fire Brigade Parade (Dezome-shiki)

3201 3331. **Date** 6 Jan.
In celebration of the city's firefighters a display is put on by the Preservation Association of the old Edo Fire Brigade, at Tokyo Big Sight (*see p304*). They dress in traditional *hikeshi* firefighters' garb and perform acrobatic stunts at the top of long ladders.

New Year Grand Sumo Tournament (Ozumo Hatsu Basho)

3623 5111/www.sumo.or.jp/eng/index.html.
Date mid Jan.
The first of the year's three full 15-day sumo tournaments (*basho*) held in Tokyo. The tournaments take place at the Kokugikan (*see p273*) from the second to the fourth Sundays of January, May and September. The other three *basho* take place in Osaka, Nagoya and Kyushu in March, July and November respectively.

Coming of Age Day (Seijin no Hi)

3201 3331. Meiji Shrine & other locations.
Date 2nd Mon of Jan.
Those reaching the age of 20 in the 12 months up to April head to shrines in their best kimonos and suits for blessings and photos. Some areas organise a ceremony at local school halls; in recent years these have been interrupted by drunken youngsters (20 is the legal drinking age). The traditional date of 15 January generally coincides with New Year's Day under the old lunar calendar, so the ceremonies are held at this time to maintain a tie with the old system.

Chinese New Year

045 641 4759/www.chinatown.or.jp/info/schedule. html. Yokohama Chinatown. Ishikawacho station (Keihin Tohoku, Negishi lines), Chinatown exit.
Date Jan/Feb.

Cymbals crash as dragon dancers weave their way along the restaurant-lined streets of Yokohama Chinatown for the local community's annual festival. The restaurants get packed, so be prepared for a long wait to get a table.

Toray Pan Pacific Open Tennis Tournament

www.toray-ppo.co.jp/web/pc/.
Date late Jan-early Feb.
This women-only indoor tennis tournament, played at the Tokyo Metropolitan Gymnasium (*see p274*), is usually well attended by the biggest names in the women's game. Martina Hingis beat Ana Ivanovic in the final of the 2007 event.

Setsubun

3201 3331. **Date** 3 Feb.
Much hurling of soybeans to cries of *oni wa soto, fuki wa uchi* ('demons out, good luck in') as the last day of winter – according to the lunar calendar – is celebrated in homes, shrines and temples. The tradition is to eat one bean for every year of one's age. Sumo wrestlers and other celebrities are among those doing the casting out in ceremonies at well-known Tokyo shrines, including Senso-ji (*see p68*) and Zojo-ji (*see p106*).

Valentine's Day

Date 14 Feb.
Valentine's was introduced to Japan by confectionery companies as a day when women give chocolates to men. There are heart-shaped treats for that special someone, plus *giri choko* (obligation chocs) for a wider circle of male associates. These are reciprocated by men giving women chocolates on White Day (*see p212*) a month later.

Plum Blossoms

3836 0753. Yushima Tenjin Shrine, 3-30-1 Yushima, Bunkyo-ku. Yushima station (Chiyoda line), exit 3. **Date** mid Feb-mid Mar.
These delicate white blooms arrive a little earlier than the better-known cherry blossoms, and are usually celebrated in a more restrained fashion, possibly because the weather is still on the cold side. Yushima Tenjin Shrine, a prime viewing spot south of Ueno Park, holds a month-long festival featuring traditional arts such as *ikebana* and tea ceremonies.

Daruma Fair

0424 86 5511. Jindai-ji Temple, 5-15-1 Jindaiji Motomachi, Chofu-shi. Chofu station (Keio line), north exit then bus to terminus at Jindai-ji Temple.
Date 3-4 Mar.
After meditating in a cave for nine years, Bodhidharma, a Zen monk from ancient India, is reputed to have lost the use of all four limbs. The cuddly red figure of the Daruma doll, which is modelled after him, also lacks eyes. The first eye gets painted in when a difficult task is undertaken for good luck, the second when the task is successfully completed. Jindai-ji's Daruma Fair is one of the biggest and most crowded.

Children

The big city for small fry.

There's no shortage of stimuli for children in Tokyo. From amusement parks to zoos, and playgrounds to toy emporiums, there are myriad outlets aimed specifically at youngsters. Large stores provide small (unstaffed) play areas, allowing parents to shop without worrying that their brood might be getting bored. Government-run children's halls provide purpose-built, free entertainment, and Tokyo's restaurants increasingly welcome families.

Public transport is free for kids under six and half-price for under-12s. Most stations and major commercial facilities in the downtown areas are equipped with lifts and escalators – although you may need help to locate them, particularly in the large and crowded terminal stations.

Nappy-changing facilities are available in indoor public toilets, although not in parks or playgrounds. Most commercial outlets have nursing facilities. You should be aware, however, that the Japanese do not breastfeed in public, so be prepared to brave curious stares if you do.

If you have to carry a pushchair up a long flight of steps, it's best to ask a woman for help. Japanese men are apparently too timid to offer such assistance, particularly to foreigners. Avoid the weekday rush hours, when trains and stations are usually horribly packed. Facilities for kids can get very crowded at weekends and during school holidays (21 March-7 April, 20 July-31 August and 23 December-7 January), especially on wet or cold days.

For useful information and child-oriented tips, visit **www.tokyowithkids.com**, an online forum for English-speaking families living in Japan. Click on 'Discussions' at the top of the home page to link to a decent list of topics that includes shopping, education and playgroups.

For children's clothes and toy shops, *see pp187-210* **Shops & Services**.

Amusement parks

Visiting amusement parks can be a pricey business, so it's worth noting that tickets are often available cheaply at *kinken* shops – discount ticket stores – sometimes at a fraction of the regular prices. In addition to the places listed below, the small **Hanayashiki** park (*see p69*) has lots of old-fashioned charm and a 1953 rollercoaster, while **Toshimaen** (*see p91*) offers hours of

splashing fun at its water park in summer and a spa in winter. For the **Tokyo Disney Resort**, out in Tokyo Bay, *see p136*.

Joypolis

Decks Tokyo 3F-5F, 1-6-1 Daiba, Minato-ku (5500 1801/www.sega.co.jp/joypolis/tokyo_e.html). Odaiba Kaihin Koen station (Yurikamome line) or Tokyo Teleport station (Rinkai line). **Open** 10am-11pm daily (last entry 10.15pm). **Admission** *1-day passport* ¥3,300; ¥3,100 7-14s. *Entry only* ¥500; ¥300 7-14s; each ride then costs ¥300-¥600. **Credit** AmEx, DC, JCB, MC, V. **Map** Odaiba p101.

You can simulate snowboarding in the half-pipe canyon or ride a virtual hang-glider through tropical islands at this indoor park in Odaiba that is packed with Sega's virtual-reality games. Bilingual instructions are provided for each game. The – non-virtual – highlight is the Spin Bullet, a whirling rollercoaster.

Kidzania

Lalaport Toyosu 2-4-9 Toyosu, Koto-ku (0120 924 901/www.kidzania.jp). Toyosu station (Yurakucho, Yurikamome lines). **Open** 10am-3pm, 4-9pm daily. **Admission** ¥800 Mon-Fri; ¥1,000 Sat, Sun. *4-15s* ¥1,200 Mon-Fri; ¥1,500 Sat, Sun. *2-3s* ¥600 Mon-Fri; ¥750 Sat, Sun. **Credit** AmEx, DC, JCB, MC, V.

If your kids have been misbehaving, why not reprimand them with a day at Kidzania, where they can spend time in a miniaturized, fully branded Coca-Cola bottling plant, a burger store or a bank, or they can emulate more exciting careers such as firefigher or magician. And if child labour and brand indoctrination aren't dubious enough themes, your offspring can spend their mock earnings via a Kidzania credit card. Kidzania is a Japanese-language theme-park, and some 'careers' require Japanese fluency to participate, but staff can assist international visitors. Activities are designed for ages 2-12.

Tamatech

5-22-1 Hodokubo, Hino-shi (042 591 0820/ www.tamatech.com). Bus from Tama Dobutsu Koen station (Keio line). **Open** 9.30am-5.30pm daily. **Admission** *All rides* ¥4,000; ¥3,000 7-12s; ¥2,200 3-6s. *Entry only* ¥1,600; ¥800 3-12s; each ride then costs ¥200-¥800. **Credit** JCB, MC, V.

Children can drive a train, a car or a motorcycle at this Honda-run amusement park an hour from the city centre. There are 700m and 1,200m go-kart loops and a 500m racing circuit; kids need to be nine years old to participate. Other standard amusement park fare includes a free fall and a rollercoaster.

Creative play is the name of the game at the **National Children's Castle**. *See p220.*

Tokyo Dome City

1-3-61 Koraku, Bunkyo-ku (5800 9999/www. tokyo-dome.co.jp). Suidobashi station (Chuo line), west exit; (Mita line), exits A3, A4 or Korakuen station (Marunouchi, Nanboku lines), exit 2 or Kasuga station (Mita, Oedo lines), exit A1. **Open** *Dome City 10am-10pm daily. LaQua Spa 11am-9am daily. Toys Kingdom 10am-6pm Mon-Fri; 9.30am-7pm Sat, Sun.* **Admission** *Dome City multi-ride ticket ¥3,000; individual rides ¥200-¥1,000. LaQua Spa ¥2,565 Mon-Fri; ¥2,680 Sat, Sun; ¥4,455 midnight-6am. Toys Kingdom 1st 3hrs ¥700-¥1,000; every subsequent 30mins ¥300-¥400.* **No credit cards**.

The amusement park formerly known as Korakuen reopened in 2003 as part of an amusement complex, with baseball stadium Tokyo Dome (*see p270*) at its centre. The ultra-modern section, called LaQua, comprises a shopping centre, restaurants, the world's first spokeless Ferris wheel and a hot mineral bath theme park where spring water is pumped up from an incredible 1,700m (5,670ft) below ground. Restaurants include a Hawaiian-Japanese place run by retired sumo star Konishiki. Topping it all off is the Thunder Dolphin, a stunning urban rollercoaster that starts off higher than the Dome, leaps to the roof of the main LaQua building and plunges through the centre of the Ferris wheel. For small kids, there's Toys Kingdom, with room after room of toys and educational equipment, making the place a great rainy-day solution.

Tokyo Sesame Place

600 Kamiyotsugi, Akiruno-shi (042 558 6511/ www.sesameplace.co.jp). Akikawa station (Itsukaichi line) then bus or taxi. **Open** *July-Sept daily. Oct, Nov,* *Mar-June Mon-Wed, Fri-Sun. Dec-Feb Sat, hols. Hrs vary.* **Admission** *Summer ¥2,200; ¥1,200 2-12s. Winter ¥2,000; ¥1,000 2-12s.* **No credit cards**.

This theme park based on the *Sesame Street* TV series has reproduced some of the most exciting attractions of the original park in Pennsylvania, including big ball pools, a gigantic air mattress, cargo nets, tunnels and climbs. Various interactive shows, including English play-along and musical revues, will keep the kids entertained. A small water section (open in summer) includes a paddling pool and a water maze. It's about an hour by train from Shinjuku station.

Aquariums & zoos

There's also an aquarium inside Sunshine City in Ikebukuro; *see p91* for details.

Inokashira Nature & Culture Park

1-17-6 Gotenyama, Musashino-shi (042 246 1100/ www.tokyo-zoo.net/english). Kichijoji station (Chuo line), park (south) exit. **Open** *9.30am-5pm Tue-Sun (last entry 4pm).* **Admission** *¥400; ¥150 13-15s; free under-13s.* **No credit cards**.

A five-minute walk from Kichijoji station, this zoo is set in splendid Inokashira Park (*see p136*), with a pond, woods, playground and outdoor pool all close by. The zoo comprises two sections: one near the pond, housing an aviary and freshwater aquarium; the other near the wood, containing a zoo with a petting area, greenhouse and small amusement park. The entrance fee gets you tickets for both sections, which can be used separately.

Arts & Entertainment

Shinagawa Aquarium

3-2-1 Katsushima, Shinagawa-ku (3762 3431/ www.aquarium.gr.jp). Omori Kaigan station (Keihin Kyuko Line), east exit or Sujo water bus from Hinode Pier. **Open** 10am-5pm Mon, Wed-Sun (last entry 4.30pm). **Admission** ¥1,300; ¥600 7-12s; ¥300 4-6s. **No credit cards.**

Tokyo's best aquarium is in a rather inconvenient location, on the western edge of Tokyo Bay. The best feature is the water tank tunnel, which lets you walk under swimming green turtles, stingrays and scores of other fish. From another tank, huge sand tiger sharks peer out with cold, steely eyes. The aquarium also offers Tokyo's only dolphin shows, which take place at the outdoor stadium four or five times a day. They always attract huge crowds, so check the show schedule on arrival.

Tama Zoo

7-1-1 Hodokubo, Hino-shi (042 591 1611/www. tokyo-zoo.net/english). Tama Dobutsu Koen station (Keio line). **Open** 9.30am-5pm Mon, Tue, Thur-Sun (last entry 4pm). **Admission** ¥600; ¥200 13-15s; free under-13s. Free 29 Apr, 5 May, 1 Oct. **No credit cards.**

The animals at this zoo in Hino City (an hour by train from central Tokyo) are displayed in a more natural setting than at Ueno Zoo (*see below*). Built over several low hills, Tama Zoo is divided into three ecological areas: Asiatic, African and Australian. The main attractions include koalas, lions in a 'safari' setting and, above all, a huge insectarium with butterflies, beetles and other creepy-crawlies. Enjoy the sensation of butterflies coming to rest their weary wings on your hand.

Tokyo Sea Life Park

6-2-3 Rinkai-cho, Edogawa-ku (3869 5152/ www.tokyo-zoo.net/english). Kasai Rinkai Koen station (Keiyo line) or Sujo water bus from Hinode Pier. **Open** 9.30am-5pm Mon, Tue, Thur-Sun (last entry 4pm). **Admission** ¥700; ¥250 13-15s; free under-13s. Free 29 Apr, 1 Oct, 10 Oct. **Credit** (giftshop only) JCB, MC, V.

Newer than Shinagawa Aquarium and located on the other side of Tokyo Bay, this place was built on the 77ha (190 acres) of reclaimed land that constitute Kasai Seaside Park. The main attraction is a large doughnut-shaped water tank, home to 200 tuna. Tokyo Disney Resort (*see p136*) is nearby.

Ueno Zoo

9-83 Ueno Koen, Taito-ku (3828 5171/www.tokyo-zoo.net/english). Ueno station (Yamanote, Ginza, Hibiya lines), park exit. **Open** 9.30am-5pm Tue-Sun (last entry 4pm). **Admission** ¥600; ¥200 13-15s; free under-13s. Free 20 Mar, 29 Apr, 1 Oct. **Map** Ueno & Yanaka p123.

Japan's oldest zoo, established in 1882, is also Tokyo's most popular, thanks mainly to its central location in Ueno Park and its range of beasts, including a giant panda and a Sumatran tiger. You'll find the panda in the eastern section, along with elephants, lions, gorillas, sea lions and assorted

bears. Don't be discouraged by the crowds, though; the western section across the bridge is less busy and offers opportunities to interact with animals in a petting zoo and to watch a huge alligator relaxing in the reptile house.

Children's halls

Run by the local authorities, children's halls (*jidokan*) are free indoor play facilities for residents (not short-term visitors). Designed to supplement formal education, they provide weekly play classes for pre-schoolers, and daily after-school programmes for school-age children of working parents. There are more than 500 *jidokan* within Tokyo's 23 wards, including one run by the Tokyo Metropolitan Government, and another built by the welfare ministry, the National Children's Castle (the only one that charges a fee). For information about other *jidokan*, contact the Tokyo Metropolitan Government Foreign Residents' Advisory Centre (*see p307*).

0123 Kichijoji

2-29-12 Kichijoji Higashi, Musashino-shi (0422 20 3210/www1.parkcity.ne.jp/m0123hap/kichijoji/ index.html). Kichijoji station (Chuo line), north exit. **Open** 9am-4pm Tue-Sat. **Admission** free.

This *jidokan* caters specifically for under-threes. Converted from a former kindergarten, it's a spacious building with a garden and a sandbox. Children can paint, and play with clay and a variety of toys handmade by the staff.

National Children's Castle (Kodomo no Shiro)

5-53-1 Jingumae, Shibuya-ku (3797 5666/www. kodomo-shiro.or.jp). Shibuya station (Yamanote, Ginza, Hanzomon lines), Miyamasuzaka (east) exit or Omotesando station (Chiyoda, Ginza, Hanzomon lines), exits B2, B4. **Open** 12.30-5.30pm Tue-Fri; 10am-5.30pm Sat, Sun. **Admission** ¥500; ¥400 3-17s. **No credit cards. Map** Shibuya p109.

A fabulous play hall halfway between Shibuya and Omotesando. Facilities include climbing equipment and a playhouse on the third floor, and a music lobby on the fourth floor where children can indulge their love of noise. The playport on the fifth-floor roof garden is the biggest attraction, combining a jungle gym with large ball pools. Kids must be over three to use the playport, which closes on rainy days. **Photo** p219.

Tokyo Metropolitan Children's Hall

1-18-24 Shibuya, Shibuya-ku (3409 6361/ www.fukushihoken.metro.tokyo.jp/jidou/English/ index.html). Shibuya station (Yamanote, Ginza, Hanzomon lines), Miyamasuzaka (east) exit. **Open** *July, Aug* 9am-6.30pm daily. *Sept-June* 9am-5pm daily. Closed 2nd & 4th Mon of mth. **Admission** free. **Map** Shibuya p109.

Handily located not far from Shibuya station, this six-storey hall is packed with recreational and educational facilities. The second floor is reserved for pre-schoolers, with large climbing frames and wooden toys. The third floor has a handicraft section, the 'human-body maze' and a ball pool. There's a library on the fifth floor, while on the roof kids can try roller-skating and unicycling. Each floor has plenty of lockers to stash belongings.

Museums

Other child-friendly museums include the **Transportation Museum** (*see p98*), **Japan Science Foundation Science Museum** (*see p97*) and **Fire Museum** (*see p119*).

National Science Museum

7-20 Ueno Koen, Taito-ku (3822 0111/www. kahaku.go.jp/english). Ueno station (Yamanote line), park exit; (Ginza, Hibya lines) Shinobazu exit. **Open** 9am-5pm Tue-Thur; 9am-8pm Fri; 9am-6pm Sat, Sun. **Admission** ¥500; ¥70 concessions; free under-12s. **No credit cards. Map** Ueno & Yanaka p123.

At this museum inside Ueno Park, the exhibits of fossils, specimens and asteroids are now supplemented with touch screens providing videos and multilingual explanations. After checking out dinosaur bones and a prehistoric house built with mammoth tusks, you may want to taste the speciality of the museum's Musée Basara restaurant: a 'dinosaur's egg' croquette. All displays are currently in the new building, which opened in November 2004, while the main building is being refurbished.

Tama Rokuto Kagakukan

5-10-64 Shibakubo, Nishi-Tokyo-shi (042 469 6100/ www.tamarokuto.or.jp). Hana-Koganei station (Seibu Shinjuku Line), north exit then 18mins walk, or take bus bound for Tama Rokuto Kagakukan from Hana-Koganei station (Seibu Shinjuku line), south exit (Sat, Sun & holidays) or Kichijoji station (Chuo line), north exit (Sun & holidays). **Open** 9.30am-5pm (last entry 4pm) Tue-Sun. **Admission** ¥500; ¥200 4-18s. *Planetarium shows* ¥500; ¥200 4-18s. **No credit cards.**

Visitors can climb inside the life-size model of a space shuttle that stands upright in the middle of this science museum an hour from Shinjuku. You can practise moving cargo with a robot arm simulator, while a moonwalker simulator recreates the low-gravity environment of the moon's surface. Star shows are held at the planetarium, one of the world's largest. While astronomy is the major focus, there are also geology and biology sections. The major drawback is poor public transport access, with infrequent bus services from local train stations.

Parks & playgrounds

Apart from **Yoyogi Park** (*see p84*) and **Shinjuku Gyoen** (*see p119*), parks in central Tokyo are few and far between. Furthermore,

they are often not ideal for picnics or playing – Ueno Park is more concrete than grass, for example. To find the best green spaces, you're better off grabbing a map and a rail pass and heading to the suburbs.

Koganei Park

1-13-1 Sekino-machi, Koganei-shi (042 385 5611/ www.tokyo-park.or.jp/english). Musashi Koganei station (Chuo line), north exit then any bus from bus stop 2 or 3; get off at Koganei Koen Nishi-Guchi. **Open** 24hrs daily. **Admission** free.

You can explore the central part of this spacious park in western Tokyo by bicycle; about 120 bikes are available for pre-schoolers and their parents (¥100-¥200/hr). If your child tires of pedalling, they can try sledging down an artificial, turf-covered slope that's built into one of the park's grassy knolls. The 17° slope is wide enough for at least a dozen sledges to race down at the same time. Kids love it. You can buy a sledge or borrow one of the park's by queuing at the bottom of the slope. The park also houses the open-air branch of the Edo-Tokyo Museum (*see p68*).

Nogawa Park

6-4-1 Osawa, Mitaka-shi (042 231 6457/www. tokyo-park.or.jp/english/park/detail_03.html). Shin-Koganei station (Seibu Tamagawa line) then 15mins walk (follow railway tracks south until you reach Nogawa river). **Open** *Park* 24hrs daily. *Nature centre* 9.30am-4.30pm Tue-Sun. **Admission** free.

A natural spring on the northern side of the Nogawa river bisects this picturesque park. The area around the spring is a popular paddling spot in summer. Upstream is a small nature centre where you can listen to recorded sounds of birds in Tokyo and learn about various insects. Climbing frames and other wooden play equipment dot the extensive grassy areas. It's a half-hour train ride from Shinjuku, followed by an easy walk.

Showa Kinen Park

3173 Midori-machi, Tachikawa-shi (042 528 1751/www.showapark.jp). Nishi-Tachikawa station (Ohme line). **Open** 9.30am-4.30pm/5pm daily (last entry 1hr before closing); closing time varies during year. **Admission** *Park* ¥400; ¥80 6-14s. *Park & Rainbow Pool* ¥2,200; ¥1,200 6-14s; ¥300 4-5s. **No credit cards.**

A paradise for athletic children, this 1.8sq km (0.7sq miles) park 40 minutes from Shinjuku has a large play area called Children's Forest, with giant trampoline nets, bouncy domes and 'foggy woods' that – as the name implies – get covered by clouds of artificial fog. The Forest House in the centre sells snacks and drinks and provides a resting space. If it's too hot to walk to the Children's Forest from the main gate, pop into the Rainbow Pool for a paddle. Three pools contain waterfalls and squirt fish; bigger children have the choice of a current pool, a wave pool and water slides. The park also has some lengthy cycling tracks; bike rental for three hours costs ¥250 for under-15s, ¥410 for adults.

Trim Sports Centre (Jingu Gaien 'Jido Yuen')

1-7-5 Kita-Aoyama, Minato-ku (3478 0550/ www.meijijingugaien.jp/child/index.html). Shinanomachi station (Sobu line). **Open** 9.30am-4.30pm/5pm daily (last entry 30mins before closing); closing time varies during year. **Admission** ¥200; ¥50 2-12s. **No credit cards.**

Despite its compact size and central location, this popular playground within the Outer Garden of the Meiji Jingu has more play equipment than any other park in Tokyo. Children can try swings, slides and climbs of various sizes and shapes, and picnic at beautiful log houses equipped with large tables and chairs. The park has three areas, each for a different age group, but children are allowed to wander anywhere under parental supervision.

Resources

Babysitting & nurseries

Staff at more reputable hotels may be able to arrange babysitting. Alternatively, the following outfits come highly recommended by Tokyo parents. Expect to pay between ¥1,500 and ¥2,800 per hour. Some agencies demand a minimum of two hours at a set rate; you then pay for each additional hour, with different rates for late-night and early-morning services.

Japan Baby Sitter Service

3423 1251/www.jbs-mom.co.jp. **No credit cards.**
One of the oldest services in Tokyo, specialising in grandmotherly types. Bookings must be made by 5pm on the preceding day.

Kids Square

West Walk 6F, Roppongi Hills, 6-10-1 Roppongi, Minato-ku (5772 1577/freephone 0120 086 720/ www.alpha-co.com/english/index.html). Roppongi station (Hibiya, Oedo lines), exit 1. **Open** 11am-7pm daily. **No credit cards.** **Map** Roppongi p103.

Located conveniently in the middle of the Roppongi business district, this is a spacious, well-equipped nursery. You can check your child via mobile phone or computer by hooking up to video cameras installed in the nursery. Book by 4pm the day before. **Other locations:** Ark Hills Side 3F, 1-3-41 Roppongi, Minato-ku (3583 9320); Tokyo Dome Hotel 7F, 1-3-61 Koraku, Bunkyo-ku (5805 2272).

Kids World

Pigeon Shoto Takada Bldg 2F, 1-28-11 Shoto, Shibuya-ku (5428 3630/www.pigeonhearts.jp/ kidsworld). Shibuya station (Yamanote, Ginza, Hanzomon lines), Hachiko exit or Shinsen station (Keio Inokashira line). **Open** 9am-6pm Mon-Fri. **No credit cards.** **Map** Shibuya p109.

This English-language school for children also provides nursery care at its many branches in the city, including this one in Shibuya. Pigeon Hearts, which runs the school, can also arrange a babysitting service for those able to communicate in Japanese; phone for more details on freephone 0120 764 154. **Other locations:** throughout the city; details on 0120 001 537.

Little Mate

045 712 3253/www.tokyolm.co.jp. Nurseries at Hotel Okura, Roppongi (3586 0360), Keio Plaza Intercontinental, Shinjuku (3345 1439), Sheraton Grande Tokyo Bay Hotel, near Tokyo Disneyland (047 355 5720). **Open** 10am-6pm daily. **No credit cards.**
You can drop off your kids for an hour or more at a day nursery at one of the three hotels listed above. Reservations are required by 6pm the previous day (4pm at the Hotel Okura).

Poppins Service

3447 2100/www.poppins.co.jp/english/index.html. **Open** 7am-9pm Mon-Sat. **No credit cards.**
Expect either a young lady trained in early childhood education or a retired veteran teacher when you request a sitter from Poppins. Non-members pay a flat rate of ¥2,500 per hour (¥3,200 6-10pm), and bookings must be made two days in advance. If Japanese is not your – or your children's – strong point, speakers of English, German, French or Italian can be provided.

Royal Baby Salon

Ginza Kosumion Bldg 7F, 1-5-14 Ginza, Chuo-ku (3538 3238/www.royalbaby.co.jp). Ginza-Itchome station (Yurakucho line), exit 6. **Open** 10am-6pm daily. **Credit** (incurs extra charge) AmEx, DC, JCB, MC, V. **Map** Ginza p75.
An upmarket nursery in Ginza that also offers a babysitting service. Bookings must be made by 5pm on the preceding day.

Equipment rental

Duskin Rent-All

0120 100 100/www.kasite.net.
If you don't have access to second-hand childcare equipment, try Duskin. It hires out all sorts of kit, from car seats to cots, at very reasonable rates, and will deliver to your home. There are also ten central outlets, but you'll need to speak Japanese.

Hairdressing

Choki Choki

Aqua City Odaiba 6F, 1-7-1 Minato-ku (3528 4005/www.choki-choki.com). Daiba station (Yurikamome line). **Open** 11am-9pm daily (last appointment 7.30pm). **Credit** AmEx, DC, JCB, MC, V. **Map** Odaiba p101.
Located in the Aqua City shopping mall in Odaiba, this is Japan's largest hair salon for children. Junior customers are covered in a plastic cape printed with cartoon pictures, and sit on a chair that's actually a pedal car. While they are 'steering' and watching a video shown in a side mirror, the hairdressers go about their business. Clever, huh?

Clubs

Put on your dancing shoes: Tokyo's club scene is stronger than ever.

Tokyo is arguably one of the most exciting club scenes in the world right now. The city's nightlife has the breadth and quality to match any of the major clubbing capitals, but avoids the pretentiousness and pomposity that plague many comparable scenes. Thanks to some heavy corporate investment, there are now enough top-level venues, and sufficient clubbers, to bring the big European and US DJs to play every weekend. The promoter's balance sheets are also healthy enough for them to invite emerging talents to entertain the eager crowds.

The sheer number of performing visitors, however, does seem to point to an indigenous weakness – finding a quality home-grown event on a weeknight, for example, is close to impossible. With few exceptions, people are still wary of celebrating domestic talent until it's been validated with acclaim abroad (à la Satoshi Tomiie or DJ Krush). As a result, it's rich pickings for the superstars, who make regular trips to venues like **Yellow** (*see p227*), **Womb** (*see p231*) **Ageha** (*see p231*), and **Air** (*see p224*).

Amusingly, at the time of writing, the person voted 'best Japanese DJ' by readers of *Loud* – Japan's equivalent of *Mixmag* – is 100 per cent British. Hailing from Stoke Newington, London, Mike McKenna has held the crown three years in succession, beating more famous names including Ken Ishii, Kimura Ko (*see p226* **Local view**) and Yohji Biomehanika.

Any reticence to nurture home-grown talent is more than made up for by the mind-blowing variety of sounds on offer, and the open-minded approach of Tokyo's club crowds. Keb Darge on Friday, Jeff Mills and Co Fusion on Saturday, then Japanese dancehall on Sunday afternoon? Not a problem. Tokyo's clubbers care more about quality than cliquey consistency.

Tokyo's current nightlife sweet spot isn't just about economics. It's also benefiting from a globalisation of tastes, Japan's rising international profile and a music industry finally waking up to the profit potential in something other than J-pop. Undeniably, most clubs also benefit from a licensing regime that would be unthinkable in countries where binge drinking is synonymous with violence. Japan's club laws are technically draconian – no drinking under 20, no dancing after midnight – but the rules are widely

ignored. The occasional crackdown never seems to affect the scene as a whole, and in the more party-oriented areas (Shinjuku, Shibuya, Roppongi) that messy all-nighter can easily go on until mid afternoon.

Clubs are scattered across the capital, but generally follow the feel of their locality. So Shibuya's venues are young, cool and cover all the main musical bases. Aoyama is more moneyed, less edgy but a good choice if you fancy dressing up or going dancing after dinner in the area. Daikanyama is Aoyama's chilled-out younger sister and a good area for those who want a taste of Shibuya cool without the grime. Shinjuku offers an eclectic mix of rowdy DJ bars, quirky little dancefloors and one vast venue in **Club Complex Code** (*see p231*). And then there's Roppongi: seedy, cheesy and drunk 24-7. English is practically the local language – as is tequila – and while it certainly isn't the snobs' choice, it can be a lot of fun, especially as a warm-up or cool-down to an event in nearby Azabu (Yellow is the stand-out choice here). Other locations include Harajuku (home to some good smaller clubs), Ikebukuro (Shinjuku-lite), and Shimokitazawa (mainly live houses, many of which double as clubs). Last, but certainly not least, Shinkiba – a warehouse district in the middle of nowhere – is home to Japan's biggest club, the gargantuan Ageha.

One major recent change is that drugs are no longer the taboo they once were (though many non-clubbers are still very shocked by them). Potent ecstasy pills, cocaine (often highly adulterated) and amphetamines of various kinds are regular fixtures on the faces of sweaty clubbers. Do not be deceived by this apparent ubiquity: police periodically search people in the street, with a clear preference for foreign faces. They also occasionally operate undercover in clubs.

INFORMATION AND HOURS

For event listings, the website **Higher Frequency** (www.higher-frequency.com) is a good place to start. Meanwhile, internet radio station **Samurai** (www.samurai.fm) not only highlights the pick of upcoming parties but usually has on-demand streaming of the DJs. In Japanese there are various websites that are worth exploring (www.clubberia.com, www. ciajapan.com and Heineken's www.hmusic.jp).

Arts & Entertainment

Stylish but never snooty, **Air** really is a breath of fresh air.

Also in Japanese (but not hard to figure out) are the clubbing and event magazines *Floor* (¥300) and *Juice* (free), which can be found in major music stores. In English, *Metropolis* magazine offers good insights and can also be found online at www.metropolis.co.jp. MySpace has only just launched its Japanese language version, so it doesn't have much by way of event info yet (its Japanese rival **Mixi**, at www.mixi.jp, is much better), but it's still a good way to meet local clubbers who are the very best source of information.

Expect to pay ¥1,000-¥2,000 for entry to a DJ bar on the weekend (often free weekdays) and ¥3,000-¥4000 (occasionally more) for one of the big clubs. Many venues include drink tickets with admission.

Bars and small clubs get going early, especially if there's a band on first. The bigger places don't get busy until at least midnight, winding down at around 5am (often much later).

Ebisu & Daikanyama

The legendary **Liquid Room** (*see p258*) has shifted its focus to live acts but still hosts clubbing events on occasion.

Air

Hikawa Bldg B1F-B2F, 2-11 Sarugakucho, Shibuya-ku (5784 3386/www.air-tokyo.com). Daikanyama station (Tokyu Toyoko line). **Open** 10pm-5am Mon, Thur-Sat. **Admission** ¥2,500 (incl 1 drink). **No credit cards**.

One of Tokyo's best-designed clubs. Large but intimate, stylish but never flash, and run by staff without the snootiness that seems de rigueur for major venues, Air draws big-name international DJs, as well as the best local talent. Hungry clubbers can pop upstairs for some decent late-night food in the stylish Frames café.

Milk

Roob 6 Bldg B1F-B2F, 1-13-3 Ebisu-Nishi, Shibuya-ku (5458 2826/www.milk-tokyo.com). Ebisu station (Yamanote line), west exit; (Hibiya line), exit 2. **Open** 10pm-5am; days vary. **Admission** from ¥2,500. **No credit cards**.

Milk's mission when it opened in 1995 was to bring the best of rock, punk and hardcore to Tokyo. These days, even it has succumbed to the techno and house sound that has swept Tokyo clubland, though it still frequently hosts rock gigs. Despite a capacity of around 400, the venue has neglected to devote much space to one essential amenity: on busy nights there is often a longer queue for the toilet than the bar.

Harajuku & Aoyama

Ever

KY-NYK Bldg, 6-2-9 Minami Aoyama, Minato-ku (5774 1380/www.ever-site.com). Omotesando station (Chiyoda, Ginza, Hanzomon lines), exit D1. **Open** 10pm-5am Fri, Sat. **Admission** ¥2,500. **No credit cards**.

This venue was once home to the hugely popular club Blue. Reopened in 2006 as Ever, it hasn't yet taken Tokyo by storm, but it does offer a stylish

It's like the Bubble never burst. Tokyo's extravagant '80s get a rerun at this new venue, where crystal chandeliers and antique French furnishings try to disguise the narrow dimensions. The swanky setting has made it a popular venue for unashamedly glitzy events by the likes of *Dazed & Confused* magazine and various fashion brands. The space operates as an unremarkable restaurant on Mondays, Tuesdays and Thursdays. **Photo** *p227*.

Ikebukuro

Bed
Fukuri Bldg B1F, 3-29-9 Nishi-Ikebukuro, Toshima-ku (3981 5300/www.ikebukurobed.com). Ikebukuro station (Yamanote line), west exit; (Marunouchi, Yurakucho lines), exit 1A. **Open** 10pm-5am daily. **Admission** ¥2,000 (incl 2 drinks) Mon-Thur, Sun; ¥2,500 (incl 2 drinks) Fri, Sat. **No credit cards**. **Map** Ikebukuro p87.
As you descend into Bed, you will be greeted by photo montages of previous, presumably satisfied, customers. The clientele is on the young side, and the music is mainly hip hop, with the occasional spot of techno and house.

Roppongi & Azabu-Juban

328 (San Ni Pa)
B1F, 3-24-20 Nishi-Azabu, Minato-ku (3401 4968/ www.3-2-8.jp). Roppongi station (Hibiya, Oedo lines), exit 1. **Open** from 8pm daily. **Admission** ¥2,000 (incl 2 drinks) Mon-Thur, Sun; ¥2,500 (incl 2 drinks) Fri, Sat. **No credit cards**. **Map** Roppongi p103.
You'll spot 328's large neon sign from the Nishi-Azabu crossing. A real veteran of the club scene, it opened way back in 1979. Expect a mix of genres, from soul to dance classics, and an older crowd. On Saturday the focus turns to rare groove, and 328 gets packed (it's small), so arrive early. It usually stays open past midnight on weekends.

setting with several lounge spaces and a good sound system. Try the monthly 'Love' events for some sexy house and even sexier patrons.

Fai
Hachihonkan Bldg B1F-B2F, 5-10-1 Minami-Aoyama, Minato-ku (3486 4910/www.fai-aoyama.com). Omotesando station (Chiyoda, Ginza, Hanzomon lines), exit B1. **Open** 10pm-5am daily. **Admission** ¥2,000 (incl 1 drink) Mon-Thur; ¥2,500 (incl 2 drinks) Fri-Sun. **No credit cards**.
Fai specialises in sounds from the 1970s and '80s, notably disco, funk, soul and jazz. It's an unpretentious spot staying just the right side of cheesy.

Mix
B1F, 3-6-19 Kita-Aoyama, Minato-ku (3797 1313/ www.at-mix.com). Omotesando station (Chiyoda, Ginza, Hanzomon lines), exits A1, B4. **Open** 10pm-5am; days vary. **Admission** ¥2,000 (incl 2 drinks) Mon-Thur, Sun; ¥2,500 (incl 2 drinks) Fri, Sat. **No credit cards**. **Map** Harajuku & Aoyama p82.
This tiny, narrow club makes full use of its limited space, somehow managing to fit a seating area between the dancefloor and bar, and get some interesting art up on the walls to boot. It's usually rammed at the weekends and has been that way for over a decade. Expect a mixed, friendly crowd grooving to sounds that tend towards reggae, dub, hip hop and dancehall.

Velours
Almost Blue B1, 6-4-6 Minami Aoyama (5778 4777/ www.velours.jp). Omotesando station (Chiyoda, Ginza, Hanzomon lines), exit B3. **Open** 10.45pm-4am Wed; varies Fri; 11pm-4am Sat. **Admission** ¥2,000- ¥3,500. **Credit** AmEx, DC, MC, V.

The best Clubs

Best for serious clubbers
Womb (*see p231*).

Friendliest club
Ruby Room (*see p230*).

Best for glitz and glamour
Velours (*see p225*).

Best meat market
Muse (*see p226*).

Best sound system
Shibuya Nuts (*see p230*).

Arts & Entertainment

Alife

1-7-2 Nishi-Azabu, Minato-ku (5785 2531/www.e-alife.net). Roppongi station (Hibiya, Oedo lines), exit 2. **Open** *Lounge & restaurant* 11pm-5am Mon-Sat. *Club* from 9pm Thur-Sat. **Admission** ¥2,000-¥3,500. **No credit cards. Map** Roppongi p103.

This big club is fairly well appointed, with a spacious party lounge on the second floor, a stylish café on the ground floor and a large dance area in the basement. It has a hedonistic atmosphere and is a haven for hard-core clubbers, with guest DJs playing trance or house on Sunday mornings.

Bar Matrix

Mizobuchi Bldg B1F, 3-13-6 Roppongi, Minato-ku (3405 1066). Roppongi station (Hibiya, Oedo lines), exit 3. **Open** 6pm-4am daily. **Admission** free. **Map** Roppongi p103.

Named after the Keanu Reeves movie, this Roppongi bar/club has a futuristic, metallic interior and a cyber feel. It could be considered emblematic of Tokyo, or at least of what travellers expect Tokyo to be. The music is a mishmash of everything, but tends towards hip hop and R&B.

Bullet's

Kasumi Bldg B1F, 1-7-11 Nishi-Azabu, Minato-ku (3401 4844/www.bul-lets.com). Roppongi station (Hibiya, Oedo lines), exit 2. **Open** 10pm-5am Fri; 11pm-5am Sat. **Admission** ¥2,000 Fri; ¥1,500 Sat. **No credit cards. Map** Roppongi p103.

If nothing else, this is the cosiest venue in Tokyo. Half the place is carpeted, and guests are asked to remove their shoes. There are also sofas and mattresses to lounge on while you listen to an often experimental line-up of DJs.

Club Jamaica

Nishi-Azabu Ishibashi Bldg B1F, 4-16-14 Nishi-Azabu, Minato-ku (3407 8844/www.club-jamaica.com). Roppongi station (Hibiya, Oedo lines), exit 1.

Open 10pm-5am Thur-Sat. **Admission** ¥1,000 (incl 1 drink) Thur; ¥2,500 (incl 2 drinks) Fri, Sat. **No credit cards.**

Opened by a reggae fanatic in 1989, Club Jamaica blasts out roots reggae on Thursday nights, then pulls in a younger crowd at the weekend with dancehall sounds. It's a small venue with a hard-to-find entrance, but the atmosphere is friendly and the sound system has some serious bass – the back wall is piled high with speakers.

Colors Studio

Barbizon Bldg B3F, 2-25-23 Nishi-Azabu, Minato-ku (3797 5544/www.growcreation.com/colorsstudio). Roppongi station (Hibiya, Oedo lines), exit 2. **Open** 10pm-5am Mon-Sat. **Admission** ¥2,000-¥3,000 (incl 1 drink). **No credit cards.**

The winding staircase descends three flights to a booming club that contains only the essentials: a bar, a dancefloor and a very loud sound system. Their Sunday morning after-hours party offers techno from 6am to midday.

Core

TSK CCC Bldg B1F-B2F, 7-15-30 Roppongi, Minato-ku (3470 5944/www.clubcore.net). Roppongi station (Hibiya line), exit 4B; (Oedo line), exit 7. **Open** from 10pm Wed-Sun. **Admission** usually ¥2,500 (incl 1 drink). **No credit cards. Map** Roppongi p103.

Yet another club apparently too shy to hang a sign. This one is a mid-size venue with a very varied line-up, although house and techno dominate. It's classier than most of Roppongi's night-time options, but that's faint praise. The bar snacks are impressive (for a club), and drinks start at ¥600.

Muse

4-1-1 Nishi-Azabu, Minato-ku (5467 1188/www.muse-web.com). Roppongi station (Hibiya, Oedo lines), exit 1. **Open** from 7pm Mon-Thur, Sun; 7pm-5am

Local view Ko Kimura

Agaru Sagaru Nishi Iru Higashi Iru (meaning 'Go north, south, west and east') is one of Tokyo's best restaurants for authentic Japanese dining – and not just because of the food. The plates they serve on – mostly traditional Japanese ceramics and lacquerware – and presentation are also really impressive. There's a set menu that changes on the 15th of each month, making it a great place to enjoy the seasonal flavours of Japan.

For after-dinner entertainment, try **Space Lab Yellow** (*see p227*), one of the best and longest-running clubs in Tokyo. It attracts internationally renowned stars and makes quality music its priority. Yellow is a real must-visit.

Agaru Sagaru Nishi Iru Higashi Iru

Takeyama Bldg B1, 3-25-8 Jingumae, Shibuya-ku (3403 6968/http://r.gnavi.co.jp/g508401). Harajuku station (Yamanote line), Takeshita exit. **Open** noon-2pm, 5.30-11pm daily. **Credit** DC, MC, V.

One of the very first first house-music DJs in Japan, Ko Kimura has been playing professionally for over two decades. His flagship event, 'Kool', has been running at Yellow for over nine years. He also runs Japan's first house-music label, Futic Recordings Tokyo.

Fri, Sat. **Admission** ¥2,000 (incl 2 drinks) Mon-Thur, Sun; ¥3,000 (incl 2 drinks) Fri, Sat. **No credit cards. Map** Roppongi p103.

This three-level club features a stellar bar, cave-like areas, and billiards and ping-pong tables in the basement. So it's a shame that it's just a massive meat market. It's located at the Nishi-Azabu crossing; walk past Hobson's ice-cream parlour towards Hiroo on Gaien-Nishi Dori and look to your right. It's also worth noting that there's a 'not too casual' dress code.

Space Lab Yellow

Cesaurus Nishi-Azabu Bldg B1F-B2F, 1-10-11 Nishi-Azabu, Minato-ku (3479 0690/www.club-yellow.com). Roppongi station (Hibiya, Oedo lines), exit 2. **Open** 10pm-5am; days vary. **Admission** ¥3,000-¥4,000. **No credit cards. Map** Roppongi p103.

Better known as simply 'Yellow', this is the original hip venue in Japan; everyone from 808 State to Laurent Garnier and Timo Maas have played here. It faces stiffer competition than it used to, and from more conveniently located venues, but Yellow still draws the megastars, and then tests how many people it can squeeze in.

Vanilla

TSK Bldg, 7-15-30 Roppongi, Minato-ku (3401 6200/ www.clubvanilla.com). Roppongi station (Hibiya, Oedo lines), exits 4A, 4B. **Open** 7pm-5am Thur-Sat. **Admission** usually ¥3,000-¥3,500 (incl 1 drink). **No credit cards. Map** Roppongi p103.

Probably the most underused space in Tokyo. Vanilla is a vast club that can accommodate over 5,000 people, yet it never attracts a name big enough to lure such a crowd. When all the rooms are open – their decor ranges from traditional Japanese to carpeted playboy lounge – it's a fun place to party. Most of the time, though, the best rooms are closed, and punters are herded to the huge dancefloor to rub shoulders with office crowds while no-name DJs play cheesy house.

Warehouse

Fukuo Bldg B1F, 1-4-5 Azabu-Juban, Minato-ku (5775 2905). Azabu-Juban station (Nanboku, Oedo lines), exits 4, 7. **Open** 8pm-1am Mon-Thur, Sun; 8pm-3am Fri, Sat. **Admission** usually ¥2,500-¥4,000 (incl 1 drink). **No credit cards.**

A spacious venue that hasn't quite managed to capture clubbers' hearts as its predecessor Luners did. It is, however, still a decent alternative to the less salubrious offerings up the hill in Roppongi, and pulls in the occasional international DJ. Warehouse also hosts gay events.

Shibuya

Ball

Kuretake Bldg 4F, 4-8 Udagawacho, Shibuya-ku (3476 6533/www.club-ball.com). Shibuya station (Yamanote, Ginza lines), Hachiko exit; (Hanzomon line), exits 3, 6. **Open** 10pm-5am Mon-Sat; varies Sun. **Admission** ¥2,000 (incl 2 drinks). **No credit cards. Map** Shibuya p109.

Velours. *See p225.*

Club Camelot. *See p229.*

There's a great night view of Shibuya to be had from this little venue, but sadly that is its best feature, despite the moderately priced bar (drinks from ¥600). The sound system simply isn't up to scratch – and given that the choice of music is house, this is a very serious shortcoming indeed. The tiny dancefloor is another drawback.

Club Asia

1-8 Maruyamacho, Shibuya-ku (5458 2551/www. clubasia.co.jp). Shibuya station (Yamanote, Ginza lines), Hachiko exit; (Hanzomon line), exit 3A. **Open** usually from 11pm. **Admission** ¥2,000-¥3,500 (incl 1 drink). **No credit cards. Map** Shibuya p109.

Club Asia offers three bars and two dancefloors, with a high ceiling that looks spectacular but doesn't always do the sound any favours. It is increasingly being used as a live venue rather than as a club, and is a favourite space with private-party organisers, so check the schedule.

Club Atom

Dr Jeekahn's Bldg 4F-6F, 2-4 Maruyamacho, Shibuya-ku (5428 5195/www.clubatom.com). Shibuya station (Yamanote, Ginza lines), Hachiko exit; (Hanzomon line), exit 3A. **Open** 9pm-5am Thur-Sat. **Admission** ¥3,000 (incl 2 drinks). **No credit cards. Map** Shibuya p109.

There are two reasonably open dancefloors at this roomy venue. The one on the fifth floor focuses on mainstream trance or house, while the cave-like fourth floor offers R&B and hip hop. It's wildly popular with the heavily made-up, super-tanned Shibuya 'gals' and, as such, is more interesting from a sociological perspective than a musical one.

Club Bar Family

Shimizu Bldg B1F, 1-10-2 Shibuya, Shibuya-ku (3400 9182). Shibuya station (Yamanote line), Miyamasuzaka (east) exit; (Ginza line), Inokashira, Tamagawa exits; (Hanzomon line), exit 11. **Open** 10.30pm-4am Mon-Thur; 10.30pm-5am Fri, Sat. **Admission** ¥2,000 (incl 1 drink). **No credit cards. Map** Shibuya p109.

A tiny space pouring out heavy bass sounds, Family features ground-level hip hop at its best. Perfect if you like thundering rap beats. It's rare to see a non-Japanese face here, but that can mean a warm reception to any visitor who does venture inside. Drinks are a good deal at around ¥600.

Club Camelot

1-18-2 Shibuya, Shibuya-ku (5728 5613/www. camelotcourt.jp). Shibuya station (Yamanote line, Ginza line), west exit; (Hanzomon line), exit 12. **Open** 7pm-5am Thur-Sat. **Admission** ¥2,500-¥3,000 (incl 1 drink). **Credit** AmEx, DC, MC, V. **Map** Shibuya p109.

While Camelot wants to court the well-heeled and more mature trendsetters, its dress code is never enforced, and the weekend crowd varies from scruffy young Shibuya kids to dressed-up business-people looking to wind down. The smaller of the two floors holds 300 and specialises in hip hop, R&B and

reggae. Downstairs in the main area 700 people can gather on the marble floor or lounge on the white leather sofas. Try 'Ultimate Saturday' for a mix of house and hip hop. **Photos** *p228.*

Club Hachi

Aoyama Bldg 1F-4F, 4-5-9 Shibuya, Shibuya-ku (5766 4887). Shibuya station (Yamanote line), Miyamasuzaka (east) exit; (Ginza line), Inogashira, Tamagawa exits; (Hanzomon line), exit 11. **Open** 10pm-5am Mon-Sat; 5-11pm Sun. **Admission** ¥2,000 (incl 1 drink) Mon-Thur, Sun; ¥2,500 (incl 1 drink) Fri, Sat. **No credit cards. Map** Shibuya p109.

This dingy but funky club occupies the whole of a run-down, four-storey building on Roppongi Dori. The first floor contains a yakitori bar, the second a DJ bar, the third the main dance area, and the fourth a lounge bar. The monthly schedule ranges widely, from drum 'n' bass to R&B, house, techno, hip hop and jazz. Hachi was once the regular haunt of globally fêted DJ Ken Ishii.

La Fabrique

Zero Gate B1F, 16-9 Udagawacho, Shibuya-ku (5428 5100/www.lafabrique.jp). Shibuya station (Yamanote, Ginza lines), Hachiko exit; (Hanzomon line), exit 6. **Open** 11am-2am Mon-Thur; 11am-5am Fri, Sat. **Admission** ¥3,000-¥4,000 (incl 1 drink). **No credit cards. Map** Shibuya p109.

This branch of a Parisian dining club offers French dining in the daytime and dancing by night. The weekend events draw quality local acts and the odd visiting star, and usually kick off at around 11pm. Downtempo sounds are usually played during the week; but by the weekend the music speeds up to include a mix of house and disco.

Harlem

Dr Jeekahn's Bldg 2F-3F, 2-4 Maruyamacho, Shibuya-ku (3461 8806/www.harlem.co.jp). Shibuya station (Yamanote, Ginza lines), Hachiko exit; (Hanzomon line), exit 3A. **Open** 10pm-5am Tue-Sat. **Admission** ¥2,000 (incl 2 drinks) Tue-Thur; ¥3,000 (incl 2 drinks) Fri, Sat. **No credit cards. Map** Shibuya p109.

Located in the same building as Club Atom (*see above*), Harlem has been the mecca of hip-hop culture in Japan since the mid 1990s. If you want to see B-boys and fly girls shakin' it, as well as some of Japan's up-and-coming MCs, this is the spot. The tunes are basically straight-up rap with a little R&B mixed in. DJ Hasebe and other well-known Japanese spinners often play here.

Loop

B1F, 2-1-13 Shibuya, Shibuya-ku (3797 9933/www. club-loop.com). Shibuya station (Yamanote line), Miyamasuzaka (east) exit; (Ginza line), Inokashira, Tamagawa exits; (Hanzomon line), exit 11 or Omotesando station (Chiyoda, Ginza, Hanzomon lines), exit B1. **Open** 10pm-5am daily. **Admission** ¥2,000 (incl 1 drink) Mon-Thur; ¥2,500 (incl 1 drink) Fri-Sun. **No credit cards. Map** Shibuya p109.

Located between Shibuya and Omotesando stations, Loop has a stylish, bare-concrete interior and is an ideal hideout for dance-music aficionados. The dance-floor has moody lighting, an excellent sound system (music is mainly deep house, tech house and techno) and a friendly vibe. For local talent, check out 'Smoker' (Wednesday) and 'In the Mix' (Saturday).

Module

M&I Bldg B1F-B2F, 34-6 Udagawacho, Shibuya-ku (3464 8432/www.clubmodule.com). Shibuya station (Yamanote, Ginza lines), Hachiko exit; (Hanzomon line), exits 3, 6. **Open** from 10pm Mon-Sat. **Admission** ¥2,000 (incl 1 drink) Mon-Thur; ¥2,500 (incl 1 drink) Fri, Sat. **No credit cards.** **Map** Shibuya p109.

There's a relaxing split-level bar on the first floor and a marked contrast when you get downstairs to the second level. Here you'll find a loud sound system that causes the foundations to shudder below a small, pitch-black dancefloor, with only a glitter ball for light. Module pulls a much better selection of DJs and a more knowledgeable crowd than many of its peers. Being owned by Yellow (*see p227*) helps.

Neo

TLC Building 5F, 2-21-7 Dogenzaka, Shibuya-ku (5459 7230/www.clubasia.co.jp). Shibuya station (Yamanote, Ginza lines), Hachiko exit; (Hanzomon line), exit 3A. **Open** 11pm-5am; days vary. **Admission** ¥3,000-¥3,500. **No credit cards.** **Map** Shibuya p109.

Neo's location among Shibuya's biggest clubs (Womb, Vuenos, Club Asia) means it's often overlooked by clubbers, but it can offer a more chilled-out experience. The venue has no music policy – so you could be listening to dancehall, reggae or progressive house.

Organ Bar

Kuretake Bldg 3F, 4-9 Udagawacho, Shibuya-ku (5489 5460/www.organ-b.net). Shibuya station (Yamanote, Ginza lines), Hachiko exit; (Hanzomon line), exit 6. **Open** 9pm-5am daily. **Admission** ¥2,000 (incl 1 drink) Mon-Sat; ¥1,000 Sun. **No credit cards.** **Map** Shibuya p109.

Another small joint in the same building as Ball (*see p227*). What the tiny dancefloor lacks in space, it makes up for in atmosphere. The focus is on soul, jazz and bossa nova, all of which attract a slightly older crowd. All drinks cost ¥700.

Rockwest

Tosen Udagawacho Bldg 7F, 4-7 Udagawacho, Shibuya-ku (5459 7988). Shibuya station (Yamanote, Ginza lines), Hachiko exit; (Hanzomon line), exit 6. **Open** 10pm-5am daily. **Admission** ¥2,000-¥2,500. **No credit cards.** **Map** Shibuya p109.

Formerly a happy hardcore venue, Rockwest moves to a slower beat these days, with hip hop and soul dominating the schedule. Plus points are the air-conditioning, good sound system, relatively roomy dancefloor and re-entry system.

The Room

Daihachi Tohto Bldg B1F, 15-19 Sakuragaoka, Shibuya-ku (3461 7167/www.theroom.jp). Shibuya station (Yamanote line), south exit; (Ginza line),

central exit; (Hanzomon line), exit 8. **Open** 10pm-5am Mon-Sat. **Admission** ¥1,000-¥2,000 (incl 1 drink) Mon-Thur; ¥2,500 (incl 1 drink) Fri, Sat. **No credit cards.** **Map** Shibuya p109.

The Room is well hidden, so look for a red street light poking out from the basement. Owned by members of Kyoto Jazz Massive, it's a small venue split in two: one half is a concrete-walled bar, the other a pitch-black dancefloor. The flavour is usually house, jazz, crossover or breakbeats. Top DJs sometimes come here to try out new sets on their nights off, much to the delight of the clientele.

Ruby Room

Kasumi Bldg 4F, 2-25-17 Dogenzaka, Shibuya-ku (3780 3022/www.rubyroomtokyo.com). Shibuya station (Yamanote, Ginza lines), Hachiko exit; (Hanzomon line), exit 3A. **Open** 7pm-5am daily. **Admission** free Mon-Thur, Sun; ¥1,500 (incl 1 drink) Fri, Sat. **No credit cards.** **Map** Shibuya p109.

A little box of a venue that punches well above its size. Ruby Room holds around 150 people, yet has drawn acts including Basement Jaxx, Hernan Cattaneo and Belle & Sebastian to play impromptu sets. It remains a hugely popular spot for expats and club-conscious Tokyoites, despite a bizarre renovation in 2006 that saw a huge chunk of the floor space given over to a semi-private booth that looks very much like a toilet. Events are varied, but the monthly breaks party 'Deck 'n' Effect' is always reliable and busy.

Shibuya Nuts

B2, 2-17-3 Shibuya, Shibuya-ku (5466 8814/www.clubnuts.net). Shibuya station (Yamanote, Ginza lines), west exit; (Hanzomon line), exit 8. **Open** 10pm/11pm-5am Tue-Sun. **Admission** ¥2,000-¥3,000 (incl 1 drink). **No credit cards.** **Map** Shibuya p109.

It didn't take long for the younger sister of Roppongi Nuts to pick up a regular posse of its own fans. Hip hop and reggae dominate here, with breakbeats and house getting an occasional look in. A genuine, and much friendlier, rival to the larger Harlem (*see p229*) on the opposite side of Shibuya, Shibuya Nuts sometimes pulls in remarkably big international names. Sunday's 'Raga Nuts' is a Tokyo phenomenon – a rammed Sunday night, with locals bouncing off the walls to Japanese and visiting Jamaican MCs.

Vuenos Bar Tokyo

1F-B1F, 2-21-7 Dogenzaka, Shibuya-ku (5458 5963/www.clubasia.co.jp). Shibuya station (Yamanote, Ginza lines), Hachiko exit; (Hanzomon line), exit 3A. **Open** 11pm-5am; days vary. **Admission** ¥2,500-¥3,000. **No credit cards.** **Map** Shibuya p109.

Across from and owned by Club Asia (*see p229*), Vuenos opened in 1998 with a mission to spread the word about Latin, soul and dance music. On many levels it succeeded, though, at weekends, the line-up tends to focus more on hip hop, R&B and reggae. Vuenos attracts a younger crowd and is very popular, so you'll need to be prepared to queue to get in, especially later in the evening.

Womb

2-16 Maruyamacho, Shibuya-ku (5459 0039/ www.womb.co.jp). Shibuya station (Yamanote, Ginza lines), Hachiko exit; (Hanzomon line), exit 3A. **Open** usually 10pm-5am Thur-Sat. **Admission** usually ¥2,000-¥4,000. **No credit cards. Map** Shibuya p109. Womb is a top-flight club with a vast dancefloor, great lighting, a super-bass sound system and what claims to be 'Asia's largest mirror ball'. House, techno and drum 'n' bass are the usual sounds here. Womb's schedule is packed with foreign names, but DJ Aki (drum 'n' bass) is one local hero who plays here.

Shinjuku

Club Complex Code

Shinjuku Toho Kaikan 4F, 1-19-2 Kabuki-cho, Shinjuku-ku (3209 0702/www.clubcomplexcode.com). Shinjuku station (Yamanote, Chuo, Sobu lines), east exit; (Marunouchi line), exit B12; (Oedo, Shinjuku lines), exit 1. **Open** from 7pm daily. **Admission** ¥3,000 (incl 2 drinks) Mon-Thur, Sun; ¥3,500 (incl 2 drinks) Fri, Sat. **No credit cards.** With three dancefloors, one of which takes 1,000 people, this is in theory quite a venue. But it enjoys nothing like the stellar reputation of other mega-clubs in town and is starting to scrape the creative barrel with 'cyber trance' nights. Still, it's always worth a peek at its schedule.

Garam

Dai-Roku Polestar Bldg 7A, 1-16-6 Kabuki-cho, Shinjuku-ku (3205 8668). Shinjuku station (Yamanote, Chuo, Sobu lines), east exit; (Marunouchi line), exit B12; (Oedo, Shinjuku lines), exit 1. **Open** 9pm-6am daily. **Admission** ¥1,000-¥1,500 (incl 1 drink). **No credit cards. Map** Shinjuku p117. This swinging, foreign-owned Jamaican dancehall and reggae club could double as a walk-in closet. Still, the staff are very friendly, and Garam's become something of an institution, with Japanese MCs, sharp DJs and pounding vibes. To find it, head out of the east exit of Shinjuku station and down the pedestrianised street next to the Studio Alta TV screen. Cross Yasukuni Dori, and it's the third building on the right.

Izm

J2 Bldg B1F-B2F, 1-7-1 Kabuki-cho, Shinjuku-ku (3200 9914/www.clubizm.net). Shinjuku station (Yamanote, Chuo, Sobu lines), east exit; (Marunouchi line), exit B12; (Oedo, Shinjuku lines), exit 1. **Open** 10pm-5am daily. **Admission** ¥2,000 (incl 1 drink) Mon-Thur, Sun; ¥2,500 (incl 1 drink) Fri, Sat. **No credit cards. Map** Shinjuku p117. Sitting incongruously in the seediest part of Kabuki-cho, this small venue attracts a teenage clientele for a diet of hip hop, with a touch of R&B and reggae.

Open

2-5-15 Shinjuku, Shinjuku-ku (3226 8855/http:// club-open.hp.infoseek.co.jp). Shinjuku-Gyoenmae station (Marunouchi line), Shinjuku Gate exit. **Open** 5pm-5am Mon-Sat. **Admission** ¥1,000-¥1,500 (incl 1 drink). **No credit cards. Map** Shinjuku p117.

Open is the proud inheritor of the roots reggae tradition in Japan. It was set up by the staff of 69 – the country's very first reggae bar/club – when it closed down about a decade ago.

Oto

2F, 1-17-5 Kabuki-cho, Shinjuku-ku (5273 8264/ www.club-oto.com). Shinjuku station (Yamanote, Chuo, Sobu lines), east exit; (Marunouchi line), exit B12; (Oedo, Shinjuku lines), exit 1. **Open** 10pm-5am daily. **Admission** ¥2,000 (incl 1 drink) Mon-Thur, Sun; ¥2,500 (incl 1 or 2 drinks) Fri, Sat. **No credit cards. Map** Shinjuku p117. Oto (meaning 'sound' in Japanese) lives up to its name, with a PA that would do a much larger place credit. This long, thin venue isn't the cosiest place in town, but if you're there to dance, it's great. The sounds span the dancier end of the club-music spectrum.

Rags Room Acid

Kowa Bldg B1F, 2-3-12 Shinjuku, Shinjuku-ku (3352 3338/www.acid.jp). Shinjuku-Gyoenmae station (Marunouchi line), Shinjuku Gate exit. **Open** from 10pm; days vary. **Admission** usually ¥2,000 (incl 2 drinks). **No credit cards. Map** Shinjuku p117. Finding the entrance to Rags Room Acid (formerly Club Acid) is a challenge in itself – a small sign on Shinjuku Dori provides the only hint of its existence. The best method is to pay attention to the stairways of neighbouring buildings and follow your ears: you can hear anything booming out of here, from ska to rock, hip hop to Latin, R&B to techno to drum 'n' bass.

Further afield

Club Que (*see p260*) in Shimo-Kitazawa becomes a rock-oriented club at weekends.

Ageha

2-2-10 Shinkiba, Koto-ku (5534 2525/www.ageha. com). Shinkiba station (Rinkai, Yurakucho lines). **Open** 11pm-5am Thur-Sat. **Admission** usually ¥4,000 (incl 2 drinks). **No credit cards.** The biggest club in Tokyo, Ageha suffers from a far-flung location and dimensions that can feel a bit too cavernous. It offers three dancefloors, a pool area, numerous bars and chill-out spaces, and the best sound system in town. Women should check out the cubicle nearest to the toilet entrance – it leads to a secret, lockable room. The club provides a free bus from Shibuya every half hour. Board at the bottom of Roppongi Dori; you'll need photo ID featuring your birth date to be allowed on.

Bar Drop

2F-B1F, 1-29-6 Kichijoji-Honcho, Musashino-shi (0422 20 0737/www.drop.co.jp). Kichijoji station (Chuo, Sobu lines), central exit. **Open** from 9.30pm Mon-Thur; from 11pm Fri, Sat; varies Sun. **Admission** usually ¥1,500 (incl 1 drink) Mon-Thur; ¥2,000 (incl 1 or 2 drinks) Fri-Sun. **No credit cards.** This Kichijoji club features 1990s US and UK pop music on its two dancefloors, and a large lounge space for when you need a breather.

Film

A city of silver screens.

Cinema Rise rises to the challenge of bringing independent film to the masses. *See p234.*

Hollywood remakes have planted Japanese cinema firmly in the global consciousness, and added murderous videotapes and vengeful houses to the register of cinematic icons. But Japan's film industry stretches way back to the 19th century and a documentary entitled *Geisha no Teodori* ('Geisha's hand dance'). Mass viewing of film began in the early 20th century with imported foreign silent movies. Since the audience could not understand the foreign language inter-titles, a narrator (or *benshi*) was employed to explain things. *Benshi* soon became valued artists who narrated both Japanese and foreign work. A film of particular note from this early era is *A Page of Madness* (*Kurutta Ippeiji*, 1926) by Kinogasa Teinosuke, about a janitor in a mental asylum. Its images and techniques remain gripping today, testament to Kinogasa's vision, as well as to the sophistication of early Japanese film.

THE 'GOLDEN AGE'

The 1930s marked the dawn of the 'golden age' of Japanese cinema. Gifted directors such as Ozu Yasujiro, Mizoguchi Kenji, Naruse Mikio

and the less-heralded Shimizu Hiroshi produced work that exhibited a remarkable mastery of the craft. Although Ozu is best known for his post-war films, such as the famous *Tokyo Story* (*Tokyo Monogatari*, 1953), his pre-war work is edgier, more varied and equally accomplished. This period also saw the rise of the Japanese studio system. Much like their Hollywood counterparts, large studios such as Shochiku, Toho, Daiei and Nikkatsu started to put directors under contract and control the content of their work. Filmmaking was a thriving and extremely profitable business, and the studios ruled it with an iron fist.

The hiccup of Word War II limited film production to mainly jingoistic dreck, but the industry recovered its poise afterwards. General consensus holds that the golden age continued into the mid to late 1950s with Ozu, Mizoguchi and Naruse still active. In addition, new stars such as Kurosawa Akira – a man who would define Japanese cinema for the next 40 years – were rising fast. This period saw the emergence of talented auteurs Ichikawa Kon, Masumura Yasuzo and Teshigahara Hiroshi.

NUBERU BAGU

In the late 1950s and early '60s the studio system thrived as never before, but it was challenged by youthful and radical directors of the 'nuberu bagu' (from the French term *nouvelle vague*, or new wave) movement, despite the fact that major studio Shochiku had launched this movement to attract younger fans. Oshima Nagisa, Imamura Shohei, Hani Susumu, Yoshida Yoshige and others made films exposing Japan's social problems, questioning the assumption of Western values and materialism, and addressing taboo subjects like sexuality. In addition, they broke the studios' grip on directors, eventually venturing out on their own and also forming the artistically noteworthy independent production company Art Theatre Guild (ATG).

The tapering-off of the nuberu bagu in the mid '70s triggered a crisis in Japanese cinema. Attendances had been falling for years, and there were few new acclaimed directors appearing (although Kurosawa, Oshima and Imamura, among others, were still active). The situation continued in this vein for much of the 1980s. Although nearly half of Japanese box-office receipts still derived from locally made fare (a claim that few countries could make), the studios continued to churn out formulaic, melodramatic pieces and were suffering financially – in 1972 Daiei went bankrupt and Nikkatsu turned to making soft-core porn.

REBIRTH

Japanese cinema underwent an energetic rebirth in the 1990s with the arrival of young and/or fresh directors such as Kitano 'Beat' Takeshi – the most internationally successful of contemporary Japanese filmmakers – Iwai Shunji, Kurosawa Kiyoshi, Tsukamoto Shinya, Shinozaki Makoto and Ichikawa Jun. In addition, Japanese *anime* (animation), led by the genius of Miyazaki Hayao, started to conquer foreign markets and take huge profits at home – Miyazaki's *Spirited Away* (2001) is the highest-grossing film of all time in Japan. Hollywood has also jumped on the bandwagon, winning box-office success with remakes of a number of domestic hits, such as Nakata Hideo's horror mysteries *Ringu* (1998), *Ringu 2* (1999) and *Dark Water* (2002) and Shimizu Takashi's *Ju-on: The Grudge* (2003).

TICKETS AND INFORMATION

Visiting a cinema in Tokyo is expensive, with most cinemas charging a standard ¥1,800 for on-the-day admission (¥1,000-¥1,500 concessions). If you want to save money, you can buy advance tickets at convenience stores and ticket agencies for around ¥300-¥500 less

(or go on the first day of the month, when admission is usually ¥1,000). The problem with this system is that tickets are sold for the film, not the cinema – so in theory any number of people can arrive to catch the latest blockbuster. Seats are not allocated, so people regularly arrive an hour in advance and then charge in as soon as the doors open to grab the best places. The cluster of Japanese cinemas in Shinjuku, Ginza, Shibuya and other busy areas all operate this system. Seats can be reserved through agencies such as Pia (*see p251* **Tickets**), but this adds an extra ¥200-¥1,000 to the price. Some cinemas are cheaper; we've given ticket prices for those below. Hope also comes in the form of the new breed of multiplexes, which offer allocated seating at point of sale for no extra cost.

Most Hollywood or other foreign films are screened in their original version with Japanese subtitles. Cinemas occasionally screen a Japanese film with English subtitles (usually the last showing on a Sunday). If you visit in the autumn, you may catch one of the two international film festivals – the **Tokyo International Film Festival** (*see p216*) and **Tokyo Filmex** (www.filmex.net) – both of which show Japanese films with English subtitles. For film listings, check *Metropolis*, *Japan Times* and Tokyo Q (www.tokyoq.com).

Independent & repertory

Athénée Français Cultural Center

4F, 2-11 Kanda Surugadai, Chiyoda-ku (3291 4339/www.athenee.net/culturalcenter). Suidobashi station (Chuo, Sobu lines), east exit; (Mita line), exit A1. **Tickets** vary. **Seats** 80.
Screens classics and discovers new filmmakers.

Ciné Amuse

Fontis Bldg 4F, 2-23-12 Dogenzaka, Shibuya-ku (3496 2888/www.cineamuse.co.jp). Shibuya station (Yamanote, Ginza lines), Hachiko exit; (Hanzomon line), exit 3A. **Seats** *East Screen* 132. *West Screen* 129. **Map** Shibuya p109.
Programming ranges from Japanese classics such as *Ai no Corrida* to new international films.

Le Cinema

Bunkamura 6F, 2-24-1 Dogenzaka, Shibuya-ku (3477 9264/www.bunkamura.co.jp). Shibuya station (Yamanote, Ginza lines), Hachiko exit; (Hanzomon line), exit 3A. **Seats** *Screen 1* 150. *Screen 2* 126. **Map** Shibuya p109.
This two-screener in the giant Bunkamura arts complex offers mainly French fare. It's the principal venue for the Tokyo International Film Festival (*see p216*).

Cinema Artone Shimo-Kitazawa

Suzunari-Yokocho 2F, 1-45-15 Kitazawa, Setagaya-ku (5452 1400/www.cinekita.co.jp). Shimo-Kitazawa

station (Keio Inokashira, Odakyu lines), south exit.
Tickets ¥1,500; ¥1,000-¥1,300 concessions. ¥1,000
1st of mth (not Jan). **Seats** 50.
Independent films from around the world.

Cinema Rise

*13-17 Udagawacho, Shibuya-ku (3464 0051/www.
cinemarise.com). Shibuya station (Yamanote, Ginza
lines), Hachiko exit; (Hanzomon line), exit 6.* **Seats**
Screen 1 220. Screen 2 303. **Map** Shibuya p109.
A champion of independent cinema, this is where
Tokyoites watched *Buena Vista Social Club* and
The Corporation. Foreign students (who must
show ID) pay only ¥1,000. **Photo** *p232*.

Cinema Square Tokyu

*Tokyu Milano Bldg 3F, 1-29-1 Kabuki-cho,
Shinjuku-ku (3202 1189/www.tokyucinemas.net).
Shinjuku station (Yamanote, Chuo lines), east exit;
(Marunouchi line), exit B12; (Oedo, Shinjuku lines),
exit 1.* **Seats** 224.
The pioneer of art-house cinemas in Tokyo, show-
ing mainly recent independent films.

Ciné Pathos

*4-8-7 Ginza, Chuo-ku (3561 4660). Ginza station
(Ginza, Hibiya, Marunouchi lines), exit A6.* **Seats**
Screen 1 177. Screen 2 130. Screen 3 72. **Map**
Ginza p75.
A three-screener with new films and classic revivals.

Ciné Quinto

*Parco Part 3 8F, 14-5 Udagawa-cho, Shibuya-ku
(3477 5905/www.parco-city.co.jp/cine_quinto).
Shibuya station (Yamanote, Ginza lines), Hachiko
exit; (Hanzomon line), exit 6.* **Seats** 227.
Map Shibuya p109.
Quinto often screens new British films, and offers
bizarre film-based discounts. For example, when
Hong Kong film *The Eye* was on, anyone carrying
a photo of a ghost got a discount of ¥800. Different
rules are stipulated for each film. Keep your ticket
stub to enter for just ¥1,000 on your next visit.

Ciné Saison Shibuya

*The Prime 6F, 2-29-5 Dogenzaka, Shibuya-ku
(3770 1721/www.cinemabox.com). Shibuya station
(Yamanote, Ginza lines), Hachiko exit; (Hanzomon
line), exit 3A.* **Seats** 221. **Map** Shibuya p109.
Revivals, mini festivals and independent productions are the lifeblood of this comfortable cinema.

Ciné Switch Ginza

*Ginza-Hata Bldg B1F, 4-4-5 Ginza, Chuo-ku
(3561 0707/www.cineswitch.com). Ginza station
(Ginza, Hibiya, Marunouchi lines), exit B2.* **Seats**
Screen 1 273. Screen 2 182. **Map** Ginza p75.
Recent European and American films.

Ebisu Garden Cinema

*Ebisu Garden Place, 4-20-2 Ebisu, Shibuya-ku
(5420 6161/www.gardencinema.jp/yebisu). Ebisu
station (Yamanote line), east exit; (Hibiya line),
exit 1.* **Seats** Screen 1 232. Screen 2 116.
A mix of American indies and foreign films are
shown here. Film-goers are summoned in numbered

batches, according to when they bought their tickets,
so there's never any stampede for seats.

Euro Space

*Q-AX Bldg, 1-5 Maruyama-cho, Shibuya-ku
(3461 0211/www.eurospace.co.jp). Shibuya station
(Yamanote,Ginza lines), Hachiko exit; (Hanzomon
line), exit 5.* **Seats** Screen 1 91. Screen 2 144.
Map Shibuya p109.
An art-house specialist with a lifespan of over two
decades, playing independent films from Europe
and Asia, and in a new location since January 2006.

Ginza Théâtre Cinema

*Ginza-Théâtre Bldg 5F, 1-11-2 Ginza, Chuo-ku
(3535 6000/www.cinemabox.com). Kyobashi
station (Ginza line), exit 2 or Ginza-Itchome
station (Yurakucho line), exit 7.* **Seats** 150.
Map Ginza p75.
Late-night shows with interesting programmes.

Haiyu-za

*4-9-2 Roppongi, Minato-ku (3470 2880/www.haiyuza
gekijou.co.jp). Roppongi station (Oedo line), exit 6;
(Hibiya line), exit 4A.* **Tickets** vary. **Seats** 300.
Map Roppongi p103.
Roppongi's venerable old fleapit opens irregularly,
but when it does, its speciality is weird and avant-
garde films from all continents. A Tokyo treasure
that is worth a visit, if you can catch it open.

Hibiya Chanter Ciné

*1-2-2 Yurakucho, Chiyoda-ku (3591 1511/www.
chantercine.com). Hibiya station (Chiyoda, Hibiya,
Mita lines), exit A5.* **Seats** Screens 1 & 2 226.
Screen 3 192. **Map** Ginza p75.
Mainly recent European and American films.

Iidabashi Ginrei Hall

*2-19 Kagurazaka, Shinjuku-ku (3269 3852/
www.cam.hi-ho.ne.jp/ginrei). Iidabashi station
(Chuo, Sobu lines), west exit; (Oedo, Namboku,
Tozai, Yurakucho lines), exits B4A, B4B.* **Tickets**
¥1,500; ¥1,000-¥1,200 concessions; ¥1,000 1st of
mth. **Seats** 206.
Special double features offer interesting combinations of second-run films. Pay ¥10,500 to join the
Cinema Club and you can go as often as you like for
a whole year without paying another yen.

Institut Franco-Japonais

*15 Ichigaya-Funagawaramachi, Shinjuku-ku
(5206 2500/www.ifjtokyo.or.jp/services/cinema.
php). Iidabashi station (Chuo, Sobu lines), west
exit; (Oedo Nanboku, Tozai, Yurakucho lines),
exit B3.* **Tickets** ¥1,000. **Seats** 115. **Map**
Marunouchi p93.
A pearl in the Japanese cinema scene, this French
culture centre shows contemporary French films at
the weekend, often with English subtitles.

Iwanami Hall

*Iwanami Jinbocho Bldg 10F, 2-1 Kanda-Jinbocho,
Chiyoda-ku (3262 5252/www.iwanami-hall.com).
Jinbocho station (Hanzomon, Mita, Shinjuku lines),
exit A6.* **Seats** 220. **Map** Marunouchi p93.

Weeper reapers

The Japanese movie industry may not get as much press internationally as its counterparts in China, Korea and Hong Kong, but it beats them all in the number of films it produces – nearly 400 in 2006 alone – and its domestic box office netted $699 million in 2005.

Japanese films come in all genres, with a far broader range than those renowned abroad: samurai swashbucklers, yakuza actioners, animation and J Horror. But what's hot among Asian movie geeks in London is not always what's hot in Japan. J Horror, for example, has had only patchy success in Japan in recent years, while Hollywood continues to pay millions for the remake rights.

The films that really fill seats in Tokyo fit no one template, but many do an excellent job of stirring tender emotions. The Japanese enjoy a good, heart-cleansing sob at the movies – and the Japanese film industry knows better than Hollywood how to deliver it.

The most popular young actress right now, Nagasawa Masami (*pictured*), made her breath-through in the aptly titled 2004 smash *Crying Out for Love in the Centre of the World* (*Sekai no Chushin de Ai o Sakebu*), playing a bubbly, rosy-cheeked teenager with a fatal disease who haunts the dreams of her romantically bumbling boyfriend decades after her death. Audiences wept buckets, the film made $73 million and a star was born.

Nagasawa has since played variations of her loveable *Crying Out* character in film after film, most recently in *Nada Soso – Tears for You*, whose appeal for the local audience is summed up in its English subtitle.

The story, which is set in the subtropical island of Okinawa but could have been penned by Dickens, describes the struggles of a brother (Satoshi Tsumabuki) and sister (Nagasawa) who are alone in a cruel world, but utterly devoted to each other. Tragedy then strikes (and strikes and strikes), climaxing in a typhoon that nearly carries off poor Masami, until her brother makes the ultimate sacrifice in saving her. The audience got its tears, and the film's producers got their millions – more than $50 million to be exact. In Japanese movies today, wet is hot.

This highbrow cinema has been screening international works of social realism since the 1970s. The focus is on female directors and political work.

Kichijoji Baus Theatre

1-11-23 Kichijoji-Honmachi, Musashino-shi (0422 22 3555/www.baustheater.com). Kichijoji station (Chuo line), north exit. **Seats** *Screen 1* 220. *Screen 2* 50. *Screen 3* 106.

Everything from Hollywood blockbusters to Japanese independent films, but with an emphasis on mainstream stuff these days. There are discounts for men on Mondays, women on Wednesdays and couples on Fridays – plus anyone celebrating a birthday.

Kineca Omori

Seiyu Omori 5F, 6-27-25 Minami-Oi, Shinagawa-ku (3762 6000/www.cinemabox.com). Omori station (Keihin-Tohoku line), east exit. **Seats** *Screen 1* 134. *Screen 2* 69. *Screen 3* 40.

Three screens showing predominantly Asian films from all genres.

Laputa Asagaya

Laputa Bldg 2F, 2-12-21 Asagaya-Kita, Suginami-ku (3336 5440/www.laputa-jp.com). Asagaya station (Chuo, Sobu lines), north exit. **Tickets** ¥1,200; ¥1,000 concessions; ¥1,000 Wed. **Seats** 50.

Uplink Factory.

A charming, tiny cinema that shows everything from Japanese indies to experimental fare – stuff that's usually not shown anywhere else in Tokyo.

National Film Centre
3-7-6 Kyobashi, Chuo-ku (5777 8600/www.momat. go.jp). Kyobashi station (Ginza line), exit 1 or Takaracho station (Asakusa line), exit A4. **Tickets** ¥500. **Seats** *Screen 1* 310. *Screen 2* 151. **Map** Marunouchi p93.
Part of the National Museum of Modern Art, this venue has two cinemas, a gallery, a library and a café. It holds a collection of 19,000 films, and often revives Japanese classics.

Sanbyakunin Gekijo
2-29-10 Hon-Komagome, Bunkyo-ku (3944 5451/ www.bekkoame.ne.jp/~darts). Sengoku station (Mita line), exit A1. **Seats** 302.
Art-house specialist: classic features, revivals and cinema marathons. A place for serious cinephiles.

Sangenjaya Chuo Gekijo
2-14-5 Sangenjaya, Setagaya-ku (3421 4610). Sangenjaya station (Tokyu Denentoshi line), Setagaya Dori exit. **Tickets** ¥1,300; ¥800-¥1,100 concessions. ¥1,100 Fri; ¥1,000 1st of mth. **Seats** 262.
Second-run cinema with interesting double features.

Shimo-Takaido Cinema
3-27-26 Matsubara, Setagaya-ku (3328 1008/ www.ne.jp/asahi/kmr/ski/shimotakaido_cinema. html). Shimo-Takaido station (Keio line), east exit. **Tickets** ¥1,600; ¥1,000-¥1,300 concessions; ¥1,000 women Wed, 1st of mth. **Seats** 126.
A repertory cinema with a varied programming policy, from revivals to recent major films.

Shin-Bungeiza
Maruhan-Ikebukuro Bldg 3F, 1-43-5 Higashi-Ikebukuro, Toshima-ku (3971 9422/www.shin-bungeiza.com). Ikebukuro station (Yamanote, Yurakucho lines),
east exit; (Marunouchi line), exit 30. **Tickets** ¥1,300; ¥900-¥1,200 concessions. **Seats** 266. **Map** Ikebukuro p87.
A legendary repertory house in Ikebukuro showing a wide range of films, from Japanese classics to Hollywood no-brainers.

Theatre Image Forum
2-10-2 Shibuya, Shibuya-ku (5766 0114/www.image forum.co.jp). Shibuya station (Yamanote, Ginza lines), east exit; (Hanzomon line), exit 12. **Tickets** vary. **Seats** *Screen 1* 64. *Screen 2* 108. **Map** Shibuya p109.
Cutting-edge contemporary films, classics, avant-garde features and experimental work.

Tollywood
2F, 5-32-5 Daizawa, Setagaya-ku (3414 0433/http:// homepage1.nifty.com/tollywood). Shimo-Kitazawa station (Keio Inokashira, Odakyu lines), south exit. **Tickets** ¥600-¥1,500. **Seats** 46.
Art-house cinema specialising in shorts, famous directors' early works and new independent films.

Uplink Factory
Totsune Bldg 1F, 37-18 Udagawacho, Shibuya-ku (5489 0750/www.uplink.co.jp). Shibuya station (Yamanote, Ginza lines), Hachiko exit; (Hanzomon line), exit 3A. **Tickets** vary. **Seats** 70.
A fascinating mix, from Roman Polanski's early works to Eurotrash, plus lots of experimental and short work thrown in. Uplink also holds film workshops and live performances.

Multiplexes

Cinema Mediage
Mediage, Aqua City 1F/2F, 1-7-1 Daiba, Minato-ku (5531 7878/www.cinema-mediage.com). Daiba station (Yurikamome line). **Seats** 13 screens seating 114-612. **Map** Odaiba p101.
The home of the super-premium love seat, designed for canoodling couples (¥6,000), Warners-owned Mediage provides a superior film-going experience, with all seats reserved at no extra charge.

Shinagawa Prince Cinema
Shinagawa Prince Hotel, Executive Tower 3F, 4-10-30 Takanawa, Minato-ku (5421 1113/www.prince hotels.co.jp/info1/shinagawa-executive/cinema_imax/ site/cinema/index.html). Shinagawa station (Yamanote line), Takanawa exit. **Seats** 10 screens seating 96-219.
All the latest hits appear at this ten-screen giant. Premium screens have wide, high-backed seats (¥2,500), and parents can leave kids in the hotel's day nursery (9am-6pm; call ahead to get a place).

Virgin Toho Cinemas Roppongi Hills
6-10-2 Roppongi, Minato-ku (5775 6090/www.toho cinemas.co.jp/roppongi/index.html). Roppongi station (Hibiya line), exit 1C; (Oedo line), exit 3. **Seats** 9 screens seating 81-652. **Map** Roppongi p103.
Virgin's nine-screen multiplex in Roppongi Hills offers all-night screenings on Thursdays, Fridays, Saturdays and days preceding national holidays. Very comfortable seats (¥1,800-¥3,000).

Arts & Entertainment

Galleries

The cream of the creative capital.

Things move fast in Tokyo's contemporary art scene. As this guide went to press, a handful of significant new venues were set open in Roppongi, joining the roughly 1,000 existing galleries in the capital. The Kuma Kengo-designed **Suntory Museum of Art** (www.suntory.com/culture-sports/sma/index.html) in the new **Tokyo Midtown** complex (*see p107*) handles the traditional side of things, with collections of Japanese craft and treasures. Elsewhere in Midtown, **21_21 Design Sight** (www.2121designsight.jp; *see p107*) is a promising design research centre-cum-exhibition space, with Issey Miyake among its directors. But the most significant new arrival is likely to be the **National Art Center** (6812 9900, www.nact.jp), a 14,000 square metre exhibition space that plans to borrow wide-ranging collections from major international galleries, kicking off with an exhibition looking at the effects of materialism on art.

Handily for art lovers, many of Tokyo's best galleries are clustered together. Ginza boasts a diverse range of diminutive spaces (*see p242* **Local view**), and in the unassuming little area of Kiyosumi, a short distance from Tokyo station, you'll find some of the capital's best-known gallery complexes, housing **ShugoArts**, **Taka Ishii Gallery**, **Hiromi Yoshii Gallery** and the hugely influential **Tomio Koyama Gallery**. And Roppongi, the area once known only for all things lowbrow, now looks like one of the best destinations for art lovers. Alongside the three new spaces there's **Ota Fine Arts**, **roentgenwerke** and **Taro Nasu Gallery** in the Complex, and the always impressive **Mori Art Museum** (*see p102*). Across town in Omotesando, the white **Galeria Building** is home to Art-U Room, Promo-Arte and Gallery Gan, while other venues of interest nearby include **Gallery 360°** and **Spiral**.

INFORMATION

You'll find listings in *Metropolis*, the weekly art sections of newspapers – the *Japan Times* on Thursday, the *International Herald Tribune* on Friday and the *Daily Yomiuri* on Saturday – and the quarterly *Tokyo Journal*. Websites to check include TAB (www.tokyoartbeat.com) and Real Tokyo (www.realtokyo.co.jp/english). Real Tokyo are also the people behind *Art-it*, the first English-language print magazine

dedicated to Tokyo's art scene. The major commercial galleries have a free pamphlet that's entitled *New Favorite*, released every two months as a guide to the biggest contemporary art exhibitions.

Note that many of the galleries below open only when they have an exhibition on, so it's wise to call in advance or check online.

Asakusa

Gallery ef

2-19-18 Kaminarimon, Taito-ku (3841 0442/ www.tctv.ne.jp/get2-ef). Asakusa station (Asakusa line), exit A5; (Ginza line), exit 2. **Open** noon-7pm Mon, Wed-Sun. **Map** Asakusa p63.
The beamed ceilings and lacquered floors of this extremely rare example of a 19th-century earthen-walled warehouse are tough competition for the contemporary art that is shown here. The shows are mainly by lesser-known but interesting Japanese artists, with some international names joining in. There's a nice café too; *see p182*.

Ginza

Galleria Grafica Tokyo

Ginza S2 Bldg 1 2F, 6-13-4 Ginza, Chuo-ku (5550 1335/www2.big.or.jp/~adel/grafica.html). Ginza station (Ginza, Hibiya, Marunouchi lines), exit A3. **Open** 11am-7pm Mon-Sat. **Map** Ginza p75.
Two distinct spaces are housed within Galleria Grafica. The ground floor is a rental space for up-and-coming artists, while the second floor is home to works by the likes of Picasso, Miró, Giacometti, Matisse and Man Ray, and concentrates mainly on lithographs and prints.

Gallery Koyanagi

1-7-5 Ginza, Chuo-ku (3561 1896). Ginza station (Ginza, Hibiya, Marunouchi lines), exit A13 or Ginza-Itchome station (Yurakucho Line), exit 7. **Open** 11am-7pm Tue-Sat. **Map** Ginza p75.
This long-standing gallery may have a reputation for photography, but that's been by chance rather than design. It still represents photographer Sugimoto Hiroshi as well as animation queen Tabaimo, and works with notable foreign artists such as Thomas Ruff and Sophie Calle.

Ginza Graphic Gallery

DNP Ginza Bldg 1F, 7-7-2 Ginza, Chuo-ku (3571 5206/www.dnp.co.jp/gallery). Ginza station (Ginza, Hibiya, Marunouchi lines), exit A2. **Open** 11am-7pm Mon-Fri; 11am-6pm Sat. **Map** Ginza p75.

Mori Art Museum. *See p237.*

One of Japan's largest printing companies presents contemporary design and graphics here. Japanese designers are prominent, but major international talents appear from time to time.

INAX Gallery

INAX Ginza Showroom 9F, 3-6-18 Kyobashi, Chuo-ku (5250 6530/www.inax.co.jp/Culture/gallery/1_tokyo. html). Ginza-Itchome station (Yurakucho line), exit 7 or Kyobashi station (Ginza line), exit 2. **Open** 10am-6pm Mon-Sat. Closed 1wk Aug. **Map** Ginza p75.

Major ceramics-maker INAX runs an architecture bookshop on the ground floor here and two galleries upstairs. One gallery caters for emerging artists with a craft edge, while the other deals with exhibitions of traditional craft techniques from around the world.

Maison Hermès

Maison Hermès 8F Forum, 5-4-1 Ginza, Chuo-ku (3289 6811). Ginza station (Ginza, Hibiya, Marunouchi lines), exit B7. **Open** 11am-7pm Mon, Tue, Thur-Sun. **Map** Ginza p75.

The rounded glass-block walls of this beautiful, Renzo Piano-designed building both filter daylight and magnify neon at night. The gallery on the eighth floor holds shows of Japanese and international contemporary art and crafts, organised according to annual themes, such as 'The Hand'.

Nishimura Gallery

3rd Floor, Nihombashi Nikko Bldg, 2-10-8 Nihonbashi Chuo-ku (5203 2800/www.nishimura-gallery.com). Nihonbashi station (Ginza, Tozai lines), exit B1. **Open** 10.30am-6.30pm Tue-Sat. **Map** Ginza p75.
Yokoo Tadanori, Oshie Chieko and David Hockney are among the artists, both Japanese and international, appearing here.

Shiseido Gallery

Tokyo Ginza Shiseido Bldg B1, 8-8-3 Ginza, Chuo-ku (3572 3901/www.shiseido.co.jp/gallery/ html). Shinbashi station (Yamanote line), Ginza exit; (Asakusa line), exit A3; (Ginza line), exit 1. **Open** 11am-7pm Tue-Sat; 11am-6pm Sun. **Map** Ginza p75.
Like Maison Hermès (*see p238*), this place – run by cosmetics giant Shiseido – is more of a *kunsthalle* than a commercial gallery. It hosts important group and solo shows by contemporary Japanese and international artists such as Nakamura Masato and Roman Signer, as well as occasional retrospectives (Man Ray, for instance) and fashion-related shows. The gallery is located in the basement of the company's Ricardo Bofill-designed headquarters.

Tokyo Gallery

Daiwa Shunya Bldg 7F, 8-10-5 Ginza, Chuo-ku (3571 1808/www.tokyo-gallery.com). Shinbashi station (Yamanote line), Ginza exit; (Ginza line), exit A3; (Ginza line), exit 1. **Open** 11am-7pm Mon-Fri; 11am-5pm Sat. **Map** Ginza p75.
Tokyo Gallery shows modern and contemporary Japanese, Chinese and Korean artists. It opened a Beijing branch in 2003.

Wacoal Ginza Art Space

Miyuki No.1 Bldg B1, 5-1-15 Ginza, Chuo-ku (3573 3798/www.wacoal.co.jp/company/artspace). Ginza station (Ginza, Hibiya, Marunouchi lines), exit C2. **Open** 11am-7pm Mon-Fri; 11am-5pm Sat. Closed 1wk Aug, 2wks Dec-Jan. **Map** Ginza p75.
Underwear manufacturer Wacoal sponsors this space for exhibitions of contemporary art in fabric and other media, including ceramics.

Harajuku & Aoyama

Canadian Embassy Gallery

B2, 7-3-38 Akasaka, Minato-ku (5412 6200/ www.canadanet.or.jp). Aoyama-Itchome station (Hanzomon, Ginza, Oedo lines), exit 4. **Open** 9am-5pm Mon-Fri; 1-5pm Sat.
Canada's best artists appear in the spacious, high-ceilinged granite basement of the distinctive, award-winning Canadian Embassy building, designed by Moriyama & Teshima Architects.

Galeria Building

5-51-3 Jingumae, Shibuya-ku. Omotesando station (Chiyoda, Ginza, Hanzomon lines), exit B2. **Open** 11am-7pm Tue-Sun; hours can vary. **Map** Shibuya p109.
This building houses three galleries: Promo-Arte (3400 1995, www.promo-arte.com), Tokyo's main Latin-American art space; Art-U Room (5467 3938, www.mmjp.or.jp/art-u/index.html), specialising in contemporary Asian art; and Gallery Gan (5574 8178, www.presskit.co.jp), which represents mainly Japanese artists.

Gallery 360°

2F, 5-1-27 Minami-Aoyama, Minato-ku (3406 5823/www.360.co.jp). Omotesando station (Chiyoda, Ginza, Hanzomon lines), exit B4. **Open** noon-7pm Tue-Sun. **Map** Harajuku & Aoyama p82.
This well-located space emphasises works on paper and multiples by the likes of Lawrence Wiener and Homma Takashi, as well as examining the work of Fluxus, Buckminster Fuller and others.

Nadiff

Casa Real B1F, 4-9-8 Jingumae, Shibuya-ku (3403 8814/www.nadiff.com). Omotesando station (Chiyoda, Ginza, Hanzomon lines), exit A2. **Open** 11am-8pm daily. **Map** Harajuku & Aoyama p82.
The city's best art bookstore (the flagship shop in a chain) has a small gallery showing hot young Japanese artists, often in order to promote their latest book.

Sign

Yamazaki Bldg B1, 2-7-18 Kita-Aoyama, Minato-ku (5474 5040). Gaienmae station (Ginza line), exit 3. **Open** 10am-3am Mon-Fri; 11am-3am Sat, Sun.
This hip little café fills its awkwardly shaped basement gallery with photography and illustrations from up-and-coming young artists.

Spiral

Spiral Bldg 1F, 5-6-23 Minami-Aoyama, Minato-ku (3498 1171/www.spiral.co.jp). Omotesando station (Chiyoda, Ginza, Hanzomon lines), exit B1. **Open** 11am-8pm daily. Closed 1wk Aug, 1wk Dec-Jan. **Map** Harajuku & Aoyama p82.
A ramp spirals around the circular open space at one end of this Maki Fumihiko-designed building, hence its name. A wide range of fashion, art and design shows appears here. There's also a café, bar, interior goods store and record/CD shop.

Marunouchi

Base Gallery

Koura Bldg 1 1F, 1-1-6 Nihonbashi-Kayabacho, Chuo-ku (5623 6655/www.basegallery.com). Kayabacho station (Hibiya, Tozai lines), exits 7, 8 or Nihonbashi station (Asakusa, Ginza, Tozai lines), exit D2. **Open** 11am-7pm Mon-Sat. **Map** Marunouchi p93.
This well-established space represents blue-chip contemporary Japanese artists, such as painter Ohtake Shinro, and younger names, including photographer Yokozawa Tsukasa.

Arts & Entertainment

Forum Art Shop

B Block 1F, Tokyo International Forum, 3-5-1 Marunouchi, Chiyoda-ku (3286 6716/http://paper.cup.com/forum). Yurakucho station (Yamanote line), Tokyo International Forum exit; (Yurakucho line), exit A4B. **Open** 10am-8pm daily. **Map** Ginza p75.

Inside architect Rafael Vinoly's stunning landmark convention and performance centre (*see also p95*), this space showcases contemporary Japanese objets, arts and crafts. It also combines as a shop, selling a range of funky gifts.

Zeit-Foto Salon

Matsumoto Bldg 4F, 1-10-5 Kyobashi, Chuo-ku (3535 7188/www.zeit-foto.com/). Tokyo station (Yamanote, Marunouchi lines), Yaesu exit or Kyobashi station (Ginza line), exit B6. **Open** 10.30am-6.30pm Tue-Fri; 10.30am-5.30pm Sat. Closed 1wk Aug, 2wks Dec-Jan. **Map** Marunouchi p93.

This space behind the Bridgestone Museum of Art (*see p95*) claims to be the first photography gallery in Japan (it opened its doors back in 1978). It's certainly one of the strongest, with over 3,000 works in its possession. Expect inspired, reliable and wide-ranging exhibitions by both Japanese and international photographers.

Roppongi

Gallery Ma

Toto Nogizaka Bldg 3F, 1-24-3 Minami-Aoyama, Minato-ku (3402 1010/www.toto.co.jp/gallerma). Nogizaka station (Chiyoda line), exit 3. **Open** 11am-6pm Tue-Thur, Sat; 11am-7pm Fri. Closed 3wks Dec-Jan. **Map** Roppongi p103.

Sponsored by bathroom appliance-maker Toto, Gallery Ma holds some of the city's best modern and contemporary architecture shows. Foreign architects featured recently include Angelo Mangiarotti (from Italy), Seung H-Sang (Korea) and Yung Ho Chang (China). There's a small bookshop on site too.

Ota Fine Arts

Complex 1F, 6-8-14 Roppongi, Minato-ku (5786 2344/www.jade.dti.ne.jp/~aft/home.html). Roppongi station (Hibiya, Oedo lines), exits 3, 5. **Open** 11am-7pm Tue-Sat. **Map** Roppongi p103.

Some of Japan's best-known contemporary artists – such as Kusama Yayoi, Ozawa Tsuyoshi and others who deal with the politics of identity – show at this well-established gallery.

roentgenwerke

Complex 3F, 6-8-14 Roppongi, Minato-ku (3475 0166/http://roentgenwerke.com). Roppongi station (Hibiya, Oedo lines), exits 3, 5. **Open** 11am-7pm Tue-Sat. **Map** Roppongi p103.

Roentgen (German for 'X-ray') was first the largest and then the smallest gallery in Tokyo. Now the place is of a happy medium-small size, holding exhibitions of conceptual work, mostly by Japanese artists, such as Yanobe Kenji.

Taro Nasu Gallery

Complex 2F, 6-8-14 Roppongi, Minato-ku (5411 7510/www.taronasugallery.com). Roppongi station (Hibiya, Oedo lines), exits 3, 5. **Open** 11am-7pm Tue-Sat. **Map** Roppongi p103.

Works by young and emerging Japanese and international artists – the likes of Matsue Taiji – are displayed here, under Taro Nasu's unusually thin fluorescent strip lighting.

Shibuya

Gallerie Le Déco

Le Déco Bldg, 3-16-3 Shibuya, Shibuya-ku (5485 5188/http://home.att.ne.jp/gamma/ledeco). Shibuya station (Yamanote line), east exit; (Ginza line), Toyoko exit; (Hanzomon line), exit 9. **Open** 11am-7pm Tue-Sun. Closed 2wks Dec-Jan. **Map** Shibuya p109.

Regular exhibitions of work by young Japanese artists working in a range of media fill the six floors of this rental space. There's also a café and lounge area on the ground floor.

Nanzuka Underground

Shibuya Ibis Bldg B1F, 2-17-3 Shibuya, Shibuya-ku (3400 0075/www.nug.jp). Shibuya station (Yamanote line), east exit; (Ginza line), Toyoko exit; (Hanzomon line), exit 12. **Open** 1-8pm Wed-Sun. **Map** Shibuya p109.

Nanzuka presents new generation art with a hip, urban edge. Illustrations, futuristic fashion and vintage record sleeves have all adorned the walls of this gallery, located appropriately in Tokyo's yoof centre of Shibuya.

Tokyo Wonder Site

1-19-8 Jinnan, Shibuya-ku (3463 0603/www.tokyo-ws.org/english/shibuya/index.html). Shibuya station (Yamanote, Ginza lines), Hachiko exit; (Hanzomon line), exit 7. **Open** 11am-7pm Tue-Sun. **Map** Shibuya p109.

The most significant and convenient of a trio of government-funded sites that aim to nurture young creatives with gallery space, regular seminars, a café and an art market.

Other locations: Cosmos Aoyama South 3F 5-53-67 Jingumae, Shibuya-ku (5766 3732); 2-4-16 Hongo, Bunkyo-ku (5689 5331)

Shinjuku

Public art is relatively scarce in Tokyo, but near the west exit of Shinjuku station is **Shinjuku I-Land**, a collection of outdoor pieces by such big names as Daniel Buren, Luciano Fabro and Roy Lichtenstein.

epSITE

Shinjuku Mitsui Bldg 1F, 2-1-1 Nishi-Shinjuku, Shinjuku-ku (3345 9881/http://epsite.epson.co.jp). Nishi-Shinjuku station (Marunouchi line), exit 1. **Open** 10.30am-6pm daily. Closed 1wk Aug, 1wk Dec-Jan. **Map** Shinjuku p117.

Enjoy a soak in some culture, at bathhouse-turned-gallery **SCAI The Bathhouse**.

Epson uses its latest digital technology to create the enormous, impressively detailed photo prints displayed in its showcase gallery.

Kenji Taki Gallery
3-18-2 Nishi-Shinjuku, Shinjuku-ku (3378 6051/ www2.odn.ne.jp/kenjitaki). Hatsudai station (Keio New Line), east exit. **Open** noon-7pm Tue-Sat.
Kenji Taki and Wako Works are neighbours in the shadow of Tokyo Opera City. Taki exhibits contemporary artists from home (Watanabe Eiji) and abroad (Wolfgang Laib).

Tokyo Opera City Art Gallery
3-20-2 Nishi-Shinjuku, Shinjuku-ku (5353 0756/www. operacity.jp). Hatsudai station (Keio New Line), east exit. **Open** 11am-7pm Tue-Thur; 11am-8pm Fri, Sat.
With money from Odakyu Railways, NTT and other giant corporations, Opera City is one of the city's largest and best-funded private contemporary art spaces. As well as its own exhibitions of Japanese and international artists, it brings in touring shows from around the world. Hori Motoaki, former curator at the Museum of Modern Art in Kamakura, has recently taken the helm.

Wako Works of Art
3-18-2-101 Nishi-Shinjuku, Shinjuku-ku (3373 2860). Hatsudai station (Keio New Line), east exit. **Open** 11am-7pm Tue-Sat.
Wako shows blue-chip and/or conceptual contemporary artists, both Japanese and foreign. Among the big names to appear are Gerhard Richter and Wolfgang Tillmans.

Kagurazaka

Yamamoto Gendai
Minato 3 Bldg 4F, 3-7 Nishi-Gokencho, Shinjuku-ku (5225 3669/www.yamamotogendai.org). Kagurazaka station (Tozai Line), exit 1 or Ushigome Kagurazaka station (Oedo line) exit 3A. **Open** 11am-7pm Tue-Sat.
Located in an old printing factory, Yamamoto Gendai is the largest and best known of the four galleries that opened here in 2004. Visit to see up-and-coming Japanese talent such as Motohiko Odani. The gallery also stages the occasional live performance and symposium.

Yuka Sasahara
Takahashi Bldg 3F, 3-7 Nishi-Gokencho, Shinjuku-ku (5228 5616/www.yukasaharagallery.com). Kagurazaka station (Tozai Line), exit 1 or Ushigome Kagurazaka station (Oedo line) exit 3A. **Open** 11am-7pm Tue-Sat.
This gallery presents a younger generation of talent than is usually found at Tokyo's more established galleries. Though Sasahara holds the same address as Yamamoto Gendai, it is actually located in the building behind. Look for the spiral staircase and head to the third floor.

Yanaka

SCAI The Bathhouse
Kashiwayu-Ato, 6-1-23 Yanaka, Taito-ku (3821 1144/www.scaithebathhouse.com). Nippori station

Arts & Entertainment

(Yamanote line), south exit. **Open** noon-7pm Tue-Sat. Closed 2wks Aug, 2wks Dec-Jan. **Map** Ueno & Yanaka p123.

Formerly a bathhouse (the building is over 200 years old), this high-ceilinged space in a charming neighbourhood near Ueno Park features contemporary Japanese artists (Miyajima Tatsuo) and international practitioners (Lee Bul, Julian Opie).

Further afield

Depot

2-43-6 Kami-Meguro, Meguro-ku (5773 5502). Naka-Meguro station (Hibiya line). **Open** hours vary Tue-Sun.

Tokyo's media and arts movers and shakers gather in this fashionable new café/gallery space in Naka-Meguro. Located beneath rumbling railway arches, Depot has a distinct downtown New York feel, with exhibitions focusing on graphics, illustration and street culture.

Hiromi Yoshii Gallery

6F, 1-3-2 Kiyosumi, Koto-ku (5620 0555/www. hiromiyoshii.com). Kiyosumishirakawa station (Hanzomon, Oedo lines), exit A3.
Open 11am-7pm Tue-Sat.

Yoshii specialises in two areas: very young Japanese artists and new talent from art fairs abroad.

Mizuma Art Gallery

Fujiya Bldg 2F, 1-3-9 Kami-Meguro, Meguro-ku (3793 7931/www.mizuma-art.co.jp). Naka-Meguro station (Hibiya, Tokyu Toyoko lines). **Open** 11am-7pm Tue-Sat. Closed 2wks Dec-Jan.

This Naka-Meguro gallery presents some of Japan's hottest contemporary artists, among them Aida Makoto and Ujino Muneteru.

ShugoArts

5F, 1-3-2 Kiyosumi, Koto-ku (5621 6434/ www.shugoarts.com). Kiyosumishirakawa station (Hanzomon, Oedo lines), exit A3. **Open** noon-7pm Tue-Sat.

One of three major galleries in Kiyosumi's must-see art complex is ShugoArts, showing an eclectic range of contemporary Japanese and international artists, such as Shimabuku and Candice Breitz.

Soh Gallery

2-14-35 Midori-cho, Koganei City (042 382 5338/ www.soh-gallery.com). Higashi-Koganei station (Chuo line), north exit. **Open** 1-7pm Fri-Sun; by appointment Wed, Thur. Closed 1wk Dec-Jan.

Soh Gallery has long-standing relationships with top Japanese artists such as Morimura Yasumasa, Suga Kishio and Yoshizawa Mika.

Taka Ishii Gallery

5F, 1-3-2 Kiyosumi, Koto-ku (5646 6050/ www.takaishiigallery.com). Kiyosumishirakawa station (Hanzomon, Oedo lines), exit A3. **Open** 11am-7pm Tue-Sat.

Taka Ishii shows photography by major international and Japanese artists (Araki Nobuyuki, Hatakeyama Naoya, Thomas Demand).

Tomio Koyama Gallery

7F, 1-3-2 Kiyosumi, Koto-ku (6222 1006). Kiyosumishirakawa station (Hanzomon, Oedo lines), exit A3. **Open** 11am-7pm Tue-Sat.

One of Japan's most powerful contemporary galleries, Tomio Koyama has the clout to pick and choose whom it represents. It has chosen major Japanese artists, including Murakami Takashi and Nara Yoshitomo, as well as international figures such as American Dennis Hollingsworth. This is the fourth of the main spaces in the Kiyosumi complex.

Local view Paul Baron

For every interesting shop in Ginza, there is certainly an interesting gallery, which means thousands of different itineraries are possible.

My favourite route usually takes me from the main crossing of Ginza Yon-chome to the **Ginza Graphic Gallery** (*see p237*), one of the rare spaces showing graphic design in Tokyo. Then, on my way to the **G8**, a gallery specialising in Japanese illustrative or poster art (8-4-17, 1F Recruit Ginza 8 Building, Ginza, Chuo-ku. 3575-6918/www.recruit. co.jp/GG), I'll stop at the **House of Shiseido** (7-5-5 Ginza, Chuo-ku, 3571 0401, www. shiseido.co.jp/house-of-shiseido) for a look at art nouveau perfume-bottle design or a retrospective of their cosmetics advertising. Next, **Guardian Garden** (Recruit GINZA 7 Bldg

B1F, 7-3-5 Ginza, Chuo-ku, 5568-8818, www.recruit.co.jp/GG), a small basement space displaying contemporary photography or painting by Japanese artists, followed by a visit to the **Shiseido Gallery** (*see p239*) to catch some installation art. The **Tokyo Gallery**'s (*see p239*) numerous Chinese contemporary artists complete the Asian flavour of the walk, which I often finish off with a visit to the **Vanilla Gallery** (4F 6-10-10, Ginza, Chuo-ku. 5568 1233/www.vanilla-gallery.com/index.html), one of the few erotic-art galleries in Tokyo.

Paul Baron is a co-founder of Tokyo Art Beat (www.tokyoartbeat.com), a non-profit bilingual website listing events for over 500 of the city's art and design venues.

Gay & Lesbian

The closet's bigger than it looks.

Appearances can be deceiving, especially when it comes to homosexuality in Japan. Despite the growing visibility of celebrities who are openly (or seemingly) gay, a flourishing gay culture has yet to emerge at street level. The high pressure of social conformity keeps most Japanese gays and lesbians in the closet.

Strictly speaking, Tokyo doesn't have any gay neighbourhoods, if a neighbourhood is a place where people actually live. But don't despair, the metropolis does have its full share of gay bars, clubs and even brothels (called 'host clubs'). The main gay district, **Shinjuku Ni-chome**, is home to approximately 200 gay bars, yet remains a virtual ghost town until evening falls. But when the lights come on, the fun begins. When the nation's gays and lesbians are away from the prying eyes of family and co-workers, life is a cabaret.

It is not, however, a seminar. The power of the closet means that gay political and social organisations are tiny and few, and related awareness is low. For instance, while Western gays and lesbians almost universally support gender and racial equality, it is not unusual for queer establishments in Japan to exclude people because of race, gender or age.

Most bars for gay men in Tokyo can't comfortably hold more than 20 people, which makes visiting one an intimate experience; it's akin to being in the owner's living room. The atmosphere and decor are very much a reflection of his personality, and every visitor will have to speak to him – or a member or his one- or two-person staff – personally. The same holds true at the far smaller number of bars that cater specifically to women.

In such environments it's not foreigners as such who cause unease so much as people who don't speak Japanese. But if you know just enough for some rudimentary Q&A about your name, age, country and job, you should do fine. A polite, if clueless, smile will be the only communication skill you'll need for the rest of the evening. You may also be required to graciously purchase a mandatory *otoshi* bowl of snacks (*see p171*).

When you walk into a gay bookshop, you'll see another effect of the closet. Since being gay in Japan is largely about getting laid, gay bookshops are devoted almost exclusively to pornography, with none of the volumes on more wide-ranging subjects you'd find at gay bookstores in the West. That said, modern Japanese erotica can be interesting, thanks to its manga influences. Try **Books Rose** in Ni-chome (2-14-11 Shinjuku, 3352 7023, www.books-rose.com), which also accepts overseas orders on its bilingual website.

One hopeful sign for gay culture in Tokyo is the annual **Tokyo International Lesbian & Gay Film Festival** (*see p214*). The festival lasts several days, showcasing films from both home and abroad, and usually squeezes in at least one big party.

Another positive development is the recent appearance of Japan's first sexual-minority politicians. Transsexual Aya Kamikawa was elected to the local assembly in Tokyo's Setagaya ward in 2003. Kanako Otsuji won a seat in the Osaka prefectural assembly the same year, and came out as a lesbian in 2005.

INFORMATION

You can find more in *Otoko Machi Map (OMM)*, an annual guide to gay bars and venues nationwide, with thousands of listings and numerous maps. Since the 1990s *OMM* has evolved from a staple-bound booklet into a glossy paperback of more than 300 pages. In 2004 it received the sincerest form of flattery when an imitator called *Gay Navi* appeared. Both are available at any gay bookshop, as are *G-Men*, *Samson* and *Badi*, brick-sized magazines whose photos, cartoons and classified ads will give you some idea of the scene. They're worth a look even if you don't read Japanese. These resources are aimed at men, but queer women in Tokyo now have a valuable resource of their own, in the form of the bilingual lesbian website **Out Japan** (www.outjapan.com).

Bars & clubs

Advocates Bar

7th Tenka Bldg B1F, 2-18-1 Shinjuku, Shinjuku-ku (3358 8638). Shinjuku-Sanchome station (Marunouchi, Shinjuku lines), exits C7, C8. **Open** 8pm-4am daily. **No credit cards. Map** Shinjuku p117.

This small, smoky basement dance bar has a separate entrance around the corner from its sister, Advocates Café (*see p244*). Weekend DJ nights are hit and miss; follow the crowds from Advocates Café. There is sometimes a cover charge.

Advocates Café

7th Tenka Bldg 1F, 2-18-1 Shinjuku, Shinjuku-ku (3358 3988). Shinjuku-Sanchome station (Marunouchi, Shinjuku lines), exits C7, C8. **Open** 6pm-4am Mon-Sat; 6pm-1am Sun. **Credit** AmEx, DC, JCB, MC, V. **Map** Shinjuku p117.

With its zebra-striped walls and mirrored disco balls, this is not your average pavement café. But then Tokyo doesn't really do average pavement cafés: such places are still very rare, and this is one of the few spots in the city where punters spill out on to the street. Happy hour is 6-9pm Monday to Friday, and there's also a 'beer blast' on Sunday (6-9pm; all the beer you can drink for ¥1,000). Open to all sexes and sexualities. A good place to find out where the crowds are heading.

Arty Farty

Dai 33 Kyutei Bldg 2F, 2-11-6 Shinjuku, Shinjuku-ku (3356 5388/www.arty-farty.net). Shinjuku-Sanchome station (Marunouchi, Shinjuku lines), exits C7, C8. **Open** 7pm-midnight Mon; 7pm-5am Tue-Fri; 5pm-5am Sat, Sun. **Admission** ¥800 Mon-Thur; ¥900-¥1,000 Fri-Sun. **Credit** AmEx, DC, JCB, MC, V. **Map** Shinjuku p117.

This bar with a dancefloor offers DJs on weekends and mint-flavoured beer any time. Arty Farty is very popular among foreigners, including members of Gay Friends Tokyo (http://groups.yahoo.com/group/gayfriendstokyo/), an international English-speaking social group that often meets here on Wednesdays. Women are allowed 'with their gay friends' on Fridays and Sundays.

Backdraft

Tenka Bldg 6, B1F, 2-10-10 Shinjuku, Shinjuku-ku (5269 8131). Shinjuku-Sanchome station (Marunouchi, Shinjuku lines), exits C7, C8. **Open** 8pm-5am daily.

Admission *Men* ¥1,500 (incl 1 drink). *Women* ¥3,000 (incl 3 drinks). **No credit cards. Map** Shinjuku p117. The decor of this cosy, rock-walled den reflects the Japanese owner's past as a firefighter on a US military base. He and some of his all-bear staff speak English, and foreigners are welcome. A food menu of about 20 items is posted on the wall.

Chestnut & Squirrel

Ooishi Bldg 3F (Minx), 3-7 Shibuya, Shibuya-ku (090 9834 4842/http://2d-k.oops.jp/cs/cs.html). Shibuya station (Yamanote line), east exit; (Ginza line), Toyoko exit; (Hanzomon line), exit 9. **Open** 7pm-midnight Wed. **No credit cards. Map** Shibuya p109. Although open only one night a week, this small lesbian bar serves good food and draws a lively international crowd, including the occasional man. Mistress Chu speaks English and was one of the organisers of Team Japan at the 2002 Gay Games in Sydney. The name is a mischievous bilingual pun, as 'chestnut and squirrel' in Japanese is 'kuri to risu' – a homophone for 'clitoris'.

Dragon

Accord Bldg B1F, 2-12-4 Shinjuku, Shinjuku-ku (3341 0606). Shinjuku-Sanchome station (Marunouchi, Shinjuku lines), exits C7, C8. **Open** 7pm-4am Mon-Thur, Sun; 8pm-5am Fri, Sat. **Admission** free Mon-Thur, Sun; ¥1,000 (incl 1 drink) Fri, Sat. **No credit cards. Map** Shinjuku p117. Dragon is an aggressively male space in which women may not feel entirely welcome. On the other hand, its muscular, revealingly attired staff and dancefloor are major selling points. Be warned that it can get very crowded and sweaty if no other specifically gay event is happening in the city on a Friday or Saturday night. The dancefloor becomes a dark-room on Sunday afternoons and some weekdays.

Arty Farty.

Love father, love son

Same-sex marriage may be a hot issue in the Western world, but it's not even a faint blip on Japan's political radar. However, gays and lesbians here do have a way to form legally recognised families, and it's been around for generations. *Yoshiengumi*, or adult adoption, is a legal device whereby two men become father and son, or two women become mother and daughter. The older partner officially becomes the parent and the younger one the child, no matter what the age difference.

The adoption of infants is rare in Japan, but families seeking heirs – to run the family business, for instance – have often adopted adults. The same legal device is used by same-sex couples as a non-marital route to forming a family. One famous example was lesbian novelist Nobuko Yoshiya (1896-1973), who made a daughter of her beloved live-in 'secretary' Chiyo Monma, only three years her junior.

Otsuka 'Tac' Takuya (owner of Tac's Knot bar; *see p248*) has published an introductory guide to the subject. He tells of a gay couple who bought a house together but could register only one owner. When that partner died, his blood relatives claimed the property, and the survivor lost everything. According to Otsuka, same-sex couples who apply for adoption do it mainly to avoid such negative outcomes, but there are also positive aspects to the arrangement. Many Japanese companies offer employee benefits that extend to immediate family members. More importantly, an adoptive relationship guarantees a partner's right to make hospital visits and have a voice in medical decision-making, which might otherwise be vetoed by blood kin.

One of the drawbacks of adoption as an alternative to marriage is the unequal status of the partners, with one partner becoming the 'parent'. In their memoir *Love Upon the Chopping Board*, bi-national lesbian couple Marou Izumo and Claire Maree write that that they considered adoption, but found the idea of one addressing the other as 'Mom' to be just a little too weird.

Another drawback to adoption is that it involves a name change for one partner. This essentially means coming out to one's family and – more significantly in Japan's conformist society – also to one's employer.

Inheritance laws also complicate the issue, with the outcome depending on whether it's the 'parent' or the 'child' who dies first. And trying to circumvent the laws by filing complementary wills doesn't necessarily work in Japan since, according to Otsuka, local officials who review the wills must reject anything contrary to the public interest – but the definition of 'public interest' is left to their discretion. Some couples' wishes tally with the public interest, others are less fortunate. In contrast, adult adoptions must be accepted if the paperwork is in order.

Adoption seems to hold more appeal for older couples. Younger ones tend to put it off in the hope that real marriage will one day be available. But until then, at least gay and lesbian couples in Japan have a plan B.

Fellow

2-63-5 Ikebukuro, Toshima-ku (3971 5756). Ikebukuro station (Yamanote line), north exit; (Marunouchi, Yurakucho lines), exits 20A, 20B. **Open** 7pm-2am Mon-Wed, Fri, Sat. **No credit cards. Map** Ikebukuro p87.

Drawing mainly middle-aged athletes, this is a good place for a refreshing cool-down drink after a workout at the Toshima Ward Sports Center, just one block away across the tracks. Master Naka is a very good cook, and walking through his door means you have ordered a plate of food that is likely to include quiche. Clientele and staff are friendly, but you'll need to speak at least some Japanese to make yourself understood.

Fuji

B1F, 2-12-16 Shinjuku, Shinjuku-ku (3354 2707). Shinjuku-Sanchome station (Marunouchi, Shinjuku lines), exits C7, C8. **Open** 8.30pm-3am Mon-Thur, Sun; 8.30pm-5am Fri, Sat. **No credit cards. Map** Shinjuku p117.

After recent renovations this long-standing basement karaoke bar has begun to draw a younger, more international crowd than in the past. Grab yourself a microphone and show them what you're made of.

GB

Shinjuku Plaza Bldg B1F, 2-12-3 Shinjuku, Shinjuku-ku (3352 8972/www.techtrans-japan.com/GB/index. htm). Shinjuku-Sanchome station (Marunouchi, Shinjuku lines), exits C7, C8. **Open** 8pm-2am Mon-Thur, Sun; 8pm-3am Fri, Sat. **No credit cards. Map** Shinjuku p117.

Shinjuku's GB has long been the most famous bar in Tokyo for East/West encounters of the gay kind, and is also handily attached to a 'business hotel'. A large venue by Tokyo standards, GB has a less relaxed atmosphere than many places but is

24-hour party people

Tokyo's gay bars tend to be tiny and intimate, and its sex clubs tend to be tiny and cramped. One astonishing exception is the 24 (Niju-Yon) Kaikan, a sexual 'theme park' so big it occupies three whole buildings in Asakusa, Ueno and Shinjuku. One foreign customer calls it 'Tokyo's best-kept secret'. Check the website – **www.juno.dti.ne.jp/~kazuo24/ index.htm** – for details (in Japanese, English and Korean) of the three venues.

The procedure is the same at each establishment. Put your shoes in a small locker out front, then hand in the key and the entrance fee (¥2,300 to ¥2,800 depending on the time and location) in exchange for a towel, bathrobe and key to a bigger locker for the rest of your clothes. Once inside, the first item on your agenda is a Japanese-style communal bath.

At the five-storey building in Asakusa, this means sitting between paintings on opposite walls by Tagame Gengoroh, the famous Japanese erotic artist. Both show fierce,

heavily muscled men in loincloths riding *mikoshi* portable shrines (a reference to the annual Sanja Festival in Asakusa). The hyper-masculine Tagame type is unlikely to be seen in person, though, as the Asakusa clientele tends towards grey-haired, older men and a few long-haired 'new halfs' (transsexuals). The bath area also includes two saunas (one dark) and a suffocatingly hot steam room, as well as several two-man shower stalls with latching doors.

Over at the ten-storey building in Ueno, the baths are bigger and so are the men, with lots of bodybuilders and robust blue-collar types. (In fact, most of the tenth floor is a large, well-equipped weights room.) The wall above the main tub is adorned with a Tagame mural of seven virile men in various states of traditional undress. It gives the place a slight Baths of Pompeii atmosphere in which you can imagine that burly fellow with the ripples lapping his nipples to be a horny centurion. The shower area has double-occupancy stalls.

always pretty busy. It's located opposite Dragon (*see p244*) and admits men only, except for one day of the year – Halloween.

Go Round

Satake Bldg 1F, 2-16-12 Shinjuku, Shinjuku-ku (3350 1050/http://www.bar-goround.com), Shinjuku-Sanchome station (Marunouchi, Shinjuku lines), exits C7, C8. **Open** 7pm-3am Mon-Thur, Sun; 6pm-5am Fri, Sat, holidays. **Credit** AmEx, DC, JCB, MC, V. **Map** Shinjuku p117.

Opened in 2006, this is one of the newest additions to Ni-chome's ever-changing gay bar scene. At least one of the staff, a Japanese guy who used to live in New York, speaks English. Go Round is smaller inside than its corner location and wide, windowless façade suggests. Its two-tone decor includes a black chandelier, a white merry-go-round horse, black and white walls and floors, and Guinness on tap. The latter goes for ¥500 until 8pm daily.

Hijouguchi

1F, 2-12-16 Shinjuku, Shinjuku-ku (3341 5445/ http://www.hijouguchi.com), Shinjuku-Sanchome station (Marunouchi, Shinjuku lines), exits C7, C8. **Open** 7pm-1am Mon-Sat. **No credit cards**. **Map** Shinjuku p117.

Hijoguchi means 'Emergency Exit', but the English signage at this side-street bar just says 'Exit'. Signs in both languages are done in factory-issue style, making them easy to miss. The bartenders' island inside the main entrance leaves barely enough room

for customers to squeeze around the edges. Make your own 'emergency exit' through the unmarked door at the rear to find a second bar area. Here, the drinks counter hugs one wall, and a DJ booth clings to another, leaving a surprisingly spacious (by Ni-chome standards) dancefloor in the middle. Hijouguchi has little personality of its own, but hosts a chameleon-like array of events, sometimes including the women-only floating disco 'Goldfinger'. The food menu includes *izakaya*-style snacks such as spring rolls and sautéed gizzards.

Hug

2-15-8 Shinjuku, Shinjuku-ku (5379 5085). Shinjuku-Sanchome station (Marunouchi, Shinjuku lines), exits C7, C8. **No credit cards**. **Map** Shinjuku p117.

A women-only karaoke bar that tends to attract a clientele aged 30 and above.

Kinsmen

2F, 2-18-5 Shinjuku, Shinjuku-ku (3354 4949). Shinjuku-Sanchome station (Marunouchi, Shinjuku lines), exits C7, C8. **Open** 8pm-1am Tue-Thur; 7pm-1am Fri-Sun. **No credit cards**. **Map** Shinjuku p117.

A fixture on the anglophone gay scene for more than two decades, this spacious bar has been run since Christmas 2002 by a jovial pair of guys who go by the unlikely names of Nori and Ebi (Seaweed and Shrimp). Beyond its famous, giant *ikebana* flower arrangements, you'll find scented candles, tiny cacti, antique-looking Western furniture and a piano that

The seven-storey Shinjuku operation – which opened in 2003 – has the largest bath area of all, including more double shower cubicles than the other two places combined, some communicating with neighbouring stalls via glory holes. There are two saunas, a steam room, a mist room and a sling room equipped with showerheads. No artwork, but there's plenty to look at in terms of your fellow customers. It's a younger crowd on the whole, with the greatest variety in terms of age, nationality and body type.

All three buildings have car parking at street level, sunbathing on the roof and a free condom at the front desk (plus condom-vending machines). They also offer bunkrooms and open, futon-floored rooms where you may sleep, cuddle or 'play', as well as hotel-style private rooms available for an extra charge. Asakusa has a public room set up like a peephole-riddled maze, and Shinjuku has a 'starlight room' where ultraviolet light turns bodies into stark black shapes against glowing white bedding. You'll also find snack bars, tanning beds and multiple TV lounges, and a large karaoke bar at Asakusa. All three are open 24 hours a day; credit cards are not accepted.

24 Kaikan Asakusa

2-29-16 Asakusa, Taito-ku (5827 2424). Asakusa station (Asakusa line), exit A3; (Ginza line) exits 7, 8. **Admission** ¥2,300 5am-9pm; ¥2,800 9pm-5am. **Map** Asakusa p63.

24 Kaikan Shinjuku

2-13-1 Shinjuku, Shinjuku-ku (3354 2424). Shinjuku-Sanchome station (Marunouchi, Shinjuku lines), exits C7, C8. **Admission** ¥2,600 up to 13hrs. **Map** Shinjuku p117.

24 Kaikan Ueno

1-8-7 Kita-Ueno, Taito-ku (3847 2424). Ueno station (Yamanote line), Iriya exit; (Ginza, Hibiya lines), exit 9. **Admission** ¥2,400 5am-9pm; ¥2,800 9pm-5am. **Map** Ueno & Yanaka p123.

sometimes actually gets played. Men, women and foreigners are made to feel equally welcome at this very laid-back place.

Kinswomyn

Daiichi Tenka Bldg 3F, 2-15-10 Shinjuku, Shinjuku-ku (3354 8720). Shinjuku-Sanchome station (Marunouchi, Shinjuku lines), exits C7, C8. **Open** 8pm-3am Wed-Sun. **No credit cards.** **Map** Shinjuku p117.

Kinswomyn (a sibling of the nearby men's bar; *see p246*) is Tokyo's most popular women-only bar. Old-guard butch-femme types occasionally drop by, but for the most part it's a cosy, relaxed crowd.

Kusuo

Sunflower Bldg 3F, 2-17-1 Shinjuku, Shinjuku-ku (3354 5050/www5.ocn.ne.jp/~kusuo), Shinjuku-Sanchome station (Marunouchi, Shinjuku lines), Exits C7, C8. **Open** 8pm-4am Mon-Fri, Sun; 8pm-5am Sat. **No credit cards.** **Map** Shinjuku p117.

A karaoke cathedral and one of the biggest gay bars in Tokyo, Kusuo not only has plenty of room to dance the night away but sometimes offers tango or square-dancing lessons in the afternoon too. What it lacks in refined decoration – the walls and ceiling are sloppily painted black – it more than makes up for in abundant breathing room and an exuberant, foreigner-friendly staff. Another plus is that women are officially welcome, though their first drink will cost ¥1,500, compared to ¥1,000 for men.

Monsoon

Shimazaki Bldg 6F, 2-14-9 Shinjuku, Shinjuku-ku (3354 0470). Shinjuku-Sanchome station (Marunouchi, Shinjuku lines), exits C7, C8. **Open** 3pm-6am daily. **Credit** AmEx, MC, V. **Map** Shinjuku p117.

A small, inexpensive, formerly men-only bar that now admits everyone. Unusually long opening hours make it one of the few places in Ni-chome where you can get a drink before sunset. The artwork on the walls changes every few months.

New Sazae

Ishikawa Bldg 2F, 2-18-5 Shinjuku, Shinjuku-ku (3354 1745/http://new_sazae.tripod.co.jp/open.htm). Shinjuku-Sanchome station (Marunouchi, Shinjuku lines), exits C7, C8. **Open** 9pm-6am Mon-Sat; 10pm-6am Sun. **Admission** ¥1,000 (incl 1 drink). **No credit cards.** **Map** Shinjuku p117.

Despite the 'new' in its name, this is a blast from the past – specifically the 1970s – in terms of both music and decor. It gets going late and has a great attitude-free, anything-goes atmosphere. Fabulous, old, seen-it-all drag queens can sometimes be found propping up the bar.

Papi Chulos

M&T Bldg 8F, 2-12-15 Shinjuku, Shinjuku-ku (3356 9833). Shinjuku-Sanchome station (Marunouchi, Shinjuku lines), exits C7, C8. **Open** 6pm-5am daily. **No credit cards.** **Map** Shinjuku p117.

One of Ni-chome's newest bars (opened in summer 2004), Papi Chulos is a friendly place, welcoming all genders and nationalities. The agreeable, young, English-speaking master, Masa, enjoys experimenting with cocktail recipes; an early success is the lime-cranberry Haychini, named after a regular customer. A small open-air balcony and a loft with fur-draped sofas make this an unusually comfortable bar, while the window-box installation art makes it a quirky one as well.

Snack 24

2-28-18 Asakusa, Taito-ku (3843 4424). Asakusa station (Asakusa line), exit A3; (Ginza line), exits 7, 8. **Open** 6pm-2am daily. **Admission** ¥2,800 (incl 3 drinks). **No credit cards. Map** Asakusa p63.

This bar, associated with the nearby branch of 24 Kaikan (*see p246* **24-hour party people**), consists of two sections, with street clothes worn in one area and traditional Japanese loincloths in the other. Regular customers bring their own loincloths, but these can also be rented for ¥500, and first-timers will be taught how to tie one on. Occasional patrols by a flashlight-wielding barman ensure minimal hanky-panky in the main areas – but there is a back room. The crowd tends to be mostly middle-aged or older. Wednesday nights are particularly popular as they offer all-you-can-drink deals for ¥2,800.

Tac's Knot

3-11-12 Shinjuku, Shinjuku-ku (3341 9404/ www.asahi-net.or.jp/~Km5t-ootk/tacsknot. html). Shinjuku-Sanchome station (Marunouchi, Shinjuku lines), exits C7, C8. **Open** 8pm-2am daily. **Admission** ¥1,200 (incl 1 drink). **No credit cards. Map** Shinjuku p117.

Each month the walls of this tiny cocktail bar display the work of a different local gay artist. Master Tac is a local gay community leader and an artist of some note himself – his bejewelled reliquaries for pubic hair caused a stir back in the 1990s. Tac speaks some English, but prefers to get warmed up first in Japanese. **Photo** *p249.*

Tactics

Princess Ichiban-kan Bldg 3F, 3-22-3 Shinbashi, Minato-ku (070 5086 8839/www2c.airnet.ne.jp/ tactics), Shinbashi station (Yamanote line), Karasumori exit. **Open** 6pm-midnight Mon-Thur, Sat; 6pm-5am Fri; closed Sun, holidays. **No credit cards.**

West and south of Shinbashi station are hundreds of bars where hard-working Japanese businessmen drown the stresses of their day to relax. At least 50 of those bars, including Tactics, are gay. The clientele here consists mostly of salarymen in their 30s, direct from the office in their suits and ties, while the staff are predominately younger guys in T-shirts. Foreign visitors are made to feel welcome, and long-term expats are also sometimes part of the scene. The first drink here costs ¥1,500, and ¥800 thereafter.

Other location: 1F, 2-7-3 Shinjuku, Shinjuku-ku (3354 5050), Shinjuku-Sanchome station (Marunouchi, Shinjuku lines), exits C7, C8.

Sex clubs

Dozens of Tokyo *hattenba* (sex clubs) are listed in *OMM*. They're usually small apartments or offices turned into 'cruising boxes', with flimsy partition walls, dim lighting and dodgy music. Some have themes (naked, swimwear, jockstraps and so on) on different nights – but the real theme is always the same. Those listed below accept foreign customers.

Pay close attention to the addresses, as external signage is often minimal or non-existent. Condoms are generally provided at the door, but it's wise to bring your own. When you arrive, a voice behind the counter may ask if you speak Japanese. Just say 'hai'.

For details about the 24 Kaikan mega sex clubs, *see p246* **24 hour party people**.

Jinya

2-30-19 Ikebukuro, Toshima-ku (5951 0995). Ikebukuro station (Yamanote line), west exit; (Marunouchi, Yurakucho, lines), exit C1. **Open** 24hrs daily. **Admission** ¥2,200. **No credit cards. Map** Ikebukuro p87.

This gay bathhouse may be smaller than the three 24 Kaikan (*see p246* **24-hour party people**), but it certainly dwarfs ordinary *hattenba*. Facilities include a refreshment/television room, a communal bath, a sauna, private rooms with beds and locking doors, futon rooms with curtained doorways, and a large porn-viewing lounge with sofas and futons. You'll be issued with a towel and bathrobe upon entering the premises.

Spartacus

MK Bldg 4F, 2-14-3 Ikebukuro, Toshima-ku (5951 6556). Ikebukuro station (Yamanote line), west exit; (Marunouchi, Yurakucho, lines), exit C1. **Open** 24hrs daily. **Admission** ¥1,500; ¥1,000 5am-11am. **No credit cards. Map** Ikebukuro p87.

The adverts for Spartacus say nobody 'over 40 or ill-mannered' will be admitted. As the club is on the fourth floor of a lift-less building, your physical state on arrival may reveal whether you're over the age limit. Then the cashier can reveal whether he is being ill-mannered. On weeknights the maze-like interior can be as dark and silent as a tomb, but it gets much busier at weekends. Rikkyo University is nearby. Dress code: nude.

Treffpunkt

Fukutomi Bldg 4F, 2-13-14 Akasaka, Minato-ku (5563 0523). Akasaka station (Chiyoda line), exits 2, 5A, 5B. **Open** noon-11pm daily. **Admission** ¥1,000. **No credit cards.**

A small club near Tokyo's business areas, laid out in such a way that it takes a while to explore all the nooks and crannies (including one alcove with a newly installed sling). Even on a Sunday evening, when the surrounding area is dead, Treffpunkt is likely to be busy, with many foreigners in the mix. Underwear is forbidden at weekends. It is worth

Tiny **Tac's Knot** proves the best things really do come in small packages. *See p248.*

noting that unlike most sex clubs, which are open 24 hours a day, Treffpunkt closes at 11pm.

Host clubs

'Host bar' is Japanese English for a place to hire rent boys. Japan's prostitution laws – at least as applied – pertain only to certain heterosexual acts, leaving gay bordellos free to operate openly. There are at least 14 such establishments in Nichome alone. At the two listed below, hosts will service foreigners. Step inside, have a drink at the bar, look over the assembled staff and take your pick.

Janny's

Tenka Bldg 3 2F, 2-14-8 Shinjuku (3341 3333/ www.jannys.net). Shinjuku-Sanchome station (Marunouchi, Shinjuku lines), exits C7, C8. **Open** 6pm-5am daily. **Admission** ¥1,300. **Credit** DC, JCB, MC, V. **Map** Shinjuku p117.
Easy to find, with a sign located just across the street from popular Advocates Café (*see px227*), Janny's boasts that all its hosts are aged between 18 and 25; photos of the current crop can be seen on the sign outside or checked out online before your visit. They cost ¥12,000 an hour, plus ¥2,500 for a room on the premises.

King of College

2-14-5 Shinjuku, Shinjuku-ku (3352 3930/www. kocnet.jp). Shinjuku-Sanchome station (Marunouchi, Shinjuku lines), exits C7, C8. **Open** 6pm-4am daily. **Credit** AmEx, DC, JCB, MC, V. **Map** Shinjuku p117.

Friendly, English-speaking staff make this place ideal. You can rent hosts (starting at ¥13,000 for 60 minutes on top of the ¥1,500 one-drink cover charge) in a free private room at the club or to take to your own home or hotel. The bilingual website has staff photos on the Japanese side.

Love hotels

Business Hotel S

2-12-3 Shinjuku, Shinjuku-ku (5367 2949). Shinjuku-Sanchome station (Marunouchi, Shinjuku lines), exits C7, C8. **Open** 24hrs daily. **Admission** ¥4,200 2hrs; ¥8,800 overnight. **No credit cards**. **Map** Shinjuku p117.
The word 'business' fools no one. Formerly known as Business Hotel T, this is a gay love hotel, pure and simple, conveniently located above GB (*see p245*). Rooms here are small and spartan, but include a coin-operated minibar full of beer, and *yukata* bathrobes, presumably for more modest post-coital lounging.

Hotel Nuts

1-16-5 Shinjuku, Shinjuku-ku (5379 1044). Shinjuku-Sanchome station (Marunouchi, Shinjuku lines), exit C8. **Open** 24hrs daily. **Admission** ¥5,800-¥7,400 2hrs. **Credit** AmEx, JCB, V.
The best known of Tokyo's smattering of gay love hotels, located just outside Shinjuku's main gay bar area. The basic rooms are pink, spotlessly clean and have decent bathrooms. Be aware that the management has been known to refuse entry if neither customer is Japanese.

Music

The best of the West, and lashings of local talent.

Suntory Hall. *See p251.*

Whatever your taste in music, you'll find a scene for it in Tokyo. From hip hop to opera, funk to punk, northern soul to old-time rock 'n' roll, there's a thriving live scene, specialist record shops and great domestic acts for genres as unlikely as afrobeat or ska. The venues run the gamut from tatty fleapit to state-of-the-art hall. All you have to do is pick your listening pleasure.

Classical & opera

Tokyo has an outstanding collection of classical music venues. Flush with Bubble-era cash, corporate titans and politicians hired brand-name architects and launched them on a building spree that has left 21st-century Tokyo with a number of gleaming entertainment venues, including the **Tokyo Opera City** and **New National Theatre, Tokyo** (NNTT) complex (Tange Kenzo, 1996) and the **Tokyo International Forum** (Rafael Vinoly, 1996).

Perhaps less thought was given to how to fill these new halls, but with dozens of amateur and professional orchestras, Tokyo claims to offer more classical music events than any other city in the world. Classical music has been popular in Japan since the country opened to the outside world in the 19th century, and it has produced

its own legitimate stars – from conductor Ozawa Seiji and composer Takamitsu Toru to pianist Uchida Mitsuko and violinist Midori.

Tokyo has no fewer than five symphony orchestras; the most distinguished are the **NHK Symphony Orchestra** (founded in 1926, www.nhkso.or.jp) and the **Tokyo Symphony Orchestra** (founded in 1946, www.tokyo symphony.com). As is common elsewhere in Japan, most are led by star conductors from overseas, but native conductors like Takaseki Ken are beginning to make their mark.

Opera is represented by the venerable **Fujiwara Opera Company**, founded in 1934 and specialising in Western opera, and the **Nihon Opera Kyokai**, specialising in Japanese opera; both operate under the auspices of the Japan Opera Foundation (www.jof.or.jp). The government-run New National Theatre, Tokyo has its own chorus and presents operas in conjunction with the Tokyo Symphony Orchestra. The NNTT's high-profile artistic director, Austrian Thomas Novohradsky, recently ruffled feathers by abolishing the double-cast system that paired foreign and domestic singers in lead roles. This has reduced opportunities for local singers, but raised the overall quality of performances by importing top international guest stars.

INFORMATION

Check out the free weekly magazine *Metropolis* for the most up-to-date English-language listings. Most of the larger venues have detailed listings in English online.

Main venues

New National Theatre, Tokyo

1-1-1 Honmachi, Shibuya-ku (5352 9999/ www.nntt.jac.go.jp). Hatsudai station (Keio New line), central exit. **Capacity** *Opera House 1,814. Playhouse 1,038. The Pit 468.* **Box office** 10am-7pm daily. **Credit** AmEx, JCB, MC, V.

The National Theatre (*see p265*) focuses on traditional dance and theatre, while the New National Theatre (NNTT) caters to the modern generation. It calls its spaces the Opera House, the Playhouse and the Pit. The last two cater for mostly modern dance and drama, while the Opera House was purpose-built for opera, but sometimes hosts classical ballet performances. The complex that houses the spaces is worth a visit in its own right. Opera tickets cost from ¥3,150 to ¥21,000.

NHK Hall

2-2-1 Jinnan, Shibuya-ku (3465 1751/www.nhk-sc.or.jp/nhk_hall). Harajuku station (Yamanote line), Omotesando exit or Meiji-Jingumae station (Chiyoda line), exit 1. **Capacity** *3,677.* **No credit cards**.

Located next to Yoyogi Park, the main auditorium of national broadcaster NHK is home to the NHK Orchestra, but also hosts a range of other productions from opera to ballet to pop concerts. The modern hall is serviceable but lacks the grandeur and audacity of Tokyo's newer performance spaces.

Orchard Hall

Bunkamura, 2-24-1 Dogenzaka, Shibuya-ku (3477 9999/www.bunkamura.co.jp). Shibuya station (Yamanote, Ginza, Hanzomon lines), Hachiko exit. **Capacity** *2,150.* **Box office** 10am-5.30pm daily. **Credit** AmEx, JCB, MC, V. **Map** Shibuya p109.

This is the largest shoebox-shaped hall in Japan, designed to produce the best possible acoustics – though some complain it's rather echoey. Classical, opera and ballet are the norm, but works in other genres are also staged.

Sumida Triphony Hall

1-2-3 Kinshi, Sumida-ku (5608 1212/www.triphony. com). Kinshicho station (Hanzomon, Sobu lines), north exit. **Capacity** *Large Hall 1,801. Small Hall 252.* **Box office** 10am-7pm daily. **No credit cards**.

Situated just across the Sumida river, this venue has a beautiful, old-fashioned lobby and a warm atmosphere. It's the home of the New Japan Philharmonic Orchestra, and you'll also find international artists and events.

Suntory Hall

1-13-1 Akasaka, Minato-ku (3505 1001/ www.suntory.co.jp/suntoryhall/english). Roppongi-Itchome station (Nanboku line), exit 3. **Capacity**

Large Hall 2,006. Small Hall 432. **Box office** 10am-7pm Mon-Sat; 10am-6pm Sun. **Credit** AmEx, JCB, MC, V. **Map** Roppongi p103.

Run by local drinks company Suntory, this two-space venue is used mainly for orchestral concerts and recitals. The huge, Austrian-made pipe organ is the most striking visual feature of the Large Hall, giving it an almost church-like appearance. The acoustics are superb, with legendary conductor Herbert von Karajan describing the place as 'truly a jewel box of sound'. Soloists and chamber groups appear in the Small Hall. **Photo** *p250.*

Tokyo Bunka Kaikan

5-45 Ueno Koen, Taito-ku (3828 2111/www.t-bunka.jp). Ueno station (Yamanote, Ginza, Hibiya lines), park exit. **Capacity** *Large Hall 2,303. Small Hall 649.* **Box office** 10am-7pm Mon-Sat; 10am-6pm Sun. **Credit** JCB, MC, V. **Map** Ueno & Yanaka p123.

Located in historic Ueno Park, these halls were Tokyo's classical music mecca in the post-war period. Now more than 40 years old, they were refurbished at the end of the 1990s to make up for ground lost to newer, flashier venues. The main hall is one of the city's largest, and it is high enough to have four balconies. On the fourth floor of the building is Tokyo's main music library (open to the public).

Tokyo Opera City

3-20-2 Nishi-Shinjuku, Shinjuku-ku (5353 0770/ www.operacity.jp). Hatsudai station (Keio New line), east exit. **Capacity** *Main Hall 1,632. Recital Hall 286.* **Box office** 10am-6pm Tue-Sun. **Credit** AmEx, JCB, MC, V.

Part of the same huge complex as the NNTT (*see above*), Tokyo Opera City presents all sorts of classical music events, but not – despite its name – much opera. The lobby's fusion of architectural styles is a sign of what's to come in the Main Hall; the base of

Tickets

Agencies throughout Tokyo sell tickets for rock gigs, classical concerts, theatre shows, films, sporting events – and plenty more. The main agency is **Ticket Pia** (0570 029 111/http://t.pia.co.jp), which has numerous outlets throughout the city, often in department stores, and publishes a weekly magazine listing thousands of events. Other agencies include **CN Playguide** (5802 9999/www. cnplayguide.com), **e-plus** (http://eplus.jp/ sys/main.jsp) and convenience-store chain **Lawson** (www2.lawsonticket.com), which has ticket vending machines in most stores. None of the websites is in English, but Pia operators can handle enquiries in English.

the hall is in the prevalent shoebox shape but rises into a soaring pyramid topped by a glass skylight. Built for the most advanced sound technology, the auditorium has a bright oak interior with a 3,826-pipe organ as its centrepiece. There's a space for solo performances too, which has also been designed to give the best acoustics.

Other venues

Casals Hall
1-6 Kanda-Surugadai, Chiyoda-ku (3294 1229/ www.nu-casalshall.com). Ochanomizu station (Chuo, Marunouchi, Sobu lines), Ochanomizubashi exit. **Capacity** 511. **No credit cards**. **Map** Marunouchi p93.
This beautiful hall in the heart of Tokyo's university and bookshop district was designed exclusively for chamber music and small ensembles, and is recognised for its great acoustics.

Hakuju Hall
1-37-5 Tomigaya, Shibuya-ku (5478 8700/ www.hakujuhall.jp). Yoyogi-Hachiman station (Odakyu line) or Yoyogi-Koen station (Chiyoda line). **Capacity** 300; when reclined 162. **Box office** 10am-6pm Tue-Sat. **Credit** JCB, MC, V.
Opened in 2003 by health-products company Hakuju, this small hall aims to provide an unrivalled musical experience. The acoustics are first rate, and every seat can be reclined (a world first!). You'll find mainly recitals, chamber groups and some world music. The open-air terrace on the ninth floor, open only to concert-goers, offers great views over Yoyogi Park and Shinjuku.

Kan'i Hoken Hall
8-4-13 Nishi-Gotanda, Shinagawa-ku (3490 5111/ www.u-port.kfj.go.jp). Gotanda station (Yamanote, Asakusa lines), west exit. **Capacity** 1,803.
A mainstay of the scene for more than 20 years, this acoustically impressive venue presents mainly classical music and ballet, but musicals, rock and jazz concerts, plus crooners both local and international, also make the bill.

Sogetsu Hall
7-2-21 Akasaka, Minato-ku (3408 1129/ www.sogetsu.or.jp/hall). Aoyama-Itchome station (Ginza, Hanzomon lines), exit A4. **Capacity** 530.
This smallish venue, which belongs to the *sogetsu-ryu* school of *ikebana* (flower arranging), stages classical music events, as well as Japanese music recitals, poetry readings and even film previews. The funnel-shaped design can be frustrating for concert-goers with sharp ears, but it provides a much more intimate experience than other halls.

Tokyo International Forum
3-5-1 Marunouchi, Chiyoda-ku (5221 9000/ www.t-i-forum.co.jp/english). Yurakucho station (Yamanote, Yurakucho lines), Tokyo International Forum exit. **Capacity** A Hall 5,000. C Hall 1,500. **Map** Ginza p75.

This soaring, ship-like edifice of concrete and glass was opened in 1997 by the Tokyo Metropolitan Government, in the middle of the Marunouchi business district. Designed by award-winning architect Rafael Vinoly, it's a huge, multi-purpose complex used for everything from conventions and trade fairs to exhibitions and pop concerts. Classical concerts are usually held in halls A and C; the former is vast, with seating for 5,000, but still manages to offer superb acoustics and a warm atmosphere.

Tokyo Metropolitan Art Space
1-8-1 Nishi-Ikebukuro, Toshima-ku (5391 2111/ www.geigeki.jp). Ikebukuro station (Yamanote line), west exit; (Marunouchi, Yurakucho lines), exit 2B. **Capacity** *Main Hall* 1,999. *Medium Hall* 841. *Small Hall 1* 300. *Small Hall 2* 300. **Box office** 10am-6pm daily. **Credit** JCB, MC, V. **Map** Ikebukuro p87.
The first thing that strikes you about this building is the long escalator, travelling from the ground floor up to the fifth floor. Not to be outdone, the halls also have some unusual features – the Middle Hall's UFO-like shape is especially peculiar. Full-scale orchestras play in the Large Hall, while the Middle Hall is used for musicals, plays and ballets as well as classical music.

Jazz

Jazz was once banned in Japan, as the nation's wartime leaders worried about the cultural

Back to basics

Traditional Japanese music, or *hogaku*, has seen a resurgence of interest in recent years, as the Japanese shake off their inferiority complex about the West and begin to reappraise their own culture. The **Yoshida Kyodai** (Yoshida Brothers) – who play the *shamisen*, a lute-like instrument with three strings – have achieved rock-star status, while **Togi Hideki** has done much to popularise the rarified form known as *gagaku* (court music); he's a former member of the notoriously exclusive Imperial Palace Gagaku Orchestra. Artists such as **Yagi Michiyo**, mistress of the zither-like *koto*, and legendary *taiko* drum troupe **Kodo** are reinventing their traditions by experimenting with a range of contemporary musical contexts. The drummers even appeared at Japan's top rock event, the **Fuji Rock Festival** (www.fujirockfestival.com), in 2006.

Sadly, Tokyo's Waon Club, which hosted the best traditional acts, closed in 2005, but the performances continue elsewhere. Check local listings for venues.

influence of this American import. The ban had limited success at the time, and six decades later the genre is arguably more popular in Japan than in its homeland. There are over 30 large clubs and 20 smaller ones devoted to some form of the genre, and they're crowded every night of the week.

In a comprehensive and diverse scene, you'll find Latin, bop, free, big-band, swing, fusion, experimental, jazz-funk and blues events, plus various open-air gigs during the summer. Club jazz has been a success story in recent years, with home-grown acts such as Jazztronik, Kyoto Jazz Massive and Soil and 'Pimp' Sessions building large followings among young Tokyoites. And for something more eclectic, the Shibusa Shirazu Orchestra (literally: 'no sense of cool orchestra') is a loose-knit troupe of around 20 talented musicians whose shows veer across genres and incorporate *butoh* dance performance (*see p266*). They were the first unsigned band ever to play the main stage of the UK's Glastonbury festival.

Unlike rock or classical music venues, where the admission price reflects the performer's pulling power, jazz clubs tend to have fixed entry charges (included below where available). Doors usually open at least 30 minutes before the music starts. Many clubs have two live sessions per evening, so check beforehand whether the entry fee covers you for both. Some of the bigger clubs accept credit cards, but in general expect to pay cash. In addition to the clubs, there are hundreds of jazz bars dotted around the city, with Shinjuku and Kichijoji boasting more than 25 such places between them. Many have extensive vinyl collections and bartenders who are happy to take music requests.

Also look out for the weekend **Tokyo Jazz** festival (www.tokyo-jazz.com) in late August. Past headliners have included Herbie Hancock, Chick Corea and Dave Holland.

INFORMATION

Metropolis magazine tends to list only the bigger clubs. For wider coverage, the Shinjuku branch of record shop **Disk Union** (*see p210*) has an excellent jazz section, with flyers and jazz magazines advertising upcoming events. The haphazardly published *JazzNin* magazine is half-English, half-Japanese and worth seeking out, while Japanese-only magazines *Swing Journal* and *Jazzlife* are great sources if you've mastered the language.

Venues

Akai Karasu

Shirakaba Bldg 4F, 1-13-2 Kichijoji Honcho, Musashino-shi (0422 217594/www.akaikarasu.co.jp).

Kichijoji station (Chuo line), north exit. **Shows** 7.30pm-midnight daily. **Admission** from ¥2,000. The 'Red Crow' has been around more than 25 years and is a relaxing, unpretentious place with a good bar (drinks start at ¥730). The music is usually straight-ahead, with an emphasis on vocalists. It's best to book ahead (talk to the manager, Sugitasan) for seats at the front.

Aketa no Mise

Yoshino Bldg B101, 3-21-13 Nishi Ogi Kita, Suginami-ku (3395 9507/www.aketa.org). Nishi-Ogikubo station (Chuo, Marunouchi lines), north exit. **Shows** 7.30-11pm Mon-Fri; 7.30pm-1.30am Sat. **Admission** ¥2,500 (incl 1 drink).
The name means 'open shop', and this place has been welcoming jazz fans for three decades. Old photos and posters line the dark walls of the basement space, creating an intimate atmosphere for some proper jazz listening. There is no set style for the acts; expect anything from free improv to Latin to piano trios. Shimada-san is the relaxed proprietor. Drinks start at a decent ¥400.

Alfie

Hama Roppongi Bldg 5F, 6-2-35 Roppongi, Minato-ku (3479 2037/http://homepage1.nifty.com/live/alfie). Roppongi station (Hibiya, Oedo lines), exit 1. **Shows** 8pm-4am daily; jam sessions after midnight. **Admission** ¥3,500. **Map** Roppongi p103.
A jazz oasis in drunken Roppongi, Alfie has a sleek interior and an upscale audience paying upscale prices to hear international musicians as well as top-flight local bands.

B Flat

Akasaka Sakae Bldg B1F, 6-6-4 Akasaka, Minato-ku (5563 2563/www.bflat.jp). Akasaka station (Chiyoda line), exit 5A. **Shows** from 7.30pm daily. **Admission** ¥2,500-¥7,000. **Map** Roppongi p103.
A large operation that also serves decent food (sandwiches, pizza and Japanese dishes). The groups are often the best in the city, and bands from the US and Europe perform a couple of times a month.

Blue Note Tokyo

Raika Bldg, 6-3-16 Minami Aoyama, Minato-ku (5485 0088/www.bluenote.co.jp). Omotesando station (Chiyoda, Ginza, Hanzomon lines), exit B3. **Shows** from 7pm & 9.30pm. Mon-Sat; from 6.30pm & 9pm Sun. **Admission** ¥6,000-¥10,000.
The largest jazz club in Tokyo – with prices to match – is part of the international Blue Note chain and well supported by the local music industry. Jazz, Latin, world and soul acts all appear. Expect short sets, expensive food and strangers sharing your dining table, but the quality of international talent keeps the crowds coming.

Blues Alley Japan

Hotel Wing International Meguro B1F, 1-3-14 Meguro, Meguro-ku (5496 4381/www.bluesalley. co.jp). Meguro station (Yamanote, Mita, Namboku lines), west exit. **Shows** from 7.30pm daily. **Admission** ¥3,500-¥6,000. **Map** Meguro p71.

Blues Alley showcases everything from jazz, big band, Latin, Brazilian, fusion and soul to pop and, yes, blues. The service is impeccable, the sound system crisp and the food tasty, but the atmosphere can be a bit on the sterile side.

Body & Soul

Anisu Minami Aoyama B1, 6-13-9 Minami Aoyama, Minato-ku (5466 3348/www.bodyandsoul.co.jp). Omotesando station (Chiyoda, Ginza, Hanzomon lines), exit B1. **Shows** *from 8.30pm daily.* **Admission** ¥3,500-¥6,000.

Jazz and jazz only at this great but pricey club, which has been in business since 1974. The best musicians in the city love to play to the savvy crowd here. Good food and wine too.

Buddy

Futaba Hall B2F, Asahigaoka 1-77-8, Nerima-ku, (3953 1152/www.buddy-tokyo.com). Ekoda station (Seibu Ikebukuro line), south exit. **Shows** *7.30pm-midnight daily.* **Admission** ¥1,500-¥4,000.

This largish venue is a little out of the way – a few stops from Ikebukuro – but worth the trip. The main focus is jazz, but tango or prog-rock groups are almost as common.

Gate One

Maruishi Bldg B1F, 2-8-3 Takadanobaba, Shinjuku-ku (3200 1452/www.h3.dion.ne.jp/~gateone). Takadanobaba station (Yamanote, Tozai lines), Waseda exit. **Shows** *from 7pm daily.* **Admission** from ¥1,000.

Gate One is a small basement jazz bar owned by a husband-and-wife guitarist/vocalist duo. The decor is nothing special, but the music is great (with an emphasis on vocalists), and there are frequent jam sessions.

GH Nine

UNO Bldg 9F, 4-4-6 Ueno, Taito-ku (3837 2525/http://homepage1.nifty.com/ghnine). Okachimachi station (Yamanote line), north exit or Ueno-Hirokoji station (Ginza line), exit 3. **Shows** *from 8pm daily.* **Admission** ¥3,000. **Map** Ueno & Yanaka p123.

A rare beast indeed – a jazz spot in east Tokyo – this futuristic space at the top of a postmodern building is always a little eerie in feel, but the music is of a consistently high quality.

Hot House

Liberal Takadanobaba B1F, 3-23-5 Takadanobaba, Shinjuku-ku (3367 1233/www2.vc-net.ne.jp/~winning/menu/hothouse/hothouse.html). Takadanobaba station (Yamanote, Tozai lines), Waseda exit. **Shows** *from 8.30pm daily.* **Admission** ¥3,500 (incl 1 drink).

As cosy as it gets. Hot House holds fewer than ten punters, but still crams in live acts. The diminutive space means that once the pianist is seated, customers can't enter, so be on time. **Photo** *p255.*

Intro

NT Bldg B1F, 2-14-8 Takadanobaba, Shinjuku-ku (3200 4396/www.intro.co.jp). Takadanobaba station (Yamanote, Tozai lines), Waseda exit. **Shows** *from 6.30pm daily.* **Admission** from ¥1,000.

Small, dark and with a great vinyl collection stacked above the bar, Intro is one of the best jazz bars in Tokyo. It doesn't have scheduled music performances every night, but the Saturday jam session (which goes on until 5am) is not to be missed, and is also great value at only ¥1,000.

J

Royal Mansion B1, 5-1-1 Shinjuku, Shinjuku-ku (3354 0335/www.jazzspot-j.com). Shinjuku station (Yamanote, Marunouchi, Oedo, Shinjuku lines), east exit or Shinjuku-Sanchome station (Marunouchi, Shinjuku lines), exit C7. **Shows** *from 7.15pm daily.* **Admission** ¥1,500-¥2,000.

A 15-minute walk from central Shinjuku, this basement club is a classic Tokyo jazz spot. It specialises in up-and-coming talent, with vocalists particularly well represented.

Jirokichi

Koenji Bldg B1, 2-3-4 Koenji-kita, Suginami-ku (3339 2727/www.jirokichi.net). Koenji station (Chuo line), north exit. **Shows** *from 7.30pm daily.* **Admission** ¥2,100-¥4,000.

Jirokichi presents everything from klezmer to didgeridoo, jive blues or jazz piano trios. The place is well run and good fun, with a young and hip atmosphere. There's barely any room to dance, but people do anyway.

JZ Brat

Cerulean Tower Tokyu Hotel 2F, 26-1 Sakuragaoka-cho, Shibuya-ku (5728 0168/www.jzbrat.com). Shibuya station (Yamanote, Ginza, Hanzomon lines), south exit. **Shows** *from 7.30pm daily.* **Admission** *from* ¥4,200. **Map** Shibuya p109.

This smart club, housed inside the sprawling Cerulean Tower Tokyu hotel, is expensive but worth it. The booking policy is consistently good, with occasional overseas players performing. The space is large, so you can move and chat while the music plays. Plus point: the bar is open until 4am on Fridays and Saturdays.

Naru

Jujiya Bldg B1, 2-1 Kanda Surugadai, Chiyoda-ku (3291 2321/www.jazz-naru.com). Ochanomizu station (Chuo, Marunouchi, Sobu lines), Ochanomizubashi exit. **Shows** *from 7.30pm daily.* **Admission** from ¥2,500.

At this medium-sized venue, young, hot players predominate, but you'll also find straight-ahead, satisfying old faves doing their stuff. There's a good selection of food and wine too.

Rooster

Inoue Bldg B1, 5-16-15 Ogikubo, Suginami-ku (5347 7369/www.rooster.jp). Ogikubo station (Chuo, Marunouchi lines), west exit. **Shows** *from 7pm daily.* **Admission** ¥1,600-¥2,500.

A small, intimate spot, Rooster features the best blues (and bluesy jazz) from all over Tokyo, including acoustic, electric, New Orleans, East Side Chicago, slide and all points in between. Master Sato's collection of vintage posters lines the walls.

Hotfoot it to the **Hot House**, where seats are at a premium. *See p254.*

Shinjuku Pit Inn

*Accord Shinjuku B1F, 2-12-4 Shinjuku, Shinjuku-ku
(3354 2024/www.pit-inn.com). Shinjuku-Sanchome
station (Marunouchi, Shinjuku lines), exit C5.*
Shows from 7.30pm daily. **Admission** ¥3,000-
¥5,000. **Map** Shinjuku p117.
All chairs here face the stage, in reverence to the
most respected jazz groups in town, who offer their
latest to the adoring crowd. It's not a place for
lingering or lounging – the atmosphere is too hallowed for that – but the music is always first class.
An irregular afternoon slot at 2.30pm offers the
stage to newly emerging bands.

Someday

*1-20-9 Nishi Shinbashi, Minato-ku (3506 1777/
www.someday.net). Shinbashi station (Yamanote,
Asakusa, Ginza lines), Karasumori exit.* **Shows**
from 7.45pm daily. **Admission** ¥2,500-¥3,700.
Map Ginza p75.
Someday specialises in big-band and Latin groups.
The atmosphere isn't particularly notable, though
the crowd is always knowledgeable and enthusiastic. There's an extensive (as well as expensive)
selection of whisky to choose from, along with the
usual Japanese snacks and small pizzas to satisfy
any hunger pangs.

Sometime

*1-11-31 Kichijoji Honcho, Musashino-shi (0422
216336/www.sometime.co.jp/sometime). Kichijoji
station (Chuo line), north exit.* **Shows** from 7.30pm
daily. **Admission** from ¥1,600.
A Tokyo institution in jazz-filled Kichijoji. The
stage at this place sits in the centre of the club, so
that you can see and hear performers up close.
Make sure that you don't arrive late and get stuck
sitting below the band; it's cramped, and the sound
is not as good. Almost every top-notch player
comes through Sometime sometime, and the management has kept the admission price reasonable
for years. In the daytime (from 11am), the venue
operates as a café.

STB139

*6-7-11 Roppongi, Minato-ku (5474 1395/http://
stb139.co.jp). Roppongi station (Hibiya, Oedo lines),
exit 3.* **Shows** from 8pm Mon-Sat. **Admission** from
¥5,000. **Map** Roppongi p103.
Combine wining and dining with world-class jazz.
The only competition to Blue Note Tokyo (*see
p253*), STB139 does some things better: the layout
is much friendlier and the atmosphere a bit more
relaxed. There's more variety in the music too,
which veers towards soul, Latin, R&B and classics
rather than just plain jazz.

Strings

*TN Clum Bldg B1F, 2-12-13 Kichijoji-Honcho,
Musashino-shi (0422 285035). Kichijoji station
(Chuo line), north exit.* **Shows** from 8pm daily.
Admission from ¥2,000.
A small venue with an emphasis on vocalists, plus
Latin/bossa nova and some soul acts. If you're hun-
gry, try the great, reasonably priced Italian food.

Tokyo TUC

*Tokyo Uniform Center, Honsha Biru B1F,
2-16-5 Iwamotocho, Chiyoda-ku (3866 8393/www.
tokyouniform.com/tokyotuc). Akihabara station
(Yamanote, Hibiya lines), Showa Dori exit or Kanda
station (Yamanote, Ginza lines), north exit.* **Shows**
from 7.45pm Fri; from 7pm Sat. **Admission** ¥3,500-
¥12,000. **Map** Marunouchi p93.
An excellent club, although it doesn't have jazz playing every night. When it does (and if you can find a
place to sit or stand), expect to hear the best musicians from Japan and overseas.

Rock & pop

The sickly sweet sound of J-pop is by far the
biggest music market in Tokyo, but there
are passionate, vibrant scenes for all the less
saccharin sounds too. Rock, reggae and hip hop
are the most conspicuous forms, but you won't
have to look far to find first-rate electronica,

Big in Japan

Tokyo draws international bands of all statures, but there's plenty of great domestic talent vying for local ears. Here are four of the best live acts right now.

Halcali

The sound: The Spice Girls meet Salt-N-Pepa.
The band: A manufactured female hip-hop duo (*pictured*) comprised of Haruka and Yukari, who were handpicked from auditions. But don't hold that against them. The judges were two fully fledged members of Japanese hip-hop royalty: Ryo-Z and DJ Fumiya of mega-selling act Rip Slyme, and Halcali have earned a following with their unique vocabulary, coining new terms in their lyrics for everyday teenage concerns like dating and dieting.
Why you should see them: Because Halcali combine the campy, barely choreographed dance routines and earthy dress sense of J-pop queens Puffy AmiYumi with catchy rhymes and rhythms that are part old-skool, part Tamla Motown and part *pico pico* (video-game-influenced pop music).
Listen to: Debut album *Halcali Bacon* (Epic, 2003) – bubblegum hip hop meets J-pop at its finest.

Osaka Monaurail

The sound: The 21st-century JBs.
The band: Formed in Osaka, now based in Tokyo, this nine-piece picks up where the late, great James Brown left off. Their driving, horn-heavy rhythms caught the ear of First Lady of Funk Marva Whitney, who invited them to tour with her as her backing band.
Why you should see them: They're the undisputed Kings of Funk in Japan, and arguably one of the top five live acts of their genre in the world right now. Their military-style uniforms, choreography and hard-nosed funk are all as tight as it's possible to be.
Listen to: *Reality for the People* (Shout, 2006) – uses the best of late '60s funk to create a 21st-century groove.

Tucker

The sound: Easy-listening meets manic drum 'n' bass and everything in between.

The artist: Tucker is a multi-instrumentalist who has toured with compatriots Cornelius and the Tarantino-approved 5,6,7,8s. He samples himself on drums and bass, scratches with his tongue and plays the ivories with his elbows before setting the instrument alight.
Why you should see him: Everyone needs to see Tucker once in their life. At his frenetic live shows, this one-man band regularly covers the *Sesame Street* theme tune, *Swan Lake* and the northern-soul classic 'Sunny'.
Listen to: *Electoon Wizard* (Oddjob Records, 2005). Stays just about the right side of kitsch to be cool.

Yura Yura Teikoku

The sound: Singer/guitarist Sakamoto Shintaro idolizes Marc Bolan. Mix in some 1960s psychedelia and Krautrock, and you're close.
The band: Three-piece Yura Yura Teikoku gained a rabid following during the 1990s playing Tokyo's tiniest toilet venues. So rabid, in fact, that when Sakamoto once shaved his eyebrows, his devoted army of fans followed suit. Despite signing to major label Sony in 2005, the band still refuses to appear on TV or radio. Yet 'Yura Tei' has matched more experimental sounds with increasing sales.
Why you should see them: Because every Yura Yura Teikoku show has at least one transcendental moment where an extended jam takes off – as does the amp-hopping, scissor-kicking Sakamoto.
Listen to: *Yura Yura Teikoku III* (Midi, 2001) thrillingly showcases the band's power-trio dynamics and pop sensibility.

soul, metal or pretty much any genre you can think of. Venues run the whole gamut, from relaxed wine-and-dine seating to trashy underground pits, from tiny crammed spaces to enormous stadiums, with just about every shape, size and ambience in between.

The larger places host whoever wants to book them, but the smaller venues – known locally as 'live houses' – often focus on a particular genre to build a following, making it possible to take a gamble on a gig by virtue of the venue alone.

Gigs often start at 7pm, even at weekends, and you can often expect to be heading home as early as 9.30pm. At a few live houses, events kick off at 11pm or midnight. Smaller venues often host three to four bands a night. Expect to pay ¥2,000-¥4,000 for a local gig, somewhat more for established medium-sized bands, and as much as ¥14,000 for the international legends.

Japan has two massive music festivals – both within easy reach of Tokyo. The biggest and best is **Fuji Rock Festival** (www.fujirock festival.com), held on the last weekend of July. Inspired by Glastonbury, it attracts a diverse range of big names to the scenic mountains of Niigata, around 90 minutes' travel from Tokyo. Fuji's rival is the more accesible **Summer Sonic** (www.summersonic.com), held each August at the **Makuhari Messe** convention centre (*see below*). The line-up is more rock-oriented, and the drab venue offers none of Fuji's atmosphere, but it still draws impressive names, including the Beastie Boys, Metallica and Daft Punk in recent years.

INFORMATION

Metropolis provides pretty complete listings of upcoming events, while *Tokyo Journal*, published quarterly, does a decent job with bigger events. The city's two biggest promoters also have useful gig guides, in English, on their websites: **Creativeman** (www.creativeman.co. jp/index.html) and **Smash** (http://smash-jpn. com/gig_guide.html).

Stadiums & large venues

Other venues sometimes used for rock and pop concerts include the **NHK Hall** (*see p251*) and **Tokyo International Forum** (*see p252*).

Makuhari Messe

2-1 Nakase, Mihama-ku, Chiba-shi, Chiba-ken (043 296 0001/www.m-messe.co.jp/index_e.html). Kaihin Makuhari station (Keiyo line), south exit. **Capacity** approx 4,000.
The acoustics at this huge convention complex in Chiba City are generally bad, the place is impersonal and it's some distance from downtown

Tokyo. Still, it's the home of the Summer Sonic rockfest, and big bands such as the Prodigy have entertained full houses here.

National Yoyogi Stadium

2-1-1 Jinnan, Shibuya-ku (3468 1171/www. naash.go.jp/). Harajuku station (Yamanote line), Omotesando exit or Meiji-Jingumae station (Chiyoda line), exit 1. **Capacity** *Gymnasium 1* 13,600. *Gymnasium 2* 3,200.
Built for the 1964 Olympics, this place is used rarely and mainly for big-selling J-pop stars, though Oasis picked this venue recently, and exhibitions are held from time to time. More interestingly, the adjacent public space near NHK has a live stage with irregular free gigs.

Nippon Budokan

2-3 Kitanomaru-koen, Chiyoda-ku (3216 5100/ www.nipponbudokan.or.jp). Kudanshita station (Hanzomon, Shinjuku, Tozai lines), exit 2. **Capacity** 14,950. **Map** Marunouchi p93.
The classic Tokyo live venue (think 'Dylan at the Budokan'). Unfortunately, this lasting reputation allows what is a horrible space to continue to host major rock shows. Built for martial-arts competitions at the 1964 Olympics, it's still used for sports events. The acoustics are poor, the vibe sombre, and the huge, ever-present Japanese flag hanging from the centre of the hall does not inspire a rock 'n' roll atmosphere. And if you're up in the balcony, you might as well be outside.

Tokyo Bay NK Hall

1-8 Maihama, Urayasu-shi, Chiba-ken (047 355 7007/www.nkhall.co.jp). Maihama station (Keiyo line). **Capacity** 6,500.
This structure manages to combine the ambience of a Roman coliseum with state-of-the-art style. The oblong interior offers good sight lines and great acoustics while still being capacious. It is inconveniently situated in Chiba City, but lots of popular foreign acts appear here (Beck, Massive Attack, the Chemical Brothers and so on).

Tokyo Dome

1-3-61 Koraku, Bunkyo-ku (5800 9999/www. tokyo-dome.co.jp). Kasuga station (Mita, Oedo line), exit A1 or Korakuen station (Marunouchi, Namboku lines), exit 2 or Suidobashi station (Chuo line), west exit; (Mita line), exits A3, A4, A5. **Capacity** 55,000-63,000.
Japan's first domed stadium opened in 1988, though it existed before that without the roof (it's the home of the Yomiuri Giants baseball team). Its moniker 'the big egg' is rarely used these days. With a capacity of between 55,000 and 63,000, it's the biggest music venue in the Tokyo area, and used for the biggest acts (the Rolling Stones, David Bowie, Michael Jackson and Madonna have all appeared here). Tickets for performances usually cost in excess of ¥10,000. The acoustics are atrocious. The huge complex also includes a spa, amusement centre and other attractions; *see p219*.

Arts & Entertainment

Yokohama Arena

3-10 Shin-Yokohama, Kohoku-ku, Kanagawa-ken (045 474 4000/www.yokohama-arena.co.jp/english). Shin-Yokohama station (Yokohama, Shinkansen, Tokaido lines), north exit. **Capacity** 17,000.

An increasingly popular venue with good acoustics. In 2004 the first Rock Odyssey bash was held here.

Medium venues

Studio Coast/Ageha hosts the occasional international rock act (Arctic Monkeys and Weezer in 2006), *see p231.*

Club Citta Kawasaki

1-26 Ogawacho, Kawasaki-ku, Kawasaki-shi, Kanagawa-ken (044 246 8888/http://clubcitta.co.jp). Kawasaki station (Keihin Tohoku, Tokaido lines), east exit. **Capacity** 1,300.

Halfway to Yokohama, Club Citta Kawasaki, thoroughly renovated in 2003, is a great hive of activity, with a large hall for gigs. The lighting gear and stageside speaker stacks are put to good use, mainly by loud and proud rock acts. Club Citta is an aggressive promoter too; some foreign bands only play this venue. Sometimes it turns into a cinema with all-night festivals.

Hibiya Yagai Ongakudo

1-3 Hibiya Koen, Chiyoda-ku (3591 6388). Kasumigaseki station (Chiyoda, Hibiya, Marunouchi lines), exits B2, C4. **Capacity** 3,100. **Map** Ginza p75.

Used since 1923, this outdoor theatre in Hibiya Park puts enjoyment at the mercy of the weather. Umbrellas are not allowed, but turn up on a nice day and enjoy one of Tokyo's few open-air venues. Unfortunately, it is an ode to concrete, including the seats, even though it was rebuilt 20 years ago.

Koseinenkin Kaikan

5-3-1 Shinjuku, Shinjuku-ku (3356 1111/www.kjp.or.jp/hp_20). Shinjuku-Sanchome station (Marunouchi, Shinjuku lines), exit C7. **Capacity** 2,000.

An early 1960s construction that went through major refurbishment a decade ago, this classical music hall is an enduring venue known for its great acoustics. The place where Bowie, Led Zep and many other '70s legends once played, it's still the venue of choice for many.

Liquid Room

3-16-6 Higashi, Shibuya-ku (5464 0800/www.liquidroom.net). Ebisu station (Yamanote, Hibiya lines), west exit. **Capacity** 1,100.

This live music and club venue is often described as 'legendary' in international publications. It was born as a scruffy venue for gigs and club nights in Shinjuku's seedy Kabukicho district, but after a move to the more upmarket Ebisu, it now offers fewer club nights and more straight-up live events. A long, rectangular room with a few seats in the back, it's a great place to catch a show. You can pick up a free monthly schedule from Tower Records or HMV.

Nakano Sun Plaza Hall

4-1-1 Nakano, Nakano-ku (3388 1151/www.sunplaza.or.jp/hall). Nakano station (Chuo, Tozai lines), north exit. **Capacity** 2,200.

An unassuming venue located a few stops from Shinjuku, this hall has hosted top bands, including the Clash, PiL and the Pogues, as well as many blues, folk rock (Suzanne Vega) and world-music artists. The list of prohibitions recited before any concert is far more suited to a classical music hall, but the venue does still offer popular stuff. The acoustics are quite good.

Unit. *See p261.*

Shibuya AX

*2-1-1 Jinnan, Shibuya-ku (5738 2020/www.
shibuya-ax.com). Harajuku station (Yamanote
line), Omotesando exit or Meiji-Jingumae station
(Chiyoda line), exit 1.* **Capacity** 1,000.

Conveniently located on the edge of Shibuya, this
venue regularly hosts hot indie acts, both foreign and
local: Sigur Ros and Hard-Fi are two recent bookings.
The acoustics and sight lines are good.

Shibuya CC Lemon Hall
(Shibuya Kokaido)

*1-1 Udagawacho, Shibuya-ku (3463 3022/www.
shibuko.com). Shibuya station (Yamanote, Ginza,
Hanzomon lines), Hachiko exit.* **Capacity** 2,300.

Known as Shibuya Kokaido before an advertising
agency rebranded it in celebration of a lemon-
flavoured fizzy drink – most locals still use the old
name. This is another 1964 Olympics structure, surviving four decades of rock thanks to great acoustics.

Shibuya O-East

*2-14-8 Dogenzaka, Shibuya-ku (5458 4681/
www.shibuya-o.com). Shibuya station (Yamanote,
Ginza, Hanzomon lines), Hachiko exit.* **Capacity**
1,300. **Map** Shibuya p109.

The O-East complex (opened mid 2004) houses a
number of clubs and bars. The biggest venue is simply called Shibuya O-East and is where international
rock bands and DJs play. The complex also houses a
small bar, the Red Bar.

Stellar Ball

*Epson Shinagawa Aqua Stadium (Shinagawa Prince
Hotel), 4-10-30 Takanawa, Minato-ku (3440 1111/
www.princehotels.co.jp/shinagawa/aquastadium/liveh
all/index.html). Shinagawa station (Yamanote line),
Takanawa exit.* **Capacity** 1884.

The Shinagawa Prince Hotel – part of the huge Prince
chain – opened this concert hall in 2005. A long, thin
stage allows a great view from any part of the room,
and high-quality lighting and acoustics add to the
appeal. Jack Johnson and Belle & Sebastian both
picked Stellar Ball for their Tokyo gigs in 2006.

Zepp Tokyo

*Palette Town 1F, 1 Aomi, Koto-ku (3599 0710/
www.zepp.co.jp/tokyo). Aomi station (Yurikamome
line) or Tokyo Teleport station (Rinkai line).*
Capacity 2,700. **Map** Odaiba p101.

Part of a chain with locations in four other cities in
the country, this large and rather sterile venue in
Odaiba has become a well-used spot for more popular foreign rock and electronic acts, including Primal
Scream and Franz Ferdinand. It is, however, less convenient and characterful than similar venues.

Small venues

In addition to the venues listed below, club
Milk (*see p224*) regularly hosts live gigs.

440

*SY Bldg 1F, 5-29-15 Daizawa, Setagaya-ku
(3422 9440/www.club251.co.jp/440). Shimo-
Kitazawa station (Keio Inokashira, Odakyu lines),
south exit.* **Capacity** 100-180.

440 takes a softer approach to live music, and is one
of very few café-style live houses outside the jazz circuit. It's part of the same group as Club 251 (*see
below*; only two minutes down the road) and is
always booked weeks in advance. Open for food and
drinks the rest of the time.

Antiknock

*Ray Flat Shinjuku B1F, 4-3-15 Shinjuku, Shinjuku-ku
(3350 5670/www.music.ne.jp/~antiknock). Shinjuku
station (Yamanote, Marunouchi lines), new south
exit; (Oedo, Shinjuku lines), exits 1, 2.* **Capacity** 300.
Map Shinjuku p117.

A small club near Takashimaya Times Square,
where Tokyo's colourful punks gather. It aims to
present 'original' music, but, more importantly, the
music has to rock. Need to vent your frustration with
the Shinjuku-station hordes? Pop down here.

Astro Hall

*New Wave Harajuku Bldg B1F, 4-32-12 Jingumae,
Shibuya-ku (3401 5352/www.astro-hall.com).
Harajuku station (Yamanote line), Takeshita
exit or Meiji-Jingumae station (Chiyoda line),
exit 5.* **Capacity** 400. **Map** Harajuku &
Aoyama p82.

When it opened in 2000 this was the venue of choice
for many local indie bands, and it's been holding
steady ever since. Some foreign acts trying to break
Japan also play here. Very intimate and generally
well laid out, it's a good place to catch a show.

Cave-be

*Kitazawa Plaza B1F, 2-14-16 Kitazawa, Setagaya-ku
(3412 7373/www.cave-be.com). Shimo-Kitazawa
station (Keio Inokashira, Odakyu lines), south exit.*
Capacity 150.

Opened in 2003 next to the Japanese indie music
shop High Line Records, the tiny but busy Cave-be
in Shimo-Kitazawa presents local amateur acts
playing all strands of rock.

Cay

*Spiral Bldg B1F, 5-6-23 Minami-Aoyama,
Minato-ku (3498 5790). Omotesando station
(Chiyoda, Ginza, Hanzomon lines), exit B1.*
Capacity 600. **Map** Harajuku & Aoyama p82.

A restaurant that regularly turns into a live (sometimes all-night) venue. Cay is located in the Spiral
Building (*see p239*), a centre for contemporary arts
and design, and the music matches the setting,
with new electronica, world music-influenced and
'fusion' acts such as Karsh Kale or the home-
grown Dakini Nights.

Club 251

*SY Bldg B1F, 5-29-15 Daizawa, Setagaya-ku
(5481 4141/www.club251.co.jp/index2.html).
Shimo-Kitazawa station (Keio Inokashira, Odakyu
lines), south exit.* **Capacity** 350.

Arts & Entertainment

One of the main venues in Shimo-Kitazawa and a reliable place to drop in. There are no restrictions on musical styles, but gigs tend to be rock-oriented. It's a black, bare place showing its age, but that's a sign of popularity rather than neglect.

Club Quattro

Parco 4F, 32-13 Udagawa-cho, Shibuya-ku (3477 8750/www.club-quattro.com). Shibuya station (Yamanote, Ginza, Hanzomon lines), Hachiko exit. **Capacity** 750. **Map** Shibuya p109.
On the top floor of the Parco 4 fashion store, Club Quattro is a superior venue with high-quality performers. It's not limited by genre, offering varied overseas acts, plus some of the best local bands, even ones that would usually prefer to play at bigger venues. Despite some view-restricting pillars on the main floor, this is one of the most appealing music venues in town.

Club Que

Big Ben Bldg B2F, 2-5-2 Kitazawa, Setagaya-ku (3412 9979/www.ukproject.com/que). Shimo-Kitazawa station (Keio Inokashira, Odakyu lines), south exit. **Capacity** 250.
This place has built a strong reputation over the past decade and, despite its small size, some not-so-small local indie bands sometimes appear. Irregular, early-afternoon gigs are held on weekends and holidays, and the place becomes a late-night DJ club on weekends.

Cotton Club

Tokyo Building Tokia 2F, 2-7-3 Marunouchi, Chiyoda-ku (3215 1555/www.cottonclubjapan. co.jp). Tokyo station (Yamanote, Chuo, Sobu lines), Marunouchi South exit; (Marunouchi line), exit 4. **Shows** 5.30pm, 8.30pm Mon-Sat; 4pm, 6.30pm Sun. **Capacity** 180. **Map** Marunouchi p93.
This sister venue of the Blue Note opened in late 2005 and operates in much the same way: pay ¥8,000-¥10,000 to enter, order your pricey dinner, then sit back for just under an hour of Tito Jackson or Sheena Easton. The artists span the soul/funk/disco/R&B spectrum, though the emphasis seems to be on international has-beens.

Crocodile

New Sekiguchi Bldg B1F, 6-18-8 Jingumae, Shibuya-ku (3499 5205/www.music.co.jp/~croco). Harajuku station (Yamanote line), Omotesando exit or Shibuya station (Yamanote, Ginza, Hanzomon lines), Miyamasuaka (east) exit or Meiji-Jingumae station (Chiyoda line), exit 4. **Capacity** 120-200. **Map** Harajuku & Aoyama p82.
Although Crocodile bills itself as a modern music restaurant, it's best to skip the food and stick to the sounds. The venue presents anything from salsa to country, rock and jazz, plus combos of any of these.

DeSeO

Dai 2 Okazaki Bldg 1F, 3-3 Sakuragaoka-cho, Shibuya-ku (5457 0303/www.deseo.co.jp). Shibuya station (Yamanote, Ginza, Hanzomon lines), south exit. **Capacity** 250. **Map** Shibuya p109.

This small live house along the JR tracks is another spot for bands warming up for bigger things. Some more established acts perform intermittently too.

Eggman

1-6-8 Jinnan, Shibuya-ku (3496 1561/www.eggman. jp). Shibuya station (Yamanote, Ginza, Hanzomon lines), Hachiko exit. **Capacity** 350. **Map** Harajuku & Aoyama p82.
Eggman is a Shibuya institution. Most nights you'll find local bands playing, particularly those with one eye on a record deal, so you should be able to catch some upcoming talent. A good venue for assorted rock-oriented music styles.

Gear

Tokyo Bldg B1F, 4-25-4 Koenji-Minami, Suginami-ku (3318 6948). Koenji station (Chuo line), south exit. **Capacity** 150.
The place for bands that might not be allowed to play anywhere else, Gear serves all sorts of 'core' offerings, with event names like 'Fangs Anal Satan'. A small venue with a big following.

Gig-antic

Sound Forum Bldg 2F, 3-20-15 Shibuya, Shibuya-ku (5466 9339/www.gig-antic.co.jp). Shibuya station (Yamanote, Ginza, Hanzomon lines), Miyamasusaka (east) exit. **Capacity** 150. **Map** Shibuya p109.
Gig-antic is a small (despite the name) venue located by the JR tracks that presents bands from around Japan. Expect a mix of hardcore and punk, with some events sold out in advance.

Heaven's Door

Keio Hallo Bldg B1F, 1-33-19 Sangenjaya, Setagaya-ku (3410 9581/www.geocities.jp/xxxheavensdoorxxx). Sangenjaya station (Tokyu Denentoshi line), south exit. **Capacity** 300.
Heaven's Door is another institution, in a rites-of-passage sense, for many loud Tokyo bands. Only a few established acts play here, yet everybody knows about it. There's not much decoration, but the speakers are huge, and that's what matters.

La.mama Shibuya

Premier Dogenzaka B1F, 1-15-3 Dogenzaka, Shibuya-ku (3464 0801/www.lamama.net). Shibuya station (Yamanote, Ginza, Hanzomon lines), south exit. **Capacity** 120-250. **Map** Shibuya p109.
La.mama has been presenting bands at the start of (one hopes) successful careers for more than 20 years. It tends to host more J-pop and commercial rock than other venues in the area.

Live Inn Rosa

Rosa Kaikan B2F, 1-37-12 Nishi-Ikebukuro, Toshima-ku (5956 3463/www.live-inn-rosa.com). Ikebukuro station (Yamanote line), west exit; (Marunouchi, Yurakucho lines), exit 12. **Capacity** 100-300. **Map** Ikebukuro p87.
Proudly J-pop, this Ikebukuro venue does also present other types of music – including events combining live bands and DJs, and many artists on their first appearances.

Live Spot 20000

*Dai 8 Tokyo Bldg B2F, 4-25-4 Koenji-Minami,
Suginami-ku (3316 6969). Koenji station (Chuo
line), south exit.* **Capacity** 180.

Another institution, 'Niman Volt', as it's known, is
the place for hard listening, with more than a nod
to the experimental and noise set. Current local
stars play here, as do big names in lesser-known
incarnations, such as Sonic Youth's Thurston
Moore, who appeared here as the Diskaholics
Anonymous Trio.

Mandala 2

*2-8-6 Kichijoji Minami-cho, Musashino-shi (0422
421579/www.mandala.gr.jp/man2.html). Kichijoji
station (Chuo line), south exit.* **Capacity** 60.

More of a music venue than its sister in Minami-
Aoyama, this branch of the mini Mandala empire
specialises in experimental music. It's a hotbed of
activity (one of the live CDs on John Zorn's Tzadik
label was recorded here), where local stars sometimes show up unannounced for one-off gigs with
friends. Check out Cicala Mvta, playing a mix of
chingdon (Japanese marching music), klezmer and
Eastern European folk.

Other locations: Mandala Minami-Aoyama MR
Bldg B1F, 3-2-2 Minami-Aoyama, Minato-ku (5474
0411/www.mandala.gr.jp/aoyama.html).

Shelter Shimo-Kitazawa

*Senda Bldg B1F, 2-6-10 Kitazawa, Setagaya-ku
(3466 7430/www.loft-prj.co.jp). Shimo-Kitazawa
station (Keio Inokashira, Odakyu lines), north exit.*
Capacity 250.

Part of the Loft group, this smallish venue in
Shimo-Kitazawa is always booked with up-and-
coming or even established local bands that might
usually play bigger venues. Overseas acts also perform here on occasion. Shelter has been around for
more than a decade and is exceedingly popular, so
it's best to arrive early.

Shibuya O-West

*2-3 Maruyama-cho, Shibuya-ku (5784 7088/
www.shibuya-o.com). Shibuya station (Yamanote,
Ginza, Hanzomon lines), Hachiko exit.* **Capacity** 500.
Map Shibuya p109.

Across the street from the Shibuya O-East complex
(*see p259*), this space usually hosts better-known
Japanese indie bands with concentration on alt
and mainstream rock. There are also two smaller
venues within the building: O-Nest (3462 4420,
capacity 250) presents on-the-way-up Japanese bands
and electronic music creators, and can tend towards
the edgy or experimental; while intimate O-Crest
(3770 1095, capacity 200) holds acoustic and more
low-key events.

Shinjuku Loft

*Tatehana Bldg B2F, 1-12-9 Kabuki-cho, Shinjuku-ku
(5272 0382/www.loft-prj.co.jp). Shinjuku station
(Yamanote line), east exit; (Marunouchi line), exit
B12; (Oedo, Shinjuku lines), exit 1.* **Capacity** *Main
stage* 550. *Sub-stage* 100. **Map** Shinjuku p117.

Loft has been around for more than 25 years and
is a dedicated promoter. Inside are two areas: one
is the main space for gigs, the other is a bar with
a small stage. Expect loud music of any genre
here. At times Loft offers more than just gigs, with
all-night events that include DJs. Nearby sister
venue Loft Plus One (1-14-7 Kabukicho, 3205
6864) is an unusual place that specialises in live
talk events. The entertainment ranges from political discussion to porn stars performing erotic
games. Needless to say, the language barrier only
affects some events.

Shinjuku Marz

*Daiichi Tokiwa B1F, 2-45-1 Kabuki-cho,
Shinjuku-ku (3202 8248/www.marz.jp). Shinjuku
station (Yamanote line), east exit; (Marunouchi
line), exit B13; (Oedo, Shinjuku lines), exit 1.*
Capacity 300.

Funk, rock and J-pop – what the bands here have in
common is the ambition to set off on a musical
career. Opened in 2001, Shinjuku Marz is doing well
despite stiff local competition.

Star Pine's Café

*1-20-16 Kichijoji-Honcho, Musashino-shi (0422
232251/www.mandala.gr.jp/spc.html). Kichijoji
station (Chuo line), central exit.* **Capacity** 350.

The biggest of the three Mandala venues (*see also
above*). The artists who perform here are mostly
experimental, and genres range from jazzy to progressive to avant-garde and dancey. Most of the
music is of high quality. It's also the venue du jour
for obscure-ish overseas acts. All-night events usually follow weekend gigs.

Studio Jam

*Central Bldg 1F, 2-3-23 Kabuki-cho, Shinjuku-ku
(3232 8169). Shinjuku station (Yamanote line),
east exit; (Marunouchi lines), exits B6, B7; (Oedo,
Shinjuku lines), exit 1.* **Capacity** 200.

In operation since 1980, Studio Jam, located in
Shinjuku's red-light district, specialises in 1960s-70s
music, with a bit of guitar pop thrown in.

Unit

*Za House Bldg, 1-34-17 Ebisu-Nishi, Shibuya-ku
(3484 1012/www.unit-tokyo.com). Daikanyama
station (Tokyu Toyoko line).* **Capacity** 600.

A medium-sized space that hosts everything from
Japanese indie-rock bands to international stars
such as Bloc Party or the New Mastersounds. Unit
managed to nab the former booking manager of
the old (Shinjuku) Liquid Room, so it's worth taking
a look at its schedule. **Photo** *p258*.

Y2K

*Aban Bldg B1F, 7-13-2 Roppongi, Minato-ku
(5775 3676/www.explosionworks.net/y2k). Roppongi
station (Hibiya line), exit 4A; (Oedo line), exit 7.*
Capacity 450. **Map** Roppongi p103.

Opened in 1999 in the heart of Roppongi with a mission to bring live music to clubbers, this venue
concentrates on smaller, local, rock-minded bands.

Performing Arts

From gender-bending stage shows to English-language comics.

Kabuki remains the most famous, and perhaps the most accessible, of Japan's dramatic media, with the stunning **Kabuki-za** theatre a must-visit for anyone. But Tokyo boasts a performance-art bill to rival any metropolis. Other home-grown forms include *bunraku*, a form of puppeteering that takes 30 years to master, and *takarazuka*, an all-female answer to *kabuki* (with extra camp). Western shows are also growing in popularity, with musicals leading the way. Even Shinjuku's bastion of entertainment for the elderly, **Koma Gekijo**, has succumbed to the popularity of a foreign sing-song, swapping its old-time variety shows for *We Will Rock You*.

TICKETS AND INFORMATION

The three English-language daily newspapers, as well as weekly magazine *Metropolis*, all list the most notable performances. Many of the theatre websites listed below have English schedules. You can buy tickets direct from the venue, or at convenience stores and department stores, or by telephone from ticket agencies. It's a good idea to book ahead.

Traditional Japanese theatre

Fearsome masks, silken costumes, stylised dialogue, intricate choreography and the piquant tones of exotic instruments: these are only a few of the elements that beckon the curious into the mysterious world of traditional Japanese performing arts. Often impenetrable to the outsider, ancient forms such as *Noh*, *bunraku* and *kabuki* employ archaic language and can even be difficult for locals to understand.

However, there is much to appreciate on an aesthetic basis alone, and many of the themes – clan battles, servant-master loyalty, revenge and justice, conflicts between duty and loyalty, unrequited love – are universal. Additionally, English programmes and simultaneous translations are increasingly available.

As with other traditional theatre forms throughout Asia, Japanese theatre integrates dance, music and lyrical narrative. In contrast to Western theatre's preoccupation with realism, the emphasis is on beauty, the mythic and the ritualistic. Another distinguishing feature is *ma*, perhaps best translated as a 'pregnant pause'. More than just silence, *ma* is the space

that interrupts musical notes or words and is used to intensify the power of the dramatic moment.

The Japanese theatre-going experience is also markedly different from that in the West. Cast aside all notions of hushed reverence and fur coats: a trip to the theatre is a social outing here, and many people come for an afternoon at, say, Ginza's Kabuki-za, armed with flasks of hot drinks, packed meals and bags full of goodies, which are noisily chomped throughout the performance. Spectators often comment on the action as it happens, for example calling out the stage name of the performer at significant moments. A particularly fine tableau may well elicit a burst of spontaneous applause.

BUNRAKU

While puppetry in Japan goes back at least to the 11th century, modern *bunraku* takes its name from the Bunraku-za organised in Osaka in the early 19th century, and was developed by city-dwelling commoners of the Edo period (1600-1868). The puppets used in *bunraku* are a half to two-thirds human size and require great skill and strength to operate. Each puppet is operated by two assistants and one chief puppeteer. Becoming a master puppeteer is a lengthy process, beginning with ten years' operating the legs, followed by another ten on the left arm before being permitted to manipulate the right arm, head and eyebrows.

Four main elements comprise a *bunraku* performance: the puppets themselves; the movements they make; the vocal delivery of the *tayu*, who chants the narrative and speaks the lines for every character, changing his voice to suit the role; and the solo accompaniment by the three-stringed, lute-like *shamisen*.

KABUKI

Kabuki is said to have originated with Okuni, a female attendant at the Izumo shrine in Kyoto, who first led her mostly female company in performances on the dry bed of the Kamogawa river in 1603. *Kabuki* means 'unusual' or 'shocking', and it quickly became the most popular form of theatre in 17th- and 18th-century Japan. However, concerns over the sexual antics of the entertainers, on and off stage, meant that women performers were banned in 1629; now all *kabuki* actors are male. Women's parts are taken by *onnagata* (specialists in female roles), who portray a stylised feminine beauty. There

Watch the master puppeteers in action, at a *bunraku* performance. *See p262.*

is no pretence of realism, so the actor's real age is irrelevant – there is no incongruity in a 75-year-old man portraying an 18-year-old maiden.

Of all the traditional performing arts in Japan, *kabuki* is probably the most exciting. The actor is the most important element in *kabuki*, and everything that happens on stage is a vehicle for displaying his prowess. *Koken*, stage hands dressed in black, symbolising their supposed invisibility, hand the actor props, make running adjustments to his heavy costume and wig, and bring him a stool to perch on during long speeches or periods of inactivity.

Most *kabuki* programmes feature one *shosagoto* dance piece, one *jidaimono* and one *sewamono*. *Jidaimono* are dramas set in pre-Edo Japan. They feature gorgeous costumes and colourful make-up called *kumadori*, which is painted along the lines of the actor's face. The actor uses melodramatic elocution, but because *jidaimono* originated in the puppet theatre, the plays also feature accompaniments from a chanter who relates the storyline and emotions of the character, while the actor expresses them in movement, facial expressions or poses. *Sewamono* are stories of everyday life during the Edo period and are closer in style to Western drama.

Every *kabuki* theatre features a *hanamichi*, an elevated pathway for the performers that runs through the audience from the main stage to the back of the theatre. This is used for entrances and exits, and contains a trap door through which supernatural characters emerge.

NOH AND KYOGEN

Japan's oldest professional theatre form, *Noh*, dates back to 14th-century Shinto and Buddhist religious festivals and was used both to educate and entertain. The ritualistic nature of *Noh* plays is emphasised by the masks worn by the principal character. Plays are grouped into categories, which can be likened to five courses of a formal meal, each with a different flavour. Invigorating celebratory dances about gods are followed by battle plays of warrior-ghosts; next are lyrical pieces about women, then themes of insanity, and finally demons. Presentation is mostly sombre, slow and deliberate. Plays explore the transience of this world, the sin of killing and the spiritual comfort to be found in Buddhism.

There are no group rehearsals: there is a pre-performance meeting, but the actors and musicians do not play together until the performance. This spontaneity is one of the appeals of this kind of theatre.

Kyogen are short, humorous interludes that show the foolishness of human nature through understated portrayal. They are interspersed for comic relief with *Noh* pieces, but are intended to produce refined laughter, not boisterous humour.

Noh future?

Noh is unarguably the origin of all forms of traditional Japanese theatre. Both *kabuki* and *bunraku* puppet theatre borrow heavily from the current 240-play repertoire of *Noh* and would likely not exist were it not for the slower-paced, highly dramatised and symbolic performance art.

Noh was the brainchild and life's work of a father and son named Kan-ami and Zeami. When Kan-ami (b. 1333) performed for a shogun in 1374, he so entranced Japan's political leader that his own future as a favoured (and thus financially sponsored) actor was assured. His son Zeami (b. 1363) took on his father's mantle and became far more prolific with the pen, producing around 100 plays that are still performed today.

In 1434 Zeami fell foul of a later shogun and was sent into exile, leaving *Noh* in an uncertain state. For centuries it remained the preserve of the ruling classes, with the odd show staged at shrines during festivals. The drama almost vanished completely when

Japan looked West in the turbulent early years of the Meiji era (1868-1912).

Saved from extinction by imperial patronage, the art form-cum-entertainment nevertheless remained off the radar until the mid 20th century when renowned novelist Mishima Yukio (1925-70) produced his famous *Five Modern Noh Plays*.

Nowadays interest in *Noh* lags far behind that of *kabuki*, partly due to high ticket prices and the use of archaic language and references. The **National Noh Theatre** (*see p265*) holds only around 600 when full. But things are changing slowly. Increasing numbers of younger Japanese can be seen at performances, numerous universities and private schools now have *Noh* clubs, well-known actors recruit and raise their own entourage of disciples and even kids and women's groups (professional *Noh* actors are all male) are starting to take root. The National Noh Theatre hosts periodical performances by the kids of today, adult actors of tomorrow.

Thirty theatres across Japan are now used for various *Noh* performances, with 13 of these in Tokyo. Performance lists, schedules and ticket information are all available in English. For the locals or the language-proficient, special 'Guide to *Noh*' performances in modern Japanese are increasing the popularity of this uniquely Japanese form of theatre. Anchored in the past, *Noh* is finally looking to the future.

Cerulean Tower Noh Theatre

Cerulean Tower Tokyu Hotel B2F, 26-1 Sakuragaoka-cho, Shibuya-ku (5728 0168/www. ceruleantower.com). Shibuya station (Yamanote, Ginza, Hanzomon lines), south exit. **Capacity** 185. **Box office** tickets sold at Cerulean Tower Tokyu Hotel (3476 3000). **Tickets** from ¥5,000. **Credit** AmEx, DC, JCB, MC, V. **Map** Shibuya p109.
Housed in the basement of the Cerulean Tower hotel (*see p47*), this is the city's newest venue for Japanese theatre. It hosts both professional and amateur *Noh* and *kyogen* performances – without English translation.

Kabuki-za

4-12-15 Ginza, Chuo-ku (information 3541 3131/box office 5565 6000/www.shochiku.co.jp/play/kabukiza/ theater/index.html). Higashi-Ginza station (Hibiya, Asakusa lines), exits A3, A6. **Capacity** 1,866. **Box office** 10am-6pm daily. **Tickets** ¥2,520-¥16,800. **Credit** AmEx, DC, JCB, MC, V. **Map** Ginza p75.
Japan's number-one *kabuki* theatre. The schedule changes monthly, with matinées starting around 11am and evening performances around 4.30pm. Shows can last up to five hours, including intervals. You can also buy tickets to watch just one act from the fourth floor; these go on sale from one hour

beforehand and often sell out. An English-language programme (¥1,000) and audio guide (¥650, plus a refundable deposit of ¥1,000) are invaluable. Note that the restaurants and souvenir shop are not accessible to fourth-floor visitors. **Photo** *p267*.

National Noh Theatre

4-18-1 Sendagaya, Shibuya-ku (3230 3000/www. ntj.jac.go.jp/english/index.html). Sendagaya station (Chuo, Sobu lines) or Kokuritsu-Kyogijo station (Oedo line), exit A4. **Capacity** 591. **Box office** 10am-6pm daily. **Tickets** ¥2,300-¥6,000; ¥1,700 concessions. **Credit** AmEx, DC, JCB, MC, V.
Noh performances are normally staged here four or five times a month. A one-page explanation of the story in English is available.

National Theatre

4-1 Hayabusa-cho, Chiyoda-ku (3230 3000/www. ntj.jac.go.jp/english/index.html). Nagatacho station (Hanzomon, Nanboku, Yurakucho lines), exit 4. **Capacity** *Large Hall* 1,610. *Small Hall* 590. **Box office** 10am-6pm daily. **Tickets** *Large Hall* ¥1,500-¥12,000. *Small Hall* ¥1,500-¥6,000. **Credit** AmEx, DC, JCB, MC, V. **Map** Marunouchi p93.
Kabuki is staged seven months a year in the National Theatre's Large Hall, while *bunraku* is staged in the Small Hall four months a year. Programmes include the story in English, and English audio guides are available (¥650, plus a refundable ¥1,000 deposit).

Modern dramas & musicals

Modern theatre productions often portray historical themes, such as *jidai geki* – samurai dramas set in the Edo period. Unlike in *kabuki*, female roles are played by women. No matter how tragic, *jidai geki* must end with a satisfactory resolution, whether it is the successful revenge of a murder or the ascent into heaven of the dead heroine aloft a podium. However, influenced by Western drama, plays with happy endings are on the increase.

Famous Western plays and musicals, translated into Japanese, are also common. The **New National Theatre, Tokyo** (*see p251*) provides a forum for the most respected Japanese directors, who take a contemporary approach to Western classics. Artistic director of both **Theatre Cocoon** (*see p268*) and the Saitama Arts Centre in suburban Tokyo, Ninogawa Yukio has made a notable splash with his trademark fusions of Japanese and Western aesthetics in productions such as *Hamlet*. **Gekidan Shiki** (Shiki Theatre Company), founded in 1953, currently has seven theatres around the country, where it stages long-running Japanese versions of such well-known faves as *Cats, Beauty and the Beast* and *A Chorus Line*.

In a city as cosmopolitan as Tokyo, it may come as a surprise to learn that only a handful of productions in English are available each year, and some of these are thanks to touring troupes from the US or Britain, such as the Royal Shakespeare Company. The city has been seeing more avant-garde productions from the likes of Robert Wilson, while the **Tokyo International Arts Festival** (www.anj.or.jp) showcases cutting-edge overseas and domestic work. It celebrated its 11th anniversary in 2005.

There is also a thriving avant-garde theatre subculture in the suburb of Shimo-Kitazawa, which has dozens of small venues.

TAKARAZUKA

Featuring an all-women, oft-moustachioed cast, the **Takarazuka Kagekidan** (Takarazuka Opera Company) is another uniquely Japanese creation. Created in 1913 by entertainment tycoon Kobayashi Ichizo to attract people to his Takarazuka resort near Osaka, *takarazuka* was to provide 'strictly wholesome entertainment suitable for women and children from good families'. It is another expression of the Japanese fixation with androgynous performers. Its famously disciplined stars perform campy revues combining elements of musicals, opera and Japanese classics in gaudy productions that drive its mostly female audience wild with pleasure. The recent rebuilding and reopening of Hibiya's **Tokyo Takarazuka Theater** testifies to the continued vigour of this unusual art.

Dentsu Shiki Theatre Umi (SEA)

1-8-2 Higashi-Shinbashi, Minato-ku (0120 489 444/www.shiki.gr.jp/siteinfo/english/). Shiodome station (Oedo line), Shiodome-kaisatsu exit; (Yurikamome line), Dentsu exit. **Capacity** 1,200. **Box office** 10am-8pm daily. **Tickets** ¥3,150-¥11,550. **Credit** DC, JCB, MC, V.
The newest Western-style theatre in Tokyo – part of the Shiki Theatre Company's empire – opened in December 2002 in advertising giant Dentsu's new headquarters in the Shiodome area of Tokyo. Its remit is to provide Western musicals, sung in Japanese. *Phantom of the Opera* opened in January 2005.

Koma Gekijo

1-19-1 Kabuki-cho, Shinjuku-ku (3200 2213/ www.koma-sta.co.jp). Shinjuku station (Yamanote, Shinjuku lines), east exit; (Marunouchi, Oedo lines), exit B7. **Capacity** 2,100. **Box office** 9.30am-7pm daily. **Tickets** ¥3,000-¥8,500. **Credit** JCB, MC, V. **Map** Shinjuku p117.
This well-known theatre in Tokyo's red-light district has long been the host of the kind of variety shows that lure the pension crowd and bemuse tourists. However, since 2006 it has drawn a different audience as the home of Ben Elton's Queen musical *We Will Rock You*.

Meiji-za

2-31-1 Nihonbashi-Hamacho, Chuo-ku (3660 3900/ www.meijiza.co.jp). Hamacho station (Shinjuku line),

Arts & Entertainment

exit A2. **Capacity** 1,400. **Box office** 10am-5pm daily. **Tickets** ¥5,000-¥12,000. **Credit** DC, V.
Usually stages samurai dramas, often starring actors who play similar roles on TV. No English.

Shinbashi Embujo
6-18-2 Ginza, Chuo-ku (3541 2600/www.shochiku.co. jp/play/index.html). Higashi-Ginza station (Asakusa, Hibiya lines), exit A6. **Capacity** 1,400. **Box office** 10am-6pm daily. **Tickets** ¥2,100-¥15,750. **Credit** AmEx, DC, JCB, MC, V. **Map** Ginza p75.
Ichikawa Ennosuke's 'Super-Kabuki', a jazzed-up, modernised version of the real thing, is staged here in April and May and at the Kabuki-za (*see p264*) in July. Samurai dramas are performed during the rest of the year.

Tokyo Takarazuka Gekijo
1-1-3 Yurakucho, Chiyoda-ku (5251 2001/http:// kageki.hankyu.co.jp/english/index.html). Yurakucho station (Yamanote, Yurakucho lines), Hibiya exit or Hibiya station (Chiyoda, Hibiya, Mita lines), exit A13. **Capacity** 2,000. **Box office** 10am-6pm Mon, Tue, Thur-Sun. **Tickets** ¥3,500-¥10,000. **Credit** JCB, MC, V. **Map** Ginza p75.
Performances are in Japanese only.

Expat theatre

With the limited number of English-language performances by companies touring from abroad, Tokyo's expatriate community has stepped up to fill the gap. There are currently no fewer than four English-language theatre groups in Japan, three of them based in Tokyo.

The most venerable – with over a century of history – is the **Tokyo International Players**, while **Intrigue Theatre** (www. intriguetheatre.com) is a more recent creation. Canadian director Robert Tsonos's **Sometimes Y Theatre** has recently relocated to Japan from Toronto and been staging challenging productions, such as Michael Healey's *The Drawer Boy* at the Canadian Embassy. Finally, Australian director Dwayne Lawler's **Rising Sun Theatre**, based in Nagoya, has shaken up the Tokyo theatre scene with a number of controversial shows. These include a cross-cultural re-envisioning of *Macbeth*, set to death-metal music, at the New National Theatre.

Tokyo International Players
TIP information 090 6009 4171/www.tokyoplayers. org. Performances held at the Tokyo American Club, 2-1-2 Azabudai, Minato-ku (3224 3670/ www.tokyoamericanclub.org). Kamiyacho station (Hibiya line), exit 2 or Azabu-Juban station (Nanboku, Oedo lines), exit 6. **Box office** 7.30am-11pm daily. **Tickets** ¥4,000; ¥2,500 concessions. **No credit cards. Map** Roppongi p103.
A keen group of amateur and professional actors, TIP usually stages productions at the long-running Tokyo American Club near Roppongi.

Dance & performance art

Tokyo is currently experiencing an explosion of contemporary performing arts. Companies such as the *butoh*-influenced **Kim Itoh & the Glorious Future** (www.geocities.co.jp/ Hollywood-Miyuki/3773/index_e.html), the comedic mime-based **Muzutoabura** (www. mizutoabura.com) and choreographers like **Yamada Un** (www1.ocn.ne.jp/~yaun/english. htm), who has transformed her joint disease into a source of inspiration are integrating Eastern and Western aesthetics to create challenging and engaging spectacles.

Festivals, including the **Park Tower Next Dance Festival** (www.ozone.co.jp/parktower hall) in February, the **Tokyo Performing Arts Market** (www.tpam.co.jp) in August, and two biennial offerings, **Die Pratze Dance Festival** and **Dance BiennaleTokyo**, are increasingly ambitious, with new works by provocative Japanese and foreign choreographers.

Classical ballet also possesses a devoted audience in Japan. The country has recently begun to churn out dancers noted for their technical proficiency, while visits by overseas groups such as the Leningrad State Ballet and the New York City Ballet occur regularly. Tokyo's own companies include the celebrated **Asami Maki Ballet** (www.ambt.jp), which stages productions ranging from *Swan Lake* to modern works such as the jazz-based *Duke Ellington Suite*, which grew out of the company's long-standing relationship with legendary French choreographer Roland Petit. Meanwhile, dancer and heart-throb **Kumakawa Tetsuya** – back from his position as soloist with the Royal Ballet in London – has been making waves with innovative productions from his **K-Ballet Company** (www.tbs.co.jp/kumakawa).

Anything Western and extroverted is also the rage in Tokyo. Tap dancing seems to be the latest fashion, while Latin dance forms from tango to salsa are trendy; the **Asakusa Samba Carnival** (*see p214*) in late August regularly draws crowds close to half a million.

BUTOH
Japan's greatest contribution to performing arts in the 20th century was the inimitable and enigmatic avant-garde dance form known as *butoh*. Differing from both classical Japanese and Western modern dance, but utilising aspects of both, *butoh* is immediately recognisable by the (mostly) shaved heads, white body paint and slow, often tortured movements of its performers.

Created by Hijikata Tatsumi and his fellow pioneers, *butoh*, originally termed by Hijikata *ankoku butoh*, or 'dance of darkness', scandalised Japan in the late 1950s. It's inspired by Japanese folk dance and German Neue Tanz, and is spiritually associated with *Noh* – but looks like none of them. Dancers contort their bodies to express emotions ranging from pain and despair to absurdity and ecstasy. Sometimes they hardly move at all; a *butoh* spectacle can be simultaneously enthralling and exhausting.

Since the 1980s, when *butoh* began to startle overseas audiences, companies such as **Dairakudakan** (www.dairakudakan.com) and **Sankai Juku** (www.sankaijuku.com) have toured abroad on a regular basis. The recent closure of Asbestoskan means Tokyo no longer has a specialist theatre for *butoh*, but the dance

form is still widely performed at venues such as the ambitious **Setagaya Public Theatre** or the more intimate **Azabu Die Pratze**.

As well as the venues listed below, the **New National Theatre, Tokyo** (*see p251*) presents mainly modern dance and drama in its two smaller spaces, the Playhouse and the Pit.

Aoyama Round Theatre

5-53-1 Jingumae, Shibuya-ku (3797 5678/box office 3797 1400/www.aoyama.org). Omotesando station (Chiyoda, Ginza, Hanzomon lines), exit B2. **Capacity** 1,200. **Box office** 10am-6pm daily. **Tickets** prices vary. **No credit cards.** **Map** Shibuya p109.

Kabuki-za. See p264.

As its name suggests, this is a theatre that can be used in the round – one of very few in Tokyo. It attracts leading contemporary performers.

Azabu Die Pratze

1-26-6 Higashi-Azabu 2F, Minato-ku (5545 1385/ www.geocities.jp/azabubu). Akabanebashi station (Oedo line), Akabanebashi exit. **Capacity** 100. **Box office** 6-11pm daily. **Tickets** ¥3,000. **No credit cards.**
This cosy space is a locus for cutting-edge dance, performance and *butoh*, as well as the host of the annual Die Pratze Dance Festival.
Other locations: Kagurazaka Die Pratze 2-12 Nishi-Gokencho, Shinjuku-ku (3235 7990).

Galaxy Theatre

2-3-16 Higashi-Shinagawa, Shinagawa-ku (5460 9999/www.gingeki.jp/index.html). Tennozu Isle station (Tokyo Monorail), Chuo exit; (Rinkai line), exits A, B. **Capacity** *Art Sphere* 746. *Sphere Mex* 200. **Box office** 10am-6pm daily. **Tickets** prices vary. **No credit cards.**
Formerly known as the Art Sphere, this theatre rebranded itself as Galaxy in late 2006. It caters to the whims of well-off young fans of contemporary modern dance, booking things that are considered 'in', but not too avant-garde or risqué. The venue's location, on Tennozu Isle, makes it one of the more interesting – and less accessible – of Tokyo's theatrical venues.

Session House

158 Yaraicho, Shinjuku-ku (3266 0461/www. session-house.net). Kagurazaka station (Tozai line), exit 1. **Capacity** 100. **Box office** 10am-10pm daily. **Tickets** ¥2,000-¥2,500. **No credit cards.**
Dancer Itoh Naoko established Session House in order to give solo dancers the opportunity to experiment. The aim is to showcase pure dance without the extensive use of theatrical props and high-tech lighting.

Setagaya Public Theatre

4-1-1 Taishido, Setagaya-ku (5432 1526/www. setagaya-ac.or.jp/sept/). Sangenjaya station (Tokyu Denentoshi line) Sancha Patio exit. **Capacity** *Public Theatre* 600. *Theatre Tram* 200. **Box office** 10am-6pm daily. **Tickets** prices vary. **No credit cards.**
Like the New National Theatre (*see p251*), this venue is a favourite with fans and performers. The main auditorium is modelled on a Greek open-air theatre, but can be changed to proscenium style. The smaller Theatre Tram is a popular venue for dance. The building is the adopted home of the Sankai Juku *butoh* troupe, when it's in town.

Theatre Cocoon

Bunkamura, 2-24-1 Dogenzaka, Shibuya-ku (3477 9999/www.bunkamura.co.jp). Shibuya station (Yamanote, Ginza lines), Hachiko exit; (Hanzomon line), exit 3A. **Capacity** 750. **Box office** 10am-7pm daily. **Phone bookings** 10am-5.30pm daily. **Tickets** prices vary. **Credit** AmEx, DC, JCB, MC, V. **Map** Shibuya p109.
The medium-sized venue of the giant Bunkamura arts centre in Shibuya is used mainly for musicals, ballet, concerts and opera.

Comedy

Japan has a tradition of humorous storytelling called *rakugo*, which can be seen at a few venues, including the **Asakusa Engei Hall** (1-43-12 Asakusa, Taito-ku, 3841 6545) and the **National Engei Hall** (4-1 Hayabusa-cho, Chiyoda-ku, 3230 3000, www.ntj.jac.go.jp/ english/index.html). However, you'll need to speak Japanese; nowhere in Tokyo offers English translations of such events.

Punchline Comedy Club

Shows at Pizza Express 3F, 4-30-3 Jingumae, Shibuya-ku (5775 3894/www.punchlinecomedy. com/tokyo). Harajuku station (Yamanote line), Meiji-Jingumae exit or Meiji-Jingumae station (Chiyoda line), exit 5. **Shows** selected days Jan, Mar, June, Sept. **Tickets** ¥8,500 incl dinner & 2 drinks. **Credit** AmEx, DC, JCB, MC, V. **Map** Harajuku & Aoyama p82.
John Moorhead started the Tokyo branch of this pan-Asian comedy club in 2001. Its mission is to bring top comedians from around the world, many from the UK, to perform before an expat crowd.

Suehiro-tei

3-6-12 Shinjuku, Shinjuku-ku (3351 2974/ www.suehirotei.com). Shinjuku-Sanchome station (Marunouchi, Shinjuku lines), exits B2, C4. **Capacity** 325. **Box office** noon-8.15pm daily. **Tickets** ¥2,200-¥2,700. **No credit cards.** **Map** Shinjuku p117.
A charming old theatre that looks alarmingly like a bathhouse, Suehiro-tei hosts performances of Japan's traditional *rakugo* comedy. No English translation.

Tokyo Comedy Store

Bar, Isn't It, MT Bldg 3F, 3-8-18 Roppongi, Minato-ku (3746 1598/www.tokyocomedy.com). Roppongi station (Hibiya line), exit 5. **Shows** 1st & 3rd Fri of mth. **Tickets** ¥2,000 incl 1 drink. **No credit cards.** **Map** Roppongi p103.
Tokyo's best-organised English-language comedy group may have the same name as the celebrated venue in London, but the similarity ends. Performers are keen amateurs, ranging from the hilarious to the dire. New material is always sought, from both Japanese and foreign performers. The Comedy Store also holds improv classes and workshops in Japanese and English.

Tokyo Cynics

The Fiddler, Tajima Bldg B1F, 2-1-2 Takadanobaba, Shinjuku-ku (3204 2698/www.thefiddler.com). Takadanobaba station (Yamanote line), Waseda exit; (Tozai line), exit 3. **Shows** 2nd Tue of mth. **Admission** free.
A ramshackle bunch of English-speaking amateur comics and outright eccentrics who regularly enliven evenings at one of Tokyo's longest-established and most popular British-style pubs. They also perform in the Maple Leaf sports bar in Shibuya on the last Sunday of the month.

Sport & Fitness

Gargantuan grapplers, world-class pitchers and hydroplane gambling.

If you've come to Japan for sporting reasons, there's a strong chance you're heading to the dojo for training in one of Japan's renowned martial arts. But there's plenty more to this city. Japan is shaking off its inferiority complex in terms of team sports. The national football team still regularly underperforms, as do the capital's league teams, but the baseball stars won the inaugural World Baseball Classic, and players of both sports have impressed abroad. But while internationalism is celebrated when a local player signs for the Yankees or Red Sox, it's a different story in sumo, where the foreigners are winning, much to the chagrin of the men behind this traditional sport (*see 273*).

Sports facilities abound within the capital but are not always easy to use. Public swimming pools, in particular, have strict, confusing and often amusing rules (such as enforced cool-down periods).

Spectator sports

American football

Gridiron in Japan has a surprisingly large presence. There is a strong university league and even a company league, known as the X-League (where firms import top players and give them 'jobs'), which finishes with the **X Bowl** in Kobe in mid December. The climax of the domestic season is the brilliantly named **Rice Bowl**, at the **Tokyo Dome** (*see p270*) in early January, when the college champions take on the winners of the X-League. The same venue also hosts regular NFL pre-season tour matches in August under the American Bowl banner.

Athletics

The IAAF Japan Grand Prix is held every spring in Osaka. The International Super Track & Field event, the Tokyo area's main annual taste of top-class competition, usually takes place on 23 September (a national holiday) at the **Nissan Stadium** in Yokohama (*see p270*).

Japan's real athletics obsession has long been the marathon. The last two female Olympic champions were Japanese, and they quickly became household names. The **Tokyo International Marathon** is held in February, and the **Tokyo International Women's**

Marathon (the world's first marathon for women) in November; both start and finish at the **National Stadium** (*see p270*). Both have strict entrance requirements (no fun runs here) and attract some of the world's top runners.

Baseball

Introduced to Japan in 1873, baseball has long held a firm grip on local hearts and minds. The first pro side, the Yomiuri Giants, was founded in 1934, and by 1950 a professional competition had been set up. The league eventually split into two divisions (the Pacific League and the Central League) with six teams in each.

Demand from both players and fans led to inter-league play since 2005, meaning Pacific League sides have been able to milk the cash cow known as the Yomiuri Giants – the New York Yankees of Japanese baseball. Each side plays 140 games a season (late March to October), with the winners of the Central and Pacific leagues meeting in the Japan Series to decide the championship.

Two teams are based in central Tokyo: the **Yomiuri Giants** at the **Tokyo Dome** (the salaryman's favourite, ergo somewhat dull) and the **Yakult Swallows** at **Jingu Stadium** (open-air, crazy fans and beer on tap – Jingu is the place to go). The **Hokkaido Nippon Ham Fighters** also play some games at the Tokyo Dome, their former home. In the Tokyo area you can also see the **Yokohama Bay Stars**, **Chiba Lotte Marines** and the **Seibu Lions**.

Worryingly for the future of the professional game in Japan has been the recent drain of local superstars to the US major leagues and the growing audiences for live broadcasts from across the Pacific. Matsui Hideki of the New York Yankees and Suzuki Ichiro of the Seattle Mariners are huge in Japan, and most of their games are broadcast live. In late 2006 the Boston Red Sox signed Seibu's superstar pitcher Matsuzaka Daisuke for a trans-Pacific record fee, which should compound the problem domestically.

Jingu Stadium

13 Kasumigaoka-machi, Shinjuku-ku (3404 8999). Gaienmae station (Ginza line), exit 2 or Kokuritsu-Kyogijo station (Oedo line), exit A4 or Sendagaya station (Chuo line). **Capacity** 46,000. **Tickets** ¥1,500-¥4,500.

This large open-air stadium is part of the complex that includes the National Stadium and was built for the 1964 Olympics.

Tokyo Dome

1-3-61 Koraku, Bunkyo-ku (5800 9999/www.tokyo-dome.co.jp). Kasuga station (Mita, Oedo line), exit A1 or Korakuen station (Marunouchi, Namboku lines), exit 2 or Suidobashi station (Chuo line), west exit; (Mita line), exits A3, A4, A5.
The Dome, or Big Egg, is home to the Central League's Yomiuri Giants. In the past the Giants have claimed that every game was sold out, but the growing number of empty seats suggests that tickets are much easier to acquire than before.

Football

The 2002 World Cup saw the eyes of the football universe focused on Japan and co-hosts South Korea, although the closest Tokyo came in terms of venues was suburban Saitama and nearby Yokohama, which hosted the final. Tokyo was also left on the sidelines when the J.League was founded in 1993, but the capital now has two top-flight teams, **FC Tokyo** and **Tokyo Verdy 1969**, who share a ground in the west of the city. The **Urawa Reds** and **Omiya Ardija** in Saitama to the north, **JEF United Ichihara** to the east, and **Kawasaki Frontale** and **Yokohama F Marinos** to the west are the other major local clubs. The J.League's official website (www.j-league.or.jp/eng) has English-language details of clubs, players and fixtures.

From 2005 the league expanded to 18 teams and has changed to a single-stage season. The **Emperor's Cup** (Japan's FA Cup) takes place in December, with the final (*see p217*) on New Year's Day. The **Nabisco Cup** (the equivalent of the League Cup) runs throughout the season with the final in early November. International matches take place year-round and include Asian Cup and World Cup qualifiers, as well as the midsummer Kirin Cup. The **Japan Football Association**'s English website (www.jfa.or.jp/e/index.html) has info on forthcoming matches.

Ajinomoto Stadium

376-3 Nishimachi, Chofu (0424 40 0555/www.ajinomotostadium.com). Tobitakyu station (Keio line). **Capacity** 50,000. **Tickets** *J.League matches* ¥1,200-¥6,000.
The large and impressive home of FC Tokyo and Tokyo Verdy 1969 opened in 2001.

National Stadium

15 Kasumigaoka-machi, Shinjuku-ku (3403 4150). Kokuritsu-Kyogijo station (Oedo line), exit A4 or Sendagaya station (Chuo line) or Gaienmae station (Ginza line), exit 2. **Capacity** 60,000.
The 1964 Olympic Stadium still hosts many major events, including the start and finish of marathons,

some international and J.League football matches, the Emperor's Cup final, the Nabisco Cup final and major rugby matches.

Nissan Stadium

3300 Kozukue-cho, Kohoku-ku, Yokohama-shi (045 477 5000/www.hamaspo.com/stadium). Shin-Yokohama station (Tokaido Shinkansen, Yokohama lines), north exit then 15mins walk. **Capacity** 70,000.
Home of Nissan-sponsored Yokohama F Marinos. You can also take a World Cup tour; *see also p281.*

Saitama Stadium 2002

500 Nakanoda, Saitama (048 812 2002/www.stadium2002.com). Urawa-Misono station (Nanboku, Saitama Railway lines). **Capacity** 63,700. **Tickets** *J.League matches* ¥2,000-¥4,500.
The country's largest soccer-only stadium. It's a 20-minute walk from Urawa-Misono station, which gets extremely crowded after major events.

Golf

Like much else in Japan, golf has suffered from the bursting of the economic bubble in the 1990s. At its peak, the Japan Golf Tour (JGTO) was the richest in the world; lucrative enough, in fact, to keep local golfers from playing abroad, so it developed into a major, if isolated, tour. But the Tiger factor, among others, has enabled America's PGA Tour to reclaim its pre-eminent position in world golf.

Reduced sponsorship has seen the Japanese tour contract slightly, but it retains very high standards. There are many professional events in the Tokyo area, and many foreign stars visit Japan after the end of the PGA and European tours. The biggest event in the Tokyo area is the **Sumitomo VISA Taiheiyo Masters** in Gotemba, an hour west of Tokyo – check out the JGTO website on www.jgto.org.

The Women's Tour has also produced its fair share of stars, notably Okamoto Ayako and Kobayashi Hiromi. In 2003 high-school student Miyazato Ai won a JLPGA tournament, turned pro and caught the imagination of the country, revitalising the waning Women's Tour. Yuri Fudo has also dominated, and British golfer Samantha Head has been a regular fixture.

Horse racing

The **Japan Racing Association** (JRA) manages the ten national tracks and stages the country's big races, while the **National Association of Racing** (NAR) oversees local courses. Racetracks are one of the few places in the country where gambling is legal. For details in English, visit the website of the **Japan Association for International Horse Racing** at www.jair.jrao.ne.jp.

Straight outta Mongolia

Sumo is more than a sport; it's a symbol, reflecting cultural, spiritual and even religious aspects of Japan. Too bad, then – at least for the nationalists – that it's been dominated by foreigners in recent years. By the end of 2006, almost 10 per cent of all professional sumo wrestlers (or *rikishi*) and a third of the 42 members of the elite Makunouchi division were non-Japanese.

Foreigners have been entering the iconic Japanese sport for the better part of half a century, but most were Mongols, Koreans or Chinese, whose physical differences were muted. Today, national sumo associations have been established in approximately 85 nations across six continents, and tournament changing rooms in Japan are bulging with Bulgarian, Brazilian, Russian, Estonian, Georgian, Tongan and even Kazakhstani wrestlers. The league's lone *yokozuna* (Grand Champion) is a notorious bad-boy Mongolian called Asashoryu.

All of which should be healthy for a sport that is applying for Olympic recognition of amateur sumo and *shinsumo* (literally 'new sumo', but meaning women's sumo). But there's palpable concern on the part of Old Japan about the changing demographics of their sport. There's been no Japanese-born *yokozuna* since the great Takanohana retired in January 2003. A pair of Americans preceded Asashoryu, and – with no Japanese wrestler currently showing the calibre to make

it – the smart money says he'll be joined in the next year or so by another Mongolian.

To counter the foreign invasion, the Japanese Sumo Association has introduced an 'unwritten' rule limiting the numbers of foreign wrestlers to one per stable in the foreseeable future. The aim is to protect the 'Japanese-ness' of the sport, but the more likely effect is a drop in its quality and appeal.

Half a dozen years into the 21st century, sumo is a sport with global potential, but also a sport dragging around the weighty ball and chain of traditional Japanese views. To learn more about sumo's historical and religious aspects, check out one of the annual dedicatory ceremonies. Two are held at the Meiji Shrine (*see p86*), in early January and at the end of September; and one in April at the Yasukuni Shrine (*see p98*), with 500 wrestlers, including *yokozuna*, taking part. Contact the tourist offices (*see p313*) for details.

Arts & Entertainment

Oi Racecourse

2-1-2 Katsushima, Shinagawa-ku (3763 2151). Oi Keibajomae station (Tokyo Monorail).
Run by the NAR, with some 120 race days every year. Twinkle Races, evening events that Oi pioneered in the 1990s, have proved very popular with office workers.

Tokyo Racecourse

1-1 Hiyoshi-cho, Fuchu-shi (042 363 3141/www. jra.go.jp/turf/tokyo/index.html). Fuchu-Honmachi station (Musashino line) or Fuchukeiba-Seimonmae station (Keio line).
Run by the JRA, Tokyo Racecourse hosts 40 days' racing a year, all at weekends. Many of the country's

most famous races are held here, including November's Japan Cup (*see p216*), an international invitational that attracts top riders and horses from around the world.

Hydroplane racing

After horse racing, *kyotei* is the second-most popular focus for betting in Japan (bets start at just ¥100). The race itself involves six motor-driven boats in what is essentially a very large swimming pool; they go round the 600-metre (1,970-foot) course three times,

K-1 combatants mash it up. Martial arts for the next generation?

regularly reaching speeds of over 80km/h (50mph). **Edogawa Kyotei** is the favourite Tokyo venue. The schedule is published in sports newspapers and at www.edogawa-kyotei.co.jp.

Edogawa Kyotei

3-1-1 Higashi-Komatsugawa, Edogawa-ku (3656 0641/www.edogawa-kyotei.co.jp). Funabori station (Shinjuku line), south exit. **Admission ¥50.**

Ice hockey

The economic recession has hit the **Japan Ice Hockey League** hard in recent years. The league came close to folding, but fought back with a novel mode of expansion: importing teams from overseas. So now there is an Asian League (www.alhockey.com) consisting of the four remaining Japanese teams (Oji, Kokudo, Nikko Ice Bucks and Nippon Paper Cranes), two teams from China, and one each from Russia and South Korea.

Higashi-Fushimi Ice Arena

3-1-25 Higashi-Fushimi, Hoya-shi (0424 67 7171). Higashi-Fushimi station (Seibu Shinjuku line).

National Yoyogi Stadium 1st Gymnasium

2-1-1 Jinnan, Shibuya-ku (3468 1171). Harajuku station (Yamanote line), Omotesando exit or Meiji-Jingumae station (Chiyoda line), exit 2. **Map** Harajuku & Aoyama p82.

Shin-Yokohama Prince Hotel Skate Centre

2-11 Shin-Yokohama, Kohoku-ku, Yokohama-shi, Kanagawa (045 474 1112). Shin-Yokohama station (Tokaido Shinkansen, Yokohama lines), north exit then 10mins walk.

K-1

People are often surprised to learn that the record attendance (74,500) for a sports event at Tokyo Dome is held by K-1, a mishmash of martial arts. It's basically a combination of boxing and kick-boxing, with bouts consisting of three three-minute rounds (if there are no knockouts). It has all the appearance of a real sport – bouts take place in a ring with a referee and three judges; doctors are in attendance; rules are enforced; it has a competitive structure – but is not taken completely seriously by all sports fans.

Events are held most months at venues such as the **Nippon Budokan** (*see below*), **Yoyogi Gymnasium** (*see p272*) and **Tokyo Dome** (*see p270*).

Martial arts

Nippon Budokan

2-3 Kitanomaru-koen, Chiyoda-ku (3216 5100/ www.nipponbudokan.or.jp). Kudanshita station (Hanzomon, Shinjuku, Tozai lines), exit 2. **Map** Marunouchi p93.

The Budokan stages the All-Japan Championships or equivalent-level demonstration events in all the martial arts except sumo. Advance tickets are not required, and in many cases admission is free. The stadium is also used for concerts; *see p257.*

Motor sports

Motor sports have a devoted following in Japan. The **Fuji Speedway** (0550 78 1234/www.fsw.tv), in the foothills of the famous mountain, hosts the annual Formula 1 Japan Grand Prix. It's a two-hour train ride from Tokyo. The **Twin Ring Motegi** in Tochigi prefecture, a couple of hours north-east of the capital, boasts two types of circuit, including an oval course that's suitable for US-style motor sports. The permanent circuit hosts local Formula 3 and Formula Nippon races, the latter seen as a major stepping stone towards Formula 1.

Motorcycle racing is also a big draw in Japan, and several top riders are home-grown. The Japanese Grand Prix is held in September at the Motegi circuit.

Twin Ring Motegi
120-1 Hiyama, Motegi-machi, Haga-gun, Tochigi-ken (0285 64 0001/www.twinring.jp/english/index.html). Motegi station (Moka line) then bus.

Pride

Pride competes for attention with K-1 in the mixed martial arts field, and is similar to the Ultimate Fighting Championships in the US. Pride's selling point is that it is 'as close as you can get to street fighting'; everything goes, almost – there's no biting or testicular activity. The sport contains elements of karate, boxing, judo, wrestling and kick-boxing. Fights can include some sporty moments of punching and kicking, and other moments where one fighter sits on the other and beats him to a pulp. It's not for the faint-hearted.

Rugby

Japanese rugby underwent a major upheaval in 2003 with the introduction of a national professional league. Cynics would say Japan already had a professional operation for many years in the form of the corporate league; however, the game was amateurish and in dire need of reform. Now there is a national league, a national championship (which includes the top university teams) and a knockout trophy – and the **Japan Rugby Football Union** (JRFU) are keen to bring the 2011 World Cup to Japan.

Tokyo's Waseda University is one of the most popular sports 'franchises' in the country; matches are often held before 60,000 fans at the **National Stadium** (*see p270*). **Prince Chichibu Memorial Stadium** is the official home of rugby and is slap bang in the centre of town, next to Jingu Baseball Stadium. Ticket information is available at the JRFU website: www.jrfu-members.com.

Prince Chichibu Memorial Stadium
2-8-35 Kita Aoyama, Minato-ku (3401 3881). Gaienmae station (Ginza line), exit 2 or Kokuritsu-Kyogijo station (Oedo line), exit A4 or Sendagaya station (Chuo line).
Internationals and other big rugby matches not held at the National Stadium are played here.

Sumo

With a history dating back 2,000 years, Japan's national sport uniquely blends tradition, athleticism and religion. Its rules are simple: each combatant must try to force the other out of the ring (*dohyo*) or make him touch the floor with a part of his anatomy other than his feet. Tournaments take place over 15 days, with wrestlers fighting once a day. Those who achieve regular majorities (winning more than they lose) progress up through the rankings, the top of which is *yokozuna* (grand champion). Wrestlers failing to achieve a majority are demoted. *Yokozuna* must achieve a majority in every tournament or are expected to retire.

Three of the six annual tournaments take place in Tokyo (in January, May and September) at the **Ryogoku Kokugikan**, which also hosts one-day tournaments and retirement ceremonies. For ticket information, results and interviews, see the websites of the **Sumo Association** (www.sumo.or.jp/eng) and *Sumo World* magazine (www.sumoworld.com). *See also p271* **Straight outta Mongolia**. For information on visiting a sumo stable, *see pp67-8*.

Ryogoku Kokugikan
1-3-28 Yokoami, Sumida-ku (3623 5111/balcony seats booking 5237 9310). Ryogoku station (Oedo line), exits A3, A4; (Sobu line), west exit. **Tickets** ¥3,600-¥14,300.
Advance tickets go on sale about a month before each tournament. They're not difficult to get hold of (apart from the most expensive box seats) – though weekends generally sell out. Some unreserved, back-row balcony seats (one per person) are always held back for sale from 8am on the day of the tournament. Many spectators watch bouts between younger fighters from downstairs box seats until the ticket holders arrive in the mid afternoon. There's also a small museum (closed on tournament days).

Tennis

In professional tennis, it's the women's game that gets the most attention in Japan. A number of female players have won Grand Slam doubles titles, and Japan's most successful player of all time, Kimiko Date, made the semi-finals in the singles at Wimbledon. Current favourite among fans is Sugiyama Ai.

The biggest event is the **Toray Pan Pacific Open** (*see p217*), a Tier I WTA tournament held in the week following the Australian Open at the end of January at the **Tokyo Metropolitan Gymnasium**. The biggest men's event is the **Japan Open** (*see p215*) in October, which is held at the **Ariake Tennis Forest** on Odaiba and also features a Tier III WTA event.

Ariake Tennis Forest/ Ariake Colosseum

2-2-22 Ariake, Koto-ku (3529 3301/www.tptc.or.jp/ park/ariake.htm). Ariake station (Yurikamome line) or Kokusai-Tenjijo station (Rinkai line). **Open** 9am-9pm daily. **Admission** ¥1,800 1hr Mon-Fri; ¥3,600 2hrs Sat, Sun. **Map** Odaiba p101.

Tokyo Metropolitan Gymnasium

1-17-1 Sendagaya, Shibuya-ku (5474 2111/ www.tef.or.jp/tmg/index.html). Kokuritsu-Kyogijo station (Oedo line), exit A4 or Sendagaya station (Chuo line).

Active sports & fitness

Aussie Rules football

The **Tokyo Goannas** (www.tokyogoannas. com) satisfy the Australian community's need for sport and drink.

Boxing

There are various gyms around Tokyo, and boxercise fitness training is available at several sports clubs. Also try **Nitta Boxing Gym** (044 932 4639, www.nittagym.com).

Cricket

Decent cricket is available in Tokyo, notably among certain expat communities – check out the **Tokyo Wombats** (www.tokyowombats. com) and the **Indian Engineers** (www. ieccjapan.com/kantocup.htm). The **Japan Cricket Association** site is at www.jca-cricket.ne.jp/index.php.

Football

There's quite a lot of soccer action in Tokyo, with several competitions for all levels. Major organisations are the **Tokyo Metropolis League** (www.metropolis-league.com) and the **International Friendship Football League** (http://home.att.ne.jp/sun/iffl/).

Golf

With time and expense posing substantial obstacles to the capital's legion of would-be golfers, driving ranges dot the city. The cost of membership at private golf clubs can easily run to millions of yen, while green fees run from ¥8,000 on weekdays to ¥30,000 at weekends. The least expensive courses are those along built-up riverbanks to the west and north of the capital. There are online reservation sites (try www.golfyoyaku.com), but only in Japanese. The **Tokyo Metropolitan Golf Course** (18

holes at par 63) is the cheapest of the city's public courses; booking is essential at weekends.

Golf in Japan is usually a game of two halves, broken up by an hour-long lunch break.

Tokyo Metropolitan Golf Course

1-15-1 Shinden, Adachi-ku (3919 0111). Oji-Kamiya station (Nanboku line). **Open** dawn-dusk daily. **Rates** *Mon-Fri* ¥5,000; *Sat, Sun* ¥6,000.

Gyms

Membership of private gyms can be very expensive. Large hotels may have swimming pools or gyms, but sometimes charge extra for using them. If you are in need of some muscle-pumping action, head for one of the following – or, more cheaply, visit one of Tokyo's public sports centres (*see p276*).

Esforta

Shibuya Infoss Tower B1F, 20-1 Sakuragaokacho, Shibuya-ku (3780 5551/www.esforta.com). Shibuya station (Yamanote line), south exit; (Ginza, Hanzomon lines), Hachiko exit. **Open** 7am-10.30pm Mon-Fri; 9.30am-7pm Sat, Sun. Closed 1st Sun of mth. **Joining fee** ¥10,000 membership, then ¥15,000 per mth. **Map** Shibuya p109.
Facilities typically include aerobics, sauna, weight machines and sunbeds. The Suidobashi and Akasaka branches have swimming pools.
Other locations: throughout the city.

Gold's Gym Harajuku

V28 Building 3F, 6-31-17 Jingumae, Shibuya-ku (5766 3131/www.goldsgym.jp). Harajuku station (Yamanote line), Omotesando exit or Meiji-Jingumae station (Chiyoda line), exit 6. **Open** 24hrs daily; closed 8pm Sun-7am Mon. **Membership** ¥5,250, then plans up to ¥8,400/mth. **Credit** AmEx, DC, JCB, MC, V. **Map** Harajuku & Aoyama p82.
All the facilities you would expect from this world-wide gym chain. **Photo** *p275*.
Other locations: throughout the city.

Tipness

Kaleido Bldg 5F-7F, 7-1 Nishi-Shinjuku, Shinjuku-ku (3368 3531/freephone 0120 208 025/www.tipness. co.jp). Shinjuku station (Yamanote, Chuo, Sobu lines), east or west exit; (Marunouchi line), exit A18 or Shinjuku-Nishi station (Oedo line), exit D5. **Open** 7am-11.15pm Mon-Fri; 9.30am-10pm Sat; 9.30am-8pm Sun. Closed 15th of each month. **Membership** ¥3,150 membership, then plans up to ¥15,000/mth. **Credit** AmEx, DC, JCB, MC, V. **Map** Shinjuku p117.
Tipness has 25 branches within Tokyo. Most of them have a pool, aerobics classes and weights gym.
Other locations: throughout the city.

Horse riding

Tokyo Horse Riding Club

4-8 Yoyogi Kamizono-cho, Shibuya-ku (3370 0984/ www.tokyo-rc.or.jp/). Sangubashi station (Odakyu

line). **Open** *Mar-Nov* 9am-5.45pm Tue-Sun. *Dec-Feb* 9am-4.45pm Tue-Sun. **Rates** *Tue-Fri* ¥6,500; *Sat, Sun* ¥7,500. ¥3,000 surcharge for beginners. **No credit cards.**
Japan's oldest riding club boasts 45 horses and seven instructors. Visitors don't, thankfully, have to pay the annual membership fee of ¥96,000 (to join the Tokyo Horse Riding Club you must be recommended by two members and pay a fee of ¥2 million). Booking is necessary.

Gold's Gym Harajuku. *See p274.*

Ice skating

Championship events are held at the **National Yoyogi Stadium Gymnasium** (*see p272*).

Meiji Jingu Ice Skating Rink

Gobanchi, Kasumigaoka, Shinjuku (3403 3458/ www.meijijingugaien.jp/ice/). Kokuritsu-Kyogijo station (Oedo line), exit A2 or Sendagaya station (Chuo, Sobu lines). **Open** noon-6pm Mon-Fri; 10am-6pm Sat, Sun. (Last entry 5pm.) **Admission** ¥1,000-¥1,300; ¥500-¥900 children. Skate rental ¥500. **No credit cards.**

Takadanobaba Citizen Ice Skating Rink

4-29-27 Takadanobaba, Shinjuku-ku (3371 0910/ www.h2.dion.ne.jp/~c.i.s/). Takadanobaba station (Yamanote line), east exit; (Tozai line), exit 1. **Open** noon-7.45pm Mon-Sat; 10am-6pm Sun. **Admission** ¥1,000-¥1,300; ¥600-¥800 children. Skate rental ¥500. **No credit cards.**

Martial arts

Almost five million people practise martial arts in Japan. There are nine recognised modern forms – aikido, judo, *jukendo*, karate, kendo, *kyudo*, *naginata*, *shorinji kempo* and sumo – and a series of more traditional forms, known collectively as *kobudo*. The national associations of each discipline may have training facilities where spectators can view sessions. They may also know of dojos (gyms) that welcome visitors or potential students.

Aikido *Aikikai Federation, 17-18 Wakamatsucho, Shinjuku-ku (3203 9236/www.aikikai.or.jp).* Also check out the English website www.tokyo seidokan.com – the organisation was established by American teacher Chris Koprowski.
Judo *All-Japan Judo Federation, 1-16-30 Kasuga, Bunkyo-ku (3818 4199/www.judo.or.jp/English www.kodokan.org).*
Jukendo *All-Japan Jukendo Federation, 2-3 Kitanomaru Koen, Chiyoda-ku (3201 1020/ www.jukendo.or.jp).*
Karate Be warned: there are three governing bodies for karate, and they could be reproducing even as we speak. Try www.wpka-kobukan.org (which has a dojo in Nakano, Tokyo; www.karate-world.org (in Shinjuku); and the Japan Karatedo Federation (3503 6637, www.karatedo.co.jp) in Minato-ku.

Kendo *All-Japan Kendo Federation, Yasukuni Kudan Minami Bldg 2F, 2-3-14 Kudan-Minami, Chiyoda-ku (3234 6271/www.kendo.or.jp).* Wooden-sword fighting, which is held, to some extent, in similar esteem to sumo. Favoured by rightists, politicians, gangsters and the police.
Kobudo *Nippon Kobudo Association, 2-3 Kitanomaru Koen, Chiyoda-ku (3216 5114).*
Kyudo *All-Japan Kyudo Federation, Kishi Kinen Taiikukaikan, 1-1-1 Jinnan, Shibuya-ku (3481 2387/www.kyudo.jp).*
Naginata *All-Japan Naginata Federation (Tokyo Office), Kishi Kinen Taiikukaikan, 1-1-1 Jinnan, Shibuya-ku (3481 2411/http://naginata.jp).* Wooden spear fighting, popular with girls.
Shorinji Kempo *Shorinji Kempo Federation (Tokyo Office), 2-17-5 Otsuka, Toshima-ku (5961 3950/www.shorinjikempo.or.jp).* Fascinating karate-type martial art created after the war 'with the aim of educating people with strong senses of compassion, courage and justice'.
Sumo (amateur) *Japan Sumo Federation, 1-15-20 Hyakunincho, Shinjuku-ku (3368 2211/English www.sumo.or.jp/eng).*

Running

The big events for hobby runners, held close to the date of the Tokyo Marathon (February), are the ten-kilometre (6.2 mile) and 30-kilometre (18.6 mile) road races in Ome in north-west Tokyo prefecture (information on 0428 24 6311). Those looking for a little gentle jogging might

Arts & Entertainment

want to check out the five-kilometre (3.1 mile) route marked out at 100-metre intervals around the Imperial Palace. There is also a branch of the **Hash House Harriers** (http://tokyohash. org) for those runners in need of a serious drink at the end of their efforts.

Skiing & snowboarding

Just 90 minutes by train from Shinjuku lies a wide range of slopes that are snowy in winter. Between December and March, JR ticket windows offer all-in-one deals covering ski pass and day-return transport for the destination of your choice, with weekday prices starting from under ¥10,000. Also visit **Snodeck** (www. snodeck.net) an après-ski place run – and populated – by foreigners, which can fix up transport and/or accommodation and provide English-language snowboarding lessons. There are also year-round indoor slopes.

Sayama

2167 Kamiyamaguchi Tokorozawa-shi, Saitama (04 2922 1384/www.seibe-group.co.jp/rec/sayama). Seibu Kyujomae station (Seibu Ikebukuro line). **Open** 10am-9pm Mon-Fri; also 10pm-6am occasional weekends. **Admission** *Mon-Fri* ¥3,500; *Sat, Sun* ¥4,000. **Credit** JCB, MC, V.
A 320m (1049ft) slope for skiers and snowboarders, with clothing, boots, board and ski rental available.

Snova Mizonokuchi-R246

1358-1 Shimo-Sakunobe, Takatsu-ku, Kawasaki-shi, Kanagazawa (044 844 1181/www.snova246.com). Tsudayama station (Nanbu line). **Open** 10am-11pm Mon-Fri; 9am-11.30pm Sat, Sun. **Admission** *Mon-Fri* ¥2,300 90mins, ¥3,500 4hrs; *Sat, Sun* ¥2,800 90mins, ¥4,000 4hrs. ¥1,000 membership payable on 1st visit. **Credit** JCB, MC, V.
For skiers and snowboarders, although lessons are for snowboarders only. Equipment rental is available.

Sports centres

Each of Tokyo's 23 wards has sports facilities, with bargain prices for residents and commuters. Except for those in Shibuya-ku, sports centres are also open to non-residents and non-commuters, but at higher prices.

Chiyoda Kuritsu Sogo Taiikukan Pool

2-1-8 Uchi-Kanda, Chiyoda-ku (3256 8444/www. city.chiyoda.tokyo.jp/sisetu/sports.htm#01). Kanda station (Yamanote line), west exit or Otemachi station (Chiyoda, Hanzomon, Marunouchi, Mita, Tozai lines), exit A2. **Open** *Pool* noon-9pm Mon, Tue, Thur, Sat; 5.30-9pm Wed, Fri; 9am-5pm Sun. *Gym* 9am-noon, 1-5pm, 6-9pm Mon-Sat; 9am-noon, 1pm-5pm Sun. Closed every 3rd Mon. **Admission** *Pool* ¥600 2hrs. *Gym* ¥350. **No credit cards.** **Map** Marunouchi p93.

This centre consists of a swimming pool and gym within a weight's throw of Tokyo's business district.

Chuo-ku Sogo Sports Centre

Hamacho Koen Nai, 2-59-1 Nihonbashi-Hamacho, Chuo-ku (3666 1501). Hamacho station (Hibiya, Shinjuku lines), exit A2. **Open** *Pool* 9am-9.10pm daily. *Gym* 9am-8.40pm daily. Closed every 3rd Mon. **Admission** *Pool* ¥500. *Gym* ¥400. **No credit cards.**

Ikebukuro Sports Centre

Kenko Plaza Toshima Bldg 9F, 2-5-1 Kami-Ikebukuro, Toshima-ku (5974 7262). Ikebukuro station (Yamanote line), north exit; (Marunouchi, Yurakucho lines), exits C5, C6. **Open** 8.30am-9.30pm daily. Closed 2nd Mon of mth. **Admission** ¥600; ¥300 concessions. **No credit cards.** **Map** Ikebukuro p87.
A 25m pool on the 11th floor and a well-equipped gym on the tenth floor. Both offer great views.

Minato-ku Sports Centre

3-1-19 Shibaura, Minato-ku (3452 4151/www. anox.net/minato/sports/sp01.html). Tamachi station (Yamanote, Keihin Tohoku lines), Shibaura exit. **Open** 9am-9pm daily. Closed 1st & 3rd Mon of mth. **Admission** ¥700. **No credit cards.**
Pool, sauna, weights gym and aerobics classes.

Shinagawa Sogo Taiikukan Pool

5-6-11 Kita-Shinagawa, Shinagawa-ku (3449 4400/ www1.cts.ne.jp/~ssa/index.html). Osaki station (Yamanote line), east exit. **Open** hours varies. **Admission** *Pool* ¥350 2hrs. **No credit cards.**
No-frills pool, as well as tennis and badminton.

Shinjuku-ku Sports Centre

3-5-1 Okubo, Shinjuku-ku (3232 0171). Shin-Okubo or Takadanobaba stations (Yamanote line), Waseda exit; (Tozai line), exit 3. **Open** 9am-9pm daily. Closed every 4th Mon. **Admission** *Pool* ¥400 2hrs. *Gym* ¥400 3hrs. **No credit cards.**

Tokyo Metropolitan Gymnasium Pool

1-17-1 Sendagaya, Shibuya-ku (5474 2111/ www.tef.or.jp/tmg/index.html). Kokuritsu-Kyogijo station (Oedo line), exit A4 or Sendagaya station (Chuo line). **Open** 9am-11pm Mon-Fri; 9am-8pm Sat; 9am-9pm Sun. **Admission** *Pool* ¥600. *Gym* ¥450 2hrs. **No credit cards.**
Run by the Tokyo Metropolitan Government, this centre has both 25m and 50m swimming pools, a weights gym, arena and athletics field. The smaller pool is not open to the public every day and rarely before 1.30pm; phone to check before you go.

Tennis

Municipal courts exist for those who want a game, but applications are often by lottery and sometimes require a minimum of four players. Log on to www.tokyotennis.com for information in English. There's also the huge **Ariake Tennis Forest** (*see p274*).

Trips Out of Town

Hokoku-ji. *See p291*.

Yokohama

Parks, shopping and the nation's biggest Chinatown.

Minato Mirai.

With a population of 3.6 million, Yokohama is Japan's second-largest city and yet also one of its newest. Until 150 years ago it was a sleepy fishing village on Tokyo Bay, but that all changed after the US-Japanese Treaty of Amity of 1858. Designated one of the first ports open to foreign trade, the village expanded rapidly to become the country's biggest commercial port.

Thanks largely to its waterside location, Yokohama has a spacious feel – especially in the futuristic new landfill development area known as Minato Mirai (literally, 'Port Future'). It also has a cosmopolitan, outward-looking atmosphere and a more relaxed tempo than Tokyo. And although a modern city, it has some historic buildings, traditional gardens and museums to go with its bayside views. It's perfect for a day trip from the capital, being less than 30 minutes by train from Shibuya station, and relatively compact to boot.

ORIENTATION

There are five main areas of note in Yokohama, strung along the side of the bay. The commercial district around Yokohama station is worth skipping, unless you need to use the shopping malls, department stores or pick up an airport limousine bus at Yokohama

City Air Terminal (YCAT). **Minato Mirai** offers entertainment and views, and it also houses some major hotels. **Kannai** and **Bashamichi** form the city's administrative centre. The upmarket **Motomachi** shopping district lies next to **Chinatown**. And the historic **Yamate Bluff** area offers parks and views.

The city's two main stations, both easily reached from central Tokyo, are Yokohama and Shin-Yokohama (where the bullet trains stop; a 20-minute train ride from the city centre). The JR Keihin Tohoku line trains continue from Yokohama station to Sakuragi-cho station, which is convenient for Minato Mirai, while Tokyu Toyoko trains continue to Minato Mirai itself and on to Motomachi-Chukagai station (convenient for Chinatown) via the new Minato Mirai extension. Both Yokohama and Sakuragi-cho stations have tourist information booths.

You can get around the touristy part of the city by boat. **Sea Bass** (045 671 7719, www.yokohama-cruising.jp) has services linking Yokohama station east exit and Yamashita Pier via Minato Mirai every 20 to 30 minutes from 10am until 7.25pm daily. The full trip costs ¥600; ¥300 concessions.

For a more sedate view of the harbour, cruise ships depart from Yamashita Pier and tour the bay. Try **Marine Rouge**, **Marine Shuttle** (both with the same contact details as Sea Bass) or **Royal Wing** (045 662 6125, www.royalwing.co.jp). The 90-minute cruises start from ¥1,600. More pricey dinner cruises are also available.

YOKOHAMA IN A DAY

Minato Mirai, a massive complex built on landfill reclaimed from old dockland, makes a good place to begin exploring the city.

From Sakuragi-cho station, take the moving walkway outside the Minato Mirai exit and head towards the area's central feature, the aptly named **Landmark Tower** – the tallest building in Japan and home to the world's fastest lift. The lower floors house restaurants and designer boutiques, as does the adjoining **Queen's Square** shopping centre (045 682 1000, ww.qsy.co.jp/english/index.htm, shops 11am-8pm, restaurants 11am-10pm daily), a giant shopping and dining complex consisting of several separate but linked tower blocks. (If you arrive by the Tokyu Toyoko/Minato Mirai line, the station is right under the shopping centre.)

This whole area is built on the port's old dry docks, one of which has been preserved for use as a public amphitheatre, adjacent to Queen's Square. Behind the Landmark Tower is the **Yokohama Museum of Art**, with its collection of modern art and photography.

Retracing your steps past the *Nihon Maru*, a preserved pre-war sailing ship once known as the 'Swan of the Pacific', you reach the **Kisha-Michi Promenade** (almost directly in front of the tourist centre outside Sakuragi-cho station). Built along the route of an old freight railway track, this will take you towards the giant Ferris wheel in the **Yokohama Cosmoworld** amusement park.

Skirting around **Yokohama World Porters** (045 222 2000, www.yim.co.jp), another giant shopping centre, themed around the concept of international trade and housed in a former dockside warehouse, follow the signs for the **Red Brick Warehouses** (Aka Renga Soko; www.yokohama-akarenga.jp). Yokohama landmarks, these two 100-year-old buildings lay empty from 1989 until they reopened, fully refurbished, in 2002. The smaller Warehouse One is home to an arts centre and exhibition space, and several crafts shops. Warehouse Two houses three floors of shops and restaurants, and top-notch jazz club **Motion Blue** (045 226 1919, www.motionblue.co.jp). The paved plaza between the two warehouses leads down to the water's edge and is a pleasant place for an aimless stroll.

From a road bridge just behind Warehouse One, take a pedestrian walkway along an old elevated railway line to Yamashita Park. The red metal tower you can see in the distance is Marine Tower, once the highest structure in Yokohama and still the world's tallest inland lighthouse. Shortly before the walkway deposits you close to the park, you will see **Osanbashi Pier** on your left, jutting out into the sea. This is the terminal for international cruise ships and was extensively remodelled in 2002. The passenger terminal at the end of the pier has a platform with panoramic views of the harbour.

Yamashita Koen itself is a pleasant area of seaside greenery with 1930s cruise ship the *Hikawa Maru* moored alongside. The ship is no longer open to the public, but the park is popular with courting couples. Buildings overlooking the park include the **Silk Museum** (045 641 0841, www.silkmuseum.or.jp, open 9am-4.30pm Tue-Sun, ¥500), which examines the history of silk production and clothing. There's also the Kenmin Hall concert hall and the graceful old Hotel New Grand, whose main building maintains one room exactly as it was when used by General Douglas MacArthur, the commander of the US occupation forces after World War II. The nearby **Yokohama Archives of History** (045 201 2100, www.kaikou.city.yokohama.jp, open 9.30am-5pm Tue-Sun, ¥200) has an exhibition devoted to the history of the city.

Red Brick Warehouses.

Trips Out of Town

Eat, drink and shop in Japan's largest **Chinatown**.

From the far end of the park, the walkway continues past the **Yokohama Doll Museum** in the direction of **Harbour View Park**, which lies at the top of a hill called Furansu (France) Yama. It's quite a steep climb, but worth it for the view of Yokohama Bay and its bridge. This park represents the boundary of one of the most historic areas of Yokohama.

Leave the park by the gates near British House, cross the road at the traffic lights to the right and continue straight on until you arrive at the **Foreign Cemetery**, which was established in 1854 to bury sailors who had accompanied Commodore Perry on his mission to open up Japan to foreign trade. It's the final resting place of 4,500 people from 40 countries who died in the city. Regrettably, the historic graves are off-limits, but you can stroll around the park area at the top and look at the small museum, which displays reproductions of documents, prints and photos.

Looking down the road from the cemetery, you will notice that this area of Yokohama bears a strong resemblance to an English village, complete with its own picture-postcard church. Well above the damp lowlands, this was considered a desirable address ever since the first British settlers started putting down their roots. An intriguing overview of the history of the area is provided at the **Yamate Museum**, located just before the church, while the young at heart might prefer the 3,000 tin toys from the 1890s to the 1960s on show at the lovely **Tin Toy Museum** (045 621 8710, www.toys club.co.jp/muse/tintoy.html, 9.30am-6pm Mon-Fri; 9.30am-7pm Sat, Sun, ¥200) to the east of the church.

Dotted around the Bluff area are other houses built by early foreign settlers in Japan, although in many cases the houses have been moved here from elsewhere. A map is available from the museum, and most of the houses are open to visitors. Facing the museum is **Motomachi Koen**, at the top of which stands the Ehrismann Residence, built in 1925 by Antonin Raymond, a Czech assistant of American architect Frank Lloyd Wright. It was moved here in 1990 when its original site was turned into condominiums.

You can skirt the park and continue south-west towards the Yamate hills and the **Diplomat's House**, one of the most fetching houses in the area. Alternatively, head downhill from the park, and the road will eventually lead you to the pedestrianised **Motomachi** shopping street (www.motomachi.or.jp), the most upmarket stretch of shops and restaurants in Yokohama. Walk down towards the canal and make for the bridge on your left.

On the other side of the bridge stands the Suzaku-mon, one of the ceremonial gates to Yokohama's **Chinatown** (Chukagai in Japanese). The biggest such community in Japan, it is home to hundreds of restaurants and Chinese shops, some selling spectacular souvenirs. Needless to say, you can eat well here after wandering the colourful streets. Leaving Chinatown by the Choyo-mon gate, near the Holiday Inn, turn right to find the entrance to Motomachi-Chukagai station. From here you can take a train directly back to Shibuya, or to Yokohama if you want to change to the JR line. Alternatively, you can walk down to Yamashita Park and take the Sea Bass ferry across the harbour to Yokohama station (or Sakuragi-cho).

Trips Out of Town

If you've got more time to explore, visit **Nissan Stadium**, venue for the 2002 World Cup final, which is a short walk from Shin-Yokohama station; or, further north, the **Kirin Yokohama Beer Village** near Namamugi station (1-17-1 Namamugi, Tsurumi-ku, 045 503 8250, www.kirin.co.jp/ about/brewery/factory/ yoko, open June-Sept 10am-5pm daily, Oct-May 10am-4.30pm Tue-Sun). There are free tours of the brewery every half hour. Near Negishi station to the south – about 40 minutes by bus from Yokohama station – are the beautiful **Sankeien** garden and the **Negishi Memorial Racetrack** park.

Diplomat's House

16 Yamate-cho, Naka-ku (045 662 8819). Ishikawa-cho station (Negishi line), Motomachi (south) exit. Open July, Aug 9.30am-6pm daily. Sept-June 9.30am-5pm daily. Closed 4th Wed of mth. **Admission** *free.*
Part of the Italian Garden, a collection of period dwellings, this 1910 house was once the family home of Japanese diplomat Uchida Sadatsuchi.

Harbour View Park (Minato-no-Mieru Oka Koen)

114 Yamate-cho, Naka-ku (045 622 8244/ British House 045 623 7812/Osaragi Jiro Memorial Museum 045 622 5002). Motomachi-Chukagai station (Minato Mirai line). Open Park 24hrs daily. British House 9.30am-5pm daily. Closed 4th Wed of mth. Osaragi Jiro Memorial Museum Oct-Mar 10am-4.30pm daily; Apr-Sept 10am-5.30pm daily. Closed 4th Mon of mth. **Admission** *Park & British House free. Osaragi Jiro Memorial Museum ¥200; ¥100 concessions.* **No credit cards.**
One of the city's first attempts at redevelopment, Harbour View Park opened in 1962. The building that housed the first British legation to Japan – now called British House Yokohama – still stands near the rose garden beside one of the park gates. The park also contains a museum dedicated to local novelist Osaragi Jiro (1897-1973).

Landmark Tower

2-2-1-1 Minato Mirai, Nishi-ku (Sky Garden 045 222 5035/www.landmark.ne.jp). Minato Mirai station (Minato Mirai line), exit 5. Open Sky Garden Mid July-Aug 10am-10pm daily. Sept-mid July 10am-9pm Mon-Fri, Sun; 10am-10pm Sat. **Admission** *Sky Garden ¥1,00; ¥200-¥800 concessions.* **No credit cards.**
Take the world's fastest lift (45km/h, 28m/h) to the top of Japan's tallest building (296m/972ft) to feast on the spectacular views. On a clear day, you can easily make out Mt Fuji to the west, Tokyo to the north and the Boso Peninsula to the east. The rest of the building is devoted to offices and a hotel.

Negishi Memorial Racetrack & Equine Museum

1-3 Negishi-dai, Naka-ku (045 662 7581/www. bajibunka.jrao.ne.jp). Negishi station (Negishi line) or Sakuragi-cho station (Negishi line) then bus 21 to Takinoue. Open Park 9am-5pm daily. Museum
10am-4.30pm Tue-Sun. **Admission** *Park free. Museum ¥100; ¥30 concessions.* **No credit cards.**
A wonderful park built on the site of Japan's first Western-style racetrack – having served as a US naval base in the interim. (There is still some naval accommodation beside the park.) A derelict grandstand survives from its 19th-century glory days, and a museum examines horsey history and man's relationship with the creatures.

Nissan Stadium: World Cup Stadium Tours

3300 Kozukue-cho, Kohoku-ku (045 477 5000/www. nissan-stadium.jp). Shin-Yokohama station (Tokaido Shinkansen, Yokohama lines), north exit then 15mins walk. **Tours** *(except when stadium is in use) 10.30am, noon, 1.30pm, 3pm daily.* **Admission** *¥500; ¥250 concessions.* **No credit cards.**
The venue that hosted the Germany v Brazil final in 2002 has started to offer tours, taking in the dressing rooms, practice area and pitch. See the Brazilians' tactic-covered whiteboard, take a shot at a silhouette of famously fumbling German goalie Oliver Kahn and gaze in awe at the rubbish the teams left behind. There's also a chance to run out on to the pitch (well, as far as the running track) with the World Cup anthem blazing. The stadium hosts international matches and home games for the Yokohama Marinos.

Sankeien

58-1 Honmoku-Sannotani, Naka-ku (045 621 0635/ www.sankeien.or.jp). Yokohama station, east exit then bus 8 or 125 from bus stop 2 to Honmoku Sankeien-mae. **Open** *Outer Garden 9am-5pm daily. Inner Garden 9am-4.30pm daily.* **Admission** *¥500; ¥200 concessions.* **No credit cards.**
A beautiful, traditional Japanese garden that was laid out by a silk merchant in 1906. When religious relics were being torn down as religion fell from official favour in the Meiji era, the local merchant decided to save the treasures from the bulldozer, importing them from across Japan. The grounds now house a three-storey pagoda from Kyoto, and a feudal lord's residence among many other priceless structures. The park is open in the evening during cherry-blossom season (April) and for Moon Viewing (September). **Photo** *p283.*

Yamashita Koen

Yamashita-cho, Naka-ku (Hikawa Maru 045 641 4362/www.hmk.co.jp). Motomachi-Chukagai station (Minato Mirai line), exit 5. **Open** *24hrs daily.* **Admission** *free.*
Verdant Yamashita Park is a popular dating spot. The statue in the middle depicts the *Little Girl in Red Shoes*, based on a Japanese song about the real-life story of Iwasaki Kimi. Born in 1902, she was adopted by American missionaries and thought destined for a life of luxury in the US. But, in fact, Kimi never left Japan: abandoned by her foster parents, she died alone, aged nine, of tuberculosis. Moored beside the park is the 1930s ocean liner *Hikawa Maru*, whose most famous passenger was Charlie Chaplin.

Yamate Museum

247 Yamate-cho, Naka-ku (045 622 1188).
Motomachi-Chukagai station (Minato Mirai line),
exit 5. **Open** 11am-4pm Tue-Sun. **Admission** ¥200;
¥150 concessions. **No credit cards**.
Housed in the last Western-style wooden building
still in its original setting, this museum provides a
fascinating insight into the early days of
Yokohama's development, and the thriving foreign
community that grew here.

Yokohama Cosmoworld

2-8-1 Shinkou, Naka-ku (045 641 6591/www.senyo.
co.jp/cosmo). Minato Mirai station (Minato Mirai
line), exit 5. **Open** *mid Mar-Nov* 11am-9pm Mon-Fri;
11am-10pm Sat, Sun. *mid Nov-mid Mar* 11am-8pm
Mon-Fri; 11am-9pm Sat, Sun. **Admission** free.
The Ferris wheel at the centre of this small amusement park, with its giant digital clock, is a true
Yokohama landmark. At 112.5m (369ft) high and
with room for 480 passengers, it's one of the largest
in the world. The park has 27 rides in all, including
a water rollercoaster.

Yokohama Doll Museum

18 Yamashita-cho, Naka-ku (045 671 9361/
www.welcome.city.yokohama.jp/eng/doll).
Motomachi-Chukagai station (Minato Mirai line),
exit 5. **Open** 10am-6.30pm daily. Closed 3rd Mon
of mth. **Admission** ¥500; ¥150 concessions.
No credit cards.
Home to nearly 10,000 dolls from 140 countries, this
museum appeals to children and serious collectors
alike. It also holds occasional puppet shows.

Yokohama Museum of Art

3-4-1 Minato Mirai, Nishi-ku (045 221 0300/www.
yma.city.yokohama.jp). Minato Mirai station (Minato
Mirai line), exit 5. **Open** 10am-6pm Mon-Wed, Sat,
Sun; 10am-7.30pm Fri. **Admission** ¥500; ¥100-¥300
concessions; additional fee for special exhibitions.
No credit cards.
One of the region's major fine art museums, this
Tange Kenzo-designed building is set on a prime,
tree-lined plaza in Minato Mirai. Abundant light
pours in through a huge skylight above the courtyard
in the centre of the entrance hall. To the right of the
court, temporary exhibitions range from Leonardo da
Vinci to contemporary artist Nara Yoshitomo. To the
left there are regularly changing exhibitions drawn
from the permanent collection of European, American
and Japanese modern art and photography.

Where to eat & drink

Chinatown

Manchinro Honten

153 Yamashita-cho, Naka-ku (045 681 4004/www.
manchinro.co.jp). Ishikawa-cho station (Negishi line),
Chinatown (north) exit or Motomachi-Chukagai
station (Minato Mirai line), exit 2. **Open** 11am-10pm
daily. **Average** ¥2,500 lunch; ¥3,500 dinner. **Credit**
AmEx, DC, JCB, MC, V.

With a history dating back to 1892, this Cantonese
restaurant is one of the oldest in Chinatown. It
burned down in a fire but reopened in 2002 as the
grandest, most lavish restaurant in the area.

Peking Hanten (Beijing Fandian)

79-5 Yamashita-cho, Naka-ku (045 681 3535).
Motomachi-Chukagai station (Minato Mirai line),
exit 2. **Open** 11.30am-2am daily. **Average** ¥1,500
lunch; dinner set meals from ¥4,000. **Credit** AmEx,
DC, JCB, MC, V.
This charming restaurant by Choyo-mon –
Chinatown's main gate – claims to be the first in
Japan to have served Peking duck.

Tung Fat (Dohatsu Honkan)

148 Yamashita-cho, Naka-ku (045 681 7273/www.
douhatsu.co.jp). Ishikawa-cho station (Negishi line),
Chinatown (north) exit. **Open** 11.30am-9.30pm Mon,
Wed-Sun. Closed 1st, 3rd Tue of mth. **Average**
¥5,000. **Credit** DC, MC, V.
This place is popular for its Hong Kong-style
seafood dishes. So popular, in fact, that lunchtime is
a spectacle, with customers jostling for position
while the strict *mama-san* tries to keep everyone in
check. While waiting, look at the window display of
mouth-watering meats, whole chickens and ducks,
sausages and other less recognisable animal parts.

Yokohama Curry Museum

1-2-3 Isezaki-cho, Naka-ku (045 250 0833/www.curry
museum.com). Kannai station (Negishi line), north exit.
Open 11am-9.40pm daily. **Admission** free.
This small museum to the west of Chinatown traces
the history of curry in Japan since its arrival in the
19th century. The main reason to visit is the seven
curry restaurants.

Minato Mirai

Kihachi Italian

Queen's East 2F, Minato Mirai 2-3-2, Nishi-ku (045
222 2861/www.kihachi.co.jp). Minato Mirai station
(Minato Mirai line), Queen's Square exit. **Open**
Lunch 11.30am-4pm, *tea* 2.30-5.30pm, *dinner* 6-11pm
Mon-Sat ; *lunch* 11.30am-4pm, *tea* 2.30-5.30pm, *dinner*
6-10pm Sun. **Average** lunch ¥2,625; dinner ¥4,200.
Credit AmEx, DC, JCB, MC, V.
This casual modern restaurant looking out towards
the Museum of Art is one of the best places to eat in
the area. The Italian food, popular with a mostly
young, female clientele, is produced with all the
aplomb you would expect from the ever-professional
Kihachi group.

Motomachi

Aussie

1-12 Ishikawa-cho, Naka-ku (045 681 3671/www.
juno.dti.ne.jp/~aussie). Ishikawa-cho station (Negishi
line), Motomachi (south) exit. **Open** 5pm-1am Mon,
Wed-Fri; 3pm-1am Sat; 3-11pm Sun. **Average**
¥3,500. **Credit** AmEx, JCB, MC, V.

the south. Highly recommended is the miso ramen at Sumire – the shop with the longest queue.

Yokohama station

The Green Sheep
2-10-13 Minami-Saiwai, Nishi-ku (045 321 0950/ www.foodcom.jp). Yokohama station, west exit. **Open** 11am-2am Mon-Thur; 11am-4am Fri, Sat; 11am-midnight Sun. **Credit** AmEx, DC, JCB, MC, V.
Yokohama's newest Irish pub serves a predictable mix of beers and big-screen football. The food menu is better than most – the shepherd's pie and lamb burger come recommended – and staff are friendly.

Kinrinmon
Sky Bldg 29F, 2-19-12 Takashima, Nishi-ku (045 441 4888). Yokohama station, east exit (above YCAT). **Open** 11am-3pm, 5-9.30pm daily. **Average** ¥2,000 lunch; ¥7,000 dinner. **Credit** AmEx, DC, JCB, MC, V.
Besides offering good seafood dishes, this sophisticated Cantonese-style restaurant provides fantastic views over the city to the mountains in the west (often including Mt Fuji). The plentiful dim sum lunch menu (¥2,635) is always popular.

Getting there

By train
The opening of the Minato Mirai subway extension has made Yokohama even easier to get to from Tokyo. A super-express on the Tokyu Toyoko line from Shibuya station takes 27mins to reach Yokohama station (¥260 single) or 34mins to its terminus at Motomachi-Chukagai (¥460).
Those with JR rail passes may prefer to take the JR Keihin Tohoku line to Sakuragi-cho from Tokyo, Shinbashi or Shinagawa stations; or take the Shonan Shinjuku line from Shinjuku, Shibuya or Ebisu, then change at Yokohama on to the Negishi line for local stops. Bullet trains on the JR Tokaido Shinkansen line take about 15mins from Tokyo station to Shin-Yokohama station.

Tourist information

The **Yokohama Convention & Visitors Bureau** (YCVB) has four information booths, plus an excellent English-language website – www.welcome.city.yokohama.jp/eng/tourism – with downloadable maps and a hotel guide.

YCVB Sakuragi-cho station *1-1-62 Sakuragi-cho, Naka-ku (045 211 0111). Sakuragi-cho station (Negishi line).* **Open** 9am-7pm daily.
YCVB Sangyo Boeki Centre *2 Yamashita-cho, Naka-ku (045 641 4759). Kannai station (Negishi line).* **Open** 8.45am-5.15pm Mon-Fri.
YCVB Shin-Yokohama station *2937 Shinohara-cho, Kohoku-ku (045 473 2895). Shin-Yokohama station, Shinkansen exit.* **Open** 9am-7pm daily.
YCVB Yokohama station *2-16-1 Takashima, Nishi-ku (045 441 7300). Yokohama station, on the east–west walkway.* **Open** 9am-7pm daily.

Park life at **Sankeien**. *See p281.*

As the name suggests, this restaurant serves all things Australian, the most popular dishes being barbecued kangaroo and crocodile.

Mutekiro
2-96 Motomachi, Naka-ku (045 681 2926/www. mutekiro.com). Motomachi-Chukagai station (Minato Mirai line), exit 5. **Open** noon-3pm, 5-10pm daily. **Average** ¥4,000 lunch; ¥8,000 dinner. **Credit** AmEx, DC, JCB, MC, V.
Motomachi's most celebrated and upmarket French restaurant has the motto 'Mode française, coeur japonais'. This means that dishes often contain typical Japanese ingredients, especially seafood, but are prepared in a French way. Booking essential.

Shin-Yokohama

Shin-Yokohama Ramen Museum
2-14-21 Shin-Yokohama, Kohoku-ku (045 471 0503/ www.raumen.co.jp). Shin-Yokohama station (Tokaido Shinkansen, Yokohama lines),north exit. **Open** 11am-11pm Mon-Fri; 10.30am-11pm Sat, Sun. **Admission** ¥300; ¥100 concessions. **No credit cards.**
A couple of floors are devoted to the history of the variety of noodle that has become a national obsession in Japan, but the main attraction is the eight ramen shops in the basement. Each shop sells a different style of ramen, ranging from Sapporo ramen (miso-based soup) from the north, to Hakata ramen (pork- and chicken-based soup) from

Trips Out of Town

Hakone

Hot springs with a view of Fuji.

Hakone is where Tokyo comes to relax and get a taste of the countryside. Around one and a half hours from Shinjuku station by the Odakyu line train, this mountainous area offers convenient transportation, beautiful scenery, a host of attractions and, best of all, a natural hot-spring bath, or *onsen*, around virtually every bend of the roads that twist through the mountains.

The best way to see Hakone is to buy the **Hakone Free Pass** (*see p287*), available at all Odakyu railway stations. The pass covers all public transport in Hakone – and what public transport it is. As well as a picturesque railway and a bus service, the Hakone area also has a funicular railway, a cable car and a boat that crosses Lake Ashinoko at its centre. All of these means of transport are interlinked, making it possible to 'do' the whole of the Hakone area in a day from Tokyo.

THE HAKONE CIRCUIT

Those in a hurry can make the most of their time by trying the Hakone Circuit. Get off the train at either Odawara or Hakone-Yumoto. From there, transfer to the Tozan mountain railway for the 50-minute ride to its terminus at Gora. At Gora, transfer on to the funicular railway up to the end of the line at Sounzan. Here, transfer to the cable car, which takes you down to the banks of Lake Ashinoko at Togendai station. To get across the lake, board one of the pleasure boats and stay on until Hakone-Machi or Moto-Hakone, from where you can take a bus back to where you started, at Hakone-Yumoto or Odawara. The round-trip should take about three hours, although in the busy summer months it may take longer.

THE FULL HAKONE

While the circuit will give you your fill of glorious scenery, you'll be missing out on a lot of what Hakone has to offer. If you decide to start your journey at Odawara, it's worth making a detour out of the east exit of the station to take the ten-minute walk to **Odawara Castle**, perched on a hill overlooking the town. First built in 1416, and rebuilt in 1960, this picturesque castle was for centuries an important strategic stronghold.

Back at the station, get on the old-fashioned Tozan railway for the next major stop (or the starting point for some), Hakone-Yumoto station.

'Yumoto' means 'source of hot water', which should give you some clue as to what this small town is about. First mentioned in eighth-century poetry as a place to bathe, Hakone became a great favourite in the time of the Tokugawa shogunate (1600-1868), with bathers travelling two or three days on foot from Tokyo (then Edo) along the Tokaido Way, portions of which can still be seen over the other side of the river from the modern railway station. The station houses a small tourist office, but the main office is up the hill on the left. Here, you'll find English-speaking assistants, who'll be happy to hand out maps and pamphlets. Restaurants and souvenir shops also line the same street; this is the place to buy the local speciality: small boxes and other objects made using *yosegi-zaiku*, a mosaic-style marquetry technique.

For dedicated modern bathers, the day may end in Hakone-Yumoto. Although the modern town is unremarkable, it is dotted with hot-spring baths: just about every building of any size is a hotel, or *ryokan*, and many allow non-guests to use their facilities. One of the locals' favourites is situated on the steep hillside on the other side of the tracks from the station. The **Kappa Tengoku** has segregated open-air baths surrounded by dense woodland, and a steady army of bathers can be seen trooping up the steps to the baths well into the night. Bring your own towel and wash cloth if you want to save money.

Up the hill from the *onsen* is the delightful **Hakone Toy Museum**, crammed with old-fashioned Japanese and foreign tin toys from the 1890s to the 1960s. The souvenir shop sells wind-up robots and charmingly retro goods imported from China and elsewhere.

Back on the train from Hakone-Yumoto, take some time to enjoy the ride itself. It's claimed that this is the world's steepest train line, and so sharp are the bends that at three points the train enters a switchback, going forward and then reversing out of a siding in order to continue its ascent. As you climb the mountain you will see water pouring out of the hillside and cascading under the tracks, some of it still hot.

The next station of any note is Miyanoshita. This is home to one of the highest concentrations of *onsen* baths in the area and is where the first foreigners in Japan came to bathe in the 19th

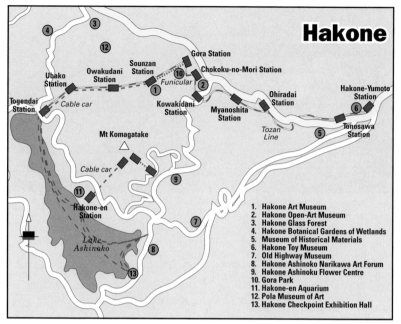

Hakone

Owakudani Station · **Sounzan Station** · **Gora Station** · **Chokoku-no-Mori Station**

Ubako Station · **Togendai Station** · **Kowakidani Station** · **Myanoshita Station** · **Ohiradai Station** · **Hakone-Yumoto Station** · **Tonosawa Station**

Funicular · **Mt Komagatake** · **Cable car** · **Hakone-en Station** · **Lake Ashinoko** · **Tozan Line**

1. Hakone Art Museum
2. Hakone Open-Art Museum
3. Hakone Glass Forest
4. Hakone Botanical Gardens of Wetlands
5. Museum of Historical Materials
6. Hakone Toy Museum
7. Old Highway Museum
8. Hakone Ashinoko Narikawa Art Forum
9. Hakone Ashinoku Flower Centre
10. Gora Park
11. Hakone-en Aquarium
12. Pola Museum of Art
13. Hakone Checkpoint Exhibition Hall

century. To cater for them, the **Fujiya Hotel** was built in 1878. Miraculously, it's still standing today, a wooden mix of Japanese and Western styles. Non-residents are free to pop in for a coffee, a bite to eat or something stronger in the bar.

Two stops up the line, at Chokokuno-Mori station, is one of the great glories of Hakone. The **Hakone Open-Air Museum** must be one of the most spectacular in the world. Set on a mountainside overlooking a series of valleys leading to the sea, the museum is dedicated to modern sculpture from all over the globe. Exposed to the elements is a world-class collection of works by Moore, Rodin, Antony Gormley, Alexander Calder, Takamichi Ito and Niki de St Phalle. It's a great place for kids. There's also a display of ceramics by Picasso in a separate pavilion.

From here, it's a ten-minute walk to the next station, Gora, the terminus of the Tozan railway and the start of the funicular that climbs the mountainside. If you're changing from the train, there will be a carriage waiting for you. The first stop on the funicular, Koen Shita, provides a pleasant diversion in the shape of **Gora Park**, a landscaped hillside garden that makes great use of the natural hot water in its hothouses. A walk uphill through the park will bring you to the next stop on the funicular.

This is a good point to visit the **Pola Museum of Art**, deep in the surrounding forest. The museum houses 9,500 works by the likes of Renoir, Picasso and Monet. To avoid damaging the beauty of the countryside, the building is constructed three floors underground, and is only eight metres (27 feet) tall on the surface. To reach the museum, take a bus from Gora station bound for Shisseikaen.

The funicular terminates at Sounzan station, and it's here that many people's favourite part of the Hakone experience begins: the cable car, or Hakone Ropeway, as it's known. Riding over the peaks and valleys of Hakone, this 4.3-kilometre (2.7-mile) route is Japan's longest cable-car route. Around halfway along its length is **Owakudani** ('big boiling valley'), one of the most breathtaking sights in Hakone. The car passes over, at a height of around 60 metres (200 feet), a smoking hillside streaked with traces of sulphur from the volcanic activity below. The air simply reeks of rotten eggs.

On top of a mountain peak sits Owakudani station, the centre of a large tourist complex of restaurants and gift shops. On a clear day – a rarity, since it's often too cloudy – you can see the peak of Mt Fuji looming over the mountain range in the distance. You can also walk to the source of some of the steam that rises out of the mountain, the ancient crater of

Trips Out of Town

The 'big boiling valley' of **Owakudani**, with the peak of Mt Fuji in the distance. *See p285.*

Mt Kamiyama, the pathway passing over hot streams of bubbling water. The air is thick with hydrogen sulphide, and signs warn of the dangers of standing in one place for too long for fear of being overcome by fumes. If you feel like a snack, try a hard-boiled egg at the top of the path. Sold by the half-dozen for ¥500, the eggs have been cooked in the hot-spring water, the sulphur turning their shells black.

From Owakudani, the Hakone Ropeway passes over several more valleys before descending to terminate at Togendai, on the banks of Lake Ashinoko. The lake is believed to be in the crater of a volcano that blew its top 400,000 years ago. The volcanic activity that goes on beneath the waters to this day ensures that it never freezes over. From here, a pair of incredibly tacky pleasure boats, one done out as a Mississippi steamer, the other as a Spanish galleon, cross the lake to Hakone-Machi and Moto-Hakone. Only 500 metres or so (1640 feet) separate the two destinations, but for ease of walking, get off at Hakone-Machi and turn left (with the lake behind you) to head for Moto-Hakone. On the way is the site of the **Old Hakone Checkpoint**, where travellers to and from Edo would be stopped and often interrogated by border guards. Ruins of the original checkpoint still stand, while other buildings have been reconstructed and opened to the public as a museum. Set back a little from the modern road is what's left of a cedar avenue, planted along the Tokaido Way in the early 17th century. Paved sections of the Tokaido Way are still extant, and keen walkers can take a short hike from here along one such section, away from the lake towards Hatajuku.

On a promontory into the lake between the two boat stops is the **Hakone Detached Palace Garden**. The garden of an 1887 villa

that once belonged to the imperial family but was destroyed in an earthquake, it has been open to the public since 1946. Further along, past Moto-Hakone and down the side of the lake, is the **Hakone Shrine**, its history going back 1,200 years. The site is clearly marked by a red *torii* (gate) that stands in the lake.

Once you've walked your fill of the area – and there's lots more to see in the Hakone vicinity – head back to Moto-Hakone and take a bus back to Odawara. All buses to Odawara stop in Hakone-Yumoto too.

Gora Park

1300 Gora, Hakone-Machi, Shimogun (0460 22825/ www.hakone-tozan.co.jp/gorapark). **Open** 9am-5pm daily. **Admission** ¥500; free concessions. **No credit cards**.

Hakone Detached Palace Garden

171 Moto-Hakone, Hakone-Machi, Ashigara-Shimogun (0460 37484). **Open** *July, Aug* 9am-5pm daily. *Sept-June* 9am-5pm Mon, Wed-Sun. **Admission** free.

Hakone Open-Air Museum

1121 Ninotaira, Hakone-Machi, Ashigara-Shimogun (0460 21161/www.hakone-oam.or.jp). **Open** *Mar-Nov* 9am-5pm daily. *Dec-Feb* 9am-4pm daily. **Admission** ¥1,600; ¥800-¥1,100 concessions. **No credit cards**.

Hakone Toy Museum

740 Yumoto, Hakone-Machi, Ashigara-Shimogun (0460 56121). **Open** 9am-5pm daily. **Admission** ¥800; ¥400 concessions. **Credit** AmEx, DC, JCB, MC, V.

Kappa Tengoku

777 Yumoto, Hakone-Machi, Ashigara-Shimogun (0460 56121). **Open** 10am-10pm daily. **Admission** ¥750. *Towel* ¥900 (to buy), ¥150 (to rent). **No credit cards**.

Odawara Castle

6-1 Jonai, Odawara-shi (0465 231373). **Open** 9am-4pm Tue-Sun. **Admission** *Park* free. *Castle* ¥400; ¥150 concessions. **No credit cards.**

Old Hakone Checkpoint

1 Hakone, Hakone-Machi, Ashigara-Shimogun (0460 36635). **Open** 9am-4pm daily. **Admission** ¥300; ¥150 concessions. **No credit cards.**

Pola Museum of Art

1285 Kozukayama, Sengokuhara, Hakone-Machi, Ashigara-Shimogun (0460 42111/www.pola museum.or.jp). **Open** 9am-5pm daily. **Admission** ¥1,800; ¥700-¥1,300 concessions. **Credit** AmEx, DC, JCB, MC, V.

Where to eat & drink

Since most of the area's activity centres around the hotels, it's hardly surprising that there are remarkably few independent restaurants worth seeking out – though the village of Sengokuhara has more options than most. For the truly hungry, there are snack bars serving curry, noodles and the like at Owakudani and Togendai stations, and on the lake at Hakone-Machi. The **Bella Foresta** restaurant in the Open-Air Museum serves a decent buffet lunch for ¥1,680, while all the large hotels have at least four restaurants that are open to non-guests. At the **Pola Museum** there's a café serving snacks and drinks (10am-4.30pm daily) and an upmarket French-style restaurant (11am-4pm daily).

Where to stay

There are hundreds of places to stay in Hakone, ranging from cheap *ryokan* to top-class hotels. All have their own hot springs. Many have separate rates for weekdays and weekends, the former being cheaper. Expect top prices at peak periods such as New Year and Golden Week in May.

If you intend to use Hakone-Yumoto as a base, cheap options include the **Kappa Tengoku** (*see p286*): a double room here costs from around ¥7,000 per night on weekdays, although its proximity to the railway tracks might mean an earlier awakening than you'd bargained for.

Up in the mountains, the **Fujiya Hotel** (359 Miyanoshita, 0460 22211, www.fujiyahotel.co.jp) is peerless, with a range of rooms in five historic buildings; doubles start at ¥18,780 on weekdays, rising to ¥30,330 during peak season. In Sengokuhara, the small *ryokan* **Fuji-Hakone Guest House** (912 Segokuhara, 0460 46577, www.fujihakone.com, twin room ¥10,500-¥12,600) is a good budget choice. The friendly proprietor, Takahashi Masami, speaks English

and is happy to offer sightseeing advice. You can get to the inn by bus direct from Odawara or Hakone-Yumoto stations; alight at the Senkyoro-mae bus stop. Sister outfit **Moto-Hakone Guest House** (0460 37880, same website, twin ¥10,000) is on the other side of Lake Ashinoko.

Overlooking the lake is the **Palace Hotel** (1245 Sengokuhara, Hakone-Machi, 0460 48501, www.hakone.palacehotel.co.jp), where doubles start at ¥18,900 during the low season. This luxury hotel often advertises special-stay plans in the Tokyo press, which can bring the price down further.

Getting there

By train

There are two types of **Hakone Free Pass**, available at all Odakyu stations and many travel agents. The weekday pass gives you unlimited journeys for two days and costs ¥4,700 from Shinjuku station. The weekend pass gives three days' unlimited transport and costs ¥5,500 from Shinjuku station. The ticket price also covers the basic fare on an Odakyu train from Shinjuku to Hakone. If you want to travel in comfort on the super-express Romance car, you will need to pay a supplement of ¥870.

If you hold a JR Pass, the most cost-effective way of reaching the area is to take a JR Tokaido *shinkansen* to Odawara station, then buy your Hakone Free Pass there. As this pass does not include transport to Tokyo, it costs ¥3,410 (weekdays) or ¥4,130 (weekends). The Free Pass also gives discounts at many local attractions. Look out for the Hakone Free Pass sticker.

Tourist information

Hakone-Yumoto Tourist Information

Kankou Bussankan, 698 Yumoto, Hakone-Machi, Ashigara-Shimogun (0460 58911). **Open** 9am-5pm daily.

Odakyu Sightseeing Service Centre

Ground-floor concourse near west exit, Odakyu Shinjuku station (5321 7887/www.odakyu-group.co.jp/english/center.html). **Open** 8am-6pm daily. The Odakyu train line's information counter inside the station is aimed at foreign visitors (staff speak English). You can buy the Hakone Free Pass here and make hotel reservations.

Odawara Tourist Information

1-1-9 Sakaemachi, Odawara-shi (0465 222339). Odawara station, east exit. **Open** 9am-5pm daily.

Kamakura

The scenic one-time capital.

For 150 years, from the 12th to the 14th centuries, Kamakura was Japan's military and administrative capital, and the factors that made it a strategic location for the first military government – hills on three sides, Sagami Bay on the other – have also protected it from the encroaching sprawl of Yokohama. It's less than an hour by train from central Tokyo, but the atmosphere is a world away.

The Minamoto family picked Kamakura for its new base after vanquishing the Taira clan in 1185 and setting up Japan's first military government – marking the start of 700 years of domination by shoguns. The new military rulers encouraged Zen Buddhism, which appealed due to its strict self-discipline, and temples of various sects were established in the area. While traces of the government and military rule faded quickly after the Minamoto clan and their regents were defeated in 1333, the religious influence endures to this day.

There are still more than 70 active temples and shrines dotted around Kamakura, from the large and eminent to the small and secluded. They represent different Buddhist sects, among them Rinzai, Pure Land and Nichiren. Over the years the buildings and grounds of most temples have been lost to fires and earthquakes, the slow encroachment of housing or to make way for the railway line. Few buildings remain intact from the Kamakura period, but many temples and shrines appear unspoilt, giving visitors a rare glimpse of old Japan.

Kamakura is now a major tourist destination, and the temples are well looked after. Most temples require a small entry fee (¥100-¥300) – a contribution towards upkeep rather than an admission charge. The main attractions are scattered around, but most are within walking distance of Kamakura or Kita-Kamakura stations and can be covered in a day trip from Tokyo. Directions and distances to temples in each vicinity are marked in English at intervals around town. You can pick up a free map (partly in English) from the tourist information window at Kamakura station (just to the right of the station gates at the east exit). Most temples are open daily, from 9am until 4pm, but museums and treasure houses (and some shops) are usually closed on Mondays.

The town and the main sites are surprisingly busy at weekends and holidays. Festival days are especially crowded; the main ones are the Grand Festival (14-16 Sept) and the Kamakura Festival (2nd Sun to 3rd Sun in April). Both take place at Tsurugaoka Hachiman-gu – the town's main shrine and focal point – which is also immensely popular on the first few days of the New Year, when hordes of worshippers converge to make their auspicious, first shrine visit of the year. Each temple and shrine also holds its own festival, and the fireworks on the second Tuesday of August attract massive crowds to the beach area. Recently, the summer months have seen temporary bars pop up on beaches in and around Kamakura.

GETTING AROUND

Walking is the best way to see the city. Narrow streets take you through quiet residential areas with well-tended gardens, old wooden houses, coffee shops and teahouses. There are also some hiking routes along the ridges of the hills, linking different parts of town. After the initial ascent, they are generally fairly easy walks, some leading to picnic areas and parks. The starting points are indicated on the road, as are destinations and estimated durations.

Bikes can be rented from an office (0467 24 2319) behind the police box on the right as you leave the east exit of Kamakura station (open 8.30am-6pm daily; ¥500 first hour, ¥250 extra hour, ¥1,500-¥1,600 full day; bring photo ID). Or you can rent a mountain bike for ¥3,250 a day from Grove (0467 23 6667), a specialist cycle shop on the left side of the main street (Wakamiya Oji) as you walk down towards the sea.

For a more leisurely mode of transport, take a rickshaw – look for the men in traditional garb outside the west exit of Kamakura station and on Wakamiya Oji, by the big *torii* (shrine gate). For half an hour, it costs ¥5,000 for one person, ¥8,000 for two (one hour ¥9,000/¥15,000).

Taxis can be caught from either side of the station. There are also regular bus services departing from the east exit. And no visit to Kamakura can be considered complete without a short trip on the venerable tram cars of the Enoden line (Enoshima Electric Railway), which winds from Kamakura station, past Hase station (the stop for Hase Kannon and the Great Buddha), down along the coast to Enoshima island and Fujisawa.

For information on more sights or special events, check with the tourist office.

The red *torii* at **Tsurugaoka**, one of Japan's foremost Shinto shrines.

TSURUGAOKA HACHIMAN-GU

Kamakura's main shrine, **Tsurugaoka Hachiman-gu**, is a ten-minute walk from Kamakura station. Hachiman is seen today as the god of war, but in the past he was regarded as the guardian of the whole nation. As one of the most important Shinto shrines in eastern Japan, this is an essential stop for all visitors.

To reach the shrine, head for the red *torii* in the left corner of the square outside the station's east exit. This leads into Komachi Dori, a narrow pedestrian street lined with souvenir and craft shops, boutiques, food stalls and shops, and numerous restaurants. At the far end of this street, turn right to the shrine entrance. Alternatively, walk directly away from the station to Wakamiya Oji. This broad avenue forms a north–south axis from central Kamakura down to the sea. Turning left, make your way along the cherry-lined walkway up the centre of the street; the blossom here (early to mid April) is gorgeous.

The shrine and grounds of Tsurugaoka (Hill of Cranes) were built to subtle and strict specifications, the most striking example of which is found near the half-moon bridge at the entrance. On the right (the east, the rising sun) is a large lotus pond with three islands (a propitious number) symbolising the Minamoto family. On the left (the west, the setting sun) is a smaller pond with four islands (the number representing death) symbolising the defeated Taira clan. Going straight on, you'll come to a dancing stage, then the steps to the main hall. The venerable

gingko tree on the left is said to have stood here for 1,000 years (pre-dating the shrine, which was moved to the site in 1180); it is famous for having concealed the murderer of the third Minamoto shogun, who was taken by surprise and killed as he was climbing the steps. The main shrine at the top is reached through a gate with two guardian figures (Yadaijin and Sadaijin). The steps descending to the right lead to other buildings and the treasure house, where historic, religious artworks from the area are displayed.

WEST OF TSURUGAOKA HACHIMAN-GU

Eisho-ji, the only active Buddhist nunnery in the area, allows access to parts of its grounds, as does nearby **Jufuku-ji**, reached by a long approach lined with maples. The quiet ancient cemetery behind, reached by the path to the left of the gate, has many burial caves, some dating from the Kamakura period.

A 20-minute stroll into the hills on this side of the city will bring you to **Zeniarai Benten**, the 'Money-Washing Shrine' dedicated to one of the seven lucky gods. A visit to this atmospheric site is highly recommended. A tunnel going through the mountainside leads into a mysterious area with waterfalls, ponds and small shrines carved into the cliff face, the air filled with incense and ethereal music. Inside the main cave, place your money, notes and all, into bamboo baskets that you then dip in the water. The truly faithful will find their assets have doubled in value.

Slightly back towards the town, a turn-off to the right leads up through a tunnel of more than 100 small red *torii* to the **Sasuke Inari** shrine.

There's not much to see up here apart from the semi-tame squirrels, but it is a peaceful glade.

From here, a 20-minute walk will bring you to Kotokuin temple, home of the **Daibutsu** statue, aka the Great Buddha – the best known of Kamakura's attractions. The temple dates from 741, and the bronze statue of Buddha from 1252. Over 36-feet (ten metres) high and weighing 125 tonnes, the figure appears ungainly and top-heavy from a distance, but from close up the proportions seem perfect. It was originally housed inside a hall, but fires and earthquakes destroyed the building several times before it was demolished for good by a tsunami in 1495. The Daibutsu was unscathed. For ¥20 you can go inside the statue.

Hase-dera (also known as **Hase Kannon**) temple is just down the road. The main feature here is the 11-faced statue of Kannon (goddess of mercy and compassion). Over nine metres (30 feet) tall, it was carved in 721 out of a single camphor tree. The temple is also famous for its thousands of small Jizo figurines offered in memory of deceased children and babies (including those who were never carried to full term). Hase-dera also has a revolving library containing Buddhist sutras – worshippers causing the library to rotate receive merit equivalent to reading the entire Buddhist canon – and a small network of caves with statues carved out of the rock. The treasure house contains artefacts excavated from the temple during rebuilding. From Hase-dera there's a panoramic view of the town, the beach and Sagami Bay.

EAST OF TSURUGAOKA HACHIMAN-GU

Although none of the main sights are in this area, which thus attracts fewer crowds, there are still many smaller temples worth seeing. The first shrine as you come from Tsurugaoka Hachiman-gu is **Egara Tenjin**, founded in 1104. Tenjin is the patron deity of scholarship and learning, and every 25 January there is a ritualistic burning of writing brushes.

Nearby is the **Kamakura-gu** shrine, founded by the Meiji emperor in 1869. From here, turn left up a lane to **Kakuon-ji**. This small temple offers 45-minute tours by a priest (¥300) on the hour from 10am to 3pm (except noon on weekdays), unless it is raining. The tour is in Japanese only, but the thatched buildings and old wooden statues do not need much explanation.

A 15-minute walk from Kamakura-gu takes you to **Zuisen-ji**, famous for its trees and flowers, especially the plum blossoms in February. This small temple has a Zen garden created in the 14th century by the celebrated priest and landscape gardener Muso Soseki.

From the intersection near Kamakura-gu, head along the main road to reach **Sugimoto-dera**, the oldest temple in Kamakura. It's a beautiful place, with white banners lining either side of the well-worn stone steps. Both the gate and temple have thatched roofs and were originally built in 734. Further along, on the other side of the road, is lovely **Hokoku-ji**, known as the 'bamboo temple' for its extensive grove of giant bamboo, where you can sit and contemplate while sipping whisked green tea. From here it's a short walk to the **Shakado tunnel**, one of the original entrances to the ancient city cut through the hills. Only passable by pedestrians, this dark (and reputedly haunted) spot is very atmospheric.

Closer to the station is **Hongaku-ji**, a small temple whose ancient gate and guardian statues gaze out towards the entrance to **Myohon-ji**, the oldest and largest of the Nichiren sect temples in Kamakura. Founded in 1260, it nestles deep into a fold in the hills and is surprisingly quiet, given its proximity to the town centre. Another 15 minutes or so away is **Myoho-ji**, also known as the Moss Temple, where the priest Nichiren once resided. The ancient steps lead up to a hilltop vantage point that remains a favourite spot.

The only major temple close to the sea is **Komyo-ji**, established in 1243, which has a huge wooden *sanmon* gate and an attractive lotus pond with carp and terrapins. A path behind the main prayer hall (on the right next to the playground) leads up the hill, giving views on clear days down the coast to Enoshima island and the Izu Peninsula, with Mount Fuji behind.

At this end of the bay are the remains of **Wakaejima**, the first artificial harbour in Japan. Built in 1232, it went into decline after the capital reverted to Kyoto, and now the stones are only visible at low tide. **Zaimokuza Beach**, the eastern half of the bay, is favoured by dinghy sailors, windsurfers and ever-hopeful weekend surfers (the waves are usually minuscule). The western section, **Yuigahama Beach**, is more popular with sunbathers. In summer, temporary huts are built along the sand to provide showers, changing facilities and deckchair rentals, as well as snacks and drinks.

KITA-KAMAKURA

This area north of the town centre is home to many Rinzai sect temples, among them the famous **Engaku-ji**, the largest Zen temple in Kamakura, situated bang in front of Kita-Kamakura station. The temple was founded in 1282, although the main gate was reconstructed in 1780. The precincts, which extend a long way up into the hills, house more than 15 smaller sub-temples. To the left of the main entrance you can often see people practising Zen archery. On the hill to the right is the famous temple bell – the biggest in Kamakura.

Hokoku-ji. *See p290.*

On the narrow road next to the railway tracks is the **Kamakura Old Pottery Museum** (10am-5pm Tue-Sun, ¥500), housed in a pleasant compound of old and reconstructed half-timbered buildings. Across the tracks is **Tokei-ji**, for a long time a nunnery that offered asylum to women seeking refuge from abusive husbands. It's worth a visit for its lovely garden and grounds, as well as the treasure house (entrance ¥300 extra), which keeps old sutras and scrolls.

Nearby is **Jochi-ji**, a Zen temple noted for the small, ancient bridge and steps at its entrance, its bell tower, the burial caves at the back and a tunnel between the cemeteries. A mountain path leading back to Kamakura station starts from the left of the entrance. On the other side of the main road is a pleasant street winding up to **Meigetsu-in**, a temple noted for its hydrangea gardens (in full bloom in June).

Heading towards Kamakura brings you to **Kencho-ji**, the oldest Zen temple in Japan. It's an imposing place with large buildings and grounds, although only ten of the 49 original sub-temples survive. Many of the halls have been rebuilt, but their arrangement hasn't changed for over 700 years. The second floor of the majestic *sanmon* gate houses 500 statues of *rakan* (Buddha's disciples), although they are not on view. Behind the last building there's a garden, from which a path leads to steps climbing to **Hanso-bo**, a shrine where statues of *tengu* (goblins) protect the temple. From here you can follow the Ten-en hiking path, which follows the hilltop ridge as far as Zuisen-ji temple in the east of Kamakura.

Back on the main road, a short flight of stairs near the tunnel marks the entrance to

Enno-ji, a very small temple housing statues representing the ten judges of Hell.

Where to eat

Around Kamakura station, there are many restaurants along Komachi Dori, the narrow shopping street near the east exit. Friendly **T-Side** (Kotobuki Bldg 2F, 1-6-12 Komachi, 0467 24 9572, lunch sets ¥1,000-¥1,500) serves great Indian food. Around the corner is **Nakamura-an** (1-7-6 Komachi, 0467 25 3500, www.nakamura-an.com, closed Thur, from ¥800), a cosy noodle shop that serves hearty, hand-chopped soba.

In Kita-Kamakura, you can try a Japanese *kaiseki* meal at **Koko-tei** (605 Yamanouchi, 0467 46 5467, lunch from ¥3,150), a quiet, rustic restaurant hidden away in the hills. For a taste of Zen, **Hachinoki Honten** (7 Yamanouchi, 0467 22 8719, lunch from ¥2,310) serves the elegant vegetarian meals of *shojin ryori* close to the main entrance of the Kencho-ji temple. **Sasanoha** (499 Yamanouchi, 0467 23 2068, lunch from ¥1,300) offers delicious (but not entirely vegetarian) meals with brown rice.

Facing the ocean in Inamuragasaki (on the Enoden line) is **Taverna Rondino** (2-6-11 Inamuragasaki, 0467 25 4355, set meals ¥1,800-¥5,250), an Italian restaurant as good as most in Tokyo. It also has a small outside terrace.

Getting there

By train

Kamakura is less than an hour by train from Tokyo. Both Kita-Kamakura and Kamakura stations are on the JR Yokosuka line from Tokyo (¥890 single), Shinbashi (¥780) and Shinagawa (¥690) stations; trains run every 10-15mins. There's a more limited service on the JR Shonan-Shinjuku line from Shinjuku (¥890), Shibuya (¥890) and Ebisu (¥780). A special one-day return, including unlimited rides on the Enoden line, is the Kamakura-Enoden Free Ticket (¥1,970 from any station inside the Yamanote line). A cheaper but longer (90mins) option is to take the Odakyu line from Shinjuku to Enoshima (¥610; ¥1,210 by express), then transfer on to the Enoden line (¥250 to Kamakura). Special-price day-trip tickets (also with unlimited rides on the Enoden) are available for ¥1,430. If you don't have a ticket for the return journey to Tokyo, get one as soon as you arrive at Kamakura, as there are always queues later in the day.

Tourist information

Kamakura City Tourist Information Service

1-1-1 Komachi, Kamakura Eki Konai, Kanagawa-ken (0467 22 3350/www.city.kamakura.kanagawa.jp). **Open** 9am-5pm/5.30pm daily.
Also check out http://kamakuratoday.com/e/.

Trips Out of Town

Nikko

Historic beauty just north of the capital.

If you haven't seen Nikko, then you can't say you've really lived – or so says a Japanese adage that's been popular since the Edo period. For over 1,200 years this area of mountains, lakes, forests and hot springs has been considered a centre of great beauty and spiritual significance. But Nikko's main claim to fame is that it's where the first Tokugawa shogun, Ieyasu, is enshrined and buried. The impressive scale and lavish ornamentation of his mausoleum make Nikko one of the most fascinating sites in the country.

In Japanese, Nikko means 'sunlight', but the name also derives from that of the sacred mountain behind the city, Futara, which is now known as Mt Nantai. It was here that the priest Shodo Shonin established a centre for Esoteric Buddhism in 782, and Mt Nantai remains a centre of pilgrimage for religious ascetics.

Ieyasu's mausoleum, the Toshogu, is surrounded by numerous temples and shrines, including the equally ornate Taiyu-in, the mausoleum of his grandson, Iemitsu, the third Tokugawa shogun. The entire complex, a UNESCO World Heritage site, can be seen in half a day. Most visitors, though, stay overnight so they can also see the area above Nikko, including Lake Chuzenji, the dramatic Kegon Falls, Yumoto Onsen and the vast Oku-Nikko national park, with its *onsen* (hot springs), hiking, camping, boating, skiing and skating facilities.

Nikko lies at the foot of the mountains on the edge of the Kanto plain, about two hours by train due north of Tokyo. It is a small city (population circa 20,000), with souvenir shops, antiques dealers and restaurants lining the main street, which runs from the two train stations up to Shinkyo, the sacred bridge that marks the entrance to the shrines and temples.

This handsome, red-lacquered bridge that spans the Daiyagawa gorge marks the spot where legend says Shodo Shonin was carried across by two huge serpents. The first bridge was built here in 1636, as the main approach to the Toshogu. Destroyed by floods in 1902 and rebuilt five years later, the second bridge carried such vast numbers of tourists that it had to be rebuilt again, its third incarnation opening in April 2005.

Cross the road in front of the bridge and follow the steps into the forested national park to reach the Toshogu complex, ten minutes away.

The road to the left leads to Lake Chuzenji, via the sprawling newer part of Nikko, with its unsightly hotels and souvenir shops.

The cluster of religious buildings on the far side of Shinkyo bridge includes the Rinno-ji temple, the Toshogu, the Futarasan Shrine and the Taiyu-in Mausoleum. Entrance fees are ¥900, ¥1,300, ¥200 and ¥550 respectively, but if you want to see them all it's much cheaper to buy the combined ticket for ¥1,000 (this can be bought as you enter the Rinno-ji or at the Tobu bus counter in the station on arrival). This also allows entry to the Yakushido (inside the Toshogu), though not to the Sleeping Cat (a well-known carving), Oku-sha (Ieyasu's tomb) or the shrines in the grounds of Futarasan Jinja.

The buildings are generally open daily from 8am to 5pm (4pm from December to March).

RINNO-JI

The **Rinno-ji**, founded in 766, is the largest of the Buddhist temples in the area. Its main hall is called the Sanbutsu-do, after the trinity of Buddhas that are the main attraction. Over five metres (16 feet) high, these gilt-covered wooden statues depict Amida Nyorai, the Thousand-Armed Kannon and the Horse-Headed Kannon – a Buddhist representation of the gods of Nikko's three sacred mountains. Off to one side is a tall pillar, Sorinto, built in 1643 to repel evil.

In front of the Sanbutsu-do is the temple's treasure house and the **Shoyo-en**, a beautiful Edo-style strolling garden (admission ¥300), with a 200-year-old cherry tree that has been declared a national monument. To the left of the Sanbutsu-do stands a black gate, the Kuremon, and the path that leads to the Toshogu.

TOSHOGU

Even if you forgo the other buildings in the complex, the **Toshogu** is a must-see. Because of its popularity, it is advisable to arrive first thing in the morning, before the tour buses converge, or late in the afternoon. It's also very busy during its three annual festivals. On 17 May horseback archery in medieval hunting attire takes place in front of the shrine, while on 18 May the Sennin Gyoretsu procession recreates the transfer of the remains of Ieyasu. The 1,000 participants dress as samurai, priests and others in the style of the days of the shogun. A festival on 17 October combines both, but on a smaller scale.

The dramatic **Kegon Falls**. *See p294.*

The Toshogu was completed in 1636, during the reign of the third shogun, Iemitsu, according to instructions left by Ieyasu, who had died in 1616. The finest craftsmen were brought in and it's said that as many as 15,000 people were involved. Unusually, the mausoleum blends both Shinto and Buddhist elements, and its flamboyant decorations owe more to Chinese and Korean influences than native Japanese design. Nearly all the surfaces are brightly painted, with ornate and intricate carvings.

Inside the first gate (*torii*) is a five-storey pagoda built in 1818, and the ticket office. A short flight of stairs leads you through the **Otemon**, also known as the Deva Gate after its fearsome statues, said to scare away evil spirits. The building on the left after the gate is the **Shin-kyusha** (Sacred Stable), where a sacred white horse is housed most of the year. This unpainted building is famous for its monkey carvings, including the renowned San-saru (Three Monkeys) representing the ideal way of life ('hear no evil, see no evil, speak no evil'). The three buildings on the right of the Otemon are repositories for costumes and other festival items. Keep an eye out for the carving of the phantasmagorical elephants.

Another flight of stairs takes you up to the spectacular **Yomeimon** (Twilight Gate). With its 500 Chinese-style carvings of giraffes, sages, dragons and other imaginary creatures, it is the most elaborate edifice of its kind in Japan. Off to the left before this gate is the Yakushi-do, famous for the large painting of a dragon on the

ceiling and for the roaring echo, which the priest regularly demonstrates. There are also 12 ancient statues inside, representing the years of the Chinese zodiac.

Just above the Yomeimon is the similarly ornate **Karamon**, leading to the Oratory and Main Hall. The dragon motif continues in the Oratory, with more carvings at the entrance, and another 100 on the ceiling. To the right of Karamon is the entrance to the **Oku-sha**, the shogun's tomb (an extra ¥520 if you hold the combined ticket). Over the door by the ticket booth is the carving of the **Nemuri-neko** (Sleeping Cat). The stairs lead up the mountain to a quiet and secluded area with two small buildings simply painted in blue and gold – behind these is the tomb.

The path leading to the left before the entrance *torii* goes to the **Toshogu Treasure Museum** (¥500), where a small selection of the treasures is exhibited on rotation.

The second path to the left (between the pagoda and the Otemon) leads to the **Futarasan Jinja**. This shrine has three other sites: the summit of Mt Nantai, the shore of Lake Chuzenji, and the bank of the Daiyagawa river. There is little to see inside the shrine, but the sacred spring and other buildings at the back (admission ¥200) are quite atmospheric.

TAIYU-IN MAUSOLEUM

Further into the hills is the **Taiyu-in Mausoleum**, where the third shogun, Iemitsu, is buried. Built in 1652, the gates and buildings are rather more restrained in scale and style than Toshogu and definitely worth visiting. Many people prefer the black-and-gold colour scheme and relatively quiet atmosphere.

The first gate has Nio (heavenly kings) guardian figures; soon after comes the Nitenmon, with statues of Komokuten and Jikokuten, two Buddhist guardians. The next gate is the Yashamon, with statues of four demons known as Yashan, and the last is the Karamon, before the main hall of worship. A few artefacts and old treasures are displayed inside. A walk around the main hall leads to the Kokamon gate and towards the shogun's actual burial site, though this is locked at all times.

Back near the Shinkyo bridge, there's a trail leading upstream along the Daiyagawa river to the Ganmangafuchi Abyss, famous for a series of old mossy statues along a stretch of the river filled with large volcanic rocks.

LAKE CHUZENJI AND MT NANTAI

To see the area's famed natural beauty, be sure to visit **Lake Chuzenji**, situated high above Nikko. The Iroha-zaka road zigzags to an altitude of 1,300 metres (4,265 feet) – watch out for the aggressive monkeys alongside the road. The lake offers swimming, fishing and boating, and the surrounding area has many campsites and hiking trails.

Most tourists come to view the **Kegon Falls**, where the lake's waters plunge 100 metres (328 feet) into the Daiyagawa river. The waterfalls, which include 12 minor cascades, are some of the finest in Japan – and especially photogenic in midwinter, when they occasionally freeze over. A lift (¥520) takes you down to an observation platform level with the bottom of the falls. The nearby Chanoki-daira ropeway gives views of the lake, Kegon Falls and Mt Nantai. There's also a botanical garden with alpine plants.

North of the lake, **Mt Nantai** rises to almost 2,400 metres (7,877 feet). There is a crater at the top, but most climbers making the five-hour ascent (May to October only) do so for religious reasons, to visit Okumiya Shrine. The side of the mountain gets crowded with worshippers during its festival (31 July-8 August).

Further north from Chuzenji is **Yumoto Onsen**, a hot-spring resort by Lake Yumoto with a good range of accommodation. The road passes through gorgeous sub-alpine meadows and has great views of the mountains.

Where to stay & eat

Although it's possible to see Nikko in a day, there are several good hotels for those who want to take things slowly. Prices below are for double rooms.

One of the oldest hotels in Japan, the **Nikko Kanaya Hotel** (1300 Kami-Hatsuishi, 0288 54 0001, www.kanayahotel.co.jp, ¥11,550-¥49,820) opened in 1873. It's a five-minute ride from either station of Nikko's two stations on a Tobu bus (¥190) heading for Nishisando, Kiyotaki, Okuhosoo, Chuzenji or Yumoto Onsen; get off at the Shinkyo stop. Another option is the **Nikko Tamozawa Hotel** (2010 Hanaishimachi, 0288 54 1152, www.tobu.co.jp/kogyo/tamozawa/, from ¥12,000), a 12-minute ride on the same buses. Alight at Rengeseki Tamozawa.

There's also the **Turtle Inn Nikko**, a small inn by the river near Shinkyo (2-16 Takumi-cho, 0288 53 3168, www.turtle-nikko.com, ¥4,800-¥5,600). It also has an annex called **Hotori-an** (8-28 Takumi-cho, 0288 53 3663, ¥12,400) a few minutes away. Get off at the Sogo Kaikanmae bus stop for either. Staff speak English.

There are plenty of hotels and pensions in the Lake Chuzenji area, and many of these have natural hot-spring baths (*onsen*). One of the crop is the **Chuzenji Kanaya Hotel** (2482 Chugushi, 0288 51 0001, www.kanaya hotel.co.jp, from ¥17,325). The bus to Yumoto Onsen stops right in front of the hotel.

It would be a definite shame to leave Nikko without trying the local speciality, *yuba* (soya milk skin). **Gyoushin-Tei** (2339-1 Yama-uchi, 0288 53 3751, closed Thur) is set in a 12th-century garden and serves *yuba* in *shojin ryori* (¥3,500) or *kaiseki ryori* (¥5,000) courses (*see pp142-3*). There are also numerous noodle shops serving soba (including *yuba* soba) along Nikko's main street, and up at Lake Chuzenji. **Enya** (443 Ishiyamachi, 0288 53 5605, www. nikko-enya.co.jp, closed Mon) offers a selection of Japanese and Western meat dishes and over 80 different world beers.

Getting there

By train

Both Tobu and JR trains go to Nikko, terminating at different but nearby stations in the centre of town. The Tobu trains are faster and cheaper, and their bus service to the sights is more regular.

By Tobu: From Tobu Asakusa station, limited express trains go directly to Tobu Nikko station (¥2,740 single; journey 1hr 50mins). Regular (*kaisoku*) trains cost ¥1,320 and take 20mins longer. *Kaisoku* tickets are always available from ticket machines, but seats on limited express trains must be reserved; book in good time, especially at weekends and holidays. Check with Tobu in Tokyo (3623 1171). **By JR**: Take the *shinkansen* (bullet train) from Tokyo station (1hr) or regular train from Ueno (90-110mins) to Utsunomiya; from there it's 45mins on a local train to JR Nikko station. Single fare: ¥2,520 regular; ¥4,920 by bullet train. There are also some trains from Shinjuku (¥2,520, 2hrs 25mins).

From both stations it's a few minutes by bus (¥190) to Shinkyo bridge and the entrance to the Toshogu, or a 25-minute walk. Tobu runs buses to Lake Chuzenji (30mins, ¥1,100; a two-day ticket allowing unlimited use of the buses is ¥2,000). There are also occasional buses to Yumoto Onsen.

Tourist information

Nikko Tourist Information Centre

591 Gokomachi, Nikko-shi, Tochigi-ken (0288 54 2496/www.nikko-jp.org/english/index.html). **Open** 9am-5pm daily.
The office is located just off Nikko's main street. The website has a detailed guide to all the sights.

Sightseeing Inquiry Office

Inside Tobu Nikko station, 4-3 Matsubara-cho, Nikko-shi, Tochigi-ken (0288 53 4511). **Open** 8.30am-5pm daily.

Other Trips

A more leisurely Japan is within easy reach.

Below are some less well-known options for day trips from Tokyo. The first offers a glimpse of Edo-era Japan; the second takes you on a pleasant walk to an ancient hilltop temple; the third to a stone-quarrying region. In midsummer, you can also join the hordes climbing Mt Fuji.

Kawagoe

With inner-city rice paddies, wide streets and an overall slower pace of life, Kawagoe – less than an hour by train west from central Tokyo – is, in many ways, typical of the suburbs that encompass the city. But the place also has a distinctive side, as hinted at in its nickname, 'Little Edo'. Kawagoe boasts one of Japan's most extensive collections of intact merchants' houses dating from the 19th century.

The collection isn't huge – fewer than 30 buildings – and they owe their survival (ironically) to the Great Kawagoe Fire of 1893, which destroyed more than a third of the city. As Kawagoe was rebuilt, merchants chose fire-resistant mortar walls and elaborately tiled *onigawara* roofs in the style of the *kura* (the traditional Japanese warehouse) as a safeguard against future disaster. The surviving structures, known as *kurazukuri*, offer a rare glimpse of a Japan long disappeared.

Conveniently for the visitor, most of the remaining *kurazukuri* are situated along one street, Ichiban-gai, a ten-minute walk from Hon-Kawagoe train station. Impressively designed, with elaborately carved shutters and supports, some of the buildings are now shops, which are worth entering as much for their interiors as for the goods on sale. Original furnishings and decorations remain, and shopkeepers won't mind if you choose not to come away with a bamboo flute or a kimono.

In between are some stately Western-style buildings erected at the beginning of the 20th century, as well as a number of *kurazukuri* reproductions. The latter are not as crass as they may sound, and they offer a viable alternative to the 'concrete box' school of modern Japanese architecture.

Beyond Ichiban-gai is a maze of narrow, winding streets where a clutch of traditional sweet shops vies for attention with ten or

so temples. The generations-old method of preparing the hard candies is on show for all who are curious to get a glimpse of a near-extinct craft.

Back towards the station is **Kita-in** temple (0492 22 0859, open Sept-Feb 9am-4pm daily, Mar-Aug 9am-4.30pm daily, admission ¥400), built in 830 and rebuilt in the 17th century using structures from the original Edo Castle. A side yard contains around 540 *rakan*, stone statues of Buddha's 500 mythical disciples. They're quite a sight; each face is different, representing a host of emotions, from joy to serenity to grief to madness.

Looming majestically above all this is the symbol of Kawagoe, the three-storey **Tokino Kane Tower**. Originally constructed in 1624, and rebuilt after the Great Fire, the wooden tower houses a bell that still chimes four times a day, serving to remind all of Kawagoe's place of importance in historical Japan.

Where to eat

Located near Kita-in temple, Kotobukian (0492 25 1184, open 11.30am-5pm, until 8pm Sat, Sun, closed Wed) specialises in *wariko-soba*, a concoction of green tea buckwheat noodles served with five different toppings, and served in a five-tiered box. For snacks, seek out Kurazukuri Chaya (0492 25 5252, open 9am-7pm daily) on Ichiban-gai. Oni (0492 25 4179, open 6-11.30pm Mon-Sat), also located in a *kurazukuri*, near Kawagoe station, offers locally brewed beer and good food. Don't miss the sunken fireplace.

Getting there

By train

The Seibu Shinjuku train leaves every 15mins from Seibu Shinjuku station to Hon-Kawagoe station (journey 65mins, ¥480 single; 47 mins, ¥890 express single). Kawagoe station, slightly further from the city's sights, is on the Tobu Toju line from Ikebukuro (fastest route: 30mins, ¥450); an express train departs every 15mins. Kawagoe is also on the JR Saikyo line from Shinjuku station (53mins, ¥740); trains run every 20mins. The 'Co Edo Loop Bus', a vintage-style shuttle bus, connects Kawagoe and Hon-Kawagoe stations with the main sights. Single trips cost ¥340.

Climbing Mt Fuji

Japan's most famous and highest mountain (at 3,776 metres/12,388 feet) is renowned for its beauty and spiritual significance. For centuries pilgrims have made their way to the summit, with shrines on the way up doubling as inns; they would pray and rest at each stage before reaching the top in time for sunrise. For years this was a men-only affair; women were only allowed to join in a few years after the Meiji Restoration of 1868.

Religious travellers are few and far between these days, but climbing Fuji remains very popular. People still go up to see the sunrise, but most use transport to the fifth stage,

where the road stops. Since the mountain is covered in snow most of the year, the official climbing season is limited to July and August, although there is transport to the fifth stage from April until November (out of season the trails are open, but facilities are closed). The best time is the middle four weeks of the climbing season; the most crowded time is Obon Week in mid August. The climb is worthwhile but not easy: a saying goes that there are two kinds of fools, those who never climb Fuji and those who climb it twice.

Choosing which side to tackle Mt Fuji from affects how easy the climb is. Most people

Tourist information

Kawagoe City Tourist Information Bureau

Inside Kawagoe station, 39-19 Wakita Honcho, Kawagoe-shi (0492 22 5556/www.city.kawagoe. saitama.jp). **Open** 9am-4.30pm daily.

Jiko-ji Temple

The oldest temple in the Kanto region outside Tokyo sits on a hilltop in the middle of a green landscape about 70 kilometres (44 miles) north of the capital. Infrequent transport connections

mean it takes pretty much all day to get there and back – but the slow journey, followed by a peaceful hour-long walk to the temple itself, is a perfect antidote to the chaos of the capital.

From Ikebukuro station, the Tobu Tojo line maps a course through sprawling suburbia to its terminal at **Ogawamachi**, just over an hour away. Surrounded by rolling hills, the town was once noted as a centre for *washi* (Japanese paper) manufacturing, and today families still carry on the gruelling task of turning pulped wood into the uniquely textured material.

From Ogawamachi, the JR Hachiko line has little diesel trains on the hour to the next follow the Yoshidaguchi Trail from the Kawaguchiko side (north), which offers a 7.5-kilometre (4.7-mile) climb that takes five hours, plus three for the descent. You can also head from the south-west side, starting at one of two new fifth stages, one near Gotemba (6.5 hours up and three down) or another further west (five hours up and 3.5 down).

There are two ways to tackle the volcano. One is to set off at nightfall, timing the ascent to arrive in time for sunrise. More sensible souls climb in daylight and rest in one of the lodges near the peak. With up to 600 people crammed into the huts, arriving and departing constantly, you won't get a sound sleep but you will appreciate the break. Lodges at the eighth stage on the Kawaguchiko side include **Hakuunsou** (0555 24 6514, ¥5,250-¥8,400 per person) and **Honhachigo Tomoekan** (0555 24 6511, ¥7,350-¥8,400). At the seventh stage on the Gotemba side, try **Hinodekan** (0550 89 2867, ¥6,000).

The temperature at the summit can be 20°C (68°F) lower than at the base; the average in July is 4.8°C (40.5°F) and in August 5.8°C (42.5°F). It's often below zero before sunrise. Essential items include good shoes, rainwear, a torch, water and food (available at huts, but overpriced). Don't forget toilet paper and some bags for your rubbish.

Once you reach the peak, you might be slightly disappointed to find it is no longer a place of solitude and contemplation. Restaurants, souvenir shops, vending machines, portaloos, a shrine and several hundred people will be waiting for you; and the spectacle of the sunrise is not necessarily enhanced by loudspeakers blasting dramatic music. But it is still an amazing feeling to be standing atop Japan's most iconic peak.

Getting there

Details below are for July and August; in other months, transport connections are fewer.

By bus

The fastest and cheapest way to Kawaguchiko is by bus from Nishi-Shinjuku's Keio Shinjuku Expressway Bus Terminal (1hr 45mins, ¥1,700 single). From the Keio bus terminal at Kawaguchiko station to the fifth stage it takes 50mins (¥1,700 single, ¥2,000 return); there are five buses a day. There are also six daily buses from Shinjuku direct to the fifth stage (2hrs 25mins, ¥2,600).

By train

Take the JR Chuo line from Shinjuku to Otsuki station (1hr 20mins, ¥1,280). From there, take the Fuji-Kyuko line to Kawaguchiko (50mins, ¥1,110) – timetables can be checked with JR in Otsuki (050 2016 1600) or Fuji-Kyuko in Kawaguchiko (0555 72 2911). From Kawaguchiko station to the fifth stage by bus takes another hour.

If you want to start the climb from Gotemba, there are four direct trains (express Asagiri) daily from Shinjuku on the Odakyu line (2hrs, ¥2,720). From Gotemba there are three to four buses to the new fifth stage (1hr, ¥1,500 single, ¥2,000 return).

Tourist information

Kawaguchiko Tourist Information

In front of Kawaguchiko station, 3631-5 Funatsu, Kawaguchiko-Machi (0555 72 6700). Open 8.30am-6pm daily.

station, **Myokaku**. From there it's a ten-minute bus ride to the sleepy hamlet of **Nishi-Daira**, where old houses with their adjoining *kura* (warehouses) are the norm, and hens appear to outnumber people. From the bus stop, a two-minute walk into Nishi-Daira will bring you to a crossroads. Here, turn right on to the steep road that disappears into the forested hills above. Where the village ends there is a small temple called **Nyonindo** that is worth a look if only for its historical significance. During the Kamakura era (1185-1333), this was the final stop for women pilgrims. Beyond, as far as Jiko-ji at the top, it was a men-only affair.

The climb is spectacular, with breathtaking views of the opposing hills as they emerge in hazy layers. But the walk is far from exhausting and offers an absorbing hour of peace before the tiled roofs of Jiko-ji come into view.

Like most temples throughout Asia, **Jiko-ji** commands a stunning location. Half-hidden between groves of thick blue bamboo, the various temple buildings are connected by a maze of stone steps. At the entrance stands an old wooden tower supporting a huge bell (dating from 1245) that is rung twice a day. Above are the main structures, many displaying intricately carved designs.

Pre-dating the Late Nara period (710-94), Jiko-ji is believed to have been established in 673 by a priest called Jiko (hence its name). The advent of the Kamakura era saw the temple's rise in prominence, and it quickly became the religious centre for 75 satellite temples that mushroomed across the adjoining hills.

The modern treasure house (open 9am-4pm daily, ¥300) contains a number of valuable items, including the Lotus Sutra, a scroll-like masterpiece of calligraphy painstakingly transcribed by Emperor Gotoba (1183-98), and now a national treasure. Kannondo, which stands at the highest point in the compound, also guards a collection of treasures, the principal one being an image of Senju Kannon, the main deity of the area. The image is only open to public viewing on 17 April, the day of the temple's annual festival.

From Jiko-ji, the walk back to Nishi-Daira takes less than half an hour. If time allows, retrace your steps into the village and drop by **Tategu Kaikan** (0493 67 0014, open 9am-4.30pm Tue-Sun), a souvenir shop that stocks an array of locally made food and woodcraft.

Where to eat

There's nowhere to eat near Jiko-ji. Best to bring a packed lunch or try Myokaku or Ogawamachi, where there are lots of *unagi* (freshwater eel) restaurants. Futaba Honten (0493 72 0038, www.futaba.to, open 11am-2.30pm, 4-8pm Tue-Sun; closed 1st Mon of mth), five minutes along the shopping street from Ogawamachi station, has belonged to the same family for 250 years and specialises in *chushichi-meshi*, a soup of rice in green tea, and the ubiquitous *unagi*.

Getting there

From Ikebukuro station take the Tobu Tojo special express to Ogawamachi station (journey 73mins, ¥780 single), then the JR Hachioji line to Myokaku (8mins, ¥200), then the Tokikawa Son'ei bus to Nishi-Daira (10mins). Services are infrequent – this is rural Japan – so it's best to check timings in advance.

Oya-machi

It is no coincidence that the small town of Oya-machi, lying 110 kilometres (68 miles) north of Tokyo, in Tochigi prefecture, has at its heart a 27-metre (89-foot) statue carved from a sheer rock face. The town sits on a mountain of volcanic stone and has been a mining centre for centuries.

Oya-machi is reached by a dusty road that leads to an expansive stone atrium. Huge doorways have been cut into the surrounding cliffs with staggering precision. Within this area is the deceptively small **Oya Stone Museum** (028 652 1232, open 9am-4.30pm Mon-Wed, Fri-Sun, admission ¥600). On display are a number of miners' tools, early photos of the quarrying process, and an exhibit about Frank Lloyd Wright's Imperial Hotel in Tokyo (demolished in 1968), for which he insisted on using Oya stone. Then things get really interesting: you descend a stairwell into a vast underground ex-quarry 60 metres (197 feet) deep and large enough to swallow Tokyo Dome. The quarry has been used as an aircraft factory in World War II, a mushroom farm and, more recently, a concert hall.

From the museum, it is a short walk back to the bus stop and into Oya-machi proper. There are a handful of shops and houses, many made entirely of stone. At the top of the slope that leads off to the left of the main street are the red gates of **Oya-ji** temple (0286 52 0128, open Apr-Oct 8.30am-5pm daily, Nov-Mar 9am-4.30pm daily, closed 2wks Dec and some Thur, ¥300), a small, ornate structure wedged beneath a bulging cliff.

Founded in 810, the temple has been a tourist destination ever since, largely because of its remarkable reliefs. The first you encounter is the 42-armed Senju Kannon. Carved directly into the rock wall, it dates to the early part of the Heian era (794-1185) and is believed to have originally been lacquered and painted with gold leaf. On the adjoining wall are another nine reliefs of varying sizes and quality, created between 600 and 1,000 years ago. A small museum contains little of interest except the remains of an 11,000-year-old skeleton discovered in the grounds during restoration.

Across the street, flanked by souvenir shops, stands a massive rectangular entrance cut through the hill. Head through here, and you reach the towering 17-metre (56-foot) **Heiwa Kannon** (Goddess of Peace) statue. Completed in 1954, she hangs from the cliff, gazing benevolently out over the town.

Where to eat

Oya's tourist cafeterias are uninspiring, so better to bring a packed lunch or eat near Utsunomiya station before boarding the bus.

Getting there

From Ueno station take the JR Tohoku line to Utsunomiya station; journey times and prices vary from 50mins/¥4,800 by bullet train to 1hr 40mins/¥1,890 by regular train. Take the west exit at Utsunomiya and catch bus 45 from bus stop 8 to Oya Shiryokan (also called Shimin no Ie, ¥300) – pay as you get off. When you leave, it's best to use the Heiwa Kannon bus stop. Oya-machi is a tiny place, so it's hard to get lost.

森美術館
Mori Art Museum

展望台
Observatory

入口
Entrance

Directory

Directory

Getting Around

By air

Two airports serve Tokyo. Most overseas flights arrive at **Narita International Airport**, which is nearly 70 kilometres (45 miles) from Tokyo and well served by rail and bus links to the city. It's less likely that you'll arrive at **Haneda International Airport**, closer to the city and to the south, which handles mainly internal flights.

Narita International Airport

Flight information 0476 34 5000/ www.narita-airport.jp/en/index.html. The **Narita Express train** (050 2016 1603, www.jreast.co.jp/e/nex), run by Japan Railways (JR), is the fastest way to get into Tokyo from Narita, but it's also the most expensive. All trains go to Tokyo station (¥2,940), with some also serving Shinjuku (¥3,110), Ikebukuro (¥3,110), Omiya (¥3,740) and Yokohama (¥4,180). Trains depart every 30 to 40 minutes, and seats can be reserved up to a month in advance.

The **Keisei Skyliner** (Narita 0476 32 8505, Ueno 3831 0989, www.keisei.co.jp/keisei/tetudou/keisei_us/top.html), operated by a private rail company, is a cheaper option. Trains on this line will take you into Ueno or Nippori station (¥1,920) in around an hour. Cheaper still is a Keisei limited express (tokkyu), a regular train that makes a few stops on its 75-minute route to Ueno station (¥1,000).

Limousine buses (3665 7220, www.limousinebus.co.jp) also run regularly to various key points and certain hotels in the city. There are ticket counters inside the arrivals halls near the exits of both terminals 1 and 2; the buses depart from just outside. Fares are ¥3,000.

Taxis are recommended only for those with bottomless wallets: they cost from ¥30,000 and are often slower than the train.

Haneda International Airport

Flight information 5757 8111/ www.tokyo-airport-bldg.co.jp. Haneda is served by the **Tokyo Monorail** (www.tokyo-monorail.co.jp), which leaves every five to ten minutes from 5.01am to 11.50pm, linking up to Hamamatsucho station (¥470) on the Yamanote line in a little over 20 minutes. The **Keikyu line** (5789 8686, www.keikyu.co.jp) can take you to Shinagawa, also on the Yamanote line, in 19 minutes (¥400). From here you can link up with major JR lines.

Limousine buses to central Tokyo cost in the region of ¥1,000, depending on which part of the city you want to go to. A **taxi** will cost a minimum of ¥6,000.

By train

Most of Japan's vast and efficient rail network is run by **Japan Railways** (JR). One of the fastest but most expensive ways to travel Japan's elongated countryside is by *shinkansen* (bullet train), which travels at speeds up to 270 kilometres (168 miles) per hour. Tickets can be purchased at JR reservation 'Green Window' areas or travel agents, or online at www.world.eki-net.com. Call the **JR East Infoline** (*see p301*) for information in English.

Trains depart from different stations depending on destination; most leave from Tokyo or Ueno stations. Slower, cheaper trains go to many destinations. Marks on the train platforms show where the numbered carriages will stop. Most carriages have reserved seats only (reservations cost extra), but some carriages are set aside for unreserved seating

on each train. Arrive early if you want to sit down.

By coach

Long-distance buses provide one of the cheapest ways to travel through Japan, although anyone over 5ft 6in (1m 68cm) may find the seats small. Most of these buses leave at midnight and arrive early the next morning; all are air-conditioned and have ample space for luggage. Seats can be reserved through a travel agent. Long-distance buses are run by the railway companies; for information, *see p301* **JR trains** and **Private train lines**.

Tokyo has one of the most efficient train and subway systems in the world: in the rare event of delays in the morning rush, staff give out apology slips for workers to show their bosses. Services are fast, clean, safe, reliable and – with a little thought and the right map – remarkably easy to use. Almost all stations have signs in English, and signs telling you which exit to take. Subways and train lines are colour-coded.

Subways and trains operate from 5am to around midnight (JR lines slightly later). Rush hours are 7.30-9.30am and 5-7pm, and the last train of the day can be extremely uncomfortable.

Tokyo's rail network is run by several different companies, and changing trains between competing systems can mean paying for two tickets.

Transfer tickets are usually available to take you from one line to another, but cost the same as buying two separate tickets and can be tricky to figure out. To simplify things, it's a good idea to type a pair of prepaid travel passes. Armed with a **Suica** and a **Passnet** (*see below* **Tickets & passes**), you can ride on any regular train in Tokyo.

The user-friendly **Jorudan** website (www.jorudan.co.jp) is in English and allows you to type in your starting point and destination to learn routes, times and prices. For a map showing the (huge) rail and subway network across Greater Tokyo, *see p332-3*.

JR trains

Overland trains in Tokyo are operated by **Japan Railways East** (www.jreast.co.jp/e), part of the main JR group. It's impossible to stay in Tokyo for more than a few hours without using JR's **Yamanote line**, the loop that defines the city centre – and with which all Tokyo's subway and rail lines link at some point (for connections at each station on the loop, *see p336*). The main stations on the Yamanote line (colour-coded green) are Tokyo, Ueno, Ikebukuro, Shinjuku, Shibuya and Shinagawa. It's very foreigner-friendly, with an infoline in English (*see below*) and information centres at major stations (look for the question mark symbol) that offer help in English.

JR's other major lines in Tokyo are: **Chuo** (orange), **Sobu** (yellow), **Saikyo** (turquoise) and **Keihin Tohoku** (blue). Because of its notoriety for gropers (*chikan*), the insanely crowded Saikyo line offers women-only cars during peak hours.

JR East Infoline
050 2016 1603.
Open 10am-6pm daily.

Subways

There are 12 subway lines in Tokyo. Most are run by **Tokyo Metro** (3941 2004 9am-9pm daily, www. tokyometro.jp/e), formerly the Teito Rapid Transit Authority (Eidan). Its eight colour-coded lines are: **Chiyoda** (dark green), **Ginza** (orange), **Hanzomon** (purple), **Hibiya** (grey), **Marunouchi** (red), **Nanboku** (light green), **Tozai** (turquoise) and **Yurakucho** (yellow), which includes **New Yurakucho** (brown), called Shin-Sen in Japanese.

Four – slightly pricier – subway lines are run by the metropolitan government, **Toei** (3816 5700 9am-7pm daily, www.kotsu.metro. tokyo.jp). They are: **Asakusa** (pale pink), **Mita** (blue), **Oedo** (bright pink) and **Shinjuku** (green). If transferring from Tokyo Metro to Toei trains, buying a transfer ticket is ¥70 cheaper than buying separate tickets.

Subway maps posted in stations are in Japanese. For a subway map in English, *see p334-5*; you can also get one at tourist offices (*see p313*).

Private train lines

Tokyo's private railway lines mainly ferry commuters to the outlying districts of the city. Because most were founded by companies that also run department stores, they usually terminate inside, or next to, one of their branches.

The major private lines are run by **Keio** (www.keio.co.jp), **Odakyu** (www.odakyu.jp), **Seibu** (www.seibu-group. co.jp/railways), **Tobu** (www. tobuland.com), **Tokyu** (www. tokyu.co.jp), **Keisei** (www.

keisei.co.jp) and **Keikyu** (www.keikyu.co.jp).

You can pick up a full map showing all lines and subways from the airport information counter on arrival. Keio lines offer women-only cars during peak hours: look for the pink window stickers (or the hundreds of grinning faces in the train if you've entered by mistake).

Tickets & passes

Standard tickets
Standard single tickets for adults (under-12s pay half-price, under-6s travel free) can be bought at automatic ticket machines at any station. Many machines feature a symbol saying which notes they accept. Touch-screen ticket machines can display information in English, but should you be unsure of your destination (or unable to read it from the Japanese map), buy a ticket for the minimum fare (¥160) and settle up in a fare adjustment machine (or window) at your destination. These machines, usually bright yellow, are found just before the exit barriers of all stations. Travellers with incorrect tickets do not have to pay punitive fines.

Transferring from one line to another, provided it is run by the same operator, will be covered by the price of your ticket. If your journey involves transferring from one network to another, you will have to buy a transfer ticket (if available) or buy another ticket at the transfer point.

If you're in town for any length of time you're better off buying a travel pass.

Suica
Suica is a prepaid travel pass issued by JR, distinctive for its bright green colour and penguin logo. It can be used on all JR lines. It contains an integrated circuit detected

at ticket gates when the pass is swiped over the right point. The minimum fare is automatically deducted from your balance on entry to the station, with the balance being picked up on exit at your destination. Suica cards can be purchased at JR 'Green Window' areas or at JR ticket machines. A card costs ¥2,000, including a ¥500 returnable deposit. Credit on the card can be topped up at ticket machines (up to ¥10,000).

With a Suica card you don't have to queue, nor do you have to try to find your destination station on a map in order to work out the required fare – you just walk up to the gates and go through. You can also use it for purchases at most station kiosks, some vending machines and the occasional shop.

Passnet

This prepaid travel pass covers all of Tokyo's railway lines (subway and overland) – *except* for JR. Available in denominations of ¥1,000, ¥3,000 or ¥5,000, it allows you to transfer from one operator's line to another without buying new tickets. The fare is automatically deducted from your remaining credit at the computerised ticket barriers. Unlike the Suica, this card must be inserted into the ticket gate. It only saves a small amount of cash, but it does save you time fiddling for change and trying to figure out the maps.

Frequent travel tickets

There's a huge variety of frequent travel tickets available, from prepaid cards to 11-for-the-price-of-ten trip tickets. There are also combination tickets and one-day passes for one, two or three networks. For more details in English, call the **JR East Infoline** (*see p301*).

JRPasses

The **Japan Rail Pass** (www.japanrailpass.net) provides for virtually unlimited travel on the entire national JR network, including *shinkansen* and all JR lines in Tokyo, including the Yamanote line. It cannot, however, be used on the new 'Nozomi' super-express *shinkansen*. It costs from ¥28,300 for seven days, about the same price as a middle-distance *shinkansen* return ticket. It's essential if you're planning to travel much around Japan.

The JRPass is available only to visitors from abroad travelling under the entry status of 'temporary visitor', and must be purchased *before* coming to Japan. You buy an Exchange Order abroad, which is then changed into a pass on arrival in Japan at an exchange office (you'll need to show your passport).

JR East, which runs trains in and around Tokyo, has its own version of the pass (www.jreast.co.jp/e/eastpass), which costs from ¥20,000 for five days. If you are not intending to travel beyond the JREast area (Tokyo and the area to the north and east), this makes a sensible choice. The same conditions apply.

Exchange Orders can be bought at overseas offices of the Japan Travel Bureau International, Nippon Travel Agency, Kinki Nippon Tourist, Tokyu Tourist Corporation and other associated local travel agents, or at an overseas Japan Airlines office if you're travelling by Japan Airlines. Check the Japan Rail Pass website for overseas locations.

Buses

Like the trains, buses in Tokyo are run by several companies. Travelling by bus can be confusing if you're new to Japan, as signs are rarely in

English. Toei and Keio bus fares cost ¥200, other buses are ¥210 – no matter what the distance (half-price for kids). Get on the bus at the front and off at the back. Drop the exact fare into the slot in front of the driver. If you don't have it, use the change machine, usually to the right, which will deduct your fare from the money. Fare machines accept ¥50, ¥100 and ¥500 coins and ¥1,000 notes. Stops are usually announced by a pre-recorded voice. A Toei bus route guide in English is available at Toei subway stations and hotels.

Tokyo Bus Association
5360 7111/www.tokyobus.or.jp.
The website and phone line provide information on all bus routes within and leaving Tokyo, in Japanese only.

Cycling

The bicycle remains the most common form of local transport in Tokyo, but unattended bikes should always be locked as these, along with umbrellas, are the only things that get stolen in Japan. Areas in and around stations are usually no-parking zones for bikes, a rule that locals gleefully ignore, but which can result in your bike being impounded. Some hotels will loan bicycles to guests.

Driving

Rental costs for garages are equivalent to those for small apartments in Tokyo, so if you rent a car you will have to pay astronomical parking fees (usually around ¥100 for 30 minutes, more in the centre). If you do decide to hire a car, you'll need an international driving licence backed up by at least six months' driving experience. English-speaking rental assistance is available at many of the large hotels as well as at the airport.

The **Japan Automobile Federation** (www.jaf.or.jp) publishes a 'Rules of the Road' guide (¥1,000) in English. Request one from their Shiba branch office: 2-2-17 Shiba, Minato-ku (6833 9100). A Metropolitan Expressway map in English is available from the **Metropolitan Expressway Public Corporation**, (www.shutoko.jp).

If you want to drive outside the capital (which is definitely a much safer option), JR offers rail and car rental packages. Call the **JR East Infoline** (*see p301*) for details.

Toyota Rent-a-lease

Narita International Airport Terminals 1 & 2 (0476 32 1020/fax 0476 32 1088/http: //rent.toyota.co.jp). **Open** 7am-10pm daily. **Other locations:** throughout the city.

Walking

Tokyo is great for walking. There are no no-go areas, and the whole place is 99.9 per cent safe 24 hours a day. Walking is the best way to discover the hidden nooks and crannies that exist in nearly every district. The **Tokyo TIC** (*see p313*) offers information on free walking tours of parts of Tokyo.

The worst thing about walking in Tokyo is the crowds. Because it's so safe and so crowded, Japanese people have a different sense of personal space and are often unaware of what's going on behind them. This results in colossal 'people jams'. People also tend to walk at speeds associated with village fêtes rather than capital cities, sometimes while sending mail from their mobiles; be prepared to experience some frustration.

When crossing the road, always do so at marked crossings and wait for the green man. If you cross on red, urban legend says that you could be held responsible for the death of those behind you, who may blindly follow you into the traffic.

Taxis

Taxi fares begin at ¥660 for the first two kilometres; then ¥100 for every 350 metres. Prices rise at weekends and between 11pm and 5am. Stands are located near stations, most hotels, department stores and major intersections. Tipping is not expected.

Hinomaru Limousine

Ark Hills Mori Bldg, 1-12-32 Akasaka, Minato-ku (3212 0505 24 hrs/www.hinomaru.co.jp). Roppongi-Itchome station (Chiyoda line), exit 3. Stretch limos and the like.

Understanding addresses

Only the largest streets in Tokyo boast names, and even they don't appear in addresses. Navigating this metropolis takes a little more work than, say, New York, but it's not nearly as impenetrable as it first appears. The Japanese system uses numbers in place of names. Central Tokyo is divided into 23 wards, or *ku*. Within each *ku*, there are many smaller districts, or *cho*, which also have their own names. Then come the numbers. The first number is the main area, or *chome*, then a second number signifies which block, and finally a third number points you to the specific building. Most buildings are named, but this name is used more for confirmation than navigation. Japan uses the continental system of floor numbering. The abbreviation 1F is the ground floor; 2F means the second floor, or first floor English style. And B1 or B2 refer to the basement levels.

Thus, the address of the Office bar – **Yamazaki Bldg 5F, 2-7-18 Kita-Aoyama, Minato-ku** – means that it's on the fifth floor of the Yamazaki Building, which is the 18th

building of the seventh block of the second area of Kita-Aoyama, in Minato ward.

To track down an address, first invest in a detailed bilingual atlas, such as the *Tokyo City Atlas* (Kodansha), which contains numbered *cho* and *chome*. Then follow your progress towards your destination by monitoring the metal plaques affixed to lamp posts or the front of some buildings. Alternatively, ask a policeman. It's what the locals do, and it's one of the main functions of the local *koban* (police box), all of which have detailed maps of their area.

In addition, most station exits in the Tokyo metropolitan area have detailed bilingual street plans of the vicinity posted, with the numbers clearly marked. Maps can also often be found on the streets themselves (though these are usually only in Japanese).

While the system isn't as tricky as it sounds, few Tokyoites leave home without a map of any new destination. Virtually all websites have maps to print, or if you have access to a fax machine, it's common practice to phone your destination and ask them to fax you a map of how to get there.

Directory

Resources A-Z

Age restrictions

There is no age of consent in Japan, and the legal age for smoking and drinking is 20; the ubiquity of vending machines, however, makes the law virtually impossible to enforce. The minimum voting age is also 20.

Attitude & etiquette

Japanese people are generally forgiving of visitors' clumsy attempts at correct behaviour, but there are certain rules that must be followed to avoid offending your hosts. For how to behave in a bathhouse, *see p64* **Old soaks**. For business etiquette, *see below*.

Business

Etiquette

Doing business in Japan is a very different proposition from doing it in the West. The Japanese place great emphasis on personal relationships between business partners, and socialising before and after the deal is done is de rigueur. Here are some basic business tips:

● Carry plenty of business cards. You will be spraying them around like confetti.
● Always pass business cards with two hands. Do not write on another person's business card, fold it or put it in your back pocket. When in meetings, read the cards that you have just received carefully and leave them face up on the table throughout, in a neat column according to hierarchy of position.
● If you need an interpreter, hire one of your own and ask them to interpret body language for you.
● Crossing your legs at the knee or the ankle indicates disrespect.
● When out eating with a group, wait for your comrades to indicate your seat.

● Never offer to split a restaurant bill. Just say thank you ('Gochiso sama') if someone else pays.
● If you receive a gift from your host, do not open it in front of them. If you give a gift, make sure it is professionally wrapped.
● Be prepared to give details of your personal life in a way that would be inappropriate elsewhere.

Conventions & conferences

Japan hosts more conventions and exhibitions than any other Asian country. Many larger hotels have conference and business rooms for hire. For Tokyo's major annual trade fairs, *see p212-17*.

Makuhari Messe

Nippon Convention Center, Nakase 2-1 Nakase, Mihama-ku, Chiba-shi (043 296 0001/www.m-messe.co.jp). Kaihin-Makuhari station (Keiyo line), south exit.

Tokyo Big Sight

Tokyo International Exhibition Center, 3-21-2 Ariake, Koto-ku (5530 1111/www.bigsight.jp/english/). Kokusai-Tenjijo Seimon station (Yurikamome line) or Kokusai-Tenjijo station (Rinkai line) or Ariake terminal (Suijo water bus). **Map** *Odaiba p101.*

Tokyo International Forum

3-5-1 Marunouchi, Chiyoda-ku (5221 9000/www.t-i-forum.co.jp/ english). Yurakucho station (Yamanote, Yurakucho lines), Tokyo International Forum exit. **Map** *Ginza p75.*

Chambers of commerce

American Chamber of Commerce *3433 5381/fax 3433 8454/ www.accj.or.jp.*
Australian & New Zealand Chamber of Commerce *5157 5615/fax 5157 5616/ www.anzccj.jp.*
British Chamber of Commerce *3267 1901/fax 3267 1903/ www.bccjapan.com.*
Canadian Chamber of Commerce *5775 9500/ fax 5775 9507/www.cccj.or.jp.*

Copy shops

Kinko's *0120 001 966/ www.kinkos.co.jp.*
A complete range of print services, and internet access. Check the website for details of 24-hour locations.

Couriers

Federal Express *0120 003 200/www.fedex.com.*
Hubnet *0120 881 084/www.hub-net.co.jp.*
UPS Yamato Express *0120 271 040/www.ups.com.*

Office space

Servcorp *5288 5100 /www.servcorp.net.*
Has several locations in Tokyo with executive service starting from ¥250,000 per month plus deposit.

Public relations

IRI *Hatchobori Bldg 7F, 2-19-8 Hatchobori, Chuo-ku (5543 1221/www.iri-japan.co.jp). Hatchobori station (Hibiya, Keiyo lines), exit A5.*
Kyodo PR *Dowa Bldg 7F, 7-2-22 Ginza, Chuo-ku (3571 5171/www.kyodo-pr.co.jp). Ginza station (Ginza, Hibiya, Marunouchi lines), exit C3.*

Secretarial service

Telephone Secretary Centre *5413 7320/ gh6m-situ@asahi-net.or.jp.*
An answering service starting at ¥10,000 a month, including bilingual secretaries, word processing and typing. Japanese lessons for new customers are thrown in for free.

Telephone answering service

Bell24 System *3590 4646/www.tas.bell24.co.jp.*
Services start from ¥15,000; bilingual at a slightly higher cost.

Translators

Simul International *Toranomon 34 MT Bldg 1F, 1-25-5 Toranomon, Minato-ku (3539 3900/www.simul. co.jp). Toranomon station (Ginza line), exits 1, 4.*

Transpacific Enterprises
Asunaro T Bldg 3F, 2-2-5 Shibasaki,
Tachikawa-shi (042 528 8282/
www.transpacific.jp). Tachikawa
station (Chuo line), south exit.

Useful organisations

JETRO (Japan External
Trade Organisation)
3582 5511 /www.jetro.go.jp.
Japanese-only automated
phone menu.

Customs

The duty-free allowances
for non-residents coming into
Japan are: 400 cigarettes or
100 cigars or 250g of tobacco;
three 750ml bottles of spirits;
57g (20oz) of perfume; gifts
or souvenirs up to a value of
¥200,000. There is no limit
on the amount of Japanese
or foreign currency that can
be brought into the country.

Penalties are severe for drug
importation: deportation is the
lenient option. Pornography
laws are very strict too and
anything showing pubic hair
may be confiscated.

For more information,
visit **Japan Customs** at
www.customs.go.jp.

Disabled

Tokyo is not easy for those
with disabilities, particularly
when it comes to public
transport. Stations, especially
the bigger ones, have long
corridors and many staircases,
and only some have escalators,
lifts or wheelchair-moving
facilities, though train workers
will assist those in need.
More common are raised
dots on the ground, to guide
the visually impaired, and
pedestrian crossings that
make a variety of noises.
Trains have 'silver seats' near
carriage exits for use by the
disabled, elderly or pregnant.

The best resource in
English for travellers with
disabilities is an online service,
Accessible Tokyo:
http://accessible.jp.org.

Club Tourism Division Barrier-
free Travel *Centre Kinki Nippon*
Tourist Co, Shinjuku Island Wing
10F, 6-3-1 Nishi-Shinjuku, Shinjuku-
ku (5323 6915/www.club-t.com).
Nishi-Shinjuku station (Marunouchi
line), Island Wing exit. **Open** 9.30am-
5.30pm daily.
Organises tours that take into
account the special needs of disabled
travellers. Make an appointment to
guarantee you speak with an
English-speaking staff member.

Drinking

In Japan, you can legally drink
– and smoke – when you reach
20. Tokyo's licensing laws
are virtually non-existent,
and many bars in livelier
areas stay open all night,
with customers staggering
home on the first train. Public
drunkenness is common, and
late Friday-night trains can
be unpleasant. Intoxication is
considered a valid excuse for
behaviour, particularly sexual

Cycle the city

It's not quite Amsterdam, but Tokyo is a
relatively cycle-friendly place, and taking
two wheels around the city is one way to
avoid the overcrowded trains.

There are no bicycle lanes; technically
cyclists are required to ride to the left of
vehicles on the roads. In reality, nobody
pays any attention to this and all but the
couriers use the pavements. At time of
writing the government were discussing
changing the law to allow pedallers to
do this with their legal blessing, but
the decision is unlikely to affect cyclists'
behaviour either way. The only real issue
to note is that night riders must wear
lights and reflectors.

You can carry your bike on a train,
as long as you follow the bizarre rule of
carrying it in a bag. This rule is enforced
with greatly varying degrees of fervour,
but if your itinerary requires riding a rail,
it's a good idea to take a bin liner to
appease any overly eager station staff
you might encounter on your journey.

Rental shops

Mujirushi

3-8-3 Marunouchi, Chiyoda-ku (5208 8241/
www.mujiyurakucho.com). Ginza Itchome
Station (Yurakucho line), exit A1.
Open 10am-9pm daily.
Rent regular or electric bikes in Muji's
distinctive minimal designs. Rental costs
are just ¥525 per day on weekdays; double
at weekends. A ¥3,000 deposit and photo
ID are required. Reservations accepted.

Y's Bike Academy

2-10-1 Akasaka, Minato-ku (5545 1525/
www.jitensya.co.jp/group/shops/academy/
mise_top.htm). Tameike-Sanno station
(Ginza, Nanboku lines), exit 11.
Open 11am-8pm Mon-Sat; 10am-7pm Sun.
Y's charges by the day (¥1,260) or half-day
(up to four hours for ¥735). Reservations are
advised. A credit card is required as a deposit.

Directory

harassment, that would be cause for a lawsuit in the West – the next day, all is forgotten, or at least avoided. Beware: foreigners are expected to have a higher alcohol tolerance than their Japanese drinking pals.

Drugs

Drugs can be found in Tokyo, but penalties for possession are severe. Expect deportation or imprisonment.

Electricity & gas

Electric current in Japan runs like the USA's, at 100V AC, rather than the 220-240V European standard. Plugs have two flat-sided prongs. If bringing electrical appliances from Europe, you need to purchase an adapter.

Electricity in Tokyo is provided by **Tokyo Electric Power Company** (TEPCO, 4477 3099); gas by **Tokyo Gas** (5722 0111).

Embassies

Embassies are usually open 9am to 5pm Monday to Friday; opening times for visa sections may vary.

Australian Embassy *2-1-14 Mita, Minato-ku (5232 4111/ www.australia.or.jp). Azabu-Juban station (Nanboku, Oedo lines), exit 2.*
British Embassy *1 Ichibansho, Chiyoda-ku (5211 1100/ www.uknow.or.jp). Hanzomon station (Hanzomon line), exit 4.*
Canadian Embassy *7-3-38 Akasaka, Minato-ku (5412 6200/ www.canadanet.or.jp). Aoyama-Itchome station (Ginza, Hanzomon, Oedo lines), exit 4.*
Irish Embassy *2-10-7 Kojimachi, Chiyoda-ku (3263 0695/www.embassy-avenue.jp/ireland). Hanzomon station (Hanzomon line), exit 4.*
New Zealand Embassy *20-40 Kamiyamacho, Shibuya-ku (3467 2271/www.nzembassy.com/japan). Yoyogi-Koen station (Chiyoda line), exit 2.*
South Africa Embassy *Zenkyoren Bldg 4F, 2-7-9 Hirakawacho, Chiyoda-ku (3265 3366/www.rsatk.com). Nagatacho station (Hanzomon, Nanboku, Yurakucho lines), exit 4.*

US Embassy *1-10-5 Akasaka, Minato-ku (3224 5000/ http://tokyo.usembassy.gov). Tameike-Sanno station (Ginza, Nanboku lines), exit 13.*

Emergencies

To contact the police (*keisatsu*) in an emergency, call **110**; to call an ambulance (*kyukyu-sha*) or fire department (*kaji-shoubou*), call **119**. From a public phone, press the red button first. The person answering should, in theory, speak English, but if you are with a Japanese speaker, get them to call.

Japan Help Line (*see p307*) offers 24-hour, English-language support but is not equipped to deal with time-sensitive emergencies.

For emergency rooms at hospitals, *see below* **Accident & emergency**.

Health

For the Japanese, medical insurance provided by employers or the state covers 70 per cent of the cost of medical treatment; those aged over 70 pay only ten per cent. Visitors will be expected to pay the full amount for any treatment received, so should take out medical insurance before leaving their own country. Calls to hospitals (except those to **Tokyo Medical Clinic**; *see below*) are answered in Japanese, but say '*Eigo o hanaseru kata ni kawatte kudasai*' ('May I speak to an English speaker?') and you'll be transferred. No vaccinations are required to enter Japan.

Tokyo Metropolitan Health & Medical Information Centre

5285 8181 9am-8pm Mon-Fri/5285 8185 5-8pm Mon-Fri; 9am-8pm Sat, Sun/www.himawari.metro.tokyo.jp. The *himawari* service provides medical and health information in English, Chinese, Korean, Thai and Spanish and can direct you to the most suitable clinic. The out-of-hours

number provides interpretation to help foreign nationals get emergency care. If you get to the hospital and can't communicate with the doctor, call them. But if you're at home bleeding, call 119.

Accident & emergency

The following offer regular appointments, deal with 24-hour emergencies and have English-speaking staff.

Japan Red Cross Medical Centre

4-1-22 Hiroo, Shibuya-ku (3400 1311/ www.med.jrc.or.jp). Hiroo station (Hibiya line), exit 3. **Open** 8.30-11am Mon-Fri.

St Luke's International Hospital

9-1 Akashicho, Chuo-ku (3541 5151/ www.luke.or.jp). Tsukiji station (Hibiya line), exits 3, 4. **Open** 8.30-11am Mon-Fri; appointments only from noon.

Seibo International Catholic Hospital

2-5-1 Naka-Ochiai, Shinjuku-ku (3951 1111/www.seibokai.or.jp). Shimo-Ochiai station (Seibu Shinjuku line), north exit. **Open** 8-11am Mon-Sat; appointments only from 12.30pm. Closed 3rd Sat of mth.

Tokyo Medical Clinic & Surgical Clinic

Mori Bldg 32 2F, 3-4-30 Shiba-koen, Minato-ku (3436 3028/www.tmsc.jp). Shiba-Koen station (Mita line), exit A2. **Open** 8.30am-5.30pm Mon-Fri; 8.30am-noon Sat.
Doctors hail from the UK, America, Germany or Japan, and all speak English. The clinic also has a pharmacy on the first floor.

Contraception & abortion

Condoms reign supreme in terms of contraception in Japan, largely because until 1999 the Pill was available only to women with menstrual problems, and taking it is still generally considered risky. Condoms are sold in most convenience stores, and in vending machines, often near pharmacies. Abortion is legal, and is generally seen as a sad necessity, not a morally controversial issue. The signature of the 'father' is required. Clinics have different rules regarding how far into the pregnancy they will perform abortions. Medical abortions are not available.

Dentists

Both of the following listings have English-speaking staff.

Dr JS Wong
1-22-3 Kami-Osaki, Shinagawa-ku (3473 2901). Meguro station (Yamanote, Mita, Nanboku lines), east exit. **Open** by appointment only Mon-Wed, Fri, Sat.

Tokyo Clinic Dental Office
Mori Bldg 32 2F, 3-4-30 Shiba-Koen, Minato-ku (3431 4225). Kamiyacho station (Hibiya line), exit 1 or Akabanebashi station (Oedo line), Tokyo Tower exit. **Open** by appointment only Mon-Thur, Sat. Japanese insurance accepted.

Doctors

Both have English-speaking staff.

Tokyo Adventist Hospital
3-17-3 Amanuma, Suginami-ku (3392 6151/www.tokyoeisei.com). Ogikubo station (Chuo, Marunouchi lines), north exit. **Open** 8.30-11am Mon-Fri; by appointment afternoons Mon-Thur. No emergencies.

Tokyo British Clinic
Daikanyama Y Bldg 2F, 2-13-7 Ebisu-Nishi, Shibuya-ku (5458 6099). Ebisu station (Yamanote, Hibiya lines), west exit. **Open** 8.30am-5.30pm Mon-Fri; 8.30am-12.30pm Sat.
Run by a British doctor, this clinic caters for most aspects of general practice, including paediatrics.

Opticians
See p207.

Pharmacies
See p207.

Helplines

The following helplines offer information in English.

AIDS Hotline
5780 1113. **Open** 10am-6pm daily.
Alcoholics Anonymous
3971 1471 (taped message)/ www.aatokyo.org.
HELP Asian Women's Shelter
3368 8855. **Open** 10am-4pm Mon-Fri; in Japanese and English.
Immigration Information Centre
5796 7112. **Open** 9am-5pm Mon-Fri.
Japan Help Line
0570 000 911/www.jhelp.com. **Open** 24hrs daily.
A non-profit-making worldwide assistance service. Among other services, it produces the Japan Help Line Card, which contains useful telephone numbers and essential information for non-Japanese speakers, as well as a numbered phrase list in English and Japanese for use in emergencies.
Tokyo English Life Line (TELL) *5774 0992/www.telljp.com.* **Open** 9am-11pm daily.
Counselling and assistance service run by trained volunteers.
Tokyo Foreign Residents' Advisory Centre
5320 7744. **Open** 9.30am-noon, 1-5pm Mon-Fri.
Run by the Tokyo Metropolitan Government, this will help newcomers adjust to Japanese life.

ID

It's most unlikely, but foreign visitors can, in theory, be arrested for not carrying ID (a passport) at all times. Long-term residents should carry their Alien Registration Card.

Internet & email

Many of Tokyo's venerable 24-hour manga coffee shops (*manga kissa*) also offer cheap internet services. They are usually clustered around train stations; for the GeraGera chain, *see p186*.

The chain of cafés run by Yahoo! Japan in collaboration with Starbucks has been whittled down to a mere four branches, including one each at Narita and Haneda airports. For all locations, see http://café.yahoo.co.jp.

Internet cafés seem to open and close in the blink of an eye, so your best bet is to try a Kinkos, which has 24-hour locations all around the city.

(www.kinkos.co.jp). For a list of internet cafés ordered by station, check out www.tcvb.or.jp/en/guide/09cafe.html.

Personal computers fitted with wireless LAN cards that meet the 802.11b WiFi standard (such as Apple's Airport card) can access the internet in many locations around Tokyo, including Ben's Café (*see p184*). An up-to-date list of wireless hotspots in the city can be found at www.hotspot-locations.com.

Language

For information on Japanese language and pronunciation, and a list of useful words and phrases, *see p318-321*.

There are hundreds of schools in Tokyo running courses in Japanese. Most of these offer intensive studies for those who want to learn as quickly as possible or who need Japanese for work or school. They may offer longer courses too.

Private schools tend to be expensive, so check out lessons run by your ward office. Ward lessons cost from as little as ¥100 a month – a bargain compared to the average ¥3,000 an hour for group lessons at schools.

Arc Academy *1-9-1 Shibuya, Shibuya-ku (3409 0391/www.arc-academy.net/nihongo/Eindex.asp). Shibuya station (Yamanote, Ginza, Hanzomon lines), east exit.*
Offers a wide variety of courses.
Meguro Language Centre *NT Bldg 3F, 1-4-11 Meguro, Meguro-ku (3493 3727/www.mlcjapanese.co.jp). Meguro station (Yamanote, Mita, Nanboku lines), west exit.*
A wide range of courses, from private lessons to group lessons.
Temple University *2-8-12 Minami-Azabu, Minato-ku (0120 861 026/www.tuj.ac.jp). Shirokane-Takanawa station (Mita, Nanboku lines), exit 2; Azabu-Juban station (Nanboku, Oedo lines), exit 1.*
Temple University offers fairly cheap evening classes as part of its continuing education programme.

Directory

Legal advice

Legal Counselling Centre
*Bar Association Bldg, 1-1-3
Kasumigaseki, Chiyoda-ku (3581
2255/www.niben.jp). Kasumigaseki
station (Chiyoda line), exit C1;
(Hibiya line), exit A1; (Marunouchi
line), exit B1.* **Open** *by appointment
only 1-4pm.*
Consultations in English (¥5,000 for
first half hour, ¥2,500 for subsequent
half hours). Free for the
impoverished on Thursday
afternoons. Topics cover a range of
issues including crime, immigration
and labour problems. Appointments
are on a first-come, first-served basis.

**Tokyo Human Rights
Counselling Centre**
*Iidabashi Joint Government Bldg 6F,
1-9-20 Koraku, Bunkyo-ku (5689
0518). Iidabashi station (Chuo, Mita,
Nanboku, Yurakucho lines), exit C2;
(Oedo line), Suidobashi exit.* **Open**
1.30-3.30pm Tue, Thur.
Free counselling is given in English
over the phone.

Libraries

Each ward has a central
lending library with a limited
number of English-language
titles; you need an Alien
Registration Card to borrow
books. The following reference
libraries have a healthy
number of books in English.
All close on national holidays.

**British Council Library
& Information**
*Centre 1-2 Kagurazaka, Shinjuku-ku
(3235 8031/www.uknow.or.jp).
Iidabashi station (Chuo, Mita,
Nanboku, Yurakucho lines), exits
B2A, B3; (Oedo line), west exit.*
Open *9am-9pm Mon-Fri;
9.30am-5.30pm Sat.*
Information on the UK, plus internet
access, and BBC World is always on.
For ¥500 a day you can use all the
facilities. Library loans for members
only. Under-18s not admitted.

Japan Foundation Library
*Ark Mori Bldg, West Wing 20F, 1-
12-32 Akasaka, Minato-ku (5562
3527/www.jpf.go.jp/e/learn/library/lib
index.html). Roppongi-Itchome
station (Nanboku line), exit 3.*
Open *10am-5pm Mon-Fri. Closed
last Mon of mth.*
Books, mags and reference material.
Specialises in humanities and social
sciences, and also has translations of
Japanese novels. Houses about 25,000
books and 300 magazine titles.
Lending as well as reference.
Under-18s not admitted.

JETRO Library *Ark Mori Bldg 6F,
1-12-32 Akasaka, Minato-ku (3582
1775/www.jetro.go.jp). Tameike-
Sanno station (Ginza, Nanboku
lines), exit 13.* **Open** *9am-5pm
Mon-Fri. Closed 3rd Tue of mth.*
Houses information about trade,
the economy and investment for
just about any country in the world.
Lots of statistics, as well as basic
business directories. Under-18s
not admitted.

National Diet Library *1-10-1
Nagatacho, Chiyoda-ku (3581
2331/www.ndl.go.jp). Nagatacho
station (Hanzomon, Nanboku,
Yurakucho lines), exits 2, 3.*
Open *9.30am-5pm Mon-Fri.
Closed 3rd Wed of mth.*
Japan's main library, with the
largest number of foreign-language
books and materials. Over two
million books, 50,000 mags and
1,500 newspapers and periodicals.
Under-20s not admitted.

**Tokyo Metropolitan Central
Library** *5-7-13 Minami-Azabu,
Minato-ku (3442 8451/www.library.
metro.tokyo.jp). Hiroo station
(Hibiya line), exit 1.* **Open** *1-8pm
Mon; 9.30am-8pm Tue-Fri; 9.30am-
5pm Sat, Sun.*
This is the main library for the
Tokyo government, with the largest
collection of books about Tokyo.
Over 150,000 titles in foreign
languages. Under-16s not admitted.

Litter

Foreign visitors are often
impressed by how clean
Tokyo is in comparison to
their home cities.

After the subway sarin gas
attack in March 1995, most
litter bins were removed from
subway stations. JR stations,
however, have bins near the
exits. They are divided into
three sections: cans, magazines
and newspapers, and other
rubbish. If you can't find a bin,
take your rubbish home.

Domestic rubbish is usually
divided into four categories:
burnable, unburnable,
recyclable and large items,
but this varies by ward, so
contact your local ward office
or check the signs at the street
collection points.

Lost property

If you leave a bag or package
somewhere, just go back: it

will probably still be there.
If you left it in a train station
or other public area, go to the
station-master's office or
nearest *koban* (police box)
and ask for English-language
assistance. Items handed in
at the station are logged in a
book. You will have to sign in
and show ID in order to receive
your item. Alternatively, ring
the general JR/police
information numbers below.
If you leave something in a
taxi on the way to or from a
hotel, try the hotel reception –
taxi drivers often bring the
lost item straight back.

Eidan subway *3941 2004*
Japanese only.
JR (Yamanote line) *3423 0111*
English-speaking service.
Metropolitan Police *3501 0110*
English-speaking service.
Narita Airport *0476 322 802*
Taxi *3648 0300.* Japanese only.
Toei subway & buses *3861 5700*
Japanese only.

Media

Newspapers

The Japanese are among the
keenest newspaper readers in
the world, with daily sales of
over 70 million copies. *Yomiuri
Shimbun* is the world's largest
circulation newspaper, with a
daily circulation of 16 million.
For English readers the choice
is limited to three newspapers:
the *Daily Yomiuri*, the *Japan
Times* and the *International
Herald Tribune*, which
incorporates the English
version of the *Asahi Shimbun*.
All cost ¥120-¥150 and are
available at most central
Tokyo station kiosks.

Daily Yomiuri
www.yomiuri.co.jp/index-e.htm.
Produces supplements together with
other world newspapers, including
the *London Times* (Sunday) and the
Washington Post (Friday). There's a
what's-on supplement on Thursdays.
**International Herald
Tribune/Asahi Shimbun**
www.asahi.com/english.
Launched in April 2001 as a joint
venture between the *International*

Herald Tribune and the *Asahi
Shimbun*, and the only English-
language paper in Tokyo to read
like English is its first language.
Japan Times
www.japantimes.co.jp.
The longest-established English-
language newspaper in Japan.
Consists mainly of agency reports.
Heavy on business. It's motto 'All
the news without fear or favour'
could read 'All the news without
fear or flavour'. Reprints two
pages of features from the UK's
Observer each Saturday.
Nikkei Weekly
www.nni.nikkei.co.jp.
The Japanese *Financial Times*
equivalent produces this weekly
digest from the world of finance.

Free reads

EL Magazine
www.elmagazine.com.
'Entertainment and lifestyle' just
means movie and music reviews.
Japanzine
www.japan-zine.com.
This humorous magazine takes
an irreverent look at some of the
quirkier aspects of Japan life.
It includes both Tokyo and
Kansai listings.
Metropolis
www.metropolis.japantoday.com.
Formerly known as *Tokyo Classified*,
this is Tokyo's biggest and best free
weekly magazine, with listings and
adverts galore. It's distributed at
foreigner-friendly bars, clubs, shops
and hotels every Friday.
Tokyo Notice Board
www.tokyonoticeboard.co.jp.
The most visible rival to *Metropolis*,
but smaller and less slick.
Tokyo Weekender
www.weekender.co.jp.
Can be tricky to find. Contains
bland expat community gossip
and news.

Magazines

If you read Japanese, there's a wealth
of what's-on details in weekly
publications such as *Pia* and *Tokyo
Walker* (both ¥320). If not, there's
Tokyo's only paid-for English-
language listings monthly, *Tokyo
Journal* (www.tokyo.to).

Radio

InterFM
www.interfm.co.jp.
Broadcasting on 76.1MHz, this is
Tokyo's main bilingual station. Plays
rock and pop.
NHK Radio Japan
www.nhk.or.jp/rj.

Television

Japanese state broadcaster
NHK runs two commercial-free
terrestrial channels: NHK
General (channel 1) and NHK
Educational (channel 3) – and
two satellite channels: BS1 and
BS2. Tokyo's five other
terrestrial channels – Nihon
TV (channel 4), Tokyo
Broadcasting System (channel
6), Fuji Television (channel 8),
Television Asahi (channel 10)
and TV Tokyo (channel 12) –
show a constant stream of
unimaginative pap, relieved
occasionally by a worthwhile
documentary or drama series.

NHK General news at 7pm
and 9pm daily is broadcast
simultaneously in both English
and Japanese: to access the
English version you'll need a
bilingual TV set (most big
hotels have them). Many non-
Japanese TV series and films
are also broadcast bilingually.

Japan's main satellite
broadcaster is Rupert
Murdoch's SkyPerfect! TV,
which offers a host of familiar
channels, including CNN, BBC
World and Sky Sports.

Money

The yen is not divided into
smaller units and comes in
denominations of ¥1, ¥5,
¥10, ¥50, ¥100 and ¥500
(coins) and ¥1,000, ¥2,000,
¥5,000 and ¥10,000 (notes).
The ¥2,000 note is rarely seen.

Prices on display must
include the five per cent
sales tax. Some places list
that figure below a much
larger price that doesn't
include the tax. If you see
two prices, you'll be paying
the higher one.

ATMs & credit cards

Japan is still a cash-based
society, and restaurants and
bars may refuse credit cards.
Larger shops, restaurants and
hotels accept major cards, but

you should always keep
some cash on you.

ATMs are rarely open after
7pm and often close at 5pm on
Saturdays. Many banks charge
for withdrawals made after
6pm, and on Sundays and
public holidays. Still, there is a
growing number of 24-hour
ATMs in Tokyo, mostly round
major train stations. All ATMs
have logos showing which
cards are accepted, but most
will not take foreign-issued
cards. Among the banks,
Citibank is the most useful,
with 24-hour ATMs all over
Tokyo (information 0120 50
4189). Of the domestic banks,
Shinsei has the most
customer-friendly reputation,
with 24-hour free ATMs.

Post offices (*see p311*) are
also convenient for cash: their
ATMs allow you to withdraw
money by foreign Visa, Plus,
MasterCard, Eurocard,
Maestro, Cirrus, American
Express, Diners and JCB cards,
and have instructions in
English. Some of their ATMs
are open 24 hours a day.

The ATMs at Narita Airport
only work during banking
hours. Ensure you have some
Japanese cash if arriving early
in the morning or late at night.

To report lost or stolen
credit cards, dial one of these
24-hour freephone numbers:

American Express *0120 020 120.*
English message follows Japanese.
Diners Club *0120 074 024.*
MasterCard *00531 11 3886.*
Visa *00531 44 0022.*

Banks

Banks are open 9am to 3pm
Monday to Friday. Do not go
to a bank if you're in a hurry –
queues are long, especially on
Fridays, and you have to take
a number and wait.

Opening a bank account is
usually easy if you have an
Alien Registration Card. For
savings accounts you will be
issued a book and card.
Getting a card can take up to

Directory

Average climate

	Temp (°C/°F)	Rainfall (mm/in)	Sunshine (hrs per day)
Jan	6/42.8	50/2	6
Feb	7/44.6	60/2.4	5.7
Mar	9/48.2	100/3.9	5.1
Apr	14/57.2	130/5.1	5.5
May	18/64.4	135/5.3	5.8
June	21/69.8	165/6.5	4.0
July	26/78.8	160/6.3	4.7
Aug	28/82.4	155/6.1	5.7
Sept	23/73.4	200/7.9	3.8
Oct	18/64.4	165/6.5	4.2
Nov	13/55.4	90/3.5	4.7
Dec	7/44.6	40/1.6	5.5

two weeks; it's usually delivered to your home and you must be there to sign for it. Alternatively, ask the bank to tell you when it arrives, and pick it up. If the bank insists you use a *hanko* (seal stamp), walk out and try another branch. You can also open an account at a post office and withdraw money from any other post-office branch.

Changing money

You can cash travellers' cheques or change foreign currency at any authorised foreign-exchange bank (look for the signs). If you want to exchange money outside regular banking hours, some large hotels change travellers' cheques and currency, as do large department stores, which are open until about 8pm. Narita Airport has several bureaux de change staffed by English speakers, open daily from 7am to 10pm.

Natural hazards

The Great Kanto Earthquake of 1923 destroyed much of Tokyo, and the chances of a future disaster remain high. Despite precautions, the 'Big One' could cause terrible damage. The Kobe Earthquake

of 1995 left over 6,000 dead, and the tremor in Niigata in October 2004 killed 30 and left many thousands homeless.

Every year on 1 September, the anniversary of the 1923 quake, Tokyo practises how to cope with a major earthquake. Residents are advised to keep a small bag handy, containing essentials such as a bottle of water, preserved foodstuffs, some cash and a torch. If you are caught up, try to shut off any stoves and gas mains, secure an exit, and look for a table or similar to protect you.

Opening hours

Department stores and larger shops in Tokyo are open daily from 10am (sometimes earlier, sometimes later) to around 8pm or 9pm. Smaller shops are open the same hours six days a week. Mondays and Wednesdays are the commonest closing days; Sunday is a normal shopping day. Convenience stores offer 24-hour shopping at slightly higher prices than supermarkets, and are found all over the city. The major chains are 7-Eleven, AM-PM, Family Mart and Lawson's.

Most restaurants open at around 11am and close around 11pm, though some bars and *izakaya* are open till 5am. Some

of them don't close until the last customer has gone.

Banks are open 9am to 3pm Monday to Friday. Main post offices are open 9am to 7pm weekdays, and often on Saturdays (usually 9am-3pm) or even Sundays; smaller post offices close at 5pm Monday to Friday, and at weekends.

Office hours are 9am to 5pm. On national holidays, many places keep Sunday hours (closing earlier), but most are closed on 1 and 2 January.

Police

For a foreign visitor or resident, the most frequent contact with the police is usually through the *koban* – the police boxes dotted around every neighbourhood (marked by two red lights with a gold seal in-between), from which officers patrol the area by car and bicycle. Each major *koban* has four officers on duty at any one time to deal with enquiries and complaints from the public. It's estimated that the *koban* outside Shibuya station's Hachiko exit receives around 3,000 visitors a day.

Common causes of friction between Japanese police and foreign nationals are being drunk and aggressive, having noisy parties at home, traffic violations and bicycle theft (if you buy a bike, take careful note of the registration number – you'll need it).

Police officers are only legally entitled to stop people if they are behaving suspiciously, but this can be liberally interpreted. If you are stopped by police officers in Tokyo, present your passport or Alien Registration Card (you're legally required to carry it with you at all times). If detained at a police station, ask to speak to someone from your embassy. Claim you speak no Japanese, even if you do, and don't sign anything you can't read.

To contact the Tokyo police in non-emergencies, call **3501 0110** (English service). For emergencies, *see p306*.

Postal services

The postal system is run by **Japan Post** (www.post. japanpost.jp). Sending a postcard overseas costs ¥70; aerograms cost ¥90; letters under 25g cost ¥90 (Asian countries), ¥110 (Europe, North America, Oceania) or ¥130 (Africa, South America). Post boxes are red; the slot on the left is for domestic mail, the one on the right is for other mail. When writing addresses, English script is acceptable, as long as it's clearly written. Larger department stores can arrange postage if you buy major items. You can purchase stamps at convenience stores. For couriers, *see p304*.

Post offices

Post offices (*yubin-kyoku*) – indicated by a red-and-white sign like a letter 'T' with a line over it – are plentiful. Local post offices open from 9am to 5pm Monday to Friday, and are closed at weekends and on public holidays. Larger post offices close at 7pm on weekdays, and may open on Saturdays (usually 9am-3pm) or even Sundays. Post office ATMs accept foreign bank and credit cards.

Poste restante

Poste restante is available at the following post offices; mail is held for up to 30 days. You'll need to show your passport to collect mail.

International Post Office

3-5-14 Shinsuna, Koto-ku, Tokyo 138-8799 (5665 4200/ www. yuubinkyoku.com). Minami Sunamachi station (Tozai line), exit 3. **Open** 9am-7pm Mon-Fri; 9am-5pm Sat; 9am-12.30pm Sun.

Tokyo Central Post Office

2-7-2 Marunouchi, Chiyoda-ku, Tokyo 100-8799 (3284 9537/ www.yuubinkyoku.com). Tokyo station (Yamanote, Marunouchi lines), South Marunouchi exit. **Open** 8am-8pm Mon-Fri; 8am-5pm Sat; 9am-12.30pm Sun.

Religion

The *Religion Yearbook* issued by the Agency for Cultural Affairs suggests that 208 million Japanese are members of religious organisations – and that's almost twice the population of the country. It's not unusual for a family to celebrate birth with Shinto rites, tie the knot with a Christian marriage, and pay last respects at a Buddhist ceremony. Freedom of worship is a constitutional right.

For more information on Japan's two major religions, Shinto and Buddhism, and on visiting religious sites, *see p80* **Gotta have faith**.

Safety

Japan is one of the safest countries for foreign visitors. Theft is still amazingly rare, so it's not unusual to wander around with the equivalent of hundreds of pounds on you without giving it a second thought. Of course, crime does occur from time to time, and it's best to take the usual precautions to keep money and valuables safe.

There are certain areas, such as Roppongi or Shinjuku's Kabuki-cho, as well as airports and crowded trains, where you should be particularly wary.

Smoking

Around 40 per cent of the adult population in Japan smoke, more than in any other similarly industrialised nation, and cigarettes are relatively cheap, at around ¥280 per packet, and readily available from vending machines and convenience stores. Smoking is common in restaurants and cafés, although a growing number of venues have started to offer no-smoking areas; very few restaurants are entirely smoke-free. In October 2002 central Tokyo's Chiyoda-ku became the first area in Japan to ban smoking on the streets, because cigarettes posed a danger to clothes and babies' heads in the area. Smoking is banned on the platforms of all private train lines in Tokyo, although JR station platforms still have smoking areas.

Telephones

The virtual monopoly enjoyed by **NTT** (Nippon Telegraph & Telephone) on domestic telephone services was broken in 2001 with the introduction of the Myline system, which allows customers to choose phone-service providers for local and long-distance calls. If you have your own phone line in Tokyo, call the **Myline Information Centre** (0120 000 406, www.myline.org) to register your choice of provider (English-speaking operators are available).

Repair Service *113*.
Moving & Relocating *116*.

Dialling & codes

The country code for Japan is 81. The area code for Tokyo is 03. Throughout this guide, we have omitted the 03 from the beginning of Tokyo telephone numbers, as you don't need to dial it when calling from within the city. If you're phoning from outside the city, you need to use the area code. If you're phoning from outside Japan, dial the international access code plus 81 plus 3, followed by the main eight-digit number.

Numbers that start with 0120 are **freephone** (receiver-paid or toll-free).

International calls

Different companies provide international call services, and charge roughly the same rates. Dial 001 (KDDI), 0041 (Japan Telecom), 0033 (NTT Communications) or 0061 (Cable & Wireless IDC), followed by your country's international code, area code (minus any initial zero) and the phone number. The cheapest time to call is between 11pm and 8am, when an off-peak discount of 40 per cent applies.

To use a public phone you need to buy a prepaid card or have a lot of change (some old phones refuse all prepaid cards). Find a booth with 'ISDN' or 'International' on the side – usually a green or grey phone. Blue 'credit phones' allow you to make calls using your credit card. Instructions should be given in English as well as Japanese.

If you set up the 'home country direct' service before leaving home, you can dial from most public phones and charge it to your home bill.

The international code for the UK is 44; 1 for the US and Canada; 353 for the Irish Republic; 61 for Australia; 64 for New Zealand; and 27 for South Africa.

Public phones

NTT still controls nearly all public phones in Tokyo. These are widely available, found in all stations, department stores and on the street, but different varieties will keep most visitors concentrating.

Green phones take flexible phone cards and ¥10 and ¥100 coins, but don't always allow international calls; grey phones are the same, but usually allow international calls; grey and orange phones only take IC cards (snap off the corner before use) and coins, but you can always make international calls; the blue credit phones require a credit card to make international calls and are hard to find. The old pink phones, sometimes the only option even in touristy towns, only take ¥10 coins and cannot make international calls.

Domestic calls cost ¥10 for the first three minutes and ¥10 for every subsequent minute.

Prepaid phone cards

Before the advent of mobile phones, everyone used these in the ubiquitous green phones, and they are still useful if you're not getting a mobile. Several kinds of international phone card can be bought in Tokyo, and you can often find promotions in free English magazines like *Metropolis*.

KDDI (0077 7111, www.kddi.com/english) produces a 'Super World' prepaid card for international phone calls, sold at most major convenience stores. They come in four values (¥1,000, ¥3,000, ¥5,000 and ¥7,000) and can be used with any push-button phone.

NTT East (0120 364 463, www.ntt-east.co.jp/ptd_e/index.html) produces two cards, one mainly for the domestic market, the other – an IC card – for both national and international calls. Both cards cost ¥1,000 and are available from vending machines in some phoneboxes and convenience stores.

Mobile phones

Mobile phones (*keitai denwa*) are a way of life in Tokyo. Japanese mobiles can be used to take photos, surf the net, send email, photos and movies. And you can talk on them too.

While it's possible to take a Japanese mobile phone abroad and use it, it's not as simple the other way around. There are three major mobile phone networks in Japan – the biggest, **DoCoMo** (0120 005 250, www.nttdocomo.com; from NTT), plus **Softbank** (0088 21 2000 (press '8' for English), http://mb.softbank.jp.mb) and **Au** (0077 7111, www.au.kddi.com). They all use technologies incompatible with each other and with phones from overseas. Information and maintenance are covered by the store selling the phone.

Residents can buy a phone on a long-term contract, but visitors will have to either buy a prepaid phone or rent one. For both you'll need to produce your address while staying in Japan (a hotel will be fine). Check in advance whether your phone has bilingual menus and voicemail.

Buying a contract phone

Go to one of the outlets operated by the mobile-phone companies or an electronics store. You will have to show your Alien Registration Card and passport. Applications will not be accepted if your visa is due to expire within 90 days.

Buying a prepaid phone

You can purchase a phone for ¥5,000 to ¥10,000 and a prepaid card for ¥3,000 or ¥5,000 from any phone or electronics store. You will need to bring your passport.

Renting a phone

Smart hotels will often rent phones to guests, or you can do it yourself at a rental outlet or at Narita Airport.

DoCoMo Shop *Shin-Otemachi Bldg 1F, 2-2-21 Otemachi (freephone 0120 680 100/http://www. docomosentu.co.jp/Web/product/ rental/index.html). Tokyo station (Yamanote, Marunouchi lines), North exit.* **Open** 10am-7pm Mon-Fri; 10am-5pm Sat. Rates start at ¥10,500/wk plus ¥60/min domestic calls.

SoftBank Global Rental *3560 7730, http://www.softbank-rental.jp/en/index.php.* Has counters in the departure and arrival halls of terminals 1 and 2 at Narita. **Open** 7am-9pm daily. Rates start at ¥535/day, plus ¥105/min for domestic calls plus insurance.

Telephone directories

Unless you're fluent, using a Japanese phonebook is out of the question. NTT publishes an English-language version, 'TownPage', available free from **English TownPage Centre** (0120 460 815) or at http://english.itp.ne.jp.

Useful numbers

Domestic operator **100**; domestic directory enquiries **104**; international directory enquiries **0051**. These numbers are non-English-speaking. The following numbers are for information and maintenance for land lines:

Japan Telecom
0088 41/www.japan-telecom.co.jp/english.
KDDI Information service
0057.
NTT Communications
0120 506 506/www.ntt.com.
English information follows the Japanese.

Telegrams

Domestic telegrams – 115 (in Japanese). International telegrams – 005 3519 or freephone 0120 445 124.

Time

Japan is nine hours ahead of Greenwich Mean Time (GMT). Daylight Saving Time is not used but is a recurring topic.

Tipping

Tipping is not expected in Japan and people will often be embarrassed if you try. If you leave money at a restaurant, for example, a member of staff may try to return it. At smart establishments, a service charge is often included.

Toilets

Public toilets can be found in and around most stations, often near the entrance or just outside the exit. Station toilets usually offer Japanese-style commodes where you squat facing the back wall.

Many public toilets have no toilet paper. Buy it from machines or take it (for free) from the workers handing out tissues on the street. The packets are ads for local companies and services.

Western-style toilets are the norm in large shops. In some women's toilets there may be a small box with a button: pushing it produces the sound of flushing. Many Japanese women flush the toilet to cover the sounds they make, and the fake flush was designed to save water.

If you're staying in a Japanese home or good hotel, you may find that your toilet looks like the command seat on the Starship Enterprise. Controls to the right of the seat operate its heating and in-built bidet. Don't push the buttons unless you like surprises – and if surprised, do *not* jump up!

Tourist information

The **Japan National Tourist Organisation (JNTO)** is the national English-language tourist service for visitors coming to Japan. It has various offices abroad, plus a **Tourist Information Centre** (TIC) next to Yurakucho station. Its website, **www.jnto.go.jp**, is packed with useful info.

There's also the **Tokyo Tourist Information Centre**, run by the Tokyo Metropolitan Government in its HQ building in Shinjuku.

Tokyo TIC

Tokyo Kotsu Kaikan 10F, 2-10-1 Yurakucho, Chiyoda-ku (3201 3331). Yurakucho station (Yamanote line), Kyobashi exit; (Yurakucho line), exit A8. **Open** 9am-5pm daily. Friendly, multilingual staff and a wealth of information are on offer here: there are maps, event booklets, books on Japanese customs, even NTT English phonebooks, plus a useful budget hotel booking service via the Welcome Inn Reservation Centre. There's nothing on the outside of the building to indicate the tourist office is here – just take the lift to the tenth floor, where there is a sign.
Other locations: *Arrival floor, Terminal 1, Narita Airport (0476 30 3383); Arrival floor, Terminal 2, Narita Airport (0476 34 6251).* **Open** 8am-8pm daily.

Tokyo Tourist Information Centre

Tokyo Metropolitan Government Bldg No.1 1F, 2-8-1 Nishi-Shinjuku, Shinjuku-ku (5321 3077/ www.kanko.metro.tokyo.jp/public/center.html). Tochomae station (Oedo line), exit 4. **Open** 9.30am-6.30pm daily.

Travel advice

For up-to-date information on travel to a specific country – including the latest news on safety and security, health issues, local laws and customs – contact your home country government's department of foreign affairs. Most have websites packed with useful advice for would-be travellers.

Australia
www.smartraveller.gov.au

Canada
www.voyage.gc.ca

New Zealand
www.mft.govt.nz/travel

Republic of Ireland
http://foreignaffairs.gov.ie

UK
www.fco.gov.uk/travel

USA
www.state.gov/travel

Directory

If you're visiting the observation deck in the Tokyo Metropolitan Government Building, pop into this ground-floor office.
Other locations: 1-60 Ueno-Koen, Taito-ku (3836 3471). In front of the Keisei Ueno station ticket gate 60.

JNTO (UK)

Heathcoat House, 20 Savile Row, London W1S 3PR (020 7734 9638/ fax 020 7734 4290/www.seejapan. co.uk). **Open** 9.30am-5.30pm daily. Contact JNTO for free maps, guides and brochures – but not hotel bookings. Check the website for details of other overseas offices.

Japan Travel Phone

3201 3331. **Open** 9am-5pm daily. A free nationwide service for those in need of English-language assistance and travel information on places outside Tokyo and Kyoto.

Odakyu Sightseeing Service Centre

Ground-floor concourse, Shinjuku station (5321 7887). **Open** 8am-6pm daily. Staff speak English, Chinese and Korean.

Visas

Japan has general visa-exemption arrangements with the UK, the USA, Canada and the Republic of Ireland, whose citizens may stay in Japan for up to 90 days. Japan also has working holiday visa arrangements with Australia, Canada, New Zealand and the UK for people aged 18 to 30. For information, go to the **Ministry of Foreign Affairs** (www.mofa.go.jp/ j_info/visit).

The following types of visa are available:

Tourist visa
A 'short-term-stay' visa, good for those not intending to work in Japan.
Working visa
It's illegal to work in Japan without a visa. If you arrive as a tourist and work, your company has to sponsor you for a work visa. You generally must then go abroad to make the application (South Korea is the cheapest option). If you plan to stay in Japan for more than 90 days, you need an Alien Registration Card. For this, you need to provide

two passport-sized photographs, a passport, an address and a signature.

Immigration Information Centre

Tokyo Regional Immigration Bureau, 5-5-30 Konan, Minato-ku (5796 7112/www.moj.go.jp/ENGLISH/IB/ib -18.html). Shinagawa station (Yamanote line), east exit then bus (follow signs). **Open** 9am-noon, 1-4pm Mon-Fri.

Weights & measures

Japan uses the metric system – although some room sizes are measured by how many tatami (straw mats) they can hold.

When to go

Spring begins with winds and cherry-blossom viewing. The rainy season for Honshu (the main island) begins in June. This is followed by the hot, humid days of summer. Autumn sees the changing of the leaves, while winter brings clear skies, cold days and the occasional snowstorm. Temperatures range from around 3°C (37°F) in January to 35°C (95°F) in July/August.

Summer in Tokyo can be unbearable for those not used to humidity. Carry a fan, some water and a wet cotton cloth with you. Fans are often handed out in the street for advertising campaigns. Spring (March to May) and autumn (September to November) are the nicest times to visit Tokyo.

The two big holiday periods, when much of Tokyo shuts down, are **Golden Week** (29 April-5 May) and the **New Year** (28 Dec-4 Jan). For annual festivals, *see p212-7.*

Public holidays

Japan has 14 public holidays: New Year's Day (Ganjitsu) **1 January**; Coming of Age Day (Seijin no Hi) **second Monday in**

January; National Foundation Day (Kenkoku Kinen no Hi) **11 February**; Vernal Equinox Day (Shumbun no Hi) **around 21 March**; Greenery Day (Midori no Hi) **29 April**; Constitution Day (Kempo Kinenbi) **3 May**; Children's Day (Kodomo no Hi) **5 May**; Marine Day (Umi no Hi) **20 July**; Respect for the Aged Day (Keiro no Hi) **15 September**; Autumnal Equinox Day (Shubun no Hi) **around 23 September**; Sports Day (Taiiku no Hi) **second Monday in October**; Culture Day (Bunka no Hi) **3 November**; Labour Thanksgiving Day (Kinro Kansha no Hi) **23 November**; Emperor's Birthday (Tenno Tanjobi) **23 December**.

Saturday remains an official workday, but holidays falling on a Sunday shift to Monday. If both 3 May and 5 May fall on weekdays, then 4 May also becomes a holiday.

Women travellers

The crime rate in Japan is very low compared to that in many countries.

Women should exercise standard precautions, but the risk of rape or assault is not high, and, in general, women can ride the subways at night or wander the streets with little concern. A woman alone might find herself the subject of harassment by staggering, drunken salarymen, but they are rarely serious; ignoring them generally does the trick.

This said, Tokyo is not totally immune from urban dangers. You should certainly not let fear spoil your holiday, but do exercise caution at night, particularly in busy nightlife areas such as Roppongi and Shinjuku's Kabuki-cho.

A less serious, but still nasty, type of assault occurs every day on packed rush-hour trains, where women are sometimes rubbed against, groped (or worse). Many Japanese women ignore the offence, hesitant to draw attention to themselves, but shouting in English can be effective.

Further Reference

Books

Fiction

Abe, Kobe *The Woman in the Dunes*
Weird classic about a lost village of sand.
Birnbaum, Alfred (ed) *Monkey Brain Sushi*
Decent selection of 'younger' Japanese writers.
Erickson, Steve *The Sea Came in at Midnight*
American novel set partly in a Tokyo 'memory hotel'.
Howell, Brian *Head of a Girl & others*
Elegantly weird short story by expat English writer based close to Tokyo.
Kawabata, Yasuwari *Snow Country*
Japan's first Nobel Prize-winner for literature.
Mishima, Yukio *Confessions of a Mask & others*
Still Japan's most famous novelist, 37 years after his suicide.
Mitchell, David *Ghostwritten & Number9Dream*
Ambitious novels by expat UK writer teaching English in Hiroshima.
Murakami, Haruki *Norwegian Wood & others*
Most of Murakami's many books are set in Tokyo.
Murakami, Ryu *Coin Locker Babies & others*
Hip modern novelist, unrelated to Haruki.
Oe, Kenzoburo *A Personal Matter & others*
Japan's second winner of the Nobel Prize.
Yoshimoto, Banana *Kitchen & others*
Modern writer who's made a splash in the West.

Non-fiction

Birchall, Jonathan *Ultra Nippon*
British journo follows Japanese soccer team, and fans, for a year.
Bird, Isabella *Unbeaten Tracks in Japan*
Amazing memoirs of intrepid Victorian explorer.
Bix, Herbert P *Hirohito and the Making of Modern Japan*
Post-war Japan.
Bornoff, Nicholas *Pink Samurai: Love, Marriage and Sex in Contemporary Japan*
All you ever wanted to know about the subjects.

Cavaye, Ronald, Griffith, Paul & Senda, Akihiko *The World of the Japanese Stage*
All you need to know about traditional Japanese performing arts.
Chang, Iris *The Rape of Nanking: The Forgotten Holocaust of World War II*
The Japanese Imperial Army's atrocities in China revealed in all their horror.
Dower, John W *Embracing Defeat: Japan in the Wake of World War II*
Award-winning account of the American-led post-war reconstruction of Japan.
Evers, Izumi & Macias, Patrick *Japanese Schoolgirl Inferno: Tokyo Teen Fashion Subculture Handbook*
An illustrated guide to the quirkiest teen tribes past and present.
Ferguson, Will *Hokkaido Highway Blues*
One man's manic mission to hitchhike through Japan following the progress of the cherry blossom.
Galbraith, Stuart *Giant Monsters Are Attacking Tokyo: Incredible World of Japanese Fantasy Films*
The ultimate guide to the weird and wacky world of the city-stomping giants of Japanese cinema.
Gravett, Paul *Manga: Sixty Years of Japanese Comics*
Beautifully illustrated, large-format survey of the history of the art form that's taking over the world.
Harper, Philip *The Insider's Guide to Sake*
Readable introduction to Japan's national libation.
Kaplan, David & Dubro, Alec *Yakuza: Japan's Criminal Underworld*
Inside look at the gangs who control Japan's underworld.
Kaplan, David & Marshall, Andrew *The Cult at The End of The World*
Terrifying story of Aum and the subway gas attacks.
Kennedy, Rick *Little Adventures in Tokyo*
Entertaining trips through the offbeat side of the city.
Kerr, Alex *Dogs and Demons: Tales from the Dark Side of Modern Japan*
Bestselling account of Japan's self-destructive streak.
Martin, John H & Phyllis G *Tokyo: A Cultural Guide to Japan's Capital City*
Enjoyable ramble through Tokyo with two amiable authors.
Okakura, Kazuko *The Book of Tea*
Tea as the answer to life, the universe and everything. Which, as every Japanese knows, it is.

Ototake, Hirotada *No One's Perfect*
True story of a boy who overcame handicaps and prejudice. A record-breaking bestseller.
Richie, Donald *Public People, Private People and Tokyo: A View of the City*
Acclaimed writer and long-time Japan resident on the Japanese and their capital.
Richie, Donald *Tokyo*
That man again, with a beautifully produced work from Reaktion Books.
Satterwhite, Robb *What's What in Japanese Restaurants*
An invaluable guide to navigating the menu maze.
Schilling, Mark *Encyclopedia of Japanese Pop Culture*
From karaoke to Hello Kitty, ramen to Doraemon.
Schilling, Mark *The Yakuza Movie Book: A Guide to Japanese Gangster Films*
A testament to the enduring appeal of the gangster in Japanese movies.
Schlesinger, Jacob M *Shadow Shoguns: The Rise and Fall of Japan's Postwar Political Machine*
Pretty good, non-academic read.
Schodt, Fredrick L *Dreamland Japan: Writings on Modern Manga*
Leading Western authority on Japan's publishing phenomenon.
Schreiber, Mark *Tabloid Tokyo: 101 Tales of Sex, Crime and the Bizarre from Japan's Wild Weeklies*
Japan laid bare through translated magazine stories.
Seidensticker, Edward *Tokyo Rising & Low City, High City*
Eminently readable histories of the city.
Sharnoff, Lora *Grand Sumo*
Exhaustive account, if a little on the dry side.
Sinclair, Joan *Pink Box: Inside Japan's Sex Clubs*
A stunning photographic portrait of the secrets behind those neon doors.
Tajima, Noriyuki *Tokyo: Guide to Recent Architecture*
Pocket-sized guide with outstanding pictures.
Tajima, Noriyuki & Powell, Catherine *Tokyo: Labyrinth City*
LP-sized guide to more recent projects.
Takemoto, Tadao & Ohara, Yasuo *The Alleged 'Nanking Massacre': Japan's Rebuttal to China's Forged Claims*
The right-wing Japanese take on the Imperial Army's actions in China.
Twigger, Robert *Angry White Pyjamas*
Scrawny Oxford poet trains with Japanese riot police.

Walters, Gary *Day Walks Near Tokyo & More Day Walks Near Tokyo*
No surprises here: detailed routes for walkers wanting to escape the city's crowds.
Whiting, Robert *Tokyo Underworld: The Fast Life and Times of an American Gangster in Japan*
An enthralling story of underworld life in the bowels of modern Japan.
Whiting, Robert *You Gotta Have Wa*
US baseball stars + Japan = culture clash. The template for many sports books written since.

Language

Three A Network/Minna no Nihongo Shokyuu
Book 1 for beginners, 2 for pre-intermediate.
Integrated Approach to Intermediate Japanese
Well balanced in grammar, reading and conversation.
A Dictionary of Basic Japanese Grammar
Standard book from the *Japan Times*.
The Modern Reader's Japanese-English Dictionary
Known affectionately as Nelson, this is the definitive tool for students of the written language.

Maps & guides

Shobunsha Tokyo Metropolitan Atlas
Negotiate those tricky addresses with confidence.
Japan As It Is
Eccentric explanations of all things Japanese.
Asahi Shinbun's Japan Almanac
The ultimate book of lists, published annually.

Films

Akira
(Otomo Katsuhiro, 1988)
The film that started the West's *anime* craze. Freewheeling youth gangs try to stay alive in Neo-Tokyo.
Audition
(Takashi Miike, 1999)
A lonely widower, a beautiful actress: another Japanese shocker.
Diary of a Shinjuku Thief
(Oshima Nagisa, 1968)
A picaresque trip through 1960s Tokyo with a master director.
The Eel
(Imamura Shohei, 1996)
Yakusho Koji in a bizarre tale of love in the aftermath of murder.
Gamera 3
(Shusuke Kaneko, 1999)
Countless Tokyo dwellers' dreams

are realised when a turbo-powered turtle demolishes Shibuya.
Ghost in the Shell
(Mamoru Oshii, 1995)
Complex, animated look at a future society where computers house human minds – and vice versa.
Godzilla, King of the Monsters
(Honda Inoshiro, 1954)
The big green guy makes his debut following an atomic accident, and smashes up Ginza. Subtext: Japan recovers from the blast of Hiroshima.
Hana-Bi
(Kitano Takeshi, 1997)
Kitano's best film won him a Venice prize, but in his native country he is still better known as a TV comedian.
House of Bamboo
(Samuel Fuller, 1955)
A gang led by an American pulls off raids in Tokyo and Yokohama.
Lost in Translation
(Sofia Coppola, 2003)
Bill Murray and Scarlett Johansson reach across the generations to form an unusual bond. Shot in and around Shinjuku and Shibuya.
Mononoke Hime (Princess Mononoke)
(Miyazaki Hiyao, 1997)
Record-breaking animated fable of man's butchery of the environment.
Rashomon
(Kurosawa Akira, 1951)
Influential tale of robbery from Japan's most famous filmmaker.
The Ring
(Nakata Hideo, 1998)
Chilling urban ghost story that has spawned a seemingly endless boom of psycho-horror movies.
Sakuran
(Ninagawa Mika, 2007)
Visually stunning debut feature from photographer Ninagawa tells of an Edo-era concubine.
Spirited Away
(Miyazaki Hayao, 2001)
Oscar-winning animated feature from the same studio as *Princess Mononoke*.
Tampopo
(Itami Juzo, 1986)
The idiosyncratic and sadly missed director's trawl through the Japanese obsession for food, with particular reference to ramen noodles.
Tokyo Pop
(Fran Rubel Kazui, 1988)
Aspiring artiste can't make it in New York, so heads off to Tokyo.
Tokyo Story
(Ozu Yasujiro, 1953)
Life in the metropolis and the generation gap it produces are explored in Ozu's masterpiece.
Une avenue à Tokyo
(Tsunekichi Shibata, 1898)
One of the earliest short films showing Meiji-era life in Japan.
Until the End of the World
(Wim Wenders, 1991)

William Hurt and Sam Neill lurk briefly around Shinjuku in Wenders's worthy but dull SF epic.
The Yakuza
(Sydney Pollack, 1974)
Robert Mitchum stars in writer Paul Schrader's tribute to the Japanese gangster movie.
You Only Live Twice
(Lewis Gilbert, 1967)
Connery's 007 comes to Tokyo. The New Otani Hotel doubles as the HQ of the malevolent Osato Corporation.

Music

Denki Groove *A*
A multi-faceted band that does pop, dance music and techno. One member, Takkyu Ishino, has toured in Europe as a DJ.
Dragon Ash *Morrow*
One of the most popular rap groups in Japan.
Hajime Chitose *Konomachi*
Born on Amami Oshima island. She sings poppy versions of traditional local songs in a unique warble.
Hamasaki Ayumi *A Ballads*
Top-selling female vocalist in Japan.
Misia *Misia Greatest Hits*
The Japanese queen of ballads.
Quruli *The World is Mine*
One of Japan's most talented bands.
Rovo *Flage*
Heavy, progressive rock, with a pronounced jazz influence. Great live.
Sheena Ringo *Karuki Zamen Kuri no Hana*
Top female rocker.
SMAP *Sekaini Hitotsudake no Hana*
Only in Japan would a group of pop stars host their own cookery show.
Tokyo SKA Paradise Orchestra *A Quick Drunkard*
The name says it all: innovative music bases on ska beats.
Utada Hikaru *Colors*
Japan's answer to Sade. **Yoshida Brothers** *Soulful*
Two young *shamisen* players play traditional music to modern backing tracks.

Websites

Getting around

Hyperdia
www.hyperdia.com
Very useful interactive route planner. Enter Japanese cities or Tokyo stations, and you will be given recommended routes between them.
Japanese Guest Houses
www.japaneseguesthouses.com
Guide to traditional *ryokan* accommodation in Tokyo, Kyoto and other cities, with online booking.

Japan Guide
www.japan-guide.com
User-friendly online guide to travelling and living in Japan. Practical information covering the whole of the country.
Japan Travel Updates
www.jnto.go.jp
Site of the Japan National Tourist Organisation (JNTO), featuring a selection of useful travel information, tips, an online booking service and several sketchy reference city maps.
NTT Townpage
http://english.itp.ne.jp
NTT's English-language phonebook.
Subway Navigator
www.subwaynavigator.com
Interactive subway-route planner. Enter your departure and destination stations, and it'll provide the route as well as how much time to allow for your journey.
Tokyo Life Navigator
www.ima-chan.co.jp/guide/index.htm
The place to start if you know nothing about Tokyo and want to swot up before you get here.
Tokyo Subway Maps
www.tokyometro.jp/e
Up-to-date maps of the sometimes baffling subway system.

Lesbian & gay

Film Festival
www.tokyo-lgff.org
Home page of the queer film festival staged annually in July.
Gay Net Japan
www.gnj.or.jp
English and Japanese forums, classifieds and support groups. Especially good for making short-term friendships.
Utopia
www.utopia-asia.com/tipsjapn.htm
Useful, fun and informative page of listings, links and more from this Asian gay portal site.

Media

Daily Yomiuri
www.yomiuri.co.jp/index-e.htm
Tokyo's second English-language newspaper's site (after the *Japan Times*) is smaller but prettier.
Debito's Home Page
www.debito.org
Amusing and informative home page of one Arudou Debito, a former US citizen called David Aldwinkle (Debito is David in Japanese), now a Japanese national.
i-mode
www.nttdocomo.com
Company home page linking to information on the successful Japanese mobile internet system.

Japan Inc
www.japaninc.com
Online version of the monthly magazine tracking Japan's progress in the so-called 'New Economy'.
Japan Times
www.japantimes.com
The most comprehensive news about Japan available on the web. The events section of the site is only sporadically updated.
Japan Today
www.japantoday.com
Tabloid news about Japan.
Mainichi Daily News
http://mdn.mainichi.co.jp
Formerly a printed English-language newspaper, now internet only. Great for quirky stories.

Music & clubs

CIA (Club Information Agency)
www.ciajapan.com
Online version of this monthly guide to club events in Tokyo has listings and party pictures.
CyberJapan
www.cyberjapan.tv
Stylish youth-culture site has fashion reports, news and streaming videos from Tokyo clubland.
Higher Frequency
www.higher-frequency.com
The most comprehensive site for clubbers, with news, interviews, listings and DJ charts.
Samurai FM
www.samurai.fm
Tokyo's best online radio station, with sets from local and international DJs.
Smash
www.smash-jpn.com
Home page in Japanese and English of one of Tokyo's biggest concert promoters.
Tokyo Record Stores
www.bento.com/rekodoya.html
A decent, but dated, guide to the capital's record stores.

Offbeat

Engrish
www.engrish.com
Hundreds of prime examples of the Japanese mutilation of the English language. And surprisingly amusing.
Quirky Japan
www.quirkyjapan.or.tv
Offbeat home page 'dedicated to digression, kitsch, eccentricity and originality', with alternative things to do in Tokyo when you're 'tired of shrines and temples'.
Ramen
www.worldramen.net
All the best ramen noodle restaurants in the world, rated and reviewed in English.

Sake World
www.sake-world.com
Everything you ever wanted to know about Japan's national tipple, put together by sake columnist John Gauntner.
Tokyo DV
www.tokyodv.com
One for broadband users, with full-length films to download. Check out the penis-worshipping festival. Also features gossip from the world of Japanese showbiz.

Portal sites

Japan Reference
www.jref.com
Extensive database with over 10,000 Japan-related links, plus tourism and culture guides, and forums.
Tokyodoko
www.tokyodoko.com
Portal with an easy-to-use and relatively in-depth reference search facility.
Tokyo Pop
www.tokyopop.com
Cute site covering Japanese pop culture from every angle.
Yahoo Japan
www.yahoo.co.jp
Yahoo is a big success in Japan: the nation's most popular search engine and information provider.

What's on

Metropolis
www.metropolis.co.jp
Metropolis is the most reliably updated English-language source for what's-on listings for clubs, concerts and art galleries, as well as feature articles and classified ads.
PingMag
www.pingmag.jp
The latest from Tokyo's design scene, in English and Japanese.
Real Tokyo
www.realtokyo.co.jp/english/index
Previews the pick of the city's upcoming cultural events.
Ski Japan
www.skijapanguide.com
During the winter, it's more than possible to head off for a day's skiing and be back in Tokyo by nightfall. This page tells you exactly how to go about it.
Superfuture
www.superfuture.com
Hyper-stylish site mapping out shops, bars and restaurants.
Tokyo Art Beat
www.tokyoartbeat.com
A bilingual site with comprehensive gallery listings and visitor reviews.
Tokyo Food Page
www.bento.com
An awe-inspiring restaurant guide.

Directory

Getting by in Japanese

JAPANESE LANGUAGE
Pronunciation
Japanese pronunciation presents few problems for native English speakers, the most difficult trick to master being the doubling of vowels or consonants.

Vowels
a as in bad
e as in bed
i as in feet
o as in long
u as in look

Long vowels
aa as in father
ee as in fair
ii as in feet, but longer
oo as in fought
uu as in chute

Consonants
Consonants in Japanese are pronounced the same as in English, but are always hard ('g' as in 'girl', rather than 'gyrate', for example). The only exceptions are the 'l/r' sound, which is one sound in Japanese, and falls halfway between the English pronunciation of the two letters, and 'v', which is pronounced as a 'b'. When consonants are doubled, they are pronounced as such: a 'tt' as in 'matte' (wait) is pronounced more like the 't' sound in 'get to' than in 'getting'.

Reading the phrases
When reading the phrases below, remember to separate the syllables. Despite the funny way it looks in English, the common name Takeshita is pronounced Ta-ke-shit-ta. Similarly, made (until) is 'ma-de', not the English 'made', and shite (doing) is 'shi-te', rather than anything else. When a 'u' falls at the end of the word, it is barely spoken: 'desu' is closer to 'dess' than to 'de-su'.

Reading and writing
The Japanese writing system is fiendishly complicated and is the main deterrent to learning the language. Japanese uses two syllabaries (not alphabets, because the letters represent complete sounds), *hiragana* and *katakana*, in conjunction with *kanji*, characters imported from China many centuries ago. The average Japanese person will be able to read over 6,000 *kanji*. For all but the most determined visitor, learning to read before you go is out of the question. However, learning *katakana* is relatively simple and will yield quick results, since it is used mainly to spell out foreign words (many imported from English). For books on learning Japanese, *see page 316*.

USEFUL WORDS AND PHRASES

Numbers
1 *ichi*	9 *kyuu*
2 *ni*	10 *juu*
3 *san*	11 *juu-ichi*
4 *yon*	12 *juu-ni*
5 *go*	100 *hyaku*
6 *roku*	1,000 *sen*
7 *nana*	10,000 *man*
8 *hachi*	100,000 *juu-man*

Days
Monday *getsu-yoobi*
Tuesday *ka-yoobi*
Wednesday *sui-yoobi*
Thursday *moku-yoobi*
Friday *kin-yoobi*
Saturday *do-yoobi*
Sunday *nichi-yoobi*

Time
It's at ...o'clock *...ji desu*
Excuse me, do you have the time?
sumimasen, ima nan-ji desu ka?
noon/midnight *shougo/mayonaka*

Months
January *ichi-gatsu*
February *ni-gatsu*
March *san-gatsu*
April *shi-gatsu*
May *go-gatsu*
June *roku-gatsu*
July *shichi-gatsu*
August *hachi-gatsu*
September *ku-gatsu*
October *juu-gatsu*
November *juu-ichi-gatsu*
December *juu-ni-gatsu*

Dates

this morning/this afternoon/this evening
kesa/kyoo no gogo/konban
yesterday/today/tomorrow
kinoo/kyoo/ashita
last week/this week/next week
sen-shuu/kon-shuu/rai-shuu
the weekend *shuumatsu*

Basic expressions

Yes/no *hai/iie*
Okay *ookee*
Please (asking for a favour) *onegai shimasu*
Please (offering a favour) *doozo*
Thank you (very much) *(doomo) arigatoo*
Thank you (for having me) *osewa ni
narimashita*
Hello/hi *kon nichi wa*
Good morning *ohayoo gozaimasu*
Good afternoon *kon nichi wa*
Good evening *kon ban wa*
Goodnight *oyasumi nasai*
Goodbye *sayoonara*
How are you? *ogenki desu ka?*
Excuse me (getting attention) *sumimasen*
Excuse me (may I get past?)
shitsurei shimasu
Excuse me/sorry *gomen nasai*
Don't mention it/never mind
ki ni shinai de kudasai
It's okay *daijoobu desu*
My name is…
watashi no namae wa… desu
What's your name?
o namae wa nan desu ka?
Pleased to meet you *doozo yoroshiku*
Cheers! *kampai!*

Communication

Do you speak English?
eigo o hanashi masu ka?
I don't speak (much) Japanese
nihongo o (amari) hanashi masen
Could you speak more slowly?
yukkuri itte kudasai?
Could you repeat that?
moo ichido itte kudasai?
I understand *wakari mashita*
I don't understand *wakari masen*
Do you understand? *wakari masu ka?*
Where is it? *doko desu ka?*
When is it? *itsu desu ka?*
What is it? *nan desu ka?*

Eating out

See also p168 **Menu Reader**.
bar *izakaya/nomiya*
canteen *shokudoo*
coffee shop *kissaten*
noodle stall *ramen-ya*
restaurant (smart) *ryotei*

May I see the menu?
Menyuu onegai shimasu?
Do you have an English menu?
eigo no menyuu wa arimasu ka?
I'm a vegetarian
watashi wa bejitarian desu
Please can we have the bill?
okanjoo onegai shimasu?

Hotels

Do you have a room? *heya wa arimasu ka?*
I'd like a single/double room *shinguru/
daburu no heya o onegai shimasu*
I'd like a room with…
…tsuki no heya o onegai shimasu
a bath/shower *furo/shawaa*

Reception

I have a reservation
yoyaku shite arimasu
Is there… in the room?
heya ni… wa arimasu ka?
air-conditioning *eakon*
TV/telephone *terebi/denwa*
We'll be staying… *…tomari masu*
one night only *ippaku dake*
a week *isshuu-kan*
I don't know yet *mada wakari masen*
I'd like to stay an extra night
moo ippaku sasete kudasai
How much is… ? *…ikura desu ka?*
including/excluding breakfast
chooshoku komi/nuki de
Does the price include…?
kono nedan wa… komi desu ka?
sales tax (VAT) *shoohi zee*
breakfast/meal *chooshoku/shokuji*
Is there a reduction for children?
kodomo no waribiki wa arimasu ka?
What time is breakfast served?
chooshoku wa nan-ji desu ka?
Is there room service?
ruumu saabisu wa arimasu ka?
The key to the room…, please
…goo-shitsu no kagi o kudasai
I've lost my key *kagi o nakushi mashita*
Could you wake me up at…?
…ji ni okoshite kudasai?
bathtowel/blanket/pillow
basu taoru/moofu/makura
Are there any messages for me?
messeeji wa arimasu ka?
What time do we have to check out by?
chekkuauto wa nan-ji made desu ka?
Could I have my bill, please?
kaikei o onegai shimasu?
Could I have a receipt, please?
reshiito o onegai shimasu?
Could you order me a taxi, please?
takushii o yonde kudasai?

Shops & services

pharmacy *yakkyoku/doraggu sutoaa*
off-licence/liquor store *saka-ya*
newsstand *kiosuku*
department store *depaato*
bookshop *hon-ya*
supermarket *suupaa*
camera store *kamera-ya*
I'd like… *…o kudasai*
Do you have…? *…wa arimasu ka?*
How much is that? *ikura desu ka?*
Could you help me? *onegai shimasu?*
Can I try this on? *kite mite mo ii desu ka?*
I'm looking for… *…o sagashite imasu*
larger/smaller *ookii/chiisai*
I'll take it *sore ni shimasu*
That's all, thank you *sore de zenbu desu*

Bank/currency exchange

dollars *doru*
pounds *pondo*
yen *en*
currency exchange *ryoogae-jo*
I'd like to change some pounds into yen
pondo o en ni kaetain desu ga
Could I have some small change, please?
kozeni o kudasai?

Health

Where can I find a hospital/dental surgery?
byooin/hai-sha wa doko desu ka?
I need a doctor *isha ga hitsuyoo desu*
Is there a doctor/dentist who speaks English?
*eego ga dekiru isha/ha-isha wa
imasu ka?*
What are the surgery hours?
shinryoo jikan ga nan-ji desu ka?
Could the doctor come to see me here?
ooshin shite kuremasu ka?
Could I make an appointment for…?
…yoyaku shitain desu ga?
as soon as possible *dekirudake hayaku*
It's urgent *shikyuu onegai shimasu*
I'm diabetic *watashi wa toonyoobyoo desu*
I'm asthmatic *watashi wa zensoku desu*
I'm allergic to… *…arerugi desu*
contraceptive *hinin yoo piru*

Symptoms

I feel faint *memai ga shimasu*
I have a fever *netsu ga arimasu*
I've been vomiting *modoshi mashita*
I've got diarrhoea *geri shitemasu*
It hurts here *koko ga itai desu*
I have a headache *zutsuu ga shimasu*
I have a sore throat *nodo ga itai desu*
I have a stomach ache *onaka ga itai desu*
I have a toothache *ha ga itai desu*
I've lost a filling/tooth
tsumemono/ha ga toremashita
I don't want it extracted *nukanaide kudasai*

Sightseeing

Where's the tourist office?
kankoo annai-jo wa doko desu ka?
Do you have any information on…?
…no annai wa arimasu ka?
sightseeing tour *kankoo tsuaa*
Are there any trips to…?
…e no tsuaa wa arimasu ka?
gallery *bijutsukan*
hot springs *onsen*
mountain *yama*
museum *hakubutsukan*
palace *kyuuden*
park *kooen*
shrine *jinja*
temple *tera*

On tour

We'd like to have a look at the…
…o mitain desu ga
to take photographs
shashin o toritain desu ga
to buy souvenirs
omiyage o kaitain desu ga
to use the toilets *toire ni ikitain desu ga*
Can we stop here? *koko de tomare masu ka?*
Could you take a photo of us, please?
shashin o totte kudasai
Are we allowed to take photos?
shashin o totte mo ii desu ka?

Travel

Where's the nearest underground station?
chikatetsu no eki wa doko desu ka?
Could I have a map of the underground?
chikatetsu no rosenzu o kudasai?
To…, please *…made onegai shimasu*
Single/return tickets
katamichi/oofuku kippu
Where can I buy a ticket?
kippu wa doko de kaemasu ka?
I'm going to… *…ni ikimasu*
on my own *hitori*
with my family *kazoku to issho*
I'm with a group *guruupu de kimashita*
I'm here on holiday/business
kankoo/shigoto de kimashita
How much…? *…wa ikura desu ka?*
When does the train for… leave?
…iki no densha wa nan-ji ni demasu ka?
Can you tell me when we get to…?
…ni tsuitara oshiete kudasai?
ticket office *kippu-uriba*
ticket gate *kaisatsu-guchi*
ticket vending machines *kenbai-ki*
bus *basu*
train *densha*
bullet train *shinkansen*
subway *chikatetsu*
taxi *takushii*

SIGNS

General

左 *hidari* left

右 *migi* right

入口 *iriguchi* entrance

出口 *deguchi* exit

トイレ/お手洗い *toire/o-tearai* toilets

男/男性 *otoko/dansei* men

女/女性 *onna/jyosei* women

禁煙 *kin-en* no smoking

危険 *kiken* danger

立ち入り禁止 *tachiiri kinshi* no entry

引く/押す *hiku/osu* pull/push

遺失物取扱所 *ishitsu butsu toriatsukai jo* lost property

水泳禁止 *suiei kinshi* no swimming

飲料水 *inryoosui* drinking water

関係者以外立ち入り禁止 *kankeisha igai tachiiri kinshi* private

地下道 *chikadoo* underpass (subway)

足元注意 *ashimoto chuui* mind the step

ペンキ塗り立て *penki nuritate* wet paint

頭上注意 *zujoo chuui* mind your head

Road signs

止まれ *tomare* stop

徐行 *jokoo* slow

一方通行 *ippoo tsuukoo* one way

駐車禁止 *chuusha kinshi* no parking

高速道路 *koosoku dooro* motorway

料金 *ryookin* toll

信号 *shingoo* traffic lights

交差点 *koosaten* junction

Airport/station

案内 *an-nai* information

免税 *menzee* duty free

入国管理 *nyuukoku kanri* immigration

到着 *touchaku* arrivals

出発 *shuppatsu* departures

コインロッカー *koin rokkaa* luggage lockers

荷物引き渡し所 *nimotsu hikiwatashi jo* luggage reclaim

手荷物カート *tenimotsu kaato* trolleys

バス/鉄道 *basu/tetsudoo* bus/train

レンタカー *rentakaa* car rental

地下鉄 *chikatetsu* underground

Hotels/restaurants

フロント *furonto* reception

予約 *yoyaku* reservation

非常口 *hijyo guchi* emergency/fire exit

湯 *yu* hot (water)

冷 *ree* cold (water)

バー *baa* bar

Shops

営業中 *eegyoo chuu* open

閉店 *heeten* closed

階 *kai* floor

地下 *chika* basement

エレベーター *erebeetaa* lift

エスカレーター *esukareetaa* escalator

会計 *kaikee* cashier

Sightseeing

入場無料 *nyuujoo muryoo* free admission

大人/子供 小人 *otona/kodomo* adults/children

割引（学生/高齢者）*waribiki (gakusei/koureisha)* reduction (students/senior citizens)

お土産 *o-miyage* souvenirs

手を触れないでください *te o furenai de kudasai* do not touch

撮影禁止 *satsuei kinshi* no photography

Public buildings

病院 *byooin* hospital

交番 *kouban* police box

銀行 *ginkoo* bank

郵便局 *yuubin kyoku* post office

プール *puuru* swimming pool

博物館 *hakubutsu-kan* museum

Note: page numbers in **bold** indicate section(s) giving key information on topic; *italics* indicate illustrations.

Place of interest	
Park	
Hospital/university	
Post office	⊠
Temple	⚲
Shrine	丌
Railway station	▮
Subway station	**S**
District	GINZA
Ward	**SHIBUYA-KU**
Hotel	◻
Sightseeing	◼
Restaurant	●
Bar	●
Coffee shop	●
Shops & services	●
Children	○
Clubs	⬠
Film	⬠
Galleries	⬠
Gay & Lesbian	△
Music	⬠
Performing Arts	⬠
Sport	⬠

Maps

Mainland Japan

Trips Out of Town

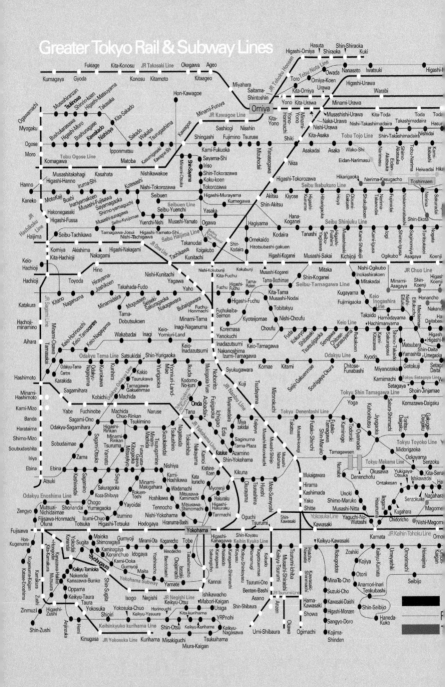

Greater Tokyo Rail & Subway Lines

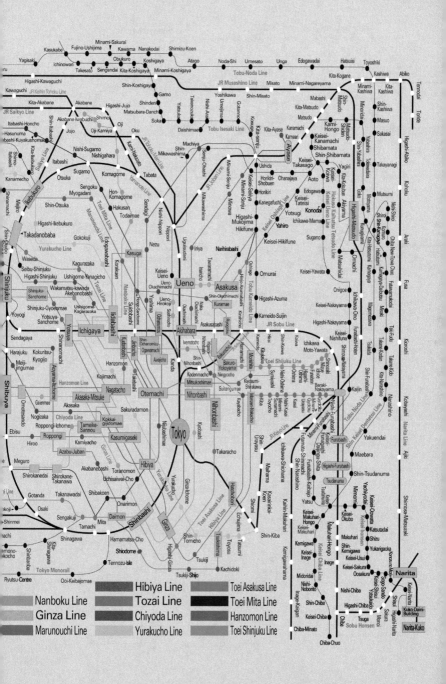

Nanboku Line
Ginza Line
Marunouchi Line
Hibiya Line
Tozai Line
Chiyoda Line
Yurakucho Line
Toei Asakusa Line
Toei Mita Line
Hanzomon Line
Toei Shinjuku Line

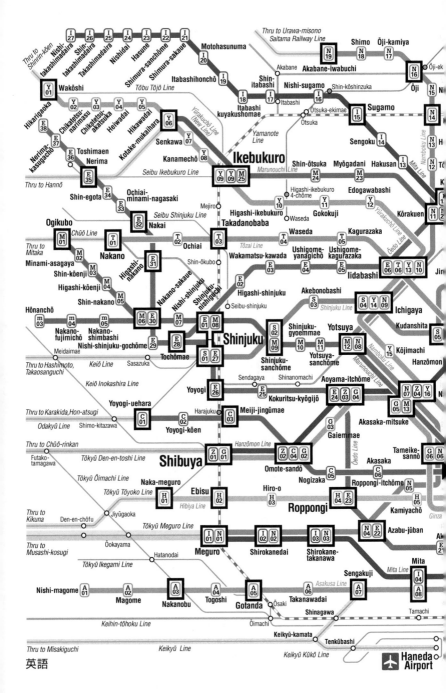

英語

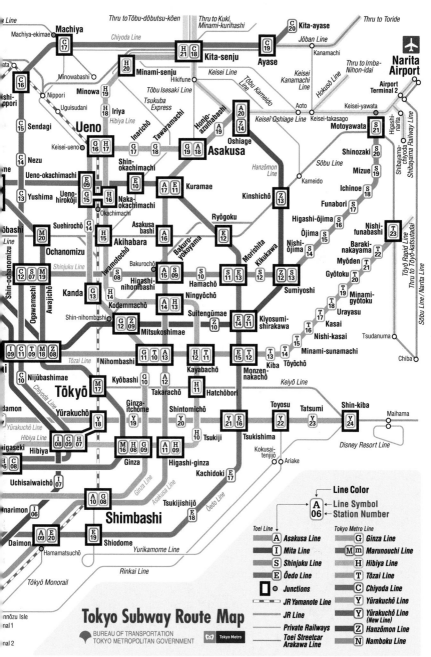

Tokyo Subway Route Map

BUREAU OF TRANSPORTATION
TOKYO METROPOLITAN GOVERNMENT

Line Color

Toei Line		**Tokyo Metro Line**
A Asakusa Line		**G** Ginza Line
I Mita Line		**Ⓜ m** Marunouchi Line
S Shinjuku Line		**H** Hibiya Line
E Ōedo Line		**T** Tōzai Line
Junctions		**C** Chiyoda Line
JR Yamanote Line		**Y** Yūrakuchō Line
JR Line		**Y** Yūrakuchō Line (New Line)
Private Railways		**Z** Hanzōmon Line
Toei Streetcar Arakawa Line		**N** Namboku Line

Ⓜ BUREAU OF TRANSPORTATION TOKYO METROPOLITAN GOVERNMENT Tokyo Metro Co., Ltd. ©2006.3 ℞100

Yamanote Line Connections

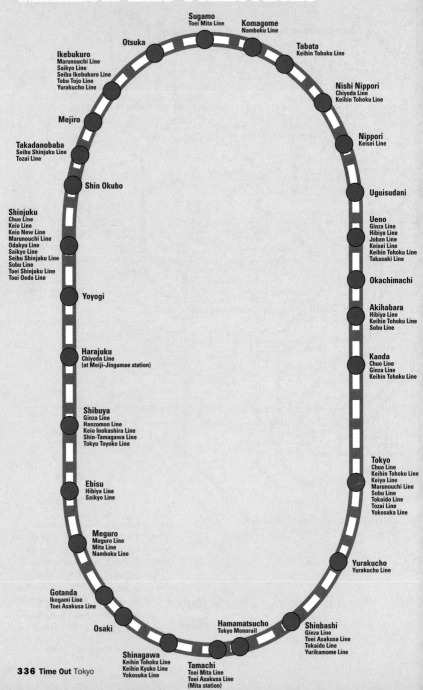

Sugamo
Toei Mita Line

Komagome
Namboku Line

Otsuka

Tabata
Keihin Tohoku Line

Ikebukuro
Marunouchi Line
Saikyo Line
Seibu Ikebukuro Line
Tobu Tojo Line
Yurakucho Line

Nishi Nippori
Chiyoda Line
Keihin Tohoku Line

Mejiro

Nippori
Keisei Line

Takadanobaba
Seibu Shinjuku Line
Tozai Line

Shin Okubo

Uguisudani

Shinjuku
Chuo Line
Keio Line
Keio New Line
Marunouchi Line
Odakyu Line
Saikyo Line
Seibu Shinjuku Line
Sobu Line
Toei Shinjuku Line
Toei Oedo Line

Ueno
Ginza Line
Hibiya Line
Joban Line
Keisei Line
Keihin Tohoku Line
Takasaki Line

Okachimachi

Yoyogi

Akihabara
Hibiya Line
Keihin Tohoku Line
Sobu Line

Harajuku
Chiyoda Line
(at Meiji-Jingumae station)

Kanda
Chuo Line
Ginza Line
Keihin Tohoku Line

Shibuya
Ginza Line
Hanzomon Line
Keio Inokashira Line
Shin-Tamagawa Line
Tokyu Toyoko Line

Tokyo
Chuo Line
Keihin Tohoku Line
Keiyo Line
Marunouchi Line
Sobu Line
Tokaido Line
Tozai Line
Yokosuka Line

Ebisu
Hibiya Line
Saikyo Line

Meguro
Meguro Line
Mita Line
Namboku Line

Yurakucho
Yurakucho Line

Gotanda
Ikegami Line
Toei Asakusa Line

Shinbashi
Ginza Line
Toei Asakusa Line
Tokaido Line
Yurikamome Line

Osaki

Hamamatsucho
Tokyo Monorail

Shinagawa
Keihin Tohoku Line
Keihin Kyuko Line
Yokosuka Line

Tamachi
Toei Mita Line
Toei Asakusa Line
(Mita station)